The Great Issues
of Politics

FOURTH EDITION

The Great Issues
of Politics

AN INTRODUCTION TO
POLITICAL SCIENCE

LESLIE LIPSON

*Professor
of
Political Science*

*University of California
Berkeley*

PRENTICE-HALL, INC.

Englewood Cliffs, N.J.

Current printing (last digit):

8   7   6   5   4   3

PRENTICE-HALL INTERNATIONAL, INC., *London*
PRENTICE-HALL OF AUSTRALIA, PTY. LTD., *Sydney*
PRENTICE-HALL OF CANADA, LTD., *Toronto*
PRENTICE-HALL OF INDIA PRIVATE LTD., *New Delhi*
PRENTICE-HALL OF JAPAN, INC., *Tokyo*

Contents

1

Introduction to
the Study of Politics   *1*

Man and His Environment, *1;* The Social Framework, *2;* The Ant's-
Eye View of Society, *4;* Information and Understanding, *6;* Human
Nature in Politics, *8;* American Foreign Policy as an Example, *9;*
Permanent Problems, Changing Solutions, *12;* The Great Issues, *13;*
Analysis of the Great Issues, *15;* Synthesis of the Great Issues, *16;* The
Method and Its Implications, *17;* Politics and Ethics, *20;* Humanism
and Politics, *21*

2

Individuals, Groups
and Society   *26*

The Social Character of Man, *28;* Why Men Live in Groups, *30;*
Restraints upon Actions that Harm Others, *31;* Cooperation plus Com-
petition, *33;* Contrasted Views of Human Nature, *34;* The State of
Nature and the Nature of Society, *37;* The Common Interest and the
Clash of Interests, *40;* Relations Between People in a Group, *41;* The
Uniqueness of the Human Group, *50;* The Variety of Groups, *51;*
Components of Groups, *52;* The Unity of Society, *55;* Divided Loyal-
ties of the Individual, *56;* The Search for Social Harmony, *57*

3

The Origins of the State   *59*

Politics, State, and Government, *59;* The Primary Function of the
State, *60;* The Universal Drive for Protection, *61;* The Evidence of
Language and History, *63;* The Nucleus of the State, *66;* Protection,
Order, and Justice, *70;* The Use and Monopoly of Force, *71;* Officials
and the Public, *74;* Force and Consent, *75;* Power and Authority, *76;*
The Evolution of Political Ends and Governmental Means, *80;* Abuse
of Force, *81;* Confusion of Politics with Power, *85;* The Ethics of
Power, *86*

4

FIRST ISSUE:

–1– The Rule of Privilege   *89*

Citizens or Subjects, *89;* Aristotle's View of Citizenship, *89;* The Argument for Inequality, *91;* A Classification of Elites, *94;* The Myth of Racial Superiority, *95;* The Cult of Ancestors, *100;* Submission to the Elders, *104;* The Unfair Sex, *105;* Discrimination Through Religion, *107;* Control by Conquest, *109;* The Claims of Cultural Leadership, *111;* Money Power, *113;* The Rule of the Wise, *117*

5

FIRST ISSUE:

–2– "All Men Are
Created Equal"   *119*

The Humanity that Unites Us All, *119;* The Case for Equalitarianism, *121;* The Classical Roots of the Doctrine of Equality, *122;* The Modern Rebirth of Equality, *126;* The English, American, and French Revolutions, *126;* Gains for Equality in the Nineteenth Century, *129;* Extension of Voting Rights in Britain, *129;* The Suffrage in American Democracy, *133;* Incompleteness of Black Enfranchisement, *137;* The Revolution in Race Relations, *138;* Toward Equality in Education, *140;* Economic and Social Equality, *143;* Controversies over Means and Ends, *143;* Constructive Steps and Comparisons, *145*

6

SECOND ISSUE:

–1– The State and Society   *149*

The Unity of Society, *149;* Pluralism versus Monism, *150;* Unity Through the Family, Church, or Business, *152;* Defects of a Single-Track Society, *154;* The State's Relation to Society, *157;* The Graeco-Roman City-State: an Experiment in Monism, *159;* The Christian Revolution: Church-State Dualism, *163;* The Theory of Dualism versus the Condition of Unity, *165;* The Papal Rejection of Dualism, *166;* Attack on Dualism by the State, *167;* The Reconstruction of Unity, *169;* Uniformity or Toleration?, *170;* Monism Again: the Theory of Sovereignty, *173*

7

SECOND ISSUE:

–2– Politics and Economics   175

The Economists' Case for Limited Government, *175;* State Control of the Economy in Antiquity, *177;* The Medieval Subordination of Economics to Ethics, *178;* Mercantilism and National Power, *180;* Laissez-Faire—The Economists' Declaration of Independence, *181;* The Bias Against the State, *185;* Business Policy in Victoria's Britain, *187;* Jeffersonian Ideals and the American Frontier, *189;* The Consequences of Industrial Capitalism, *191;* The Power of Business in State and Society, *195;* The Rise of Organized Unions, *197;* Emergence of Big Government, *200;* The Contemporary Trend, *209;* From Justice to Welfare, *211;* The Primacy of the State, *212*

8

THIRD ISSUE:

–1– Authority and the
Authoritarians   215

The Justification of Authority, *215;* Domination versus Accountability, *217;* Types of Authoritarianism, *218;* The Power of the Elite, *224;* The Normalcy of Authoritarianism, *224;* The Modern Revolution, *225;* Dictatorship in Modern Dress, *226;* Fascism and Nazism, *228;* The Communist Dictatorship, *229;* Transfer of Power Under Communism, *232;* The Khrushchev Period, *235;* The Stigmata of Dictatorship, *240*

9

THIRD ISSUE:

–2– The Freedom of
the Governed   243

Foundations of Freedom, *243;* The Athenian Democracy, *243;* The Roman Sacrifice of Liberty to Empire, *246;* The Medieval Order: Fictions and Facts, *248;* The Struggle Between Kings and Nobles, *249;* Rise of the English Parliament, *250;* The Revolution in England, *252;* Principles of the American Revolution, *253;* Supremacy of the Constitution, *255;* The Practice of Judicial Review, *256;* The Rule of Law, *257;* Conformance of Law to Custom, Nature, or Utility, *259;* Constitutions and Constitutionalism, *260;* The Political Roots of the American Constitutional System, *262;* The Politics of the British Constitution, *266;* The American and British Systems Compared, *268;*

The French Case, as a Contrast, *271;* The Key to Freedom, *273;* The Requirement of Two or More Parties, *275;* The Ins and the Outs, *276;* Flaws in the "Iron Law" of Oligarchy, *278;* Civil Liberties, *281*

10

FOURTH ISSUE:

–1– Concentration of Power

Versus

Dispersion of Powers   *284*

Power, Functions, and Institutions, *284;* Centralism or Localism, Separation of Powers or Integration?, *285;* The Contrast Between Athens and Rome, *286;* The Medieval Dispersion of Powers, *288;* Sovereignty and Absolutism in the Nation-State, *289;* Parliamentary Supremacy in Britain, *290;* The French Pattern of Unified Power, *291;* Separation of Powers in the United States, *292;* The Ideas of Montesquieu, *294;* Design of the American Constitution, *295;* The Tradition versus Modern Dynamics, *297;* Effect of Political Parties on Institutions, *300;* Government by Party and Civil Service, *302;* New Role of the American Presidency and Governorship, *302;* Cabinet Dominance in Britain, *304;* The Legislature and the Courts, *307;* The Power Pattern of Dictatorship, *308*

11

FOURTH ISSUE:

–2– Localism, Centralism,

and Federalism   *310*

Areas and Government, *310;* The Community of Interest, *311;* Boundaries and Psychology, *313;* Local Liberties versus Centralized Dictatorship, *314;* The Special Case of Yugoslavia, *316;* Freedom at, or from, the Center?, *319;* Unitary and Federal States, *320;* Centralization in Britain, *321;* American Federalism, the Start of an Invention, *324;* Variations on the Federal Theme, *326;* Centralization in American Government, *327;* Evolution of Other Federal Systems, *331;* The Experience of Brazil, *333;* The National Enforcement of Equality, *335;* The Military Impact on Federalism, *336;* The Revolt of the Individual, *337*

12

FIFTH ISSUE:

–1– The Size of States
and the Relations
Between Them

340

Territorial Basis of the State, *340;* Kinship the Earlier Basis, *341;* The Optimum Area for the State, *343;* The Greek Polis, *344;* Anarchy and Imperialism in Classical Greece, *345;* The Roman Peace, *348;* Limits of the Roman Empire, *350;* The Medieval Dream of Universal Order, *352;* The Cracks in Medieval Unity, *355;* Birth of the Nation-State, *357;* Components of Nationality, *360;* Building the American Nation, *361;* Nationhood in the British Commonwealth, *363;* The Problem in Europe, *364;* Nationalism and the Arts, *368*

13

FIFTH ISSUE:

–2– Nation-States
and International Order

371

The Crisis of the Nation-State, *371;* Imperialism and Sea Power, *372;* Contradictions of Sovereignty, *374;* Anarchy Among Nations, *377;* The Consolidation of Land Masses, *378;* Collective Insecurity, *380;* The Remedies of International Law, *381;* The Growth of International Institutions, *383;* The League of Nations, *385;* The United Nations, *387;* The East-West Split, *389;* International Relations in a Double-Standard World, *391;* Problems of International Cooperation, *393;* Region-States in the Making?, *395;* Contours and Contents of Region-States, *398;* Divisions Within East and West, *400*

14

The Dynamics of
Political Change

405

The Unity of the Political Process, *405;* Permanent Problems, Changing Solutions, *407;* Interaction Between the Great Issues, *407;* Applications of the Great Issues, *416;* The Classification of States, *417;* The Great Issues Applied to Democracy, Totalitarianism, Fascism, and Communism, *421;* Historical Perspective on the Great Issues, *422;* The Uniqueness of Twentieth-Century Politics, *423;* Equalitarianism Today, *424;* The Twilight of Pluralism, *427;* Problems of the

Monistic State, *428;* States in Space, *430;* The Methods of Political Change, *434;* The Nature of Revolution, *435;* Dictatorship in a Time of Change, *437;* From Protection to Perfection, *438;* Politics and the Good Life, *440*

Bibliography   *443*

Index   *449*

to
DAVID

Preface

TO THE FOURTH EDITION

In the five years since this book appeared in its third edition, besides two cruelly tragic wars in Nigeria and Vietnam a series of upheavals, marked by varying degrees of violence, have erupted in country after country. What is significant about these events is their worldwide extensiveness and the active participation of young persons, many of them highly idealistic.

These convulsions in our contemporary society express the indignation aroused by continuing social injustices—for example, the discrimination between sexes, races, religions, and economic classes—and the anxiety over such new phenomena as the threat of nuclear annihilation, the population explosion, the technological revolution, and the destruction of our physical environment. As a result, the values by which we should live are being reexamined, and the gap between society's pretensions and its practices is being exposed.

Governments everywhere lie in the eye of the storm, since they must bear a large measure of responsibility—whether for change or the failure to change. Consequently, all political systems are simultaneously challenged today in a manner which has few parallels in history.

To such developments, the theme of this book, in order to be valid, must have relevance. A study of politics in terms of the fundamental issues which form its constant core must be able to explain the political implications of the social revolution now unfolding. This edition, the fourth, makes that attempt. Hence the reader will find new treatments of the racial confrontation, the worldwide protests of submerged minorities or majorities, the revolt of the young, and similar phenomena which marked the history of the late 1960s. What is happening, in my judgment, is the rejection of the type of government which has been the fashionable model for at least a century—the sovereign, independent, centralized nation-state. Everywhere the institutions of that political system are under attack because they are being found inadequate for coping with the problems which now beset humanity, as the following chapters will seek to show.

In preparing the fourth edition, I have been greatly helped by the suggestions and comments of Elizabeth Monroe Drews, both on the general theme and on points of detail. She has shared with me her vivid perception of the forces which are now transforming our culture and her insight into the psychological aspects of contemporary politics.

Preface

TO THE THIRD EDITION

A French prime minister of the Fourth Republic once commented: "To govern is to choose." That statement captures exactly the spirit in which this book approaches the subject of politics. What I have attempted here is to indicate the basic problems and the possible lines of solution.

In this third edition I have retained the fundamental analysis that is my central theme and present an interpretation of the subject, which is not merely confined to our own century, but enables the whole of mankind's political experience to be understood in historical perspective. At the same time, I recognize that the treatment of politics in terms of its central issues, if it has validity, must be directly applicable to our own age. Eleven years have elapsed since the publication of the first edition, and in that decade we witnessed momentous events and have been able to distinguish more clearly some long-term trends. I have sought, therefore, in the third edition to bring within the framework of the general analysis such developments as the progressive liquidation of the older colonial empires, the movement for equality of civil rights in the United States, the domestic evolution of the Soviet system, Sino-Soviet relations, the unity and the fissures in the Atlantic Community, and so forth.

For their helpful comments and criticisms, I am indebted to Professor Alvin Z. Rubinstein and Professor Garold W. Thumm.

Preface

TO THE SECOND EDITION

It is the theme of this book that politics consists of certain fundamental issues. These do not change, but their solutions do. In this respect, the treatment of this second edition resembles the operation of the Great Issues themselves. Basically, the elements of politics are presented through the same analysis as in the first edition. But there are many changes in the method of argument and application. The discussion has been strengthened by inclusion of more examples from modern American politics, which are balanced by new illustrations from other contemporary systems and from earlier periods. Since the analysis of politics in terms of its constituent issues is meant to be universal in scope, I have felt it should be applied to the major political developments of the six years (1953–1959) since the book was written. Attention has therefore been paid to such topics as race relations in the United States and abroad, the success of anticolonial movements, the post-Stalin era in Russia, and the implications of moon rockets and space satellites.

Some of the alterations are based on critical suggestions which I have received from several scholars. In particular, my thanks are due to Professors Avery Leiserson, Arthur Maass, and Richard M. Rosecrance. One ingenious friend has proposed that the title of a second edition should be reworded: "The *Greater* Issues of Politics." I was tempted to make that change, but realized that such a revision, while logically permitting extension to a possible third edition, would preclude anything beyond that. Optimistically, therefore, I have kept the original title. Finally, I record my warm appreciation to the publishers whose continuous cooperation and technical advice have been invaluable.

Preface

TO THE FIRST EDITION

Every book should capture and, as far as possible, reproduce the spirit of its subject matter. As interpreted here, politics is the arena of controversy about some permanent issues which must be faced constantly but may be variously solved. The solutions differ in method as they do in substance. Sometimes the method is to use violence, though at a more mature level discussion is employed. Discussion captures the essence of controversy by its appraisal of alternatives, presentation of pros and cons, and review of practice and experiment.

The best way to discover truth, as ancient philosophers observed, is through the interplay of viewpoints and exchange of information which discussion supplies. Books are the next best substitute for direct discussion face-to-face, and this book explores the nature of politics by engaging in a discussion with the reader. Although plenty of factual material is contained in these pages, it is not my primary intention to cram the reader's mind with masses of descriptive data concerning the structure of government and the operations of the state. That method, though leaving the reader with a sense of repletion of a sort, can be harmful to one's intellectual digestive system. Learning facts is not identical with understanding their significance, and of the two the latter is far more important.

To understand politics it is necessary not only to know what has happened and is happening, but, even more, to grasp its meaning. The materials of politics consist of historical events, of opinions about them, and of ideal aspirations for what might be. Such data become significant when marshaled and classified in terms of the basic problems that form the kernel of the political process, for neither the actual nor the ideal makes sense unless it is fitted into a conceptual framework.

My aim in writing this book has been to suggest to those who are concerned about politics a method of analysis which I have found helpful in understanding a complex subject and which I hope will be helpful to others. What is attempted here is to explain the character of politics by a systematic treatment of its fundamental issues, which first are analyzed separately and then are studied in unison. Throughout this work the alternative solutions to the several issues are illustrated by examples chosen from different historical periods, by comparisons of contrasted types of government, and by the arguments between rival philosophies. Each issue, however, is discussed in the manner that seems most appropriate to its elucidation rather than in accordance with a stereotyped, uniform pattern. The organization of some chapters, therefore, is primarily analytical; of others, chronological. In some cases, history predominates over philosophy; elsewhere, it is the reverse.

A survey chart of the great issues of politics is provided at the end of the book.

A number of friends were generous of their time in reading the whole manuscript or sections of it and have given me valuable criticisms. I record here my debt to the late Lloyd H. Fisher and to Pedro Muñoz Amato, Roy C. Macridis, Peter H. Odegard, Frank M. Russell, and Robert A. Scalapino. To William A. Pullin of Prentice-Hall I am grateful for expert editorial guidance. My wife has given me many fruitful suggestions and her constant encouragement. The dedication to the youngest of my family is inadequate recompense for all those occasions when priorities of writing deprived father and son of each other's company.

LESLIE LIPSON

Acknowledgments

Quotations from the works of other writers have been reprinted in this book with the consent of the following publishers whose kind permission is herewith acknowledged:

Jonathan Cape, Ltd., London; Doubleday & Company, Inc., New York; and the Trustees of the T. E. Lawrence Estate; for the excerpt from *The Seven Pillars of Wisdom* by T. E. Lawrence.

The Clarendon Press of Oxford, England, for the excerpt from W. Hamilton Fyfe's translation of Tacitus' *Germania*.

J. M. Dent & Sons, Ltd., London, and E. P. Dutton & Co., Inc., New York, for passages from the *Republic* by Plato, translated by A. D. Lindsay; *Leviathan* by Hobbes; *Second Treatise of Civil Government* by Locke; *Discourse on Political Economy* by Rousseau, translated by G. D. H. Cole; *The Federalist* by Hamilton, Madison, and Jay; *Utilitarianism, Liberty and Representative Government* by Mill; all printed in Everyman's Library.

Hafner Publishing Co., Inc., New York, for the excerpt from Montesquieu's *Spirit of the Laws*, translated by Thomas Nugent and introduced by Franz L. Neumann, in the Hafner Library of Classics.

Harcourt, Brace & World, Inc., New York, and John Murray, Publishers, Ltd., London, for the excerpt from *Religion and the Rise of Capitalism* by R. H. Tawney.

Holt, Rinehart & Winston, Inc., New York, for the excerpt from *American Government* by William Anderson.

Houghton Mifflin Company, Boston, for excerpts from the English translation of *Mein Kampf* by Adolf Hitler.

Alfred A. Knopf, Inc., New York, for a passage from *Man and His Works* by Melville J. Herskovits and one from *Mutual Aid* by Peter Kropotkin in the English translation.

Longmans, Green & Co., Inc., New York, for an excerpt from *Illustrated English Social History* by G. M. Trevelyan.

The Macmillan Company, New York, for passages from *Economic Interpretation of the Constitution of the United States* by Charles A. Beard, *The Web of Government* by Robert M. MacIver, and *The Encyclopedia of the Social Sciences.*

John Murray, Publishers, Ltd., London, for the extract from *An Arab Philosophy of History,* edited by Charles Issawi in The Wisdom of the East Series.

W. W. Norton & Company, Inc., New York, for the passage from *The Revolt of the Masses,* by Ortega y Gasset.

Oxford University Press, Inc., New York, for excerpts from *The English Constitution* by Walter Bagehot, printed in *World's Classics,* and *The Modern Democratic State* by A. D. Lindsay.

Pantheon Books, Inc., New York, for the quotation from Boris Pasternak's *Doctor Zhivago.*

Penguin Books, Inc., Baltimore, for the passage from *What Happened in History,* by V. Gordon Childe.

The Round Table of London, for the quotation from the issue of June, 1954.

St. Martin's Press, Inc., New York, and Macmillan & Co., Ltd., London, for the passage from *The Golden Bough* by James Frazer.

Mrs. George Bambridge, Doubleday & Company, Inc., New York, Macmillan Company of Canada, and Methuen & Co., Ltd., London, for the quotation from *The Seven Seas* by Rudyard Kipling.

The Great Issues
of Politics

As I was born a citizen of a free State and a member of the Sovereign, I feel that, however feeble the influence my voice can have on public affairs, the right of voting on them makes it my duty to study them.

ROUSSEAU

But howsoever, an argument from the Practise of men, that have not sifted to the bottom, and with exact reason weighed the causes, and nature of Common-wealths, and suffer daily those miseries, that proceed from the ignorance thereof, is invalid. For though in all places of the world, men should lay the foundation of their houses on the sand, it could not thence be inferred that so it ought to be. The skill of making, and maintaining Common-wealths, consists in certain Rules, as doth Arithmetique and Geometry; not (as Tennis-play) on Practise only: which Rules, neither poor men have the leisure, nor men that have had the leisure, have hitherto had the curiosity, or the method to find out.

HOBBES

In so complicated a science as political economy no one axiom can be laid down as wise and expedient for all times and circumstances and for their contraries.

JEFFERSON

1

Introduction to
the Study of Politics

MAN AND HIS ENVIRONMENT

Understanding is the beginning of freedom. For freedom consists in being masters of our fates; and never, except by luck or accident, can we control what we do not understand. There is a part of the environment that has come to us from nature and exists, as we exist, without our having created it. The rest is the product of human effort both in past generations and in the present. As yet, neither the physical environment nor the man-made portion is wholly known to us. Perhaps some ultimates are not completely knowable. But yearly, as research advances and experience accumulates, the areas that are known grow broader and deeper.

Even so, extensions of knowledge, while they augment our understanding, do not always enlarge the capacity for control. Particularly this holds true for our relation to nature, some of whose phenomena are alterable by man while others are not. To the latter we must adapt ourselves; the former we can learn to use intelligently and not abuse. For instance, a geologist studies the nature of earthquakes, until conceivably he may fully comprehend them. But he can neither cause them nor prevent their occurring. The astronomer and physicist observe the sun and planets and discover the shape and motions of the earth. Yet despite all increases in our information about heavenly phenomena, these lie entirely beyond human influence. Never shall we change the stars in their courses or slow the cooling of the sun or stop this earth from spinning in its orbit. In such matters, the best way open to us (in fact, the only way) is to accept the given necessities, adjust to their requirements, and design our patterns of life accordingly. In other cases, however, we are ourselves the determinants of nature, since our use or abuse of natural forces produces results that we have caused. Here it is our own actions that work for our weal or woe. Though we cannot arrest a hurricane or divert a tidal wave, we can control and harness a river. We did not make the soil off which we live. But we can exhaust or restore its fertility, provoke erosion or reclaim a desert, or even, as the Dutch do, snatch land from the ocean.

Granted these facts, what does it require to relate ourselves to nature in a rational manner? Our first task has to be an exercise of intellect. We must learn the operation of the physical forces that manifest themselves in the universe and understand the connections of cause and effect. At an unsophisticated level, people have tried to do this by methods that are erroneous because their users are misinformed about the nature of things. A primitive man, who thinks an eclipse of the sun is the work of demons, beats a drum or sounds the temple gongs to scare away the evil spirits. He is assuming connections that do not exist in reality. Not comprehending the cause of the phenomenon, he mistakes its "cure" and believes in his own ability to influence an event over which he has no control. The same mistake, in reverse, is made today by the equally primitive persons who consult astrologers. They think that the location of stars and planets at a particular moment has the effect of shaping a personality and molding an individual's life. Neither of these attitudes is rational. They leap beyond the available evidence, they take fictions for facts, they assume causes and powers that are mythical. The rational method consists in acquiring accurate knowledge about physical forces and how they function. Human freedom vis-à-vis nature depends on learning to conform where we must and to control where we can. Against earthquakes, buildings can be so constructed that they will withstand shocks more readily, serving to mitigate the danger. In other spheres, applying scientific data through technology, we can navigate a ship across an ocean or fly an airplane around the globe. Further than that, we can launch a satellite into orbit around the earth, propel a rocket beyond the reach of terrestrial gravity, and send human beings to the moon.

THE SOCIAL FRAMEWORK

Do the same considerations apply to the other part of our environment—the part that is made by man? Is the same combination to be found here as in the physical environment? Is the social order also a mixture of the inevitable to which we must somehow adjust and the malleable, which we can make and remake? The answers to these questions are fundamental. Upon them hinges our picture of social man either as flotsam drifting along the stream of events or as a regulator directing their flow. From them derive two views of political man: as the creature of his institutions or their creator. Both positions have their supporters—which should indicate that there is some plausible evidence to be argued on each side. Since this is a book about the political aspect of the man-made environment, it involves, as does any attempt at systematic treatment, a series of assumptions about the nature of man and his social context. These assumptions, whether concealed or explicit, will color the conclusions that follow. It is best, therefore, to mention at the outset some of the concepts that permeate this work, so that the reader may know how the trail is constructed and where it may lead.

In brief, the concepts that underlie the following discussion are these. Our relations with the social environment and the physical are not the same. In physics there are some necessities; in politics there are none. The study of politics can never arrive at more than generalizations, to which there are always exceptions—whether more or less. Such words as "inevitable," "insoluble," and "never" are inappropriate to the vocabulary of politics. Nothing in this sphere is predetermined for us beyond the human power to change it. Nothing that we have inherited or are now doing is exempt from our capacity to keep or eventually alter. All social conduct, social organization, and social institutions are the product of human activity, past and present. Being wholly man-made, they are not necessitated for us by external, and partly uncontrollable, forces. Rather are they molded through causes that originate in man himself. Hence they do not contain anything which could not be changed by human will. Whatever blessings we enjoy in civilization are the fruits of man's own work. By the same logic, so too are many of the curses. Poverty, ignorance, unemployment, despotism, and war—which are among the worst scourges that afflict humanity—generally wreak more disaster than do hurricanes, droughts, earthquakes, or volcanoes. But, whereas the latter are not of our making, the causes of the former lie within humanity's power when our own doings turn to our undoing. A fortiori, therefore, where the causes spring, resides the cure. This no one should doubt: men can change what men have made.[1]

---

[1] It is a basic human trait that we apply intelligence to reorder our environment with a purpose. That this was characteristic of primitive men has recently been stressed by an archaeologist in his introduction to a monumental comparative survey of the earliest known societies: "All these assaults by man upon his surroundings, every exploitation of his fellow-animals or of the familiar plants around him, each intrusion of human will

All this implies that society can be made intelligible and that politics is a sphere of purposeful behavior through which we seek to live better than we do now. Treated as a subject of study, the content of politics can be clarified by rational analysis. Conducted as a practical art, the substance of politics may be improved by the values we choose to apply. When the results of understanding enlarge our powers, the use of reason can bring self-liberation. Before there can be action, however, there must be decision; before decision, a choice among alternative values; before choice, deliberation; before deliberation, knowledge. Our minds must analyze before our will decides.

THE ANT'S-EYE VIEW OF SOCIETY

But it will be apparent that this picture of political man, while it depicts what he sometimes does and ideally should always do, is far from being a portrayal of customary political behavior. There are times, indeed, when we seem, not the masters of our social fate, but the slaves of circumstance; when the paths of rationality and freedom are blocked by obstacles; when politics, far from yielding inspiration and betterment, bears all the stigmata of cruelty, chaos, and chance. For a variety of reasons we are less successful than we might be in treating the maladies of a disordered world. First is a mass inertia that arises from widespread passivity. There are many who fear the disturbances that accompany the process of innovation and doubt their ability to control its course. Frequently, therefore, they resign themselves to known evils rather than risk the unpredictable chances of change. Second, to a much larger extent than we consciously realize, we are creatures of habit and captives of the past; and though it is to the past that we also owe whatever freedoms we enjoy, the sanctity of age has the effect of prolonging many practices which restrict the opportunity to invent and improve. Our home upbringing, our school education, our civic training, tend to stamp on each of us an imprint of the surrounding social order, to whose design the adult behavior of the great majority generally conforms. Moreover, that design has resulted from the slow accumulation of labors which occupied many centuries and deposited their legacy in the institutions, procedures,

---

into the natural order of things, mark the emergence of man as an animal differentiated from the rest of his kind by the deliberate intention behind his acts, rather than a blind response to instinct. Civilization, however defined, is something essentially artificial and man-made, and to that extent self-conscious. A human community is one deliberately organised, and not the outcome of such a pattern of reflexes as produced the ant-heap or the bee-hive." Stuart Piggott in *The Dawn of Civilization* (London: Thames and Hudson, Ltd., 1962), p. 12.

and ideas which we inherit. All our yesterdays have shaped us into what we are, and that makes it difficult for a single generation to undo or speedily refashion the work of so many. When the philosopher Diderot proposed his ideas for governmental reform, the Empress Catherine of Russia responded to him in these words: "Ah, my dear friend, you write upon paper, the smooth surface of which presents no obstacle to your pen. But I, poor Empress that I am, must write on the skins of my subjects which are sensitive and ticklish to an extraordinary degree."[2]

Nor is the paralysis of the will that stems from habit or timidity the only impediment to progress. Action can also be inhibited by paralysis of the intellect. Before we act, most of us want to be reasonably sure about what we are doing or whither we intend to move. Not only do we disagree about our objectives and the means of realizing them, but we cannot always be sure about our diagnosis of current ills and their causes. We may be dedicated to fine ideals which we call democracy, freedom, justice, welfare. But we dispute their definition because each can mean different things to different people, and the applicability of an abstract notion to particular circumstances is always arguable. We dislike depressions. We condemn injustice. We hate wars. We want to prevent these from starting, or, when they begin, we want to end them. But do we know for certain what their causes are and can we confidently prescribe how they may be avoided in the future? Considering that so much is at stake in the policies which governments choose, how high is the probability that our answers will be correct?

Many of the puzzles that confront us when we face the problems of our social system and seek remedies for them have a common source in this fact: human society is composed of millions of persons and social processes are the sum-product of numberless individual actions. In order to decipher this confusing network of contacts between people, we study the past; we keep note of contemporary events; we look around at our fellow men and at ourselves placed in their midst. But seeing is not the same as having insight. Sometimes we feel as bewildered as if we gazed, uncomprehending, at an ant heap and saw a swarm whose movements we observe but whose meaning we do not fathom. It is hard to obtain an overall view of a complex society, to detect the details that are significant and relate those that are causally connected with others. It is even hard for an individual to be certain of his own position within the group to which he belongs or to recognize what quota he contributes, in however infinitesimal a degree, to

---

[2]Quoted in R. H. Murray, *Studies in English Social and Political Thinkers of the Nineteenth Century* (Cambridge: Heffer and Sons, 1929), I, 157.

a general social mosaic which all have helped to piece together but none has planned. At a time when the economy undergoes inflation, the majority seek to protect themselves by boosting prices, pressing for higher wages, charging bigger fees. Yet, if too many behave alike, the net effect is that nobody benefits since no one, relatively, is better off. The same can happen in an armaments race, where governments that distrust one another pursue security severally by methods that yield collective insecurity. Rather than act blindly, we search for a rationale, a principle of cause and effect, a set of laws perhaps, that will make the relationships plain. Failing that, the behavior of a mass of men often reenacts the tragedy of Hamlet. For our doubts bring indecision and lead to postponement and delay.

> And thus the native hue of resolution
> Is sicklied o'er with the pale cast of thought,
> And enterprises of great pith and moment
> With this regard their currents turn awry
> And lose the name of action.

INFORMATION AND UNDERSTANDING

The price we pay for ignorance about ourselves and our works is to be placed in servitude to others or to circumstance. Several thousand years ago a revolution occurred in politics when law was first committed to writing, instead of being deposited in the memory of a few and passed on from mouth to mouth. Once written, it could more easily be known and studied, its interpretation disputed, and officials punished for not adhering to the text. How significant was that change is shown by the example of contemporary states where the decisions of government continue to be shrouded in mystery and ordinary people are in the grip of tyranny. If "the proper study of mankind," therefore, "is man," as Pope said, the primary duty of Man the Citizen is to learn about the state. This is something that each owes to himself for the simple reason that government touches everybody and consequently all of us have a common interest in its actions. But an understanding of the state is also our duty to society, because the isolationist from politics is like the tax evader who dodges his share of public responsibility.

Even in states that make a virture of publicity and expect their citizens to participate in politics, the difficulties in the path of understanding, and thus controlling, a modern government are truly formidable. Not only are its operations obscured by their vastness and complexity, but the information about it is now so detailed and voluminous as well-nigh to baffle the inquiring intellect. Anybody who wants visual proof of this fact has only to observe the size of the catalog at the Library of Congress or visit the ever-expanding collections of public archives or scan the corridors of records in the filing division of a great department. The single episode of General MacArthur's dismissal by President Truman in 1951 occasioned a congressional inquiry whose hearings and testimony filled over 8,000 pages of print. The assassination of President Kennedy was exhaustively investigated for ten months by a commission that set forth its findings in a report of 300,000 words and in 26 bulky volumes of testimony. Year by year, the task of digesting these enormous amounts of material—all the statutes and statistics, debates and directives, opinions and orders—becomes increasingly difficult. Our civilization sinks neck-deep in paper, and those who would think about its problems risk being crushed by the sheer weight of documentation.

Paradoxically, therefore, the sense of helplessness that overwhelms a citizen when government vests its works in secrecy may be repeated under the opposite conditions. Though public acts are subject to public scrutiny, an individual who contemplates the mass of data awaiting his observation and study is apt to feel dwarfed in the presence of his subject. How is he to encompass, for instance, such a phenomenon as the American political system, wherein the federal government alone operated in 1969 on an annual budget approaching two hundred billion dollars and employed a civil service of nearly three million persons? How can he grasp all the ramifications of so much money, of so many officials? He is consequently tempted to shrug his shoulders in disgust and, abandoning the search for insight, to lapse into indifference. Or, thinking that reason has failed him and that politics is incapable of rational explanation, he may escape into uncritical worship of a leader or into notions that government is determined, independently of his willing, by some uncontrollable forces—whether he supposes them materialistic or supernatural. The result in either case will be the same: the governed will lie at the mercy of their rulers.

In the field of technology, necessity has been called the mother of invention. Necessity in politics is the mother of defeatism. Indeed, many doctrines advanced during the last hundred years have invited this fatalistic attitude. The Marxian concept of economic determinism, for instance, regards the form of government as something that is necessitated by basic productive relationships, in which view politics is considered an epilogue to economics.[3] To like effect are the teach-

---

[3] In the *Communist Manifesto* Marx asserted: "The executive of the modern State is but a committee for managing the common affairs of the whole bourgeoisie." See also Chap. 4, pp. 113–14.

ings of many a contemporary psychologist, sociologist, and anthropologist, whose principal concern is to explain how we behave in terms of the influences exerted upon us and to emphasize what the environment does to us rather than what we can do with the environment. Thus, whether they intend it or not, their image of man is a puppet who struts and grimaces according to the pulls of external compulsion. Nor can it be denied that such explanations have some color of plausibility if men are seen only in the light of their past ancestry and the present pressures that limit their opportunities to choose. But the net effect of such theorizing, when unqualified, is not so much to set men free as to persuade them to resign themselves to their lot.

HUMAN NATURE IN POLITICS

Rousseau's political classic *The Social Contract* opens with the words: "Man is born free, yet everywhere he is in irons." He would have been nearer to the truth, however, had he written: "Men are born helpless, but everywhere they have the capacity to become free." Also, one should add, they have the capacity to conduct their lives better than they now do. In politics, everything can be found that is contained within man himself—love, will, passion, and hatred, as well as memory, learning, and logical thought; kindness and mercy along with cruelty and evil. Many contemporary students of society have derived their image of man from those schools of psychology, Freudian psychoanalysis included, which interpret mankind in mechanistic, behavioral, and manipulative terms. There is however, another school of contemporary psychologists (known as the third force) who reject such pessimistic assumptions. They see in every human being a vast reservoir of potentialities, most of which are untapped and, therefore, wasted. Those rare individuals who succeed in attaining the highest level of development are the self-actualized. They are distinguished for their own creative growth and their humanitarian concern for their fellowman. The lives of such persons consist in a ceaseless quest for the higher values—goodness, truth, beauty—whose formulation endows our species with its uniquely human quality.[4]

Up to a point, our understanding of politics can be, and is, susceptible to a strictly rational analysis. Reason alone does not encompass everything, however, nor does it possess a monopoly of truth. Knowledge about human nature will come to the psychologist in the clinic

---

[4]On this subject, see the forthcoming book by Elizabeth Monroe Drews on *The Creative Intellectual Style* (to be published by Prentice-Hall, Inc.).

or to the psychoanalyst from the couch. But insights undiscoverable by the methods of science have no less surely been divined by poets, artists, and moral philosophers. Our ultimate assumptions about man—especially about his potentiality for creative growth and ethical advance—must always be a blend of reason and faith.

Since the state is constructed entirely of, by, and for human beings, its study is a kind of self-analysis. Complete detachment of view is, therefore, impossible. Because the political scientist is personally involved in his subject matter, his understanding will be colored to some extent by his own preferences. Nor is this necessarily a fault. Personal involvement may sometimes contribute to clearer insight. If each of us is aware of how he responds to war, taxes, elections, the flag, and so on, and is honest with himself in recognizing his own attitudes, he has some clues to help gauge the responses of others. Hence, being a participant should not disqualify a person from also acting as an interpreter. Even so, to be spectator and critic of a play while one is also in the cast imposes a special problem of orientation. From what angle of vision should the action be viewed, and how are its speed and direction to be estimated? Can we pass judgment or reach a wise decision when we ourselves are immersed in the midstream of events?

AMERICAN FOREIGN POLICY AS AN EXAMPLE

To illustrate these difficulties, some examples will help. If we refer to one or two of the burning issues of our time, we should be able to discern the implications they contain. Take the recent controversies over American foreign policy. These originated in a choice between isolationism or an active role of international leadership. The basic facts and their explanation are not obscure. Upon achieving independence, the people of the United States acquired the power to choose their own form of government and initiate their own policies both at home and abroad. Under the system then in vogue, mankind was divided politically into nation-states whose jurisdiction was complete and self-contained. The bigger, more powerful states did, it is true, make others their subjects. But the accepted ideal was to become autonomous or, as it was called, sovereign, and to this ideal the United States expressed its adherence when emancipating itself from colonial rule.

During its first century of nationhood the principal influences exerted upon the United States combined to underscore the virtue of independence, and to envisage it within a context of isolation. The energies of Americans were directed to their initial task of filling a continent and deploying the principles of the Constitution from the

Atlantic to the Pacific. Preoccupied with internal problems and expanding westward, the country focused its attention on the New World and turned its back upon the Old. This attitude came naturally to immigrants, many of whom, escaping from poverty and persecution, wished to be rid of Europe. In the economic sphere, isolation was a practicable policy, as long as there were abundant resources still to be exploited in the continental United States and the technology of production did not yet require the importation of basic raw materials. In its military aspects, too, the policy was adequate to the needs of people who were sheltered by two oceans, who faced no military rival on the American continent, and who had achieved a reconciliation with Britain. The proof of its adequacy, moreover, lies in the fact that between the War of Independence and World War I, the United States was embroiled in only one major holocaust which endangered its security and survival—and that war was a civil one.

The twentieth century has subjected traditional concepts to the challenge of new situations in all corners of the globe. The decline of British power, due to that country's loss of its earlier industrial lead and the growing maturity of its former colonies; the rise of an aggressively militaristic Germany and Japan; the revolution in Russia and the spread of Communist party dictatorships; the interlocking of American and foreign economies in wider union; and finally the advent of the airplane, rocket, and atomic bomb—such developments, by changing the character of the world, reformulated the conditions of American security and prosperity. The United States participated in World War I because it was not in its interest to see the eastern Atlantic controlled by an expansionist undemocratic power, but subsequently the U.S. relapsed into its former isolation. From this wishful but ineffective detachment, the American people were roughly shaken by Hitler's subjugation of the European continent and the Japanese onslaught against Southeast Asia and our positions in the Pacific. Hence at the conclusion of World War II, the United States took care not to repeat the mistake it had made a quarter of a century earlier. Not only did this country join the United Nations, which it helped to found, but soon thereafter, in the face of Stalinist expansion, it participated in a network of alliances, both bilateral and multilateral, seeking to establish systems of collective security in Western Europe, Southeast Asia, the Pacific Ocean, and Latin America.

In this new role of international leadership, the United States moved in the 1950's as far in accepting commitments all around the globe as it had previously gone in avoiding them. By the end of that decade this country had undertaken to participate in protecting some 44 states whose governments ranged along all degrees on a scale from the reputable and reliable to the chaotic and corrupt. Abandonment of the earlier isolationism led quickly to the opposite excess—a policy of interventionism, which realized its disastrous climax in the squalid war in Vietnam. Consequently, at the beginning of the 1970's Americans were asking these basic questions about our foreign policy: What are the vital interests of the United States abroad for whose protection we should be prepared to commit American manpower? What are our other interests which, however important, are not vital to this country's security and survival? Since we are not omnipotent, what are the limits of our power? Where should we draw the line between leadership and restraint?

Such a summary of how American foreign policy evolved from the Declaration of Independence to recent declarations of interdependence touches upon a wide variety of problems. If we are to say what policy is "right" or "best," we must first ask what are the objectives which a nation pursues in its external relations. Do those objectives remain constant or do they alter? When a people expands in territory, numbers, and economic and military might, when means of destruction and speed of communication with other powers are revolutionized, do these changed circumstances explain—and do they justify—a shift from avoidance to acceptance of international commitments? If so, how many commitments are enough? What issues are involved here? By what criteria do we decide? By what compass can we steer?

Some other changes, equally momentous, can also be mentioned. In the United States over a century ago, individual freedom was restricted by the existence of slavery in one-half of the Union. Nor had equality of political rights for citizens yet been achieved. Women were nowhere permitted to vote. In certain states, men could qualify for the suffrage only if their property or income reached a specified amount. From such limitations it is a far remove to the vast electorate[5] that makes its choice nowadays between the Democratic and Republican candidates for the presidency. What human values are involved in this numerical increase of the voting public? What political considerations prompted the extension of the suffrage? How has that change affected other sectors of the governmental system? In view of the fact that the same period which witnessed the movement toward greater equalitarianism has also experienced an enlargement of the functions of government, it is natural to ask whether the two changes are connected, and, if so, which has been responsible for the other. Furthermore, what is at stake in the different attitudes with which men

---

[5]Even today, however, the potential electorate exceeds the number of registered voters. See Chap. 5, pp. 133–37.

regard the spread of state activity? Some maintain that the least governed are governed best, while others deem it the responsibility of the state to provide for its citizens' welfare. In the early decades of American nationhood the commercial interests, represented by the Federalist party and by Alexander Hamilton, favored a vigorous extension of federal authority. In recent decades, the policy of businessmen in general has been opposed to the federal government's expansion. Many of those who were on the liberal side of the political spectrum in Jefferson's day were distrustful of government and suspicious of any powers it wielded. Many contemporary liberals, on the other hand, argue for a positive conception of the state, giving it plenty to do and requiring much power to do it.

PERMANENT PROBLEMS, CHANGING SOLUTIONS

Changes of this kind, which sometimes appear mystifying, do not necessarily indicate that the political process is one of random caprice or that politicians are hopelessly opportunistic. There are reasons for such differences of policy and for shifting from one choice to another. Indeed, the very fact that alternatives are possible suggests a method of analyzing the state and understanding its politics. This book is written in the belief that political history and contemporary government exhibit certain patterns which render them meaningful. If once these patterns are made clear, numerous events, which otherwise appear chaotic and confusing, fall into place. The remark has been made by a student of military affairs that weapons and equipment may change, but the principles of strategy remain constant. For example, whether one fights with bows and arrows or with jet-driven airplanes and atomic bombs, there are always identical problems of morale, training, discipline, and supplies; of deploying the right amount of strength in the right place at the right time; and so on. The subject of politics can be approached in similar fashion. Because our lives are spent amid such flux and turmoil, what tends nowadays to impress us most is a continuous need to adjust, individually and collectively, to technological invention, social innovation, rapidity of movement, economic instability, threats of war, and doubting of long-held ethical values. Nobody would deny the importance of this element of change or the need to explain it. But at the same time it is incumbent on the political scientist to discover, if he can, any factors that are constant.

The analysis offered in this book attempts to fill these two requirements. It supplies an interpretation of politics in terms of certain ever-present fundamentals and it reveals the rhythms of their variations and mutations. There are, to put it briefly, certain basic issues which all governments face and must somehow settle. These issues form the substance of politics. They are permanent. They never disappear. They cannot be evaded. They do allow, however, for alternative solutions which leave mankind with the possibility of choosing and of substituting one preference for another. Because changes occur in the context within which these problems are tackled, change itself is as constant a factor as the issues. Conditions, techniques, methods, and institutions are highly variable. Political systems resemble one another, or differ, according to their respective preferences for solving each basic issue and combining the solutions. In this way it is possible to distinguish intelligibly between the political characteristics of broad historical periods, such as classical antiquity, the Middle Ages, the modern nation-state; and of contrasted systems, such as dictatorship or democracy, class rule or equalitarianism, nationalism or international organization.

THE GREAT ISSUES

The issues which form the core or content of the political process are five in number. The first issue concerns the people who are the subjects and objects of political activity. Because they are associated within the state, they must stand in some kind of relation to each other. What is that to be? Are all members placed on an equal footing? Or are some superior to the rest? The same question may be differently phrased. Is citizenship exclusive or all-inclusive? If the former, then the people who make up a state are divided into two groups: one having rights of full citizenship, and the other treated as inferiors or subjects. If citizenship is all-inclusive, however, then everybody enjoys the same basic status without discrimination or limitation. The governing principle is a regime of privilege in one case, of equality in the other.

The next issue arises from controversy over the functions that the state performs for its members. Originating in the need for protection,[6] the state has traditionally widened the sphere of its activities. The question is thus inevitably presented, whether there are, or are not, any limits to what the state can effectively, and should rightfully, undertake. On this point schools of philosophy, as well as practices of politics, have been opposed from times ancient to the present. Some have held that no social activity and no group can, or should, be exempt from the jurisdiction of the state. Others maintain that somewhere a boundary line must be set within which the state may freely move, but outside of which it trespasses on alien ground.

[6]This point is developed in Chap. 3, pp. 61–66.

Both the third and fourth issues deal with the subject of authority, which enables the state to perform its functions, but they are occupied with different aspects of it. One problem is that of determining the source from which authority is derived. This question has become acute because, in order to provide services to its citizens, the state needs to acquire and exercise power. Since its powers are funneled into the hands of the government, and since the officials who compose the latter are numerically fewer than the rest of the community, the relation of government to governed becomes a debatable issue. Those who govern, besides claiming authority, seek to justify their use of it; the governed may try to retain the ultimate control over political power. If the distribution of power within the state is conceived in terms of a pyramid,[7] the government can be likened to the apex, and the remainder of the people to the base. Authority can then be imagined either to stem from the base and travel upward to the apex, or to originate in the apex, like the goddess Athena in the ancient myth springing fully armed from the head of Zeus, and flow downward to the base. Under the first view, the government would be controlled by, and be responsible to, the people. Under the second, the people are subjects to those who govern and are duty-bound to obey their commands.

The query about its source, however, is not the only fundamental issue which the existence and establishment of authority evoke. Irrespective of where it originates—from the base of the pyramid or its apex—another issue concerns the manner in which authority, however derived, is subsequently organized. It is possible, on the one hand, to have power concentrated at a single focal point. Or power can be subdivided into powers which are dispersed and diffused. These can be parceled out among separate branches of the government and distributed between different levels. Either the introduction of checks and balances or their removal may be sought, and the machinery of government will vary accordingly.

There remains as the fifth basic political issue the problem of magnitude—both of the area which the state covers and the population it contains, and the connected problem of relations between separate states. How large or small should be the unit of government? What is the optimum size for a state? Are there limits to its dimensions which the state should not exceed? How are independent states related? These are vexing questions in the cogitations of political theorists and the calculations of statecraft. Since the Western world has already experimented with units as diverse as the city-state, nation-state, and

[7] As Robert M. MacIver suggests in *The Web of Government* (New York: The Macmillan Company, 1947), Chap. 5.

empire-state, and continues to strive for new forms of international organization, it is evident that much can be learned from comparing governments of small, middle, large, and mammoth scale, and observing the patterns of interstate politics.

ANALYSIS OF THE GREAT ISSUES

These five issues can be summarized as follows:

1. The coverage of citizenship: Should this be exclusive or all-inclusive?
2. The functions of the state: Should its sphere of activity be limited or unlimited?
3. The source of authority: Should this originate in the people or the government?
4. The structure of authority: Should power be concentrated or dispersed?
5. The magnitude of the state and its external relations: What unit of government is preferable and operable? What interstate system is desired?

Logically, each is distinct from the rest. Each, moreover, can be analyzed alone because each is pivoted around a unique problem. The first issue deals with the reciprocal rights and duties of members of the state; the second, with the scope or ambit of governmental functions; the third, with the birthplace and legitimizing of authority; the fourth, with the institutionalizing of power; and the last, with the size of territory and population. The significant feature in all these issues is that they present an opportunity to choose between at least two possibilities. This is self-evident in a sense, because the factor of choice marks the essence of the problem. If there were no room to choose, there could be no issue. The breadth of the choice which is presented under the various issues can be envisaged in the form of this series of contrasts:

The First Issue is the choice between equality and inequality.

The Second Issue is the choice between a pluralist and a monistic state.

The Third Issue is the choice between freedom and dictatorship.

The Fourth Issue is the choice between a dispersion of powers and their unification.

The Fifth Issue is the choice between a multitude of states and a universal state.

Thus described, the choice appears to lie between two alternatives in every case. In actuality, however, as will appear later, there are usually more than two possibilities, because several issues permit solutions at various intermediate stages between the opposite poles. Thus the functions undertaken by government can be more or less limited. Powers can be more or less dispersed. There may be more or less freedom, and so on.

Here, therefore, is a way to make the political process intelligible. The key to its understanding is that five basic issues are involved, and that all admit a choice. The types of government, and the consequent character of the state, vary with the respective decisions. Since there are so many issues, and at least two solutions for each, the permutations and combinations of political patterns are numerous indeed. It is this variety which constitutes the fascination and the challenge alike to those who practice the art of politics, and to those who systematize its study into a body of organized knowledge. No group of men can establish a government without being confronted by these five issues, nor can they avoid the necessity of including some decision about each in the pattern of the state they choose. Every kind of state embodies an institutionalized answer to the basic problems with which the five issues are concerned. A student of politics cannot find any governmental system of nonnomadic peoples in any place or at any period that does not provide its solution of these issues. Wherever the Great Issues are, there is found the political process. Wherever the political process is, there are the Great Issues. Such an analysis, moreover, has the merit of interpreting this process in terms of dynamic motion. For no solution is ever fixed or final. All government has a touch of the experimental and the temporary. Men change their preferences. They oscillate between one pole and another. Ceaselessly they reconstruct the outer facade and inner floor plan of their state.

SYNTHESIS OF THE GREAT ISSUES

Such changes are conditioned, however, by another fact. It was suggested above that each issue is unique and can be distinctly analyzed. In logic that holds true, but only in logic. Reality does not correspond perfectly to its principles; neither, therefore, can the analysis of its character. For elucidating the nature of politics, one should take a cue from the comment of Marc Chagall on the painting he had executed for the ceiling of the Paris Opera: "There is nothing precise in it. One cannot be precise and still be true." In the practice of politics, the issues are never entirely isolable and separate. Instead, they are connected, and in life they interact. Nobody is able, therefore, to say precisely where one stops and another begins. Their edges are ragged, not sharp. Somewhere, their contents merge together. Analysis of political complexities into five issues, each having its varying solutions, is an aid in simplification. Yet it would be oversimplification, and hence distortion, if politics was finally represented as an amalgam of five categories tacked on to each other. The analogy of a watch may help to explain this. We divide the dial arbitrarily into 12 hours and 60 minutes. These partitions are needed because they show the time at a given moment. But time itself is a continuum. It is a ceaseless, unbroken flow. And so it is with politics. When all analysis is done, the need remains for resynthesis. As governments operate in reality, the five issues act upon and interact with each other, just as the second and minute hands move simultaneously with the hour hand. Indeed, whatever choice is adopted in politics, under the heading of any issue, can scarcely fail to have some effect on the decisions concerning the remainder. Thus a change anywhere tends to promote accompanying changes elsewhere. The history of politics, described in one sentence, consists in trying out alternative solutions for the basic issues in altered combinations.

THE METHOD AND ITS IMPLICATIONS

This approach to the subject involves not only a definite picture of the content of politics, but also a certain way of studying it. As between matter and method, nobody can doubt the relative priority. In any field of learning the substance to be understood must determine the methodology. That order should never be reversed, nor should a commitment to a particular method be allowed to dictate one's view of the subject. In this particular case, the characterization of politics as an arena of controversial choices in five substantive topics invites an appropriate methodology.

To begin with, since it is the nature of politics which we seek to comprehend, we would be mistaken in limiting our attention to the contemporary period or to events of recent memory. One cannot properly grasp the meaning of the present—still less chart a course of action for the future—without delving into the past. There is a valid point in the response of General de Gaulle to a historian who suggested that the problems of present-day France dated back to 1936. "Why not to 1513," said de Gaulle, "or, if you prefer, to 1425?" And in more general terms, the relation between the study of politics and history was thus expressed by a British historian, J. R. Seeley, who helped to develop the discipline of political science late in the nineteenth century:[8]

> History without political science has no fruit;
> Political science without history has no root.

Such an approach to politics supplies a corrective to an undue concen-

---

[8] *Introduction to Political Science* (London: Macmillan & Co., Ltd., 1919), p. 4.

tration on the more pressing problems of the moment. Otherwise we tend to forget that what may seem a major problem to us (for example, the relation of the state to the economic order) was not always so, and that controversies over which our ancestors shed blood (for instance, the relations of church and state) do not move us to acts of violence today. To understand politics, it is necessary to step, as it were, outside our immediate context in space and time, to see our world as a whole and, in Spinoza's phrase, "under the guise of eternity." For the most part we not only accept but take for granted the prevailing ideas, the dominant institutions of our environment; and, if on the whole these serve our needs, we judge them good. But does this mean that what we are familiar with and approve is right and good only for ourselves, and only here and now? Are our practices and principles equally appropriate for contemporary peoples elsewhere in this troubled world? How does our particular system of government resemble those which existed in earlier periods of history? Does it exhibit any novel features that are distinctive or even unique? In either case, how do we explain both the continuation of the old and the invention of the new?

The logic contained in these questions also suggests the wisdom of employing a comparative approach in order to find the answer. If it is bad to restrict our scrutiny to our own century, so would we be at fault in failing to look beyond our own country. To learn about the government of a single state, and at a particular phase of its history, is not the same as analyzing the political process. The seamless web of human politics is woven continuously from past to present and repeats its design from state to state. The fundamental issues which are its content must therefore be observed from the perspective of space as well as time. Insight into the significance of each choice and into the relative merits of alternative solutions requires that governments be studied by a comparative method. The politics of a particular country may sometimes be best understood by comparisons with its own politics in earlier periods; sometimes, however, by comparisons with the governments of other peoples, past or present. In this way it becomes feasible to distinguish between what is accidental or transitory and what is fundamental or permanent. In this way, too, the causes of political phenomena may be more accurately divined than would be the case if no such comparisons were attempted. Anyone who wishes, for example, to know why the United States is a federal union may obtain clues to the answer by looking at the United States alone. But, since Switzerland, Canada, and Australia are also federal unions, it is likely that a study of the reasons why they too possess this form of government will lead to valid generalizations about the causes of federalism; and such generalizations will then be more securely founded, since they will rest upon a broader base.[9] Hence, throughout this book, the comparative method is widely employed, and the problems of politics are illustrated by examples drawn from any era or continent whose experience is relevant to the issue. We can learn about the nature of government not only by observing modern America or Britain or Russia, but also by studying the lessons of the birth of the nation-state, the medieval experiment in church-state dualism, the growth and collapse of the Roman Empire, and the legacy of ancient Athens.

But that is not all. The reference to earlier periods of time and the use of comparisons contribute to a more intelligent understanding by means of classification and clarification. Since the core of politics, however, consists in controversy and choice, the orderly analysis of data forms the prelude to an act of judgment. In politics men are perennially arguing pro and con, debating the merits and demerits of alternative policies, disputing the wisdom of ultimate goals, and weighing the efficacy of possible means. In short, they are engaged in a struggle about values. The political process—not only as discussed in philosophical treatises, but as actually conducted in daily life—abounds with invocations of this, that, or the other, ideal. Men dedicate their governments to life, liberty, and the pursuit of happiness; to equality, to justice, to peace and good order; and to similar noble purposes. But how are these defined? How is democracy itself to be interpreted so that we shall know when we have it? What happens, moreover, if one ideal appears to conflict with a second? Life is sometimes sacrificed for liberty. Liberties can be lessened for the sake of equality. The public safety may clash with the rights of the individual. At one stage of their history, people are embattled for private enterprise; at another, for the general welfare. At one time they prize their freedom from the state; at another, their security through the state. It may be their union that they hold most dear; or states' rights and local independence. The glittering generalities have their place in politics because human beings identify their particular interests with these wide symbols; and then, since conduct is influenced by beliefs, the choice of the symbol, the agreement about what it means, and its application in future instances, affect the course of history.

Theorizing about values, though a speculative activity, is not independent of reality. The idealizations of philosophy have a habit of becoming the currency of the marketplace. Conversely, ideas grow out of experience; and when they are developed into a coherent

[9]As is the theme of Kenneth C. Wheare's *Federal Government,* 4th ed. (New York: Oxford University Press, Inc., 1964).

whole—which is what a philosophy is supposed to be—they serve as a signpost to further experience. Thus Rousseau, repelled by the spectacle of French society in Paris and Versailles in the middle of the eighteenth century, wrote a doctrine of protest to which the architects of the French Revolution appealed for much of their justification. The men who framed the Constitution of the United States adopted many of their principal ideas from the English tradition of constitutionalism and the structure of colonial government. But they went further and hammered out the new design of a federal union, containing governments of limited jurisdiction, which has provided the model for extensive imitation and further speculation and experiment. Political doctrines do not hover weightless in a sealed chamber removed from political actuality. They are an integral part of the living reality of government. Consequently, they help us to understand the state and render it intelligible to reason. Theory is, in part, a form of mental shorthand, compressing a multitude of connected facts into a few short symbols; and, in part, it is also an aspiration for a future that we should like to see realized.

POLITICS AND ETHICS

It follows from this that the formulation of political ideals is central to the conduct of politics, and hence the study of the subject embraces the concepts of political philosophy. As Bismarck defined it, politics is "the art of the possible." As here conceived, however, politics is the art of selecting the most worthwhile among whatever policies are possible. The essence of politics is choice, and this implies a deliberate preference for one set of values over another.[10] Nor does this imply that the values themselves are taken for granted or are somehow determined apart from the political process, so that the latter is concerned only with the methods of attaining them. Politics is a search for ends as well as means. It is through practical politics that values are disputed, their relevance is tried, and their validity is tested. Likewise it is the striving for values that injects into politics a purpose and a rationale. Indeed, that precisely is the significance of the issues this book seeks to analyze. For these are the points of focus for the controversies between rival values whose adoption and fulfillment make the core of politics.

But if the issues present a choice between opposing values, and if every value aspires to an ideal, how is the latter related to the actual?

---

[10]"To govern is to choose," said Pierre Mendès-France, a former prime minister of France, who knew whereof he spoke.

What kind of alternatives do these issues present? Do they enlighten us about what actually occurs, or do they guide us toward what ideally should occur? Or can they help in both respects?

Though many aspects of these questions are perplexing, some points are clear beyond doubt. Ideals are rooted in reality, but always project beyond it. Commencing with what is, they extrapolate to what ought to be. They can be thought of as yardsticks which measure the gap between what we have and should have, or as signposts which point the direction and tell the mileage from where we are to where we should like to be. This does not mean, however, that the world of reality can or will ever conform exactly to the dreamland of the ideal. For one thing, the laws of logic are not the laws of politics or ethics. In pure thought ideas can be developed beyond the point that practice can attain.[11] Moreover, ideals are bound to come into conflict with other ideals, as in so obvious a case as the contrast between liberty and order. If either of these be completely extended, the other vanishes. Practical politics, therefore, requires an intermixture of the two in moderate amounts.

All this is true, but nevertheless the formulation of ideals serves a useful and important purpose. Such Euclidean definitions as a point having position but no magnitude, or a line having length but no breadth, are concepts which no actual line or point can match. Yet it is the ideal that sets the standard whereby we test and judge the real. The same could be said about the markings on a compass. In practice, the navigator on the sea or in the air seldom, if ever, steers his course due south or due north—unless he expects to arrive at a Pole. But it is such points on the compass that help him to fix his other directions.

The Great Issues occupy a similar role in politics. They constitute direction-points or ultimate goals that are ideally conceivable. They therefore serve as a measuring stick for testing reality. It is thus that we may judge how closely we approximate the ideal and, conversely, how far we are falling short. Pure and perfect equality or liberty cannot be realized in practice. But to envisage the concepts supplies some sense and significance for policy and action. Whenever we contemplate what should be, we also illuminate what is.

HUMANISM AND POLITICS

Throughout its long history as a field of scholarship, the study of politics has fluctuated between the two tendencies which can be in-

[11]As Ralph Barton Perry has written: "It is of the essence of ideals that they should be unattainable. They define not what men possess but what they seek." *The Humanity of Man* (New York: George Braziller, Inc., 1956), p. 99.

ferred from the logic of the preceding discussion. Some have thought that the political process derives its character from recurrent qualities in human nature. Faced with similar situations, men are supposed to react in similar ways. If enough instances are observed, these can be gathered into generalizations enabling us to describe the fashion in which people ordinarily behave and to predict their future behavior with reasonable probability. Such generalizations are the laws of politics. To formulate them is political science; to apply them is the art of government. On this view, both the content of politics and the categories of analysis are rooted in the actual and restricted to the probable. Politics, so practiced, is independent of morals. Ethics is therefore irrelevant to its study.

By contrast, there are those who affirm the union of politics with ethics, which the former view denies. They argue that politics is the pursuit of human betterment by organized public means, just as ethics aims at the same end by private means. It is true that men in politics struggle for power, that groups are mobilized to press for special interests, that systems are at times tyrannically administered, and institutions are deflected from their proper purposes. Nobody would gainsay these facts. But it is no less true that politics also embraces the judgment on such facts. People look, appraise, and then evaluate what they see in moral terms of good and bad, of right and wrong. Ethical judgment is an integral part of actual political behavior. Moreover, is there not more to politics than its seamy, sordid side? Altruism and benevolence, self-sacrifice, dedication to the public good, a solicitude for human welfare—these too can be exemplified from political history as readily as the cruder pathology which makes the stock-in-trade of "hard-boiled" writers. Hence, if ethical factors enter the substance of politics, must not an ethical appraisal also apply to its understanding?

These two approaches have just been stated as antithethical extremes, for that indeed is how they are usually argued. In the first great systematic treatise on politics written in Europe, the Greek philosopher Plato put these contrasted views into the mouths of his two protagonists in the *Republic*—Socrates and Thrasymachus—and the debate has been continuing ever since. It has proceeded with vigor and plausibility, because each position contains its element of truth and both, when exaggerated, go over the edge from common sense to nonsense. Those who react against an excess of empirical data, unleavened by the yeast of judgment, will echo the protest of Thomas Hobbes: "For though in all places of the world, men should lay the foundation of their houses on the sand, it could not thence be inferred that so it ought to be."[12] On the

---

[12]*Leviathan*, Part II, Chap. 20. For the fuller quotation, see p. XXII of this book.

other hand, the moral philosophers can plunge so deep into formal abstractions or soar to such impractical utopias that they lose touch with
reality. Machiavelli has voiced a well-founded complaint in these much-
quoted words: "But my intention being to write something of use to
those who understand, it appears to me more proper to go to the real
truth of the matter than to its imagination; and many have imagined
republics and principalities which have never been seen or known to
exist in reality; for how we live is so far removed from how we ought to
live, that he who abandons what is done for what ought to be done, will
rather learn to bring about his own ruin than his preservation."[13]

Both warnings are highly pertinent to the situation we confront
today. Conflicts between opposing political systems and their supporting philosophies have become more, rather than less, intense in the
wake of the four major revolutions of the last three hundred years—
the English, American, French, and Russian. Men have justified the
existing order or they have risen in revolt, they have defended their
privileges or argued for reform, generalizing their points of view in
terms of an array of doctrines—conservatism or liberalism, capitalism
or socialism, fascism or communism, aristocracy or democracy. These
rivalries are continued in the contemporary competition between
democratic and communist systems, and similarly between the Chinese and Indian methods of engrafting the technology of Western
science upon Asian societies of ancient traditions. It is as true now,
therefore, as it has ever been that politics forms the arena where men
choose the values by which they organize their social systems. Hence
the nature of the subject indicates the method of its study. Politics is
the search of a society for public ethics. The study of politics is a
research into the results, ethically judged.

To say this is to reject an approach to the subject that is followed
in many quarters today. In the fields of learning which study human
society—the social sciences, as they are usually called—there has been
a vogue of late to concentrate attention on actual behavior. The
behavioral method records the details of what men do and seeks to
explain why they do it. What they ought to do, or what values they
should hold, is regarded as a separate line of inquiry which leads
beyond the province of social science. Politics is defined as the decision-making process. The political scientist examines the persons who
make the decisions, explores how they make them, and interprets
why. The passions that permeate the subject he considers with the
clinical detachment of a doctor and charts with dispassionate neutrality.

[13] *The Prince*, Chap. 15.

The objection to this approach is not that it gathers empirical data. On the contrary, we need abundant collections and analyses of human behavior in politics as in other social activities. For its contributions to realism—to the description and classification of how people tend to behave—one may be grateful for some of the research of behavioral scientists. Where they are seriously at fault, however, is in their unwillingness to admit as belonging to the subject those aspects which their method is incapable of elucidating. Thus they become the prisoners of their own methodology.[14] Anything which cannot be fitted within its narrow limitations they rigidly exclude from their field of inquiry and then from their eventual comprehension of the subject itself.

This subordination of the substance to a methodological purism drives a cleft into the heart of political studies, compelling the inquiry to cease just where some of the most interesting questions begin. Naturally, decisions are taken in politics. But we must also debate the content of the decisions and argue their merits. We must ask what is the right decision or what decision ought to be taken. The amassing of details concerning how men behave is a dead weight of intellectual lumber unless it eventually suggests how men ought to behave. Politics indeed consists in more than a decision-making process, and those who so define the field are failing to do it justice. Even a surgeon would not describe his work as the incision-making process. After all, he has a concept of health, the goal to which his surgery is directed. The best method to follow is that which enters into the spirit of the subject and recaptures its essence. This must be a combination of empirical analysis and ethical evaluation. Both are needed in mutual support; each is complementary to the other. The factual data of politics must be judged and appraised by moral criteria. The ideals must be realistically reviewed in terms of their practicability and observed results. The actual and the ideal are the dough and the yeast. It is in unison that they become a fit food for consumption.

Finally, as the trend of this argument shows, the word "science" in the title "political science" can be misleading if it is taken too seri-

---

[14]This posture is reminiscent of a technique which hunters employ for trapping monkeys. They take a jar with a wide base and a long narrow neck just barely large enough for a monkey's hand and arm. At the bottom of the jar, they place some fresh slices of apple; then, they tie the jar to the branch of a tree and wait. Along comes a monkey, which smells the apple and wants it. It inserts its arm, grabs the apple, and tries to withdraw. But the paw holding the apple is now so wide that the monkey can only withdraw his arm if he releases the apple. Being a monkey, it will not do this. So there it stays, the self-trapped prisoner of an unattainable desire, until the hunter throws a net over it. Students of human behavior, who clutch at the methodology of science and will not let it go, are similarly trapped.

ously and pressed too far. The study of politics can be considered "scientific" only to the extent that we seek to know the truth, to discover the facts with accuracy, and to correlate causes with their consequences. Beyond that, the methods that have yielded such fruitful results in the understanding of physical phenomena do not apply to the study of society because the content and material are different in kind. With the aid of modern instruments, a student of art can learn a great deal about a painting by Rembrandt. He can test the pigmentation, make detailed photographs of the brush technique, and conduct a microscopic analysis of the materials and their use. But when all this is done, what does it add up to? It still does not penetrate to the heart of the painting. It cannot explain the sensibilities and intuition of the artist or tell us why the rendering on canvas of an elderly wrinkled face or a scene such as that in "The Night Watch" can move our emotions.

And it is the same with politics. All the measurements and quantification, the polls and samples, the games and models, which are so much in vogue in contemporary research, will yield some information and perhaps provide some good guesses. But they do not reach the core of the subject. There is more to politics than can be reduced to a linear flow from the id to the IBM. All of the complexities of human nature, its many-sidedness, its good and evil, attractiveness and repulsiveness, are present in actual politics. Of all this, science can explain only so much. The rest, indeed the most important part of the subject, is one of human interpretation. Thus in any political study we must consider not only the categories of true or false but also those of good or bad, of wise or foolish. In short, since politics constitutes an organized human activity, its study comes closer to the humanities than to the sciences. Our chief preoccupation is with choices, values, and issues—to which institutions, procedures, and power are secondary. Politics includes, but reaches beyond, the making of decisions. The character and quality and results of the decision are what count most. It is these which make of politics a continuing adventure in the process of civilization.

2

Individuals, Groups, and Society

Before the issues that form the content of politics can be studied, there are two preliminary topics to consider which will run, as unbroken threads, through the ensuing discussion. The subject of politics is not what some writers have affirmed it to be: power, or institutions, or the state, or sovereignty, or decision making, or the analysis of a system. It is Man himself, functioning as a social creature. Moreover, it is the whole man, complete with all his actions, aspirations, and aberrations; not a part of a man, with one aspect of his nature (for example, the drive for power) picked out of context and exaggerated out of focus. There is no such creature as Political Man—any more than there exists an Economic Man, a Religious Man, an Academic Man, or any such abstraction. There is simply Man—the whole of him—who happens to act politically, legally, militarily, and so on.

The study of Man as a social creature means the study of our relations with our fellowmen, and the entire network of all such relations constitutes what we call society. Since politics is one aspect of Man's social activity, it is self-evident that the political system must be considered in its social context, and that any aspect of Man's social being may acquire political relevance. It is therefore a precondition to the understanding of politics that we form some generic picture of society as a whole, and then observe the genesis of the political process within the social matrix. These two matters supply the contents of the present chapter and the next. This chapter is concerned with certain principles of social action, the organization that arises from the principles, and some theories which attempt to explain them. Chapter 3 will then explore the emergence of a political function and, therewith, the birth of the state and its government.

A few reflections will quickly remind us how closely our political attitudes are connected with the rest of our social life and how impossible it is, under even the most exact analysis, completely to disentangle the one from the other. The outlook people display on political issues and the judgments they express on the actions of their government are shaped by the whole social amalgam, any one of whose many facets may temporarily assume prominence. Everybody is influenced, for example, by his occupation, by the manner in which he earns a livelihood, and by the monetary return that this brings. The teacher, the farmer, the trade unionist, the businessman, and the civil servant cannot be expected to hold identical views on economic matters. They produce differently, render different services, respond to different social demands, are vulnerable to different risks, and are differently rewarded. Thus one can understand why in some countries, such as Denmark, the pluralism of economic life is reflected in the politics of a multiparty system, so that there is one party for the industrial wage earners, another for the urban businessmen, a third for the small farmers, and a fourth for the big. Or it may happen that the principal bond of social cohesion is provided by religious belief and the organization that sustains it. In this case, Protestants may be grouped together because they are Protestants, and Catholics because they are Catholics, a fact directly relevant to politics in Switzerland, the Netherlands, Ulster, Canada, and elsewhere. The division thus caused may even provoke such political separation and animosities as occurred in Ireland, Palestine, and India. Likewise, where a society is composed of different races, politics will be preoccupied with their relationship. Miscegenation may then be accepted, as in Brazil or Hawaii; or some form of coexistence more or less tolerant, may prevail with a tendency for the relations between the races to become more egalitarian; or, again, the official policy may be to maintain segregation with its normal accompaniment of supremacy on the part of those who support it, which has been the traditional arm of the ruling oligarchies in Alabama and Mississippi and is the system in favor in South Africa.

These examples could, of course, be multiplied manyfold. But they suffice to illustrate the truth that politics is deeply involved in the fundamentals of the social order and shares in its characteristics. Any or all of these factors, and more besides, may explain why people are liberals or conservatives, why they vote for this candidate or that one if indeed they vote at all, why they support or oppose a bond issue to construct new schools, why they advocate a foreign policy of firmness or conciliation. Hence the analysis of politics should begin where society itself begins—that is, with the formation of groups. Society is a congeries of groups, and these are the breeding ground for politics.

Since all human beings live in groups, and since the state is one form of organized grouping among many, certain initial questions arise, the answers to which should throw some light on the issues of politics.

For what purposes do groups exist?

How are the members associated with one another and with the whole group?

What is the relation between the various groups?

THE SOCIAL CHARACTER OF MAN

Any generalization which comes close to universality must be the product of circumstances that are fundamental to human nature. Hence the fact that mankind everywhere lives in groups supplies a starting point for social inquiry. There are admittedly some exceptions, but these are so few and are such special cases that they serve to reinforce the rule. The hermit who would renounce the world and would mortify the flesh to fortify the spirit has generally suffered a blow to his personality which has wounded him emotionally. He escapes into hatred of humanity or into mystic communion with a super-human force. Yet the act of a permanent[1] withdrawal, which seems to deny the ties of society, positively acknowledges the power of his fellowmen, even while he rejects them, to mold his way of life. The tragic side of his character has been portrayed in Shakespeare's *Timon of Athens.* Indeed it is because the few persons who become hermits are victims of mental sickness that the question of what a human being would be like without any social bonds is necessarily a puzzle. The problem of depicting him has therefore been removed from social analysis because the empirical data are lacking. But this task has yielded a theme for imaginative fiction or philosophical fancy, both of which conceive of nonsocial man as being either subhuman or super-human—never as human. Thus, in an oft-cited passage of the *Odyssey,* the Greek epic poet Homer described his hero's encounter with the Cyclops, one-eyed giants who "have no government, nor councils, nor courts of justice: but live in caves on mountain tops, each ruling his wives and children and a law unto himself, regardless." Yet even in that case the family formed a social bond; and when he was blinded

---

[1] A temporary withdrawal, on the other hand, has offered in some outstanding cases the leisure and the opportunity for reflection that have been the prelude to intense social activity.

in his cave by Odysseus, the Cyclops shrieked for the assistance of his neighbors, who rallied to his support.[2] Daniel Defoe, narrating the adventures of Robinson Crusoe, depicted an isolated man who has been a lasting favorite of certain economic theorists. In him they have seen the archetype of their favorite character, "the individual," functioning in his purest individualism and rationing his scant resources among conflicting needs. Crusoe however did bring to his island the knowledge he had acquired within society, plus some materials salvaged from a shipwreck. And anyhow, as soon as the man Friday appeared, a social relationship began.

Perhaps the grimmest picture of how human beings would behave if there were no bonds to unite them is that drawn by an English philosopher of the mid-seventeenth century. Thomas Hobbes, having sought security in France while civil war between Royalists and Parliamentarians ravaged his native land, proceeded during the 1640's to write his celebrated *Leviathan.* In somber hues he sketched the outline of a presocial stage wherein, more genuinely than the Homeric Cyclops, man is truly revealed as an "imaginary atomic individual." Hobbesian men are driven by their "naturall passions," of which fear is uppermost, to preserve themselves against attack. Because of their all-pervading suspicions and distrust, they are unable to combine. They search for security in isolation or by getting their blow in first. Thence ensues "a warre of every man against every man. . . . In such condition," he writes, "there is no place for industry; because the fruit thereof is uncertain: and consequently no culture of the Earth, no navigation, nor use of the commodities that may be imported by sea . . . no arts; no letters; no society; and which is worst of all, continuall feare, and danger of violent death; and the life of man, solitary, poore, nasty, brutish, and short." Hobbes concedes that such a state of affairs "was never generally so, over all the world," but he asserts "that there are many places, where they live so now." As evidence he mentions "the savage people in many places of America," who "except the government of small families . . . have no government at all"—an erroneous view of the nature of Indian tribal structure, but one that

---

[2]The source is bk. ix of the *Odyssey,* 11. 112–15, p. 123 in T. E. Lawrence's translation (New York: Oxford University Press, Inc., 1932). This passage was cited by Plato (*Laws,* iii, Sec. 680) to illustrate an earlier patriarchal society in which the family was the important group, and the male ruled the family. Aristotle, too, quotes it in *Politics,* i, Chap. 2, Sec. 1252 b, to repeat the identical point. The Cyclops has provided a stock quotation ever since. Arnold J. Toynbee, writing before the age of atom bombs when the adjective "atomic" signified a self-sufficient, indivisible unit, refers to him as "the classic picture of an imaginary atomic individual" [ed. D. C. Somervell, *Study of History,* abridgement. Vols. 1–6 (New York: Oxford University Press, Inc., 1947), p. 209], which is misleading since the Cyclops, though imaginary, was not, in view of the family relationship, a self-sufficient unit.

was widespread in the seventeenth and eighteenth centuries. Hobbes claims to see other analogies in the dissolution of authority through civil war and in the international relations of independent states, though in such cases he confuses the absence or breakdown of the state with the absence or breakdown of society.[3] No doubt, Hobbes allowed his intellect to be carried away by his imagination, but he underlined the truth that each requires association with his fellows. The life of man is accurately described as a life lived in groups.

WHY MEN LIVE IN GROUPS

The reason for this fact can be readily stated. There are two fundamental aspects of human nature which keep us associated with our kind. We must live in groups in order to satisfy for one and all the needs which nobody can fulfill alone. Also, we must control any actions of an individual whose effects are too harmful to others. Groups derive, therefore, from our cooperating in matters of common concern and competing in what concerns the individual. These two principles, as is evident, spring from opposite sides of our nature and carry different implications for the resulting groups.

The needs we satisfy by cooperation with our fellowmen are not only the elemental necessities of food, shelter, and clothing, but also the ever-broadening demands that mark a progressive civilization. There are large areas of the world where it is still idle to speak of achieving the good life, since life itself is precarious and hazardous for millions. However, in communities where people have eliminated the perils of death from hunger or exposure, the social order is directed to many objects which are not necessary to life, but which may contribute to a better or more comfortable life. As society evolves from a preoccupation with necessities to the satisfaction of a vast range of desires, men undergo a profound change psychologically as well as materially. This is signalized above all by the enlargement of their field of choice and by the exercise of critical judgment. It is the earmark of a necessity to be predetermined and inescapable. If men wish to live, for instance, they must have food. Within limits, they may choose what to eat and when; where to find their food, or how. But their goal is fixed without their willing it, since eat they must.

With wants, however, in the broader sense, the area of selection extends both to the means and to the formulation of ends which can be altered, expanded, and arranged in order of priority. The structure

[3]For this distinction, see Chap. 6, pp. 167–68. The quotations are from the *Leviathan*, Part I, Chaps. 13 and 17.

that was adequate to provide a rough shelter from wind and rain later evolves into a house with an architectural style. Those who dwell in it develop the institution of the family and by living together infuse into a building the emotional attachments of a home. Food and drink acquire the sophisticated and highly selective character of dining or diet. Clothing is designed for comfort or fashion. In an advanced culture men can take their pick and decide whether they want most to have better orchestras, better automobiles, or better schools and parks. A preoccupation about bare existence belongs to a level of thought and discussion less complex than a concern about a standard of living, for a standard involves comparisons and consequent valuations. The distinction will be readily appreciated by a generation which suddenly found in the experience of total war that its major anxiety had switched from the maintenance of its living standards to the maintenance of life itself. Men whose wants have reached the stage of inquiry and reflection about standards of living are making intellectual comparisons and taking ethical choices. When they select their pattern of life from the available alternatives, their preferences are transmuted into terms of good and bad, of right and wrong—in a word, of values.[4] Thus it happens that upon the foundations of vital necessities man, the value-selecting animal, rears this elaborate structure of choices which stamp him as a rational and moral being. In large measure this whole process of formulating and attaining wants is social in character. "The gains of commonwealths," as Charles E. Merriam has written, "are essentially mass gains."[5] Without associating together in groups, men would never have become, nor could they remain, humanized. Cooperation is the source of civilization.

RESTRAINTS UPON ACTIONS THAT HARM OTHERS

But cooperation to satisfy our needs is not the only reason why groups are formed. A second reason is the simple fact that people behave in ways that produce consequences for others besides the doer. When an act is done, it is as uncontrollable as a stone that has left the thrower's hand; and its results, direct and indirect, near and remote, are like the widening ripples in a pool. An individual's actions create relationships between persons and thereby become socially relevant.[6] Anybody who

[4]According to the Book of Genesis, it was after Adam and Eve tasted the fruit of the tree of knowledge of good and evil that they first became specifically human.

[5]*The New Democracy and the New Despotism* (New York: McGraw-Hill Book Company, Whittlesey House publication, 1939), p. 37.

[6]John Stuart Mill, the British exponent of mid-nineteenth century liberalism, draws a distinction between actions that affect only oneself and those that also involve others [*Essay on Liberty*, Everyman's Library (New York: E. P. Dutton & Co., Inc.), pp. 72–75,

is affected by another's action has a concern in the conduct that touches him. Now the effect of one's actions upon others may be beneficial or harmful. The former possibility suggested itself to Adam Smith, the Scottish master of laissez-faire economics. He thought that, while pursuing their own self-interest, men may, without knowing or intending it, be "led by an invisible hand" to promote simultaneously the interest of society.[7] How these good effects are produced or whose is the invisible hand, he failed to indicate. In any case, consequences that are generally beneficial create few serious problems since scarcely anybody will object to others for promoting his welfare. It is the opposite, however, with acts that prejudice the interests of persons besides the doer. In that event, whoever is harmed seeks protection from conduct that hurts him. Therefore, as Mill concedes and Dewey insists, regulation becomes socially justifiable or necessary. Men organize themselves into groups to control the sort of behavior from whose results they suffer. In this way the desire for self-protection leads to group restraint.

Nor is this all. Social relationships are created not only when some persons act and others are passively affected, but also when people interact with one another. While independently pursuing their various aims, men clash and collide. Different persons wish to do the same thing or possess the same object. Their ambitions bring them into conflict. Each seeks to gain the advantage and outdo his rival, since it is impossible for all to obtain equal satisfaction. Under such circumstances three alternatives are possible. The competitors may be left to battle it out, let come what may. Or people may organize into groups and determine by an established procedure what settlement is due or just to all parties. Third, as an intermediate course, the group may refuse to decide the outcome; but, like a referee in the ring, may prescribe the rules by which the contest shall be conducted. The first of these possibilities is merely Hobbes' "warre of every man against every man" all over again. Its results are so wasteful and mutually destructive that men generally prefer a less disorderly solution. The two latter methods (though one confines itself to the regulation of means and the other embraces the regulation of both means and ends) have in common the fact that each recognizes the desirability of employing group authority to eliminate or lessen the perils of anarchy.

136–37]. It is very doubtful, however, whether such a distinction is tenable. For are there any actions whose effects are confined solely to the self? Mill recognized and raised this difficulty in the *Essay*, but his answer is not to the point. See also the discussion in John Dewey, *The Public and Its Problems* (New York: Holt, Rinehart & Winston, Inc., 1927), p. 12.

[7]Adam Smith, *The Wealth of Nations*, IV, Chap. 2. For a discussion of laissez-faire, see Chap. 7, pp. 180 ff.

COOPERATION PLUS COMPETITION

The discussion to this point may now be briefly summarized. Mankind lives in groups, which are formed for one or both of two reasons: to satisfy needs through concerted action and to afford protection against the harmful effects of behavior by others. Thus the basic causes of the organization of groups are cooperation in the quest of common aims and competition in pursuit of divergent ones.

Men must and do cooperate. Men also compete. To say this seems a paradox. Cooperation unites; competition divides. Both principles help to explain the formation of groups, yet they mutually contradict. To the extent that men cooperate they cannot compete. Conversely, to the extent that they compete, they can scarcely cooperate. The same persons in the same group cannot simultaneously be competing and cooperating for the same objective. So much is fairly obvious. More paradoxical and more significant, however, is the truth that neither competition nor cooperation can be successful if it exists alone and completely excludes its opposite. Unchecked by the other, each tends toward an extreme position where its very success is suicidal. For example, the practice of competition presupposes that there should be not one monopolist but two or more competitors. If these are truly to compete, they must be matched equally or nearly so. The purpose in competition, however, is to defeat the opponent and, if possible, to drive him out of business. But in that case competition necessarily ceases. Thus, wherever it be unrestrained, competition moves in the direction of monopoly and on attaining its goal destroys the conditions basic to its existence.[8] When competition is really cut-throat, the throat that is finally cut is its own.

Cooperation, though it appears totally different from competition, resembles it in one respect. Both principles seek the same end: the production of work through the stimulus of an incentive. The methods employed, however, are at variance, for competition relies upon combat, and cooperation upon harmony. In order to cooperate men must be organized, and to be organized they must obey rules. Up to a point rules and organization do stimulate incentive because they prescribe a regular pattern of behavior whereby people may work with mutual reliance and dependability. But systems, too, can be self-defeating when they stifle and frustrate the enterprise of those they control. They can be developed to a degree where human energies are no

[8]Hence the concepts of "fair competition" and "unfair competition," expressed in the antitrust policy of the United States. Much of the public regulation of business was designed not only to protect the consumer, but also to sustain the entrepreneur against his more ruthless competitors.

longer fruitfully canalized but wastefully thwarted; where, by overattention to methods, goals are lost from view; where a desire for order degenerates into a passion for orders. These results can occur in any kind of organization, but their effects are most harmful in certain fields of activity which all too easily are hampered rather than helped by efforts at concerted action. Why is it, for instance, that attempts to direct the themes and styles of creative artists, writers, and musicians are ludicrously inept? Clearly because the arts originate in an individual's imagination. They spring from the inward experience and sensibilities of the artist with a spontaneity that wilts under control.

CONTRASTED VIEWS OF HUMAN NATURE

The truth that men cannot build their lives solely on cooperation or solely on competition, and that attempts to approximate too closely to either extreme prove unworkable in practice, may be further clarified by some contrasted judgments in the fields of ethics, economics, and biology. To consider such extremes is valuable because it illumines the areas between. A temperate zone becomes more meaningful after exploration of the polar and tropical regions between which it lies.

1. *"Love Thy Neighbor as Thyself."* In the realm of ethical theory, doctrines abound that emphasize the cooperative side of human relations and prescribe a course of conduct based upon men's need for one another. Witness the injunction of the Gospels to "love thy neighbor as thyself"; or the Golden Rule to "do unto others as you would have others do unto you." In similar vein are these eloquent words of John Donne: "No man is an *iland,* intire of it selfe; every man is a piece of the *continent,* a part of the *maine;* if a clod be washed away by the *sea, Europe* is the lesse, as well as if a *promontorie* were, as well as if a *mannor* of thy *friends* or of thine owne were; any man's *death* diminishes *me,* because I am involved in *Mankinde;* and therefore never send to know for whom the *bell* tolls; it tolls for *thee."* [9] These and kindred expressions do not describe factually how most people generally feel and behave. They are statements about feeling and behavior as they might be and, in the speaker's view, ought to be. What is perhaps most significant about such doctrines is the continuing gap between the oft-repeated ideals and the persistent realities. To this, without being unduly cynical, anybody may testify who lives in this twentieth century—the most violent in recorded history. Undoubtedly the reason for the gap is that such precepts overstress human cooperativeness and allow insufficiently for men's capacity to hate and destroy.

[9] *Devotions,* No. 17. Italics in the original.

2. Let Dog Eat Dog. Opposed to universal benevolence, and equally exaggerated in the contrary direction, are dogmas of universal selfishness. In one passage of *The Prince,* Niccolò Machiavelli thus summarized his view of humanity: "For it may be said of men in general that they are ungrateful, voluble, dissemblers, anxious to avoid danger, and covetous of gain; so long as you benefit them they are entirely yours; they offer you their blood, their goods, their life, and their children, as I have before said, when the necessity is remote; but when it approaches, they revolt."[10] No less self-centered was the characterization offered by Hobbes, who considered that "of the voluntary acts of every man, the object is some *good to himselfe.*"[11] He even goes to the length of arguing that pity "ariseth from the imagination that the like calamity (of another) may befall himselfe,"[12] which is as clear a case as may be found of distorting the facts to save a theory.

In economic thought, and the policies based upon it, occur some further instances of the same tendency. During the nineteenth century the economic theory most widespread in Britain and the United States assumed that the principle of competition not only constituted the strongest stimulus to work, but also produced the greatest good for society as a whole and for its members severally. Adam Smith, who propagated this doctrine, believed the most potent motivation to be "the natural effort of every individual to better his own condition, when suffered to exert itself with freedom and security."[13] When this is harnessed to the principle of the division of labor, which forms the opening theme of the *Wealth of Nations,* there arises that peculiar link between men, the economic relation, in which each pursues and satisfies his particular interest and yet simultaneously satisfies the interest of others. Smith recognized that "man has almost constant occasion for the help of his brethren." But he goes on to say that it is in vain for a man to expect that others will help him "from their benevolence only . . . . He will be more likely to prevail," runs the argument, "if he can interest their self-love in his favor, and shew them that it is for their own advantage to do for him what he requires of them. Whoever offers to another a bargain of any kind, proposes to do this: Give me that which I want, and you shall have this which you want."[14] That

---

[10]It should be noted that elsewhere in *The Prince* and in other works Machiavelli speaks more charitably of his fellowmen.

[11]Thomas Hobbes, *Leviathan,* Part I, Chap. 14. Italics in the original.

[12]*Ibid.,* Chap. 6. This definition of pity was refuted by Bishop Butler, Sermon V, No. 1, note *a,* and by Rousseau in the "Discourse on the Origin of Inequality," in *The Social Contract and Discourses,* trans. G. D. H. Cole (Everyman's Library), pp. 196-200.

[13]Smith, *Wealth of Nations,* IV, Chap. 5.

[14]*Ibid.,* I, Chap. 2. For an excellent critique of the nature of economic exchange

is selfishness developed to a high degree, but tempered by some qualifications. For Smith concedes that even self-lovers must cooperate. This he is bound to admit, since, once the division of labor is chosen as a starting point, it follows that specialists must be interdependent.

The contrary problem is the one that has confronted the Russian Communist party. Hostile to the principle of competition because of its association with "bourgeois economics," and seeking socialism within a classless society, Marxist theoreticians and Communist policy makers were initially disposed to assume that, as soon as the exploitation of man by man was abolished, there would dawn a golden age of cooperation for the common good.[15] No longer would the state be an instrument of class coercion. Freed from their shackles and imbued with a new sense of oneness, humanity would work for the good of all. But the course of events under the Communist regime of the Soviet Union has not conformed to this pattern. Instead of the Marxian formula, "from each according to his ability, to each according to his needs," Stalin substituted, "from each according to his ability, to each according to his work." In a country whose technology was backward, whose productivity was low, and whose independence was threatened by invasion, the demand for output placed a premium upon "incentives." Hence the organization of the *Udarniki* (shock workers) who were prepared to exceed the norm; hence the Stakhanovite movement with its speedup campaign; hence the differential wage rates and grants of privileges and distinctions to exceptional workers. What is more, since theory had to be changed to suit altered needs, it was eventually discovered that there is something called socialist competition, which is supposed to differ from capitalist competition. During the 1960's the Soviet Union even experimented cautiously with changes which were revolutionary in the light of its recent past. In certain instances, instead of having to fulfill the production targets of a central plan, factory managers were permitted to determine output according to their judgment of what the consumers were demanding and would therefore buy. Nothing is better for a theory than its confrontation with the facts of life.

---

see A. D. Lindsay, *The Modern Democratic State* (New York: Oxford University Press, Inc., 1947), pp. 103–5.

[15]Some wit has suggested this definition of the difference between capitalism and communism: What you have under capitalism is the exploitation of man by man; under communism, you have the reverse.

THE STATE OF NATURE AND THE NATURE OF SOCIETY

A final pair of contrasts should be mentioned. The study of human society was profoundly influenced in the nineteenth century by the spectacular results of research in the biological sciences. As a consequence, comparisons between the life of human beings and that of other creatures were treated, not as analogies, but as part of the same order of being. Thus, from the study of "nature" mankind could derive lessons applicable to their own society. The vital questions then were: What was the nature of "nature"? What lessons did it teach? As is often the case, men looked at the same facts, selected different data, and arrived at opposite conclusions. One line of argument was composed of variations on the theme of the Greek philosopher Heraclitus, who pronounced that "strife is the parent of all things." All the world was seen as a jungle, and the jungle as a battleground. Nature's law was to use your claw. It was the lot of the weak to be dominated or exterminated by the strong or the cunning. Such doctrines were applied by Herbert Spencer to social theory in combination with the other "natural laws" of Smith's economics. The outcome was simple: let dog eat dog. Which side then did morality take? Ethics followed nature and condemned the eaten, not the eater.

On this point let Spencer speak for himself:

Pervading all nature 'we may see at work a stern discipline, which is a little cruel that it may be very kind. That state of universal warfare maintained throughout the lower creation, to the great perplexity of many worthy people, is at bottom the most merciful provision which the circumstances admit of. It is much better that the ruminant animal, when deprived by age of the vigor which made its existence a pleasure, should be killed by some beast of prey, than that it should linger out a life made painful by infirmities, and eventually die of starvation. . . . Meanwhile the well-being of existing humanity, and the unfolding of it into this ultimate perfection, are both secured by that same beneficent, though severe discipline, to which the animate creation at large is subject: a discipline which is pitiless in the working out of good; a felicity-pursuing law which never swerves for the avoidance of partial and temporary suffering. The poverty of the incapable, the distresses that come upon the imprudent, the starvation of the idle, and those shoulderings aside of the weak by the strong, which leave so many "in shallows and in miseries," are the decrees of a large, far-seeing benevolence. . . . Nevertheless, when regarded not separately, but in connection with the interests of universal humanity, these harsh fatalities are seen to be full of the highest beneficence . . . the same beneficence which brings to early graves the children of diseased parents, and singles out the low-spirited, the intemperate, and the debilitated as the victims of an epidemic.[16]

Ideas like these received an added fillip when Charles Darwin, nine years after the *Social Statics* had appeared, published his epochal *Origin of Species*. If men and monkeys were descended from a common ancestor, whatever conditions promoted the survival of the latter could not fail to be relevant to the former. Darwin, moreover, offered clues, which Darwinians were not slow to follow, in his hypotheses of "the struggle for existence" and "the survival of the fittest." Biological species had evolved by success in combat and by adaption to environment. Mankind must, therefore, subdue or be subdued; destroy or be destroyed.

Opposite inferences, however, were drawn by the Russian anarchist Prince Peter Kropotkin. While not denying the facts of struggle and competition, he felt that their significance and implications had been greatly overrated. Insufficient attention had been given, in his view, to the facts about cooperation which exists on all rungs of the ladder of evolution, and increases among the more advanced species. From his reading and observations in zoology and anthropology, he was led to the following conclusion:

"Don't compete!—competition is always injurious to the species, and you have plenty of reasons to avoid it!" That is the tendency of nature, not always realized in full, but always present. That is the watchword which comes to us from the bush, the forest, the river, the ocean. "Therefore combine—practice mutual aid! That is the surest means for giving to each and all the greatest safety, the best guarantee of existence and progress, bodily, intellectual, and moral." That is what nature teaches us; and that is what all those animals which have attained the highest position in their respective classes have done. That is also what man—the most primitive man—has been doing; and that is why man has reached the position upon which we stand now. . . . [17]

Such varied views reinforce the point that human groupings cannot be attributed to only one of their aspects or explained by a single cause. Society is, therefore, grounded in a paradox. The two principles which chiefly account for the formation of groups are mutually antagonistic. Where one advances, the other by the same measure retreats.[18] Yet they are also complementary, and each has to be mixed with its

[16]Herbert Spencer, *Social Statics*, Part III, Chap. 25, sec. 6 (London: Chapman and Hall Ltd., 1850), p. 322.

[17]Peter Kropotkin, *Mutual Aid, A Factor of Evolution* (New York: Alfred A. Knopf, Inc., 1925). The quotation is from the concluding paragraph of Chap. 2.

[18]The same point underlies Schopenhauer's parable of the porcupines, which Freud cites in *Group Psychology and the Analysis of the Ego*, Chap. 6.

antithesis to be saved from its own excesses. The oil and vinegar cannot unite; yet they blend. But this is not to say that the two principles have the same value and must be mixed in equal proportions. In fact, the contrary is the case. For of the two, cooperation is the more important. Mankind could exist without competition. It could never exist without cooperation. Even when men are acting competitively, they will form into groups where they cooperate together in order to pursue more effectively their competition against those outside the group.[19] Thus the requirements of competition do lead men into cooperation. The reverse, however, does not happen. Men do not find themselves driven into competition by the need to cooperate. Cooperation is thus the paramount principle; and though humanity must allow for the requisite element of competition, the social blend should contain a larger amount of the former and a smaller amount of the latter.

In case anyone doubts it, some confirmation of this point can be found in a comparison of groups and institutions with which we are fully familiar. Everybody would agree that of all the groupings in society the one in which cooperation is generally at its highest is the family. This is true for the great majority of families, even though there are some that contain much rivalry and tension and some that terminate in desertion or divorce. On the other hand, the business world, as its spokesmen insist, is based on a high degree of competition. In the field of government a contrast suggests itself between domestic and international politics. The former, at least in nations whose people have attained maturity and solidarity, is marked by a substantial amount of cooperation (or consensus, as it is also called). Quite the opposite holds true for the relations between states. There it is competition that predominates, so much so that humanity is still wrestling with the problem of how to restrain national policies which hurt others and to promote active cooperation in matters of mutual interest. In the family, therefore, and within the nation there is usually more emphasis on cooperation; in business and in international rela-

---

"A company of porcupines crowded themselves very close together one cold winter's day so as to profit by one another's warmth and so save themselves from being frozen to death. But soon they felt one another's quills, which induced them to separate again. And now, when the need for warmth brought them nearer together again, the second evil arose once more. So that they were driven backwards and forwards from one trouble to the other, until they had discovered a mean distance at which they could most tolerably exist."

The original can be found in Schopenhauer's *Parerga and Paralipomena* (1851) under the heading of "Parables."

[19]Plato long ago pointed out that even a band of outlaws, which seeks to plunder the rest of society, must cohere around its own principle of justice. Witness the old phrase: "Honor among thieves."

tions, the distinctive feature is competition. And who would compare the former unfavorably with the latter?

THE COMMON INTEREST AND THE CLASH OF INTERESTS

What effect does their origin have upon the nature of the groups thus formed? Within a group what relationships exist between its members? The answers may be better understood if one more question is put. What is it that induces men to cooperate and what impels them to compete? Assuredly, people cooperate because they wish to accomplish purposes which they share in common. They compete, conversely, from an awareness, and for the fulfillment, of purposes that are distinct. The genesis of groups, in other words, is to be sought not merely in certain external conditions—in mutual need and the effects of conflict—but also in the attitudes of people toward these. A group is more than a state of affairs, existing objectively. It becomes a state of mind, existing subjectively. Thus understood, a group is what results from men's recognition of how they interact with each other. If so, what forms does this consciousness take?

In seeking to satisfy those needs that call for common action, men have to recognize, discover, or even invent, a bond of union. They search for likenesses; they merge with the group; they assert their solidarity. To their separate personalities are added the ties that bind them. Major consequences now flow from their being associated, chief among which is that rights and duties become interwoven. A member of a group seeks an opportunity to act in certain ways. His desires are claims that he makes upon others of the group; his claims, when recognized by them, are his rights. The others, correspondingly, expect certain lines of conduct from him. Their expectations, which he owes in return for the rights accorded him, are his responsibilities. Recognition of rights by the group is linked up with his performance of duties toward the group, among which, of course, is respect for the rights of others. Hence group organization embodies the principle of reciprocity. He who gives takes; he who takes gives. The contrary occurs when men believe their purposes distinct and their relationship competitive. They then place the stress on differences, not resemblances; on particularity, not solidarity. Men picture themselves more as separate units than as members of an association. Instead of merging with the group, they strive to emerge from it. The self and its selfish interest loom disproportionately large, while the bonds of union become frayed amid the clash of wills.

RELATIONS BETWEEN PEOPLE IN A GROUP

These opposite attitudes are tendencies which exist in every human group to some degree, and the concepts they embody can be applied to the vexed problem of explaining the relation between a group and its membership. Whenever confronted with the difficulty of understanding something complex, such as a society of human beings, the mind seeks to make the problem intelligible by dividing it into parts and observing how they are connected. The question then arises: What is to be regarded as the whole, and what are the parts? Which, in other words, is the unit whose unity has significance? How these queries apply to the study of groups can readily be seen. According to where the emphasis is placed, one may approach the group from the standpoint of the individuals who compose it, or one may approach the individuals from the standpoint of the group to which they belong. In the latter case, human beings can be described as associated in a group. In the former, a group will be said to be made up of its members. Which is the reality that requires explanation? Is it a single human being or a group of them? And, whichever of these be taken for the unit, how should the other be understood?

As might be expected, both possibilities have found support. Some argue that the unit is the group and that we individuals are its vulgar fractions. Others say that the unit is the single human being. Each view has been defended by analogies which supposedly illustrate the nature of a social group by comparisons with other associations. For those who hold that the group is the unit, a favorite parallel is the biological organism. The members of a social body are then thought to resemble the members of an animal body, wherein all parts are functionally related and none can exist in separation from the rest. On this theory, just as the body has a natural unity, so has a social group. It then becomes a false abstraction to speak of the individual in the sense of a person divorced from relationships with others. An arm lives and moves only as part of an organic whole. Amputated from the body, it dies. An opposite conception results when the individual is taken as the unit. It is then the single human being who is viewed as a natural unity and the group which appears artificial. Society is considered an aggregate, not an organism; a collection, not a collective whole. A group of men is thought to resemble a heap of stones. They are associated, yet separable. A stone may be removed from the heap, but it remains a stone.

The first comment to be made on these contrasts is that their opposition itself needs explaining. If opinions so contrary have been formulated and propagated, each must contain some elements of truth and correspond to certain facts. Plainly there is a sense in which every human being is unique and has a distinct existence, physically and psychically. When the bell tolls for John Jones, John Donne may say that it tolls for me also. But at that moment I can hear it and John Jones cannot—and that is no small difference! Moreover, when a characteristic is attributed to a group, it should not be forgotten that groups as such do not exist, or feel and move, or act and suffer. A group is what its members are. It does only what they do. In speaking about it in the singular, one is generalizing about them in the plural. Yet in another sense a group is an intelligible and describable fact and has a meaning of its own that single human beings do not. John Jones may have died, but the group of which he was a member continues in existence with virtually the same characteristics that it possessed in his lifetime. People are united by an intricate network of connections. They do not merely move in the same direction, like traffic on a one-way street. They react and interact at countless crossroads. Man, the doer, cannot be divorced from the relationships which arise from his cooperation and competition, his needs and deeds. Each such relation is a projection from his personality, and, like a shadow, belongs both to the man who casts it and to the place whereon it falls. Unless the projections are included, their source cannot be properly understood.

But while each viewpoint reposes on the solid ground of fact, it cannot be denied that both at times have taken wing into the thin air of exaggeration and unrealism. Thus at the higher speculative altitudes theorists have jet-propelled themselves into unsupportable positions. Such errors are always likely to occur in a discussion that employs the method of reasoning from analogy. The merit of this method is that it tries to explain what is unknown or obscure by comparison with something well known and clear. But the users of analogy tend to forget that the resemblances hold good only within the limits where they overlap. The objects compared are not identical (since to compare identicals would be pointless) but possess besides their common features other traits to distinguish them. This caution is necessary for students of human society who, in elucidating their complex subject, habitually conscript analogies in their service and work them to death.

1. The Organic Theory. To compare a group with a biological organism, for example, ceases to make sense when the former is endowed with all the properties of the latter. A group of persons is not the same as a single person and the one cannot be described precisely as if it were the other. Yet how frequently does this fallacy recur! Thus Plato, arguing that the greatest good for a community is unity, thought this would be attained when all members rejoiced and sorrowed at the same happenings and what touched one touched everyone. " 'And is not this,' " runs the Socratic interrogation in the *Republic,* " 'that is nearest the condition of a single individual? For consider, when any-one of us hurts his finger, the whole fellowship of body and soul which is bound into a single organization, namely, that of the ruling power within it, feels the hurt, and is all in pain at once, whole and hurt part together. And so we say that the man has a pain in his finger. And in regard to any part of the human body whatever, may not the same account be given of the pain felt when a part is hurt, and of the pleasure felt when it is at ease?' 'Yes,' he said. 'And to return to your question, the life of the best governed city comes very near to this condition.' 'Then I fancy that when an individual citizen has any experience, whether good or bad, such a city will most certainly de-clare that experience its own, and the whole city will share his joy or his sorrow.' "[20]

Equally misleading was the judgment of Rousseau. "The body poli-tic, taken individually," he wrote, "may be considered as an organ-ized, living body, resembling that of men. The sovereign power represents the head; the laws and customs are the brain; . . . the citizens are the body and the members which make the machine live, move and work; and no part of this machine can be damaged without the painful impression being at once conveyed to the brain, if the animal is in a state of health. . . . Nor is it any more credible that the general will should consent that any one member of the state, who-ever he might be, should wound or destroy another, than it is that the fingers of a man in his senses should wilfully scratch his eyes out."[21] These notions illustrate the danger of the organic analogy when pressed too far: namely, its tendency to personify the group and then ascribe to it the behavior of a human being.

2. The Metaphysics of Descartes. The contrary doctrine—that the human being is the "true" or "natural" unit and the group an artificial aggregate—has also strayed beyond the area of relevant resemblance into a fairyland of fictions. Of such a kind are many of the assumptions and assertions which pass currently under the name of individualism. The fault they share in common is a failure to see the wood for the trees. The individualist has focused his gaze so closely on the single human being, one and indivisible, that he has difficulty adjusting his

[20]*Republic,* v, Sec. 462, trans. A. D. Lindsay (Everyman's Library).

[21]"Discourse on Political Economy," in *The Social Contract and Discourses,* trans. G. D. H. Cole (Everyman's Library), pp. 252, 264. For a literary presentation of the same doctrine, note the remarks of Menenius Agrippa in Shakespeare's *Coriolanus,* Act I, sc. 1.

vision to scan the human multitude. He sees in segments and finds it hard in consequence to unify his field. He cannot, therefore, account satisfactorily for the association of individuals in a group. Just as the organic theory is incapable of explaining the uniqueness and separability of the members of a group, so the rival view flounders in the effort to reunite what its analysis has driven asunder. The impossibility of unscrambling eggs is equaled only by that of putting Humpty Dumpty together again.

People have nevertheless sought refuge in illustrative analogies, as if these were a talisman to accomplish the impossible. Some excellent examples occur in various philosophies of the seventeenth and eighteenth centuries. Many thinkers of that period started with the sound premise that anything complex should be analyzed into simple parts. Thus in logic and psychology it was argued that all ideas and propositions, however abstruse or abstract, are reducible to what Descartes called "clear and distinct perceptions." Similarly in the study of society it was supposed that the way to understand a group is to break it down into its elements, that is, individuals. But from this premise an inference was drawn that damaged the conclusions. It was assumed that once a whole is divided into parts, everything is present in the latter that is to be found in the former. Or, to say the same in another way, nothing is to be found in the whole which does not appear somewhere in the parts.[22] When this notion is transferred to human society, one arrives at the result that a group has no qualities that cannot be discovered in its members when they are viewed severally. Expressed in mathematical symbols, this would mean that a group can be described as the sum of an addition. Thus, if S stands for Society, and the letters a, b, c, d, etc., represent its individual members, we have the equation: $S = a + b + c + d + \ldots$. An alternative view would be to regard a group as the result, not of addition, but of multiplication. The equation would then read: $S = abcd \ldots$. Seen in this light, a complex whole possesses, by the fact of association, features of its own which are not traceable to its separate parts and which only belong to it when the parts become associated. A watchmaker can take a watch apart and lay all the pieces on a table. But when you look at them, what you see is not a watch; and you cannot tell from the scattered parts what the watch will show you—namely, the time.

3. The Social Contract. There are some other false leads of this

---

[22]For examples of this mode of thinking, see Hobbes' *Leviathan* (Everyman's Library), Part I, Chap. 5, p. 18; John Locke, *Second Treatise of Civil Government* (Everyman's Library), Sec. 135, pp. 184–85; Rousseau, *Social Contract* (Everyman's Library), I, Chap. 6, p. 14.

misguided individualism which deserve mention, since they have exercised so wide an influence. In seeking to explain the mysteries of human association, the individualist theories of the seventeenth and eighteenth centuries utilized two popular parallels. One of these—the fiction of a social contract—may possibly have owed something of its vogue[23] to the contemporary spread of the joint stock company as a convenient instrument for accumulating capital and conducting business on a larger scale. Incorporation of companies produces a relation between human beings that is contractual in character. From this it is a relatively easy step—or slip—to argue that society itself rests on a contractual foundation and then to conjure up the myth of a social contract. The comparison of society with a contract has this much in its favor: a contract does confer on the contracting parties responsibilities and rights that are mutually guaranteed and recognized. Society does the same for its members. A contract involves reciprocity and is the product of a willingness to give and take. So, too, with society. But after that point any resemblances cease to be helpful. The mistake in the analogy is that not all groups are joint stock companies; not all relationships are contractual. Men do not formally enter society in the way they sign a lease or join a partnership. They do not withdraw from society as they would withdraw their money from a bank or quit a job. The bonds that unite a family; the fellowship of scholars and students in a center of learning; the faith that inspires a religious community; the work and the traditions that build a nation—can all this be explained in the language or the spirit of a deed of trust? The richness and complexities of social intercourse cannot be consigned to the four corners of a legal parchment or reduced to the items of an invoice.

4. Newtonian Physics. If the social contract suggested one means of reuniting individuals into groups, another was offered by the physicists. The publication in 1687 of Isaac Newton's *Principia Mathematica* and his formulation of the law of gravity was a great event in intellectual history. Newton's achievement lay in developing a hypothesis which could embrace and explain, as a law of the nature of matter, phenomena so diverse as the fall of an apple from a tree, the ebb and flow of the tide, the rotation of the earth and its revolution around the sun. It then appeared that there could be a system such as the universe, composed of inanimate yet interacting parts, whose union is not organic, but results from the physical properties of matter. If so, might not an association of human beings be conceived

---

[23]Though differently used to obtain different results, the social contract theory is part of the common stock-in-trade of Hobbes, Locke, and Rousseau and of lesser writers.

as an aggregate of atoms or as planets within a solar system? A group could then be explained in terms of attraction and repulsion, of balance and equilibrium, of forces and inertia.

Being novel and ingenious, this idea did not lack support. Indeed, it made its imprint on minds as eminent as those of John Locke and Thomas Jefferson. But it could never succeed in being more than a passing fashion or suggestive parallel. As an exposition of the true nature of groups, it was doomed to suffer the fate of all analogies.[24] For the conduct of human beings, though they belong to the world of physical phenomena, does not conform in all particulars to the laws of inanimate matter. Cooperation and competition are not akin to a series of positive and negative charges. Nor is it true that human actions, even though they have causes, are determined in every case by a compulsive necessity, as the ocean is pulled by the moon. Men are presented with alternative lines of action and are aware of their opportunity to make choices. At least, they think this is the case and believe that their will, though circumscribed by limits, is free within these. Such thinking and beliefs are relevant to their conduct. Human beings are self-conscious, deliberating, reasoning agents; not fully understanding themselves, and therefore not wholly predictable. They do not fall into the orbit of groups, as the moon moves around the earth or as apples fall from trees.

5. *The Iceberg Analogies.* The twentieth century has made its own contributions to these attempts to interpret the character of groups by analogies. As Darwin and Marx injected two powerful stimuli into social thought in the latter part of the nineteenth century, so, in the early decades of this century, did Freud. Significantly, the inferences to be drawn from all three converge on the same conclusion. Put in Freudian terms, it is this: the true explanation for men's actions, whether singly or in groups, does not lie on the surface. Like an iceberg, the larger part of the human psyche is concealed from the eye, and it is there that the fundamental causes of conflict or cohesion are latent. Outward appearances are deceptive, for neither individuals nor groups are what they seem.

This was the main point which the creator of psychoanalysis drove home to social analysts through his discovery of the role of the unconscious. The springs of conduct, as he postulated, lie submerged—and to a far greater extent than any of us is ever consciously aware. Patterns produced within the family in infancy and childhood reappear, in various representational modes, in the activities of the adult. The

[24]See the criticism offered by Woodrow Wilson, *The New Freedom*, ed. William Leuchtenburg (Englewood Cliffs, N.J.: Prentice-Hall, Inc., 1961), Chap. 2. Wilson is himself open to criticism, however, for accepting organic theories too readily.

affinity between such reasoning and the earlier doctrines of Marx and Darwin is clear. The former had argued that social institutions are only the superstructure conforming to the necessities which the dominant economic patterns impose. To find out what makes society tick, look behind the state to the relationships of production. It is these which control the rest. Similarly, Darwin had plumbed the depths when he investigated the origins of species. In the thought of the geneticist, man was revealed as a somewhat more sophisticated monkey. Retrace our ancestry far enough back in time, and all of us are first cousins to the chimpanzees.

Despite the profound contrasts in the subject matter on which they worked, the psychoanalyst, the biologist, and the economist produced the common effect of enlarging the perspective from which groups are viewed and understood. Each had interpreted the relations of individuals to groups in the context of a total configuration extending through time and space. For Freud, this comprises the sum of the influences which have molded one's personality since birth; for Darwin, the long process of evolution which retains elements of the savage within the folds of the civilized; and for Marx, the complex interaction between groups within a social framework determined by its economic base. Such pointers have led researchers down many dark corridors, seeking to unlock the doors to lighted rooms. We owe to these formulations the caution against taking appearance for the whole of the truth. But if much of that truth, by definition, is below the surface, our knowledge of what is real will depend ultimately as much on inference as observation, and may therefore be unprovable. Also, to the extent that the view of the superstructure is conditioned by the analyst's particular concept of the foundation, is it not possible that Freud paid more than due attention to sexuality, Darwin to the struggle for survival, and Marx to the relations of production? And does not an exaggeration in the premises yield a distortion in the conclusions?

6. Systems Analysis. In recent decades, yet another style of analogy has come into vogue—new in its language and some of its immediate inspiration, although not so original in what it has to say. This is the analysis of systems. A system is any complex whole, consisting of independent parts and interacting processes. Within it are structures which perform functions or, conversely, functions which acquire a structural form. To preserve itself, the system seeks to maintain a boundary demarcating it from other systems. Demands on raw materials are fed into the system. These are inputs. From it flow programs or products. Those are outputs.

Three points in this require comment—the substance of the

analogy, its sources, and its form. If systems analysis applied to human societies is intended to clarify what groups are and how they behave, what are we being told here that we did not previously know? To affirm that a group is a system which generically resembles other systems is a proposition whose ancestry reaches back to Plato and Aristotle. The notions of a complex whole consisting of interrelated parts and of a process dynamically producing results within a structural framework, these are implicit or explicit in the logic of several of the analogies already discussed. The only substantial difference in the case of contemporary efforts at analyzing systems in general is the range of its generality. For it aims at embracing everything—animate and inanimate, individual and social, natural and man-made. In sum, there is nothing that is not a system. In that case, however, by including everything, this reasoning ends up by explaining nothing. In order to attain such a level of generality or, perhaps, universality, the results are couched in abstractions too rarefied to be directly relevant to any particular concrete reality. Much of what is written under the rubric of systems analysis is formal and mechanistic. It has left humanity out of sight and no longer relates to flesh-and-blood people. It should, therefore, be considered for what it is—an ingenious exercise in metapolitics or social algebra.

Much of this can be explained by the sources which inspired this recent vogue. For here is a case where the impact of modern technology on social thought has been both immediate and pervasive. Computers, automation, electronics, and the aerospace industries have accomplished spectacular results by mathematical analysis and the construction of elaborate systems built by men. By analogy, similar methods are then applied to systems in general, so that human society is categorized as the social system, government as the political system, and so forth. In this way of thinking, the technology—and with it the language—of communications has been especially influential, as is notable in what one might call the telephone-exchange theory of human society. In this analogy, a community is conceived as a system of communications. It conveys messages, emits signals, supplies feedback, and may suffer from overloading. Certain components may even prove "dysfunctional" (they don't work or they work badly).

The impetus from technology has been reinforced by the contributions of sociology. This latter discipline was a latecomer to the social sciences and for that reason has not yet surmounted its identity crisis. Ever since its inauguration by Auguste Comte, the evolution of sociology has been the story of a title in search of a field. Sociologists had a choice. They could garner up the leftovers, that is, study everything social which was not earmarked by the earlier established disciplines (law, economics, politics, etc.), or they could emerge well versed in a master science enveloping everything. Since the former prospect was uninviting (for who wants to be a specialist on residues?), most have preferred the latter road—with the result that they can now subsume anything within their discipline by prefixing to it the words "the sociology of——." In an effort to unify the field of social studies, general systems analysis was admirably suited. Its very generality, the abstractness of its categories, its "over-arching theory," all fitted the bill.

Conforming to its sources in the real sciences, this mode of analysis professes to be no less scientific in the study of society. A science, as such, is objective, neutral, and independent of the values of the researcher. It discovers, describes, analyzes. It answers the questions of what, how, and why—but not the question "what for?" and never (perish the thought!) "for what good?" The analysis of human society as a general system attempts the same, and, consonant with its scientific pretensions, it clothes itself in a jargon which usually cloaks essentially simple thoughts in four-syllable words.

The great merit of system analysts is their comprehensiveness. They see and interpret everything as a whole, and, consequently, in their sense everything is interrelated and anything has relevance. That is good. But where this analogy fails is in its inability to interpret what is characteristically human in the kind of system which a society constitutes. The true flavor of the original, the special quality which one must needs comprehend, is lost in the abstractness of the analogy. Moreover, the insistence that society must be studied by the methodology of the sciences imposes a limitation on the subject which becomes self-defeating. Above all, it loses the essential—which is to recapture and interpret a human society in humanistic, not mechanistic, terms. Despite the sociologists' appeal to the authority of Max Weber, one must insist that, since man is the value-selecting animal, a study of his society which is strictly value free can never be in tune with the original.

Let us now retrace the course of the argument and see where it has carried us. After observing that men's relationships consist in striving with and against others, and that groups are born both to obtain the results of cooperation and to restrain the effects of competition, we discovered that attempts to build society on the sole basis of either the group or the individual were inadequate. The problem then resolved itself into discussing how these complementary opposites could be combined and what happened within a group when its members were united for some purposes and divided for others. At this point we examined certain interpretations of the nature of groups. Reasoning from analogies appeared to create as many difficulties as it removed. Hence theories about human association which assimilate it to an organism, a contract, the physical universe, the psyche, or a general system were rejected as either asserting too much or explaining too little. But although such theories are misleading if taken literally or if considered the complete explanation, each of them may offer a clue to the understanding of groups if it serves to highlight some aspect of an obscure subject. These clues can be threaded together if we summarize the principal points in which the various analogies are correct, and those in which they are not.

THE UNIQUENESS OF THE HUMAN GROUP

Thus, a human group resembles an organism in that its members perform various functions and are interdependent. It differs in that it has no way of thinking, feeling, and acting as one. A group is similar to a contract because those who belong to it give and receive their *quid pro quo*. But it is unlike an ordinary contractual union in that people are not always at liberty to enter or depart as they please and its aims may become multifarious and expansive. A group has in common with the physical universe the fact that both are systems in dynamic motion. But in the physical universe the parts lack the faculty of acting independently and with a purpose. A group of persons resembles the individual psyche in that its outward character is shaped by currents which run very deep. It differs in that it does not possess a personality analyzable in the same sense as a person's. A group may be classified logically in the same general category with other systems and therefore exhibit some of their characteristics. But no other system has the same specific attributes of humanity.

To what conclusion does this summary lead? Presumably to a very simple one—that a group of human beings is something unique, that it forms a class by itself, and that the best way to understand it is to see it in its own true colors. The unique quality that all human associations possess can be described as follows: A group is composed of individual members who must become parts of a whole since, unless associated, they are unable to develop themselves. Yet it is the parts, and only these, that possess a consciousness of the self and of the whole, and are thereby capable of contributing to the whole a purpose and an organization. Thus in a paradoxical manner human beings exist separately, but are inseparably united.

THE VARIETY OF GROUPS

That statement, however, does not complete the analysis of groups because there are yet further facts to observe. One reason why it is difficult to fathom the nature of a group is that we are tempted to regard it as existing by itself and to consider the relations of its members as if these were confined within its borders and did not extend beyond. But such a view is inaccurate. The truth is that all men belong to many groups. So varied are the relationships created by their needs that the same human beings, like the pieces in a kaleidoscope, form and reform, combine and recombine, into numerous associations with different patterns. If it is asked why this is so, the reply surely is that groups are no less prolific than the causes of cooperation and the consequences of competition. Groups are many in number because needs are so varied and conflict is so frequent.

The best way of describing and classifying groups is by the purpose they seek to fulfill. A great many associations, for example, are created in response to man's material necessities and wants. Such "economic" groups correspond to the innumerable phases of the system of production, distribution, and consumption. A weight has to be lifted that takes the strength of two. A fence between two farms requires repairing and the neighbors do it together. From these instances it seems a far cry to the intricate structures of a modern economy. But just as the symphonies of Beethoven or Tchaikovsky presuppose the simpler harmonics of a birdcall or tom-tom, so do underlying similarities of principle persist through the evolution of social organization from the rudimentary to the complex. A business firm is an organization of persons engaged in supplying some commodity or service on terms presumably advantageous to themselves and to the recipients. The joint stock company, the legal device of the corporation, a banking or insurance system, a cooperative store, are familiar instruments by which people pool their resources and accomplish on a larger scale results otherwise unattainable. The trade union, once regarded as a criminal conspiracy, has become a recognized and generally a conservative part of the established order. Nowadays, after the fashion of the medieval guild, it seeks to promote the security of its members both by providing a standard of skill and by eliminating mutually ruinous undercutting in the competition for jobs.

If a need like the economic, which is common to all mankind, has produced these economic associations, so other universal or widespread needs have evoked their counterparts. Man is everywhere curious about himself and his environment. He learns and he teaches. He wonders and ponders. He wishes to know and to understand. As a reasoning animal, whose mind can communicate its thoughts through the faculty of speech, man has a need for education which he can satisfy only by a cooperative endeavor. Our accumulating store of knowledge was transmitted through the generations and is bequeathed to the human race as our common intellectual heritage. To encompass its vast dimensions requires the meeting of many minds in a fellowship of learning. Hence there exists a network of institutions to provide an organized response to the desire to know. Similarly, but without laboring the point, we may cite other familiar instances where a felt need stimulates association. Belief in a Supreme Being and the wish to worship produced the world's religions. The family group gives companionship to adults and an upbringing to children. The cultural interests of like-minded people find a medium in operas, theaters, art galleries, symphony orchestras, the ballet, and so on; while fondness for recreation and physical exercise results in sporting and athletic clubs.

COMPONENTS OF GROUPS

These comparisons suggest that it is possible to subdivide a group into its components and then, as in Table I, analyze the features it shares with others and those specific to each kind. What are the elements of which a group is composed? The first is necessarily the membership, since without this there would be no group. The members are variously named and related according to the nature of the association they form. If it is a church, they are a congregation or are called, in terms of the belief they profess, the faithful. If it is a family, they are parents, children, uncles, cousins—or, all-inclusively, relatives. If a business firm, they are owners, managers, employees. If a state, they are citizens or subjects and rulers or officials. How is membership acquired in the group? Sometimes by the voluntary choice of the person who seeks admission and of the existing members who decide to admit. Thus a person may undergo conversion and then be initiated into a religious faith, or he may apply and be accepted at a school or university. He may obtain appointment to a job in a business firm, be naturalized as a citizen, marry and start a family. Sometimes the act of joining a group is involuntary, as when an infant is born into a family, is baptized into a church, and automatically receives the citizenship of the country of its birth. Similarly, membership in the group may be terminated by voluntary act of the individual or under compulsion from the group. You may sever your link with an organized religion by nonattendance at its devotions, or it may excommunicate you. You may graduate from school or college or drop out or be

Table I
THE COMPOSITION OF GROUPS

Elements Common to All Groups	Elements of Religious Groups	Elements of Educational Groups	Elements of Family Groups	Elements of Business Firms°	Elements of the State
1. Members	Congregation The Faithful	Teachers Students	Parents Children	Owners, Managers, Employees	Citizens, Subjects, Officials
a. How they join	Initiation Baptism Conversion	Appointment Admission	Marriage Birth Adoption	Purchase of shares Hiring for job	Birth Naturalization Residence
b. How they leave	Nonattendance Excommunication	Retirement Resignation Graduation Expulsion	Desertion Death Divorce	Sale of shares Resignation Dismissal	Renunciation Deportation Deprivation of citizenship
2. Functions†	Worship	Teaching Learning	Cohabitation Propagation	Manufacturing Sales	Protection, Justice, Welfare
3. Institutions	Church, Temple Mosque, Synagogue	School, College, University	The Home	Firm Corporation	The State
4. Rules	Canon law, Ritual, Mosaic law, Koran	Regulations Classroom discipline	Marriage Fidelity	Articles of incorporation Shop rules, etc.	Law Custom
5. Governing authority	Congregation Clergy	Teachers	Parents	Management Foremen	Government Officials
6. Revenue	Donations Tithes	Grants Fees	Income	Profits	Taxes, Loans, etc.
7. Ideas	Theology Creed	Pedagogy Curriculum	Monogamy Polygamy Polyandry	Property, Private ownership, Contract, Competition	Political theory

°The business firm is selected as an example of one type of economic grouping
†The functions listed in the table are not intended to be complete and exhaustive. Those stated in each case are the central and primary ones, not those that are secondary and derivative. All groups tend to acquire additional functions.

expelled; resign your job or be fired; renounce your allegiance or be deprived of citizenship.

If the members constitute the original element in any group, its functions form the second. For it is to fulfill a purpose by carrying out a certain function that members are associated. How do we describe the functions of a group? Presumably the chief function of the family is to propagate and live together; of the religious group, to worship; of the firm, to conduct a business; of the state, to protect. Functions such as these cannot be performed without organization, structure, and system. In other words, every organization that maintains its identity and retains its continuity begets a progeny of institutions. Though variously named, the latter are fundamentally alike in the role they perform. Thus education is institutionalized through schools, colleges, and universities. Religion is organized by means of temples, mosques, synagogues, and churches. Business is carried on by the firm or corporation. The family clusters round the home. Likewise the state expresses itself through government and such specialized agencies as the legislature, law court, administrative department, and civil service.

When an institution is organized, three further elements make their appearance: a body of rules, a governing authority, and revenue. Every association produces rules which define the relations of its members, allot their rights and responsibilities, and prescribe its operating procedures. In a church, this takes the form of canon law and ritual. In the family, the law of marital relations reinforces the moral code of fidelity. A business firm not only has its internal regulations, but also conforms to general trade practices and operates within the framework of laws of contract, property, corporations, and so on. The state is both creator and creature of law and custom. To enforce these rules and give general guidance to the group is the task of its governing authority. This appears under different guises, depending on the nature of the association, as the management, clergy, parents, teachers, or government. Similarly, in every group an essential ingredient is its revenue—if that term is understood to comprise the physical and material resources by which the group accomplishes its purposes. Thus a school or university is maintained by public funds or private fees and endowments; a business, by its profits; the state, by taxes and fees; the family, by its property or income.

Finally, there is one more component without which no association is complete. Every group is both producer and product of the ideas concerning it which exist in the minds of its members. These ideas are an integral part of the life of the group since they embody the hopes and aspirations of its members, expressing their conception of the group's purpose and their understandings about its processes. The ideas that sustain the group are not always explicitly formulated. In certain cases they are inarticulate, and are divined rather than defined. Even if expressed, they may not always be systematized into a coherent philosophy. For example, the kinds of family systems are numerous and various, as are the kinds of political systems. But while political theories are many, theories of the family are relatively fewer. This does not mean, however, that the family group lacks its ideology. Nor, for that matter, can religion fulfill its purposes without a theological creed for the hereafter and the herenow; a university, without an educational philosophy; or a business firm, without a theory of economic behavior.

THE UNITY OF SOCIETY

This analysis has been sufficient to show that human groups are many in number and different in purpose. But it also reveals how complex is the sum total of associations, which is best described by the word "society" because of its generality. Thus defined, society comprises the whole gamut of social relationships and organized groups. But that is not all. Besides the fact that society is made up of many groups, there is the no less significant truth that all human beings have numerous memberships. Men are by nature joiners. Each person belongs simultaneously to a collection of groups, no one of which alone embraces all his interests. Not only is society a pluralistic union of groups, but the ways in which every human being is associated are also plural. The numerous groupings into which all men enter bring them sometimes into relations with the same persons, but more usually with different ones. Thus, as a partner in a business firm, A may be associated with B, C, D, and E; as a university alumnus, with C, D, L, and M; as a worshiper in a church, with W, X, Y, and Z; and so on. As the purposes for combination vary, so each finds himself associated with different samples of his fellowmen. Neither in function nor in membership are the groups identical.

These indisputable facts produce most controversial implications. In the first place, the use of the singular term "society" to describe the sum total of relationships and groups involves a major assumption. One should raise, rather than beg, these fundamental questions: Is society truly a unity? Is there anything that embraces the plurality of groups? If so, what makes it a whole? Does this oneness occur only subjectively in our minds and emotions, or does it also appear externally in some actual structure and organization? A second difficulty arises out of the first. It can be readily seen that the processes of cooperation and competition create relations between men, and that these relations receive an orderly character through the formation of groups. But once the groups have been formed, what is it that regulates the relations between groups themselves? How is the grouping of groups arranged? Human needs and interests cannot be so sliced up as to prevent all chance of contact or overlap. When one speaks of man's economic need, his educational need, his cultural need, and so on, these are not a string of airtight compartments but the many facets of a personality that functions as a whole. Human beings have needs that interlock. They pursue objectives that conflict. So it is with the resulting groups, as some examples will indicate.

DIVIDED LOYALTIES OF THE INDIVIDUAL

Business practices, backed up by economic theory, sanction the lending of capital for interest. But the businessman's religion may frown upon this as the sin of usury. A painter interprets on canvas the world as he sees it and insists that he pursues his art for its own sake. Yet his critics may charge that he offends the moral, as well as aesthetic, susceptibilities of others, and they assert the subordination of art to ethics. Parents wish their children to be educated so that their opportunities may be broadened and improved. But the poverty of the home makes it necessary to increase the family earnings by sending the children into early employment. A man and a woman want to marry. But the church to which one of them belongs forbids the union on the ground that the other party belongs to a different church or has been divorced. A desirable piece of land in a city of expanding population is wanted by an industrial firm to erect a factory that will employ many workers. The same area is sought by educational authorities for a school and playground, by a building contractor for a housing project, by a movie exhibitor for a theater. How are such conflicts resolved? Who arbitrates the merits of the contending claims? On what principles is a just decision based?

Such cases are not hypothetical or fictitious. They are actual scenes from the tragicomedy of human life. If they possess drama, it is because any situation of conflict is inherently dramatic. Nor is this conflict one that exists solely between groups. It goes far deeper, since within each human being and inside each group a struggle develops between contrary sentiments, attitudes, habits, and ideas. Each man finds himself belonging to a number of systems that correspond with his respective interests and needs. But these interests overlap, the needs crisscross, the systems clash. As father of a family, one has an obligation to his wife and children which may be at variance with his financial circumstances. As the adherent of a religious faith, he may accept dogmas, which, as a participant in an educational program, he may be expected to question. As an artist, he may seek to portray events truthfully as they appear to him. But in so doing he may run counter to the conventions of the social order by which he is enclosed. Each of these systems—the economic, religious, cultural, family, and the rest—lays claim to the loyalty of its members. Since each system, however, covers only a segment of a man's total needs and interests, the allegiance that each can exact must itself be partial. How then can a person come to a decision when faced with antagonistic demands? Amid so many claims, how is one to know which to respect?

THE SEARCH FOR SOCIAL HARMONY

There are two possible answers to these questions. The competition of loyalties, it is arguable, may be resolved by compromise. Strictly understood, this means that neither of the rival claims is completely satisfied. Instead, an agreement is reached at some position that is intermediate. Each side succeeds on some points, and concedes on others. But if this is done, one naturally inquires: Who acts as intermediary? Who brings about the compromise? On what principles is it based? How are these determined? Even these queries, however, do not apply to conflicts which from their nature permit no compromise whatsoever. Take, for example, the demand of Roman emperors that they and their deified predecessors be worshiped as divinities by inhabitants of their empire. Between this demand and the religious beliefs of their Christian subjects, no compromise was possible. Or consider the implications of the most divisive domestic issue which has erupted in the United States since the achievement of independence: the institution of slavery. There was no midway point for settlement between one who upheld the principle that human beings may be bought, owned, and sold as the legal property of other human beings, and one who asserted the contrary principle that they may not. One view or the other had to be adopted. The twain could not be reconciled or harmonized. As the judgment of Solomon indicated when two women claimed the same child, the price of compromise was to kill the baby. The outcome of the slavery question was in fact left to the arbitrament of war; and arms decided not which view was better, but which in practice was to prevail.

As a second possibility of resolving conflict between groups, when compromise is impracticable or inadmissible, the loyalty to one group must bow before the loyalty to another. But how is this achieved? Who decides which group shall predominate and by what means it shall triumph? One method is by the use of force, with the consequent suppression or overpowering of the unsuccessful side. A second is by the voluntary submission of one side after peaceful persuasion. A third is by appealing to some larger association which will choose between opposing claims in the light of a still wider union. Thus the difficulty of harmonizing cooperation with competition, of groups with individuals, is viewed in broader focus when it is treated not simply as a matter of relations between persons within a single group, but as a complex of interrelations between numerous groups whose members are associated and reassociated in diverse ways. Consequently it is necessary to reframe the question, raised earlier, of how to describe the relation of the group to the individual. This can now be more accurately expressed as the problem of organizing many multimembered groups of human beings into one multigroup society. Can the principles of social theory and the practices of social organization devise a rationale for uniting the various groups with their many members and the various members with their many groupings? The search for this union can end only with the discovery of an interest sufficiently broad to absorb all partial, lesser interests and of an association wide enough to embrace the lesser, limited associations. It is time, therefore, to turn to the origins of the state and the contribution of government.

3

The Origins of the
State

POLITICS, STATE, AND GOVERNMENT

Of the numerous organized groups that constitute society, the state is the special concern of the student of politics. As with every human association, the state emerges and exists within society. The taproots of government reach down into the same soil which holds and nurtures the family and the church, the corporation and the trade union, the school and the club. But what is it that stimulates the state to grow in its own particular manner? What are the seeds of the political process? Why is there this institution which we call the government, and where precisely does it originate? These are some of the questions which the present chapter attempts to answer.

The way they are phrased, however, reveals a problem that confronts every analysis of this subject. The difficulty is partly conceptual and partly verbal. Our topic involves three basic terms: "politics," "state," and "government." Frequently, these are used as synonyms, and many definitions employ them interchangeably. But the facts we have to explain, and the ideas they incorporate, imply some genuine distinctions, for which different words are needed if the meaning of the argument is to be clear. Hence, the following discussion will differentiate between politics, state, and government so as to help in understanding the facts. Society was defined earlier as the broadest possible concept that embraces all human relationships and groups. If we continue to proceed from the broad to the narrow, the concept that comes next is politics. By politics I mean a process of active controversy over the merits of the alternative solutions to the five issues which were outlined in Chapter 1 and will be analyzed in Chapters 4-13.

More limited than politics is the concept of the state. This is the institution through which the dynamics of politics are organized and formalized. The state involves machinery, agencies, jurisdictions, powers, and rights. It is a network of structured relationships. The point that politics is broader than the state can be easily demonstrated. Wherever the state exists, there is also politics. But the converse is not true—that wherever politics exists, so does the state. We can speak of international politics, but we know that there is no supranational state as yet. We can talk of politics within churches or corporations or trade unions, although none of those is a state. The state, however, comprises another and narrower concept—that of government. Every state has its government, and the latter signifies specifically the persons who hold official positions and wield authority on behalf of the state. Governments in this sense will change while the same state continues. Government, therefore, implies within the state a distinction between rulers and ruled. We can visualize this series of concepts geometrically as concentric circles, where society is the outermost and government, the innermost, thus:

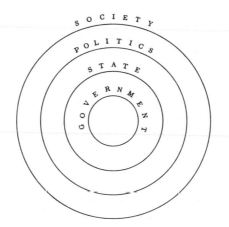

THE PRIMARY FUNCTION OF THE STATE

If all groups are organized in response to some social need, the state, because it has become a universal institution, must correspond to needs that are universal. Hence, it should be possible to infer the need to which the state responds by studying the functions it undertakes. Anybody who surveys the vast complex of activities undertaken by the state in different periods and places is bound to wonder why they are conducted by this particular association. He learns that certain functions were assumed by the state long ago, while others are more recent additions. He finds a wide measure of agreement that there are some duties appropriate for the state to undertake and much controversy about the suitability of others. Consequently he begins to ask whether the functions of government can be classified into primary and secondary, original and derivative, essential and optional, accepted and debatable. To answer such questions, the student of politics would find it a help if he could put his finger on any one function and say, "This without dispute is *the* function of the state." Or, approaching the same point from another direction, he should ask, "What is the minimum indispensable function which the state must perform in order to be a state? Is any activity of the state so vital that, were it performed by another association, the latter in effect would be or become the state?"

THE UNIVERSAL DRIVE FOR PROTECTION

To these questions the facts of government disclose an answer. Among the common concerns of all human beings is the desire for security of life and limb. All want to be safe. Everywhere men seek guarantees that they be protected from physical harm. But though the urge to ward off bodily threats is universal, different means of protection have been employed. It has not been uncommon, for example, for human beings to rely primarily on themselves. On all continents in most historical periods—and almost certainly in the prehistoric—men kept weapons in their homes and carried them on journeys. The first line of defense against attack upon one's person or possessions was also, in a sense, the last. It lay in one's own strong arm, since the help of others, even if mobilized, might arrive too late. But self-reliance was bound under certain circumstances to be inadequate. This was especially so when the likelihood of attack was constant, rather than intermittent; when the techniques available to an aggressor placed the defense at a disadvantage; and when the chief disturbance to one's peace came, not from within the group, but from the organized strength of another group outside. Effective security, therefore, had to be collective security. The protection that men could not obtain by action singly had to be found by cooperating as a group. But when a need, like this one of protection, remains constant, the method by which the group satisfies it is to develop practices and procedures that have to be continually repeated. At some stage, by virtue of repetition, these become recognized and accepted. They are then endowed with formal organization. In a word, they are institutionalized. What we call an "institution" is the outgrowth in organized form of the repetitive practices with which a group fulfills a common need. The state originates, in short, when a group of persons have institutionalized their own protection.

So far, however, this statement has consisted of assertions rather than proof. What evidence is there to prove that protection is the original function of the state? The answer can be drawn from various sources, including a review of historical data plus the analysis of present-day governmental functions. The historical evidence, though fragmentary and circumstantial, is sufficient to justify some highly probable conclusions. Thanks to the research of anthropologists, who have classified the various stages in the evolution of man and his cultures, it appears that the earliest period about which anything is known (the Lower Paleolithic) extended from perhaps 130,000 to 500,000 years back in the past.[1] Unfortunately, surviving archaeological remains and the literary heritage throw few and fitful glimpses on the manner in which men lived and governed themselves more than 5,000 years ago. In most of the world's civilizations—for example, the Chinese, Indian, Iranian, Egyptian, or European—it is not until the period roughly from 3000 B.C. to 1000 B.C. that enough is known to warrant the use of the term "history" by contrast with earlier "prehistory." At the dawn of history, however, the institution of government already existed. Its birth took place, therefore, in the prehistoric night before the dawn. Hence any assertion about the origins of the state must repose mainly on conjecture.

Nevertheless there is testimony to show that an intimate connection has always existed between the organization which a group adopts for its defense and for its government. When human beings lived as nomads, hunting or herding their food supply, their mobility necessitated a military or semimilitary organization since they transported with them their families and possessions. The able-bodied males on their mounts were already a cavalry; the carts or wagons of a caravan made a defensive post. The change from nomadism to a settled habitat, associated with the shift from hunting or tending animals to planting crops, altered the tactics of protection because the objects to be defended—the home and its source of food—were stationary, and a person who planted a seed had to remain there until he could collect his crop. Consequently, though men who became agriculturists preferred living in plains that were easier to plow and sow and reap, they

---

[1]See Melville J. Herskovits, *Man and His Works* (New York: Alfred A. Knopf, Inc., 1948), pp. 114 ff., and especially p. 120. Arnold J. Toynbee points out in his *Civilization on Trial* (New York: Oxford University Press, Inc., 1948, pp. 36–37) that the period of time about which we have some historical information is infinitesimally small in relation to the age of the earth and the evolution of man. Modern scientists estimate that the planet may have existed for some 2,000 million years and life for perhaps 500 to 800 million years. The earliest known remains of manlike creatures, the family of hominids, have been dated to two and a half million years ago. "In terms of evolutionary history," according to Dr. Louis Leakey, "man's separation from his closest cousins—the apes—is now carried back more than a million generations."

also required a defensible frontier on the rim of the plain and a fortress or citadel in the interior. It was out of this need, and the institutions occasioned by it, that the primary function of government was founded.

THE EVIDENCE OF LANGUAGE AND HISTORY

On this point language supplies illuminating evidence, since the origins of our ideas are to be found in the roots of the words that express them. Many of our oldest and commonest political expressions originally had the sense of a limited area, fortified for safety. Thus the Greek *polis,* ancestor of the term "politics," signified the strong point where scattered farmers and villagers could gather, where the women and children would be secure, and where the defense had military advantages.[2] The center of Athenian civic life, and the dominating feature of its topography, was its "high polis," or Acropolis. The city of Rome likewise commenced its history as the rallying point for scattered rural settlements in the Latin plain whose inhabitants could find protection on the seven hills beside the River Tiber. One of these hills, the famed Capitoline, was crowned, not only by the ancient temple of the Romans' ranking deity, Jupiter, but also by the *arx,*[3] or "citadel." The whole cluster of buildings atop and between the hills received the name of *urbs* (whence our adjective "urban"), which is derived from the Sanskrit root *vardh,* "to make strong." The same may be demonstrated of the institutions bequeathed by the Anglo-Saxons. Our "town" is the modern descendant of a word that variously reappears in a group of allied languages. As the Old English *tun,* it signified an enclosed place; as the Celtic *dun,* "a fortified place, or camp"; in Old High German, "a fence or hedge."[4] The borough, or burgh, comes from an uncertain source, but may be related to the old Teutonic *berg-an,* "to shelter." Its primary sense, however, is not obscure, for in German and Old Norse it chiefly denotes a "fortress or castle."[5]

To the evidence of philology is added the testimony of history. The world's oldest known city is Jericho, and it has been occupied continuously since about 7800 B.C. From early times, Jericho was strongly

[2]See Ernest Barker's introduction to *The Politics of Aristotle* (New York: Oxford University Press, Inc., 1946), p. lxv.

[3]*Arx* is an offshoot of the verb *arcere,* "to ward off."

[4]The second syllable of Lon*don* comes from this root.

[5]The original meaning of the term is well expressed in a line of a late medieval German song that became part of the Lutheran hymnal: *Ein feste Burg ist unser Gott!* (A strong citadel is our God!).

fortified with a watchtower and its famous walls.[6] Archaeological inquiries into the beginnings of civilization in Mesopotamia have thrown some light on the circumstances which explain the emergence of the state. In the area watered by the Tigris and the Euphrates urban centers evolved, controlling a river-borne commerce and an expanse of fertile fields. The social order of communities such as Akkad and Sumer was a cluster of interests in which temple officials, merchants, craftsmen, and landowners vied for position. The scattered cities, independently organized, competed for the possession of land and water. V. Gordon Childe has described what happened under these conditions: "A new institution was needed to restrain these conflicts. By the beginning of historical times the State had emerged, but it was embodied in the single person of the *city-governor* or king, who may be just 'corn-king' and war-chief amalgamated and writ large."[7]

Elsewhere in early times, not only has the duty of protecting the group devolved upon its able-bodied males, but also the privilege and responsibility of government have often been entrusted to the same hands that bear or once bore the burden of defense. From numerous examples that could be cited, a few will illustrate the truth that the organization of society for government has often been adapted, or transferred without change, from its organization for war. Under the Athenian constitution of the seventh century B.C. prior to Solon's reforms, the citizen body was divided into three classes with different rights allocated to each. The classes were determined by property qualifications; but they were also distinguished by their military functions, as two of the names indicate. In descending order of rank and wealth, they were the *Hippeis*, or cavalrymen; the *Zeugitae*, who could equip themselves for the heavy infantry; and the *Thetes*, or laborers.[8] The link between wealth and warfare is explained by the fact that it cost money to own a horse and pay for arms and armor. A parallel[9] to this Athenian example is provided by Rome, where one of the citizens' assemblies was known as the *Comitia Centuriata*. Its organization was intended to reproduce the "centuries," or "hundreds," which were the basic units in the formation of the Roman army.

As in the Graeco-Roman civilization, so in the Teutonic world the

[6]See James Mellaart in *The Dawn of Civilization* (London: Thames and Hudson, Ltd., 1962), pp. 41–58.

[7]See V. Gordon Childe, *What Happened in History* (Baltimore, Md.: Penguin Books, Inc.; Nicholls & Co., rev. ed., 1954), pp. 99–100.

[8]See E. A. Gardner and M. Cary in *Cambridge Ancient History*, Vol. III (New York: The Macmillan Company, 1923–39), p. 594, where they state, "Though the property classes were based on wealth, their original purpose certainly was not fiscal, but rather military, as was the purpose of the Roman *centuriae.*"

[9]For another Greek parallel—the government of Sparta—see Chap. 4 pp. 109–10.

same carry-over from war to government may be observed. The Roman historian Tacitus, who published in the year 97 A.D. the earliest known literary study of the Germans, thus describes their tribal organization: "On minor matters their chief men consult alone: on more important business they all meet. They provide, however, that all questions, the decision of which lies with the people, may be previously discussed by the chiefs. . . . Their love of liberty makes them independent to a fault: They do not assemble all at once or as though they were under orders: but two or three days are wasted by their delay in arriving. They take their seats as they come, all in full armour . . . if the opinion expressed displeases them, their murmurs reject it: if they approve they clash their spears."[10] Generalizing from this and similar instances, W. J. Shephard writes: "The legislative assembly of the modern state originated in the popular assemblies, the folkmoots of the barbarian peoples who inundated Roman civilization in the third and succeeding centuries. These tribal bodies included the entire soldiery of the tribe; in effect, the nation in arms. Their actions were confined to decisions on matters of supreme importance, such as peace and war."[11]

Modern experience serves on this point as a confirmation of ancient history. What happens in the twentieth century to a state that engages in a major war? When the safety and existence of the entire community are imperiled, everything is subordinated to the struggle for survival. The need to organize for defense and attack takes priority over all other activities. Centers of production are guarded and expanded. Huge military establishments are thrown together. The whole economy is diverted to the equipment and supply of the armed forces. Abruptly and compulsorily the rhythms and patterns of daily life are changed to a new design. The cells that make up the family group are plucked apart and some are killed. The home itself may suffer destruction. The citizens respond to new stimuli. They dress in uniforms, they drill, they drive toward a goal that is called victory. And to accomplish this result it is the state that assumes the responsibility. Its functions are promptly enlarged to embrace all aspects of society that have military relevance—which in the total warfare of this century means practically everything. Not only was protection the *raison d'être* of the state in ancient times; but whenever a people are momentarily preoc-

---

[10]Tacitus, *Germania*, trans. W. Hamilton Fyfe (Oxford: The Clarendon Press, 1908), Sec. 11.

[11]*Encyclopedia of the Social Sciences*, Vol. IX (New York: The Macmillan Company, 1935), p. 356. See also M. J. Herskovits, *Man and His Works*, pp. 330–31. A relic of this practice can still be seen in contemporary Switzerland. Some of the smallest cantons continue to have as their supreme governing body a mass meeting of the male citizens, called the *Landsgemeinde*, which the participants attend equipped with swords.

cupied with protecting themselves and destroying an enemy, the state literally "takes over."[12] Furthermore, the state which is defeated, since its defenses are broken, falls under the control of the victors, as happened in the military occupation of Germany, Italy, and Japan after World War II. In other words, the government of the state that cannot protect itself for the time being ceases in effect to be a government. It is not only from outside, however, that the security of the group can be menaced. Peace may also be threatened from within. The safety of one's person and security of one's possessions may be disturbed by individuals who are members of the same group. Thus the outlaw or gangster is in the group, but he places himself "out of its law." Furthermore it is possible for conflict between groups—between a corporation and a trade union, for instance—to be carried to lengths where other interests are prejudiced and where the unity of the society to which they both belong may be jeopardized. Government must, therefore, guard against the internal aggressor as well as the external. As this is phrased in the preamble to the Constitution of the United States, while one governmental function is "to provide for the common defense," another is "to insure domestic tranquillity." How does the state meet this need? And what principles are implied in its solution?

THE NUCLEUS OF THE STATE

For a starting point, consider this account by Herodotus of an actual historic event, the consolidation of the ancient kingdom of Media. According to "the Father of History," the Medes were living in anarchy and suffered the perils of insecurity. Their need presented an opportunity which a far-seeing individual was ready to grasp.

Among the Medes, there was a wise man named Deioces, the son of Phraortes. Deioces coveted absolute power and this was what he did. The Medes, at that time, were living in separate villages and there was much lawlessness throughout the whole land. Being already a person of repute in his own village, and knowing that the just is the enemy of the unjust, he became even more zealous to practice justice. His fellow-villagers, seeing how he behaved, used to choose him to judge their quarrels. In his ambition for power, he gave them just and straightforward decisions and this conduct brought him great praise from the citizenbody. Consequently when residents of other villages, who formerly had met with unfair judgments, learned that Deioces was the only man whose decisions conformed to justice, they gladly frequented his home so that they too could have him for their judge. Finally

[12]For statistical evidence on this point, expressed in budgetary terms, see Chap. 11, pp. 335–36.

they would go to no one else. As more and more litigants keep on appearing when they learned that suits were always settled with fairness, Deioces knew that everything was falling into his lap. Whereupon he announced his unwillingness to hold sessions where he had done so previously, or to continue adjudicating. For, as he put it, it was not profitable to him to settle his neighbors' disputes day after day and neglect his own business. Then when looting and lawlessness broke out among the villages to an extent even greater than before, the Medes assembled and discussed what had taken place, most of the speakers, in my estimate, being friends of Deioces. "Since we cannot live in the country in its present state," they said, "come, let us constitute somebody as our king. Thus the land will be well governed and we shall conduct our affairs without being uprooted by lawlessness." By these arguments they persuaded themselves in favor of a monarchy; and as soon as they began proposing candidates for the kingship, Deioces was the one most proposed and praised by all. So they agreed upon him for their king.[13]

Whether the details which Herodotus relates are wholly accurate or not is a matter on which opinions may differ. The present purpose in quoting the passage is not for the sake of its historical truth, but for the insight that the narrative displays into the fundamentals of the organization of the state. For the argument bores through the many strata of governmental functions until it reaches bedrock. When men conflict with one another in their mutual dealings, they need an orderly process for composing their differences, and a recognized tribunal to give decisions whose binding character they will accept. To promote cooperation and to confine competition within limits that are not injurious, society erects protective ramparts. The duties of the mediator, arbitrator, judge, and ruler are like steps on an ascending ladder of government. But the ascent is only possible under two conditions. There must be a widespread understanding that the restraints imposed through law and order are less irksome than the disturbances that erupt in their absence. Furthermore, the tribunal to which disputing parties resort must inspire general confidence on the ground that its procedures are fair and its decisions just. Deioces in the Herodotean story fulfilled these requirements. He was therefore able to found a state and become its king.

There is a celebrated episode in the history of Switzerland which further illustrates the role of the honest arbitrator in cementing the foundations of the state. During the fifteenth century the Swiss Confederation was at the height of its military power, since its citizens were then the finest foot soldiers in Europe. The country was expanding through pressure on its neighbors, some of whom became its subjects, while others joined the confederation or were associated

[13]Herodotus, *Histories,* i, Chaps. 96–98 (my translation).

as allies. The change in Swiss power and the enlargement of the state provoked internal tensions. These took the form of a conflict between urban and rural centers. The original members were principally of the latter kind, while some of the new adherents contained strong cities with manufacturing and mercantile interests. In 1481 a controversy erupted over the question of raising Solothurn and Fribourg from the status of allies to that of full confederates. The opposition of the rural cantons was voiced so strongly that there was a risk of the confederation splitting apart. At this point during a meeting of the Diet at Stans, Nicholas von der Flüe, an eminent and respected man who had retired from political life, suddenly intervened in the discussions and by sheer weight of argument, force of personality, and disinterested patriotism, composed the rivalries and achieved an acceptable settlement. Acting as arbitrator and conciliator he brought to both sides an awareness of the common interest in staying united and in making reasonable concessions to one another. The understandings thus reached strengthened the state, while enlarging its membership, and thereby saved Switzerland.[14]

More recent history again confirms these observations. Whenever human beings are uprooted from their established ways and exposed to the hazards of a new environment, a social bond has to develop anew. Their prime political need is then to organize in common for protection and physical security. The settlement of the United States by European immigrants contains many incidents of this nature. The pioneers who peopled an unmapped and untamed continent were exposed to risks at one another's hands and to the hostility of the Indians whose lands they seized and occupied. Life on the frontier was not far removed from Hobbes' characterization of life in the state of nature—solitary, poor, nasty, and brutish. At times it was also short. A man who rode within sight of another on a backwoods trail did not know whether to trust the stranger, and both had their guns ready for the draw. Wherever something essential was in short supply, such as water in the West, men fought for its control. Ranchers, like medieval barons with retainers, armed their employees to protect boundary stakes and cattle from neighboring rustlers. The conflict between an agriculture based on slaves and one employing free labor brought violence and bloodshed, as in Kansas, and ultimately a civil war. An event like the discovery of gold in California could attract an inrush of adventurers, whose aggressive individualism raised the temperature of the economic order to a fever while that of the social order dropped to zero.

[14]On this subject, see William Martin, *Histoire de la Suisse* (Lausanne: Librairie Payot, 1943), pp. 74–75, and G. Soloveytchik, *Switzerland in Perspective* (London: Oxford University Press, 1954), p. 154.

In newly settled territories if men came to work and build and stay, rather than to loot and depart. They wanted around them at least that minimum stability and security without which progress is impossible. Hence they were forced simultaneously to construct a community out of a mosaic of individuals who previously had no connecting ties, and to found a state by establishing law and enforcing order. It was necessary for the state and the community to grow together, since, until and unless political institutions were created, the soft tissue of society was formless and flabby and lacked the skeleton to hold it firmly. A state was born in the West when scattered individuals banded together and established the sheriff's office. The state did not grow up, however, until the sheriff's authority was generally obeyed. Then and only then was a framework of security organized within which other social institutions—economic, religious, educational, and so forth—could proceed about their respective tasks.

This can also be seen happening in reverse when a settled and organized community breaks down under conditions of civil war. The state holds society together in much the same way as a skeleton gives structure and form to the soft tissues of the body. Without the skeleton, all is loose and shapeless. So, when the state disintegrates and rival parties seek to capture its machinery, ordinary people may find themselves forced back to presocial and prepolitical savagery. The Russian author Boris Pasternak alluded to this in his account of some of the events that accompanied the Bolshevik Revolution and the subsequent civil war between Reds and Whites. "That period," he wrote, "confirmed the ancient proverb, 'Man is a wolf to man.' Traveller turned off the road at the sight of traveller, stranger meeting stranger killed for fear of being killed. There were isolated cases of cannibalism. The laws of human civilization were suspended. The jungle law was in force. Man dreamed the prehistoric dreams of the cave dweller."[15] A more recent, and still grimmer, example is the case of the Congo in the early 1960's after the Belgians gave up their rule. Rapidly, as tribe turned savagely against tribe, the edifice of central authority disintegrated. With anarchy substituted for order, nothing was secure and nobody was safe. The "state," under such conditions, was a fiction; its "government," a tragic farce; its politics, a process of murder. No superstructure of law, justice, and basic services can hold together when its foundations have been swept away and violence stalks the land.

[15]Boris Pasternak, *Doctor Zhivago*, trans. Max Hayward and Manya Harari (New York: Pantheon Books, Inc., 1958), p. 378.

PROTECTION, ORDER, AND JUSTICE

What are the implications of this analysis? In the first place, it demonstrates that what began as protection broadened out into something
wider. Human beings come to expect more than the physical safety of
their own persons. So that they may conduct their ordinary daily
dealings with their fellowmen, they require a minimum of stability
which can only be founded on mutual trust. Furthermore, men also
acquire relationships with material goods. Through their labors they
accumulate possessions which they regard as property and wish to
preserve. Hence the function of safeguarding life and limb is expanded to guarantee a general framework of security that surrounds
the relations of men to men and of men to things. The best term to
describe the whole system is "order." It is order that is able to grow
after protection has been firmly planted, and it is an orderly way of
life that government seeks to nurture. This is what the traditional
phrases signify that ascribe to government the provision of "law and
order" or "peace and good order." In other words, if order is to give
peace, it must rest upon law and upon agencies capable of enforcing
the law. Order is the product of common rules effectively applied
through common institutions.[16]

But that is not all. There is order in a barracks as there is in a prison.
In fact, the most orderly place on earth is a cemetery. Yet a barracks,
a prison, or a cemetery is not a state—even though admittedly the
modern dictatorship with its police state has certain features that
resemble all three! Something more than order is required for the fully
developed state. Just as order grows out of protection and is the larger
concept that embraces it, so is there a further goal that order strives
to realize. A clue to its nature may be discovered in this famous passage by Augustine: "Set justice aside, then, and what are kingdoms but
great robberies? because what are robberies but little kingdoms? for
in thefts, the hands of the underlings are directed by the commander,
the confederacy of them is sworn together, and the pillage is shared
by the law amongst them. And if those ragamuffins grow up but to be
able enough to keep forts, build habitations, possess cities, and conquer adjoining nations, then their government is no more called thiev-

[16]This point is made with characteristic clarity by Jean Monnet, the French statesman who played such a leading role in creating Western Europe's Coal and Steel
Community and the Common Market (see Chap. 13, pp. 394–98). These agencies were
invented to overcome the anarchic nationalism, economic and political, of independent
states. "To establish this new method of common action," wrote Monnet, "we adapted
to our situation the methods which have allowed individuals to live together in society:
common rules which each Member is committed to respect, and common institutions
to watch over the application of these rules." Quoted in *The Common Market,* ed.
Lawrence B. Krause (Englewood Cliffs, N.J.: Prentice-Hall, Inc., 1964), p. 44.

ish, but graced with the eminent name of a kingdom, given and gotten, not because they have left their practices, but because that now they may use them without danger of law."[17]

A society may arrive at the stage of an order based on law. It may eliminate anarchy and be systematically organized. But merely to establish order is not enough. Order, viewed ideally, must embody what men consider just. The kind of order which men prize is one wherein they feel that they are receiving justice. A system that is organized to ensure protection, but where people are not persuaded that they are justly treated, may gain obedience, but never allegiance. Justice consists both in a method and in a certain kind of result. The method is one of fair dealing. The result is to recognize equally the basic interests of all individuals and groups and promote a harmony between them. People will feel that they have justice when the community within which they live accords them an equal chance and safeguards their fundamental interests in a manner proportionate to the like interests of others. As the Herodotean story shows, a government can originate under two conditions. The understanding must be widespread that restraints imposed through order and its law are less irksome than the disturbances which erupt in their absence. Furthermore, the tribunal to which disputants resort must inspire general confidence on the ground that its procedures are fair and its decisions just. Deioces fulfilled these requirements. He was therefore able to found a state and become its king. But, as Augustine reminds us, if you remove justice, what is there to distinguish between a state and a band of robbers?

THE USE AND MONOPOLY OF FORCE

The next question is: By what methods and through what institutions are these results achieved? What happens when a community mobilizes to protect itself, then founds a system of order, and finally establishes justice? Every association of human beings must employ the methods that are indispensable, or at least are the best fitted, for performing its primary function. Thus, if an institution, such as a school or university, is designed to educate, whatever means are necessary in education are appropriate for that institution to use. The same is true of the state. If the state originates in the need for protection, to it belong initially any techniques which insure attainment of that objective, and if the state is to progress toward broader goals, the techniques of government must evolve in the process. Granted that

[17] *Concerning the City of God*, XIX, IV, 6, trans. John Healey (1610).

protection, order, and justice are ends to which the state successively aspires, what are the means for obtaining each?

Since an institution must possess the means appropriate to its function, it follows that, if it is to give protection, the state must have force[18] at its disposal. Protection against attacks from outside cannot be provided unless the group can repel force with force. Likewise, protection against attack from within calls for the establishment of agencies—for example, police, militia, army, courts, and prisons—capable of applying coercion to the disorderly and the lawless. The tribunals that are supposed to settle disputes must be able to enforce their decisions. Otherwise nobody will have assurance that the rules he obeys will be observed by his fellows. It is therefore the purpose out of which the state originates, namely to afford protection, whose character imposes on the state the necessity of employing force. Many of the problems which are peculiar to the state and distinguish it from other human associations flow from the simple, but fundamental, fact that the state must use force or it cannot even begin to be a state.[19]

Let us consider what some of these problems are. In the first place, because it must employ force, the state inevitably seeks to monopolize it. This is so because, if there exists within society any concentration of force which the state does not control, it is there that the possibility lurks of offering to the state whatever resistance that force permits. Any organized force which lies outside the ambit of the state amounts to a proportionate diminution of the power of the state. Hence in order to be unchallenged in performing its protective function, the state seeks to be the sole possessor of coercive techniques. Conversely, whenever force is available for use by associations other than the state or by persons other than the government, there exist in embryo the potential makings of a substitute state and government. An incident that illustrates this fact is cited by Augustine in the sequel to the passage quoted earlier:

For elegant and excellent was that pirate's answer to the great Macedonian Alexander, who had taken him: the king asking him how he durst molest the sea so, he replied with a free spirit, "How darest thou molest the whole world? But, because I do it with a little ship only, I am called a thief: thou, doing it with a great navy, art called an emperor."[20]

[18]Here and elsewhere, unless the context states otherwise, "force" is used in a literal, not a metaphorical sense. It means physical restraint or coercion, actual or threatened.

[19]This truth is recognized by those anarchists who condemn force as such, and argue that acting voluntarily is morally superior to acting under compulsion. Knowing that the state cannot function without possessing its agencies of enforcement, they favor the total abolition of the state in order to accomplish their goal of eliminating coercion of man by man.

[20]*Concerning the City of God,* XIX, IV, 6.

Alexander could not tolerate the pirate because the state, to maintain itself, must be a monopolist of force whose possession it then attempts to moralize by serving the ideal of the public good. The little gang appears antisocial because it preys upon the larger community and puts its private advantage before the general interest.

History presents innumerable examples of the danger that threatens the state when any force is organized within its midst to break its monopoly. On this point the testimony of the ancient, medieval, and modern worlds is uniform and conclusive. During the sixth century B.C. Peisistratus usurped power in Athens and established a dictatorial regime. To accomplish the *coup d'état* his principal means was to employ a bodyguard assigned to him by his fellow citizens after he had feigned attacks upon his life.[21] The closing century of the Roman Republic from 133 B.C. to 31 B.C. witnessed a cumulative series of futile efforts by the Senate to control its armies in the field. On the termination of victorious campaigns abroad, successive generals—such as Marius or Sulla, Pompey or Caesar, Antony or Augustus—were able to bend the government to their will or make themselves masters of the state. There were even periods when the Senate could not keep order in the streets of Rome and lay at the mercy of the vicissitudes of violence between rival gangs like those of Clodius and Milo. Then when the republic, which could not rule an empire, had given way the emperors who could, the latter, too, were at times made or unmade by the captains of the Praetorian Guard who garrisoned the capital city, or by army commanders in a distant province. In the Middle Ages when government throughout Western Europe was highly localized in keeping with the feudal system,[22] the kings of England or France found it difficult or impossible to exercise authority over powerful nobles who were secure in their castles and could place in the field a body of retainers and vassals wearing their livery. If medieval monarchs could not control what the historian Fortescue called their "overmighty subjects," it was because the latter had the backing of private armies.

The same in all essentials has been true of the modern state. When would-be dictators rise within the midst of weakly-constituted regimes, they seek to subvert the armed forces and organize militias of their own. In Italy between 1920 and 1922, Mussolini was able to overawe and paralyze the governments in office by mobilizing his

[21]Aristotle describes this in his *Constitution of Athens*, 14. See also Plato's *Republic*, viii, Secs. 505–6, where the allusion is to Peisistratus and others of his kind.

[22]See Chap. 10, pp. 287–88.

Black Shirts and obtaining the passive connivance of the army. Hitler organized thugs to capture the city streets and ended up molesting the whole world. Elsewhere, as in Perón's Argentina, or Franco's Spain, it is by launching a military rebellion that a politically ambitious officer overturns the constituted authorities and installs himself in power. Even the gangs that flourished in various cities of the United States during the Prohibition era form an aspect of the same story. When Capone dominated the Chicago underworld in the 1920's and conducted illegal rackets on a vast scale under the eyes of a complaisant mayor and police, was it not in his gunmen that a major portion of the city's power was located? Nor is it without political significance that what the gangster offers to the victims of his blackmail he calls "protection." The lesson is obvious. The state must either monopolize the force of the community or risk surrender to whoever can muster counterforce for its overthrow. The logic of coercion dictates monopoly.

OFFICIALS AND THE PUBLIC

When one speaks, however, of force being monopolized by the state, what exactly is meant? To talk of the state is to employ an abstraction. Acts of government resolve themselves in practice into acts done on behalf of everybody by a limited number. The latter may be variously described as representatives, agents, deputies, officials, or the government. It is characteristic of the state to entrust its use of force to certain known persons who are recognized by the whole community as acting on their behalf. In this sense a distinction can be drawn between public and private, official and unofficial, government and governed; and a different social significance may attach to the selfsame action according to the persons who perform it and the methods they employ. Thus it is one thing for a mob to track down and lynch a suspect and another for a sheriff to conduct an arrest. It is one thing to carry on a personal vendetta, and another to seek remedies for a wrong through a judicial process. When law reposes in the police rather than in a mob, when defense is secured by a standing army rather than by guerrilla bands, the trained professional acting under public orders is substituted for the unauthorized acts of private individuals. Save under the extreme necessity of self-defense, the citizen may no longer take the law into his own hands, once it has been entrusted to officials. If he does, his actions lack the character of law and he then becomes an "outlaw."

This latter truth was tragically brought home to the American people in the period from 1963 to 1968 when four men of national prominence were assassinated by gunshot. These were President John F. Kennedy, his brother Senator Robert F. Kennedy, the Black Muslim leader Malcolm X, and the Reverend Martin Luther King, the campaigner for civil rights who was an apostle of nonviolence and had received the Nobel Peace Prize. Such well-known victims belong within the broader context of a people with an appallingly high rate of deaths from shooting (nearly 20,000 a year). Some 200 million firearms are estimated to be in private hands in this country—more than in the armed forces of the U.S.A., the U.S.S.R., and the NATO countries combined. Is it any wonder that with guns so easily accessible too many get used and that persons in public life become targets?

On the other hand, there are occasions when an emergency arises of dimensions that place it beyond the ordinary resources of officialdom. In those cases, the principle that the official is the agent of the community is reinforced by his invoking the aid of the citizens themselves. Thus under English common law if a policeman blows his whistle when he is attacked or is trying to make an arrest, any able-bodied citizen within earshot must go to his assistance. Similarly, the sheriff in western territories in an earlier day would call out the posse to help him track an outlaw. The theory behind this is that the policeman is the agent of all the citizens. When the latter go to his aid, therefore, they are momentarily doing for themselves what he ordinarily does on their behalf. For similar reasons, under extraordinary conditions that threaten the whole community, reinforcements may be mobilized by doctors fighting an epidemic, by firemen extinguishing a conflagration, or by engineers trying to contain a flood. Finally, in the ultimate case of total warfare, the professional army is expanded through universal conscription, and all fit persons are enlisted in the service of all.

FORCE AND CONSENT

The government, as was just mentioned, is allowed to exercise the coercive force of the whole. But how does this come about? What is it that permits a few to wield the force of many? The answer can be found if one remembers that, though the functions of government begin with protection, they evolve beyond their starting point. Protection grows into order and order seeks to blossom into justice. Something similar happens with the techniques of government, since a method that is adequate at one stage of development ceases to be so at the next. Force may be sufficient for protection. But to create order, something more is required. This extra something is what is called power. What is power? It is simply force with some consent added.

How large a volume of consent is debatable. Indeed the quantity may vary, with consequential differences of great importance, as will be seen later. But for the moment it suffices that consent plus force equals power.

Let us examine more closely this relation between force and consent. All governments in the world use force, and even the most dictatorial is supported by some minimal measure of consent. People always want certain results from their government, and they are willing that their officials have the means of bringing those results to fruition. They, therefore, give their consent to the general body of law, which prescribes the order they desire; and, along with the law, they approve coercive enforcement against those who would infringe it. The nature of this relationship has been so well stated by A. D. Lindsay that his words deserve quotation in full:

Many people think that the state's use of force gives the lie to the doctrine that government can rest on consent, yet it is also clear that without some sort of consent the government's force would not exist. These puzzles confound more people than should be so confounded. Men have been accustomed so much to think of the law as restraining other people than their respectable selves that they easily think of the state's force as necessary to enable some people to restrain others. . . . But a little consideration will show us that we need and desire the power of the state to restrain ourselves. Consider a simple example from traffic control. We most of us think there ought to be laws regulating traffic, compelling us to light our lamps at a certain time and so on. Such rules have our consent and approval. Yet most of us, if we are honest, know that we are likely to break those laws on occasion and that we are often restrained from breaking them by the sanctions of the law. Most laws are like that. They will work and can be enforced because most people want usually to keep them. The state can have and use organized force because most people usually want common rules and most people want those rules to be universally observed; there must be force because there are rules which have little value unless everyone keeps them, and force is needed to fill up the gap between most people usually and all people always obeying.[23]

POWER AND AUTHORITY

Power is an ability to achieve results through concerted action. It is the product of the mobilization of support. It involves a relationship between a group and its agents. The latter may be described as delegates or representatives, in the sense that they follow the group; or as leaders, if the group follows them. The building of consent may de-

[23] *The Modern Democratic State* (New York: Oxford University Press, Inc., 1947), Vol. I, p. 206.

pend on the capacity of a group to organize itself coherently, formulate its program, and instruct its representatives; or alternatively on the capacity of a leader to attract adherents and win a following.[24] The support elicited will thus be reciprocal. A group supports its agents, while they support the group. Franklin D. Roosevelt, in a critical period of domestic economic breakdown and aggressive international militarism, confidently offered programs which gave people new hope. Thus he achieved something without precedent, being elected four times to the presidency of the United States and wielding power for more than 12 years.

But the evolution of governmental techniques does not terminate with power. As order, to be securely stabilized, attempts to gain acceptance as justice, so does power aspire toward a concept yet more advanced. If protection is sustained by force and order by power, justice requires authority. What does authority mean, and how is it distinguished from power? To understand the contrast, one must introduce a further refinement into the distinction between the government and the governed. In fact, the governed subdivide into two parts —the supporters of the government and its opponents. This means that the citizens who compose the state are really made up of three groups:

1. representatives (or leaders) and officials,
2. those who support them, and
3. those who dissent and oppose them.

Power consists in the fusion of 1 with 2. It is able to include that ingredient of force, which makes government ultimately effective, because of the support mobilized in its favor. But the claims of power to hold sway are, by definition, valid only for those who consent. Likewise, the rightness of its force is justified only in the eyes of those who render it support. Being based upon consent, power is not accepted by those who dissent. The force that power may deploy will be resented, and may be resisted, by those who disagree. Opponents may have to submit to the decisions of power; but submission is different from acquiescence. The imperatives of power may secure compliance; but this is not the same as allegiance.

What demarcates authority from power is that the former is power recognized as rightful. Authority is government that all accept as valid. Its exercise is therefore sanctioned by those who approve the

[24]A memorable witticism was pronounced during the French Revolution by a politician who saw a mob rush by in the street and dashed out of the house after them, saying, "I am their leader; so I must follow them."

particular act or agent, and is tolerated by those who disapprove. Confronted with power, the citizen has a choice: whether to support or oppose. Confronted with authority, it is his duty to obey. Resistance to power is lawful; resistance to authority, unlawful. Authority is power clothed in the garments of legitimacy.

How this transformation takes place can be illustrated in two episodes, one ancient and one modern. The former of these is the sequel, as Herodotus relates it, to the rise of Deioces to the position of king of the Medes.

Deioces ordered them to build him a palace worthy of a king and to guard it with spearmen. This the Medes did. They built him a large, strong palace on a site that he picked, and authorized him to select any of the Medes for his bodyguard. Once established in authority, he compelled the Medes to build a single capital city and equip and adorn it, devoting less care henceforth to other towns. In this, too, the Medes obeyed him, and thus he built the great strong fortress called Agbatana with its girdle of walls rising one above the other. . . . These fortifications Deioces built for himself—especially round his own palace—but the rest of the people he ordered to live outside the walls. When all was completed, Deioces instituted a ceremonial, the first of its kind. Nobody from outside could enter the royal quarters or see the king. All business was transacted by messengers. No one, moreover, could laugh or spit in the king's presence. The reason for surrounding himself with this solemn etiquette was to keep out of sight of his former companions who had been brought up with him, who belonged to equally good families, and who were as brave as he. For, seeing him, they might resent his position and plot against him; but if he were unseen, they might think of him as being of more than common clay. With this protocol arranged and his absolutism established, he was a stern watchdog for justice. . . . If he learned of anyone waxing insolent, he would send for them and punish them according to their offense. For he kept his spies and informers up and down the country that he ruled.[25]

Much political science is compressed into this narrative. A number of human beings, suffering from conditions of anarchy, sought to improve their lot. They wished to resolve their disputes by a method that would be fair to the antagonists and by conditions that could be accepted as just. Voluntarily, they turned to one of their members, their need dovetailing with his capacity and ambitions. After repeated experience of him, they found the results they wanted. Continued acceptance of his verdicts created the strongest presumption that they were binding. In order to formalize its newfound security, the group became supporters of Deioces. By these steps the influence he had acquired was converted into power. The latter, once it was recog-

[25]Herodotus, *Histories,* i, Chaps. 98–100 (my translation).

nized and sanctioned, became authority. After this, he was entitled to enforce the law that he expounded. His decisions, compliance with which was formerly optional, were thenceforth compulsory. Resistance or disobedience was visited with coercion.

A comparable modern case—the birth of a state and the erection of the authority to govern it—is described by one who saw it happen and contributed his share. In the *Seven Pillars of Wisdom,* T. E. Lawrence describes his experience during the first World War when he was attempting in conjunction with Feisal to instigate a revolt of the Arabs against the Turks. A major obstacle was to overcome the ancient tribal jealousies and feuds between the respective Arab chieftains and their followers. So that they would combine and not bicker at cross-purposes, they had to be persuaded to adjust their animosities, merge themselves into a whole larger than the tribe, and accept a superior authority as binding them. This was Feisal's occasion and his challenge. Lawrence thus relates it:

Except that all its events were happy, this day was not essentially unlike Feisal's every day. . . . The roads to Wejh swarmed with envoys and volunteers and great sheikhs riding in to swear allegiance. . . . Feisal swore new adherents solemnly on the Koran between his hands, to wait while he waited, march when he marched, to yield obedience to no Turk, to deal kindly with all who spoke Arabic (whether Bagdadi, Aleppine, Syrian, or pure-blooded) and to put independence above life, family and goods: He also began to confront them at once, in his presence, with their tribal enemies, and to compose their feuds. An account of profit and loss would be struck between the parties, with Feisal modulating and interceding between them, and often paying the balance, or contributing towards it from his own funds, to hurry on the pact. During two years Feisal so laboured daily, putting together and arranging in their natural order the innumerable tiny pieces which made up Arabian society, and combining them into his one design of war against the Turks. There was no blood feud left active in any of the districts through which he had passed, and he was Court of Appeal, ultimate and unchallenged, for western Arabia. He showed himself worthy of this achievement. He never gave a partial decision, nor a decision so impracticably just that it must lead to disorder. No Arab ever impugned his judgments or questioned his wisdom and competence in tribal business. By patiently sifting out right and wrong, by his tact, his wonderful memory, he gained authority over the Nomads from Medina to Damascus and beyond. He was recognised as a force transcending tribe, superseding blood chiefs, greater than jealousies. The Arab movement became, in the best sense, national, since within it, all Arabs were at one, and for it, private interests must be set aside.[26]

There then is a picture of the growth of authority rendered possible

[26]*Seven Pillars of Wisdom* (New York: Garden City Publishing Co., 1938), Chap. 30, pp. 175–76.

because it was being founded on consent, with force at its disposal. Feisal met the need of the Arab tribes for a wider system of order, into which he infused his concepts of justice. Thereby his power became authority; and thereby he made history.

THE EVOLUTION OF POLITICAL ENDS AND GOVERNMENTAL MEANS

It appears then from this analysis that both the ends of the state and the means of government undergo a progression. Because protection, though necessary, is not enough, human beings construct a system of order; and from order they strive for justice, because the most durable order is the one that men deem just. A similar progression occurs with the techniques that government employs to fulfill these ends. The prerequisite for protection is force. But since the latter alone cannot sustain a system of order, power is generated by the admixture of force and consent. Finally, if order is to culminate in justice, power must be transmuted into authority.

Each stage, therefore, builds upon, and develops beyond, the one preceding. Authority is a shell without a filling if it lacks power, and power may be flouted with impunity unless it can wield force. Justice enhances, yet depends upon, order, without which men could have no confidence in each other or sense of trust; while order itself must be based on the protection that makes them secure. Diagrammatically, these relationships and sequences can be expressed thus:[27]

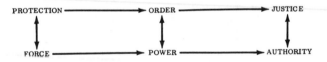

The foregoing account outlines the historical origins of government and sketches an ideal development that some states subsequently realize in practice. Manifestly it does not describe what all states are actually like or what they succeed in becoming. Certain states never reach the level of justice. Some establish it for the majority only. In that case, what the majority regards as justice the minority views as a system of "law and order" imposed unjustly by majority power; the minority may then resort to force of its own, which by definition is illegal, to resist that power. Other states advance little beyond protection. Many governments are unable to convert power into authority.

[27]It should be noted that even justice is not necessarily the final stage of this evolutionary development. Various modern states are striving for a further ideal that lies beyond justice. See Chaps. 7, pp. 209–10, and 14, pp. 438–41.

In others again, the blend that produces power consists of more force and less consent. How does this happen and what are the political consequences?

ABUSE OF FORCE

The ends of the state—protection, order, justice—are achieved by the means of government—by force, power, or authority. It has been said[28] that the end justifies the means. But this is not universally true, because there are some means which no end can justify. The truth is rather the contrary. Because men do not refrain from passing moral judgments on the methods employed, the means can stultify the end. In the field of statecraft, especially, the implications of this are far-reaching. More perhaps than any institution, the state is peculiarly affected by the nature of the means it has to employ, and their abuse may fatally vitiate its ends. The possibility of this occurring arises from two facts already mentioned: the claim of the state to monopolize force, and the choice of representatives and officials to perform the functions of government. The result, when these facts are combined, is virtually to place this monopoly in the hands of officialdom. Thus the possibility occurs that the rest of the community may be at the mercy, or under the grip, of their own officials, since the latter have means of coercion at their fingertips. Because protection depends on the opposition of force to force, a group which has institutionalized its protection cannot avoid entrusting to officials the means of physical compulsion. In that case what guarantee is there that the force, which is intended to be used for the group, may not be used against it?

Plato expounded this problem in a memorable passage of the *Republic*:[29]

"Then we are quite clear as to what must be the bodily characteristics of our guardians?"

"Yes."

"And as to their mental qualities, we know they must be spirited."

"Certainly."

"Then, Glaucon," I said, "with such natures as these, how are they to be prevented from behaving savagely towards one another and the other citizens?"

"By Zeus," he said, "that will not be easy."

"Still, we must have them gentle to their fellows and fierce to their ene-

[28]For example, by Machiavelli in *The Prince*.
[29]II, Sec. 375, p. 55, trans. A. D. Lindsay (Everyman's Library).

mies. If we can't effect that, they will prevent the enemy from destroying the city by doing it first themselves."

Even more pungently the Roman satirist Juvenal inquired in words that have become proverbial: "But who will guard the guardians themselves?"[30] Force, like fire, can be a useful servant of mankind. But it is a dangerous master; and like fire, once it goes out of control, it has vast potentialities for destruction. This perennial truth, had any doubted it, was proven once again when mass protests and demonstrations were organized during the late 1960's in many cities in many lands. The same scenario was reenacted with horrifying similarity in Chicago and New York, Paris and Tokyo, Mexico City and Berlin. Once violence is unleashed—be this the revolutionary stratagem of dissident groups or the repressive force of established authority or both—restraints vanish and brutality prevails. The resort to violence by private groups can never be justified, morally or politically, when it is directed against a system which offers a valid constitutional procedure for encompassing change by peaceful means. But when the powers that be react by unleashing what one American report described as "a police riot," the result for the individual citizen is even worse. The police are there for the public's protection against private lawbreakers. But against police excesses, how shall we protect ourselves?

THE DANGERS OF POWER

Because power consists of force plus consent, the difficulties attending the use of naked force are still present when the latter is dressed in the raiments of consent to form power. Those in power can abuse the force at their command by seeking to impose their order on the recalcitrant. Furthermore, the means lie at their disposal whenever they are so minded. Hence the existence of force and the construction of power, which are the inescapable products of man's need for protection and order, are the root-cause of government's perennial dilemma. Force and power there must be. Otherwise there can be no government; nor can some basic ends of the state be attained. But such means permit restraints upon the opponents of government, which can be extended to the point where freedom is endangered. Power is susceptible to abuse by those who possess it and is then convertible into tyranny. What originates as an instrument of service can culminate in a weapon of enslavement. Hence many of the controversies concerning the organization and functions of the state re-

[30] *Sed quis custodiet ipsos custodes? Satires*, No. VI, II. 347–48.

volve around the problem of fixing limits within which power may usefully be employed and beyond which it cannot safely be increased.

As applied to power these considerations are more complex than as applied to force. That is because the former includes the quota of consent which, by definition, is absent from the latter. If the state consisted only of an elementary bisection into government and governed, its problems would at least be more clear-cut. In fact, however, all government is an eternal triangle, whose three angles are: *(a)* those in office, *(b)* their supporters, and *(c)* their opponents. Power flows from the supporters to the government, which exercises it over both its supporters and the opposition. But what makes a vital difference in these relationships is the amount of consent that goes into power, as compared with the volume of dissent. Every government uses force and, initially at least, is supported by some consent. This is true of dictatorships as well as democracies. Lenin, Stalin, Hitler, Mussolini, and their brethren of today, could not have gained power or stayed on top without the support of other persons who accepted their ideas and were content to do their bidding. There is an enormous difference, however, in the respective quantities of force and consent which combine into power, and in the relative importance of each. As a general rule, the broader the area of consent, the less is the need or occasion to employ force. Conversely, wherever the apparatus of force bulks large in the machinery of government and is in constant use, it is reasonable to suppose that the supporters of government are not strong enough to control their opponents by other means. Every police state relies heavily on methods of coercion, because its rulers have not transformed their power into authority and are not backed by enough consent.

Furthermore, the effect on government of the lapse of time must not be forgotten. Power, and even authority, may be constructed initially upon a foundation of consent that is wide and deep. But as the years pass by, these foundations may crack. A Deioces may win a kingdom with willing acclaim. Yet he himself in later years, or his successor, may lose support through tyrannical acts. The authority, that was once legitimate and just, may then be perverted into despotism. Temporarily, a ruler or ruling group may continue to wield power with waning consent. In this they may succeed for a while because the people at large is imbued with habits of obedience, is paralyzed by inertia, and is severally inferior to the force mobilized by the ruler.[31] Once rooted, power is not easily shaken. But having consumed its

---

[31]Hence as an English philosopher pointed out in his justification of the ultimate right of a people to rebel, "People are not so easily got out of their old forms as some are apt to suggest. They are hardly to be prevailed with to amend the acknowledged faults in

initial capital of consent, it slides into the morass of despotism. Then, when the sustaining conditions of government are removed, when justice vanishes and order has to be imposed, men start inquiring into the purposes that justify acts of government, and the insolvency of political pretensions is quickly laid bare. For if the state requires force, or power, or authority to perform a service, it is the continuation of the service, and this alone, that warrants the continuation of the means.

It is force which thus enables a regime in practice to outlive the consent with which it was formerly endowed. In erecting the force to serve them, men also create a technique for dominating over them. Mobilized because of their wish, that force may later be directed against their wish. This possibility reaches the extreme point when a government has to use force, not to protect the governed, but to protect itself against them. In that case the rulers even reveal the truth about their political situation in the architectural style of their governmental buildings. When a government is on guard not only against external foes, but against some of its own people, it houses itself within a fortress for safety from its opponents. Thus in medieval Italian cities, the ruling faction would shelter behind stout walls and equip itself with lofty watchtowers, at the same time prohibiting others from doing likewise. Observe the exterior of the famous Signoria in Florence, and what you see—allowing for all the sculptural embellishment—is not a city hall but a citadel, and one designed with that end in view. So have the tyrants of Germany and Russia dwelled in their Berchtesgadens and their Kremlins, as if in a constant state of siege. The perils of their position were well understood and are thus described by Plato:

"It seems to be that in our inquiry on this matter (a good and an evil life) we must get light from the following sources."

"From which?"

"By examining each of those rich individuals in cities who own a great number of slaves; for they have this point of similarity with tyrants, that they are rulers of many. No doubt the tyrant has the best of it in point of numbers?"

"He has."

---

the frame they have been accustomed to. . . . Great mistakes in the ruling part, many wrong and inconvenient laws, and all the slips of human frailty will be borne by the people without mutiny or murmur. But if a long train of abuses, prevarications, and artifices, all tending the same way, make the design visible to the people, they cannot but feel what they lie under, and see whither they are going, it is not to be wondered that they should then rouse themselves, and endeavour to put the rule into such hands which may secure them the ends for which government was at first erected. . . . " John Locke, *Second Treatise of Civil Government,* Secs. 223, 225, pp. 230–31 (Everyman's Library).

"You know, I suppose, that they live unconcernedly, and are not afraid of their servants?"

"Well, is there anything for them to fear?"

"Nothing," I said; "but do you see why that is?"

"Yes. The whole city gives assistance to each individual."

"Excellent," I said. "But supposing one of the Gods were to take a man who possesses fifty slaves or even more and were to lift him and his wife and children out of the city and put him down with all his property and his slaves, in a desert place where there would be no free men to come to his assistance, do you not suppose that he would be in the most terrible fright in apprehension lest he and his children and his wife should be killed by their servants?"

"In the worst of frights," he answered.

"Would he not then be compelled to pay court to some of those his slaves, to make them many promises, and to set them free, quite against his desire, and stand revealed as his own servants' toady?"

"He would certainly have to do so or die," he said.[32]

CONFUSION OF POLITICS WITH POWER

For these reasons—that power, once acquired, may be transformed by abuse—the essence of the state and the nature of the governmental process are often misunderstood. Every student of the state observes that it controls the organized force of the group. Everybody knows, moreover, that those who monopolize force do misuse it at times and with success on some occasions. These are indisputable facts. But clear though they be, they have led to conflicting interpretations. Because force must be wielded by the state if it is to provide protection, and because force, to be effective, must be amassed as a monopoly, many regard this force not merely as the instrument by which the state operates, but as its principal characteristic. Seen from this viewpoint, the state is then differentiated from other associations and defined as a state by virtue of its being the sole rightful monopolist of the force available within society. Max Weber, for example, wrote this: "Ultimately, one can define the modern state sociologically only in terms of the specific *means* peculiar to it, as to every political association, namely, the use of physical force.—Of course, force is certainly not the normal or the only means of the state—nobody says that—but force is a means specific to the state. Today the relation between the state and violence is an especially intimate one."[33] When so much stress, however, is placed upon the state's exercise of force, this feature is no longer treated as a tool incidental to performing the

[32] *Republic*, ix, Secs. 578–79, p. 278.

[33] Max Weber, *From Max Weber: Essays in Sociology*, translated and edited by H. H. Gerth and C. Wright Mills (New York: Oxford University Press, Inc., 1958), pp. 77–78. Italics in original.

function of protection. Instead, force is shifted into the central position in the analysis of the state, and the latter is thereupon discussed in terms not of the needs it serves but of the methods it employs. The emphasis is moved from the ends to the means in such a way as to result in a reversal of positions. What once was considered the instrument is now conceived to be the master. Instead of using force to carry out its protective function, the government is pictured as performing that function in order to maintain its capacity to coerce.

The same logic is then extended from the narrow concept of force to the broader one of power. Because government is energized through power, how to accumulate it is described as the central problem of the state. Politics is then considered the arena where the struggle for power is conducted; and power is no longer regarded as the tool through which other results may be accomplished, but as if it were itself the objective to be attained. Under those circumstances, when power is thought of as the be-all and end-all of the state, a complete reversal of means and ends ensues. Arguments which once interpreted the state in terms of the functions it undertakes are twisted into arguments on behalf of the power it must employ. George Orwell has thus stated the point, through the mouth of one of his characters: "Power is not a means, it is an end. . . . The object of persecution is persecution. The object of torture is torture. The object of power is power."[34] The practices that follow from this attitude raise some crucial questions about the relation between power and ethics. If the political process is in truth a battle for might, what is its relevance to choices between right and wrong or evaluations of good and bad?

THE ETHICS OF POWER

Three views are possible, each of which has at some time or other found an exponent. In the first place, power may be clothed with moral approval and be upheld as good. When the accumulation of power is viewed as the business of the state, it is an obvious next step to argue that what conduces to might is right and then to conclude that might is right. Secondly, power may be thought of as unconnected with moral choice and ethical value. The sphere of the state and the processes of politics are deemed amoral or ethically neutral. They have no concern with matters of right and wrong, of good and bad. The latter belong to a different order of inquiry, much as art is

[34] *Nineteen Eighty-Four* (New York: Harcourt, Brace & World, Inc., 1949), pp. 266–67. From the speech of an Inner Party member.

often held to exist for art's sake and aesthetics are believed exempt from moral connotations. In this case it makes no sense to pass judgment on the state, except in terms of whether it succeeds in maintaining that power which is its be-all and end-all. The third possibility is that power may be condemned as evil, on the ground that its control of force involves a coercion that is morally reprehensible. If the state, then, is preeminently a power-wielding institution that can employ force, condemnation of force leads to condemnation of the state as something immoral. This value judgment is, of course, reinforced by the empirical observation that power is often abused in practice and will be employed in ways and for ends which affront a civilized conscience.

The three views lead inevitably to different deductions. The first results in glorification of power and, therefore, of the state that employs it. The second carves out spheres of interest and assigns politics to a separate compartment of life. The third seeks to combat the evils of power either by adopting the extreme position of the anarchist who says that all coercion is morally wrong and that consequently the state must be abolished; or by upholding the less drastic view that the functions of the state had better be confined to a minimum, since the fewer they are, the less power will be needed. Such divergent conclusions are made possible by the ambiguity contained in the concept of power. Since power combines some force with some consent, people's opinion of power will vary according to whether it is the force or the consent that appears uppermost in the compound. But divergent though they be, the various conclusions share a common origin and derive from the same premises. They spring from a preoccupation with the techniques that the state uses rather than the end it pursues, and they substitute the former for the latter as the essential criterion of the state. Nothing has given rise to more misconceptions about the activities of government and the place of the state in society than this false emphasis and gratuitous switching of priorities. In their correct order, those priorities may be thus expressed: Policy is what politics is about. Power always comes into politics, necessarily but secondarily, because without it no policy can be realized in practice.[35]

To help the reader in understanding the problems of politics accurately and in seeing them in an undistorted perspective is the purpose

[35]Substantially the same point was made in the opening sentences of this leading editorial in the *Times* of London: "First what, then how. First look at the merits of the question, then work at the feasibility of the best solution. First study policy, then study politics. This is and always has been the basis of all good government, and bad government inevitably results from the opposite course of looking at the political pressures first and allowing them to shape the policy" (January 16, 1968). In this phrasing, the concept of politics is virtually synonymous with that of power.

of this book. These opening chapters have inquired into the why and wherefore of social groups and have sought to explain the genesis and *raison d'être* of states and their governments. It is now possible, therefore, to begin the analysis of politics in terms of the five perennial issues which make it what it is. The next ten chapters are devoted, in pairs, to a study of these issues and the solutions, both classic and contemporary, that men have attempted in their striving for civilization.

4

FIRST ISSUE:

–1– The Rule of Privilege

CITIZENS OR SUBJECTS

Since the primary concern of the political process is with people who are organized through the institution we call the state, the first issue of politics is to select a principle to govern their relationship. The state consists of members associated together. Some rule, therefore, must determine who are to be recognized as members and how their membership is acquired. If membership produces opportunities for certain kinds of action, and expectations of certain kinds of treatment—or, what amount to the same, rights and responsibilities—these must be allotted according to principles, the choice of which endows a state with its special character. The politically inevitable division of society into government and governed raises a flock of queries about their mutual relations. What persons, for instance, should be picked to compose the government? Are all people fit and entitled to serve in that capacity? What rights do the governed possess? Should there be the same fundamental rights for everybody? Or is the community to be divided between first-and second-class citizens, between citizens and subjects? Such matters are variations upon a single theme. They involve an inquiry into the nature of citizenship and the relations between those who compose a state.

ARISTOTLE'S VIEW OF CITIZENSHIP

The first European thinker to reduce this concept to systematic analysis was Aristotle.[1] His formulation, therefore, because of its

[1] *Politics*, iii, Chaps. 1-5.

priority in time and the significance of his argument, is a suitable opening for discussion. "What makes a person a citizen?" is his initial question. He mentions, but rejects, the answers that define a citizen by residence in a certain place or by birth of parents who are citizens. Residence is not a satisfactory explanation, since aliens and slaves reside in a community, but are not its citizens. Nor is it helpful to derive citizenship from one's parents, since this will not explain how their citizenship was obtained. Aristotle makes plain that he seeks to explore citizenship in terms of functions rather than origins. By shifting the emphasis to the functional side, he invests his answer with a dynamic quality. For when a citizen is characterized by performance, it is as a participant that he is judged. What then is his function?

The reply subdivides into two parts. The citizen is "a man who shares in the administration of justice and the holding of office."[2] What Aristotle means is that citizens must be both subjects of authority and holders of it. They must serve in the twin roles of government and governed. They are to make the law, obey the law, and share the chores of enforcement. But to this doctrine, that a citizen is one· who participates in ruling and being ruled, Aristotle attaches a corollary. Those so described must possess capacities which qualify them for playing both parts. The citizen cannot be merely an obedient subject. He should also be competent to rule. The latter requirement, however, is one that in Aristotle's view calls for special abilities of character and intellect not necessarily found in all people. Some human beings he classifies as "slaves by nature." Others he considers, by reason of their occupations, incapable of leading a life of virtue. Consequently, as he insists on defining citizens functionally, his logic compels him to exclude those whose personal failings debar them from adequately performing the duties essential to citizenship. Hence the conclusion that "one need not class as citizens all those without whom there would be no city."[3] Citizens, in other words, form an exclusive group. They do not and should not embrace all members of the state. Such is the Aristotelian argument. Its main steps, briefly summarized, are contained in three assertions:

1. A citizen is a person who performs certain functions.
2. One such function is to participate actively in the exercise of authority.
3. The number of persons competent to share in this is limited.

[2] *Ibid.*, ii. Chap. 1, Secs. 5-6.
[3] *Ibid.*, iii, Chap. 5, Sec. 2.

His chain of reasoning evidently depends on the connections between the three links. A break in the sequences must bring a breakdown in the consequences.

Whether one agrees or not with Aristotle's analysis, it contains that characteristic merit of much in Greek philosophizing. Aristotle goes straight to the heart of the problem. He concentrates upon the issue that is fundamental. He asks the right question, irrespective of whether he supplies the right or wrong answer. That question may be variously phrased. Is membership in the state synonymous with citizenship? Is a common status to be given to all who are necessary to the state's existence? Is politics so different from other social activities that citizens ought to be a class separate from subjects? Let us consider more fully what is implied in these queries. For in the answers they receive everything is at stake.

THE ARGUMENT FOR INEQUALITY

Broadly speaking, one may distinguish between two contrasted answers. One line of reasoning proceeds from the assumption that government is an expert undertaking which requires a highly specialized technical competence and consequently demands of its practitioners more than ordinary qualities of character or mind. Government is not then considered an activity appropriate to the common run of men. Its "secrets of empire," insofar as these may be revealed, are variously pictured. Those who conceive of ruling as a skill that springs from intuitive imagination speak of government primarily in aesthetic terms. To them it is an art,[4] more or less fine. Others consider that politics is conducted according to a body of rules that are knowable and can be studied and learned. They therefore place it in the category of the rational and label it science. Still others, viewing human strivings in relation to a Supreme Being or superhuman forces operating in the universe, envelop their concept of politics with the aura of magic or theology. To them government is a mystery, indeed a fragment of the greater mystery of life. But, whether art, science, or mystery, government in any case is deemed the preserve of the chosen.

If these assumptions are accepted, certain conclusions flow naturally. It is evident that as soon as the process of government is viewed primarily from the standpoint of the expertise needed for its performance, only a minority of the population is likely to be judged as

[4]See Jacob Burckhardt, *The Civilization of the Renaissance in Italy* (New York: Oxford University Press, Inc., 1945), where Chap. 1 is entitled "The State as a Work of Art."

meeting the required standard. If such were not the case, the standard set and the skill prescribed would have little meaning. Thus the chosen turn out to be few in number, and government becomes—in the literal Greek sense—an "oligarchy."[5]

In opposition to this view, however, it can be urged that while the task of ruling, namely the actual making of decisions and exercise of authority, is not a job for Tom, Dick, and Harry, nevertheless Tom, Dick, and Harry are competent at least to judge and, if necessary, to criticize what their betters do. Should this be conceded, the chosen few must somehow be answerable to the vulgar many, and the way is open to argue that those who by definition are less wise and less worthy should nevertheless control their betters. In the long run this could imply the subordination of the few and their ultimate loss of caste. Those who shrink from such a conclusion resist the insertion of the wedge that cracks their logic. Not only do they argue that government must be conducted by experts, but they deny that the quality of their work can be appraised by anybody less skilled. Excluded from participation in ruling, the many cannot be allowed to judge their rulers. The chosen few are not merely the practitioners of politics. They are also the sole judges of their own handiwork.

This argument assumes a variety of guises from crude to sophisticated. An example of the former, put in earthy terms, is the reported remark of a Sudanese to a British official. The latter, in the period when the Sudan was administered by an Anglo-Egyptian condominium, was explaining to an old tribal chief a new plan for holding an election among the people of his area. "Surely, this is great nonsense," said the Sudanese chief, "this talk of consulting the people and asking them to elect their representatives. If I have a valuable herd of cattle, I do not ask them to elect a representative bull—I send a trained herdsman to watch over their welfare. Mind you, if I let them run wild, in course of time a bull will make himself the master, but only after much fighting, and in the meantime the herd will be ravaged by lions and hyenas."[6] The attitude expressed here has been common throughout history, although the statement of it is seldom as frank and ingenuous. Men in the mass are thought of as cattle, who, as such, need a herdsman. His job is to keep them in order, and to protect them against those who would prey upon the herd. In any case, should there be no herdsman, the cattle will still have to submit to a master, who will inevitably be the strongest and toughest of their number.

---

[5] *Oligarchy* means rule *(arche)* by the few *(oligoi).*
[6] Quoted in *Round Table,* June, 1954: "Cross Purposes in Egypt," p. 235.

Exactly the same thought, although its form is more refined, is contained in this opinion of Thomas Carlyle: "Aristocracy and Priesthood, a governing class and a teaching class: these two, sometimes separate, and endeavoring to harmonize themselves, sometimes conjoining as one, and the King a Pontiff King:—there did no society exist without these two vital elements, there will none exist. It lies in the very nature of man. You will visit no remotest village in the most republican country of the world, where virtually or actually you do not find these two powers at work. Man, little as he may suppose it, is necessitated to obey superiors.—He obeys those whom he esteems better than himself, wiser, braver; and will forever obey such; and even be ready and delighted to do it."[7] Frederick the Great, as might be expected, proceeded from similar assumptions. "It is necessary to show the people," he said, "as one shows a sick child, what they must eat and drink." Next to this may be placed a statement of Hitler: "The parliamentary principle of decision by majority, by denying the authority of the person and placing in its stead the number of the crowd in question, sins against the aristocratic basic idea of nature."[8] Also in this category may be placed the doctrines of the modern Spanish philosopher José Ortega y Gasset. In his book *The Revolt of the Masses* one may find the following clear-cut affirmation of inequality: "Society is always a dynamic unity of two component factors: minorities and masses. The minorities are individuals or groups of individuals which are specially qualified. The mass is the assemblage of persons not specially qualified. . . . I uphold a radically aristocratic interpretation of history. Radically, because I have never said that human society *ought* to be aristocratic, but a great deal more than that. . . . Human society *is* always, whether it will or no, aristocratic by its very essence, to the extreme that it is a society in the measure that it is aristocratic, and ceases to be such when it ceases to be aristocratic."[9]

Arguments of this character portray a certain picture of human nature. Here is one of many examples of the connection between political science and psychology. It is impossible to theorize about politics without formulating ideas about human behavior, and these embrace a psychological doctrine. The common meeting ground for all doctrines of the chosen few is the position that mankind must be separated for political purposes into two groups. These are supposed to be distinguished by certain fundamental differences which are both qualitative (that is, superiors vis-à-vis inferiors) and quantitative (that

---

[7]Thomas Carlyle, *Past and Present,* iv, Chap. 1, on "Aristocracies."

[8]*Mein Kampf* (New York: Reynal and Hitchcock, 1939), p. 103.

[9]*The Revolt of the Masses* (New York: W. W. Norton & Company, Inc., 1932), pp. 9 and 14. Italics in original.

is, the few vis-à-vis the many). Implied in this division is the belief that among the differences between human beings are some that are basic, and that should consequently weigh more heavily in politics than any overall resemblances. Inequality thus becomes the cardinal principle on which the relations between members of the state are patterned. Their rights and duties are then apportioned, not uniformly, but according to their differences in status and function. The chosen few, who constitute the ruling circle, refer to their system of government as an aristocracy.[10] Seen from the other side, the same appears a regime of privilege.

A CLASSIFICATION OF ELITES

Any theory of aristocracy, or advocacy of government by an elite, must face two associated problems. It has first to justify the power that a few exercise over many, and explain why these few are the worthier to govern. Second, it must devise a means of separating lions from lambs. This requires some criterion of inclusion in the elite and exclusion therefrom. The two problems are closely connected because the success of any justification depends largely on the nature of the criterion adopted. In practice, types of aristocracy have been numerous for the reason that so many criteria have been used at one time or other, as a list will show. Here are the principles invoked to select the chosen few and reject the inferior masses: race, ancestry, age, sex, religion, military strength, culture, wealth, and knowledge. This classification of types of aristocracy can be represented pictorially in a chart such as appears below.

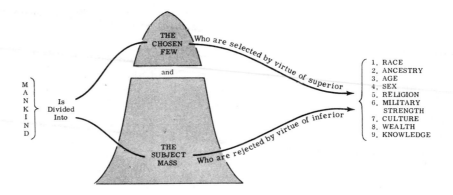

[10]Literally, "rule by the best."

So that misunderstanding may be avoided, two comments on the classification should be added. These nine criteria, though distinguishable, are not in all cases mutually exclusive. On the contrary, most elites known to history have exhibited two or more of these criteria in combination. For example, those of reputedly superior ancestry may also be the wealthiest; or a self-styled superior religion may be that of a conquering people who excel in military strength. Actual elites may thus turn out on examination to be mixed kinds, and not simple. Further, it should be noticed that, while these nine criteria and their permutations differ, all have an essential feature in common. However they may vary on other matters, they invariably glorify inequality. To this principle all doctrines of aristocracy, or "lions and lambs" formulas, are inexorably committed. With those reminders, let us now explore each of the nine criteria as postulated in theory and applied in practice.

THE MYTH OF RACIAL SUPERIORITY

One way to distinguish between individual human beings is to classify them into the racial groups of which mankind as a whole is composed. If this be tried, and if the distinctions are to be valid, the term "race" should be defined with exactitude, so that in distinguishing one race from another everybody may know what is being described. Unfortunately the word has often been employed with a looseness and imprecision—sometimes innocent, sometimes deliberately misleading —which impair its usefulness for scientific discussion. In writings, as in daily speech, examples abound of references to "the human race," "the Negro race," "the British race," "the Jewish race," "the white race," "the Indian race," and so on. It is evident that not all these usages are correct, since some include, contradict, or overlap with others. What sense can be made, for instance, of the term "British race"? If pigment be the test, then the British belong to a wider grouping of people with white skins. If the test be religion, then the British, who are overwhelmingly Christian and predominantly Protestant, can hardly be separated from other Protestant Christians. If it be language, the use of English in the British Isles (where there are many dialects and accents) does not mark off its inhabitants from the English-speaking people of the United States. If, however, the determinant be political, and "the British race" refers to a group that shares a common historical tradition and lives under the same government, at least the meaning becomes clearer—but then some other term, possibly "nation," had better be substituted.

Race can receive only one connotation which is reasonably clear, and it will be used here in that sense alone. An anthropologist has called it "a principal division of mankind, marked by physical characteristics which breed true. In this sense," he points out, "the word race is a biological term, and is restricted to the bodily characteristics that distinguish one group of human beings from another."[11] Thus defined, one may properly apply the word to Caucasians, Mongolians, or Negroes, and to subdivisions of these main stocks; and one can proceed objectively to discover and describe the physical traits peculiar to each. When all facts of this sort are collected and classified, what is revealed? That there are differences. Yes, but how should these be interpreted, and what is their social relevance? Admitting that differences do exist, can anybody assert that one kind is the superior? This is not possible except on one condition, namely that certain traits are demonstrably related to the better performance of certain functions. Take the human nose, for example. The purpose of a nose is to smell. So, if it can be shown that broader or longer nostrils are definitely correlated with a keener power of scent, then the wider or lengthier nose is manifestly superior.

But can the argument about the part be transferred to the whole? On the analogy of noses, this would be possible if men, by virtue of being human, could be shown to have a function which certain racial stocks are better equipped to perform than others. In that case—and only then—would it be arguable that a particular race is superior or supreme, a doctrine that reaches its climax in the assertions that the inferiors are not really human but subhuman, or that the master race is made up of supermen (Uebermenschen). This is exactly the reasoning of so eminent a philosopher as Aristotle when he justified the institution of slavery. According to him, a man's goal or end (telos) is to maintain happiness by leading a life of virtue under the governance of reason. Since it is reason that makes virtue possible, and virtue that makes happiness possible, anybody insufficiently endowed with reason can be neither virtuous nor happy, unless he is placed under the control of someone who is so endowed. In this way, both master and slave would benefit. The former, who needs to own property in order to develop his

----

[11]Melville J. Herskovits, *Man and His Works* (New York: Alfred A. Knopf, Inc., 1948), p. 133. A sociologist, however, points out that the anthropologists do not agree among themselves as to precisely which physical criteria constitute a race. Conceding that race "is fundamentally a biological concept," he argues that, in terms of social relevance, a group may be thought to be a race even though, in scientific fact, it is not. "Thus," Professor Herbert Blumer suggests, "it would seem that a reasonably accurate, realistic, and workable concept of race is that it is a class or group of human beings who are regarded and treated in social life as a distinctive biological group with a common ancestry." See his "Reflections on Theory of Race Relations" in *Race Relations in World Perspective,* ed. Andrew W. Lind (Honolulu: University of Hawaii Press, 1955), pp. 3 and 5.

potentialities, possesses the slave as "an animate tool."[12] The latter lives the life that is best for him by obeying the dictates of his superior in wisdom.[13] Slavery is therefore a natural institution, because it is rooted in and conforms to physiological and psychological differences in human nature. The entire argument is one that flows logically from premises to conclusion, provided that its major assumptions be accepted. These are: (1) that man, as man, has a definable function; (2) that happiness, virtue, and reason are understood in the Aristotelian sense; and (3) that differences between individuals, inherited at birth, are too great to be modified by learning afterwards.

The argument is not of interest, however, only as a theoretical exercise in logic. Its political importance lies in the efforts made to apply such principles in practice, or rather in the attempts of those who practice discrimination anyway to borrow from Aristotle the color of justification and respectability. While virtually every historical period, continent, and civilization yields its harvest of examples, some of the most significant may be gleaned from the nineteenth and twentieth centuries. The enslavement of human beings was permitted by law in the British Empire until 1833; in Russia, where it assumed the form of serfdom, until 1861; in the United States until 1863; in Brazil until 1888. In the decade or so before the American Civil War, the South's defense of its "peculiar institution" was often couched in Aristotelian terms which confidently asserted the permanent inferiority of one human group to another. At the close of the nineteenth and beginning of the twentieth centuries, when colored peoples stirred restlessly in resentment at the imposition of alien white rule, there were European and American writers who reaffirmed a belief in racial differences and their own preordained supremacy. Such was the spirit of Rudyard Kipling's ballad *The White Man's Burden,* or his *England's Answer* where he wrote:

> Truly ye come of The Blood; slower to bless than to ban;
> Little used to lie down at the bidding of any man. . . .
> Thus for the good of your people—thus for the Pride of the Race.[14]

A similar attitude inspired the Frenchman De Gobineau and two American writers, Madison Grant and Lothrop Stoddard.

But it is a twentieth-century German who sought and has rightfully

[12]*Politics,* i, Chap. 4, Sec. 2.

[13]*Ibid.,* Chap. 5, Sec. 9.

[14]From *The Seven Seas* by Rudyard Kipling. Reprinted by permission of Mrs. George Bambridge and Doubleday & Company, Inc.

earned the dubious credit of formulating the doctrine in its starkest manner and applying it with most systematic thoroughness. Before seizing power, Adolf Hitler had expressed this philosophy in *Mein Kampf:*

Any crossing between two beings of not quite the same high standard produces a medium between the standards of the parents. . . . But such a mating contradicts Nature's will to breed life toward a higher level. The presumption for this does not lie in blending the superior with the inferior, but rather in a complete victory of the former. The stronger has to rule and he is not to amalgamate with the weaker one, that he may not sacrifice his own greatness. . . . Just as little as Nature desires a mating between weaker individuals and stronger ones, far less she desires the mixture of a higher race with a lower one, as in this case her entire work of higher breeding, which has perhaps taken hundreds of thousands of years, would tumble at one blow. . . . What we see before us of human culture today, the results of art, science and techniques, is almost exclusively the creative product of the Aryan. . . . For the formation of higher cultures, the existence of inferior men was one of the most essential presumptions because they alone were able to replace the lack of technical means without which a higher development is unthinkable. The first culture of mankind certainly depended less on the tamed animal, but rather on the use of inferior people.[15]

For more than a decade, while the National Socialists ruled Germany, these beliefs were promulgated as the official policy of the government of a major European state. In their name were enacted the so-called Nuremberg laws, prescribing the conditions of citizenship and proscribing all marriages between those of "superior" and "inferior" blood. In their name were committed atrocities against people of the Jewish religion which resulted in the mass extermination of six million Jews. In their name the German government prepared and unleashed a war for the domination of Europe, in which millions of Europeans and Americans perished.

Since the downfall of that regime, another country has emerged into notorious prominence because of a government which officially promotes the supremacy of one racial group over all the others. This is the Republic of South Africa. The dominant race is of European ancestry, but it forms only one-fifth of the country's population. This group is itself subdivided into a majority (approximately three-fifths) who speak Afrikaans and a minority whose language is English. The former are the descendants of Protestants who emigrated from the Netherlands, and from France and Germany, in the second half of the seventeenth century. The forbears of the latter came to South Africa

[15]*Mein Kampf,* pp. 390, 392, 397, 404, 405.

during the nineteenth century after Britain annexed the Cape at the end of the Napoleonic Wars. The past relations of Afrikaners and British were so bitter that they led to two wars, the second of which ended in 1902. Among the seeds of discord—besides differences in Protestantism, economic technology, and political outlook—was a contrast of attitudes toward the Africans, a contrast somewhat analogous to the traditional attitudes of whites toward the American Negro in North and South respectively. Irreconcilable Afrikaner nationalists never forgave the British for emancipating their Negro slaves and for conquering the two independent Republics to which they had "trekked" in the interior.[16]

The racial majority in South Africa is composed mainly of Africans. The indigenous Bushmen, Hottentots, and Zulus have now either disappeared or are greatly outnumbered by Bantus, most of whom are descended from tribes that moved into South Africa from the north. In addition, there are one and a half million half-castes, designated there as Coloured, and 500,000 Indians who came originally to South Africa as indentured labor in the sugar plantations of Natal.

In a country where only the Europeans enjoy full political rights, the government since 1948 has been in the hands of the Nationalist party, led solely by Afrikaners and mostly by their extremists. This party has retained control in every election since 1948 with increasing support. Its major policy has been to enforce *apartheid,* or segregation. As spelled out in law and administration, this has meant complete segregation, along racial lines, of all public facilities, the classification of the entire population and assignment of identity cards to everyone in terms of race, prohibition of interracial intercourse and marriage, the enforced separation of residential areas in the cities, and discrimination in employment. *Apartheid* in principle is white supremacy in practice, since only the one group directs the separating and determines the lines of discrimination. Increasingly, therefore, as the minority attempts to prolong its privileges, the South African government assumes the character of a police state. Impelled by the politics of fear, a little band of backward-looking fanatics defies the movement of modern world history and prepares its own ultimate disaster.

But the sin of racial arrogance is certainly no monopoly of whites. Each race, it seems, fashions its idea of excellence after its own kind. There have been Chinese and Japanese spokesmen who have pro-

---

[16]The constitution of the South African Republic contained a clause that read: "The people desire to permit no equality between coloured people and the white inhabitants of the country, either in church or state." Quoted in Alexander Brady, *Democracy in the Dominions* (University of Toronto Press, 1947), p. 307.

nounced that yellow-skinned people are racially superior to others. Similar notions have not been lacking among the redskins. The Western poet[17] who wrote so condescendingly about "the poor Indian" and his "untutored mind" would have been astonished to learn that some Indians at least believed the boot to be on the other foot. Among the Cherokees, whose knowledge of mankind extended to Europeans and Negroes, this myth is related about the origin of races. The Great Spirit created man out of dough, modeling three figures which he put in an oven. Overanxious to see the results, he opened the door and took out the first figure too soon. It was whitish, half-baked, unattractive. But the act was irrevocable, and a white race descended from this sorry specimen. Next he drew out his masterpiece, a figure perfectly cooked to a rich reddish-brown, which of course became the progenitor of the redskins. So proudly did he admire his handiwork that he forgot all about number three, until alas! he smelled something burning. Too late, he removed it from the oven, a blackened cinder —ancestor of the Negroes.[18]

The Aristotelian assertion that by nature some men are masters and others are slaves lends itself too readily to the Nazi perversion: "All that is not race in this world is trash."[19] This statement of Hitler, which incidentally is a good example of his own advocacy of the "big lie," is itself pure trash and is refuted by much evidence.

THE CULT OF ANCESTORS

The doctrine which divides human beings into superiors and inferiors by virtue of inborn physical and psychological differences may take another form. The emphasis can be placed on the family, rather than the race to which a human being belongs. In other words, the line of division between human beings is still surveyed in terms of hereditary factors which are transmitted at birth and are supposedly not acquired or modified afterwards; but the smaller family group is substituted for the larger one of race. According to this way of thinking it is a person's lineage or pedigree that counts. His ancestors' merits rather than his own may secure for him, without effort on his part, a lofty position in the social order; or may relegate him, possibly contrary to his abilities, to a lowly status.[20] The lions and lambs

---

[17]Alexander Pope, in the *Essay on Man.*

[18]The story, cited in Herskovits' *Man and His Works,* pp. 68–69, was reported by a Belgian anthropologist. The identical theme has also been found among the brown-skinned Malayans.

[19]*Mein Kampf,* p. 406.

[20]See Chap. 5, pp. 129–32. The connection between the concepts of aristocracy

become the well-born and ill-born, the upper class and lower, the aristocrats and masses.

When an elite is constituted on this basis, one must distinguish between its central feature and the attendant consequences. The central fact is the perpetuation of an aristocracy over successive generations by the hereditary principle. A group of families recognize each other, and are respected by the rest, as members of a charmed circle. In any one generation the odds are heavily against the demotion of any of these families or the admission of a new one. At the outset, of course, and before its hereditary character becomes fixed,[21] such a system must originate in some alternative scheme of differentiation. Those families which eventually emerge as superior may have succeeded earlier in accumulating greater wealth or conducting a conquest. Thus they win an initial position of privilege which they pass on by inheritance. Furthermore the members of a family that belongs to the charmed circle can amass possessions through social influence, just as they may enhance their personal abilities because of their opportunities and experience. In judging the merits of a hereditary aristocracy, however, one is not primarily concerned with their wealth, their powers, their polish, or their knowledge of affairs, since these factors are either the cause or the consequence of the point that is really in issue: the acceptance of kinship as the determinant of one's status within a social classification.

The basic assumption of such an aristocracy is the belief that planned, selective breeding among human beings can produce characteristics which parents will transmit to their offspring, so that a "higher" type may be evolved and preserved. Whether this view be true or false only the specialist in genetics can venture to assert. The student of politics, however, can observe that no actual aristocracy has ever conformed to this ideal. Indeed, if experience warrants any hypothesis, it can just as well support a contrary generalization. The aristocracies that have survived the longest were those which, like the Roman and the British, were willing to accept periodic or continuous infusion of new stock; while from excessive inbreeding once-famous lines, like the Hapsburgs or Bourbons, have run to seed. But, quite apart from genetic difficulties, the hereditary principle involves social consequences which are open to major objections. One of these is its rigid application to circumstances that are highly variable. For the principle ignores the fact that no one stratum of society has a

---

and lineage is revealed in the Spanish word *hidalgo*, and the corresponding Portuguese *fidalgo*, meaning a "nobleman." The former is an abbreviation of *hijo de algo*; the latter of *filho de algo*. Both expressions mean "son of a Somebody."

[21]For the example of Venice, see p. 114.

monopoly of great ability and that its reproduction in successive generations cannot be guaranteed. A second obnoxious feature is its system of ancestor worship, which classifies the living, not for what they are, but for what their forefathers were. Too often has the luster of a noble house conferred an inflated valuation upon an ignoble scion. Too often have the talents of those less fortunately born been denied creative outlets. To base distinctions upon heredity is to predetermine the lives of all by a criterion in no way related to their personal efforts or exertions. One's parentage cannot be chosen, altered, escaped, or denied.

Be this as it may, examples of the hereditary elite may be found in almost all periods of history and all parts of the world. The Homeric poems, which present in blended fact and fiction one of our earliest literary pictures of a European society, relate the deeds of a cluster of eminent families acknowledged in war and peace as the leaders of the Hellenic World. Their prerogatives come to them by right of birth, and, since their lineage is illustrious, they may be addressed by their own name (for example, Achilles, Agamemnon, Odysseus) or by the patronymic (for example, Son of Peleus, Son of Atreus, Son of Laertes).[22] The same status which creates their rights demands connected duties. Chieftains are under obligation to be champions of the army and fight in the front line. They receive the greater rewards of an exalted position, but run the greater risks. And what of the rank and file? They are the ever-present background, but nameless and nondescript. If individualized at all, they appear in the favorable role of the faithful and humble servant (for example, the swineherd Eumaeus, who stays loyal to his master Odysseus). Only once does Homer portray them in protest, and in that single instance the poet, whose epics were composed to glorify heroes and to be chanted in princely palaces, offers an unflattering characterization. Thersites, criticizing Agamemnon in the council of the chiefs, voices the first revolt of the underdog in occidental writing. For this the poet has him thrashed by Odysseus while the onlookers laugh.[23]

In subsequent centuries, for which more exact information is available, the same pattern recurs of a ruling aristocracy which faces an acquiescent or at times rebellious populace. Athens was controlled until the seventh century B.C. by an oligarchy of families known as the Eupatridae ("of good parentage"), and most of the other Greek city-

---

[22]All of these are kings *(basileis)*. But kingship has degrees, and some chiefs are kinglier than others *(basileuteroi)*, and Agamemnon is kingliest of all *(basileutatos)*.

[23]Homer, *Iliad*, ii, 11. 211 ff. Similarly unsympathetic portrayals of spokesmen for the underprivileged are the pictures of Cleon (the fifth century Athenian) by Aristophanes and Thucydides, and that of Jack Cade in Shakespeare's *Henry VI.*

states never evolved beyond this to the more equalitarian society and politics that appear in the Athens of the fifth and fourth centuries. In the Roman Republic the most momentous domestic controversy of the fifth, fourth, and third centuries B.C. was the famous Struggle of the Orders which has enshrined the names "patricians" and "plebeians" in our everyday vocabulary. The gulf between the two consisted of differences in social status, civil rights, religious ceremonial, and political power. The aim of the plebeians was to abolish privileges in which they did not share and to win equality. But, even when this was achieved, the grant to the plebeians of substantial equality with the patricians reformulated, rather than terminated, the domination of Rome by an aristocracy. What happened was that certain plebeian families were admitted to the clique of dominant clans, who monopolized for themselves and passed around among their own number the principal offices *(honores)* of the Roman Republic. Once anybody was elected to a major office, he and his family became ennobled *(nobilis)*. Within the nobility so constituted, families were scaled in importance by the number of such officeholders they had produced and were conventionally ranked as praetorian, consular, or censorian according to whether the highest office reached by one of their members was that of *praetor, consul,* or *censor.* Thus by the second century B.C. the odds were as strongly in favor of a Marcellus, Claudius, Julius, or Metellus to secure the office he desired, as they were against a "new man" *(novus homo)* from a family outside the *nobilitas.* Cicero, the orator without equal in Rome, relates with complacent pride that he was the first new man for a long time to break through the barriers of the nobility and obtain a consulate.

Whatever variation there may be in detail, the common feature in this type of political organization is the division of the population into two classes. One is composed of relatively few members, the other contains the great majority, and the former dominates the latter. Membership in each class is hereditary. Only rarely does movement occur upward into the preferred class or downward into the lower. A division of society, however, into two levels is in many instances an oversimplification. A cross section of certain communities would show three strata and sometimes more. Indeed, it is possible for the entire community to be organized on the familiar military pattern with a ladder or scale of ranks on which people are assigned their respective places in a hierarchy. A famous example of this is the system which evolved in western Europe after the strife and turmoil following the dissolution of the Roman Empire, namely, feudalism. Its essential feature was to erect a fabric of personal relationships on the basis of land ownership and tenure. The relations of men to land governed the relations of men to men. A man received land as a fief from another, to whom he swore on his knees an oath of fealty. The two thus became lord and vassal; and while it was the responsibility of the lord to protect his vassal, it was the latter's duty to serve the former. This system of horizontal stratification was applied to both the spheres, temporal and ecclesiastical, into which medieval Christendom was split. But though government was hierarchical in state and church alike, the elite that controlled the latter was prevented from being hereditary by the requirement of celibacy. A social order so built on hierarchical principles, and extended to cover the universe, is described by Shakespeare in an eloquent speech of Ulysses in *Troilus and Cressida*.[24] The same conception is philosophically defended in the essay of a late-Victorian British ethicist A. C. Bradley, who wrote approvingly on the theme: "My Station and Its Duties."[25]

SUBMISSION TO THE ELDERS

Along with race and ancestry, two further methods for differentiating between human beings and assigning them a superior or inferior political status may be mentioned. These are, respectively, age and sex. The idea that the right to govern is a prerogative of age has underlain the practice of many communities. It is associated with the belief that ruling is an art involving a high degree of judgment; that judgment in practical matters is largely acquired by experience; and that older persons necessarily possess an experience that is longer, riper, and therefore more trustworthy. In addition, a system that entrusts government to the aged because of their age is normally built upon a social base which attaches great importance to the family and, within the family, stresses the authority of the father. The rule of the Elders is patriarchy writ large.

Examples are not lacking of political institutions whose *raison d'être* was to embody the authority of age. Such a system in a very primitive community is thus described by J. G. Frazer:

Let us begin by looking at the lowest race of men as to whom we possess comparatively full and accurate information, the aborigines of Australia. These savages are ruled neither by chiefs nor kings. So far as their tribes can be said to have a political constitution, it is a democracy or rather an oligarchy of old and influential men, who meet in council and decide on all measures of importance to the practical exclusion of the younger men. Their deliberative assembly answers to the senate of later times: if we had to coin a word for such government of elders we might call it a *gerontocracy*. The elders who in

24 Act I, Sc. 3, 11. 75 ff.
25 *Ethical Studies* (1876).

aboriginal Australia thus meet and direct the affairs of their tribe appear to be for the most part the headmen of their respective totem clans.[26]

But the authority of age is by no means confined to primitive forms of society. In the governmental machinery of Sparta there was a powerful body called the *Gerousia,* or "Council of Old Men," membership in which commenced at the age of 60. A more celebrated instance is the Roman Senate, a word that means in Latin exactly what *Gerousia* does in Greek. Composed of past and present holders of the higher offices in the Republic, this body for over four centuries was the nuclear force in the government of Rome. Likewise, the institutions of the Anglo-Saxon tribes distinguished between the Folkmoot, or meeting of male citizens, and the influential Witanagemot, or council of wise men who were the tribal elders. Modern Japan under its Meiji Constitution (adopted 1889) developed a similar council of elders, called the *Genro.* To it belonged the senior statesmen who had twice held the office of premier. The Genro acted informally as a consultative body to which the emperor might turn for advice on the formation of a new government, or on issues of high policy. Indeed, so great was the traditional Japanese respect for age that even the emperor would feel reluctant to give directions to an older man.[27] On this point, it is worth noting that the Constitution of the United States prescribes an age of 35 as the minimum for the presidential office. Political practice in the twentieth century, however, has added almost twenty years to that figure. Even allowing for John F. Kennedy who was only 43 when he took the oath of office, the average age of the 13 presidents from McKinley to Nixon at the time of assuming office was 54. During the same period in the United Kingdom, 15 men have served as premier from Salisbury to Wilson; their average age when they first began their duties was 59.[28]

THE UNFAIR SEX

More common, however, than distinctions based upon age have been those derived from sex. Although anthropological research has

[26]James G. Frazer, *The Golden Bough,* Part I, Vol. I, 3rd ed. (New York: The Macmillan Company, 1919–1935), p. 335. Italics in original. *Gerontocracy* means "government by the aged."

[27]"Baron Harada records that the emperor wished to speak to Prince Konoye, apparently to give him some advice, but was hesitant to do so directly. Remarked the emperor, 'After all, he is older than I, so I cannot very well order him specifically: "do this" or "do that." ' " *Saionji Harada Memoirs,* Sept. 3, 1936, p. 1590. Quoted in Yale Maxon, *Control of Japanese Foreign Policy* (Berkeley: University of California Press, 1957), p. 4.

[28]Like President Kennedy, Prime Minister Wilson reached the summit at an age (48) well below the average.

established the existence of some matriarchal societies, patriarchy is the more usual mode of family organization. Politics, similarly, has normally been a function or monopoly of the menfolk. This was most probably due to the primary connection between government and defense, which endows the able-bodied male with importance. But it is also to be explained in terms of the specialization that assigned child-rearing and domestic matters to the female and took the male out of the house as the hunter, farmer, or breadwinner. For over two thousand years the traditional forms of Western society excluded women from active participation in government, save when the operation of the hereditary principle conferred a crown upon one who reigned as queen in her own right (as Elizabeth I of England or Catherine of Russia). Not until the twentieth century did the fair sex begin to challenge the monopoly of government by the unfair.

Systems that arbitrarily discriminate against half the population, or more, on such grounds as age or sex, are open to the same objection as those based on heredity. They classify entire groups as politically adequate or inadequate in a wholly arbitrary manner, since they assume a connection between fitness for government and some other circumstance that may prove completely irrelevant. Of course, it can be true that older persons, with more knowledge of the ways of the world, may be more competent to run the state. Likewise, because in most societies the menfolk have traditionally done most of the work outside the home, they have acquired an experience denied to women. But this does not mean that age is synonymous with political wisdom, or that any male is fit to govern. Still less can it be argued that persons whose ages are between 20 and 45 have nothing useful to contribute to government in the way of ideas or energy. If so, how should we explain the achievements of Alexander the Great or Thomas Jefferson, of Alexander Hamilton or the younger Pitt?[29] Correspondingly, the belief that no woman has a talent for politics is a false presumption based on nothing better than male vanity and prejudice. Who, for instance, could argue thus about Queen Elizabeth I of England or Catherine the Great of Russia?[30] What makes for capacity

[29]Alexander of Macedon, born in 356 B.C., became king at the age of 20. When he died in 323 B.C., he was master of the region from Greece to the northwest portion of India. Thomas Jefferson, born in 1743, was 33 years old when he wrote the Declaration of Independence. Alexander Hamilton, born in 1757, was 30 at the time of his contributions to the convention that drafted the United States Constitution. William Pitt the younger, born in 1759, was only 24 when George III first appointed him prime minister in 1783.

[30]The first woman to head a modern government was Mrs. Sirimavo Bandaranaike of Ceylon. Others, since her, have been Mrs. Indira Gandhi of India and Mrs. Golda Meir of Israel.

in government is the merit of the individual concerned, whether young or old, man or woman, as developed by the opportunities that society affords to gain experience.

The principles examined so far are race, ancestry, age, and sex. These have been discussed first because they differ from the remainder of the list and can be appropriately grouped. The feature in which race, ancestry, age, and sex resemble each other is that all four lie beyond our control. We cannot choose our race, our ancestry, our age, or our sex; and though one's age, unlike the other three, does alter during a lifetime, the process of growing old and the rate of change lie beyond our power. A community is free to decide whether it will distinguish politically between a few superior members and an inferior majority. If it does so, it is also free to decide whether to select one of these four principles as the criterion of division. But once such a choice is taken and any of these criteria is adopted, an individual has no say about the place to which he or she is assigned and no means of influencing the assignment. The application of the rule to particular cases cannot be modified, still less overruled, by the efforts of the person concerned or the discretion of others.

In the classification of elites presented earlier in this chapter, nine types were listed. Those not yet considered are religion, military strength, culture, wealth, and knowledge. These five differ from the preceding four in that a community which selects its ruling elite by any of these criteria may conceivably permit its members to join the charmed circle by their own volition and exertions.

DISCRIMINATION THROUGH RELIGION

Religion must be considered in this connection, not for the theology or faith it adopts (that is beyond the scope of this book), but for the reason that religious movements become organized in institutions which have social consequences for human beings in this life. Many, indeed, are the instances where religion has sanctified a separation into upper and lower castes, though whether religion was the originating cause of such practices in every case is not always clear. Sometimes it would seem that religious doctrines have been responsible for introducing a stratification and rigidifying the strata with the cement of divine sanction. One illustration is the effect upon Vedic India of the invasion of Aryans from the west who brought to a darker-skinned people the creed of Brahmanism and Hinduism.[31] Under its impact,

[31]The word "Hindu" is not indigenously Indian, but came in from Iran with the invaders. It is a variant of the Iranian river name "Sindhu."

Indian society was grouped into the four classes of Brahman, Kshatriya, Daishya, and Sudra—a hierarchy in descending order of priests, rulers, artisans, and slave-laborers. These became the hereditary castes which prescribed an individual's occupation as well as his social status. The fourfold grading was based upon an authoritative text of the Hindu scriptures, the *Rigveda*.[32]

At other times, religions whose creeds were fundamentally equalitarian have condoned and conformed to preexisting social cleavages which they have helped to reinforce and justify. A case in point is the spread of Christianity. The spirit of the Christian religion in its pure form consists in emphasizing equality,[33] since affairs of the soul are held to be more important than those of the body, and all souls are deemed equally worthy in the eyes of God. But when the Emperor Constantine embraced Christianity as the official religion of the Roman Empire, the church accepted—for this world—the existence of a hierarchical society including the institution of slavery. Similarly the medieval church tolerated the system of serfdom. As R. H. Tawney has written:

The canon law appears to have recognized and enforced serfdom. Few prominent ecclesiastics made any pronouncement against it. Aquinas explains it as the result of sin, but that does not prevent his justifying it on economic grounds. Almost all medieval writers appear to assume it or excuse it. Ecclesiastical landlords, though perhaps somewhat more conservative in their methods, seem as a whole to have been neither better nor worse than other landlords. . . . The disappearance of serfdom . . . was part of a general economic movement, with which the Church had little to do, and which churchmen, as property-owners, had sometimes resisted. It owed less to Christianity than to the humanitarian liberalism of the French Revolution.[34]

Correspondingly, the catechism of the Church of England in the eighteenth century gave its blessing to the division of society into classes; serfdom was fully sanctioned by the Russian Orthodox church; slavery was defended by the southern branches of some American churches in the 1840's and 1850's, as it was also approved in South Africa by the Dutch Reformed church.

It frequently happened in the nineteenth century that persons of liberal outlook, who espoused the cause of equality, found themselves in opposition to a cluster of institutions which together defended their

[32]*Rigveda*, x, Hymn 90, Verse 12.

[33]See Chap. 5, p. 124.

[34]R. H. Tawney, *Religion and the Rise of Capitalism* (New York: Harcourt, Brace & World, Inc., 1926), Chap. 1, "The Medieval Background," Sec. iii, "The Ideal and the Reality."

vested interest in privilege. Characteristically, these institutions were the army, nobility, and church. In the Hapsburg Empire, for example, the leadership of the Catholic church was closely identified with the principles of legitimacy, autocracy, and monarchical rule, and the preservation of a static, stratified society. Likewise in France, the church, which had been a main pillar of the *ancien régime*, consistently resisted the Revolution and republicanism throughout the vicissitudes of constitutional change. Along with the king and the aristocratic landowners, it stood to lose its privileges whenever *liberté, égalité et fraternité* should triumph. So too, in Spain, amid a social order of profound inequalities, the ecclesiastical hierarchy adhered to the old ways from which it had derived great power and profit. The same was true of the Orthodox church in Russia, which, under the tsarist regime, was a prime supporter of thorough-going inequality. Indeed, one of the high officials of that church, a procurator of the Holy Synod, penned his philosophy in a book which contains the frankest expression of an elitist outlook towards the mass of mankind.[35]

There are other ways in which religion may lend itself to the political stratification of humanity. Sometimes the group which controls the government is closely identified with an ecclesiastical organization which maintains that it alone has the true faith, and that nonbelievers, or infidels, cannot commune on terms of equality with the faithful. Those who profess an alternative faith may then find themselves relegated to a position of political inferiority and be denied equality of rights. Thus, in Britain the Protestant nonconformists who dissented from the Church of England were so treated from 1689 to 1828, as were Catholics until 1829. In other countries Catholics have meted out similar treatment to Protestants by imposing disabilities, or inflicting persecution, on those regarded as heretics. Jews, even when not subject to pogroms and inquisitions, were normally denied equality of status in Christian countries until the nineteenth century.

CONTROL BY CONQUEST

Government by physical might is apparently in sharp contrast with

[35] See K. P. Pobyedonostseff, *Reflections of a Russian Statesman*, trans. R. C. Long (London: Grant Richards, 1898), p. 44. "The prevalent doctrine of the perfection of Democracy and of democratic government, stands on the same delusive foundation. This doctrine presupposes the capacity of the people to understand subtleties of political science which have a clear and substantial existence in the minds of its apostles only. Precision of knowledge is attainable only by the few minds which constitute the aristocracy of intellect; the mass, always and everywhere, is *vulgus*, and its conceptions of necessity are vulgar."

government by divine right. Yet for purposes of our present classification, they belong to the same category, since both have the result of separating humanity into a superior and an inferior group. Because of the intimate bond between the need for protection and the origin of government, prowess in war has frequently served as a basis for inclusion in the favored few.[36] A community which exists in constant fear or suspicion of hostile neighbors, and which inhabits an area where terrain and topography offer no natural barriers for defense, is likely to place a premium on fighting ability. Whoever excels in the military art will be accorded privileges by those who need his services and can exact obedience from them. No dividing line is then drawn between the military and civil sectors of government. Or rather, it is the military which absorbs and embraces the civil. Service in the armed forces then becomes not merely a vocation or career, but a high road to social influence and political power.

The warrior elite, however, while it responds to the need for protection, is liable to the defect that is the corruption of its virtues. For dominance by the military can degenerate into the excesses of militarism. The history of Prussia yields a classic illustration of this danger. Living in an exposed position in the center of the north European plain, with no obvious defensive frontier to west or east, the Prussians have traditionally thrust outward or been hemmed inward according to the relation of their striking power to that of their French and Slavic neighbors. By tight organization and by building an efficient army, the landowning Junkers contrived to be secure and strong. But the tool they had forged for safety became the instrument of their own disaster. The officers of the general staff and a succession of authoritarian rulers took the bit between their teeth. Fostering in the country a militaristic spirit of expansion, they plunged through wars of aggression to their own and their people's destruction.

Although it is the need for protection that brings a community to accept the authority of military experts, in yet another way the practice of warfare results in differentiation between human beings. The victors may follow up their conquest by imposing their rule upon the vanquished. Thus the militarily weak are subordinated to the strong; and the strong, if they seek to maintain their rule, must

[36]See the characterization of the Condottieri as state-builders in fifteenth century Italy by Jacob Burckhardt, *The Civilization of the Renaissance in Italy,* in Chap. 1, "The State as a Work of Art." Japanese history provides a similar case in point. The Shogunate was originally a military form of government; and the hereditary warriors, the *Samurai,* were a dominant influence in government from the eleventh to the fifteenth centuries.

preserve their military power.[37] A notorious example is provided by the ancient Greek state of Sparta. The people whose discipline has become a byword were trained under the regimen, and lived according to the pattern, of an army barracks. Their fighting qualities, of almost legendary renown in the Greek world, were displayed at their finest in the heroism of Leonidas and the Four Hundred, holding the narrow pass at Thermopylae in defiance of the invading Persian multitude. But what is significant about the Spartans is that they employed in their domestic affairs the kind of organization appropriate to an army in the field. The reason was that they never lived entirely at peace, but always in a condition of suspended or expectant warfare. The Spartans had migrated into Greece later than many other Greeks and made their home in the Peloponnese when it was already occupied. They took their "living space" by force, and reduced the earlier inhabitants, Messenians by name, to the level of serfs, or *Helots*.[38] From that time, under the compulsion of their own policy and in fear of their subjects who outnumbered them, the Spartans were condemned to militarize their mode of life and stay permanently on guard against uprisings. They adjudged proper all means to this end. The government maintained a secret organization *(Krupteia)*, the equivalent of a Gestapo, whose duty it was to forestall revolt. On one occasion during the Peloponnesian War the *Krupteia* was responsible for the sudden rounding up and slaughtering at night of several hundred *Helots*. Such methods were incapable of doing more than prolonging a static despotism, where the master people eventually succumbed to internal dry rot. By contrast, the most successful empires of history are those like the Roman and the British, which, though founded in large part by force, subsequently developed the policy of elevating subjects to partners, and which, at least in the case of Britain, upheld at home the supremacy of civilians over the military.

THE CLAIMS OF CULTURAL LEADERSHIP

Military conquest may be accomplished by one people at the expense of another who differ from them in culture as well as in fighting capacity. In this case the conquerors may assert their right to rule the conquered by virtue of their cultural, as distinct from their military,

[37]This is a further illustration of the point discussed in Chap. 3, pp. 81–82, that the force which is required for protection may be perverted by abuse. Internally, that takes the form of despotism; externally, of aggressive conquest.

[38]From a word meaning "captive."

superiority. Used in this context the term "culture" requires some explaining. It is perhaps best understood in contrast to the term "race," with which it is too frequently, and quite erroneously, confused. Race,[39] properly defined, describes those human traits, both physical and psychic, which are inborn and derive from heredity, while culture refers to other characteristics acquired by learning after birth and representing the influence upon the individual of his environment. To anthropologists and sociologists, culture means the whole way of life of a person or group. To them it is the broadest possible of categories, embracing all aspects of social organization—political, economic, religious, and the rest. A political scientist, however, may be content with a less inclusive formula. For him, "culture" can be defined to exclude politics, economics, and religion, which are more conveniently treated as distinct categories. Everything else, that is, the social remainder, is culture.

What is there in this remainder that is politically relevant? Among the social elements which constitute a culture are the family system, the principles and content of education, and the language which people speak and write. The relation that these bear to politics may be viewed from two angles. To the extent that people share the same family system and education and speak a common language, they belong to one community; and the sense of social identity that flows from their awareness of this fact can contribute to political union. Probably the ingredient in culture which is closest to politics is language. Since language among literate peoples supplies the medium for transmitting and communicating the shared experiences of a group, a people's literature becomes a deposit of its history. Writers, therefore (no less than statesmen, soldiers, or prophets), can be venerated as heroes. Such is the position of Shakespeare among Englishmen, Dante among Italians, Cervantes among Spaniards, Goethe among Germans, and Pushkin among Russians.

From the external standpoint, however, the features which unite a group into a community serve also to separate it from any other group that builds its families and education around different patterns and speaks another tongue. In this case, pride in one's own culture may develop into the feeling that one's own is a better culture than some other from which it happens to differ. It has commonly resulted from such attitudes that an alien ruling group has based its right to govern upon the asserted superiority of its culture and that sometimes it seeks to suppress the culture which it considers inferior. One may bear in mind the treatment which the Spanish *conquistadores* meted out to

[39]See pp. 94–95.

the Aztecs and the Incas, or that of the Manchus to the Chinese. Prior to 1918 the German-speaking Austrians had similar attitudes toward the Slavic inhabitants of their empire, and the British rulers of India felt much the same about their Hindu and Muslim subjects. Truly, the paths of empire builders are strewn with the results of vaunted cultural preeminence.[40]

MONEY POWER

If it is not leadership in culture which distinguishes the lions from the lambs, the leadership may come from wealth. In this case, the criterion by which human beings are differentiated is economic. People are classified as better or worse by reason of their possessions and according to the index of riches which happens to be in vogue within a given society. That index can be land, livestock, gold, precious stones, slaves, shares or bonds—anything, in fact, that is conventionally accepted. Whoever succeeds in accumulating a large amount of these is assured of admission to the charmed circle. Whoever has too little to qualify, or owns nothing, is assigned an inferior status and is excluded from participation in political functions. The name for this type of state is plutocracy, the Greek for "government by wealth."[41] On what theory is the ownership of riches regarded as justifying a right to rule? This question has been variously answered. Sometimes it is argued that possessions constitute "a stake in the country"—with the implied corollary that the more one owns, the greater one's stake. The wealthy not only have a large investment in the community, but stand to lose more if misgovernment occurs. Their concern to safeguard their fortunes makes them the more prudent custodians of the public interest. Or it may be argued that if government is to be conducted by "the best," then a man's possessions can be taken as an objective yardstick of his abilities as an individual and of his services to others. The wealthiest are to be adjudged the worthiest. Or again the view may be advanced that an ample fortune emancipates its owner from the daily anxieties of earning a livelihood and enables him to be more fully dedicated to public affairs. Hence the well-to-do enjoy the leisure and the detachment which make them a "natural" ruling class. Finally—and using somewhat different premises—those who call themselves realists may contend that, since wealth does in fact breed influence and power, to acknowledge the authority of the rich is merely to recognize the actual structure of power in society.

[40]For a further discussion of the relation between culture and nationhood, see Chap. 12, pp. 359–69.

[41]The Japanese term *zaibatsu*, meaning "financial clique," is similar though it does not include the notion of government.

The doctrines that the distribution of political power will tend to correspond to the distribution of wealth, and that the difference between "haves" and "have-nots" creates political as well as economic cleavage are, of course, among the well-worn commonplaces of political thought. When Plato drew up a ranking of states on a scale that proceeded from perfect goodness to utter evil, he placed plutocracy in the middle of his five types.[42] He considered its main defect an overaddiction to the amassing of wealth and a general acquisitiveness.

"Then when in a city wealth and the wealthy are honoured, virtue and the good are slighted?"
"Obviously."
" . . . Then in process of time, from men who love victory and honour they become lovers of money-getting and of money; they give their praise and admiration to the rich man, and elect him to rule over them, but the poor man they slight?"
"Certainly."
"Then they lay down a law which is the distinguishing feature of an oligarchic constitution. They prescribe a sum of money varying in amount as the oligarchy is more or less extreme, and proclaim all disqualified for office whose means do not amount to the prescribed sum. . . . Such a city must of necessity be not one but two—the city of the rich and the city of the poor—rich and poor dwelling within the same walls, and always conspiring against one another."[43]

To similar effect is the judgment expressed by James Madison:

The latent causes of faction are thus sown in the nature of man; and we see them everywhere brought into different degrees of activity, according to the different circumstances of civil society. . . . But the most common and durable source of factions has been the various and unequal distribution of property. Those who hold and those who are without property have ever formed distinct interests in society. Those who are creditors, and those who are debtors, fall under a like discrimination.[44]

However, although each was well aware that the economic distinction between rich and poor assumed a frankly political character, neither Plato nor Madison developed his analysis to the lengths that were reached by Karl Marx. For Marx and the Marxists have gone beyond their predecessors and the evidence in asserting that the eco-

[42]His ranking, from good to bad, was: (1) rule of philosopher-kings; (2) timocracy (government by soldiers conforming to a knightly code of chivalry); (3) plutocracy; (4) democracy; (5) tyranny. *Republic*, viii–ix.
[43]*Republic*, viii, Sec. 551, pp. 246–47, trans. A. D. Lindsay (Everyman's Library).
[44]*The Federalist*, No. 10 (Everyman's Library), p. 43.

nomic factor controls and determines all other aspects of society, and in interpreting all recorded history as a series of struggles between economic classes becoming more sharply differentiated into exploiters (that is, owners of the means of production) and exploited (that is, those who toil on behalf of the exploiter). This doctrine, which claims to be a descriptive statement of fact, says both too much and too little. Too much, because it exaggerates the influence of the economic factor out of proportion to its true size and significance, and because it pretends to discover in all places and in all periods of history a polarization between hostile economic classes which has existed in fact less generally than Marx imagines. It says too little, because it fails to allow for the effect upon society as a whole of factors operating independently of economics, and further because it depicts with distortion, or overlooks completely, any actual situation which does not neatly fit the doctrine.

But he who rejects the validity of the Marxian theory could easily lapse into the same error as Marx himself if he leaned too far backward and denied the existence or the political relevance of economic divisions. Many states have proceeded from the assumption that the right to participate in government should be correlated with the ownership of property. Of innumerable examples, three will suffice. The first is the government of a state that achieved splendor, power, and fame in the Middle Ages—the Republic of Venice. The Venetians owed their greatness to their skill in using the advantages of an unusual location. This cluster of islands, shoals, and mudbanks, belonging to land and water alike, had provided an early home for fishermen and a haven for the refugees who fled the invasion of the Huns. On the edge of the Italian peninsula, and at the head of the Adriatic, their seapower gave the Venetians security in defense and an avenue for commerce. Successfully combating their rivals—were they Dalmatians or Genoese—they emerged as the major commercial power of the eastern Mediterranean, commanding the access to the Middle East and forming a bridge of ships between Latins and Byzantines. The wealth that poured into Venice from the Levant enriched her merchants, and the plutocracy evolved into an aristocracy whose unequal status was derived from the profits of sea-borne trade. As these merchant-princes, whose palaces fringed the Grand Canal, became a hereditary oligarchy, they changed the constitution of the Republic in order to entrench their privileges through political control. The original authorities had been the general assembly of the citizens (concione) and the annually elected doge. But by degrees, the wealthy families—fearing the power of many and envying that of one—weakened those two institutions by reducing their functions to ceremonial formalities. In their place, they concentrated the real government in a Grand Council (whose membership was restricted after 1296 by hereditary right), a Senate, and a secretive Council of Ten which supervised public safety and forestalled conspiracies. Such bodies effectively carried over to politics the socioeconomic realities of domination by a few great commercial houses.

Another such case is the governmental system which prevailed in Britain through the eighteenth century and the first third of the nineteenth. Prior to the Reform Act of 1832, political power was concentrated in the hands of an oligarchy of landowners and merchant-financiers who had a grip on every key institution. Identifying themselves with the prerogatives of the monarchy, they were unassailably entrenched in the House of Lords through the device of hereditary peerages, as well as in the officer ranks of the navy and army and in the higher clergy of the established church. Over the House of Commons, before its reform, their control was almost as secure as elsewhere. The antiquated apportionment of districts was heavily biased in favor of rural areas and the ancient boroughs and ignored the shifts of population. The method of nominating and voting for candidates gave all the advantages to the lords and squires influential in the locality. Qualifications for the franchise were based primarily upon property, with the result that even in 1831—only four generations removed from the present—those entitled to vote in Britain numbered a bare 3 per cent of the population.[45]

A striking parallel, in the sense that it was designed to correlate political power with wealth, is the electoral organization adopted in the Kingdom of Prussia and in force there until the year 1918. Representatives to the Prussian *Landtag* were chosen in districts, each of which returned one, two, or three members. These were elected, not directly by the voters, but indirectly by an electoral college. For picking the latter body, every district was divided into subdistricts, to which was allotted one member of the electoral college for every 250 inhabitants. To choose the members of this college, the voters in the subdistrict were grouped in three classes, composed of those who paid direct taxes. The first class consisted of the wealthiest, who contributed one-third of the tax quota of the subdistrict; the second class, of those who paid another third; the third class, of the remaining taxpayers. Each class chose by absolute majority one-third of the electoral college membership of the subdistrict. Those so picked in all subdistricts, acting together as the electoral college of the district, voted for the representatives to go to the *Landtag*. The actual effect

[45]See Chap. 5, p. 129.

of these ingeniously complicated details can be seen in the figures for the year 1908, when the first class contained 293,000 voters (4%); the second class, 1,065,240 voters (14%); and the third class, 6,324,079 (82%).

THE RULE OF THE WISE

Of the types of oligarchy so far discussed, the two most likely to establish themselves in practice are government by warriors and government by wealth, for these possess ample means of "persuasion" and are the hardest to resist. There remains one final type. It is the rarest and would be very difficult to establish. This is the government of the wisest. The argument in its favor consists of a series of essentially simple points. It asserts that the process of ruling—like the art of medicine or the science of engineering—calls for the professional knowledge of experts. It supposes that there is a body of knowledge concerning the subject matter of politics that can be discovered and learned. It then calls for an educational system which will impart the "right" knowledge to the "right" people. Perhaps there is no little irony in the fact that the earliest systematic treatise of political philosophy now surviving is devoted to this hypothesis. The whole of Plato's *Republic* rests upon two fundamental assumptions. One is the metaphysical doctrine that a distinction must be drawn between knowledge and opinion; that the subject matter of the former is reality, whereas that of the latter is appearance; and that the reality that is knowable includes the true forms or models of political ideals that must serve to guide the statesman. The second is the psychological assumption that human beings differ fundamentally in their intellectual endowment, and that only a small number are qualified and can be trained to reach the highest levels of philosophical inquiry and know the ideal. It is these superior minds, in Plato's view, and these alone, that deserve to be entrusted with political power:

Unless philosophers bear kingly rule in cities, or those who are now called kings and princes become genuine and adequate philosophers, and political power and philosophy are brought together, and unless the numerous natures who at present pursue either politics or philosophy, the one to the exclusion of the other, are forcibly debarred from this behaviour, there will be no respite from evil for cities, nor, I fancy, for humanity.[46]

To judge such a system of government is impossible because it has never been tried. If it ever were instituted, doubtless it would be

[46]*Republic,* v, Sec. 473, p. 166.

authoritarian to the point of absolutism because those who are certain that they possess the truth can be quite intolerant of everybody else —witness Plato's own *Republic*! Realistically seen, the history of politics consists in an elaborate documentation of the complaint voiced to his son by Oxenstierna, who was Sweden's famous chancellor in the second quarter of the seventeenth century: "My son, you do not know how small is the amount of wisdom with which the world is governed." True, there have been sporadic instances where individuals of superb intellectual and ethical standards have held the highest office in the state, but these are few enough to count on one's fingers. Witness Marcus Aurelius and Antoninus Pius in the Roman Empire; or, in modern times, Gladstone in Britain; Masaryk in Czechoslovakia; Jefferson and Wilson in the United States; and Nehru in India. Civil services, too, when they have sought to recruit their officials according to the ability each displays in competition, have recognized the connection that should exist between powers of government and powers of mind. But nothing has ever been attempted in practice which comes anywhere near the rigorous and uncompromising logic of Plato's grandiose educational curriculum. The elite of the all-wise philosopher-ruler remains in the realm of hypothetical fantasy. There let it remain!

Enough has now been said to illustrate the point that elites or oligarchies or aristocracies appear in many guises. All constitute, however, an assertion that the best government is the one that the few best control. All take for granted the existence of a certain kind of superiority. All are dedicated to the principle of inequality, which is the law of their being. Nor are these aberrations, rarities, or deviations, that have been considered in this chapter. On the contrary, most of the governance of men that is known to history has corresponded to one or other of the major types delineated here.

5

FIRST ISSUE:

–2– "All Men Are Created Equal"

THE HUMANITY THAT UNITES US ALL

"Human beings are divided into two groups; those who divide human beings into two groups, and those who don't. I prefer the latter." This remark satirizes the attitude discussed in the preceding chapter and keynotes the contents of the present one. After a review of principles and practices which confine the right of governing to first-class citizens and demote the remainder to second-class status, let us study the alternative. This consists in rejecting the assumptions of elitists. It does not envisage the relation of government to governed as if it were analogous to that of lions to lambs, doctor to patient, brain to body, potter to clay, shepherd to sheep, or any of the countless similes of this kind. Instead, it affirms the principle that for purposes of politics the same basic rights must be accorded to all. If any are to be excluded from full participation, they should be the exceptions, not the rule. They should be as few as possible in number, and their exclusion should require special justification (that is, those under a certain age, those committed to institutions for mental illness, those serving jail sentences for a criminal conviction, those owing allegiance to a foreign state, and so forth).

The purpose of this view is to affirm and promote equality. This involves shifting the emphasis to factors the opposite of those that attracted the elitists. The elitists were preoccupied with singling out and exaggerating some features by which human beings may be distinguished and segregated. They placed their accent upon differences and wove their theories around a pattern of dissimilarities. Anything might then be called into use which could serve as an index for discrimination. The contrary doctrine puts the stress elsewhere. It searches for what men have in common. Its accent is upon likenesses, similarities, resemblances. It speaks in terms not of classes, but of humanity; not of ranks, but of equals. Within its categories there is no room for the concepts of subhuman or superman. All are placed on one level, encompassing the whole of mankind.

In describing these contrasts, let us be clear about what is in issue and at stake. Those who prefer the aristocratic doctrine do not deny that even between superiors and inferiors certain over-all similarities exist. The advocates of all-inclusiveness concede that side by side with the resemblances they observe there are also differences. The disagreement then resolves itself into a dispute over priorities. Granted that all men are alike in some respects and different in others, which factors should be considered more important? You will be an elitist if you think that the points on which people differ are the fundamental ones. You will be an equalitarian if you hold that the features wherein men resemble one another are primary. As the premises vary, so will the conclusions. The outcome of the former view is to emphasize whatever elements in human nature divide men; of the latter, those elements that unite us.

Before the philosophy of equality is examined, a word should be said about its psychological significance. For the great majority of mankind the desire to be respected as an equal, and to be treated as such, presents a potent emotional appeal. It is all too true that the record of most societies and most political systems embodies the practice of privilege. Doubtless, this is the reason why equality, when it is evoked, has so explosive an effect. When the time comes for men to raise their heads and stand erect instead of bowing in deference, when they realize that they do not have to submit permanently to a second-class status, the feelings that result can lead to a tremendous upsurge of morale and outpouring of energy. For the ideal of equal status men will undergo much sacrifice and, in concert with their peers, will set great events in motion. It is no accident, therefore, that some of the most revolutionary movements in history have been sparked by a desire to achieve equality.[1] An example, from the sphere of religion, is the spread of Christianity in its first three centuries. Likewise, the great political revolutions of the seventeenth and eighteenth centuries—the English, American, and French—succeeded in large measure because the passion for equality was one of their driving forces. More recently, the Marxist philosophy and the Communist

[1]This is recognized by such an advocate of inequality as Aristotle. Generalizing from Greek political experience, he correctly states that the prime object of many revolutions is a desire for equal treatment. *Politics*, v, Chaps. 1–2.

movement owed some of their earlier successes, not so much to the content of the theory or the attractiveness of the party organization, but to the fact that they expressed an angry indignation against the injustices of inequality. Equality, even more than liberty, is the most revolutionary of political symbols. Whoever harnesses its power can shake and change the world.

THE CASE FOR EQUALITARIANISM

However, the problem of the intellectual exposition of the equalitarian concept remains. Even when stress is laid upon unifying similarities, how and why is the right of everybody to participate in government explained and approved? If the exponents of aristocracy conceive of ruling as a science, art, or mystery, what counterformulation is offered by their opponents? In a nutshell, what gives Thersites the right to talk back to Agamemnon? When we examine the foundations of the equalitarian view, we shall find that it rests on many pillars. Just as there are numerous species of oligarchy even though their central feature is identical, so do numerous roads lead to the unique goal of universal humanism. For a start one could cite the old words: *Quod tangit omnes ab omnibus approbetur* ("Let all approve what touches all"). But to say this without proof is like asserting that the square on the hypotenuse of a right-angled triangle equals the sum of the squares on the other two sides without detailing the logical steps that led Pythagoras to such a conclusion. Foundations for equalitarianism can be outlined thus: Each has a right to determine his own welfare. Each, therefore, has the right to seek control over anything external to himself that affects his welfare. The actions of government impinge on human welfare and leave nobody unaffected. Consequently all have the right to participate in controlling the state and contributing to its decisions.

The argument is impressive. By itself, however, it is insufficient to rebut the elitists. For their attack exposes one weak link in the chain of reasoning: the statement that "each has the right to seek control over anything external to himself that affects his welfare." To affirm the right they would say, is one thing; to exercise it, another. The right to control what touches your welfare depends first on knowing how to detect it; second, on being able to master it. The mass of men, so the oligarch will argue, are not equipped intellectually to perform the first task and lack the power to carry out the second. Hence the assumed right is meaningless.

To this the equalitarian presents a countercharge. In effect he asserts that the analogy between government and science or art is not complete and can become misleading. To look only at the qualifications needed by rulers is to overlook the other side of the equation. If government consists of services provided by the rulers to the ruled, it is wrong to think only of those who produce the services and to ignore the consumers. Granted that I am not able to compose like Beethoven, write like Shakespeare, paint like Rembrandt, or invent like Edison, I can still appreciate the worth of their music, poetry, paintings, or inventions or even criticize a great master when he sometimes lapses from his highest flights. A man who could not design an automobile can nevertheless learn to drive one and can judge its performance on the road. Government, in other words, is not merely an affair of skilled technique applied by expert practitioners. It is above all else a problem of providing services to people who need them. In politics, as in economics, the start and finish of the process are consumer need and consumer satisfaction. Traditionally, this truth is summed up in the everyday saying that "only the wearer knows where the shoe pinches."[2] But the theory which embraces all men as citizens has been placed on a higher plane. For the arguments of the equalitarians involve basic beliefs concerning the nature of man. As such, they cannot be divorced from larger issues of ethics, metaphysics, and theology. If this broadening of the scope of our inquiry occasions any surprise to the student of political science, let him reflect that there are many branches to the study of mankind, that these are all related, and that no single specialization can boast all the answers.

THE CLASSICAL ROOTS OF THE DOCTRINE OF EQUALITY

1. The Stoics. In the history of Western political ideas the doctrine which emphasizes human equality is almost as old as its opposite. After Aristotle's death in 322 B.C., the most prominent star in the Greek philosophical firmament was Zeno of Citium, founder of the Stoic school. Against the background of turmoil which followed Alexander's conquests and early death, amid the breakdown of the once autonomous city-state and the overthrow of kingly dynasties, Zeno's theories were formulated to help men bear their trials with fortitude and lift their hopes towards new loyalties and wider horizons. The central theme of the Stoic philosophy was to equate rationality and deity. The divinity that shapes our ends is rational, and reason, conversely, is divine. The universe is the product of a divine purpose,

---

[2]For an excellent discussion of this, see A.D. Lindsay, *The Modern Democratic State* (New York: Oxford University Press, Inc., 1947), pp. 269 ff.

manifesting itself throughout nature in a rational plan. Deity is not something external to the universe, inscrutably watching its creation and uncomprehended by its creatures. It is instead all-pervading, since wherever there is reason is God. From these metaphysics the Stoic proceeded to draw conclusions with a social relevance. All human beings possess reason. True, the power to reason exists in different degrees in each of us. But wherever it is, and whether it shines bright or dim, the light of reason is a spark of the divine fire. All men, because they share in reason, share in the godhead. It is less important that the reasoning ability of individuals is differently developed than that everyone alike possesses some ability to reason. Thereby all mankind is differentiated from other animals and is united. On this account—and the point is fundamental to the Stoic—the concept of humanity (that is, the quality of being human) does not admit of degree. As men, all are equal. To assert that any human beings do not "belong," or to deny their equal title to consideration, is to exclude a fragment, however infinitesimal, of divinity.

2. *Roman Law.* With its various additions and popularizations, this philosophy competed successfully with the contemporary doctrines of Cynics and Epicureans and acquired a general vogue among educated and professional people in the Mediterranean world. In the period when Roman military and political power was absorbing Greece and Greek culture and philosophy were humanizing Rome, Stoicism was imported to Rome under the influence of the Scipionic circle[3] and was imparted to Roman audiences by the philosopher Panaetius and the historian Polybius. What followed is an instructive episode in political and intellectual history. The century that marked the introduction of Stoicism coincided with the extension of Roman military power over the lands that fringe the Mediterranean. Newly conquered territories —Sicily, Greece, Spain, Libya, Gaul (France), Asia (Turkey), and the rest—were organized into provinces and absorbed into the empire of Rome. The inhabitants of these areas, so diverse in their cultural traditions and political maturity, their economic resources and religious doctrines, became the subjects of Rome, but not, at first, its citizens. To enforce the peace, Rome was obliged not only to safeguard the frontiers of its empire from external menace, but to establish internally a system of order and trust in human relations. Contact and commerce between inhabitants of different provinces led to transactions involving trade, contracts, property, marriage, inheritance— transactions covering the whole gamut of social activities. A Gaul and

[3]The Scipionic circle was a group of political leaders, literary men, and philosophers, assembling in the middle decades of the second century, B.C., under the influence and patronage of the great soldier-statesman Scipio, the destroyer of Carthage.

a Spaniard, a Greek and a Sicilian, a Libyan and an Egyptian, might be involved in a dispute and seek to have their rights determined by litigation. But whose law would be applied in such cases? Not necessarily the law of Rome, for the civil law was applicable to citizens only. Confronted with a practical problem, the Romans responded in a practical manner. They established a new court to hear those cases where the rights of foreigners were involved. The presiding judge considered the legal principles that were in force in the territories of both parties to the dispute. If he could discover some common ground between them, he would adjudicate accordingly. If not, he would propose a solution based upon equity, that is, upon a conception of right and justice which conformed to an abstract standard of fairness. The decisions rendered in particular cases and the principles they embodied were readopted annually in an edict which the judge issued to govern the proceedings of his court. Eventually, the accumulation of precedents hardened into a body of case law, which Roman jurists came to call the "law of the peoples" *(jus gentium).*

The stage was then set for a brilliant climax. Acting empirically without preconceived plan or foreknowledge of their goal, the Roman jurists developed from particular cases a coherent framework of general principles. In these were included the legal concepts which the various peoples of their empire were found to possess in common, as well as principles of equity that satisfied a sense of justice. Where the Romans had been thinking inductively from the particular to the general, the Stoic philosophers worked deductively. Arguing from metaphysical assumptions and moving from the universal to the particular, the Stoics concluded that all men were united through their common possession of reason. But the two systems of the Stoic philosophy and the Roman *jus gentium,* though they set out from opposite poles, drew close together and ultimately came within hailing distance. What was then easier than to suppose that the common concepts which the Romans discovered and applied by use of reason were the product of that same all-pervading reason which the Stoics had divined as a law of the universe? It is true that the correlation was never exact. There were important points of divergence, as when the *jus gentium* condoned the institution of slavery which Stoic reason rejected. But in many areas the approximation was sufficiently close for jurist and philosopher alike to assume that their tracks were converging. Speculative metaphysics and pragmatic imperialism led jointly to the desired goal of the equality and unity of mankind.

Nor was the construction of the *jus gentium* the only way in which the Romans attempted to give effect to the principle that all men are equal. No less momentous was the extension of their citizenship, which they proceeded to grant in stages both to individuals and entire communities, first among the Latins living nearby in the center of Italy; then to their allies in the rest of Italy; and afterwards to inhabitants of the outlying provinces. The climax was reached in 212 A.D. when the notable edict of the Emperor Caracalla conferred the citizenship of Rome upon all free (nonslave) inhabitants of the empire. The nations of contemporary Europe are still far from possessing the common citizenship which Rome accomplished at the beginning of the third century. But idealistic as Caracalla's achievement sounds, it was not lacking a materialistic side. The imperial treasury at that time was depleted and required new revenues. One lucrative source was the tax on the estates of the deceased, but this was levied by Rome only on its dead citizens. Enlarging the citizenry had the result of replenishing the treasury.

3. *The Gospel of Jesus.* The trends initiated by the philosophers of Greece and the jurists of Rome were reinforced by the preachers of the Christian gospel. Jesus and the apostles, like many of their early believers, came for the most part from humble origins. The appeal of the new religion was what could be expected of those who spread its message. Christianity spoke first to the underprivileged; to the lowly of this earth, not the mighty; to those who were rich only in hope and faith. Its social teaching in consequence was inclined heavily towards equalitarianism. Human society in this life displayed the contrasts of luxury and poverty, power and weakness, eminence and lowliness. But the worth of the individual soul, which would outlive its bodily habitat, was to be judged not by man but by God, whose universal fatherhood made all men brothers. Measured on the infinite scale of divine goodness, justice, and compassion, all human distinctions were trivial. As St. Paul said to the Galatians: "There is neither Jew nor Greek, there is neither bond nor free, there is neither male nor female, for ye are all one in Jesus Christ."[4] The philosophy here is Stoic. The legal doctrine—apparent to the apostle who affirmed "I am a Roman citizen"—is Roman. The religious aura is Christian. In that trinity the intellect, politics, and faith of antiquity found their culminating union.

It should not be forgotten, however, that the equality on which Christianity insisted was more pertinent to the next world than to this. It was in terms of their souls, which could be lost or saved, that all men stood an equal chance. Indeed, it was the rich and the mighty who were handicapped in the race for salvation, since their earthly power exposed them to greater temptation and made them more lia-

[4]Epistle to the Galatians, 3:28.

ble to fall from grace. But this shift of the scene of equalitarianism to the hereafter made it possible for Christianity to accept, and either overlook or minimize, the inequalities existing here and now. Let men be content with their earthly lot, though it may be disagreeable, in expectation of glory in the life after death. Since "the powers that be are ordained of God," the Christian should submit to the wrongs inflicted by his fellowmen with the certainty of being compensated by a justice that is divine.

THE MODERN REBIRTH OF EQUALITY

In the history of the West there have been two periods in which mankind has made notable advances in the direction of equality. The one just reviewed lasted five hundred years from the rise of Stoicism to the Edict of Caracalla. The second, commencing in the mid-seventeenth century, has persisted through seven decades of the twentieth and has not yet run its course. The circumstances which started and accelerated this modern movement are as noteworthy as the theories it has evoked. Chronologically these circumstances fall into three phases. The earliest dates from the middle of the seventeenth century to the end of the eighteenth. The next corresponds more or less exactly to the ten decades (1815-1914) between the defeat of Napoleon and the German invasion of Belgium in World War I. The third phase has lasted from that time to the present. A survey of all three, by discovering whence we have come and where we now are, may help us to understand better whither we may be bound.

THE ENGLISH, AMERICAN, AND FRENCH REVOLUTIONS

The first phase coincides in time and space with the three great revolutions in the countries which are the standard-bearers of the Atlantic community: the revolution in Britain from 1640 to 1688, in the United States from 1776 to 1791, and in France from 1789 to the present day.[5] Each had somewhat similar objectives and therefore produced doctrines with many similarities. The aims of the revolutionaries, whether British, American, or French, included the overthrow of governmental regimes not controllable by the governed. To justify rebellion against the legal order, it was necessary to show that right was on the side of those who rebelled. This could be done either by arguing that the state is founded upon a contract, and by asserting that the contract had been broken by the government; or by insisting

[5] For further discussion of these revolutions, see Chap. 10, p. 289 ff.

that over the laws enacted by governing authorities there reigns some higher law, to which men may make appeal. The rebellions, furthermore, were directed against an established ruling class who based their position upon doctrines of legitimacy,[6] aristocracy, and hereditary right. To justify their replacement, it was important to contend that the authority to govern did not belong exclusively to the monarch or the nobility, but was the common birthright of mankind which had been stolen from them.

These needs explain why the philosophies of Locke, Voltaire, Rousseau, Jefferson, and Paine place so much emphasis upon the hypotheses of a social contract and a law of nature, and upon the vindication of individual rights to liberty and equality. The insertion of nature as one of the links in the chain of reasoning had a special purpose. Men who were dissatisfied with the existing order wanted a yardstick or standard of comparison. They found it helpful to suppose that a state of nature had preceded the organized civil state. This natural state was blended of a medley of advantages and inconveniences, and governments were instituted in order to escape the latter —but not so as to lose the former. Of the advantages, the greatest appeared to be the relative equality of conditions existing among men and their consequential equality of rights. As Locke expressed it: "To understand political power aright, and derive it from its original, we must consider what estate all men are naturally in, and that is a state of perfect freedom to order their actions. . . . A state also of equality, wherein all the power and jurisdiction is reciprocal, no one having more than another."[7] If the actual conditions of organized society differed from this, if there were king and subjects, masters and slaves, luxury and penury, it was not from nature that these differences derived. Rather, they existed in contravention of nature, being the handiwork of social man, not of natural man. Let mankind therefore reconstitute their governments so as to be guardians, not violators, of natural right. Such were the sentiments embodied in the great declarations of the American and French republics. The first of the truths which Thomas Jefferson pronounced self-evident in 1776 was "that all men are created equal." With similar effect the *Déclaration des Droits de l'Homme et du Citoyen,* adopted in 1793, proclaimed: "Governments are instituted to guarantee to men the enjoyment of their natural and imprescriptible rights. These rights are equality, liberty, security, and property. By nature and before the law, all men are equal."

[6]Legitimacy meant, in this context, a right to govern based upon ancestry.

[7]John Locke, *Second Treatise of Civil Government,* Chap. 2, Sec. 4 (Everyman's Library), p. 118.

It is significant that such statements were not merely enunciated by individual thinkers but were affirmed officially by public bodies: by the Continental Congress of the United States and by the National Convention in France. No less impressive is the insistence upon equality as a basic ideal, since this concept was truly revolutionary in relation to the social and political facts of the world at that time. Nor are any weakening qualifications inserted into the phrasing. All men, without reserve or ambiguity, were included. The range of equality was universal. What was highly ambiguous, however, was the appeal to nature as the basis and justification of the desired rights. Men might dispute the circumstances of the assumed state of nature (whose details were derived from imagination, rather than fact), and also about the law of nature that was supposed to prevail therein. Proof and evidence concerning natural law and natural rights were sought by reference to "reason," which was not always a sure guide to government if it gave different answers to different men; or if not to reason, then the reference was to God, the Creator of nature and, therefore, of its rights and law. Once again, however, the interpretations were at variance, since not only did Christians disagree with non-Christians, but Protestants and Catholics themselves disputed the character of the divine dispensation. There were too many prophets who claimed to have heard the voice of God and tried to translate it into the vernacular. When a state contained among its citizens adherents of various faiths, which revelation should it accept?

Problems of this kind made it desirable, if equality and universality were to be upheld, to discover alternative doctrines as substitutes or supplements for natural law. At this point aid was forthcoming from moral philosophies, which, though disagreeing in other particulars, confirmed the same central principle. This was the reassertion of the belief in the equal worth, fundamentally, of all men. In the mid-seventeenth century during the debates in Cromwell's army a Colonel Rainboro, one of the group known as the Levellers, declared: "Really I think the poorest he that is in England hath a life to live as the richest he." The same thought was echoed more than a century later by the German philosopher, Immanuel Kant, who enunciated respect for human dignity in the somewhat cryptic command: "So act as to treat humanity, whether in thine own person or in that of any other, in every case as an end withal, never as means only."[8] With greater clarity and less mysticism, the founder of the English Utilitarians, Jeremy Bentham, remarked that each person should count for one,

---

[8] *Fundamental Principles of the Metaphysic of Ethics*, 10th ed., trans. T. K. Abbott (London: Longmans, Green & Co., Ltd., 1929), p. 56.

and nobody for more than one—which is perhaps the most succinct and least equivocal formula for equalitarianism ever expressed in a few words.

GAINS FOR EQUALITY IN THE NINETEENTH CENTURY

The relation of the Stoics, who formulated the abstract principles, to the Romans, who broadened outward from the particular to the general, is paralleled in both method and timing by the relation of the nineteenth century to its two predecessors. If it was the achievement of the seventeenth and eighteenth centuries that they hammered out the fundamental philosophies and the resultant declarations, the task of the nineteenth century was to start from actualities and bring them by degrees into closer approximation with those grand abstractions. When surveying these events which are closer to our own time, we have the advantage not only of fuller historical records, but also of more precise statistical description. The concepts of an inclusive or exclusive citizenship can be measured with some precision by reference to the franchise and its gradual extension to those not previously qualified to vote. In countries where the legislature is accepted as a crucial and central agency of government, the number of citizens entitled to vote for their representatives is one of the pointers indicating whether privilege or equality prevails.

The main precipitating cause in this nineteenth century development was undoubtedly economic. The economic factor, however, assumed different guises in different places. Thus in Britain the movement to broaden the franchise was an offshoot of the Industrial Revolution, which increased the social power of the urban middle class and converted a large section of the population into factory workers. In the agrarian community of the United States, as also in Canada, Australia, and New Zealand, equalitarianism issued largely from the psychological impact on Europeans of emigrating from overcrowded lands to spacious undeveloped territories where new vistas beyond the outer rim of settlement beckoned the enterprising. There, where each could find enough, and where muscle and nerve were a man's primary resources and stock of capital, that equality of conditions existed which makes for freedom.

EXTENSION OF VOTING RIGHTS IN BRITAIN

The impact upon politics of these changes deserves description, since within a century they were responsible for writing a spectacular new chapter in the history of the state. It is relevant to include the experiences of Britain for several reasons. In the nineteenth century she was the world's most powerful nation; she was ahead of others in industrialization; and simultaneously she was extending the institutions of democracy. At the time of her mortal clash with Napoleonic France, which for two decades dammed up the domestic currents of reform, Britain already possessed a potent legislature, but one that represented only a minority of the population. The House of Lords, filled for life by hereditary peers, was the entrenched stronghold of the land-owning aristocracy who, along with a minority of merchant-financiers, enjoyed a virtual monopoly of wealth, prestige, and political skill. The control of governmental power by this oligarchy embraced a House of Commons whose personnel were in large part the kinsmen of the nobility and were elected from antiquated districts by voters with ancestral or property qualifications. That this system did not preclude the possibility of opposition to the government is proven by the rise of the party system toward the end of the seventeenth century, by the conflicts between Whigs and Tories, and by the careers of such men as the two Pitts, Burke, Fox, and Canning. But institutional change was necessary if Britain intended to absorb industrial urbanism into its politics at home and to organize its gigantic empire abroad. A decade and a half of agitation after the defeat of Napoleon led to the enactment in 1832 of the first of the Reform Acts. Its general aim was to initiate a closer relation between the Parliament and the people. With this in view, the constituencies were redistributed and the franchise was altered. While a property qualification was retained, the necessary amount was set lower than before, which resulted in the enfranchisement and formal entry into politics of the urban middle class. The electorate in 1833 was 75 per cent higher than what it had been two years earlier, but it was still a mere 4 1/2 per cent of the whole population.

During the middle decades of the nineteenth century, the suffrage remained exactly as it was defined in 1832. Indeed, as late as 1866, less than 6 per cent of the British population were registered as voters. Government was of the people; but it was certainly conducted by a minority and, on the whole, for that minority. The two major barriers which excluded the majority of adults were wealth and sex. When would the electoral law abandon the disqualifications of poverty and femininity?

The middle class could not avoid the issue of sharing with the working class the privileges which they themselves had wrested from the aristocracy. In the agitation for political reform that shook British politics to its foundations in the years 1830–1832, the working class

Table II
THE GROWTH OF THE BRITISH ELECTORATE

Date of law extending suffrage	Registered voters		Population at nearest census		Percentage of voters to population
	Date	Number (000's omitted)	Date	Number (000's omitted)	
1832	1830	440	1831	16,261	2.7
	1833	725			4.4
1867	1866	1,200	1861	23,128	5.6
	1869	2,250	1871	26,072	8.6
1884	1883	2,590	1881	29,710	9.9
	1886	5,000			16.8
1918	1910	7,200	1911	40,831	17.6
	1918	19,500	1921	42,769	45.6
1928	1924	20,650	1921	42,769	48.3
	1929	28,500	1931	44,795	63.6
	1966	36,000	1961	52,675	68.0

gave their support to middle-class demands without insisting prematurely on a share for themselves. But eventually they were bound to press for their share. It then remained to be seen whether the middle class would acquiesce and reciprocate their support or would, as radicals of yesterday who had gained their desires, become the conservatives of tomorrow. Such queries erupted in the revolutionary year of 1848, when autocratic regimes were challenged or overthrown on the continent of Europe and new constitutions were proposed or established in France, Prussia, Austria, the Italian states, and elsewhere. At a critical stage in those movements, the middle class took alarm at working-class aspirations and swung to the side of the conservative elements. Thus the liberal blossoming of Germany's Frankfurt Assembly, elected in 1848 by universal manhood suffrage, ran quickly to seed in the Bismarckian reaction. In France, the liberal-democratic constitution of November, 1848, which contained a similar suffrage, gave way to the empire of Napoleon III. Hence, a British historian has tersely commented: "The year 1848 was the turning point at which modern history failed to turn."[9]

In Britain itself the year 1848 did not witness the same upheaval as

[9] G. M. Trevelyan, *British History in the Nineteenth Century* (New York: Longmans, Green & Co., Inc., 1922), p. 292.

occurred on the opposite side of the English Channel. This was because the British had been wise enough or fortunate enough to conduct in the seventeenth century the kind of political revolution which others were attempting in the nineteenth,[10] and also because the crisis of 1832 had been weathered successfully from the reformers' standpoint. All that happened of moment in 1848 was that the Chartists, who had been pressing for further changes (including universal adult suffrage), reached the climax of their movement in the peaceful presentation of their Charter to Parliament. Liberalism was then forced to decide whether its acceptance of Bentham's precept would be extended in practice to an all-inclusive doctrine of citizenship. If the desire of the working class for equal voting rights were conceded, the middle class would have to welcome as full participants in the political process those who were poorer, less educated, and on a lower social level than themselves. The conflict in their reasons and emotions is typified in the candid avowals of the leading intellectual of mid-nineteenth century liberalism John Stuart Mill. When the first edition of the *Principles of Political Economy* was published in 1848, he stated with characteristic frankness: "Of the working classes of Western Europe at least it may be pronounced certain, that the patriarchal or fraternal system of government is one to which they will not again be subject. . . . The poor have come out of leading strings, and cannot any longer be governed like children. . . . The prospect of the future depends on the degree in which they can be made rational beings. There is no reason to believe that prospect other than hopeful."[11] To him, the ultimate goal was not debatable. Only the timing was in question; and he, for one, was prepared to consider the maturity of the working class to be conditional upon its education.

These same anxieties were repeatedly voiced in the years immediately preceding and following the second extension of the franchise in 1867. When Mill's *Considerations on Representative Government* appeared in 1861, he again expressed his fears in this way: "But even in this democracy, absolute power, if they chose to exercise it, would rest with the numerical majority; and these would be composed exclusively of a single class, alike in biases, prepossessions and general modes of thinking, and a class, to say no more, not the most highly cultivated."[12] Similarly Walter Bage-

---

[10]Macaulay, in a passage of his *History of England* that was penned in 1848, compares British and Continental experiences in a series of rhetorical contrasts that exude no little complacency. Vol. I, p. 412.

[11]John Stuart Mill, *Principles of Political Economy* (Boston: Little, Brown and Company, 1848), Vol. 2, IV, Chap. 7, Sec. 1.

[12]*Considerations on Representative Government* (Everyman's Library), pp. 276–77.

hot, who added a new introduction to the second edition of his *English Constitution* in 1872, commented with even more candor: "As a theoretical writer I can venture to say, what no elected member of Parliament, Conservative or Liberal, can venture to say, that I am exceedingly afraid of the ignorant multitude of the new constituencies. . . . Their supremacy in the state they now are, means the supremacy of ignorance over instruction, and of numbers over knowledge."[13] Nevertheless, British democracy did take the plunge, and dived into the deep seas of mass enfranchisement. In 1867 the vote was first accorded to members of the urban working class, and within less than two decades it was conferred upon their rural confreres. Two years after the Act of 1884, the enrolled voters numbered some five million, or roughly 17 per cent of the population.[14]

The barriers were now breached and the sequel of the story is a march toward the foregone conclusion. The focus of the final struggle was shifted from the working class to the womenfolk. Feminists had already pleaded their cause, as Mill had; and a nation which romanticized its Queen Victoria could not long or consistently deny to women a place in government. After the turn of the century, the suffragettes added a militant warhead to the movement, which gained its victory as one of the political offshoots of World War I. The Acts of 1918 and 1928 marked the culmination in a century of orderly evolution toward the ultimate goal of universal adult suffrage. When the British nation went to cast their ballots in the fall of 1966, nearly 36 millions of a population approaching 53 millions (68 per cent) were registered on the electoral rolls, and of these 27 1/4 millions (76 per cent) voted.

THE SUFFRAGE IN AMERICAN DEMOCRACY

The experience of the United States in the eighteen decades since the Constitution came into force has run a course parallel to that of Britain, with one country or the other taking the lead in the race for equalization of voting privileges. But the American development has been more complicated than the British. This is due in part to the greater heterogeneity of America's population, which has contained a large racial minority, and has owed much of its increase to the immigration of adults whose mother tongue was not English and whose

---

[13]Walter Bagehot, *The English Constitution*, World's Classics (London: Oxford University Press, 1928), pp. 272, 276.

[14]Enrollment of voters, be it remembered, was voluntary. There were many who could qualify to vote under the law but who for some decades neglected to register.

assimilation took time. In part, the complication has arisen from the relation between the electoral laws and the federal system. The regional diversities which have been present in America from its founding precluded the drafting of uniform qualifications for the franchise at the Philadelphia Convention of 1787. Instead, the convention adopted a provision which applied to national elections whatever franchise the states respectively chose for electing the lower houses of their own legislatures.[15] Hence every extension of the suffrage within a state has simultaneously broadened it at the federal level.[16] For this reason, and also because the systems of registration of voters in all states are voluntary not automatic, it is impossible to trace the exact stages in the growth of the American electorate with the same precision as can be done for Britain. We can therefore say how many persons were registered to vote and how many did vote in the presidential contest, but not how many were qualified to vote under the varying electoral laws of the different states.

According to the estimate of Charles A. Beard, when elections were held in 1787–1788 to choose the delegates to the state convention who would ratify or reject the United States Constitution, only a small percentage of the nation, then numbering almost four millions, participated. "It seems a safe guess to say," he summarized, "that not more than 5 per cent of the population in general, or in round numbers, 160,000 voters, expressed an opinion one way or another on the Constitution. . . . We may reasonably conjecture that of the estimated 160,000 who voted in the election of delegates, not more than 100,-000 men favored the adoption of the Constitution at the time it was put into effect—about one in six of the adult males."[17] In the presidential election of 1968, however, when the population had risen to over 190 millions, nearly 90 million citizens were registered as voters, of whom 73 millions actually recorded their ballots. What happened between 1788 and 1968 to make this possible?

One hundred and seventy years ago in America three principal barriers, besides age, excluded the majority of the people from the polls: wealth, color, and sex. The history of the equalization of the franchise is the story of the total elimination or progressive reduction of these barriers. At the beginning, all states had legal requirements

[15]"The House of Representatives shall be composed of members chosen every second year by the people of the several States, and the electors in each State shall have the qualifications requisite for electors of the most numerous branch of the State legislature." *Constitution of the United States*, Art. I, Sec. II.

[16]Conversely, any restriction of the franchise within a state automatically narrowed the federal franchise.

[17]Charles A. Beard, *An Economic Interpretation of the Constitution of the United States* (New York: The Macmillan Company, 1935), p. 250.

which confined the franchise to the well-to-do. Sometimes the method was to insist that the voter must own a minimum amount of property. Sometimes the tax assessment was used as the criterion. Such limitations, in vogue along the eastern seaboard, lost their meaning when population moved west of the Alleghenies and carved out new territories which were admitted as new states. Here was free land for the taking. Here everyone who worked could become a man of property. Here were intrepid and hardy souls who would not accept a lower class citizenship. The barriers of wealth, like the walls of Jericho, fell before the trumpet blast of the all-leveling frontier, and under the fluid social conditions of the early nineteenth century new ramparts could not long be sustained. Benthamism, firmly planted in the West, spread back to the East, bringing constitutional change and electoral amendment. As Tocqueville presciently remarked: "The further electoral rights are extended, the greater is the need for extending them; for after each concession the strength of the democracy increases, and its demands increase with its strength. . . . The exception at last becomes the rule, concession follows concession, and no stop can be made short of universal suffrage."[18] As early as 1832, when less than 5 per cent of the people were registered as voters in Britain under the new Reform Act, nearly 10 per cent of America's population actually voted in the election that gave a second term to Andrew Jackson. In the presidential contest when Abraham Lincoln was first victorious, actual voters were 15 per cent of the population, a number that compares favorably with the 5 per cent who were then registered as voters in Britain.

The failure of the property line to provide an adequate defensive position in the resistance of quality to equality was followed by inroads upon the color line. Whereas the West spearheaded the attempts to nullify the electoral predominance of the wealthy, it was the North that began minimizing the political relevance of distinctions in race and color. In the "birth certificate" of the United States was inscribed the clause: "*All* men are created equal." Written by a southerner, these words were now to receive a literal and liberal interpretation. Although the northern states did not allow slavery, they did not universally accord to the Negro the right to vote. By the time of the Civil War, this right was available to black citizens in only four of the New England states, where they were quite few in number. The most important of the legal changes resulting from the Civil War were the three new amendments inserted in the supreme law. The thirteenth abolished human slavery from the United States, making all American

[18]A. de Tocqueville, *Democracy in America*, trans. Henry Reeve, Part I, Chap. IV.

territory "free soil." The fourteenth clarified the meaning of American citizenship, which had been at issue in the Dred Scott case, and based it primarily upon the fact of birth within the United States irrespective of parentage. The fifteenth spelled out further the status of citizens in the political sphere. It affirmed that the right to vote could not be denied by the federal government or by any state for reasons of "race, color or previous condition of servitude." By these amendments the principles of the Constitution finally caught up with the philosophy of the Declaration of Independence.

What was left to be determined was whether "all men" included "all women." Again it was the West that proved itself the radical innovator, and for reasons that are well known. The women who braved the hardships of the untamed West earned the respect of their menfolk. What is more, there were fewer of the fair sex in the states and territories between the Mississippi and the Pacific, and rarity supplied a scarcity value. It was in the western region therefore that America's women were first enfranchised. The movement to nationalize what the states were doing piecemeal was stimulated by the events of World War I, which brought more women into public life and economic activity. The climax came in 1919 with the adoption of the Nineteenth Amendment.

Despite these challenges to the barriers of wealth, color, and sex, it remains true that all adults are not yet qualified to vote—or, if qualified by law, are not registered—in the contemporary United States.[19] The phrasing of the Fifteenth and Nineteenth Amendments is significantly negative. To declare that the right of citizens to vote may *not* be denied or abridged on account of race, color, previous condition of servitude, or sex, implies that this right may legally be denied or abridged on some ground other than these four. In fact, various methods are employed constitutionally for excluding some citizens from the polling booth. The age limitation is an example.[20] The requirement of a certain length of residence in the voting district is justifiable as a means of permitting proper registration and enrollment of voters and thereby of restricting a number of fraudulent practices. The literacy tests which exist in not a few states may be defended on the ground that a citizen who exercises within a democracy the precious right of the franchise should possess enough information to cast an intelligent vote. This argument applies with special force, moreover, in a nation where many citizens were sometime immigrants who became naturalized. But these tests are indefensible if the state does

[19]In 1968, when nearly 90 million voters were registered, it was estimated that Americans of voting age numbered nearly 121.5 millions.

[20]But there is nothing sacrosanct about any particular age—e.g., twenty-one.

not provide all its citizens with adequate public facilities for obtaining the requisite knowledge, or if the system is administered with the ulterior aim of establishing some preconceived pattern of discrimination. Such a pattern was clearly recognizable in the poll tax imposed as a condition of voting by the ruling oligarchies in several southern states. That tax was designed to keep from the polls the poorer citizens of any color, and it helped some unsavory political machines to prolong their stay in office. In 1964,[21] however, the Twenty-fourth Amendment, barring such taxes as prerequisites for voting in any federal elections, was added to the Constitution of the United States.

INCOMPLETENESS OF BLACK ENFRANCHISEMENT

From the national adoption of a policy and its incorporation into the fundamental law, there can be a long distance to local conformance and effective enforcement. Citizens who are unconvinced and who remain stubbornly opposed can devise ways and means, both within the law and outside it, of delaying, circumventing, and obstructing. On its face, the law may look fair. But the administrator can speak with a forked tongue. The official procedures employed in something so vital as registering a citizen to vote can be smooth and simple for some, but impossible for others. And if all else fails, society at large has extralegal weapons to bring to bear on those who would obey new law which reverses old customs. Economic boycott, loss of employment, social ostracism, and physical violence can be turned to political account by desperate men. Let him who doubts this go to Mississippi.

Despite the plain intent of the Constitution and the will of a national majority expressed in such legislation as the Civil Right Laws of 1957 and 1964, Negroes still form the largest minority in the United States whose voting rights as citizens are not yet equally respected. The statistics on this subject demonstrate two points. First, the majority of Negroes in southern states have been consistently prohibited, by one means or another, from exercising their constitutional rights—in particular, the basic one of voting. Thus, it was estimated in 1956 that eleven southern states contained five million black citizens of voting age, of whom less than a quarter were registered.[22] In 1960, the number of blacks registered in those same states was around a million and a half. Although the majority of southern Negroes cannot

---

[21]At that time five southern states still had a poll tax. This amendment however does not prohibit a state from imposing a poll tax as a condition of voting in state elections, and a few states continue to do so.

[22]See the report on *The Negro Voter in the South* by Margaret Price (Atlanta: Southern Regional Council, 1957), p. 1. Of the whites 60 per cent were registered.

yet function politically as first-class citizens, the remedies for that injustice have gathered momentum. In particular, the intensive registration drives, conducted with the assistance of Negroes and whites from the North and West, have had their effect. In 1968, according to some estimates, about two million, eight hundred thousand Negroes, out of approximately five millions of voting age, had succeeded in registering in the eleven southern states. That number is still only 57 per cent of those eligible. But it marks a tremendous change.[23] The forward trend of the last decade is unmistakable, and one may predict with certainty that similar advances in the same direction will continue during the next decade.

THE REVOLUTION IN RACE RELATIONS

For the politics of a democracy, voting is fundamental. But since men do not live through politics alone, more than a biennial trip to the polls is required if they are to maintain their essential dignity. Equality has many applications. Outside the polling booth it is pertinent to the home and neighborhood, the factory and office, the school and university, the streetcar and airplane, the restroom and restaurant. Any discrimination between human beings for the reason that they differ in race is obnoxious—and humiliating to those treated as inferiors—whether it be manifested in politics, education, employment, amenities, or local services. Alike in the body social and the body politic, black persons, who form one-tenth of the population, have traditionally been forced to remain a group apart. Northerners who have criticized the South chose to overlook—and neglected to change —the colored districts of their own cities, where Negroes are involuntarily segregated in ghettos by economic pressure and white prejudice.[24] Continuously since 1910, as Negroes have migrated from the South, the size of these ghettos has grown and, along with it, their social disorganization. From all the major metropolitan areas, whites have been moving to the suburbs, leaving the blighted central core to the blacks—many of them poor and poorly educated.[25] Never yet

[23]The most dramatic change is in Mississippi, where only 7 per cent of Negroes of voting age had registered in 1964. In 1968, the percentage had risen to 60.

[24]"Segregation and poverty have created in the racial ghetto a destructive environment totally unknown to most white Americans. What white Americans have never fully understood—but what the Negro can never forget—is that white society is deeply implicated in the ghetto. White institutions created it, white institutions maintain it, and white society condones it." *Report of the National Advisory Commission on Civil Disorders* (New York: Bantam Books, Inc., 1968), p. 2.

[25]On these points, the statistical data speak eloquently. "In 1910, 91 per cent of the nation's 9.8 million Negroes lived in the South and only 27 per cent lived in cities of 2,500 persons or more. Between 1910 and 1966 the total Negro population more than

assimilated into the community as a whole and relegated, in general, to a low social status, Negroes form the largest of the minorities[26]—others being the Indians and Mexican Americans—to which thus far the political ideals of America have been extended only in part.

But all this nowadays is challenged and changing. We are in the midcourse of a social revolution which is uprooting vested interests, plucking down exclusive privilege, and attacking ancient prejudice. What is at issue in this revolution is too far-reaching, as are its potential consequences too explosive, to submit to precise formulation or simple summary. Far more is here at stake than an enlargement of electoral registers or a reordering of social habits. Nothing less has been put to the test than the integrity of our civic conscience. On our example, as shown by our actions, will depend our influence in the world.

The march towards equality in race relations has become one of the sweeping global movements of this century. The case for its recognition, brutally denied by German National Socialists and South African Nationalists, affirms the inherent worth of all humanity to which distinctions of race, per se, have no relevance. The equalitarian principle insists that a person's opportunities be based on the capacities of each individual and not on the group to which one was born or happens inadvertently to belong. The task confronting our generation is to break down the man-made barriers of segregation, both legal and social, and to treat individuals as their merits entitle them. If there is any conclusion to which the findings of the majority of anthropologists and sociologists point, it is this: In comparing whole groups of human beings of different race, religion, culture, wealth, or sex, no proof can be offered that any one group is inherently superior and any other inherently inferior. The differences which may be observed between the average of one group and that of another are attributable to man-made, socially fostered discrimination which has enlarged for some and has restricted for others the avenues which lead to education, income, and advancement. When such discrimination is removed, however, experience proves that individual members of formerly underprivileged groups can advance according to their abilities in the same fashion as members of groups which once were privileged.

---

doubled, reaching 21.5 million, and the number living in metropolitan areas rose more than fivefold (from 2.6 million to 14.8 million). The number outside the South rose elevenfold (from 880,000 to 9.7 million)." *Ibid.*, p. 12. "In 1966 about 11.9 per cent of the nation's whites and 40.6 per cent of its nonwhites were below the 'poverty level' defined by the Social Security Administration (currently $3,335 per year for an urban family of four). Over 40 per cent of the nonwhites below the poverty level live in the central cities." *Ibid.*, p. 14.

[26]Except for the largest of all—the women of all races.

Various causes, domestic and external, have contributed in the United States to the new conditions since the end of World War II and the altered climate of opinion. For many decades the South has been changing in ways that were unavoidable in a section of an expanding and dynamic nation. Industrialization has diversified the southern economy and raised the standard of living. Enlightened federal programs, notably those of the Tennessee Valley Authority, have introduced federal aid into regions which were backward and impoverished. In addition, the character of World War II, when the United States fought against the Nazi doctrine of a master race, and our subsequent competition with Communist powers, have made this country self-conscious of its position in modern world history. The grant of independence to European colonies in Africa has instilled in men of dark skins a pride in their own race and all its attributes. When the heads of African governments attend the United Nations in New York and are treated there with diplomatic courtesies, black Americans could not fail to wonder why they should be subject to segregation. Hence they have insisted with increasing articulateness that the principles of the Declaration of Independence ("all men are created equal") and the Constitution (Thirteenth, Fourteenth, and Fifteenth Amendments) be converted from promise to practice. Finally, when this nation began observing the centennial of the Civil War, including the Emancipation Proclamation, Negroes took fresh stock of their position and demanded improvements "Now."

TOWARD EQUALITY IN EDUCATION

As this revolution runs its course, the effects pervade the social order. Understandably, a central target in the black drive for equality has been the educational system. When schools and universities are financed from public funds, their policies are subject to the public interest. Discrimination by public bodies along racial lines negates the principle of the Fourteenth Amendment, which prohibits a state from denying "the equal protection of the laws" to any person within its jurisdiction. Although the intention and the spirit of this famous formula are clear enough, 86 years elapsed between the dates when the amendment was added to the Constitution and when it was unequivocally interpreted in so vital a sphere as the education of school children. Late in the nineteenth century, in the case of *Plessy* vs. *Ferguson* the Supreme Court had adopted the "separate, but equal" doctrine. This held that in public transportation the different races must be given equal facilities, which could, however, be separate as long as they were still equal. A few years afterward, that concept was applied to schools; and the policy of the South has been to forestall social mingling between the races by providing parallel, and supposedly equal, services.

That policy, however, always rested upon a fiction. Theoretically the Constitution was observed by pretending that separate facilities could be equal and in fact were so. Reality did not support this contention, which became more and more dishonest. Not only were the two sets of facilities in most cases physically and materially different in quality and standard, but the very fact of segregation established an intentional barrier with profound results on the psychology of individuals and the ethos of society. When two races live side by side, but only one of the two determines the pattern of their coexistence and draws the lines of isolation and exclusiveness, equality is a myth and not a fact. The inescapable consequence is a relation of superiors to inferiors; and when one side of the "equation" continues to retain all the social advantages, the judge who disregards such reality makes a mockery of justice. This truth was cogently stated by a unanimous Supreme Court in its momentous decision of 1954, in the case of *Brown* vs. *Board of Education,* requiring the racial integration of public schools throughout the country. Chief Justice Warren's opinion pierced the enveloping outer-cloud of fiction and make-believe and formulated good sense with this impressive simplicity: "Segregation of white and colored children in public schools has a detrimental effect upon the colored children. The impact is greater when it has the sanction of the law; for the policy of separating the races is usually interpreted as denoting the inferiority of the Negro group. . . . Separate educational facilities are inherently unequal."

Few decisions in modern times have offered so conspicuous an example of the gap between the enunciation of a principle and its detailed enforcement. In the aftermath of that decision a bitter controversy erupted, not only involving the relations between races, but embroiling both political parties, the federal and state governments, the legislative, executive, and judicial branches at all levels, the police and the army, and the international influence of the United States. The crux of the problem has been to overcome the stubborn refusal of many whites (public officials and private individuals alike) to accept the social integration of races as required by the supreme law of the land and expounded by its supreme tribunal. That compliance would be neither easy nor automatic was recognized by the Supreme Court from the outset. It takes time to alter social practices which have long been fixed in institutions and attitudes. Private associations that are to be shorn of privileges do not promptly yield, even to public authority. A national majority can find it hard to persuade, and difficult to coerce, opponents who are geographically concentrated in local majorities. For all this the Supreme Court made due allowance when it invited the officials of the areas concerned to prepare their plans for changing "separate, but equal" facilities into "integrated and equal," requiring however that the change be consummated "with all deliberate speed."

One full decade after that decision, Negroes were asking themselves which seemed to be more deliberate—the federal speed or the local resistance. The actual results are expressed in these figures. By the end of 1964, in the eleven states of the Confederacy, 64,000 Negroes out of a total of almost 3 million (only 2.13 per cent) were enrolled in biracial schools.[27] What such figures cannot convey, of course, is the degree of strain and struggle required in producing even this amount of integration. Starting in 1957 at Little Rock, Arkansas, and continuing with successive incidents in Virginia, Louisiana, Alabama, and Mississippi, the local officials, legislatures, and governors defied the authority of the federal government and in some instances did not comply until confronted with the presence of superior force. Both Presidents Eisenhower and Kennedy had to send armed soldiers into a high school and a university to enforce the orders of the federal courts.

Similarly in the North and the West, much of the public education has been racially segregated in practice. Enforcers of this segregation have been neither the laws nor officialdom, but rather the social structure and the economy. If a school is organized to serve a neighborhood, and if all the families living there belong to the same race, *de facto* that school will be segregated. Also, if the teachers, the teacher-pupil ratio, and the facilities in the central core of a large city are of low standards, students from there will have little chance of admission to higher education or to the professions and the better-paying jobs. Since it takes so long to alter a deeply rooted pattern of segregated housing, some communities have sought instant integration of their schools by bussing children from one district to another—thereby requiring the school system to make up for social injustices which the realtors and mortgage companies have helped to perpetuate. This method has been adopted and is now functioning in a few cities; but in many, it has encountered profound hostility, even violent opposition, from white parents.

[27]Data from Southern Education Reporting Service, Nashville, Tennessee, cited in *New York Times* (Special Education Survey), Jan. 13, 1965, p. 75. By 1966 the total had risen to 690,000, the percentage, to 16.9.

ECONOMIC AND SOCIAL EQUALITY

From what has just been said about efforts to integrate the public schools and to equalize the opportunities they provide, it is clear that the problem of bringing social justice to a house divided against itself has many facets and solutions have to be sought simultaneously on many fronts. Equality, in a word, is indivisible: You cannot have it anywhere unless you achieve it everywhere. Juridical equality of rights, for instance, will have little practical effect if incomes are distributed unequally, since money is the key which unlocks many doors. Why insist that a housing tract or hotel, a golf club or restaurant, be integrated if members of a minority group cannot afford to foot the bill? At this point, it becomes clear that, while many contemporary manifestations of inequality are grounded in the fact of racial differences and the feelings these engender, the situation contains other aspects besides the racial. So wide is the social distance, so severe the economic separation, that race becomes compounded with class in a social structure which superimposes group upon group in a manner repugnant to the ultimate individualism of the American ethic.

There is thus a circularity among the conditions to be changed as among the remedies proposed. If a member of a disadvantaged minority is to qualify for the professions and for jobs requiring higher skill, he needs better education. To attain this, the segregated system must be broken down. Integrated schools properly presuppose, especially at the primary level, that housing is integrated. But renting or buying a house or apartment in the more desirable neighborhoods costs more money, which requires a higher income. There is no one lever, not even the right to vote, that can raise or remove all obstacles at once. In a revolution which is social as well as political, the underprivileged—impatient now and aroused—follow a strategy of advancing on all fronts at once. For this purpose, to the extent that politics can make laws which remake society, the passage in 1964 of the Civil Rights Act was an impressive achievement. By that legislation, the Congress at long last went officially on record with the expression of the majority will for a national policy.

CONTROVERSIES OVER MEANS AND ENDS

The course of this social revolution has accelerated, since that date, in speed and intensity. For many of the participants, not only have the objectives altered, but, with them, the leaders and their tactics. Nationally as well as locally, some genuine progress has been registered, but demands too have multiplied thick and fast. While the debate grew yearly more strident and the action more violent, America responded in fear and shock to the most profound challenge to its domestic tranquillity since the Civil War. To reach a balanced appraisal of a basic change in human relations is difficult when one is immersed in its midstream and the surge of passion rises to so high a crest. But certain points need emphasis if this drive for equality is to be seen in perspective and soberly judged.

First, it has become evident that the older tendency to make the South the nation's whipping boy was unjust. The events of the sixties proved conclusively that racial prejudice has no geographical confines. When northern and western communities found their practices challenged, many individuals in neighborhoods which until then had not explicitly faced the issue, resisted integration from a mixture of motives in which racial fears, class discrimination, and propertied interests were closely interwoven. The majority of Americans have not displayed this attitude—if they had, the Civil Rights Act could never have become law—but the minority that acted this way was sufficiently large and influential to produce an effect.

That minority has been matched by another at the opposite end of the spectrum, which gained support and publicity in the late sixties. These were the advocates of "Black Power," mobilized in such organizations as the Black Muslims and the Black Panthers. Their significance has lain in their explicit rejection of the concept of integration, and a desire to establish a community of their own as independent as possible of whites. They do not believe that black persons could be truly equal in an integrated society where they would be outnumbered ten to one. Hence they have espoused the "separate, but equal" doctrine. How far that separation should go is in dispute. Some Black Power leaders would like to make it total, including all the apparatus of an independent state. Others speak of acquiring sufficient economic strength for Negroes to live on the same standard as whites and to exercise control within the local sectors and institutions where they can predominate. But, whatever the degree of separation and whether this be conceived as partial or total, the aim is akin to the South African *apartheid*—with the difference, however, that in this case the dividing walls would be erected and enforced from both sides alike.

The implications of this viewpoint require comment. One is the conscious refusal to accept as a desirable goal the notion of a fully integrated, multiracial community. The latter solution has been that envisaged by the minority of liberal-minded people, both black and white. Their aim was ultimately to put race on the same footing as religion, that is, to create a community in which these differences would become irrelevant to social practice and public ethics. How far that ideal of mutual tolerance is removed from present actuality can be inferred from recent data which also throw light on the springs of the movement for Black Power. Whatever the Constitution may prescribe or Congress may enact, current statistical data show that American society is in fact dividing increasingly in the direction of *apartheid*. In 1968 the National Commission on Urban Problems issued a study which concluded that, if present trends continue, by 1985 the United States will be disunited through geographic, as well as economic and racial, separation.[28]

The awareness of these facts and trends, disillusionment over the slow pace of token solutions to massive injustices, and the vivid contrast between life in the ghetto and the televised image of affluent America, all of this led in the late sixties to outbreaks of mass violence, expressing both rage and despair. Convulsed in the agony of a belated social revolution, and facing a crisis of its own moral conscience, the nation witnessed the burning and pillage of the Watts district of Los Angeles, prolonged racial upheaval in Detroit, and the assassination of the most saintly of the black leaders, the Reverend Martin Luther King, apostle of nonviolence and recipient of the Nobel Prize for Peace. As always in human history, extremes assist one another; and so too in this tragic story violence begets counterviolence, and the racism of one side feeds the racism of its opposites.

CONSTRUCTIVE STEPS AND COMPARISONS

But the record is not all failure, nor do all the signs leave us without hope. Far from it. There are other facts to indicate that progress is being made and that favorable trends are in motion which could counteract divisiveness. In the five years since the last edition of this book appeared, one can record the following events: A Negro has served in the president's cabinet, and another now sits on the Supreme Court. Massachusetts has elected a Negro to the United States Senate, and Cleveland, Ohio, and Gary, Indiana, have Negro mayors. The last three cases are particularly important in what they reveal of social attitudes in a large state and large cities. Just as John F. Kennedy required Protestant and Jewish votes to win the presidency, black candidates for mayoral and senatorial office needed white support for their election. Assuredly there is prejudice among us; but there is also the fact, and the potentiality, of tolerance and mutual respect.

Spectacular outrages fill the headlines and are reprinted in the

[28]According to its figures, by 1985 American cities will lose about 2½ million whites and will gain 10 million nonwhites. In the suburbs, whites will have increased by 54 millions, nonwhites by 4 millions.

world's newspapers. The progress we make—steady, although admittedly slow—does not capture similar attention because it occurs piecemeal and often is discreetly conducted. But the gains already recorded in the name of equality are indeed noteworthy. When one considers the past, the changes that occurred in the sixties without fanfare or undue friction in such a divided state as Georgia are truly impressive. The capital city of Atlanta is a conspicuous case of what can be accomplished constructively by an intelligent civic leadership, both public and private. Moreover, those who would too loosely generalize about the United States might pause to remember that, if we have a Mississippi, we also have Hawaii, and while there are Harlems, there is also Honolulu. The fiftieth state, placed "at the crossroads of the Pacific," contains a living laboratory in which different ethnic and racial groups have learned to coexist and are combining fruitfully. This has been possible precisely because the principles of the Constitution of the United States were genuinely applied here to peoples of extraordinary dissimilarities.

Nor should we forget that if there is struggle and resistance, and even violence, this is because we are now taking positive steps to rectify existing injustices. American experience on this point is part of the world movement in the direction of greater equality; and we are not alone in discovering that when different races confront one another in new modes of social and physical proximity, the responses are highly irrational and can be dangerous. Great Britain is a country which twenty years ago had no racial problem in its midst. Since then, however, the immigration of Commonwealth citizens from the West Indies, Africa, Pakistan, and India, accentuated by their concentration in certain districts of London and other cities, has evoked some reactions similar to those long known in North America. The British Parliament has enacted a law to reverse the traditional policy of permitting unrestricted immigration from the Commonwealth and colonies and has also legislated against economic and social discrimination. In the general elections of 1964 and 1966 the friction over the presence of colored newcomers was a political factor in a number of constituencies. In India the continuation of the Hindu castes[29] provides a major impediment to modernization. Gandhi did all that one inspired humanist could do to relieve the lot of the untouchables, and Nehru, himself a high-caste Brahmin by birth, had a Jeffersonian attachment to equality. Progress in breaking down caste distinctions has been considerable, especially in the areas of urbanism. But rural India,

---

[29]Caste and race are not unrelated. Generally, the high-caste Brahmins have light skins; the untouchables are usually darker.

like rural districts everywhere, is harder to reach and slower to change. In fact, some of India's difficulties with caste are analogous to those of the United States with race, and enlightenment from the center is similarly obstructed by local backwardness. Our world indeed continues to exhibit the familiar evidence of man's inhumanity to man, and much of it still takes the form of racial hostility. Yet it should be remembered that like can devour like. The peace of mankind was marred in the late sixties by two tragically insane wars, those in Vietnam and Nigeria, and in the latter misery was inflicted by black upon black.

Inequality dies hard. Seldom do the privileged surrender their advantages without a struggle. And this is true not only of races whose contacts so often end in conflict, but of religions, linguistic groups, and nations. In world politics, no less than within states, the spokesmen for peoples who have latterly gained their independence from colonial rule demand their say in the United Nations and elsewhere.[30] Indeed, the universality of this demand is as notable as its emotional intensity; and so also, when equality is observed in historical perspective, is its rarity.

Reviewing the exclusive and inclusive notions of citizenship, one may conclude the subject of these two chapters with the reminder that most political history and most operative constitutions have been the work of oligarchies. Normally and customarily the many have been governed by the few for the benefit of the few. Humanity as a general rule has lived under regimes of inequality and privilege. Efforts to the contrary have been exceptional, but they have been made both among the ancients and among the moderns. To proclaim in theory the basic equality of all men and to establish a system which gives effect in practice to the like rights of all is unusual and abnormal. But since the trend in this direction has been more pronounced during the last hundred years than in any century of the past, there is some ground for hoping that what once was rare may yet become the fashion. Indeed, the acceptance of the principle of universal adult suffrage, not only in the United States, Britain, and India but also in many medium-sized and smaller countries, stands out as one of the political triumphs of the last hundred years in human history. It is a new fact, without precedent in earlier times, to find so many countries where virtually all adult citizens now possess the right to take part in the election of their government. Never before, if a Churchillian saying may be adapted, have so many had so much opportunity to choose so few. In those modern states where the mass of the population is

[30]On this point, see Chap. 13, pp. 388–94.

now entitled to participate in the electoral process, the formulas of Kant and Bentham, and the broad humanity of the great declarations, are being translated into practical effect.

6

SECOND ISSUE:

–1– The State and Society

THE UNITY OF SOCIETY

Governments exist because we want certain results which they are able to provide. To know, therefore, what the state is, we must look at what it does. Hence we turn from the citizens it serves to the nature of its services. All associations, as we have seen, are differentiated by the functions they perform. In the case of the state, those functions admit many alternatives and, since they embrace a wide range of choice, are debatable. Controversy thus extends beyond what the state does to what it might do. Human beings inject into discussions concerning the state their preferences about the activities that properly belong to it, which makes the study of governmental functions not merely descriptive, but normative. For the state is what its functions are, as influenced by men's conceptions of what they ought to be.

If one is to make a rational choice, the alternatives must be understood. Consequently, it is important to grasp the issues involved in the debate concerning the activities appropriate to the state. What is at stake here? Why do men struggle so strenuously to extend or confine the volume of governmental activity? Since the state germinates within the matrix of society, what is its relation to that society once it has matured? The answer to these questions can be attempted by picking up the threads of the argument begun in Chapter 2. There the point was stressed that cooperation and competition between human beings give rise to a plurality of groups, and that individuals are variously associated and reassociated according to the aims they share or the ambitions over which they clash. The fact that society is a com-

149

plex whole, wherein individuals are members of many groups, creates for each of us a problem of competing loyalties. The outward schism between the groups that compose society is reproduced internally by what Toynbee calls "schism in the soul." If people are to feel at one with themselves, and if there is to be harmony among groups, two requirements have to be met. Subjectively, human beings must feel that what unites them is superior to what separates them. Objectively, they need some institutional means for organizing those feelings. For the term "society" to be more than merely a handy generalization, something is necessary to bind the mixture. Can that "something" be identified?

PLURALISM VERSUS MONISM

The relations between the groups that make up society have been viewed in two ways. Some influential thinkers have held that associations spring spontaneously from the free play of human activity. They are not summoned by fiat, nor are they the product of one central source. In their origins they are independent of one another; and as the stimuli to associate differ, so do the associations themselves. Therefore, it is concluded, they must be allowed to operate with the same freedom that permitted their birth. Since to be free they must be equal, they are to be regarded as coordinate with one another. No association can be accorded a special prerogative of superiority over the rest. The strivings of mankind cannot, it is argued, be folded within the embrace of one supreme good or final end. Men reach out for ends in the plural, not for one end in the singular; and as their purposes are plural, the structure of society must be likewise.[1]

To the pluralists comes the rejoinder of the monists. In their view society is, or ought to be, a unity; and for it to be unified, there must be a tie that binds. While it is true that human drives spontaneously produce numerous groupings, once these exist they cannot, though independently born, act in independence. Groups impinge upon each other, as they pursue their aims, and create a need for order and harmony. Men are distracted by the conflicting claims upon their allegiance of separate, and often rival, associations. The remedy for this is to discover some highest good that includes and supersedes the lesser. Next, it is necessary to recognize one association as responsible for attaining that highest good. To this let the

[1]For examples of this viewpoint, consult Harold J. Laski, *Grammar of Politics,* 3rd ed. (London: George Allen and Unwin, 1934), pp. 25–28, 37; or Robert M. MacIver, *The Modern State* (New York: Oxford University Press, Inc., 1926), pp. 7, 182.

remaining associations be subordinated. Thus society can become, and stay, unitary in purpose as in organization.[2]

Each of these views is evidently strong where the other is weak. One lays stress on the role of society as a richly creative matrix of varied behavior. To advocates of this way of thinking, any proposal for central control or unified direction spells death to the kind of society they idealize. Spontaneity, freedom, variety, autonomy—these they consider the cardinal virtues of groups and group action; and the society they most applaud is the one in which such qualities are maximized. But the price of diversity is the impairment of unity. The more the pluralist exalts and exaggerates the independence of associations, the more "the great society"[3] vanishes—until, as with the Cheshire cat, a face lingers on without a body, then a grin without a face, and lastly the grin fades away.

Contrariwise is the position of the monist. He is all for unity and for the virtues he hopes will accompany it—order, harmony, and singleness of purpose. To attain these is impossible, as he sees it, unless the many cohere around one focus. Nor does this coherence result from subjective attitudes alone. To unify society, it is not enough for people to feel that they belong together. The sentiment must be fortified with organization that establishes orderly and harmonious relations between groups by institutional procedures. Though this consummation be devoutly wished by the monist, he too encounters difficulties which stem from his position. For he invites the question whether his insistence upon unity is so excessive that groups, other than the supreme unifying agency, will lose meaning, character, and identity to the extent that their autonomy is impaired. The penalty for unity can be the imposition of uniformity.

Moreover, each of these two views of society confronts a difficulty that is the result of its special position. Both philosophies stand unequivocally against something: the pluralist, against organized unity; the monist, against anarchic diversity. But, in a constructive sense, for what kind of society does each view positively contend?

The pluralist may argue for a multiplicity of coordinate associations, whose mutual interplay will cancel out the dangers of excessive power by any one group.[4] But, following the potentialities inherent in his own logic, he may go further. Approving the subdivision of society into its groups, he may also approve the fragmentation of the latter

---

[2]The monists, curiously enough, exhibit contrasts no less marked than the pluralists. Witness Aristotle, in the paragraph with which he commences the *Politics,* and Mussolini in *The Social and Political Doctrine of Fascism.*

[3]This is the title of a book by Graham Wallas, published in 1914.

[4]Such, essentially, is Madison's conception of society in *The Federalist,* No. 10.

into their individual members. At the logical extreme, therefore, the true pluralist is the individualist. His stress is upon individuals; and in the name of their individuality he may protest against the groups in which they combine as he does against the society that would combine the groups. Pluralism, so conceived, is the plurality of autonomous individuals, rather than that of autonomous associations. Or conversely, the pluralist may veer in the other direction. Conceding the need for individuals to be grouped and organized, he may yet be dubious about the possibilities of maintaining equilibrium and order among too many associations. He may therefore support the idea of a balance between two bodies roughly equal in weight and bulk. Afraid to risk the monopoly that the monist accepts, he therefore settles for dualism. Two great associations may be more stable than many, and safer than one. Indeed, as the discussion will show later in this chapter and the next, the pluralistic argument for society has in some cases historically assumed a dualistic form.

UNITY THROUGH THE FAMILY, CHURCH, OR BUSINESS

The monist, too, has his problems. Desiring to provide society with an integrating focus, he must designate what this should be. He must pick the institution that is appropriate to embrace, oversee, or absorb the rest. Which is he to choose? And how can its task be accomplished?

That a choice does exist, and that the answer is not cut and dried, is substantiated by historical evidence. Several social institutions have, as a matter of fact, essayed this role of being prime coordinator for society. One of these, at various places and times, has been the family. In such a case kinship becomes the chief determinant that governs every relationship. Because human beings are connected in certain ways by birth, their other group activities are cast within the mold of heredity. Thus the family serves as the economic unit, where each works for all and is entitled to a share of the total output. The family takes care of its weak, its aged, and its incapacitated. The family provides education; and, for religion, worships its ancestors. The family determines marital unions by alliance with other families. The family establishes rules and administers its discipline with rewards and punishments. In some instances it even levies a death penalty on one of its members or wages war upon some neighboring family in the form of a blood feud or vendetta.

Similarly, some religious associations have extended beyond their primary function of worship and have encompassed under spiritual authority the general direction of society. In fact, the system of government named theocracy is evidence in point. When Calvin and Calvinists controlled Geneva in the seventeenth century or when the Jesuits ruled Paraguay in the eighteenth, church-government regulated in minute detail the conduct of individuals and groups. Religious, no less than secular, bodies can declare and enforce the law by reference to divine sanction; maintain and direct an economic system as proprietors and managers; supervise the family by granting or withholding its rites; educate the youth; organize charities for the needy; and dominate the arts by control over their themes and forms. Religions can likewise launch crusades, proclaim "holy wars," and place armies in the field.[5] Men have bled and died for the Cross, the Crescent, or the *Mogen David,* as they have for Old Glory, the Union Jack, or the *Tricolore.*

The same has been true of business firms. Occasionally the association paramount over the rest is economic. A group which originated for purposes of commerce, manufacturing, or trade may discover in a certain *milieu* that it cannot fulfill these functions unless it extends its control over other institutions. Whether Napoleon was right or wrong in describing the British as "a nation of shopkeepers," or whether President Coolidge did full justice to his fellow countrymen with the remark that "the business of America is business," the fact remains that society can be integrated not by kinship, or religion, but by control of productive resources, by entrepreneurial technique, and, in Carlyle's phrase, by the "cash nexus." Indeed there have been corporations clothed in the full panoply of governments; and, if one mentions the celebrated East India Company[6] which ruled Britain's empire in India until 1858, this is merely to cite a conspicuous, and not a unique, example. When business organizes society for business ends, it too can make and apply the law, establish the ethical code and define the standards of right and wrong in relation to such concepts as "property," "profit," or "labor." By prescribing the conditions and hours and wages of work, business can make or break the family. By its influence over occupations and careers, it can mold the policies and curricula of education. By paying the artist and purchasing his products, it can regulate aesthetic style and taste. Lastly, by promot-

---

[5]"Men never do evil so completely and cheerfully," wrote Pascal, "as when they do it from religious conviction."

[6]In the course of his *Speech in the Impeachment of Warren Hastings,* 1788, Edmund Burke thus described the company: "The constitution of the company began in commerce, and ended in empire. . . . The India company came to be what it is —a great empire, carrying on, subordinately, a great commerce. . . . In fact, the East-India Company in Asia is a state in the disguise of a merchant." *Works,* VII (Boston: Wells and Lilly, 1827), 29.

ing or preserving a trading or industrial empire, business can mobilize military force and fight its battles at so much *per caput* and for such and such *per cent.*

These facts warrant an inference. Because the family, church, and corporation have made efforts of this kind with more or less success, it would appear that, in the absence of a coordinating institution, society contains a vacuum which there is an opportunity to fill. If various associations have made the attempt, it is reasonable to assume that a genuine need exists which they seek to satisfy, and that they can then be judged by how well they fill it. That need was seen earlier to arise from the competition between associations and the rival claims they make upon the allegiance of their members. The relations between groups create the occasion for control, supposedly by some superassociation. But there is more to it than that. If the unity of society means anything, and is not an empty phrase, more may be required than a mechanism that merely mitigates the effects of conflict. Since society is built upon cooperation, as well as on competition, a case can be argued for a positive policy of promoting harmony between groups.

Furthermore, since a group is more than just the sum of its separate members, so is society more than the mere addition of the component groups. The structure of society has been described by some writers as federal. This is a helpful analogy if it is understood in two senses: first, that society is not properly a collection of individuals, but rather of groups of individuals, and, second, that the groups collectively constitute more than they do separately. Considered by itself, each association is concerned with human interests that are fractional, these fractions being called economic, educational, religious, and so on. Functioning in its primary sense, an economic association performs activities that are economic, a religious association pursues aims that are religious, and similarly with the rest. No one association, if all are coordinate in rank and limited in function, has the responsibility or means to see that these fragments of human life are fused into a whole. In other words, there is no way of ensuring that the economy functions, not as a thing apart, but as the economic aspect of society; that a school or university is no cloistered academy, but a training ground for the use of intelligence in the workaday world; that the particular, in short, be treated within the framework of the general.

DEFECTS OF A SINGLE-TRACK SOCIETY

But while the monist who wants an integrated society has many weapons to use against the pluralist, at the same time he runs a risk.

If any association is to succeed in coordinating society, it must evolve from a minor part to the leading role. Thus it must broaden the necessarily narrow interest, from which it started, into a comprehensive concern for the whole. The question is whether an association will in fact be capable of growing to the stature of its wider responsibilities or will instead remain the prisoner of its origins and of the limits they impose. The problem can be illustrated by some examples that are by no means hypothetical. Suppose the institution which attempts the general coordination of society is the family.[7] Then it must be expected that a group, created by kinship and sustained by living together, will transfer to other social spheres the characteristics which spring from its primary functions. Thus relations between human beings will correspond to those between husband and wife, or parents and child, or sibling and sibling. Authority will be parental in form. Status within the family circle will determine status within the social circle. Family dictates will be the overriding consideration in the economic realm. Thus, for instance, the ownership and inheritance of the family homestead, the provision for a son to marry and support a wife, production for subsistence only or for exchange—these and similar matters will be settled by the prevailing conceptions of the family as the unifier of the social order. The great society will become an association of kinsmen, writ large.[8]

Likewise, when the integrating agency is religious, its theology will be extended to every secular activity. If the religion asserts the existence of a soul that survives the death of the body, men will be taught to prepare themselves in this world of mortal things for the eternity hereafter. The rules of daily conduct will be construed as a lifelong consecration to the Deity. The social contacts of the individual will be confined to the ranks of his coreligionists. Those who do not belong to the established communion—call them heathen, pagan, gentile, infidel, heretic, or what you will—will be the low castes or outcasts of society. These are "the stranger within thy gates," "the untouchables," "the internal proletariate,"[9] living witnesses of a house divided against itself, with religion as the divider. Holy Writ becomes law in the form of the Gospel, the Torah, the Koran, the Vedas; and the supreme lawgiver is the Holy Man, Prophet, or Son of God—a

---

[7]Some oriental cultures provide examples of the transfer of the family relationship to an entire society. See an analysis of this attempt in Japan by Robert A. Scalapino, *Democracy and the Party Movement in Prewar Japan* (Berkeley: University of California Press, 1953), pp. 120 ff.

[8]Many peoples have expressed this idea in the form of a story that they are descended from a common ancestor.

[9]This is A. J. Toynbee's phrase in his *Study of History.*

Gautama, Jesus, Mahomet, or Moses. Within this frame of reference, criticism of authority is equated with blasphemy. Opposition itself is sin.

Similar in principle is the result which befalls the economic group that seeks to integrate society. In this case the basic elements of the economic order will extend a pervasive influence throughout the social order. Thus the rights that are vested in the ownership of property, and the human relationships arising from it—such factors of production as the control of natural resources, the use of tools and equipment, the structure of the wage system—all this and more will affect the rest of man's estate. Humanity will be preoccupied with material concerns: with living standards, the distribution of goods, the struggle for acquisition, the maintenance of employment and of purchasing power. The world will be converted into a market. Language iself will take its connotations from the categories of economics. "Enterprise" will be synonymous with business; ideas that one seeks to impart will be commodities one "sells"; human beings will be specified as "managers," "consumers," "hands." The great society, if it knows no other god than Mammon, will strike the balance sheet of its civilization in pecuniary terms. For what shall it profit a man if he gain his own soul and lose a whole market?

The point of the foregoing paragraphs can thus be summarized: When an association that originates with a finite function broadens out to the indefinite horizons of society, it tends to apply to its larger task the criteria of its initial limits. To the extent that this is so, its efforts provide society with both integration and straitjacketing. To subordinate all aspects of life and all kinds of groups to the single principle of kinship, religion, or economics can yield an unwholesome monism. If its results then are to be beneficial, the unifying association must meet this acid test: While retaining its original functions, it must rise above them and change its own character. It cannot integrate society merely by refashioning every other association in its own image.

This survey of the arguments in issue between monists and pluralists and of the problems peculiar to each facilitates a better understanding of the controversy over the functions of the state. The analysis so far has indicated that the question of what activities are appropriate to the state is not narrowly political, but broadly social. It has also become clear that two questions are involved, since a choice must first be made between pluralism and monism; and, if the latter is preferred, a second choice must determine which of many associations can best coordinate the whole. The answer to the second question is, in a vital sense, relevant to the first, because, if no association can perform the job of integrating, the case for pluralism wins by default.

If, on the other hand, some one association is competent to do the job, then the case for the monist is strengthened.

THE STATE'S RELATION TO SOCIETY

In this controversy the state is directly involved. Wherever there is government, questions must arise concerning the activities it is to undertake. This means that the relations of the state to the other associations which men form must somehow be defined. If the pluralist is to have his way, he must explain (1) why it is necessary to limit the functions of the state, (2) where those limits should be placed, and (3) how society hangs together, or achieves integration, in the absence of a unifying agency. If, however, the monist is to get the better of the argument, he must demonstrate (1) that society is in need of unification, (2) that the state is able to undertake this, and (3) that any dangers which may ensue from confiding this duty to the state are either outweighed by the attendant advantages or can be safely forestalled.

Both viewpoints have been put forward at various times by those who wished to advocate or resist this or that manifestation of governmental power. Nor have the rival philosophies been confined only to the realm of theoretical debate. Under one guise or another, each has been translated into practice and has received concrete expression. Hence the discussion and evaluation of each can be based both on the reasoned hopes of their advocates and on the performance that results from their application in practice. Like the family, business, and church, the state has entered this field of controversy because there is an opportunity for it to grasp. If society is ready for integration, the state is as well placed to provide it as are associations based upon kinship, economics, or religion. Or possibly, it is even better placed. This is so because of the character of the primary function from which the state originates. Every human being is in need of protection. All, therefore, need, and to a point depend on, the association which provides this. Furthermore, the state controls the force that assures protection. Through this same force, the government is able at times to impose itself upon the other institutions of society. Indeed the state can be more effectively monistic than either businesses, families, or churches because of the sanctions it employs. Those who do not bow to family control may be excluded from the kin group. Those who defy their employers may lose their bread and butter. Those who resist sacerdotal authority may be excommunicated. Such sanctions are not completely compulsive unless the victim is left with no other alternative. But in some societies a man may survive without a family;

he may earn his living in new ways; he may embrace a new faith or do without one. Universally, however, the ultimate sanction of the state is a gun pointed at your temple. If, as is ordinarily the case, the state has a monopoly of the available force, there is no choice but to submit or die.

The modern debate over the proper sphere of governmental activity trails behind it a history of at least twenty-five centuries. For that reason the best way to understand current controversies about the functions of the state is to review them in chronological perspective. The story forms a sequence of alternating episodes, with the emphasis shifting from one pole to the other. The city-state of the Graeco-Roman period was primarily monistic in spirit and organization. The counterdoctrine, that the sphere of the state must be limited, was advanced in idea and reality by the Christian church after it became the official religion of the Roman Empire and a partner in the established order. This principle continued to prevail through the Middle Ages, but lost ground with the advent of the Reformation and the emergence of the nation-state. The ethos of the latter at its inception was as strongly monistic as the city-state had been. It remained so until the economic ferment of the Industrial Revolution once more brought into vogue the concept of the limited state, with business now cast in the role formerly played by the medieval church. The twentieth century, in this matter as in others inheriting its legacy from the nineteenth, has both imitated and reacted against its predecessor. Midway in this present century, it is certain only that both viewpoints—the one that insists on limits and the one that does not—are still embattled. It is uncertain at the moment which is dominant or likely to become so.

The five periods may be roughly identified as follows:

1. First period: approximately from the tenth century B.C. to the fourth century A.D. Monistic State.
2. Second period: from the fourth century A.D. to middle of the fifteenth century. Limited State.
3. Third period: from middle of the fifteenth century to 1776. Monistic State.
4. Fourth period: 1776 to 1914. Limited State.
5. Fifth period: since 1914. Return to the Monistic State.

A survey of these periods,[10] and a review of their problems, will

[10]This breakdown into "periods" is offered with the necessary caution that any

help to explain the advantages claimed for each doctrine and the difficulties attending its fulfillment.

THE GRAECO-ROMAN CITY-STATE: AN EXPERIMENT IN MONISM

In its fully developed form, the *polis* or city-state, such as Sparta in the sixth century B.C. or Athens in the fifth, demanded of its citizens the whole of their allegiance. All human activities and associations were either actually controlled or liable to control by the state. Society —meaning the sum total of all groups—was regarded, not as separate from the state, but as subordinate to it. Even the Greek language, that flexible instrument for conveying the subtlest nuance of thought, had no word to signify the concept of society any more than it had a term to distinguish between state and city. The one word *polis* sufficed for city, state, and society combined. Within this context of ideas, the state was the paramount social institution when and where it chose to intervene. Thus, the economic field was subject to political ordering as the public interest seemed to require. Religion consisted of state worship to the patron hero or deity of the city and to the pantheon of the Olympians. The cultural achievements which have made that age immortal were in large part evoked or produced under the stimulus of state demand. The architects, sculptors, and painters—an Ictinus, Phidias, or Apelles—dedicated their genius to the temples and other civic buildings which the state constructed for its adornment. It was the public marketplace that served as classroom for the interrogations of Socrates; the citizens' assembly that inspired the oratory of Pericles or Demosthenes; the official festivals and contests that promoted the staging of dramas by the great tragedians and of comedies by Aristophanes.

Nevertheless, although the account above correctly describes the general tendency, certain aberrations or exceptions did exist. There were religious cults, such as the Eleusinian Mysteries, which did not belong to official state ceremony. There were creative artists, lyric poets for instance, who produced their works to satisfy an inward urge rather than a public audience. In actuality, not everything was prescribed and ordered by the state, save possibly in Sparta and Crete. But what is important is that, if the state chose to extend its authority to any sphere, there was no rival institution strong enough to resist its advance and no social philosophy delimiting the bounds of state ac-

---

such subdivision contains an element of arbitrariness. The beginning and ending dates are averages, rather than precise points. Few periods, moreover, are all one thing or all another. Usually, contemporary instances of the opposite to the prevalent tendency can be discovered.

tion. Indeed, the classic pronouncements of thinkers like Plato and Aristotle are wholly couched in terms of the omnipotent state. These two men, somewhere or other in their major treatises, touch on practically every one of the great issues that occupy the forefront of political theory and practice in the modern world. Significantly, though, they omit the questions of the relation of the state to society and the possible limits of state power. The reason for the omission is that such queries did not even arise in Greek experience. It therefore never occurred to Plato and Aristotle to examine an alternative to monism. This they took for granted.

On this point, however, the distinction between state and government must be borne in mind. There was a notable Greek tradition that condemned a certain type of government as tyrannical, justified resistance to it, and made heroes of tyrannicides. Some of the men who employed this line of thought—Plato, for instance—were convinced monists. Prepared to resist a tyrannical government, they were nevertheless not prepared to circumscribe the sphere of the state. Were these viewpoints self-consistent? How can a government be termed tyrannical, and opposition to it be upheld, save on some theory that it is exceeding its limits and doing what it ought not to do? Otherwise, why call it tyranny? The answer is that the Greeks resolved their inconsistency and saved their logic by accepting another major assumption. They distinguished between true and perverted kinds of government. The former were those wherein the rulers ruled in the interests of the whole community (inclusive of the governed). The latter were those where rulers governed for their own interest only. This distinction explains why Plato and Aristotle could logically accept a monistic theory of the state provided it were of the true kind, and yet support resistance to the perverted kind.

One further clarification should be added. Both Plato and Aristotle are monists in the sense that they view the state as supreme among human associations and set no bounds to its activities. But their monism is not identical. Or, to be more precise, the supremacy of the state reveals itself in different ways. Aristotle asserts his monism in the opening paragraph of the *Politics*, where he calls the state the paramount association, embracing all the rest and pursuing the highest good. Yet this conception of the state does not lead him to undervalue, still less to abolish, the remaining associations. These retain their place within the fabric of society and even serve to strengthen the bonds of social cohesion. But ultimately, and in case a conflict arises, it is to the state that all are subordinate. Plato differs from Aristotle in his utterly uncompromising emphasis upon unity, which, in his belief, is best safeguarded by the destruction of competing associations. All loyalties and affections are to be focused on and drawn towards one center. If other institutions, such as the family or the ownership of private property, are likely to distract the individual from a single-minded dedication to the public interest, the platonic guardians must be denied a share in them. The monistic state of Aristotle is one that permits other groups to exist, but stands supreme over them. The monistic state of Plato prefers to abolish the other groups and absorb their functions.

Apart from the preferences of the philosophers, however, what were the social reasons why the practice and philosophy of the city-state were monistic? Two reasons suffice. One was the smallness of the city-state. With an area and population so confined, there was little room for parallel, coordinate systems. As the Greeks read the lessons of their own history, they could choose one of two alternatives: unity with order or faction fights with anarchy. Closeness of contact, and the pressure of small-sized communities, bred a view of the state as the paramount social organization. In the antithesis between the public and private sides of life, Greek spokesmen gave their preference to the former. Thus their term for private citizen, *idiotes,* has yielded for its modern descendant the word "idiot," and Pericles could castigate persons who did not participate in civic affairs as being useless to the community.[11] Besides smallness, a second reason for monism was the condition of insecurity that plagued the Greeks in their interstate relations. Not only was there the possibility of war between Greek and non-Greek, but the little city-states themselves were often at each other's throats, and neighboring settlements were likely to be hereditary foes. Seeking protection from these perils, the Greeks were impelled to rally around the institution whose function was to protect.

If monism was encouraged by the smallness of the unit of government and facilitated by the absence of any association rivaling the state, it could be expected that, when these conditions disappeared, the monistic state would also disappear. Early signs of this possibility were discernible in the first philosophies that emerged after the absorption of the *polis* into the larger units of kingdoms or empires. The Stoics[12] and Epicureans rejected the outlook of Plato and Aristotle which favored an all-embracing collectivism within the confines of the *polis.* Instead, they sought to reconcile opposite extremes by finding a place for the individual in the immensity of the universe. Since the politics of the three centuries between the breakup of the empire of Alexander and the consolidation of that of Rome were chaotic and turbulent, men tended to view the state with pessimism, apprehen-

---

[11]See the Funeral Oration in Thucydides' *Histories,* ii.
[12]For the Stoics, see Chap. 5, pp. 121–22.

sion, or indifference. If the good life was unobtainable through politics, it must be sought in other ways. If the ambitions of governments were prejudicial to the public peace, peace of mind must be cultivated elsewhere. Hence followed a reassessment of the relative priorities of public and private activity, and philosophers now advised that men should compensate for the insecurities around them by seeking their security inside themselves.

As occurred in the case of equalitarianism, a concept born in the minds of Greeks received institutional form through the acts of Romans. This happened after Rome had succeeded in expanding into an empire and Christianity had managed to capture Rome. Previously, when Rome was a small community beset by unfriendly neighbors, it was subject to the same internal and external forces as the city-states of Greece. No sphere of life was exempt from the power of the state, if there was occasion or demand for its exercise. None of the other groups composing society was in a position to withstand the state or claim an independent or higher allegiance. Family relations, religious cults, economic affairs, cultural advances—all could be brought within the ambit of official surveillance. The situation changed when the Roman Empire expanded to a size unparalleled in the earlier history of the Mediterranean area. The tightly knit, close-packed organization of a small community could not be transferred or reproduced across the large-scale dimensions of Rome's conquests. Given the means of communication available at that day between the central authority and peripheral regions, the extent of the area to be governed precluded any intensive direction of society by the state. As long as Rome's authority was firmly established in the three vital spheres of military power, foreign relations, and finance, much diversity and autonomy were permitted in other matters to the various provinces and municipalities.

Along with this change of scale, an empire which eventually stretched from Persia to Scotland and from the German forests to the Sahara Desert came to embrace a host of religious faiths. Out of the welter of sects, cults, rites, and deities, Christianity through three centuries of growth emerged dominant. When the Emperor Constantine was converted, the *Imperium Romanum* entered into articles of union with the church. Considered in political terms, this partnership between the Cross and the Eagle brought gain and loss to both. The state had gained, because the spiritual influence of the Christian faith could now be employed to unify the allegiance of Roman citizens. But simultaneously the state had lost something, because it surrendered its monopoly. By accepting a partner, it had admitted a separate and coordinate body to the citadel of power. The church likewise derived a benefit, but also incurred a liability. Becoming an integral part of the established order, the church ceased to be a victim of persecution and was able henceforth to do the persecuting. Indeed it could, if necessary, invoke the secular arm as its ally against heretics and infidels. This power, however, brought attendant disadvantages. Not only might the church be obliged to extend reciprocal aid and support its temporal partner, even if the latter were, to put it mildly, unsaintly, but the church could also become corrupted by its involvement in the preoccupations of its position. Dominance could even bring wealth, at least to the princes of the church, and therewith a tendency to corruption. It was Dante[13] who wrote, with a reference to the supposed Donation of Constantine to Pope Silvester:

> Ah Constantine, what evil hast thou sired!
> Not thy conversion, but that price wherewith
> The first rich father thou hast paid and hired!

THE CHRISTIAN REVOLUTION: CHURCH-STATE DUALISM

Thus a new era in political history was inaugurated. The new era was signalized by a different solution to the problem of defining the functions of the state. Where the old order had been content with a doctrine that set no limit to these functions and made the boundaries of politics coextensive with the whole range of social conduct, the crux of the new order lay precisely in the effort to delimit the field of politics within the larger area of society and thus necessarily establish an adjacent field that the state would have no right to enter. The earlier concept of a society unified by the monistic state was rejected. For it there was substituted the notion of a society split in two, with twin institutions separated by a frontier line. Philosophy was now called upon to justify, and statesmanship to operate, a division of spheres. The issues posed by this endeavor were challenging. Reasons had to be discovered for the assertion that dualism was in some ways superior to unity; a line of demarcation had somewhere to be drawn; and finally the separate spheres and the governments of each had somehow to be related to each other. These problems in all their ramifications occupied human ingenuity for over a thousand years.

Whenever it is argued that the state be shorn of a portion of its power, the proposal takes specific form from the nature of the association that offers the challenge to monism. In this case, since religion

[13]*Inferno,* Canto XIX, ll. 115–17. My translation. In this Canto, Dante is attacking the clerics who sold ecclesiastical office and religious favors for monetary gain.

assumed the offensive, it was the church that emerged as an institution coequal with the state. Relations between church and state now became a major issue for political theory and organization, which they had not been before. It is, therefore, to the social doctrines of Christianity, as these evolved from the fourth to the fourteenth century A.D., that we must turn for understanding the theory and tactics of the Dark and Middle Ages. Like all systematic philosophies, Christianity assumed or asserted a view of human nature. Man was thought to be composed of two parts, body and soul. The body, an object of sense perception and known through sensory evidence, exists as a member of the world of material things. It is born, passes through the life cycle, and dies. The soul does not belong in the sensory realm. Proof of its existence is granted by divine revelation that must be accepted on faith. Joining the body when life begins, the soul will depart on the advent of death and is immortal. The soul is therefore, on a higher plane than the body and is a man's most important possession. Hence in the scale of Christian values this world takes second place to the next one. The care of the spirit, which is everlasting, has priority over the care of the temporal and mundane. Man's greatest concern, while alive on this earth, is to save his soul for eternity.

How dualism runs through Christian thinking and theology is evident in the saying of its Founder: "Render, therefore, unto Caesar the things that are Caesar's; and render unto God the things that are God's." The same pattern recurs in the treatise of Saint Augustine, *Concerning the City of God,* where an analogous distinction is drawn between two cities, the earthly and the heavenly. Men should resist the temptations and avoid the perils of the former. Let them seek the eternal bliss of the heavenly city by obeying the counsel to be perfect "even as your Father in Heaven is perfect." To apply these attitudes to actual government was the task initiated by one of the early popes, Gelasius I, and continued by various of his successors. Since men were compounded of two natures, one mortal and the other immortal, the organization of society—so the argument ran—must correspond to the dualism implanted in humanity by the Creator. The church should be the institution charged with the salvation of souls and the preparation in this life for the life everlasting. The state should have the responsibility for this-worldly, as opposed to other-worldly, affairs; that is to say, for the mortal sphere pertaining to the body. Church and state should be constituted as separate authorities, each paramount within its own bailiwick and possessing its own government. But how were the twain, *sacerdotium* and *imperium,* the ecclesiastical power and the temporal, the spiritual and the secular, to be related? The Gelasian answer envisaged them as "two swords" that could not be grasped and wielded by one hand. As God had endowed man with a soul separate from his body, so must church and state exist independently of each other. It would therefore be as wrong for an emperor to exercise spiritual power as for a pope to hold secular sway. What God had put asunder, let no man put together.

It is evident that the application of these formulas in practice depended on the validity of two assumptions: one, that the spheres of the ecclesiastical and temporal jurisdictions could in fact be separated, and the other, that the two institutions would respectively adhere to the status of equals and coordinates. Failure to fulfill either assumption would mean the death of dualism. How did the medieval Christian world meet these tests of its dogma?

THE THEORY OF DUALISM VERSUS THE CONDITION OF UNITY

The separation of the spiritual realm from the secular was more easily stated as an ideal than realized in actuality. The things that are Caesar's may be distinguishable from the things that are God's, yet both are in many areas intertwined. Thus, there were ceremonies and official acts of the state that were accompanied by prayer or required solemnizing by some religious affirmation. Treaties between rulers, for example, were signed and sworn under oath that called for the presence of the Bible and a priest. Governments were staffed by human beings who possessed souls, and who, being Christians, were sons of the church. The church could therefore call them to account if their governmental acts violated its canons of Christian duty. By the weapons of excommunication and interdict, the popes could even subdue a temporal ruler, as in the cases of the Emperor Henry IV and King John of England. The long drawn out investiture controversy revolved around the question of whether a bishop should be invested with the insignia of his office by the secular authority of the area or by an ecclesiastical superior. Conversely, while the church was involved in various functions of the state, so was the state immersed in matters vital to the church. The church, as its power waxed, became an integral part of the established order which the state existed to protect.[14] The church acquired land and buildings and other forms of property. It had large numbers of people, including serfs, working in its employ. It used for its own needs the revenues that accrued from its possessions and claimed to be exempt from contributing to the temporal treasury. If the state failed to maintain internal order, or was unable to protect its territories from invasion, the church ran the risk of

[14]For some evidence on this point, see Tocqueville, *Ancien Régime*, Part 2, Chap. 1.

looting and pillage. Hence, in a thousand ways lay matters were inter-locked with spiritual. The two spheres were separated by a meta-physical, not an iron, curtain, and it was not practicable to make them self-contained.

Similar difficulties were encountered with the effort to place the two institutions on that footing of equality that the Gelasian theory enunciated. Each of the partners, as occasion permitted or demanded, pressed its attack on the other. Each, at one time or another, struck at the foundations of Gelasianism by attempting either to subordinate one sword to the other or to grasp both with one hand. In this tussle for supremacy between church and state, the initial advantage lay with the church, and the first major blows at the doctrine of Gelasius were dealt by his papal successors. There were various reasons why this happened. For one thing, the theoretical postulates of Christianity were not easily reconciled with the concept of equal jurisdictions. To a Christian the soul was clearly on a higher plane than the body, life in the hereafter more important than the life here and now, eternity more significant than threescore years and ten. Hence in the hier-archy of Christian values the church outranked the state. If church-men argued that the spiritual sword should precede and overpower the temporal, who could gainsay such a contention? Furthermore, quite independently of theoretical beliefs, there were practical con-siderations that favored unity rather than dualism. This was especially so in the troubled times which followed the breakdown of the Roman Empire in the West, when Teutonic peoples invaded its territories and carved out new kingdoms. While the secular power was at the worst in dissolution, or at the best in flux, the sole focus and rallying point for society often proved to be the church. If there were in-stances when popes gratuitously clutched at both swords, there were also times when the church seized both through the state's default.

THE PAPAL REJECTION OF DUALISM

The papal attacks on the Gelasian doctrine were occasioned by two of the most prolonged and harassing issues of the medieval period: one concerning the claim of secular rulers to invest bishops with the symbols of their office, and the other arising over royal demands that clergy pay taxes to the state treasury. During the former of these controversies, which at one stage witnessed the capitulation of the Emperor Henry IV to Pope Gregory VII, the latter insisted that within the church the bishops were subordinate to the pope and that in church-state relations a defiant ruler could be excommunicated and his subjects absolved from their oaths of allegiance to him. This was tantamount to claiming for the papacy a power to depose a monarch, employable at the pope's discretion. Implicit in this, of course, was the view that of the two swords the *sacerdotium* was mightier than the *imperium*, a doctrine which, whether justifiable or not, was not Gelasian. But Gregory went even further. Mindful of the distinction that St. Augustine had drawn between the city of God and the earthly city, he proceeded to suggest —which Augustine had not —that the city of God was synonymous with the church whereas the earthly city, or kingdom of the Devil, was identifiable with the state, a pair of equations that definitely concluded with a debasement of the secular sphere in the hierarchy of Christian values!

The later controversy over the taxing power was, if anything, fiercer and more embittered. It reached on the side of the church, as its relative position weakened, the ultimate in extravagant contentions. In this struggle the leading protagonists were Pope Boniface VIII and Philip the Fair, King of France. Armed with the doctrine enunciated earlier by Innocent IV that the pope enjoyed *plenitudo potestatis* ("total power"), Boniface moved into the logically final ground and expressly rejected dualism. In a bull entitled *Unam Sanctam,* whose initial word stressed unity, the Pope claimed both swords—though the temporal one could be delegated to the secular arm to be wielded at ecclesiastical bidding. This pronouncement sealed the papal rejection of the goal of a divided society.

ATTACK ON DUALISM BY THE STATE

The position of the state during these controversies was one that switched as its power changed relatively to the church. If the temporal authorities were disorganized, as was not infrequently the case during the Dark Ages; if the empire, reconstituted by Charlemagne in 800 A.D., was more shadowy than real, and the emperor was insecure in his authority; if kings were weakened by the pretensions and powers of the feudal nobility; then the secular branch was scarcely so consolidated as to withstand a determined pope. Under such conditions the state was placed on the defensive, which forced its apologists to adhere fairly strictly to the doctrines of Gelasius. Acknowledging the monopoly of the church in the salvation of souls, the defenders of the state had to assert that over temporal matters the ruler derived his power directly from God—not indirectly via the pope as an intermediary. In other words, the things that are Caesar's are entrusted to Caesar by divine dispensation. For the powers that be (and this means all of them) are ordained of God. Upon this assumption, the state could preserve its role as the equal partner of the church.

In the later phases of the conflict, however, especially during the struggles between Boniface VIII and Philip and between Pope John XXII and the Emperor Ludwig of Bavaria, the weights were tipped in the balance on the secular side. This was due to the cumulative effect of political trends operating within the medieval system which finally contributed to its downfall. One such trend was the gradual consolidation of monarchical power at the expense of the nobility.[15] Another, associated with it, was the glimmer or dawning of national[16] sentiments—particularly evident when on the tax question the French clergy supported King Philip of France against the pope at Rome. A third was the eventual political weakening of the papacy because of internal corruption and lowered prestige in the period of the schism. Thus strengthened, the state was able to launch its own offensive, and therewith attack the Gelasian theory from the opposite flank. Its line of argument contended that the function of the church is to teach and preach. As an institution organized on this earth, the church falls within the category of this-worldly affairs. Hence its property is taxable by the state, while its personnel (the clergy) are merely one vocational group within society and, as such, subject to the jurisdiction of laymen. Like the contrary attempt of Boniface VIII, this, too, was a rejection of dualism. But the advocacy of unification now issued from the other direction, with the state casting itself in the paramount role.

All in all, the medieval experiment in these two respects must be judged a failure. Dualism did not work. The two spheres were not kept separate. The two jurisdictions did not continue equal and coordinate. The two swords were not brandished in harmony and unison. Too often they clashed against each other. Like a pair of unruly oxen harnessed to the same yoke, both parties sought to be rid of the Gelasian legacy. But the impasse which medievalism had reached by the early fifteenth century marked the end, not of the story, but only of an episode. A new epoch was arriving with new facts and formulas.[17]

[15]See Chap. 10, pp. 288–89.

[16]See Chap. 12, p. 355 ff.

[17]In countries that have fallen behind in the race for progress, old notions are likely to survive when they are discarded elsewhere. Twentieth century Spain has several medieval characteristics, and among them some living relics of medieval thought. This statement made in 1954 by the Cardinal Primate, Monsignor Play Daniel, could have been said in 1154: "Collaboration between the church and the regime must not be misunderstood. The two societies, religious and civil, are independent entities, each one in its own orbit. The church, however cordial its collaboration may be, is tied to no regime. It leaves to the state the glory of success and the responsibility for failure." Quoted in an article by Richard Mowrer, *Christian Science Monitor*, August 8, 1960.

THE RECONSTRUCTION OF UNITY

It is characteristic of the political process that, when a trend in one direction has reached a point of excess, a counteraction is likely in reverse. Sometimes the latter movement, too, will be developed to excess. With the breakdown of the attempt at dualism there came a new effort, or rather a second try, to reinstate the older principle that predated Constantine's conversion. In place of two spheres, two jurisdictions, two swords, there was now to be one. Instead of the state performing limited functions that covered a fraction of society, its sphere was now to be as wide as that of society. In lieu of limits, the state's range of action was to know no bounds but those of social need or necessity.

The yearning for unity was a not unintelligible reaction to the insecurities and discords of a divided society. There were many who had had their fill of conflicting claims, clashing loyalties, and antagonistic systems. They preferred to accept, with all its risks, a single authority. Unity at least meant that you knew whose laws and which commands to obey. Hence it is that Thomas Hobbes, describing the nature of the covenant on which a state and government are founded, urges the concentration of authority in these words: "The only way to erect such a Common Power, as may be able to defend them from the invasion of Forraigners, and the injuries of one another, . . . is, to conferre all their power and strength upon *one* Man, or upon *one* Assembly of men, that may reduce all their wills, by plurality of voices, unto *one* will. . . . "[18]   In keeping with this plea for unity, Hobbes views with suspicion, distrust, or outright antipathy the development within society of associations other than the state, since these may grow from subordinates into rivals of the central authority. Upon them he vents his displeasure in a wholesale indictment that embraces "the Ghostly Authority" of the church, the accumulation of too much treasure by a few, the loyalty of an army to an ambitious general, "the immoderate greatness of a town," and also "the great number of Corporations, which are as it were many lesser common-wealths in the bowels of a greater, like wormes in the entrayles of a naturall man." For full measure he adds to his list "the Liberty of Disputing against absolute Power, by pretenders to Politicall Prudence; which though bred for the most part in the Lees of the people; yet animated by False Doctrines, are perpetually meddling with the Fundamentall Lawes, to the molestation of the Common-wealth; like the little Wormes, which Physicians call *Ascarides*."[19]

---

[18]*Leviathan*, Part 2, Chap. 17 (Everyman's Library), p. 89. My italics. See Chap. 29 (pp. 174–75) for his explicit rejection of church-state dualism.

[19]*Leviathan*, Chap. 29

If allowance is made for the extravagant language, a clear meaning emerges. Hobbes is predisposed against a plurality of associations on grounds that are akin to Plato's objection to the family and private property. The coexistence of other associations alongside the state he considers a weakness to both state and society, because it subjects each individual, as a member of many groups, to diverse affiliations and potentially rival allegiances. The Hobbesian cure-all for the disorders of pluralism is as drastic, uncompromising, and clear-cut as the Platonic. All power must go to the state, and, within the state, to its supreme ruling element. Rid yourselves, so runs his advice, of a multiplicity of associations. Rally around the great association. Finally, since not all of his readers were rationalists, with a last flourish he inserts the keystone of religious faith into the archway of his "scientific" reasons for the foundation of the state: "This is the Generation of that great LEVIATHAN, or rather (to speake more reverently) of that *Mortall God*, to which wee owe under the *Immortall God*, our peace and defence."[20]

These excerpts from Hobbes have been chosen as representative of the new trend because of the rigorous and unflinching character of their logic. They have the simple merit of hewing the issue in sharp outline and high relief. But the ideas were not, of course, carved *in vacuo* or chiseled in thin air. They were excavated from the rock strata of facts, thrown up into new convolutions by the political earthquakes of the sixteenth and seventeenth centuries. The violence of those circumstances was due to the breakdown of the Gelasian formula and the search for new solutions.

UNIFORMITY OR TOLERATION?

Since the church had been partner or rival of the state for a thousand years, and since church-state relations were a bone of contention, it was to this problem that the new era first turned its attention. The relative strength of the two institutions, already changing with the emergence of nationalism, was decisively altered in the sixteenth century as the papacy weakened. In this respect, even more important than the internal decline of its organization (which could be, and was later, reconstructed) was the defection from Rome of large areas of Western Christendom. The Protestant Reformation, whose influence was most strongly felt in north central and northwestern Europe

[20]*Ibid.*, Chap. 17, p. 89. Italics and capitals in original.

and more among Teutonic and Scandinavian peoples than among Latins, established in a Christendom already divided between the Roman and Eastern Orthodox rites a further split within the West. From
that time to the present, to be a Christian in Western Europe or its
subsequent colonial offshoots did not necessarily mean acceptance of
the Roman rite or allegiance to papal authority. The Catholic church,
whose Greek name literally means "universal," no longer possessed a
universal following. The result has been that for five centuries no one
church in the West has enjoyed a monopoly of Christianity. Furthermore, when the dissolvent acids of Protestantism commenced their
corrosion of the once monolithic church, the same chemistry could
operate within the chinks and crevasses of Protestantism itself. The
practice of dissent could react upon its instigators; and the divisive
process, once started, set in motion a train of sects and schisms. Luth-
erans, Anglicans, Presbyterians, Baptists, Quakers, Methodists, and
others besides held out to mankind the keys to the Kingdom.

The political consequences of a fragmented Christianity were momentous alike for citizens individually and for the state of which they
were members. In spiritual matters the individual was no longer faced
with the compulsions of monopoly. The doctrine that "there is no
salvation outside the Church"[21] lost most of its effect, since there was
now a variety of churches, each proffering salvation. Excommunication lacked its former terror, for there were other communions to join.
The interdict, whereby medieval popes forbade obedience to a
heretical ruler, became an obsolete weapon. Skepticism now had full
scope in matters theological, since if many churches pointed out different roads to heaven, the curious were bound to inquire which one
was right.

What effect did all this have upon the state? In what ways was
government impelled to adjust to this new situation? The political
novelty lay in the fact that Christianity, which for a thousand years
had provided a unifying force in Western Europe, was now torn asunder and became a disruptive agent. Previously, if a ruler was prepared
to accept the church as a partner in his power or as his superior, there
would at least be relative harmony. But now a Christian ruler had to
choose between different churches (it being agreed that he could not
be non-Christian or atheist); and, once his personal choice was made,
he had to decide whether his subjects could choose differently from
himself or must adhere to the same communion. Thus arose the political issue of whether a person's religious beliefs were relevant to their
citizenship and their allegiance to their sovereign. Could Protestants

[21] *Extra ecclesiam nulla salus.*

tolerate Catholics, or Catholics tolerate Protestants as equally loyal members of the same state? Could one Protestant sect even tolerate another? Should the state, confronted with the fact of differences, exercise neutrality and ennoble the tolerance of diversity as an ideal of politics? Or should it require conformity to orthodoxy, if necessary by imposing it and persecuting heretics? To find the answers to these questions took more than two centuries in which throughout Europe much blood was spilled, martyrs were tortured and burned, great treasure was squandered, savage wars were fought, and bigotry reaped its bitter harvest of bestiality.

One answer—which was everywhere the first attempt, and in some places also the final outcome—proceeded on the assumptions that a person's religion is relevant to the ruler, that church and state must be identified by merger of their controlling authority, and that heresy is therefore treason. These doctrines were summarized in the terse Latin formula: *cujus regio, ejus religio* ("who controls the region, controls its religion"). Both Protestants, in areas where the Reformation was successful, and Catholics, where the Counter-Reformation held its ground, applied this formula to their adversaries. In England, for example, the Reformation was launched when Henry VIII, wanting to divorce his wife, obtained the support of Parliament for abolishing papal authority over the church in England, dissolved the monastic orders, and established a national church with himself at its head as "Defender of the Faith." These decisive events initiated a chain reaction of aftereffects, as when Henry sought to exact from the clergy an oath of allegiance to himself as their spiritual superior; when Mary attempted to reinstate Catholicism; when policy was once more reversed under Elizabeth I, who authorized a new prayer book and a revised liturgy; and when James II, a century too late, again led England back to Rome and lost his throne in the final assertion of triumphant Protestantism.[22]

The dreadful cost of internecine strife between irreconcilables prompted England at last to apply an alternative answer: that the state, though officially committed to an orthodoxy of its own, could safely permit its subjects to profess different religious beliefs—always

---

[22]The principle of the subordination of the church to the state is thus described by G. M. Trevelyan: "Bishop Jewel, the best exponent of the ideas of the early Elizabethan settlement, declared: 'This is our doctrine, that every soul, of what calling soever he be —be he monk, be he preacher, be he prophet, be he apostle—ought to be subject to King and magistrates.' The sphere of King and magistrates covered religion. All were agreed that there could be only one religion in the state, and all except Romanists and very rigorous Puritans were agreed that the state must decide what that religion should be." *Illustrated English Social History* (London: Longmans, Green & Co., Ltd., 1950), II, 34.

provided that this concession did not diminish their political allegiance. Through the eighteenth century only members of the Church of England were allowed by law to hold political office.[23] But in the third decade of the nineteenth century the disabilities of other faiths were removed and all posts, save the monarchy, were opened to their adherents. Gradually, the principle of tolerance, at first a hard-won necessity, was elevated into a virtue. In the United States, from the beginnings of its independent nationhood, public guarantees of private religious freedom, as well as a ban upon establishing an official religion, were incorporated into the legal structure of the governmental system.[24] Jefferson was the author of Virginia's notable *Act for Establishing Religious Freedom*, passed in 1786. Its preamble affirmed that the state stands neutral where matters of faith are involved: "Our civil rights have no dependence on our religious opinions, more than our opinions in physics or geometry." A few years afterwards, when the Bill of Rights was appended to the Constitution of the United States, the opening words of the first amendment declared: "Congress shall make no law respecting an establishment of religion, or prohibiting the free exercise thereof."

MONISM AGAIN: THE THEORY OF SOVEREIGNTY

The quest for a fresh formula with which to cut the Gordian knot of church-state relations did not lack results. In the sixteenth century a new principle took shape to express the departure from Gelasianism. This is the doctrine, of which so much has been heard from that time to the present, called sovereignty. An early exposition of it comes from the Frenchman Jean Bodin, who in 1576 published his *Six Books Concerning the Republic*. He writes: "Sovereignty is a power over citizens and subjects that is supreme and above the law."[25] In this phrasing of it, as in others, sovereignty is evidently a complex, embracing several ideas. Some of these, since sovereignty has many ramifications, fall under different headings among the five classic issues and will be discussed elsewhere.[26] But one aspect is central to the issue now being considered. In rejecting the view that the functions of the state should be exercised within a limited sphere, sovereignty asserted the limitless range of governmental activity. When

---

[23] Annually, however, after 1727, Parliament passed Indemnity Acts, exempting from legal penalties those who held public office without swearing the necessary oath.

[24] Prior to independence, of course, the leading example of religious toleration, thanks to Penn and the Quakers, was to be found in Pennsylvania.

[25] *Maiestas est summa in cives ac subditos legibusque soluta potestas.*

[26] See Chaps. 10, pp. 288–90, and 13, pp. 373–74 ff.

sovereignty was pronounced to be one and indivisible, this meant that the state was to assume (or resume what it enjoyed in Graeco-Roman days) the general direction and supervision of society. The very force of the new insistence upon unity was a measure of the reaction against dualism.

But a further clarification is necessary. It is evident that when a king, like Henry VIII of England, proclaimed himself head of the church, he was unifying the two spheres. The church was then in no position to set bounds to the sphere of politics. If the state was prepared to tolerate religious dissent, however, as later happened in Britain and the United States, did the abandonment of the demand for conformity imply that the state accepted limits to its power? The answer to this question, though arguable, is probably negative. Where the state tolerated diversity, it did so upon one important condition, whether tacit or expressed. A dividing line was supposed to be drawn between matters of public, and those of private, concern. The churches—any number of them—were permitted their freedom, on condition that they confined their activities to worshiping the Deity and teaching religious doctrine. Belief in this field was ascribed to the private conscience, for which reason the state would keep its hands off. But in the public domain the state maintained its claim to be sovereign, and any church that departed from the private sphere and entered the public arena would run the risk and pay the penalty of grappling with Leviathan. Hence if toleration existed, it did so on political sufferance. The state stood neutral because the stings of the churches were drawn. They, for their part, exercised their freedom on the condition of abstaining from designs to wield political power. Any breach of this condition would call down on ecclesiastical heads the full weight of sovereignty, that is, of secular supremacy.

Thus the wheel had swung full circle. The first experiment in setting bounds to the functions of the state ended in a restoration of the *status quo*. From the Greek concept of the all-embracing *polis* to the Bodinian or Hobbesian theory of sovereignty, a connecting thread is woven across the centuries. But the first challenge to the omnipotent state was not the last. It is time now to turn to the second attempt and observe how, when, and why, the pluralist cudgels were brandished anew.

7

SECOND ISSUE:

–2– Politics and Economics

THE ECONOMISTS' CASE FOR LIMITED GOVERNMENT

The second major attempt to limit the functions of the state began with a series of presuppositions, largely different from the first, but ended with a curious and unforeseen resemblance. This was the effort to restrict the authority of government by appeal to the authority of the individual. Following the train of thought that government maintains order, order calls for law, law requires enforcement, enforcement demands coercion, and coercion is the enemy of freedom, one may reach the conclusion that government and liberty are antithetical. From this it could follow that any enlargement of the functions of government would mean a corresponding reduction of liberty, so that those who prize the latter would have to confine their government within limits. Then, once those limits were set, individual human beings would be free to apply their energies at will outside the sphere remaining under the control of the state.

Historically this doctrine, whose result was to create a power vacuum wherever the state was unable to operate, preceded the Industrial Revolution. But the latter phenomenon released new forces which rushed to fill the void. During the nineteenth century the social order of many countries was well-nigh transformed by a series of economic changes. New scientific discoveries, new techniques of production, new forms of corporate organization, made possible the accumulation of new wealth without the inhibitions of political direction. Such wealth, when amassed, formed a reservoir of power, and its owners were accordingly able to challenge the rulers of the state for the leadership of society. In this indirect fashion, owing largely to the historical timing, the individualist doctrine, which the Renaissance and Reformation initiated, laid the ground for what was tantamount to a second venture in dualism. For there arose an economic theory, suited to the interests of businessmen, that preempted the individualistic argument and supplied its own bias to the notion of opposition to state authority. The effect of the doctrine—though seldom presented as explicitly as this—was a virtual bisection of society into a political order and an economic order, alloting to business a position within society coordinate with the government and carving out an economic sphere which should function as independently as possible of the state.

The similarity between this and the medieval system resides, of course, in the common presumption in favor of a limited government. The difference, however, lies in the source of the challenge to the state's monopoly of authority. It is now economics, rather than religion, which leads the assault upon the monistic state. It is now economists, businessmen, bankers, manufacturers—not the clergy—who provide the main impetus and drive toward pluralism. Hence it is in terms of economic policy, and over the relations between economics and politics, that many arguments about the functions of the state are framed and formulated. The state and the economy; government and business; politicians (or officials) and entrepreneurs; these, whether conceived as partners or rivals, resume the controversy where popes and emperors left off. Leviathan in the second round grapples with Mammon.

As there was an element of novelty in the problem which Christianity posed for the state from Constantine onwards, so there was an innovation in this changed relationship of the political and economic orders. Prior to the close of the eighteenth century the intimacy of the connection between politics and economics was not seriously questioned. The field of economics, originating as "household management," the literal meaning of the term, became, when writ large, the management of the community of households. As such, this management was scarcely distinguishable from the government of the community. Issues of public policy and choices between alternative social values were undeniably implicit in the nature of the economy which the political order protected. The problems of the economy, though these embraced their specialized and technical aspects, were not considered separable from the sphere controlled by the state. Take any of the major economic questions prior to the so-called Industrial Revolution—the tenure of land and its distribution, the accumulation of wealth, the provision of food supply, urban-rural relations, the pricing system, the direction of foreign trade, and so forth—these were treated as aspects of "political economy" dealing with subject matters which overlapped and finally fused. Opposition might be directed against specific instances of governmental power; and controversies might arise about the equity or expediency of this or that policy, but that the power of the state could include the general control of the economy was not an article of dispute.

STATE CONTROL OF THE ECONOMY IN ANTIQUITY

From Graeco-Roman antiquity to the eighteenth century the history of all European states provides testimony to support these generalizations. The list of economic functions which the state has performed in various places and periods is lengthy. Besides waging war, three major activities which long ago drew the government into affairs of commerce were communications, currency, and food supply. There was always, of course, a military motive behind the building of highways, as well as the need for speedier transmission of official edicts and diplomatic documents. Such reasons explain the lengthy Royal Road which the Persians constructed to link their inland capital of Susa with the Mediterranean seaboard of Asia Minor. Of the same character, and far more spectacular, was the famous network of highways which the Romans flung across the provinces where their legions trod. But the roads that were of service to cavalry, phalanx, or legion were usable also by the caravan. Under state auspices they provided the means for facilitating the flow of commerce and for its control by dues and tolls. The supply and issue of currency, too, was early undertaken by the state. When the direct barter of commodities was replaced by the use of a medium of exchange, or money, the state intervened for two impelling reasons. If there was to be such a medium, men had to know it, accept it, and have confidence in it. Consequently it was best to employ a single medium, common to all transactions, and issued by authority with some recognizable stamp or imprint. Furthermore, to be accepted, it should consist of a material which was scarce, durable, and not too bulky. Thus metals were generally in demand for currency and since their mining and coining could be very lucrative, the state found an added incentive to enter and then monopolize the business of money making. The coins of Athens, Corinth, and other states with far-flung commercial interests, spread extensively through the central and eastern Mediterranean. Wider still in later centuries was the dispersion of the *denarius,* financial symbol of Rome.

The concern of the state over food is explicable in terms which are in part economic, but to a great degree political. In the era when the city-state was the unit of government,[1] in addition to the natural dangers of crop failure due to drought or flood, the man-made perils of war exposed many communities to periodic risks of undernourishment or even starvation. A small city would ordinarily obtain its wheat and olive oil from the rural area adjacent to its walls. When states were at war, the contending armies always sought to destroy the standing wheat before it ripened and to cut the slow-maturing olive trees. Even in peacetime the largest cities were vulnerable because they imported their grain and oil from distant areas (the granaries being Sicily, North Africa, and what is now southwestern Russia). There was always the chance that political disorders abroad or piracy on the intervening seas might disrupt or curtail the supply. Hence ancient states often took strict measures to control the food market by bulk purchases overseas, naval protection for transports, and regulating the domestic price. To avoid riot and insurrection among the poor, state policy frequently required the sale of wheat at subsidized low prices or even its free distribution. The politics of food, involving direct governmental intervention, was a dictate of humanitarianism, expediency, and plain necessity.

In the three fields just discussed, different factors with varying influence led to similar results. The motives for state intervention in communications were mainly military; in coinage, mainly economic; in food supply, mainly political. But regardless of variations in emphasis, the feature common to all instances was the accepted view that a widespread social need occasioned and justified action by the government. All that was necessary was for the need to arise and be felt. Given these conditions, no obstacle was presented either in the form of ideas that the state ought not to enter this field or in the form of nongovernmental institutions powerful enough to do the job themselves and to resist conduct of the enterprise by the state.

THE MEDIEVAL SUBORDINATION OF ECONOMICS TO ETHICS

The infusion of Christian doctrine into the Graeco-Roman tradition did not, in this respect, produce a change of principle. When the church argued that there were limits to secular power, it sought to define these within a theological context. As to economic problems, neither church nor state denied or ignored their existence. But both institutions stood on common ground in believing that economic

[1]See Chap. 12, pp. 343–47.

affairs were part of the general ordering of this world and were therefore merged with, or subordinate to, the jurisdiction which each exercised in its respective sphere.[2] Now this did not mean that among the
issues which divided state and church there were none with economic
relevance. On the contrary, such disputes as those over the ownership
of land, the use of revenues from its produce, and the taxation of the
clergy were economic as well as political, and they were certainly
vital to both parties. But the bone of contention was not the question
whether economics formed an independent sphere of its own, but
whether the control over particular segments of the economy should
be vested in church or state; and each institution, in facing the challenge of the other, became more desperately anxious to strengthen
and secure the control of its own economic base.

The dominance in the medieval age of theological assumptions and
a Christian ethic was a further reason to impede a recognition of
autonomy for economic factors. If to charge interest for a loan or to
exact above a certain rate was branded "usury" and deemed "un-
Christian," then an economic matter was being decided on moral
grounds. Likewise, when prices rose too high for the poor to purchase
the necessaries of life, a policy of price control could be justified by
the concept of a "fair price" *(justum pretium)*. In this doctrine, economic, legal, theological, and ethical considerations were intertwined.
But the ethical category was the most important and was adopted as
the criterion for establishing an economic standard.

In connection with this problem there is an aspect of economic
organization in the Middle Ages which must be mentioned because it
might seem to rest on a theory that the economy forms an autonomous
branch of human behavior. What was the significance of the guilds
and the place that these succeeded in occupying in medieval society?
A guild was a group of persons organized, by virtue of their common
interest, for a particular economic activity. This might be composed of
merchants, traveling together in a caravan or stationed in one spot at
some great entrepôt (at Antwerp, London, Hamburg, or the like). Or,
it could be formed, not of middlemen supplying a service but of those
who produced a commodity. In a handicraft economy, artisans might
combine together and define their articles of membership. These

[2]Tocqueville supplies some striking examples of the economic activities of the church
in *Ancien Régime*, Part 2, Chap. 1. Likewise, R. H. Tawney has written: "The Papacy
was, in a sense, the greatest financial institution of the Middle Ages, and, as its fiscal
system was elaborated, things became, not better, but worse. . . . Practically, the Church
was an immense vested interest, implicated to the hilt in the economic fabric, especially
on the side of agriculture and land tenure. Itself the greatest of land-owners, it could
no more quarrel with the feudal structure. . . . " *Religion and the Rise of Capitalism*,
Chap. 1, Secs. i and iii.

could be extended to cover the definition of their craft, the maintenance of a standard of skill, the acceptance of apprentices, the rates
to be charged, and so on. Where guilds emerged, as in Flanders, the
German states, England, and elsewhere in central and western
Europe, they came into being from various causes and under pressure
of different circumstances. In some places they developed spontaneously as voluntary groupings for mutual protection (which often meant
the establishment of a local monopoly). Elsewhere they were made
artificially and were brought into existence by the governing authorities.

But irrespective of their origins, the guilds are relevant to this present analysis in that some of them operated with a considerable measure of autonomy. The self-regulation which their members attained,
often upon the legal basis of charters granting specific rights and
privileges, was tantamount to a high degree of independence in economic affairs. To state the position of the guilds, however, in stronger
language and to equate it with the ideals expounded by nineteenth
century economists is to be guilty of exaggeration and anachronism. A
king or a municipality might recognize the right of an association of
merchants or craftsmen substantially to regulate themselves in the
provision of their service or the application of their skill. If so, this was
done for reasons of expediency or utility. The policy did not conform
to, or evoke, the notion that economics pursues laws of its own and
functions best when it is independent of the laws of politics or ethics.

MERCANTILISM AND NATIONAL POWER

While the medieval world subordinated economics to ethics, and
the latter to theology, in the following period economics was no less
emphatically subordinated to calculations of political and military
power. When, therefore, the medieval dogma of dualism was replaced
by the politico-legal concept of sovereignty, it was to be expected that
a corresponding substitution would take place in the field of economic
policy and theory. The new doctrines which emerged to supersede
those of the Middle Ages, and which provided in economics a counterpart to sovereignty in politics, have been generally known, since
Adam Smith's critique, as mercantilism. This was a system of thought
that reacted against the kind of restraints to which the medieval
economy was subject—the restraints upon production, for instance,
which the craft guilds imposed, and the numerous restraints upon
commerce in the form of customs barriers between localities and tolls
on rivers and highways. In order to augment the national wealth, the
mercantile system considered it necessary to increase the volume of

production and exchange, to which end the restrictions of the medie-val order had to be modified or eliminated. The new philosophy held that a surplus of exports over imports was a sign of strength, the surplus being measured by the importation of bullion from the pur-chasing countries. Hence an inflow of gold and silver to replace an outflow of goods was approved as the sure index of a prosperous economy.

To assess the economic pros and cons of such ideas is beyond the scope of the present inquiry. The political implications, however, are relevant. The prime objective of policy, as it seemed to the mercantil-ists, was the furtherance of national power, and their emphasis was thus placed on national, in contrast to local or regional, interests. To this goal, so preeminently political in character, economic policy was supposed to contribute. The means that the mercantilist advocated, as distinct from the ends (that is, the stimulation of exports and the desire to accumulate bullion), could, of course, be argued as essentially economic propositions. But the employment of such means led di-rectly to political consequences—to trade wars, struggles for markets and for sources of raw materials, control of colonial settlements, and the rest. Hence under the aegis of mercantilism, economics was neces-sarily the serving maid of politics. One had only to demonstrate a connection between a particular economic policy and an advantage to national power, and there was no questioning the central assumption that the state had the right to intervene in any fashion in this or that sector of the economy. The difference between the medieval and the mercantilist economies lay not in the latter's emancipation of the eco-nomic order from governmental controls, but rather in its substitution of one type of governmental control (particularly if nationwide in scope) for another.

LAISSEZ-FAIRE—THE ECONOMISTS' DECLARATION OF INDEPENDENCE

When the weather vane of economic policy turned in the sixteenth century toward mercantilism, the change of direction, though signifi-cant, was not as momentous as that which ensued two centuries later. The new winds which started to blow in the mid-eighteenth century and prevailed throughout the nineteenth veered to the opposite pole. In fact, they pointed to a quarter of the compass previously unex-plored in the social organization and theorizing of the West. Judged from the standpoint of political science, the sharpest break in the continuity of economic thought occurs in the swing from mercantilism to its successor. The newcomer, as it then was, has passed under a number of names. Nowadays it is variously called economic liberalism, conservative economics, classical economics, or laissez-faire. Without prejudice to the other terms, the last of those descriptions will be employed here. What manner of novelty did laissez-faire, as an economic doctrine, impart to views about the state?

The essence of the novelty consisted in a bias against the state. Once that central point and its implications are grasped, the rest follows with logical consistency and plausibility. The historical reasons prompting that bias are no less significant than the character of the bias itself, and they help to explain the resulting consequences. For a point of departure one may select the publication in 1690 of John Locke's two *Treatises of Civil Government.* Writing to justify the peaceful English Revolution of 1688, Locke advocates a theory of the state that substitutes constitutionalism for arbitrary[3] power and limited for omnipotent government. To support the latter position, he assumes the existence of a law of nature that "belongs to men as men"[4] and not as citizens of a state. A natural social union, according to his belief, is chronologically prior, as it is logically prior, to the establishment of a political and legal union. In this state of nature, as he calls it, men are endowed with rights which, since they derive from natural law, are also natural. The collective name for these rights is "property"—an ambiguous usage, since Locke employs it both in an all-inclusive sense embracing "life, liberty, and estate" (where "estate" means material things that one may acquire and use), and in a restricted sense that equates it with estate only and omits life and liberty.[5] It is to enjoy their property (in either or both of those senses) more securely that human beings mutually contract to institute a government.[6] The legitimate powers of government are derived from that portion of their natural rights which human beings entrust to its care, and its functions are to preserve intact the rights that the citizens retain. Such suppositions glide readily to the evident conclusion that the scope of state activity is confined within the limits of the powers delegated to it. Should the state exceed those limits, it has passed out of bounds, becoming an invader of a domain where it had no right to enter.[7]

This concept, that there is a domain which the state may not enter, carries the corollary that there is a sphere of social activity which is

[3]For the meaning of these terms see Chap. 5, pp. 125–27.

[4]*Second Treatise of Civil Government,* Chap. 2, Sec. 14 (Everyman's Library), p. 124.

[5]For these conflicting usages, compare the passages in Secs. 87, 123, 31, pp. 159, 180, 132.

[6]*Second Treatise of Civil Government,* Secs. 85, 94, 138, pp. 158, 163–64, 187.

[7]*Ibid.,* Sec. 135, pp. 184–85.

best conducted either by individuals in their private capacity or by associations other than the state. (If there was not this corollary, it would be virtually pointless to argue in favor of limiting the functions of the state.) To pursue this inference and press it to a conclusion was the preoccupation of many thinkers from the middle of the eighteenth century to the mid-nineteenth. The next step forward after Locke was taken by a French school, called Physiocrats. Their philosophy was conceived in reaction against the mercantilist system, as that was designed and developed in France by Colbert, the finance minister of Louis XIV, and his successors. Whereas the basis of national wealth and strength appeared to mercantilists to reside in foreign commerce, favorable trade balances, and international movements of precious metals, to the Physiocratic view it lay in the land. Land was the primary productive resource and the chief original creator of wealth. Hence the prosperity of agriculture was the prime indicator of the national weal, and the interests of landholders overrode those of merchants. Such an outlook confirmed the Physiocrats in an antistate bias. For one thing, their solicitude for farming was linked with the contemporary, romantic appeal for a "return to nature," since it was easy to identify farming as man's "natural" occupation.[8] Just as Rousseau in the political theory of that period assumed a contrast between man's primitive goodness in an idealized state of nature and his corruption by society and the state at Paris and Versailles, so the economic doctrine of the Physiocrats employed the same concept for an assault upon the state.

To be precise, it was against the functions of the state as Colbert planned them that the Physiocrats protested—against restraints, restrictions, requirements, both negative and positive, which the state imposed upon the economy in the mercantile interest. The Physiocrats' reaction to this was a desire to curb and confine the sphere of the state, to limit it within boundaries, and leave the (mainly agrarian) economy to the operation of "nature." Their specific protest was voiced in the cry: "Leave us alone to produce what we want and to send our products where and how we want" *(laissez nous faire, laissez nous passer).* Shortened into *laissez-faire,* this was generalized into the crisp injunction addressed to the state: "Leave us alone!" The further cultivation and final flowering of these principles took place in Britain and the United States. Let us see what happened there in the last quarter of the eighteenth century and the first half of the nineteenth.

The Bible of the British movement was *The Wealth of Nations,* which Adam Smith, a Scottish professor of moral philosophy at the

[8]The title "physiocrat" means "rule by nature."

University of Glasgow, published in 1776. The book was epoch-making because of its contribution both to intellectual thinking and to government policies. Its significance is best judged nowadays by the influences and trends it set in motion, rather than by what Smith actually says and teaches. For the contents of the work embrace much that is outdated or has been superseded. Roughly a quarter of it is devoted to an indictment of the faults of mercantilism, wherein some of the strictures are merited but others are exaggerated and, perhaps, prejudiced. Smith's theory of value, which he bases upon the cost of labor expended in the production of a commodity, was discarded by many of his followers in the second half of the nineteenth century and would today be accepted in its naked simplicity by few contemporary economists. But, such criticisms aside, the permanent importance of *The Wealth of Nations* may be found in the general picture it paints of how a social order can function well. It is this picture, whether clarified by Smith in the highlights of the foreground or veiled in the half shadows of the background, that was reproduced, filled in, and more sharply delineated by such successors as David Ricardo and John Stuart Mill. It was this that became the leading doctrine in economic thought during most of the nineteenth century. It was this that epitomized the revolution in the attitudes toward the state of the economist and businessman.

What was this picture? Essentially it depicted the individual as the true unit and society as an artificial aggregate compounded of individuals in association. Assuming that everybody desires his self-interest; that the latter, translated into economic terms, means material enrichment; that each individual can best judge and choose for himself the means appropriate to his goal—then it follows that, the larger the sphere of action left to the initiative of private persons, the better. Through the enterprise that involves taking risks in the cut and thrust of competition, individuals will reap the best rewards for themselves and, in the aggregate, for society as a whole. So strongly was Smith dedicated to this individualistic doctrine, and so thoroughly did he apply it, that his antipathy for collective endeavors extended not only to various state activities, but also to the institution of the joint stock company. The latter, which has become a major instrument of a modern capitalist economy, he deprecated as having limited usefulness and as functioning successfully only when it possesses a protected monopoly or conducts some routine operation.[9]

If these presuppositions were granted, Smith still had to demon-

---

[9] *Wealth of Nations*, Vol. 2, V, Chap. 1, Part III, Article I (Everyman's Library), pp. 242–45. Smith's attitude to the joint stock company was common to most English economists through the nineteenth century.

strate that the results of free competition between individuals could be not only beneficial, but also harmonious. For this he relied upon a belief in "nature." The economic system, if men left it to the interplay of economic forces, would act in conformity with a set of laws of its own. Certain of these were based upon psychological assumptions of universal human egoism (for example, Gresham's law that the bad money drives out the good, because people will keep reliable currency and circulate the unreliable). Others were linked to the operation of physical factors also rooted in "nature" (for example, the law of diminishing returns, which tells the farmer that if he plants the same crop in the same field year after year, without replenishing the soil, he will eventually obtain decreasing yields). The analysis and elucidation of these laws formed the substance of economic science. Thus to discover and know them would assist men in conducting their economy according to nature.

THE BIAS AGAINST THE STATE

Where did the state fit into this order of thinking? As with most doctrines which place their faith in nature, a contrast was implied between what is natural and what is man-made, conventional, or artificial. Since nature, by definition, is right and good, the actions of man, unless conformable to nature, are likely to be wrong and bad. If nature has laws of its own, they must be beneficial. Human laws, when they contravene those of nature, are by that very fact unsound and harmful. From this point it is a short and simple step to conclude that human laws have a limited use since they are fruitful only if they assist nature and fruitless if they do not. The balance is so delicately poised, the interrelations so complex, between economic factors functioning as nature intends, that state direction is likely through clumsiness and misunderstanding to disturb or destroy the natural equilibrium. Hence a policy is adjudged wise when it enlarges the spheres of private activities and correspondingly restricts the range of governmental action. Such was the reasoning that led John Stuart Mill to write:

In all the more advanced communities, the great majority of things are worse done by the intervention of government, than the individuals most interested in the matter would do them, or cause them to be done, if left to themselves. . . . The preceding are the principal reasons, of a general character, in favor of restricting to the narrowest compass the intervention of a public authority in the business of a community: and few will dispute the more than sufficiency of these reasons, to throw, in every instance, the burden of making out a strong case, not on those who resist, but on those who recommend, government interference. *Laissez faire,* in short, should be the general practice:

every departure from it, unless required by some great good, is a certain evil.[10]

This revealing passage expresses the new way of thinking without equivocation. It asserts the superiority of private over public enterprise. It places upon the state the onus of proving that its functions are justified and beneficial. It supports, prima facie, any opposition to an extension of those functions. In a word, it typifies the bias against the state.[11]

Thus was launched a new attack upon the monistic doctrine of the omnipotent state. With its ramparts battered or breached, the way was open for inroads upon its supremacy. The main assault upon the citadel of power was, of course, the one conducted by business or in its name. In the medieval period, when the sphere of the state was curtailed by the claims of the church, the limits of political activity had been drawn along a line which simultaneously marked off the extent of religious activity; now the effect of circumscribing the powers of government was to widen the powers of economic associations.[12] The strategy of the offensive against the state conformed therefore in the main to the dictates of economic policy. If you could determine how much range was required by nature for the operation of its economic laws, you were by the same logic fixing the boundaries of the laws of government. The economic and political orders were thus considered to be coordinate, and a new species of dualism was accordingly envisaged as the substitute for monism.

As was to be expected, however, the main assault upon the state was aided and reinforced by a variety of flanking movements whose goal was not so much dualism as pluralism. Educational bodies, in their reassertion of "academic freedom"; religious bodies, seizing the occasion to renew their opposition to secular supremacy; these and others, pooling their forces with the economic agitation, formulated theories of society in terms not of a simple dualism but of complex interrelations between many groups of which the state was only one. Such pluralism is evidenced in the late nineteenth century viewpoints of the German theorist Von Gierke or the British legal historian Maitland. It is continued in the twentieth century by the French authority

[10]*Principles of Political Economy*, 1st ed., V, Chap. 11, Secs. 5, 7.

[11]An even stronger bias was expressed by Herbert Spencer in his *Social Statics* (1850) and *Man versus the State* (1884).

[12]The parallelism between the medieval relation of state to church and the nineteenth century relation of state to business is epigrammatically expressed by David Ogg, "The Scarlet Woman has been immured, and the Economic Man let loose," essay on "The Renaissance and Reformation" in *Great Events in History*, ed. G. R. S. Taylor (London: Cassell & Co., Ltd., 1934), p. 335.

on jurisprudence and political science Duguit; by the British political scientist Laski, and the British economist Cole in their earlier works; and by the American sociologist Robert M. MacIver.[13]

Nevertheless, in the modern statement of the issue the argument based upon economics and its case for dualism has bulked larger than the argument based upon a multiplicity of associations and their case for pluralism. The reasons for this are significant because of what they reveal about practical politics. To impose effective limits on the monistic state, more is required than the elaboration of a doctrine. A contrary power has to be mobilized to confront the power of the state. Under no other circumstances will the state abdicate from its monistic professions. But to organize a counterforce capable of resisting the state means, in fact, that some other association has to marshal its resources and build a following. It was precisely because the church had attained this position by the fourth century A.D. that Constantine's conversion was assured and state and church, in effect, established a partnership. If the church had not succeeded in mustering a widespread allegiance, it could not have effectively pressed the case for dualism. You have to create two institutions, or you waste your breath talking about two spheres. It was because this indispensable condition was repeated in the nineteenth century that dualism was converted from a potentiality of social theory into a political actuality.

BUSINESS POLICY IN VICTORIA'S BRITAIN

What reinforced the talk of laissez-faire economists was the rise of business firms powerful enough collectively to come to grips with the state. In Britain the writings of Smith, Ricardo, Mill, and Spencer coincided with the social ferment known by the title of Industrial Revolution. Aided by a series of technological inventions, the methods of manufacturing transformed the industrial process and created an economic structure of new design. Instead of the former handicraft

[13]Some of these men provide illuminating examples of the parallelism between medieval and nineteenth century thought on the subject of the state's relation to other associations. Maitland, impressed by the social role of the business corporation, elaborated a general theory of corporate groups and their independence of the state. The sources from which he drew much historical illustration and philosophical inspiration were medieval. Cole likewise developed in his early works a socialist counterpart to the businessmen's doctrine of a division between politics and economics. The resulting concept pictured a social order divided into two spheres, one for the production and distribution of wealth and the other for governmental functions. This he called guild socialism, reviving the name, and some of the theory, of the medieval guilds. Cole later abandoned his own doctrine, realizing that a split between politics and economics would be no more practicable than the attempted medieval separation of church and state.

system, in which a worker in textile production, for example, could own his fairly simple machine and operate it in his home, the new and complicated power-driven machinery involved a big capital outlay for plant and equipment. This change divorced the workmen from ownership of their machines and necessitated their assembling in factories which were owned by their employers. The latter, being called upon to make larger investments of capital, discovered in the joint stock company a flexible device for pooling and risking the savings of other persons along with their own. Flying the flag of the corporation, the business firm sailed on the buoyant crest of the economic tide.

Being first to apply the new techniques and stimulated by the Napoleonic Wars to increased industrial exertions, the manufacturers of Britain found themselves unrivaled in their domestic market and advantageously placed for international competition. Their efforts over the course of a century made it possible for Victoria's Britain to become "the workshop of the world," to treble its population, and to establish its position as the world's top-ranking nation and the center of the most extensive empire yet known to history. But this achievement was accompanied by demands from the business community that they be emancipated both from the requirements imposed upon production and commerce by mercantilism and also from the political control of landowners with agrarian preferences. This two-pronged drive against the mercantilists and the landed interests merged into a concentrated attack upon the protective tariff which artificially maintained the price of British-grown wheat. After the Reform Act of 1832 had transferred the control of the House of Commons to the urban middle class, it needed only the succession of potato crop failures in Ireland in the 1840's to bring about the momentous Repeal of the Corn Laws in 1846. Three years later by the repeal of the Navigation Acts, which had set restrictions on the external commerce of the colonies, Britain certified her full adoption of the principles of "free trade." Henceforth, as long as Britain's manufacturers could undersell any competitors and as long as her navy dominated the oceans, in neat reciprocity Trade followed the Flag and the Flag followed Trade.

The same symbol of freedom, which in the case of foreign trade was invoked to justify abolition of a tariff on imports, was also applied to the domestic sphere, although in two different senses. In a negative sense, the entrepreneur claimed freedom from control, which meant control by the state, as that was the only association capable of restraining him. Let the economic process function in obedience, not to laws of the state, but to laws of economics—a plea that might be rephrased to read: Let the businessman be a law unto himself. Interpreted in a positive sense, freedom meant the provision of opportunity to employ initiative, to take chances, to experiment, to innovate. This was buttressed in the law courts by the special doctrine of "freedom of contract," which became applicable to a variety of economic relationships—for example, those of business partners, of seller and purchaser, of master and servant. The doctrine assumed the like freedom and equal capacity of the contracting parties, voluntarily agreeing as individuals to transactions for mutual advantage. In any case, either connotation of freedom, the negative or the positive, spelled a warning to the state to keep its hands off.

JEFFERSONIAN IDEALS AND THE AMERICAN FRONTIER

The same antistate bias found a soil fertile for growth in the United States. But the reasons and reasoning were not identical with those that prevailed in Britain. The act of acquiring independence had involved both resistance to a hereditary monarch, who still possessed wide discretion in picking his own ministers (for example, Lord North) and defiance of a Parliament in which the inhabitants of colonies were not represented. When a government of limited power, based upon the Constitution, replaced a government which appeared in American eyes autocratic and absolute, the memories of opposition to King, Parliament, and royal governors left as part of their legacy a determination to circumscribe the sphere of activity allotted to the state.[14] Hence, when he wrote the Declaration of Independence, being confronted with the same problem John Locke had faced nine decades earlier, Thomas Jefferson adopted a similar solution and used Lockian terms and thoughts. He speaks, therefore, of inalienable rights, which exist prior to the state. He assumes that, in joining the state, men surrender to it a fraction only of their rights, while retaining the rest. It then becomes the duty of government to employ its power to maintain inviolate the rights that are reserved. As a consequence, the power of the state must always be limited.

Besides these ethical and political arguments, Jefferson's thesis was strengthened by his economic philosophy. Although the *Wealth of Nations* was given to the world in the same year as the Declaration, it is probable that Jefferson in the ensuing decade and a half derived his economic theories less from Adam Smith than from the French Physiocrats. Jefferson's personal predilection for an agrarian economy and the values of rural life chimed harmoniously with

[14]See Chap. 10, pp. 291 ff.

Physiocratic doctrines about agriculture and the importance of the landed interest. This preference was stated unequivocally in the *Notes on Virginia:*

Those who labor in the earth are the chosen people of God, if ever He had a chosen people, whose breasts He has made His peculiar deposit for substantial and genuine virtue. . . . Generally speaking, the proportion which the aggregate of the other classes of citizen bears in any State to that of its husbandmen, is the proportion of its unsound to its healthy parts, and is a good enough barometer whereby to measure its degree of corruption. While we have land to labor then, let us never wish to see our citizens occupied at a work-bench, or twirling a distaff. Carpenters, masons, smiths are wanting in husbandry; but, for the general operations of manufacture, let our workshops remain in Europe. . . . The mobs of great cities add just so much to the support of pure government, as sores do to the strength of the human body.

Later on, his stay in Europe, where he served as American Minister to France (1784–1789), and his residence in the capital city of Paris and observation of its citizens confirmed in Jefferson a distaste for large urban centers, which he regarded as politically unstable, economically parasitical, and socially corrupting. Thus, all elements in his makeup—the statesman, the Virginia gentleman-farmer, and the social philosopher—combined in the conclusion that a community of farmers, owning and working their own properties, constitutes the economic base for an ideal society. Let farmers, who live close to nature, be free to follow nature's laws. Let governments intervene only to protect and enlarge the range of private activities. For are not the best governed the least governed?

The conditions prevailing in the United States during the first half of the nineteenth century made this theory immediately attractive to many Americans. For in certain respects it corresponded with their actual mode of living. Not only had the United States succeeded in opposing what it regarded as autocracy, but the young nation, with independence assured, needed to populate and develop a territory of continental dimensions. As settlers flooded west in wave after wave, Jeffersonism was reborn with each extension of the frontier. The pioneers who tamed a wilderness of forest, prairie, river, mountain, and desert were driven by the varied stimuli of quest for adventure, economic necessity, or religious belief. To them the West beckoned as an escape from a secure but humdrum existence, from poverty, from religious intolerance. Assuredly there were government agencies which assisted and promoted this westward movement in countless respects. It was the federal authority in particular which negotiated the diplomatic treaties delimiting the international boundaries, which extended the United States by military action against Mexicans and Indians, which authorized grants of land from the public domain, which organized territories and admitted new states, and which helped to plan and underwrite the spread of highways, railroads, and canals. But at the same time, in a very real sense the expansion of the United States from the Atlantic to the Pacific was also an achievement of private persons and groups. The scouts and prospectors, lumbermen and cattlemen, trappers and traders, these did not act under political directives or conform to a state plan. They were rather the forerunners, blazing a trail along which others followed to do the work of development and settlement. Their efforts took them into regions inhabited, if at all, by Indians and beyond the immediate sway of the Constitution of the United States. They were, therefore, accustomed to fend for themselves, to go armed, and to discharge as individuals some of those functions (for example, the protection of persons and property) that in a longer-established society are transferred to the state and its officials. Such conditions, however, bordered perilously close upon anarchy. When no agencies existed to enact and enforce the law, who could say which citizen was law abiding and which the outlaw? As the population grew in the West, the need increased for a system of order that only the apparatus of government could provide.

While the taming of the frontier was the work both of public and private enterprise, because the pioneers were exposed to physical hardship and danger was it not natural for them to believe that the role of the state, however indispensable, was also a limited one? Thus as the frontier moved west during the nineteenth century, the theory of laissez-faire reflected with some accuracy the psychology and the social realities of a transcontinental expansion. But this was not as true of the more developed eastern seaboard,[15] where Hamiltonian mercantilist notions continued influential. After the Civil War, however, at the time of the tremendous industrial expansion of the East and the Midwest, laissez-faire here too came into its own. This was due to the simple fact that, as in Victoria's Britain, the leaders of American business were transforming the economy and were amassing capital and the power which it brings. Hence they felt less dependent on public initiative and more disposed to rely on their own.

THE CONSEQUENCES OF INDUSTRIAL CAPITALISM

Both in the United States and in Britain, the laissez-faire doctrine,

[15]For evidence, see Louis Hartz, *Economic Policy and Democratic Thought: Pennsylvania 1776-1860* (Cambridge, Mass.: Harvard University Press, 1948).

as was noted earlier, expressed a bias against the state. What consequences ensued when these ideas were put into practice? What have been the results of proceeding on the assumption that a good society is one in which governmental functions are confined to a minimum and economic activities enjoy the maximum of independence? Without attempting a detailed analysis, one can summarize the highlights and assess their political effect.

Some of the most notable changes were those which have occurred in the field of production. Never before in history has mankind come within reach of the abundance, actual or potential, that has lain in its grasp during the last century. The techniques of mass production have increased the sheer volume of commodities available to the consumer beyond previously known levels. The freeing of the channels of trade inside the nation-state, and freer trade—when practiced—across international boundaries, have together resulted in great extensions of the market, with many accompanying benefits. The existence of so many potential customers has helped to offset the proneness of mass production to standardize and, under the stimulus of competition, has encouraged diversification of the products offered for sale. The same factors have also contributed to price reductions, so that in many instances what once were luxuries for the few have become staples for the many. In general, all this has spelled itself out in a series of changes which, from the material standpoint, have contributed enormously to human well-being and in various countries, among which the United States is the preeminent example, have made possible the highest standards of living in the world.[16]

These improvements, however, have been associated with other changes that are less beneficial. If risk taking, individual autonomy, and entrepreneurial initiative have served as stimulants or intoxicants to induce new endeavors, they have also been responsible for some less pleasant aftereffects. The constructive achievements which laissez-faire capitalism has undeniably registered in the productive sphere are not matched by an equal record in the field of distribution. The main preoccupations of the economic order have been to organize the capacity to produce and to increase the gross accumulation of capital rather than to be concerned about the equities of distributive justice. As a consequence, even the wealthiest nations, such as

[16]Great and important as these gains are, it must not be forgotten that the credit for them belongs not to the single factor of the laissez-faire doctrine, but to a combination of factors of which this was only one. In the nineteenth century the economic progress of Britain was attributable in large measure to the fact that she was first in the field with industrialization, and thus possessed a competitive advantage. The similar progress of the United States was facilitated by this country's rich endowment of natural resources that laid the foundation for agricultural and industrial wealth.

Britain before 1914 or the United States since 1919, have included within their midst a significant percentage of underprivileged people, and the gulf dividing the very rich from the very poor became dangerously large. The same may perhaps be said in another way: An immoderate emphasis on individual freedom can, and does, accentuate inequalities between individuals.

Risk taking and enterprise, similarly, can be responsible for unwelcome consequences. When millions of persons take their several calculations of profit and loss and make decisions accordingly, their actions lead cumulatively to a collective result to which all have individually contributed (though none have willed it) and which may turn out mutually ruinous. A striking example of this is the phenomenon known as the business cycle. Over many decades under the normal conditions of peace—wars being considered abnormal—statisticians have been able to trace a cyclical movement of the economy through a succession of phases. Market conditions offering opportunities for sales and profits create an atmosphere of confident buoyancy, which encourages brisk expansion and new ventures. The desire to ride the crest of the wave tempts businessmen at times to gamble on commitments beyond their immediate resources. The crash comes when too many have overreached themselves and the economy as a whole slumps into a depression, more or less prolonged, after which by a gradual recovery it returns to the opening phase. Prosperity—depression—prosperity; boom—bust—boom; growth—contraction—growth, this recurrent rhythm can be otherwise described as a chronic condition of instability and insecurity.

The application of laissez-faire doctrines, particularly to an economy in the course of change from a mainly agrarian to a mainly industrial base, has included many by-products which are not merely economic but, in the broadest sense, social. For industrialism alters the physical environment in which men move, reshapes their everyday habits of living and working, and produces effects that are more drastic, the less there is of planning and regulation. Under shelter of the maxim "leave us alone," as it was practiced in Britain and the United States during the nineteenth century, the demands for manpower for the factories, mines, railroads, and all the services linked with them, brought into existence huge and sprawling cities where masses of human beings were overcrowded, overworked, underpaid, and underfed. The cities spread upon nature's landscape their blight of dirt and pollution, and upon their human inhabitants the blights of slums, disease, and squalor.[17] For many of the urban population, and cer-

---

[17]For an analysis of modern urbanization, see Lewis Mumford, *The Culture of Cities*

tainly for the poorest, the consequences were a life of dreariness and drudgery and a helpless feeling of being imprisoned in a vast, impersonal mechanism.

In large and wealthy countries, however, perhaps the most paradoxical result of laissez-faire has been its inability to live up to its own principles in certain critical sectors of the economy. The very freedom on which the system prided itself permitted ample opportunities for any who started with an initial advantage or who were unscrupulous in their means or who enjoyed exceptional luck to become richer and more powerful than their fellows. Despite its good intentions, the doctrine of freedom paved the road to privilege. The presence, side by side, of very rich and very poor; the concentration of wealth and, with it, of social power; the organization of trusts, cartels, and monopolies; and the rise of holding companies and interlocking directorates, such practices, where prevalent, negated the ideal of free competition among equal individuals. Indeed, to apply to huge corporations, owning assets that run into eight or more figures, the rights and attributes of a single flesh-and-blood individual is a fiction that does violence to the facts.[18] The point that systems professing laissez-faire and dedicated to free competition between individuals have in reality diverged widely from their own doctrines is fraught with far-reaching implications. The central concept of laissez-faire which upheld state inaction as a virtue formed an umbrella beneath whose shelter economic organizations could luxuriate and thrive. Since their activities were subject to few restraints, the largest and strongest could press their advantage to dominate the small and weak. Thus society found itself at grips with the problem which President Grover Cleveland expressed in the words: "It is a condition which confronts us, not a theory."[19] This condition was simply the fact that business corporations of great size had come into existence, wielding incalculable power by virtue of the numbers they employed, the assets they owned, and the services or commodities they sold. In many branches of the economy and of society in general, the paradoxical outcome of a doctrine that glorified the autonomous individual and simultaneously restricted the role of the state was to subordinate the great majority of individuals to the pressure of these very corporations. Once established, moreover, they were hard to dislodge, and their ability to survive had the effect both of accentuating the differences between rich and poor and of further diminishing equality of opportunity.

(New York: Harcourt, Brace & World, Inc., 1938).

[18]For a critique of this practice, see Thurman Arnold, *The Folklore of Capitalism* (New Haven: Yale University Press, 1937).

[19]*Annual Message to Congress,* 1887. Cleveland was referring to the issue of free trade versus protection. But his words had a much wider application.

THE POWER OF BUSINESS IN STATE AND SOCIETY

In yet another respect did the results of laissez-faire belie one of its initial assumptions. Proponents of the doctrine had called for limitations upon state power and the maximum of independence for the economic order. Let government and business stick to their own spheres so that individual human beings could have a large area for personal enterprise and be equal and free. Practice, however, did not bear out the theory. For as it grew big, business spelled power, power in any sense you will—the amassing of wealth, the control of men, the dispensing of social influence, and, above all, the mastery of the state. Such, indeed, was the ultimate and inescapable consequence of the success that business had registered. The enforced contraction of the state did not leave society devoid of potent associations. When state power was dammed up, a vacuum was created into which other forces were free to flow. What resulted, then, was not the extinction or even the limitation of power, but the substitution of one form for another —that is, of economic for political power. Men were still subject to controls. Only the controllers had changed.

Nor is that all. The substitution of economic for political power can be rephrased as the conquest or absorption of the political order by the economic order, of the state by business. Power generated in the economic sphere was transformed into political power. Laissez-faire did not insist that the state wither away, but rather that its branches be pruned and its growth circumscribed; while business plants could spread around and above, cutting the state off from sunlight and water. In this way political considerations were subordinated to economic and the powers of the state, when employed, were generally made to subserve what business deemed its interest. Hence the net result of the modern attempt to limit the functions of government and subdivide society into two or more spheres was curiously akin to the comparable medieval endeavor to organize the secular and the spiritual realms in parallel compartments. Both of these historic experiments proved to be unworkable. Both came to grief in the same manner. In neither instance was it possible to establish a clear line of demarcation. The medieval priest and the nineteenth century businessman stepped out beyond their original bounds of saving souls or capital, and their respective institutions, church and corporation, became deeply involved in the control of the entire social order. Each in turn, as the moment appeared advantageous, sought to establish the supremacy of his own functions over those of the state—the church with the claim that the hereafter was of deeper importance to man than the life now, and business with the assertion that a competitive system promoted freedom whereas the work of government rested basically upon coercion. Starting as pluralists or dualists, both ended as monists—the one seeking to unify mankind through obedience to the Ten Commandments and the Sermon on the Mount, the other, through the division of labor and the laws of supply and demand.

Nor does the similarity end there. The power wielded by the strongest of the medieval popes provoked a counterassertion of secular authority by emperors and kings, so that the aftermath of state-church dualism was the rise of the "sovereign" state. What has been the sequel to the nineteenth century experiment in state-business dualism?

Karl Marx, the intellectual founder of the organized Communist movement, asserted that capitalism contained in itself the seeds of its own destruction. It would, he predicted, be destroyed from within through the irreconcilability of the classes it created. That the forecast has turned out inaccurate is proven by facts whose potentialities Marx either underrated or misunderstood. He did not, for example, envisage the prospect that capitalism would develop a capacity for continuous adaptation in an evolutionary, rather than a revolutionary, manner. He did not expect that the different economic classes of owners and employees—the relation between whom he described as the *Klassenkampf* or "class war"—might eventually draw closer together instead of drifting asunder. Nor did he anticipate that liberal democracy, in his day largely a phenomenon of the middle class, would be extended to embrace the working class through a new formula for political partnership and a redefinition of citizenship. The suggestion that remedial measures might be employed to correct demonstrable abuses in the social order was alien to Marxian diagnosis and therapy. His cure for the disease was to kill the patient.

But to say that the "inevitable" revolution did not, in the most advanced industrial societies, explode as predestined does not mean that the capitalist economy has persisted unchanged through the fiery trials of the last century. On the contrary, the continuousness of change has been the one constant factor in these dynamic decades. What has differentiated the history of various modern peoples has been the character, extent, depth, and method of changes from which none has been exempt. The prediction of Marx would have been more accurate had he stated that industrial capitalism contained within itself the seeds of its own reconstruction and reform. Let us explore the evidence for this view and see by what mechanism those seeds were watered and nurtured.

Primarily it was industrialization which created the occasion and preconditions for new and momentous changes. Two of these must be singled out, since the train of events they set in motion became directly relevant to politics. When the technology of production summoned ever more complex machines into the service of mankind, it became imperative for an increasing number of the labor force to be commensurately skilled. Many phases of the manufacturing process called for human beings who could operate, tend, and repair an intricate piece of machinery; who could understand and follow elaborate instructions, written as well as verbal; who could calculate mathematically, and so on. In a word, industrialization demanded education, and mass production necessitated mass education. The large capital investment tied down in a manufacturing plant could not prudently be entrusted to the unschooled.

The other great innovation which must be laid at the door of industrialism was the geographical redistribution of human beings. For the first time in their history, countries that felt the full effects of the Industrial Revolution contained more inhabitants in the cities than on the land, more employees in factories and urban occupations generally than in agriculture, and higher densities of population per square mile. These changes led in turn to a spreading contagion of adverse conditions: slum dwellings, unsanitary streets, high death rates, juvenile delinquency, sweated labor, and ignorance. But the physical overcrowding which aggravated these evils made it possible for their victims to combine in searching for remedies. Thus a second offshoot of industrialism was the encouragement given to combination on a large scale. Hence, while laissez-faire doctrine emphasized the virtues of individuality, the growth of an industrial society tended to negate that same philosophy. Because it demanded mass organization, industry paved the way for collectivism, first private and then public.

THE RISE OF ORGANIZED UNIONS

There were various ways of mustering opposition to the wealth and power which a relatively small number of people had amassed under the laissez-faire system. One method was to argue that, if the root cause of the current trouble was the growth of overpowerful business corporations, the solution likewise must be found in the economic field. The proper counterpoise to an economic force was a rival economic force. It is in this light that such organizations as the trade unions, farm groups, and the consumers' cooperative movement can be understood. Two of these in the sphere of production and the third in that of consumption have been designed to offset the dominating position of the captains of industry.

Take trade unions as a case in point. The trade union is an association of employees banding together for their mutual protection and for improvement in their conditions of labor. Union activities may spring out of, or develop into, a desire for higher wages, shorter hours of work, employee welfare, job security, a share in factory management and production policy, and so forth. Composed of members who are insecure, because individually they are poorer and weaker than their employers, the trade union stands or falls by the degree of solidarity it can elicit. Hence the urgent stress laid by trade unionists upon discipline and cohesion, upon the closed shop or union shop, and their resentment of those whom they designate as strikebreakers, or "scabs."

The history of organized labor has been a checkered one. It was not long ago that the trade union—now a stock character of the modern economic drama—was viewed askance as an interloper on the legitimate stage. British law at the beginning of the nineteenth century allowed workingmen to contract individually with their employers, the two parties to each such agreement being considered free and equal. Since in fact, however, the bargaining power of an individual laborer was greatly inferior to that of an employer, the former sought to equalize conditions by contracting collectively and presenting a united front to obtain better terms. The employers thereupon besought the state to intervene by prohibiting such associations. Parliament responded with a series of Combination Acts, such as those of 1800 and 1825, which pronounced collective bargaining with an employer to be a combination in restraint of trade and any union formed for this purpose to be, as such, illegal. Not to be outdone, the courts supplemented the statutes by invoking against the unions the common-law doctrine of criminal conspiracy. Labor had to wait for the Trade Union Act of 1871, sponsored by a government of the Liberal Party, and for an amended Combination Act of 1875, sponsored by a ministry of conservatives, to remove the common-law and statutory bans upon trade unions and to accord them a protected status within the law. Even more severe than in Britain was the penalty at one time imposed by the state on trade unions or *syndicats,* in France, where they were classified as "seditious"—a word only one degree removed from "treasonable." The *syndicats* of the Third Republic were not fully legitimized until the passage of liberalizing legislation by the Ferry ministry in 1884.

In the United States incipient unionism fared in one respect better, in another respect worse, than its British counterpart. Here too the unions fell victim to the criminal conspiracy doctrine. But they shook themselves free of its incubus at an earlier date, being largely helped by a decision of the Supreme Court of Massachusetts in

1842.[20] After the Civil War, however, when the rapid expansion of manufacturing multiplied the number of industrial workers and their grievances, and when interstate unionism sought to advance in step with interstate commerce, the courts gave aid to employers by drawing out of their common-law arsenal a weapon forged for other uses but easily convertible to industrial strife. This was the injunction. By means of this an employer threatened with a strike, a picket line, or other hostile tactics could go before a judge and after a summary hearing obtain a court order to enjoin—that is, forbid—the union from pursuing its course of action. Only with the passage of the Norris-LaGuardia Act of 1932 was the power of the courts to issue injunctions in labor disputes diminished.

Similarly the opposition to combinations in restraint of trade—an opposition wholly consistent with the pure philosophy of competitive individualism—was pressed into an antilabor shape. This philosophy found statutory expression in the Sherman Antitrust Act of 1890. Enacted by Congress under its constitutional authority to regulate interstate commerce, the law prohibited, without exceptions, all combinations restricting the flow of trade across state lines. While the law was originally evoked by a public agitation against the power of big business and monopolistic abuses, its phrases were sufficiently general for the United States Supreme Court in 1908 to apply it to a union that had launched a strike against a manufacturer and had organized an interstate boycott of his product.[21] Although the Clayton Act of 1914 specifically exempted labor from the operation of the antitrust laws, the federal courts were still able to devise new deterrents on any union activity that would diminish the volume of interstate commerce. Only the circumstance of the economic depression of the early 1930's, and the ensuing change of political climate, secured in 1935 the passage of the Wagner Act, definitively guaranteeing to labor its right to organize[22] and to bargain collectively with management.

Trade unions have thus come a long distance. Formerly regarded as criminals holding legitimate business up to ransom, they are now recognized as having a proper place in the industrial process. But this position raised new problems. It became necessary to determine how broad are the powers accorded the unions, what positive limits should be set to those powers, and so on. Such issues were acutely formulated in Britain in 1927 and in the United States twenty years later. In 1926

---

[20]*Commonwealth* v. *Hunt,* 4 Metc. 111 (Mass. 1842).

[21]*Loewe* v. *Lawler* (the Danbury Hatters' case), 208 U.S. 274 (1908).

[22]This right the Supreme Court, when it upheld the Act's constitutionality, pronounced "fundamental." *National Labor Relations Board* v. *Jones and Laughlin Steel Corporation,* 301 U.S. 1 (1937).

a strike of British coal miners was extended by sympathetic action of other unions into a general strike, paralyzing the nation's economy for nine days. During the next year a Conservative majority in Parliament enacted the Trades Disputes Amendment Act, which among other changes made general strikes illegal. In the United States, when price controls were removed after the end of World War II, considerable industrial unrest occurred during 1946 in the efforts of unions to obtain higher wages. Thereupon the Eightieth Congress under Republican leadership adopted the Taft-Hartley Law, imposing a number of curbs upon labor organizations and tactics. In both cases, labor has agitated for the repeal of the statutory limitations, being successful in Britain in 1945 after the electoral victory of the Labor Party, but unsuccessful in the United States. Labor's critics point, with justification, to abuses of power on the part of certain unions—for example, the calling of jurisdictional strikes, the practice known as featherbedding, domination of some unions by oligarchies or virtual dictators as well as their infiltration by gangster elements, and the corrupt use of union funds. Labor's friends argue, however, that the attention of the public has been excessively focused on such abuses to provide a pretext for weakening the labor movement as a whole and for curbing the decently run unions along with the bad. In the sphere of management the same publicity has not been given to correspondingly serious faults—that is, to nepotism in appointments and promotions, extravagant salaries and pensions, the fiction of democratic control of the corporation by its shareholders, and the willingness of some businessmen to gain advantages by bribing civil servants and union officers.

EMERGENCE OF BIG GOVERNMENT

Where has this sequence of events led? The Industrial Revolution, geared to a doctrine of individualism and sparked by the power of private capital, permitted the business corporation to wax big and strong and evoked the challenge of its economic counterpart, the union. The latter, in order to present an effective challenge, had to be as big and strong as its adversary. If and when conflict between the two affected the interests of third parties or even disrupted the economy as a whole, who was to arbitrate or override their differences? The same holds true, of course, of the farmers, who have likewise organized to further their interests. At times they have been locked in battle with bankers and industrialists, at other times with labor. Indeed, when the economy is operating under strain, as during depression, inflation, or war, the unity of the social order may be impaired by struggles between business, labor, and agriculture. In such cases a still greater force is needed to keep order among elements always spirited and potentially unruly.

The logic of these circumstances pointed to the obvious conclusion. For remedying evils and adjusting conflicts such as those described, the only institution capable of doing the job was one which embraced everybody, which concerned itself with the general welfare, and which had power to enforce a settlement among the contestants—in other words, the state. Thus, by a converging of political pressures in its direction, the state was invoked as the chosen instrument to regulate and direct the forces of social change. But not the state as conceived by the philosophers of laissez-faire! Not the kind of state where good government was equated with little government! The new state had to be strong. Its functions had to be formulated in positive, not negative, terms. If changes originating in the economic sphere set up repercussions throughout the whole society, solutions on the political level were required to mitigate their effects. Hence the attempt to carve out for economics a sphere of its own, operating under laws of its own, had broken down. The social order was forced to reassert the primacy of politics over economics, of the state over business.

This truth is exemplified in the struggle, outlined above, of trade unions for recognition. What stands out in that account is the evolving role of the state. First, it appears in a passive capacity as the underwriter of the businessman's predominance; next, as a recording or certifying agency that admits unions to their place in the sun; and finally, as an institution of active authority, arbitrating rival claims, defining spheres of influence, and enforcing at least a minimum standard of cooperation. The more intense the economic struggle, the more strenuously men seek to enlist the power of the state in their support. No major interest in society has been reluctant to appeal to the state for preferential treatment when its advantage would thereby be promoted. The same businessmen who are supposed to speak in character when voicing complaints about government "interference" in the economic process are not loath to demand a customs tariff for the political protection of their market, or to accept the services of a Department of Commerce, or to influence monetary policy for their own pecuniary benefit. Farmers similarly welcome the work of the state when the price of their produce is raised by subsidies or when rural electrification brings labor-saving appliances to their barns and kitchens. And just as labor and business both turn to the state to invoke its authority against the other party, so have farmers besought governmental aid against the railroads, banks, and insurance companies, and equally against agricultural unionism. All theories to the contrary, the truth is that the pressure to enlarge the functions of government is exerted by everybody who needs some service otherwise unobtainable or who wishes to bolster a weak competitive position. If dependence on the state is labeled sin in the decalogue of classical economics, there is none virtuous enough to cast the first stone.

All these reasons explain why in every country touched by the effects of industrialism the functions of the state have since expanded so broadly. To diagnose the causes, however, is one thing; to describe and summarize their effects, another. In so vast and intricate a subject, it is not easy to depict clearly just how the activities of government have increased and what forms that increase has assumed. Nevertheless it is possible to pick one's way through the labyrinth if guided by a map of the main routes and directions. The rest of this chapter is intended to serve as such.

The role of the state in the economy can be studied in three relationships. First, the ownership and operation of an enterprise may be vested in the state rather than in private hands. This is often referred to as socialism or nationalization. Second, the ownership and actual administration may be left to private citizens, but the state lays down its rules and conditions or insists on certain policy requirements to which the private management must conform. In addition, the state may attempt to coordinate centrally the different aspects of the economy (production, investment, consumption, wages, profits, prices, et cetera) and may prescribe an overall plan to harmonize them. This is called a system of controls or regulation or planning or a managed economy. Third, the state may accept the obligation for the welfare of its citizens and may undertake to provide them with what are known as social services. To finance these it must obtain much of its revenue through taxation, taking most from those who have most and thereby, in some measure, redistributing incomes. Each of these developments—state ownership, state regulation, and state-provided social services—must be reviewed in turn.

1. Pros and Cons of Public Ownership. As was shown at the opening of this chapter, state ownership and operation is no novelty. The element of novelty consists only in determining whether this or that specific enterprise should be under public auspices or private. Some state-owned undertakings (coining money, for example) are so long established and universally accepted that they no longer evoke the raising of an eyebrow or shrug of a shoulder. Some, such as the generation of electric power, gave rise to classic controversy in the United States several decades ago, but are now less vehemently contested. Others, like the acquisition by the state of the British iron and steel industry in 1950, its subsequent return to private owners, and its later renationalization, continue to be centers of controversy.

If these facts follow any pattern, it appears to be simply that arguments about whether the state should undertake an activity or not are waged more intensely according to the recency and infrequency of its operation by the state and the strength of the opposing private interests. In this, as in other matters political, yesterday's heresies are often tomorrow's orthodoxies.

The number and the character of the enterprises owned by the state and operated by governments vary considerably from nation to nation. In the continental United States, besides the ubiquitous post office, the federal government performs such kinds of business as making loans to corporations and home owners, production and distribution of hydroelectric power, manufacture of fertilizers, maintenance of national parks with tourist facilities, and development of atomic energy. Various states have a monopoly in retail sales of liquor; some operate harbor terminals; and North Dakota is unique in having instituted a state bank, state grain elevators, and state crop insurance. At the local level numerous instances exist of municipalities owning transit systems and supplying gas, electricity, and water. All of these, however, are dwarfed by the agency which exercises considerably more influence on the economy than any other single organization, namely, the Department of Defense. In 1967 defense expenditures cost $70 billions, or 40 per cent of the federal budget. The assets of the department were reported at $184 billions, which was more than half the total value of federally owned property. One American in ten was employed either by the department directly or in a defense industry. Some two-thirds of all the money spent in the United States on industrial research and development is supplied by the federal government, and the bulk of this is channeled through the Pentagon. Small wonder that President Eisenhower drew attention in his farewell address to the increasing power of the "military-industrial complex."

In the second largest English-speaking democracy the trend toward state ownership is quite pronounced.[23] The telegraph and telephone systems were nationalized before World War I. During the interwar decades the same was done with radio broadcasting, with London's port and passenger transport, the generation and wholesale distribution of electricity, and civil aviation. Translated into terms of party politics, these facts mean, of course, that many socialist experiments were sanctioned by governments and parliaments controlled by Lib-

[23]See Table III, p. 202.

Table III

Prior to 1945	Acquired since 1945
Post Office (including Savings Bank)	Bank of England
Telegraph	Telecommunications
Telephone	Coal industry
Radio	Railroads (and ancillary services)
London Passenger Transport	Electricity (retail distribution)
Port of London	Gas (some of this municipally owned
Central Electricity Board (generation, prior to 1945)	
transmission, and wholesale dis-	Iron and steel
tribution)	Atomic energy
Civil aviation	

erals or Conservatives. After World War II, however, while the Labor party was in office, many more programs of this character were instituted than existed previously, and they were adopted in the short space of six years (1945-1951). The state became the owner of the Bank of England, the coal industry, gas supply, retailing of electricity, the railroads and canals, some of the long-haul road freight, overseas cables, and iron and steel works. A story similar in general character but varying as to detail could be told about most of the democracies on the continent of Europe and in the South Pacific.[24]

The arguments adduced in favor of state ownership are worth exploring. One familiar line of reasoning insists that whoever owns or controls a commodity like water or a service like transportation will wield power over his fellowmen since everybody needs it, and such power should be a function of public authority. A second argument contends that certain industries (coal, for example) are essential to the functioning of all the rest, so that, if it is desirable to plan and coordinate the economy as a whole, ownership of a few "key" concerns facilitates the regulation of the remainder. A third point is that certain of these undertakings require so much capital—either to start an infant industry or modernize an old one—that the state may well be the sole source for obtaining the necessary finance. Fourth, in cases where an enterprise is already a monopoly in private hands or could operate more efficiently if turned into one, the view is advanced that the kind of monopoly least dangerous to the people is that which they own through the instrumentality of the state. This argument, which is

[24]For the example of New Zealand, a highly socialized country, see my *Politics of Equality* (Chicago: University of Chicago Press, 1948).

wholly political in character, clearly assumes that the state in question is governed democratically; it does not apply to dictatorship. Finally, it is suggested—from a standpoint which is part political, part ethical —that to substitute state for private ownership is to change the guiding motif of the management from individual profit to public service, which some consider socially preferable.

The counterarguments, too, are many and stem from different preconceptions. Some are concerned about the potential danger to individual freedom in the fusion of economic with political power. Even a state of limited functions is potent enough, especially in view of the fact that weapons of coercion are at its disposal. Entrust to the government a series of functions which make it the arbiter of its citizens' livelihood, and you are but a few steps from tyranny. Taking another tack, some maintain that an attempt by the state to conduct a business activity is foredoomed to failure. That is because they regard the quest for individual profit as the most powerful of managerial incentives. A salaried state employee will not, they assume, be as efficient as an owner of a private business, and, in any case, the enterprise of the state employee is restricted by the ultimate control of a legislature filled with party politicians. Other objections are directed not so much at the feature of state ownership, but at the inherent difficulties of size. Bigness, whether in private or public organizations, is itself a liability, and may eventually be self-defeating because of the complex structure and elaborate procedure it necessitates. As the size increases, and as an undertaking approaches or becomes a monopoly, the elimination of competition may have the effect of reducing efficiency.

2. State Regulation and a Planned Economy. When the government, instead of owning an enterprise, regulates those who own it privately, the relationship of the state to the economic order raises some different problems. Not all, however, are dissimilar. Certain regulatory activities of the state, for example, are of such long standing or satisfy so universal a demand that they are accepted without question. Codes for safeguarding public health and sanitation fall into this category, as do provisions to ensure the supply of pure food and drugs. Only a generation ago the regulation of railroads and public utilities by public agencies which fix their rates, prescribe their service, and so forth, occasioned fierce political battles in states like Wisconsin and California and in the halls of Congress. The struggle to regulate some of the conditions of industrial employment was passionately conducted by factory workers, when their unions were weak, and as passionately resisted by the majority of employers. Today, businessmen, who, when it suited their pocketbooks, have not always flinched from price-fixing among themselves, object to price controls if administered by the state, and unions which in the past have invoked the aid of the state to place a floor below wages sometimes resent its efforts to stabilize them by putting a ceiling overhead.

As with public ownership, regulation incites the most acrimonious controversy when the forms it assumes are novel and those at whom it is directed are powerful. Some examples will illustrate the point. Control of farm production, including such details as the acreage sown, crops planted, hogs raised, and cattle slaughtered; control of stock market transactions and sales of securities by an examination of company assets and prospectuses; control of investment and credit; control of prices, wages, hours of labor, essential materials, and manpower; control of foreign exchange, together with the licensing of imports and exports; control of land use together with building permits, zoning ordinances, and rent restrictions—these and more have been for three decades the battlefields or battle cries of parties and pressure groups in their struggle for place, profit, and power.

In this elaborate network of regulation, what pattern is woven? When controls reach so far, not only into broad sectors, but into cracks and crevices of the economic and social orders, what overall purpose do they serve? Do they possess a rationale which imparts a meaning and a purpose? What more need be said about controls than that they tend to expand indefinitely?

The traditional case in their favor represents the relation of the state to the economic process as that of an umpire or arbitrator laying down and enforcing the rules of a contest in which private individuals and groups are engaged. When the latter are left purely to their own devices, abuses are bound to occur. Monopolies can fleece the public. Competition can become mutually ruinous. The weak can be forced to the wall. The drive of an acquisitive society for individual gain can imperil the foundations of the commonweal. Thus arises the need for the state to brandish its big stick at the monopolies; to dull the throat-cutting edge of competition; to shield the weak from extinction; and finally to succor that orphan child of individualism—the public interest. The saintly knight who leaps to the rescue and fends off the devils and dragons is the regulatory agency, whether department, commission, or board.

A system in which the state regulates, but private persons own and operate, is often extolled for combining the best of both worlds. While private ownership contributes its vaunted efficiency, because of the profit motive and competitive[25] stimulus, state surveillance ensures that service to the public interest will be considered along with profit. Or again, regulation may be lauded as a happy compromise between two extreme positions—that of outright public ownership and that of autonomous private ownership. Thus the regulated economy is pictured as a "middle way," lying between the aberrations both of socialism on the left and of laissez-faire capitalism on the right. An additional argument, with a different slant, emanates from Socialists, who are prepared to confine public ownership within certain bounds, but desire to plan the entire economic system in order to secure such nationally important ends as the prevention of mass unemployment, improvement in living standards for the poorest, expansion of exports, and a more stabilized economy with its consequent security.

As the nature of controls is diverse, so are the criticisms leveled against them. It is only to be expected that what some consider the advantages of regulation appear disadvantages to others. Thus if regulation is praised as a compromise or middle way, it is also condemned by those who find a halfway house less satisfying than journey's end. Advocates of unrestricted laissez-faire blame the system of state regulation for hampering their initiative and limiting their authority, while proponents of socialism claim that the public interest suffers if the state confines itself to laying down conditions and leaves their application to private operators. Thus instead of a union of public responsibility and private efficiency in harmonious wedlock, the results may exhibit divided authority and jurisdictional deadlock. Furthermore, if regulation is justified as a device which facilitates a planned economy, many will be found to condemn the means by rejecting the end. Planning in their view is administratively unworkable, economically inefficient, and politically dangerous. It calls for a large number of civil servants, subordinates economic decisions to political calculations, and concentrates enormous power under the sway of the state.

3. The Social Service State. Besides altering the economy by operating businesses of its own and regulating those of others, the state further intervenes with what are called social services. Under this heading belong the activities of the state in the areas of education, health, housing, and social security—to mention only four of the principal items. All these have excited political controversy at the time of their inception because the assumption of such responsibilities by the state involved bigger public expenditures and competition or conflict with private interests. When education in primary and secondary

---

[25]Except when the regulated undertaking enjoys a monopoly.

schools was first organized under public authority on a compulsory basis, the private institutions, both lay and ecclesiastical, which hitherto had monopolized the field, did not always welcome the entry of the state into a domain they considered theirs. Even nowadays there are still many countries where conflict between state and church schools continues to be acute. The care of health has long fallen under state purview because disease knows no boundaries and major epidemics can lead to social upheaval. Modern urbanization, with its congestion, has required strict public precautions in such matters as the provision of a safe water supply, disposal of sewage, sale of food, and isolation of the victims of contagious disease. In the middle decades of the present century stiff battles have been waged around proposals to organize medical service under state financing and control, proposals that invariably encounter the opposition of the medical associations. There has been a similar situation in housing, when governments have tried to stimulate the building of low-cost homes in competition with the majority of speculative contractors, lending firms, and banks. So, too, with social security, in which field modern states have launched comprehensive insurance programs which take away business from private companies by giving the citizen alternative protection.

Decade by decade the amounts spent on purposes of this kind have increased until more people than ever before have come to depend upon the annual continuation of these outlays, and, except in periods when war or the threat of it has necessitated huge expenditures for defense, social services have accounted for rising percentages of national budgets.[26] Nor is it without significance that the term "social service state" is frequently used to characterize the modern functions of government. Perhaps this is only another way of saying that the pressures impelling the state to carry more responsibilites of this character are geared to issues which are basic to contemporary politics. The reasons advanced in favor of social services will show why this is so. It would never have been necessary for the state to undertake such duties if there had not coexisted within the bosom of a single community those "two nations" of whom Disraeli wrote in *Sybil*—the rich and the poor. Through their wealth the rich could provide for the medication of their bodies and the education of their minds. They

[26]Between 1950 and 1963 and 1964, the percentage of gross national product devoted to social security and health rose in Great Britain from 9.6 to 11.8, in Sweden from 9.7 to 13.8, in Italy from 8.4 to 13.9, in the Netherlands from 8.0 to 13.4, in France from 11.5 to 15.4, in Belgium from 11.6 to 15.2, in West Germany from 14.8 to 16.1, and in Czechoslovakia from 12.4 to 16.8. (Article by Peter Townsend in *The Guardian* [London], January 2, 1969.)

could reside in homes that were spacious and gracious. They could vacation at will and retire in comfort. The poor could do none of these things. To the rich neither unemployment nor age presented a financial crisis since the revenue from the capital they accumulated did not cease to flow. To the poor the expectation of loss of earnings through age or unemployment was an ever-haunting dread. Those to whom the price of private education, private medicine, private housing, and private insurance was prohibitive could obtain such services from one source only, namely a public agency. This meant an appeal to the state by the use of the political process.

But what was the goal to be attained? Some called it equality, since they proposed to extend uniformly to all the benefits that wealth alone had been privileged to buy. Others named it social justice, for they thought that knowledge, health, a home, and economic security were due to all men and were not to be rationed in proportion to property or income. Irrespective of label, however, the movement behind social services was concerned with raising the level of the living standard of the less fortunate nearer to that of the more fortunate, and reducing the gap between "haves" and "have-nots." For the state to adopt such policies entailed, of course, the expenditure of large sums of money which could only be obtained from the pockets of those who possessed a surplus beyond their own needs. Consequently the extension of social services was accomplished by an increase in tax levies, the rise of tax levels, and by the imposition of new taxes, generally graduated, on personal income. Thus financed, the social services have the effect, up to a point, of redistributing income. Or, in other words, private wealth becomes subordinated to general welfare; economics yields priority to ethics; and it is politics which serves as the instrument whereby such change is accomplished.

THE CONTEMPORARY TREND

Since the economic functions of the state have undergone extension for more than half a century, their cumulative effect is now observable. If one attends to reality without letting one's judgment be unduly influenced by doctrine, the logic of fact compels a clear conclusion. At the turn of the century, capitalism and socialism were debated as opposites and were considered mutually exclusive. The issue was squarely joined. You could choose one alternative or the other. But you could not have both. What is the situation today? Obviously what has evolved in the advanced economies would be anathema to both Karl Marx and Herbert Spencer. Our contemporary system is neither socialist nor capitalist; it is a blend, with many features of both. Admittedly, the ingredients in the blend, and their amounts, vary from country to country. Sweden and Switzerland are not identical. Nor are the United States and the United Kingdom. But overall, the mature societies display a similar character. We do not nowadays, if we have any sense, dispute the abstract merits of the isms. Instead, we argue about this or that specific activity, and how its particular problems— economic, social and institutional—can be solved in the best interests of society at large. Our modern economies are mixed ones. Conceptually, this is confusing. But socially, the mixture works.

This judgment[27] is confirmed in an important comparative survey of the advanced economies by Andrew Shonfield. His study opens with the assertions that "the welfare aspect of the new capitalism is its most striking characteristic" and that "the datum line in the postwar world is full employment and the existence of policies aiming to maintain it." Summarizing the major institutional features which have characterized the economy since 1945, he lists the following: that public agencies now wield vastly greater influence on the management of the economy, that public expenditure on social welfare continues to increase, that the violence of the market in the private sector has been tamed, and that it is now taken for granted that real income per head should rise noticeably every year.[28]

Indeed it is significant that in their various ways the decisive influences of the modern world converge in the same general direction— and this despite differences of ideology, tradition, and aim. In the United States there are still many, in both politics and business, who pay public lip service to the capitalist creed in its early stage of development. But what we do is always more important than what we say; and, theories to the contrary, in North America the economic functions of government show no signs of diminishing. Nor, if we attempt to forecast the future, is their decrease to be expected. As long as the growth of population results in more pressure on resources and land, as long as we maintain so high a level of military expenditures, and as long as we invest in atomic energy and the exploration of space, the operations of the state will continue to be the major influence in our economy.

That the state should occupy this role in the countries with Communist rule is also contrary to doctrine, since Marxism predicted the state would wither away when a classless society had been achieved—and the Soviet Union has now had over half a century since the Bolshevik Revolution to achieve that Utopian ideal. What decided the trend in

[27]I expressed this view in the 3rd edition of this work, published in 1965.

[28]Andrew Shonfield, *Modern Capitalism* (New York and London: Oxford University Press, 1965), pp. 7, 38, 66-67.

the Communist governments, however, was their need for the rapid development of backward communities. For that end, the state had to give the lead, and did. But it should be noted that among the countries where a Communist party prevails there is one that is considerably more openminded, experimental, and creative than the rest, namely, Yugoslavia. When the Yugoslavs discovered that Stalinism did not work, their system became highly flexible and pragmatic; it is evolving through an ingenious mixture of local initiative, community and private ownership, and central planning. A Yugoslav Marxist will be the first to insist that in his scheme of socialism the owners of each particular economic enterprise, industrial or commercial, are the people who work and produce there, and not the state.[29] This relative liberalism of the Yugoslavs has produced a contagious effect on their neighbors in Eastern Europe, who have also been impressed by the spectacular growth recorded in the six countries of the European Community[30] and in the United States and Japan. In consequence, there have been sporadic, yet repeated, attempts in one communist regime after another to modify the highly centralized system of state planning by intermixture with some elements of a market economy. In the most dramatic case, however, that of Czechoslovakia, when such changes were associated with new freedoms of political assembly and public discussion, the Soviet government and its allies in the Warsaw Pact invaded and occupied the country in August, 1968, forcing a movement in reverse.

As for the underdeveloped areas of Asia and Africa, many of which formerly belonged to Western empires, the first desire of their governments on attaining independence is to develop their economies in all possible directions at the greatest possible speed. Because of the lack of private capital, they depend overwhelmingly on the state both to obtain foreign aid—whether from other governments, international agencies, or private interests—and to plan their domestic priorities. Nor is it exaggerating to say that everywhere in the contemporary world at least half of the responsibilities of governments are economic in character. Granted the technology of today, the military perils, the complex interdependence of social groups, and the political articulateness of increasing numbers, how can it be otherwise?

FROM JUSTICE TO WELFARE

These results have an important bearing on the discussion in Chapter 3, where it was observed that the functions of the state undergo

---

[29]On this topic, see also Chap. 11, pp. 315–18.

[30]Belgium, France, Italy, Luxemburg, the Netherlands, and West Germany.

a progression. From its initial duty of providing protection, the responsibilities of the state expanded into a framework of order which involves a concept of justice. But this latter ideal, deriving from Greek social theory and Roman legal practice, did not mark the end of the quest for a better life through political means. With the advent of the Christian religion, the function of charity was much extolled in the West, and for many centuries was church administered. The system, however, whereby religious agencies provided education, hospital care, or aid to paupers and aged could cover only part of the total need, because of the limitations of finance and staff. Hence, if all the needy were to obtain relief and all the ignorant be educated, the task must devolve upon an institution that could mobilize the resources of the entire community. Thus the state entered the field, though not without challenge and sometimes stubborn resistance from churches which did not relish the loss of their monopoly. From another quarter comparable opposition was expressed by thinkers, of the Herbert Spencer variety, who saw in social services—and the tax revenues required to finance them—an interference in the "natural" operation of economic laws. The laissez-faire economists were often moral and merciful men, as individuals, but their economics, as a science, was indifferent to ethics and callous to human suffering. When economics was once more united with politics, it was at the same time subordinated to ethics.

What this means, in short, is that the state, converting charity from the private concern of the church into a public charge of government, and injecting morality into the economic order, has itself progressed from justice to the ideal of welfare. For welfare is simply humanized justice. The protective state, the law and order state, the just state, the welfare state—such has been the aspiration, and in some places an actual trend, in the upward evolution of politics through four thousand years of effort and experiment.

THE PRIMACY OF THE STATE

Thus a survey of the modern relationship between politics and economics leads to a conclusion paralleling the story of earlier relations between church and state. In both cases the same attempt was made to limit the functions of government. In both cases, doctrines were formulated to facilitate the acquisition of power by rival institutions. In both cases, a rival to the state did emerge that developed sufficient strength to make its claims effective. But what was the aftermath? The sequel to both experiments has been similar. The attempts to restrict the sphere of the state eventually broke down. In neither case was it possible to draw a dividing line which could be practicable and mutually acceptable. Instead of harmony between the respective spheres, clash and conflict, overlap and intrusion, became the order of the day. The medieval society and the modern were faced with the problem, not of maintaining coordinate spheres, but of deciding whether church or business should control the state or the state should control them. In each case the same verdict has been rendered, and therefore in the mid-twentieth century we are witnessing the repetition of what occurred in so many parts of Europe during the sixteenth, namely, the reassertion of the primacy of the state over other associations.

Now, the evidence of history must be taken into account when the relation of the state to society is considered in terms of the choices posed at the beginning of Chapter 6. What we ought to do must allow for what we can do, and what we think we can do in the future should be guided by the experience of what was tried and done in the past. Granted, we should never concede that what has previously been undesirable or impossible will necessarily be undesirable or impossible for the future. The solution of this issue, the choice between pluralism and monism, in the distant future is not predetermined by past decisions, be the latter what they may. Men may forget their history, or they may knowingly decide to disregard it, or conceivably they may fundamentally restructure their social order. In the present and for the immediate future, however, it seems most probable that the odds are against pluralism. It is unlikely after two failures that success would be achieved the third time.

Modern society becomes ever more interdependent in its functions and groupings. This interdependence posits an essential unity. The latter, if it is to be effective, must be expressed through institutional forms. The pluralism which takes the pure form of individualism has had to bow before the group needs and pressures of contemporary social organization. The pluralism that welcomes the interplay of many autonomous associations provides no solution on the occasions when they conflict. The pluralism that adopts the special form of dualism cannot in practice achieve what it sets out to do, namely, to bisect society in twain. Nowadays, therefore, one is left with monism as the more practicable solution, and with the state as the ultimate coordinator of society. The family cannot serve in this role, since its unit is too small. Religion cannot do it, because there are so many faiths and churches, and modern life, anyway, becomes increasingly secular, scientific, and skeptical. Business cannot do it, because economic considerations alone do not satisfy enough of the needs for which men are socially organized.

By elimination, therefore, one is left with the state.[31] But to say that is only to solve certain problems and simultaneously to take arms against another sea of troubles. What if the monistic state be perverted? What if it be a tyranny? What if it should outrageously abuse its powers over society? Will the actual government conform to what the state ought to be?

These questions lead us to consider the third issue.

---

[31]The discussion of the problem is resumed in Chap. 14. See pp. 426–29.

8

THIRD ISSUE:

–1– Authority and the Authoritarians

THE JUSTIFICATION OF AUTHORITY

The choice of techniques whereby the government carries out its functions for the members of the state presents the third of the great issues of politics. If the objectives of government are to evolve beyond protection, and if they are ever to arrive at welfare, the means must likewise be transformed. For the selection of means is directly related to the realization of ends. This is not the same as saying that the end justifies the means. The point is rather that, whatever are the goals which one desires to attain, the choice of the appropriate means becomes a condition of success, and furthermore, the selection of methods greatly influences the results which are actually achieved. The force that is necessary to guarantee protection is not enough by itself to establish justice, still less to promote welfare. The state must, therefore, rise to the challenge of modifying its original methods, or its usefulness to society will be vitiated. The questions whether this can be done, and how, create the issue.

Political decisions must be translated into governmental acts. These require enforcement, which admits of two alternatives: to impose coercive power or to elicit a willing support. Thus the problem, raised in Chapter 3, of the relation between force and consent becomes paramount. For it is the selection of means that helps to mold the attitudes of the governed and imparts to government much of its legitimacy and practical effectiveness. Those in office seek to convert power into authority, while the governed ask of authority that it serve their need. "By what right do you claim to do this?" "Whence comes your power?" "Who gives you authority?" These typical questions are more persistently raised concerning the state than any other human association, for the reason that its functions produce such direct effects upon everybody and are so intimately related to life and welfare. Moreover, there comes a time when those in authority or their successors lose the popular support that once brought them to office. As power slips from them, the problem arises of transferring to other hands the authority which that power once sanctioned. Can this be done peacefully? Who are to be the next inheritors of power? And how, if recognized, is their possession of it legitimized? It is precisely because of the character of the functions of government, and because abuse of power and conflicts over its transfer can be so dangerous, that controversies occur about authorization. If the state were a "do-little" body, few would care to search the validity of its title deeds. But wherever much power is concentrated, many will insist that might be adequately endowed with right.

Normally, men obey the state. That is, nearly all of us do so most of the time. For its part, the state expects this obedience, can ordinarily count upon it, and exacts its penalties for disobedience. Why does this happen? A common answer is that of certain psychologists who explain a human being as the product of his environment. His conduct consists in the main of patterns of behavior designed for him, rather than by him. His parents, teachers, friends, customers, clients, and employers help to construct within him a strong pressure to conform. To that pressure he will habitually respond both because he desires that approval and because swimming with the tide is always easier, as well as more agreeable, than battling against the current.

But this explanation, even if correct, is only partial. It describes how men behave and states, in terms of motivation, what drives them. It does not explain two important matters. One is the fact of opposition to the state, for, even if obedience to constituted authority is the normal rule, there are notable instances from every age of protest, criticism, and resistance. How are we to explain the dissenter, the nonconformist, the unorthodox, the heretic, the martyr? History would have no record of rebels or revolution, of movements for reform or independence, if its sole determinant were submission to the powers that are. Second, it should not be forgotten that conformists themselves look for reasoned justifications of what they are doing. Those who administer the state usually tell their fellow citizens or subjects that they have to obey, and also that they ought to do so. The problem, therefore, is broader in scope than a description of how people behave. It involves the moral issue: Does the state rightfully command, and ought one to obey? By what means does power acquire an ethic and officialdom its legitimacy? What is there, after all, to distinguish between two men bearing a gun—the policeman and the gang-ster?

DOMINATION VERSUS ACCOUNTABILITY

To such questions supporters of different political systems have off-ered many answers. These can be sorted into two groups, based on diametrically opposed philosophies of the relation between govern-ment and the governed. If government is thought of as a procedure whereby a small number of persons issue orders to a much larger number who are their subjects and, as such, their inferiors, then au-thority is supposedly vested in the ruling class by virtue of the superi-ority they possess and is handed down to the mass of the community from on high. Civil government, so viewed, is likened to military disci-pline. As soldiers obey their commanding officers, so the people obey the state and are accountable to it. A ruler can no more be held to account by his subjects than a general by his army. The opposite doctrine reverses this relationship. It makes the ruler answerable for his actions instead of the people for theirs. The source of authority is the mass of the community who are to be regarded as fellow citizens rather than as subjects. It is they who grant power, they who super-vise its use, they who may revoke it. Authority is not something which a few impose upon many; it is what many temporarily delegate to a few.

This disagreement leads to results that are far-reaching. The charac-ter of the state and the structure of its government are directly related to this controversy about the origins of political power. According to whether authority is believed to flow from the governed or to be exercised over them, institutions will be differently constructed. In the latter case the ruling group will organize to maintain its supremacy and will repress opposition. It will employ techniques of intimidation and coercion. Not daring to allow any challenge to its preeminence, it will use the police, prisons, and army as central organs of adminis-tration. In all these respects it will constitute a dictatorship. If the guiding principle, on the other hand, is to assert popular control, means must be discovered for making officials govern on behalf of the people, and for keeping them within the limits of their powers. The people must choose certain of their number to act as agents for them all. Systems must be devised to enforce the responsibility of the gov-ernment to the governed. For this purpose the state will be rooted in constitutionalism and the rule of law. It will institute an electoral process and welcome the existence of two or more parties which offer a variety of programs and leadership. The choice between these alternatives must be considered in some detail, since it is crucial to the distinction between dictatorship and democracy.

TYPES OF AUTHORITARIANISM

When a government is founded on the opinion that its authority does not originate with those over whom it is exercised, some alternative source must be contrived. Two possibilities suggest themselves. Authority can be imagined to descend upon the government, like manna from Heaven, as a gift of some higher power outside and above both the government and the governed. Or it can be thought to inhere in the rulers by virtue of certain qualities with which they are uniquely endowed.

1. Divine Right. The belief that the right to rule over other human beings comes from a higher than human source has lived long and dies hard. Nor must one search far for the reason why an idea of this kind should have been advanced. Often bewildered by the world around him, not fully understanding the operation of its physical laws, and therefore unable to control his environment, man has sought to erect frail shelters of security against the mysteries of the universe that dwarfs him. Before the modern age of experimental science he ventured to bend to his will the concealed and unknown forces whose effects he observed, but whose causes he did not comprehend. If drought were threatening his crops, with solemn ritual he poured water upon a stone, a symbolic act intended to draw rain from the reluctant skies. Desiring to be rid of some hated person, he fashioned an effigy which he then stabbed or mutilated, thinking thereby to bring on his enemy disaster and death.[1] But when the result did not conform to the hope, it occurred to man that he might entreat the forces which he could not command. Prayer might accomplish what magic did not. In this case, however, since man was begging a favor, he must obtain the good will of the power or powers to whom he made appeal. To attain this end certain observances were necessary on his part. He must be careful to give no offense to his deities and incur no displeasure. Thus, he must live righteously, that is, in conformity with divine will, and must approach his deity in a proper manner, that is, with the correct ritual. To know this will and ritual was of supreme importance. Indeed, in such matters as the conduct of war or the assurance of food supply, the life and death of the community might be at stake. To placate and enlist the aid of a deity was

[1]See James Frazer, *The Golden Bough*, one-volume abridgement (London: Macmillan & Co., Ltd., 1941), Chap. 3.

therefore no casual affair but an act fundamental to the general welfare.[2]

These are some considerations that explain the close connection so frequently existing between government and religion or magic. Where much depends upon maintaining the right relation with the power pervading the universe, governmental responsibilities like war and welfare become intertwined with the ceremonies of witchcraft or worship. It calls for special skills, and therefore specialized personnel, to mediate on man's behalf between the world that is seen and that which is unseen. He who holds the key to the mysteries that determine human fates wields power.

Before modern times, when communication was severely restricted and few people ever had the occasion or the means to travel far from their homes, the reality with which most persons were directly acquainted was bounded by a close and closed horizon. Beyond that little which was known, the world shaded off into the myriad gradations of the vast unknown, all endowed with equal credibility. In this vein, Doris Mary Stenton has written of the belief in the supernatural which was so natural to the Middle Ages:

The hard-headed practicality of the medieval people is nowhere more clearly shown than in their attitude to God and religion. They lived in a small world and knew nothing of its place in the universe. The conception of a globe revolving in space in a determinable relationship to other bodies had not dawned upon even the most advanced thinkers. Beyond the limits of their known world lay an unknown fringe of incalculable depth, sea or land, equally remote and full of perils. Their lives within the little medieval world were hard and brief and they accepted unquestioningly a religion that offered to the poor and hungry an eternity of satisfaction. Since so much of the world about them was unknown the invisibility of the next world did not trouble them. It was as real to them as remote lands to-day are real to the untravelled. They were equally assured of its existence.[3]

For the purpose of this analysis, it is unnecessary to inquire which kind of authority, human or superhuman, was the prior and superior. Indeed, the gaps and silences of prehistory do not allow a conclusive answer to the question: Did those who already possessed political power look for reinforcements from magic or religion, or did medicine men and priests project their influence into the general arena of government? All that can be stated with certainty is that human and superhuman authority have often been found in the closest relation to each other. The phenomenon of the priest-king or god-ruler is widely

[2]*Ibid.*, Chap. 4.

[3]Doris Mary Stenton, *English Society in the Early Middle Ages* (Baltimore: Penguin Books, Inc., 1951), p. 203.

spread among peoples at different levels of cultural development. Over the centuries and around the world the research of anthropologists and historians has discovered countless examples of rulers who perform magical or religious rites or are worshiped as living deities or trace back their lineage to a divine ancestor; of prophets who announce they have heard the word of God and administer His code of commandments; of priests whom the faithful revere as custodians of the true faith and exponents of divine will. Until 1946 the emperors of Japan claimed to be descended from the Sun God. Homeric kings traced their lineage back to Zeus the Thunderer, king of the gods. Those of the Roman emperors who did not arouse the ire of their subjects were customarily worshiped (at least in the eastern half of the empire) while alive, and after death were officially deified with the title *Divus* and placed on the ceremonial roster of gods to whom prayer was due.[4] The Dalai Lama, who until 1950 reigned over Tibet from Lhassa, was regarded by his subjects as a living reincarnation of the Buddha. Alternatively, while the human character of the ruler may be recognized, he may be considered a prophet or priest acting on behalf of the Deity, ruling by his authority and thus mediating between God and man. In that sense, the people of Israel, when governed by Eli or Samuel, were a theocratic state. Their formal transition from theocracy to secular government is described in the Book of Samuel.[5] Other such theocracies were the city of Geneva when under the control of Calvin, the Papal States in Italy before 1860, the Vatican since 1929.

What consequence does all this produce for the state? How is the authority to govern men affected by being linked with a belief in power that is more than human? The answer is that when humanity thinks its ruler is divine, or has a divine ancestor, or is divinely appointed, it is impossible to expect that the relation of government to the governed can even nearly approach equality. In the presence of deity or a representative of deity, men are accustomed to bare the head or bow the knee, to listen submissively, to avert the eye, or gaze with awe and reverence.[6] All of which effectively precluded controls

[4]Hence the famous saying of the Emperor Vespasian on his deathbed: *Ut puto, divus fio.* ("I suppose I'm becoming a god.")

[5]I Sam. 8.

[6]Montezuma, whose position combined the functions of chief and priest, was accorded such deference by the Aztecs. Cortés described it thus: "The nobles always entered his palace barefoot, and those who were bidden to present themselves before him did so with bowed head and eyes fixed on the ground, their whole bearing expressing reverence; nor would they when speaking to him lift their eyes to his face, all of which was done to show their profound humiliation and respect." *Five Letters of Cortés to the Emperor*, trans. and ed. J. Bayard Morris (New York: W. W. Norton & Company,

over government! How can a mere mortal demand an accounting from the godhead when criticism is named heresy and opposition is sin? Is not a law firmly founded when men believe it to be given by God, as when Hammurabi, king of Babylon, received the law from Shamash, or when Moses on Sinai was told the Ten Commandments from the mouth of Jehovah? Small wonder that royal monarchs in the sixteenth and seventeenth centuries attempted to fortify their authority with the doctrine of the "divine right of kings." This theory, being then in vogue, was even put into the mouth of King Claudius, when Shakespeare allowed him to exclaim:

> There's such divinity doth hedge a king,
> That treason can but peep to what it would,
> Acts little of his will.[7]

In real life, the deification of monarchy was unequivocally asserted by a reigning monarch, James I of England, in these words to Parliament: "Kings are justly called gods; for they exercise a manner of resemblance of Divine power upon earth. For if you will consider the attributes of God, you shall see how they agree in the person of a king."[8] Other rulers, without attempting so close an identification of themselves with deity, have used titles or asserted principles to invoke a divine sanctity and sanction for their office. The Fundamental Laws of the Russian Empire, as issued in 1892, proclaimed in Article I: "The All-Russian Emperor is an autocratic and unlimited Monarch. ... God Himself commands that his supreme power be obeyed, not only because of fear but also because of conscience." One may also recall such titles as Holy Roman Emperor and Most Christian Majesty; the careers of Joseph Smith and Brigham Young and the founding of the Mormon State of Deseret; and the role of the English monarch as the Head of the Church of England—a fact that used to be politically relevant. From the standpoint of those who govern, the great advantage in deriving their authority from divine will is that opposition is made to seem so fruitless. Who dares resist the government is challenging a divine dispensation which mere mortals must accept and may not amend.

   2. *"Might is Right."* A second method by which authority demands obedience is the appeal to force. The right of those in power is then

---

Inc., 1962), p. 97. This extract is from the second letter, dated October 30, 1520, describing his first conquest of Mexico.

   [7] *Hamlet*, Act IV, Sc. 5, 11. 122–24.

   [8] Quoted in G. P. Gooch, *Political Thought in England, from Bacon to Halifax* (London: Williams and Norgate, 1914), p. 14.

defended by virtue of the fact that they are in power and possess the means to enforce their will. This view, instead of arguing that might is justified by the right it serves, inverts the relationship, deriving right from might. Thus we have such assertions as "Justice is the interest of the stronger," "Obey the powers that be," and "Whatever is, is right." The most that can be said for this point of view is that it offers the governed a counsel of expediency and prudence. But on all other grounds it is open to serious objections. Any doctrine is morally indefensible which seeks to justify right by might, and legion are the crimes and cruelties which have thus been coated with a glossy polish. Furthermore, to derive a government's authority from the force it commands is to invite any opponent to test its strength and challenge it with counterforce. For those who can overthrow the existing order by violence are then entitled to succeed to its authority, and some will think the prize is worth the price.

Most states were created or have grown by violence. But the lapse of time can work a change in governments founded on force. A later generation will accept by habit and inertia what was imposed on its ancestors by conquest. Thus the power that commands by terror today may reign by hereditary right tomorrow. Ibn Khaldun of Tunis was aware of such developments, which he had studied in the history of the Arab world, and drew this distinction between new and established states: "Newly founded states can secure the obedience of their subjects only by much coercion and force. This is because the people have not had the time to get accustomed to the new and foreign rule. Once kingship has been established, however, and inherited by successive generations or dynasties, the people forget their original condition, the rulers are invested with the aura of leadership, and the subjects obey them almost as they obey the precepts of their religion, and fight for them as they would fight for their faith."[9]

An example of this transformation and of its practical results may be found in the earlier history of South America. The Incas built their empire in the Andes by the usual methods of conquest. But once their power was consolidated, the character of their rule altered, as did their subjects' submission. Consider the following description: "When the Incas set out to visit their kingdom, it is told that they traveled with great pomp, riding in rich litters set upon smooth, long poles of the finest wood and adorned with gold and silver. . . . Around the litter and alongside it came the Inca's guard with the archers and halberdiers, and behind an equal number of lancers with their cap-

[9]*An Arab Philosophy of History,* ed. Charles Issawi (London: John Murray [Publishers] Ltd., 1950), p. 110.

tains, and along the road and over the road itself went faithful runners seeing what there might be and giving word of the coming of the Inca. So many people came to see his passing that all the hills and slopes seemed covered with them, and all called down blessings upon him. He traveled four leagues each day, or as much as he wished; he stopped wherever he liked to inquire into the state of his kingdom; he willingly listened to those who came to him with complaints, righting wrongs and punishing those who had committed an injustice."[10]

3. Ancestral Lineage. Once this change has occurred, the feeling that submission to those in power is an unalterable feature of the established order can then be endowed with its own justification and rationale. It can be asserted that the authority to govern issues neither from force nor from Heaven, but from the past.[11] Government, as the argument runs, consists essentially in superiors giving orders to subjects. The continuity and stability of the state are best assured when human beings are ranked in classes and are assigned at birth the same status in society as their parents so that relationships continue unchanged in successive generations. Some are highborn, some lowborn. If my grandfather was the inferior of your grandfather, and my father of your father, then I am inferior to you and take your orders. Authority thus becomes a matter of hereditary right, an appendix to a birth certificate. The title to rule is a product of lineage and lapse of time.

Such a philosophy is not merely a conservative plea for the *status quo*. It is also a defense of a society divided into classes whose membership is determined—or rather predetermined—without any of us willing it so. Society thus visualized evolves as a loom weaving a seamless web to a pattern made long ago. By allotting to each his station in life, heredity selects his environment for him, and the latter may not be altered since it results from the unalterable circumstance of parentage. It then becomes a simple matter to discover the source of authority. Authority is ancestral—and that is that. This principle is plainly one which can operate only in a fairly static society. Furthermore, it can provide but one political advantage, namely stability of government and a sure procedure for the transfer of power, which, though desirable up to a point, is not the sole ideal for which the state exists. But in any case how does an authority founded on the past reply to critics who shout that the times are out of joint and that a sick society needs a new medicine and new medicine men?

[10]This is taken from *The Incas of Pedro de Cieza de Léon*, trans. Harriet de Onis, ed. by Victor Wolfgang von Hagen (Norman: University of Oklahoma Press, 1959).

[11]In some cases one source of power may merge with another, for example, when people worship their own ancestors, as did the Confucian Chinese.

THE POWER OF THE ELITE

The three methods just described have this in common. They justify the authority of those in power by reference to some external criterion—be it God, grandparents, or guns. But if these methods fail, or are not employed, another way is possible. This is to argue that the authority of the few over the many derives from some quality of excellence in the former which makes them inherently superior. Who are "the best" and what it is that makes them such is the problem discussed in Chapter 4, where different elites were analyzed. They have been variously identified as the oldest, wisest, wealthiest, and so on. If sufficient people accept the view that fitness to govern is associated with one of these attributes, then those who have mustered enough years or knowledge or property owe their authority to this fact. In short, once the premises are conceded, the conclusion resolves itself into a tautologous statement: The best know best how to govern. How, therefore, can their inferiors hold them accountable?

THE NORMALCY OF AUTHORITARIANISM

Throughout history, the majority of governments have been authoritarian. Indeed, the commonest type of rule has been that of oligarchies which impose their will by fiat. Now this is a fact that deserves notice. A priori, it might seem natural, and even inevitable, that majorities should rule and that they should be the donors of authority and its source. After all, the weight of numbers is on their side, and that is no small advantage. But if any generalization is warranted by the historical evidence, it points to the contrary. It has normally been easier for the few to dominate the many than the reverse, and this is as true in politics as it is in religion, economics, and the military. Most politics, in fact most social organization so far, has consisted in the subordination of the masses. The method of doing this has been a judicious blend of force and fraud. Force has meant the custody of weapons and their use by a trained and disciplined few, since a small band, well-armed and organized, can usually overpower an ill-equipped, unorganized multitude. Fraud has been practiced by playing on the superstitions and fears of the ignorant, by the use of ideas as a technique of political supremacy, or by what is nowadays called propaganda. Moreover, the mass of men in most communities of the past, occupying a lowly social status and eking out a living which left little or no margin above subsistence, were habituated to accept their condition as part of a predestined order. Custom, inertia, and ignorance have always combined to preserve the *status quo.*

To maintain traditional patterns has naturally been easiest in periods when the rate of change was so slow that society seemed, to any one generation, to be cast in a rigid mold. The majority of mankind were then resigned to political servitude as their inescapable lot. Politics appeared to be physically distant from them and to be conducted at a level high above their daily affairs and preoccupations. The capital was remote from the farm and village. The castle and the palace were places where arrogance dwelt in opulence. What most men wanted of their rulers was that they should not be oppressive.[12] When the state intruded into the lives of the common people, it generally came in an unpleasant guise. The government was the tax gatherer, soldier, or functionary. Politics, therefore, was conducted by a small cast and on a limited stage. The populace were passive spectators of a play which they were privileged to observe at a distance, a play that usually went over their heads.

THE MODERN REVOLUTION

The political and social revolution of modern times has drastically altered the conditions under which authoritarianism can be successful. One change is fundamental to all else. The masses are no longer the passive spectators they once were. In the course of the past century they have grown increasingly self-conscious and self confident. The numbers of those who are actively concerned and who actually take some part in the political process are larger than ever before in history. More and more people look to their government, make claims upon it, and expect its help. Twentieth century politics is the politics of mass action. Governments can rely no more on the passivity of subjects; they must be prepared for the activity of citizens.

This numerical difference, together with the psychological change in relationships, does not mean that authoritarianism has ceased to be possible in the sense of a minority imposing its will on a majority. Far from it. The majority of the human race still live under political dictatorships as did their ancestors. What has altered, however, is the method which authoritarianism must employ in order to succeed in the contemporary world. It has had to adapt its techniques to this vast enlargement of scale. The few can still dominate the many by doing violence to body and mind. But in both spheres the means have to be both more brutal and more refined, more coercive and more subtle, more ruthless and more calculated. What are the institutions, then,

---

[12]"The aim of the people is more honest than that of the nobility, the latter desiring to oppress, and the former merely to avoid oppression." Machiavelli, *The Prince*, Chap. 9.

which have been evolved to serve this purpose? How does modern authoritarianism resemble, and differ from, its predecessors?

DICTATORSHIP IN MODERN DRESS

Dictatorships of the twentieth century can be grouped in two broad categories. The type more closely resembling the traditional is that which has a military ruler at the head. Many such regimes have held power, the majority being of quite recent vintage. The most durable of all has been that of Chiang Kai-shek, who controlled most of China for twenty years and then, after losing to the Communists, transferred his rule to Taiwan in 1949. Franco comes second in political longevity, squatting on Spain's back for three decades. The French in 1958 wearily gave up the effort of governing in accord with the general will and resigned themselves to the will of the General, who resigned in a huff in 1969. And Greece, the birthplace of democracy, fell prey to a military junta in 1967.

Latin America, which has a long tradition of army *caudillos,* continued to yield its share—for example, Perón in Argentina, Batista in Cuba, Trujillo in the Dominican Republic, Somoza in Nicaragua, Stroessner in Paraguay, and others of their ilk in Guatemala, Honduras, Venezuela, Bolivia, and Peru. Some of these were overthrown in the late fifties and early sixties. But Brazil, the largest country of Latin America and potentially the most important, lost its fragile grip on constitutionalism in 1964 and surrendered to its own army whose "hard-line" officers stayed in the saddle by tightening the rein. Likewise, in the turbulent Middle East, Gamal Abdel Nasser dominated Egypt for more than a decade and a half, and at one time or another army men have governed in Iraq, Lebanon, Syria, and Turkey. Further to the east, when parliamentary institutions collapsed in Pakistan, Field Marshal Mohammad Ayub Khan exercised a paternalistic autocracy for a decade and then, in the face of mounting opposition, resigned in favor of still another soldier. The postimperial chaos of Southeast Asia sprouted military regimes in Burma, Thailand, Indonesia, South Korea, and South Vietnam. Finally in Africa, many of the new governments, soon after winning independence, became authoritarian and in some cases (for example, Ghana under Nkrumah) despotic. The freshly promoted army officers, having force at their command, emerged in the sixties as rulers of states and bosses of their people.

The general reasons for this spreading rash of military rulers are not difficult to detect. What are called the developing countries are characterized by backward economies, deficient technologies, and low living standards. At the same time they exhibit wide gaps between the possessions and privileges of a few and the poverty of an illiterate, undernourished mass. To modernize the inherited society and adjust to the stresses of change imposes heavy responsibilities on government—responsibilities for which, in general, the political leadership is untrained and the administrative apparatus, inadequate. Under these circumstances, when the winds of change begin at last to blow through the musty corridors of custom, the old order sways and bends and, in some instances, comes tumbling down. Amid the ensuing disorder, people will acquiesce, grudgingly or with relief, in a strong hand. Decisions of whatever kind will appear preferable to indecision; discipline, superior to chaos. What social institution then has the better claim or opportunity to be the organizer of order than the army? But notice that in these situations the military junta or generalissimo may be performing one of two contrasted roles in relation to social change and incipient revolution. Some army leaders consist of Young Turks,[13] who mean to modernize and do it fast and thoroughly. These men are innovators—often ruthless and dynamic—in soldiers' uniform. In other cases, the military ruler heads a reaction, using the coercive power of the army to dam the currents of change and shore up the established regime of privilege.[14]

There is a second species of modern dictatorship that has little in common with traditional types. Its aims are revolutionary in a more fundamental sense and certain of its methods have been invented in this century. This kind of dictatorship envisages refashioning human society in terms of some ideology or doctrine. Its instrument of power and innovation is the state, and it employs the three techniques of terror, propaganda, and the single political party. The first of these is by no means novel, since brutal men in all centuries have dealt forcibly with opposition. But the modern species of terror is more thoroughly organized. Propaganda, too, has some earlier analogies, at least to the extent that censorship negatively restricted the freedom of opinion. What distinguishes the modern version is the active propagation of half-truth and untruth, designed positively to direct people's thinking into certain molds.[15] The monopoly of political power by one dominant party is the feature that is unique to our time. It is precisely this organizational tool that has been engineered to cope with the

---

[13]This familiar term was derived from a group of younger Turkish officers who from 1908 onwards spearheaded their country's revolution. From them emerged the great Kemal Ataturk.

[14]As examples, contrast a Franco and a Nasser.

[15]The nearest parallels to this in previous systems are provided by religious fanaticism—the Spanish Inquisition, for instance.

problem of mass participation. The party is the instrument by which the masses are both driven and led, both controlled in disciplined subjection to the few and aroused to follow them as required.

These practices have been most systematically employed by the dictatorships of Right and Left, by the Fascists, Nazis, and Communists. Although these differ in their philosophy and objectives and in the groups from which they receive support, they are markedly similar in method. In fact, one can observe in chronological succession an import-export balance, or borrowing in mutual admiration which has taken place between the extremes. The first in the field was Lenin, who organized the Bolsheviks for the overthrow of the Kerensky regime and then guided Russia through the period of revolution, civil war, and foreign intervention. His methods were imitated by Mussolini, whose Blackshirt militia overawed the feeble government of Italy in 1922. After 1925 the techniques of the Fascist system came more and more to resemble those of the Communists. Next in line was Adolf Hitler, whose Nazis emulated and vied with Communists and Fascists. They established their evil dominance over a nation which had greatly vaunted its enlightenment and *Kultur*. As the Germans do everything—whether good or bad—more thoroughly than others, so in the use of brutality by the Nazis they sank back to unprecedented barbarism. Finally in the Soviet Union the efficient and cold-blooded Stalin learned many lessons from Hitler and applied them internally against his own opponents. In the mid-1930's, and again in his last phase (1947–1953) when he became morbidly suspicious and despotic, Stalin's system of terror was closely parallel to Hitler's.

FASCISM AND NAZISM

When Mussolini in 1932 wrote an article on "The Political and Social Doctrine of Fascism" for the *Italian Encyclopedia*, he asserted: "A party which entirely governs a nation is a fact entirely new to history, there are no possible references or parallels." Although this statement, referring as it does to his own Fascist party, conceals the debt that he owed to Lenin, Mussolini was correct in emphasizing the function of the party in the conduct of the dictatorship. Both fascism and nazism considered themselves programs of action. They represented their mission as the regeneration of a people demoralized by division and defeat. Theirs were regimes of crisis, injecting into the cynical and the listless the political wonder drug of enthusiastic nationalism. They were movements of combat, their adherents trained for battle, taught to hate, beating up the enemies within, "blitzing" the enemies without. Democracy they despised as weakness. Discussion spelled delay and the inability to agree. Reason was the fraud or cowardice of the intellectual. Instead of reason, they glorified will; instead of discussion, decision; instead of democracy, leadership. Leadership was the responsibility of the party, which itself took its cue from its leader, the Duce or Führer. Authority was exercised by the dominant group over the nation, as the leadership interpreted the nation's interest. The people did not delegate that authority, could not define it, dared not revoke it. Those who ran the party had mobilized force. Those who used such force gained power. Those who possessed power claimed authority.

Unswerving obedience to an ironclad autocracy was the ideal of the Nazi-Fascist state. In Italy and Germany under the regimes of Mussolini and Hitler the dictatorship of the party over the people was as intense as the preeminence within the party of the Duce or Führer. "Believe, obey, fight" was the motto prescribed by Mussolini for his countrymen. "In the name of God and of Italy I swear that I will obey the orders of the Leader without questioning"—this was part of the oath taken upon admission to the Fascist party. *Mein Kampf,* the Bible of the Nazi movement, enunciated with grotesque clarity the contempt that Hitler felt for the mass of humanity and his determination to subject them to a disciplined inferiority. "A view of life," he proclaimed, "which, by rejecting the democratic mass idea endeavors to give this world to the best people, that means to the most superior men [the Germans], has logically to obey the same aristocratic principle also within this people and has to guarantee leadership and highest influence within the respective people to its best heads." Political organization therefore requires "putting the heads above the masses" and "subjecting the masses to the heads." Mankind's interest "is not satisfied and is not served by the rule of the masses who are either unable to think or are inefficient, in any case not inspired." Such assumptions brought Hitler to formulate his principle of leadership. "The principle which once made the Prussian army the most marvelous instrument of the German people has to be some day in a transformed meaning the principle of the construction of our whole state constitution, authority of every leader towards below and responsibility towards above."[16]

THE COMMUNIST DICTATORSHIP

Dictatorships of the far Left employ the same methods as those of

[16]These quotations are all from "Personality and the Conception of the National State," *Mein Kampf,* trans. Alvin Johnson (New York: Reynal & Company, Inc., 1939), Vol. II, Chap. 4, pp. 661, 665, 670.

the far Right, although in certain respects they display a greater skill. For communism patently carries out the principle that the masses must be goaded, curbed, and led by a disciplined few, and the instrument for accomplishing this is the single dominant party, concentrating in its grip a monopoly of power and legal authority. As a technique of government, the system originated with the revolutionary movement from the Left that grew out of the central root of Marxism. The one who invented the idea and first applied it was Lenin. What he initiated was rigorously extended by the man who chose to call himself "Lenin's faithful disciple"—Joseph Stalin. Holding the Marxian view that society is irreconcilably split into two fundamentally opposed economic classes, that the relationship between these can only be one of war, and that the revolt of the submerged class and its eventual triumph are inevitable, Lenin concerned himself with the question of tactics for hastening the inevitable and guiding it into the approved Communist channels. Since the revolutionary class (called the proletariat) was large, poorly educated, and politically inexperienced, its victory required, according to him, the aid of a smaller group, firmly disciplined and iron-willed, whose members could fathom and follow the fundamental laws of "scientific" Marxism.

Such was the Communist party which Lenin set out to build and which Stalin and his followers continued in the Soviet Union or reproduced elsewhere. Its character was clearly described by Stalin at the time (1924) when he was its secretary-general. According to him the party "must first of all constitute the vanguard of the working class." As such, it "must take its stand at the head of the working class, it must see ahead of the working class, lead the proletariat and not trail behind the spontaneous movement." The similarity between a revolutionary struggle and war makes it necessary for the proletariat, like an army in the field, to have a general staff. "The Party," therefore, "is the Military staff of the proletariat." From these premises the conclusions follow that the party must be "the organized detachment of the working class"; that it is "the highest form of class organization of the proletariat"; that it serves as "the weapon of the dictatorship of the proletariat"; and that "the existence of factions is incompatible with Party unity and with its iron discipline."[17] When the "Stalin Constitution" was written and ratified in 1936, the principles outlined above were duly recorded in Article 126 as follows:

The most active and politically conscious citizens in the ranks of the working class and other strata of the toilers unite in the Communist Party of the Soviet

[17]All the above quotations are from a lecture on "Foundations of Leninism" given by Stalin in 1924 and printed in many collections of Marxist writings.

Union (Bolsheviks), which is the vanguard of the toilers in their struggle to strengthen and develop the socialist system and which represents the leading core of all organizations of the toilers, both public and state.

Using statements of this kind to explain his actions, Stalin established a remarkable triple dictatorship: that of himself over the Communist party, that of the party over the peoples of the USSR, and that of the party in the USSR over organized Communist movements elsewhere in the world, with the exception of the one which eluded his grip, Yugoslavia.

Numerically the ratio of Communist party members to the population they govern is small. Their control is maintained by various devices—by a complete grip on the machinery of government at its highest levels, by placing their members at key points in the community (in factories, collective farms, educational bodies, and so forth) to direct and report on nonmembers, by a monopoly of all media for influencing opinion, by the forcible suppression of any overt criticism, and by the terrorist activities of a dreaded secret police. Most important of all to the party is the selection and training of its own personnel. Prospective members are carefully observed during a long period of probation and preparation. Once admitted to the party, the Communist's life is dedicated to a meticulous discipline of thought and action prescribed by his official superiors. Every now and then a purge is conducted to rid the party of any who are too weak, too half-hearted, or too independent for its tasks. Because of the Communist conception of their mission as an officer class directing a revolutionary upsurge of the masses of mankind, their ethical code knows no greater sin than disunity. Their bitterest hatred is therefore directed, not at those they call their class enemies, but at other Communists who differ or deviate from the high command (as Trotsky did) and at Socialists of a democratic brand who compete with Communists for the support of the working class. Finally, since a dictatorship thrives on continuing an atmosphere of crisis, the Communist leaders have frequently pursued the policy of sowing suspicion among their subjects and implanting widespread fear of traitors within and spies from without. If systematically conducted by a watchful secret police who are backed up by concentration and forced labor camps, this policy is well calculated to keep the opponents of those in power disorganized, demoralized, and therefore harmless.

The most ruthless employer of these techniques was Stalin. After Lenin's death and the ensuing interregnum during which he fought and worsted his opponents in the party, Stalin consolidated his own power and remained supreme for a quarter of a century. Lenin had never been scrupulous in his choice of methods and had dealt mercilessly with non-Communists. But he had tolerated discussion within the ranks of his own party and always felt some attachment to the "Old Bolsheviks," who had been his fellow conspirators. Stalin, "the man of steel" as his pseudonym indicates, had none of these feelings. Aloof, secretive, and callous, he spared nobody. Communist and non-Communist, young and old—all had to toe the line. In a manner reminiscent of other Russian autocrats before him—Ivan the Terrible, for instance, or Peter the Great—he devoted his fantastic energies and powers of will and organization to strengthening his country. All else was subordinated to this aim. To achieve it, like Hitler, he killed by the millions when he deemed it necessary.

Even after 1945, when the prestige of victory in World War II might have seemed to ensure his power, Stalin actually tightened his grip on the Russian people instead of relaxing it. The party he converted into what Trotsky had once contemptuously called "the dictatorship of the secretariat." The army was prevented from rising against him by a policy of decorating the marshals who had become popular heroes, and then relegating them to minor commands outside Moscow. All individuals who had access to him were kept under watch by the secret police, whose activities were enlarged on the pretext of the cold war, which Stalin himself did so much to foment. As far as possible, Russians were effectively sealed off from contact with persons and opinions outside the Communist sphere. Moreover, what was sauce for the Russian goose was sauce for the satellite gander. The same Stalinist system, shielded by its iron curtain, was forced on the peoples of Eastern Europe whose lands had fallen under the dominion of the Red Army. Only in one place did the results backfire. In Yugoslavia the strong-willed Communist ruler Marshal Tito successfully declared and consummated his independence—one of the few cases in which Stalin failed to exterminate a foe.

TRANSFER OF POWER UNDER COMMUNISM

Every political regime faces the need to maintain its own continuity and provide for an orderly succession. For a dictatorship this creates a special problem. Can a system born of crisis and revolution develop into normalcy? Can it constitutionalize its own processes? Can it arrange for a transfer of power to new hands without reverting to internecine struggle? The danger to an oligarchy is particularly acute whenever one person accumulates great power. When he becomes feeble or dies, a sudden vacuum is created. Feuding among the few at the top can so weaken the regime as to lead to the abandonment of authoritarianism. Hereditary monarchies, founded on legitimacy, adopted an automatic solution. But how does the modern dictatorship provide for the smooth transfer of power?

In the case of Fascist Italy and Nazi Germany this problem never arose. Both regimes were overthrown by military defeat in a war which they had themselves instigated. But the Russian Communists have now confronted this problem three times—after the deaths of Lenin and Stalin, and since the ouster of Khrushchev. There are some interesting resemblances between these episodes, but there are also significant differences. Lenin's death left a Russia which had barely survived the ordeals of foreign war, revolution, civil war, and intervention, a Russia that was isolated internationally and was still in the very early phase of rebuilding and of forward development. The domestic opposition to the Communists was crushed, but the Communist party was full of "Old Bolsheviks," who were veterans of the revolutionary era. For three years (1924–27) the party was torn by internal arguments about theory and program. But finally its general secretary emerged above the heads of the rest by steering his own passage between the cliques and building a machine subservient to himself. How Stalin maneuvered himself between personalities and policies deserves a description. The chief domestic issue concerned the future direction of the economy. Under Lenin's New Economic Policy, a limited amount of capitalism had been reintroduced in order to revive production after the fighting ended. The right wing of the Communist party, under Bukharin, Tomsky, and Rykov, favored the further extension of this policy. Trotsky, however, led a left wing, where he was joined by Kamenev and Zinoviev, in proposing rapid industrialization under state auspices and a collectivized agriculture. At the same time Trotsky espoused a foreign policy of "permanent revolution," arguing that socialism could not survive in one country and that Communist revolutions must be fomented elsewhere.

Stalin had no theory, but he had two clear objectives. He wanted to build the power of Russia and his own power in Russia. Recognizing Trotsky as his leading adversary, he decided to destroy him first. For this, he utilized the collapse of Russian policy in China, as evidenced by the dismissal of Borodin and the victories of Chiang Kai-shek over the Chinese Left. He thus secured the support of the right wing of his party, advocating against Trotsky and his adherents the policy of "socialism in a single country." In 1927 the party expelled Trotsky, Kamenev, and Zinoviev. The next year, however, Stalin turned against the Right. Arguing now for a five-year plan of rapid industrial development and collectivization of agriculture, he reversed the New Economic Policy and secured the expulsion first of Tomsky and Bukharin and then of Rykov. All these, except for Trotsky whom he really feared and therefore drove into exile,[18] he subsequently readmitted on his own terms. Playing off one group against the other, and picking certain policies from each side as they strengthened Russia and himself, within a few years Stalin ruled supreme. During his long sway, and because of the fear he inspired, the adulation of his individual personality went to lengths that far exceeded the deference paid to Lenin. The truth of this is well attested by those who had most cause to hate Stalin—the men near him. At the Twentieth Party Congress in 1956, his successors spoke revealingly of the terror which had reigned at the top. Nor did they make any secret of their dislike for his despotic excesses. Mikoyan, then first deputy premier, stated: "In the course of about twenty years we, in fact, had no collective leadership. The cult of personality, condemned already by Marx and afterward by Lenin, flourished, and this, of course, could not but exert an extremely negative influence on the situation within the party and on its work."[19] Speaking in the same vein, Khrushchev delivered a lengthy report indicting Stalin for acts of despotism. "It is clear," he said, "that here Stalin showed in a whole series of cases his intolerance, his brutality and his abuse of power. Instead of proving his political correctness and mobilizing the masses, he often chose the path of repression and physical annihilation, not only against actual enemies, but also against individuals who had not committed any crimes against the party and the Soviet Government."[20]

Stalin's heirs confronted a situation which was new and which required delicate handling if their own power was to continue unimpaired and their regime was to advance in strength. Internally, the Russian people had good cause to feel more secure than in the 1920's. But they had been denied consumer goods and were sealed off from communication with the world beyond their borders. In the Communist party only a few of the "Old Bolsheviks" remained. Practically all the men at the top, and everyone in the middle ranks, were of the generation that knew only Stalin. The army leaders were anxious to have more of a say, as were the new intelligentsia, the scientists, the experts in technology, on whom the Soviet Union depended for its further progress. Moreover, the government was deeply involved in a network of relations with other Communist regimes, on which Stalin's hand had lain so heavily and roughly.

---

[18]Many years later Trotsky was murdered in Mexico by Stalin's agents.

[19]As quoted in the *New York Times,* February 19, 1956, p. 26.

[20]The text of the entire report, with commentary, is published in *Khrushchev and Stalin's Ghost,* by Bertram D. Wolfe (New York: Frederick A. Praeger, Inc., 1957). This extract is on p. 116.

THE KHRUSHCHEV PERIOD

The internal struggle for power which erupted after 1953 revolved around two axes: choice of policies and rivalries between individuals and institutions. In the sphere of policy, a decision had to be made whether to continue Stalin's programs and methods, or relax or reverse them. Depending on this decision, one person or group would emerge predominant. There were three institutions in the Soviet system that might have produced the new leadership: the party, the government functionaries, or the army. The man who came out on top, as we know, was Khrushchev. It took him about five years (1953–58) to consolidate his position—one year longer than it took Stalin—after which he remained Number One in Russia until his overthrow in October, 1964. Let us see how he went about the task.

When Stalin died, Malenkov became chairman of the government. Closely associated with him were two other powerful figures—Beria, the head of the secret police, and Molotov, the foreign secretary and long-time associate of Stalin. Meanwhile, the Presidium of the Communist Party underlined the change from the former "cult of personality" to the new "collective leadership." Khrushchev was strategically placed as general secretary of the party, and the army marshals, of whom Zhukov was the best known, were seeking an opportunity to assert themselves. All sides now began the political game of Russian roulette. Only one shot was fired, however. Its victim was Beria. As chief of the secret police responsible for internal security, he had a military force under his own command, which his "colleagues" feared and the army resented. He also had dossiers, of course, on everybody else, which he could draw on whenever he saw fit. Since he was a threat to the others, they closed ranks, with support from inside the army, and struck at him first. He was executed—the only one, as far as is known, to whom this happened in the post-Stalin period.

For nearly two years Malenkov stayed in the chair, but insecurely because he was under pressure from Molotov in the sphere of foreign policy and Khrushchev on the domestic front. How much of the budget to divert from armaments and heavy industry to consumer goods? How to increase agricultural production? How to deal with the regimes of Eastern Europe; how to handle China; whether to continue the cold war with the United States? On all these questions divisions occurred between a right wing of hard-core Stalinists and what might be called the revisionists. Malenkov, who tended to represent the government functionaries and the technological experts, suffered an erosion of his power at the hands of men who ran the party apparatus. Eventually, he resigned and was demoted to a minor position. His place at the formal head of the government was then taken by Bulganin, with Khrushchev looming large at his side. Together, for about three years, this pair paraded together, both inside Russia and outside. But increasingly, the vigorous and ebullient personality of Khrushchev stole the show from the mediocre Bulganin.

Still talking about the virtues of collective leadership and collegiality, the pair embarked on a mixed policy. They continued relaxing restrictions in Russia. Stalin's monolith began to crack, until the dictator's corpse was even removed from its place of honor in Lenin's tomb. More voices were heard; a freer movement of persons, and even ideas, was cautiously permitted. Bulganin and Khrushchev sought to satisfy the army, restoring the wartime hero Marshal Zhukov to Moscow and admitting him to the Party Presidium. Attention was given to consumer needs; the satellite regimes were treated more gently; a reconciliation was sought with Tito. For a dictatorship in transition, the beginnings of freedom are a time of danger. The new taste whets the appetite of those unfamiliar with the flavor. They want more. Hence, in October, 1956, a full-scale revolt broke out in Budapest. The Hungarians deposed their Communist regime and installed one which was not communist. At this threat to Russian hegemony, the Soviet leaders reverted to Stalinism. With guns and tanks, the Red Army reentered Budapest and reenthroned the dictatorship of the proletariat.

In the aftermath of those events, the struggle for power was renewed in Moscow. Khrushchev's rivals now had a case against him: He was endangering the solidarity of the Soviet Empire. In June, 1957, Khrushchev was outvoted in the Party Presidium. Normally that would have been the end. But this was no normal man. With tough resilience, he struck back—appealing the decision from the Presidium to the larger, parent body, the Central Committee. As it happened, this was well stacked with his supporters, for he had not used his time as general secretary to no avail. Vindicated at the higher level, he launched his counterattack on the "antiparty" group (that is, anti-Khrushchev). Out went Molotov, and with him the remaining hard-line Stalinists. Malenkov was shunted to an assignment in Siberia. Bulganin, who had wavered, was retired. Khrushchev installed himself as chairman of the government. Only one man remained as a potential challenger. Marshal Zhukov had thrown his weight on Khrushchev's side in June, 1957. The Red Army, it could be assumed, would follow him if he gave the lead. Therefore he must be in no position to do it in the future. The next year, Zhukov was despatched on a visit to Belgrade. While out of the country, he was replaced. On his return home, he found himself dropped.

Continuity and Change in the Soviet Union. Between these two instances of consolidation of power in Russia, by Stalin and Khrushchev, respectively, there are two striking parallels and two profound contrasts. The first parallel is the switch from an initial attempt at collective leadership to a subsequent cult of personality. Under Stalin this latter trend reached a despotic excess. Under Khrushchev, it did not; and his rule was not a tyranny of the Stalinist type. Nevertheless, there is no denying that from 1958 until his removal in 1964 Khrushchev held a position of personal preeminence in the Soviet system. Indeed, this point was stated in the criticisms leveled against him after his fall.[21] It is surely significant that the characteristics of power in the Soviet Union have led, in every case thus far, to the dominance of One—first Lenin, then Stalin, and latest Khrushchev. One is therefore entitled to wonder whether it will happen again. Can collective leadership be a reality in Moscow?

The second noteworthy parallel between Stalin's rise and that of Khrushchev consists in their both operating from the same base. In the tug of war between groups—the army, the government officials, and the party—the last of these has thus far proved itself the most potent. The party politicians, in fact, ran circles around the only men who had the means to depose them—the army marshals. Within the party itself, the key person hitherto has been the general secretary. Using the advantages of that post, the secretive Stalin outmaneuvered the brilliant Trotsky. From the same post the gregarious Khrushchev outsmarted Malenkov, Beria, Molotov, Bulganin, and Zhukov. It will be worth observing whether the same phenomenon recurs among Khrushchev's successors.

But the contrasts between the Stalin and Khrushchev periods are also illuminating. A personality cult will vary with the person, and the person, if he is shrewd and sensitive, will respond to changes in the society and to altered circumstances abroad. Everybody near the top was in fear for his life while Stalin ruled Russia. Since he died, it has been possible to change the leadership three times without resort to bloodshed. This has been done through votes in the Party's Presidium or Central Committee. At present, as far as we know, three former heads of the Soviet government—Malenkov, Bulganin, and Khrushchev—are still living. They were demoted, but were permitted to

[21]In the second edition of this book, published in 1960, I wrote: "As a consequence, when a party congress convened early in 1959, the patent political fact was the return to the supremacy of one man. In fact, the 'cult of personality,' for which Khrushchev had criticized Stalin, was beginning to reappear in the form of a new boss." On Friday, October 16, 1964, the day after the announcement of Khrushchev's dismissal, a *Pravda* editorial criticized "the ideology and practice of the personality cult" and demanded "collective leadership."

live.[22] For Russian communism, this is progress. The stakes in the game of roulette are changing.

The other great change is the beginning of liberalization within the system. The Russia of the early sixties was different from that of the early fifties. There was less repression, less terror, less self-imposed isolation. More Russians traveled abroad; more foreigners visited Russia. The cold war was becoming a "hot peace." The government showed more concern over the need to raise the living standards of its own people. Although censorship continued and the press and radio were still strictly controlled by the state (that is, by the party), a "public opinion" was emerging. And a similar "public opinion" was emerging in the relations between Russia and the other countries with Communist regimes. Whereas previously Moscow spoke and the rest stayed silent, now there were dialogues. Not only Belgrade but also Warsaw and Bucharest were talking out and talking back.[23] What is more, the latter two were even talking to each other. A new term was used to describe the new reality. The monolith of Stalin's day was gone. In its place was "polycentrism."

Since nothing in life is fixed and permanent, and since politics is a slice of life, nothing political remains the same. Dictatorships, too, if they survive longer than a generation, will proceed to evolve. This is what has been happening in the Soviet Union. And the events prompt the inquiry: In what direction, and at what speed, will the evolution continue? As a whole community becomes literate and higher education is extended to more persons, an intellectual curiosity is stimulated beyond the sphere of technology or the bounds of physical science. Once the human mind is endowed with the equipment to learn and think, in countless individual cases it will range afield and explore beyond the limits that a propagandist imposes. The educated ask more questions and make demands for evidence, which are often inconvenient for the monopolists of political power. All this, I emphasize, has reached only an early stage. The Soviet Union is capable of sending its cosmonauts to outer space. But it has a long distance yet to travel before it becomes an open society on this earth. On the same day, October 15, 1964, when Moscow announced to an astonished Soviet people that Khrushchev had been deposed, the people of Great Brit-

---

[22]Even after his demotion, Malenkov was sufficiently trusted by his successors to be sent on a visit to Great Britain. The late Hugh Gaitskell, at that time leader of the Labour party told me of having had this conversation with him. "Do you know, Mr. Malenkov," asked Gaitskell, "why it is that all of us here are so interested in you?" "No," replied the Russian, "why is it?" "Because you're alive!" was the reply. Gaitskell said that Malenkov enjoyed this and laughed, then remarked in seriousness: "Do realize that this is a different Russia now."

[23]For Sino-Soviet relations, see the discussion in Chap. 13, pp. 400–402.

ain went to the polls in a free election at which 27,650,000 out of
35,894,000 registered voters made their choice among three competing parties. Not until the middle of the following day, when every last
vote was counted, could the people's decision be certified. By contrast
in the Soviet Union, a country with a population then estimated at
210,000,000, an infinitesimal number of individuals at the top of the
party hierarchy, presumably with the support of leaders of the army,
initiated and engineered the steps that resulted in Khrushchev's fall.
In all of this the Russian people were merely passive spectators, who
took no part in the procedures. Only at the end of the conspiracy
were they told whom to follow and applaud next. The difference
between the democratic and dictatorial methods of transferring
power could not be more dramatically underscored.

No less dramatic has been the Soviet experience since 1964 in
failing to cope with the problem of loosening a centralized monopoly
of power. The leadership which replaced Khrushchev consisted of
two men, coequal in outward appearance: Brezhnev in charge of the
party apparatus and relations with other Communist regimes, and Kosygin, an expert in industrial management, heading the machinery of
government and serving also as the archdiplomat in contacts with the
Western and Third worlds. With this pair at the helm, the USSR had
to adjust to the urgent issues of the late sixties: the domestic demand
of its citizens for higher living standards and a freer intellectual fare,
the increased enmity of China, the restiveness of Eastern Europe as
manifested in Romania and Czechoslovakia, and the groping toward
a tacit coexistence with the United States—albeit bedeviled by the
continuing tragedy of Vietnam.

Until 1968 it seemed that a cautious liberalization, both internal and
external, would prevail and that the customary harshness of Soviet
power was being moderated. But in the summer of that year came the
turning point, and the direction chosen was backward. Confronted by
the radical measures which the new leadership of the Czechoslovak
Communist party was inaugurating under Dubcek, and spurred on by
the self-regarding fears of the Polish and East German autocrats, the
Russians moved to the Right—in Prague as well as Moscow. The pattern of their occupation of Czechoslovakia was strikingly parallel to
Hitler's actions in 1938–39, even to the extent of including East German troops among the initial invading force. The strategy behind this
move was not hard to decipher. The men in the Kremlin had set their
faces against those changes which would have spelled a greater diversity of policies and opinion. Increasingly preoccupied with the menace of China, the Bear was preparing for its duel with the Dragon by
solidifying its grip on the region in its rear and by stifling dissident

voices at home. Just like the tsarist autocracy before it, Communist autocracy was afraid to set its people free.

THE STIGMATA OF DICTATORSHIP

To discipline civilian life, to dress people's bodies in uniforms and their minds with uniformity, to have one legal party serving as the general staff or officer class of a passive population—this is the common denominator of dictatorships of extreme Left and Right. Hitler, Mussolini, Franco, Stalin, and Mao are in this respect brothers under the skin. For the governed (that is, the majority of the population) to determine policy or call their rulers to account is as impossible under communism as under fascism. Both systems, since their government is a dictatorship, exalt the value of leadership and impose the party as an aristocracy on the nation. Both are authoritarian in the sense that, as in an army, authority resides in a few who are responsible for, but not responsible to, the many. Both, when challenged, maintain their dominance by trial and terror.

Authoritarianism leaves its imprint on politics in many ways. An oligarchy, while it sharpens the distinction between ruler and subject, blurs the distinction between government and state. In order that its authority may not be challenged, the ruling class not only seeks to monopolize the actualities of power, but denies to others their right to power. An effective means to this end is for rulers to assert that those who are the government are in fact the state—thereby obliterating the difference. If their contention is accepted, an attempt to change the government becomes an effort to overthrow the state, and political opponents of those in power can be punished as traitors. When, however, the government is viewed as a group of officials authorized for the time being to act in the name of the state, then it is possible to say that the state continues in existence despite changes of government.

Hereditary aristocracies of the traditional kind, in periods when they held a monopoly of governmental power, regarded the state as a species of property that they owned. The people who were their subjects "belonged" to the privileged class by virtue of an inherited status—in much the same way as a mansion, land, crops, and cattle belonged to the individual noble. A similar outlook pervades the one-party state of the twentieth century. The elite party in a Fascist or Communist dictatorship absorbs the state, instead of merely acting on its behalf. The party does more than take over the government. It abolishes any institutions of the state that might compete for authority with the organs of the party—as the Russian Communists abolished the Duma, and Mussolini, the Chamber of Deputies. Or, instead of destroying, the party emasculates its rivals, permitting them a twilight and ineffectual existence—as Hitler allowed the Reichstag to linger on and as the Communists under Stalin treated their own Soviets. The state thereby becomes the adjunct of the party; not the party, the servant of the state. Only in this one respect can the state be said to wither away: Its life is sucked from it by the cancerous growth of the party.

Besides thus identifying the rulers with the state, authoritarianism also produces a distinctive theory of law. Since every kind of state formulates general rules for its members to obey, the sources and sanctions of law are closely related to the problem of authority. Different governmental systems advance varying answers to the question: What gives law its obligatory character? Under the dictatorship of an authoritarian regime, the answer is unambiguous. Law simply expresses the will of those with the power to issue and enforce their commands. Once the authorities have spoken, what they said is the law—and that is all there is to know. Such a doctrine is well adapted to exempt the rulers' wishes from challenge. If law must be accepted at its face value because the rulers will it so, how can anyone query its validity? As long as the ruling group remains united and speaks with one voice, no alternative is left to the subject but obedience.

The classic vice of all dictatorial systems is their basic assumption of the superiority and infallibility of those in power. Such pretensions are not justified by the facts of history. Though some absolute rulers have been benevolent, though some oligarchies have performed acts of wise statesmanship, these systems generally have been and are still productive of far too much stupidity, waste, and cruelty to merit the favor of mankind. Dictatorship exaggerates the worthiness of a few and demeans or brutalizes the remainder. With unwarranted arrogance, it identifies the general well-being of the community with the special interest of the ruling group. Even when philosophers, like Hegel, devote their services to its cause, the claims of absolutism remain bogus. Stripped of the veneer and camouflage, dictatorship is essentially a regime of privilege. As such, since it cannot evoke consent from the underprivileged, it must hold sway by force and fraud. The dominant group coheres together for fear of losing its special advantages. It is able to prolong these, because in practice the mobilized force of an equipped and disciplined minority is often superior to the potentialities of an unorganized majority. Dictatorship thus succeeds in diverting a portion of the force, which the whole community needs for its protection, to supply the government with protection from the governed. Hence arise the familiar characteristics of the "police state," which is simply an arrested stage of political development. It is a state that begins with the elementary need of protection and has advanced as far as establishing order. But there it stops, and it is unable, as long as it continues a dictatorship, to progress toward the law and ethics of justice or the humanism of welfare.

9

THIRD ISSUE:

–2– The Freedom of the Governed

FOUNDATIONS OF FREEDOM

What is the alternative to dictatorship? By what means can the authority of government be made subject to consent? How is it possible to grant powers for use and safeguard them against abuse? The beginning of an answer is to reject the doctrine that the government is the source of authority and to embrace the contrary notion that authority derives from the mass of the people who entrust the government with powers to be exercised on their behalf. Although a critical issue of the present century is the choice between these two political poles and their resulting forms of organization, the decision which confronts humanity is not new. A long tradition supports the view that authority is somehow delegated by the governed to their government, despite the fact that states founded on this principle have been rarities and continue to be the exception rather than the rule. The assertion of the principle, however, would have had little effect on practice unless institutional means were developed for placing a curb on those in authority. The doctrine that government should be responsible has to be studied in the light of historical efforts to make it so.

THE ATHENIAN DEMOCRACY

In the oldest democracy about whose institutions anything is known in detail, an elaborate system was devised to ensure that the people, or *demos*, would be self-governing in fact and would possess the upper hand over their officials. From the middle of the fifth century B.C. to the middle of the fourth, the government of Athens rested upon the belief that all power belonged to the people, who exercised it by a many-sided participation in public affairs. The price of Athenian citizenship was activity and versatility. Among the duties of a citizen were service in the army or navy, attendance at festivals and spectacles, and jury work in the courts of law. But most important of all was his presence at the monthly meetings of the Assembly, at which he helped to enact laws and decrees, settle questions of high policy, conduct foreign relations, and authorize the financial operations of his state. The work of the Assembly, however, busy though it was, required supplementing by administrative officials. These were selected in one of two ways. The Assembly filled by election offices that required special qualifications and expert knowledge. In other cases, where the duties to be performed simply needed average intelligence and the use of ordinary judgment, the Athenians employed a method which was distinctive to their democracy—the lot. Their favorite practice was to place at the head of a department or agency a board of citizens picked annually by lot. Such a system served many purposes. It ensured that government was conducted, in a literal way, *by* the people. It contributed to public education by enlarging the direct acquaintance of citizens with governmental problems. Through rotation in office, it spread a sense of civic responsibility.

Certain safeguards were added, moreover, to forestall the appointment of anybody manifestly unfit and to prevent abuse of power. Before they could assume their posts, those whom the lot selected were made to pass a scrutiny which was a mixture of qualifying test and loyalty clearance. Then ten times during the year, at one of the regular meetings of the Assembly, a standing order of business invited the populace to vote approval or censure of their officials—censure being followed by an indictment in the law courts, tantamount to impeachment. Finally, when the officeholder's year of service came to an end, he presented to a special board of auditors the accounts for any public monies of which he was collector, custodian, or disburser. It was this last requirement—the accountability of the official as enforced by a postaudit—which in Athenian eyes constituted the ultimate weapon of popular control. When Athenian statesmen and philosophers contrasted their political institutions with those of oligarchy or monarchy, two of the features which they most frequently mentioned to highlight the differences were appointment by lot and postaudit. Both practices, in their view, prevented the rise of a bureaucracy, either in the sense of an official caste aloof from and superior to the people or in the sense of an uncontrollable corps of officialdom.

There was, however, another risk to which Athenian democracy was liable. Where matters of such weight were determined at the Assembly of the citizens, much depended on the judgment that the leading orators displayed. Decisions were reached by vote of the majority after free and open discussion, and a proposal could be adopted on the motion, not of some holder of public office, but of any private citizen with a popular following. That being the case, in the absence of further safeguards, policies might be settled or reversed by snap votes; majorities could be incited by ranting orators; the heat of factional fights might inflame the community. To counteract these dangers, of which they learned through bitter experience, the Athenians instituted two more safety devices. One was the curious and drastic expedient called ostracism. When internal dissension and conflict between ambitious politicians imperiled the unity of the state, the Assembly could adopt a motion to ostracize. This was followed in two months' time by a special election where, provided at least 6,000 participated, the man who received a majority of adverse ballots was banished for ten years, after which he could return and resume all his civil, political, and property rights. A second way in which the Assembly sought protection against irresponsible leaders and against its own worse judgment was by drawing a distinction between laws, which contained rules of general application, and decrees, which dealt with particular circumstances. A law could not be amended or repealed without notice in due form and the observance of certain procedural requirements. Likewise, a decree had to fulfill some procedural checks; but in addition it must conform to existing legislation. The Athenians enforced these principles by a judicial process.[1] Within a year of the passage of any law or decree, its proposer could be indicted on a charge of unconstitutionality, the penalties for which were severe. Thus an all-powerful Assembly attempted to guarantee a government under law.

There is more than experimental novelty and a uniquely interesting structure to give merit to this Athenian constitution. It is distinguished in addition by the quality of realism. The Athenians were not content solely to proclaim the fine-sounding doctrines of citizen participation, official accountability, and rule of law. Such ideas would have been insufficient to mold political behavior, were they not reinforced with appropriate institutions and procedures. It was the latter that put teeth into theory and made democracy effective. How vital it is to install the necessary machinery, if ideas are to operate in practice, can be better understood by noting the contrast with other systems which

---

[1]Judicial process meant a trial in the courts, where the verdict was returned by a jury who were a random sample of the citizens.

neglected adequately to translate some well-meant formulas into hard fact.

THE ROMAN SACRIFICE OF LIBERTY TO EMPIRE

Consider the experience of Rome and the political testament which that city bequeathed to its successors. Between the expulsion of the monarchy at the end of the sixth century B.C. and the establishment of the Augustan Principate five centuries later, Rome was a republic. During this period of half a millennium, the Romans accomplished some remarkable achievements. They laid the groundwork for a system of civil and criminal law which is basic to the jurisprudence and legal codes of many modern nations. By the prowess of their redoubtable legions they absorbed within a single empire all the lands and peoples surrounding the Mediterranean. Under the dominion of Rome almost all southern and western Europe, North Africa, and much of the Middle East experienced a greater measure of political unity than that region had known before or has ever known since. But these organizers of law and legions; these architects of highways, aqueducts, and central heating; these Caesars and Ciceros whose craftmanship left Rome the eternal city and Latin a universal language—these men could not for all their political genius construct a democracy. The governmental tradition associated with the name of Rome was and is authoritarian. The major concepts that typify the Roman contribution to politics are expressed in these Latin-derived words: "power"— *potestas,* "authority"—*auctoritas,* "empire"—*imperium.*

The reason for this is plain. The constitution of the Roman republic did embody principles that were potentially democratic. Wanting to avoid a repetition of the tyranny they had suffered under some of their kings, the Romans adopted the device of a distribution and separation of powers and relied upon the various agencies and authorities to balance, and thereby check, each other. Their officials, from the consults on down, were elected by assemblies of citizens, and for a year at a time. Legislation, too, had to be voted upon by the citizens, whose approval converted a proposed bill into an authoritative law. From this it would seen clear that the Romans intended their government to be subordinate to the governed. But circumstances combined to defeat the intention. The republic seldom enjoyed the luxury of a long, uninterrupted peace. Its response to the challenge of nearby peoples launched it upon a tide of military conquest. Acceptance of an imperial mission, however, brought to Rome an enlargement of size and power for which its earlier institutions proved inadequate. The need for continuous direction of policy and for central supervision of outlying provinces was ill met by the poorly organized popular assemblies and annually changing magistrates.

Only one institution attempted to fill the need, the Senate. But when this body—a tightly knit oligarchy of past and present officeholders and noble families—was itself split through the growing division of Roman society into opposed classes, the state was torn apart by internal conspiracies and civil war. The last century of the republic's existence (133–31 B.C.) comprised a dismal catalog of revolution, counterrevolution, and *coup d'état*. Unable to control its powerful commanders in the field, the Senate lay successively at the mercy of Marius, Sulla, Pompey, Caesar, and Anthony and finally succumbed to Augustus. The system founded by the last of these became an autocracy centralized in the person of the emperor, who maintained his position by placating the mob in the streets of Rome and controlling the legions in their barracks on the far-extended frontiers of the empire. Only as perfumed memory of the past did the theory linger on that the emperor received his authority in a law conferring the imperial prerogatives at the beginning of his reign. That law, however, was enacted merely out of deference to an ancient form. It altered not a whit the political realities of absolutism.

A striking parallel may be observed in the medieval period. The political structure of feudalism exhibited a glaring contrast between the doctrines that government is limited by law and rulers are responsible for their actions, and the absence of effective means of enforcement. Though they acknowledged the principle that they should serve the common good, medieval governments fought shy of control by the common people. For this there is a historical explanation. The Germanic tribes, which burst the ramparts of the Roman Empire in the fifth and sixth centuries A.D. and sliced its sprawling territories into kingdoms, had formerly developed some institutions of a rough and primitive democracy in the forests of Germany. But the urge that drove them west and south was itself the result of pressure upon central Europe from other peoples farther east—the pressure of Asiatics, like the Huns, foraging for new supplies of food and plundering as they went. This migration of people, the *Völkerwanderung*, had a profound effect upon forms of government. A tribe on the march, or one that has to repel invaders, must militarize itself to survive, which always means that it becomes authoritarian. When in addition the Goths, Franks, Vandals, and the rest gradually imbibed the influence of the civilization they had overrun, they sought to assimilate their own kingdoms to the pattern of imperial Rome. The democratic folkways of the German forests, like the traditions of the Roman republic, thenceforth continued to exist in a fairyland of remembered ideas to which the brute facts of daily government gave the lie.

THE MEDIEVAL ORDER: FICTIONS AND FACTS

The medieval world which emerged from the turmoil of these Dark Ages fairly bristled with notions of law as a restraint upon government. Being a Christian, a ruler must conform to the law of God. Being custodian of   community's way of life, he must uphold and preserve its immemorial customs, to which indeed he owed his own powers and privileges. But was there anyone to say whether a ruler had in fact violated divine or human law, and, if so, how could he be called to account? The possibility of curbing a ruler depended, as always, on the existence of organized opposition. In the Middle Ages there were two sources from whence this might spring. One was, of course, the church. If it could be charged that a ruler sinned against divine law, the church could direct against him its two powerful weapons—excommunication and interdict. When employed by a masterful pope, these devices could bring to heel a king like John of England, or even such an emperor as Henry IV.

Clerical resistance to royal or imperial power, though it imposed a limitation upon the state, did not necessarily constitute a gain from the standpoint of democratic or popular control. All that happened when the papacy scored a success was the subordination for the time being of secular to ecclesiastical authority, the latter being as authoritarian in spirit and structure as the former. Hence, toward the close of the Middle Ages a movement developed for the reform of church government. Associated with the names of the Italian Marsiglio of Padua, and the Englishman William of Occam, this was called the Conciliar Movement because its aim was to place at the head of the church a general council of elected delegates representing not only the clergy but all Christian believers. The Conciliarists came near to their goal at the end of the Great Schism when, in order to heal the breach in the church and overhaul its organization, two councils were convoked and met respectively at Constance (1414–18) and Basel (1431–49). In the face, however, of opposition from the pope, the cardinals, and the higher clergy generally, this attempt to democratize the structure of the church met with failure. The "Petrine theory" of papal power, placing supreme authority in the pope who governs in consultation with the college of cardinals, was emphatically asserted. In consequence, as George H. Sabine has written: "The pope in the fifteenth century established himself as the first of the absolute monarchs, and the theory of papal absolutism became the archetype of the theory of monarchical absolutism."[2]

---

[2]George H. Sabine, *History of Political Theory* (London: George G. Harrap & Co., Ltd., 1937), p. 326. See the whole of Chap. 16 in that book.

THE STRUGGLE BETWEEN KINGS AND NOBLES

There was only one other quarter besides the church from which effective opposition to a king could come in the Middle Ages. This was the nobility. Much of the political history of those centuries consisted in struggles between the nobles and their monarch, with each side trying to curb the other. When the nobles stood solidly together, they could wring concessions from a king. A notable instance was the triumph of the English barons in compelling King John to sign the Great Charter of 1215 which reaffirmed their ancient rights and privileges against royal encroachment. Still more successful was the Polish nobility, whose prolonged resistance reduced the institution of monarchy to a weak figurehead. In their case, however, success had tragic consequences since the Polish state in the absence of strong direction fell easy prey to Russian and Prussian expansion and was erased from the map. Sometimes a powerful nobleman opposed the reigning monarch in order to dispossess him of the crown and place it upon his own or a kinsman's head. More often than not, the rivalries between great aristocrats and their clans sowed a bitter crop of strife and bloodshed. The Wars of the Roses, which for three decades tore medieval England into two hostile camps, were sparked by the clashing ambitions of the Houses of Lancaster and York, as were the political aims of papacy and empire respectively championed on the Continent by Guelphs and Ghibellines.

From this welter of discord, into which the loose-knit character of feudalism had plunged society, there emerged in one country the beginnings of a constructive achievement which was destined to endure. It was in England during the thirteenth century that the institution of Parliament took shape and acquired, at the hands of Simon de Montfort (1265) and King Edward I (1295), the form and functions which differentiated it from the earlier Great Council. During the thirteenth and fourteenth centuries that form was set into the definite mold of two chambers, one of which, the House of Lords, contained the higher nobility and higher clergy and the second, the House of Commons, represented the lesser nobles (for example, knights of the shire) and commoners. The functions of Parliament are a more complicated story. The reason for its existence in the Middle Ages may be found in two circumstances. The "loyal, trusty, and well-beloved subjects" of the king normally had various grievances of which they wished to complain to His Majesty. These could be more effectively voiced and would carry more weight if expressed through a regularized procedure. While subjects needed to approach the king for redressing their wrongs, he had a motive on his side for approaching them, since he wanted their money. Originally the king's government was considered a branch of his household. As any great landowner managed his estates and supervised the affairs of his tenantry, so was a king supposed to govern the realm and protect its inhabitants. Affairs of state were handled by secretaries and other palace officials who in a literal sense were servants of the Crown, while the costs of administration were defrayed out of the king's personal wealth. In all this, no attempt was made to separate what was public from what was private. Or rather, the concept of public interest had disappeared in the smothering embrace of private relationships. Public officials were court functionaries; the public treasury, a private purse.

Such a situation could continue only so long as the functions of the central government were few and their costs remained small. Everything changed, however, when kings endeavored to extend their authority to new fields (for example, the provision of a uniform, national system of justice) and when they embarked on the most expensive of all governmental activities—war. To pacify the Welsh, contain the Scots, crush the Irish, and conquer the French[3] meant retaining and supplying large armies in the field. No longer could a king "live off his own" as tradition expected him to do. He must now ask his subjects to contribute in his service not only their lives but that other dear possession, their money. Here then was a situation with the makings of a bargain advantageous to both sides. If the king were to appropriate his subjects' money without their consent, they would have a new and serious grievance. If he requested them, however, to contribute their money voluntarily, was not the time opportune for them to request him to remedy their wrongs, which might lead to legislative action or to changes in executive policy? Furthermore, when asking for money, the king would have to satisfy the natural curiosity of taxpayers who wished to know how equitably it would be collected and for what purposes it would be spent. Hence Parliament received its start in life from the coupling of two original functions—the exercise of the power of the purse and the need for a public forum for the ventilation of grievances. From these roots grew such other duties as the enactment of law, discussion of public policy, and control of the executive.

RISE OF THE ENGLISH PARLIAMENT

Great institutions grow slowly, however, and, like big trees which add a new ring annually, store up their annual accumulation of prece-

[3] For example, the protracted campaigns of the Hundred Years' War (1337-1453).

dents. Four centuries elapsed between Edward I's Model Parliament of 1295 and the final, decisive victory of parliamentarians over royalists in 1688. What was it that took so much time? The answer consists in a social and economic, as well as a political, explanation. When Parliament was constructed to represent wealth and social superiority, when the dominant interest in the economy was the possession of land, and when the nobles were among the biggest landowners, then an addition to the powers of Parliament with its proportionate weakening of the Crown could only mean government of the people by the nobility, for the nobility, and it was doubtful whether anything was to be gained by rejecting the king's yoke in favor of that. On the contrary, from the standpoint of the mass of the population there was much to be said in favor of a weak nobility and a powerful king, since, when a king abused his power, his oppression was likely to bear hardest upon the nobles, who were the nearest rivals to his preeminence.

The politics of this situation was reinforced by the economic developments of the fifteenth century. At that time the structure of feudalism, centering around the ownership and produce of the land, was suffering the force of a contrary interest. An expansion of handicraft industries was accompanied by increase in domestic and foreign commerce. Enterprises of this character stimulated and strengthened the craft guilds, associations of merchants, and credit and banking institutions. For mutual convenience these clustered within the walls of the trading city[4] *(Handelsstadt)*, which was indispensable as the focal point in the system of production, distribution, and communication. Such cities began to exert their influence upon the political process. What they sought was the preservation of order (because warfare disrupted trade) and emancipation from rural supremacy. On both scores urbanism pitted itself against the feudal aristocracy, whose discords disturbed the peace and whose wealth was drawn from the soil. The monarchy, natural foe of the nobility, was the natural ally of the urban *burghers* or burgesses. The grant to cities of royal charters of incorporation, as in England, enabled them to be self-governing, that is, to be rid of feudal government by the nobles who dominated the countryside. Consequently it was this urban "middle" class which rallied to the Crown, which helped to replace the decentralized disorder of feudalism by unified central power, which embodied the new concept of sovereignty[5] in the person of the sovereign (a word that became synonymous with "king"), and which reaped the economic

[4]Witness the growth in importance of the Hanseatic League (including in its membership Hamburg, Bremen, Lübeck, Bergen, Danzig, and others), the cities of northern Italy (like Venice, Milan, and Florence), and Antwerp, Amsterdam, and London.
[5]See Chap. 6, pp. 171–72.

benefits of the centrally directed policies of mercantilism.[6] In England as in France the monarchy became absolute because there were material interests approving the powers it wielded.

THE REVOLUTION IN ENGLAND

It is the style of political change, as was observed earlier,[7] to proceed from excess in one direction to counterexcess in the other. If feudal disunity was the prelude to royal absolutism, the latter too outlasted its original justification and by abuses of its own invoked new opposition. A monarch who was steering a dangerous course— witness Henry VIII piloting the English Reformation or Queen Elizabeth I holding the Spaniards at bay with zigzags of dalliance and defiance—wisely employed the institution of Parliament for enlisting public support, and Parliament's members, their appetite for authority whetted with each taste, would not willingly be denied a further share once the immediacy of crisis was past. The cooperation between Parliament and the Crown, which was fairly well maintained by Tudor monarchs, broke down under their unhappy successors, the Stuarts. A variety of circumstances turned a rift into a revolution. Chief blunders on the royal side were the decisions of Charles I to dispense altogether with Parliament, to levy taxes without parliamentary consent, and to administer secret and arbitrary "justice" in the Court of the Star Chamber. The price which England paid was a civil war of ten years' duration (1641–51). Charles paid by defeat and the loss of his head. Even this example did not deter King James II, thirty years later, from attempting to restore Catholicism to a predominantly Protestant people. Again an aroused Parliament formed the focus of opposition. In 1688 a second revolution was won without bloodshed, the King being forced to flee with his neck intact. It was Parliament which then invited William of Orange and his wife Mary to occupy the throne, and in an Act of Settlement laid down the terms and limits by which the monarchy has since been bound.

Thus was consecrated the first of the series of modern revolutions which delivered a new birth of freedom. By the end of the seventeenth century England had secured the essentials of political liberty by creating at the apex of its government an institution representative of the governed. In this way the English people established for themselves, and by their example demonstrated to others, a method through which the effectiveness of power could be legitimized with

[6]See Chap. 7, pp. 178–79.
[7]See Chap. 6, p. 167.

the moral sanction of consent. Then, with parliamentary supremacy assured, the theoretical explanation followed. These stirring events required a justification, and the occasion found the man. It was in 1690 that John Locke published his two *Treatises of Civil Government.* The first he devoted to the negative task of destroying the fatuous doctrine of the divine right of kings. In the second he constructed a positive theory to take its place. Governments, he asserted, may rightfully exercise only those powers to which the people give their consent. Authority is conferred as a trust, being simply "a fiduciary power to act for certain ends."[8] The wishes of the community are represented and formulated by the legislature which ranks supreme among the organs of the state. Should those in power abuse their trust and a conflict break out between the government and the governed, the latter retain the ultimate weapon of revolution since they can never surrender the right to save themselves.[9] In any such dispute between the citizen body and authority, no third party can serve as judge. The people are always their own final court of appeal.

The supremacy of Parliament, which had resulted from military victory in the civil war and political triumph in 1688, accorded well with these doctrines—subject to one proviso. It was one thing to assert that the monarchy should henceforth be limited, not absolute, and that Parliament (the legislature) should be paramount over the Crown (the executive). It was something else to assume that the dominance of Parliament was the same as control by all the people. The franchise at the time when Locke wrote was limited to a small number of property owners who were but a fraction of the population. Nor did Locke propose to change this. Thus the consent of the governed boiled down to the consent of a class. Nevertheless, it was Locke's achievement that, wittingly or unwittingly, he had sown a seed, and there was no stopping its growth. What is more, there were other soils besides that of England in which it could take root. This was what an English government learned in 1776.

PRINCIPLES OF THE AMERICAN REVOLUTION

"To secure these rights, Governments are instituted among Men, deriving their just powers from the consent of the governed." The key words in this sentence are "just" and "consent." Jefferson's problem, when he drafted the Declaration of Independence, was similar to what Locke had faced one century before. He was expounding the

[8] *Second Treatise of Civil Government,* Chap. 13, Sec. 149.
[9] *Ibid.*

right to rebel against any kind of authority that was unresponsive to the governed. Since liberty to him was a supreme good, he wanted a society of free men. These, he recognized, must accept certain restraints upon their behavior and must enforce their rules upon offenders. Like the other fathers of the American Revolution, Jefferson was no anarchist. His purpose was not to sweep all government away, but to substitute authority which could be held to account for authority that could not. How was this to be done? Was it possible to argue for freedom and yet acquiesce in some coercion?

Jefferson's answer began by reasserting the principle that the consent of the governed is the foundation of all legitimate government. It is consent alone which gives moral sanction and legal validity to the physical force employed by the state. Powers, therefore, which are derived from consent are just, that is, are justified. But suppose a government acts in defiance of consent. What then? "Whenever any form of government becomes destructive of these ends," continues the Declaration, "it is the right of the people to alter or to abolish it, and to institute new government, laying its foundation on such principles and organizing its powers in such form, as to them shall seem most likely to effect their safety and happiness."

To those who read them, these ideas have never ceased to yield inspiration. Their expression in this particular form was evoked at one of the turning points in modern political history and their influence on subsequent politics has been profound. Yet the concepts enshrined in the Declaration are not free from difficulties, both philosophical and practical. Designed for a solution to existing problems, they inaugurated certain new ones.

Consider, for example, some implications of the doctrine of consent. Besides the ethical force of the argument that consent lends morality to the actions of government, it made sense in the seventeenth and eighteenth centuries to contend that, when people stayed in a community, the fact of their remaining implied their consent to its functions. Englishmen who disliked their government could emigrate across the Atlantic. Colonists who wished, after 1776, to remain under the British Crown could move north to Canada. Where there was some freedom of movement, the doctrine of consent was not a pious fiction. It contained some realism. But in the twentieth century, the world is not so open. Many, having no genuine alternative and being unable to emigrate, must live within a regime to which they do not consent.

Moreover, consent must imply agreement on certain points. But agreement about what? Is it agreement only about procedures (for example, elections, voting, and majority decisions), whereby we assent in advance to abide by any result which emerges from the procedures? Or is it agreement about ends and goals as well? That is to say, do we agree in preferring a certain kind of social order, a group of values, a civilization? And do we then regard it as a duty of government not to do the things that would infringe upon such values? In the former case, there can be no restriction on how the procedures are used, provided that a "due process" is followed. In the latter case, the restrictions are very definite, since the community in question is dedicated or committed to certain goals. These will be modified only as men come to prefer new values or alter their interpretation of the old ones.

Nor is it undeniable that consent, if stated as an absolute or as *the* absolute, can never be completely realized in practice. Since unanimity never exists in big political issues, somebody's consent has to be forfeited whenever a majority has its way at the expense of a minority. On occasion, it may be in society's interest for the majority to prevail, and the minority should then submit. But cannot majorities also be tyrannical and oppressive? And, if so, is not the minority then entitled to resist? In other words, consent is not the sole pillar of a free society, though it certainly is one of the pillars that are fundamental. The problem of ensuring the freedom of the governed is not the apparently simple one of discovering what the people will and then doing it. On most matters there are many wills, since human beings belong to many groups and have so many interests. Because in actuality the support which sustains a government will be at times that of majority, at other times that of a minority, the governed may need alternately both protection by government and protection from it. To assert the inalienable right of a people to regain their freedom by revolution is excellent doctrine. But it describes an ultimate weapon for use in the last resort. Revolution can be a method—fully justified when it is directed against a despotism—of founding a government in the first instance. It is not a means of continuous popular control over regular government activities. For this, something else is required, and it is to the credit of Jefferson's generation that they not only formulated abstract ideas, but also constructed workable institutions which have yielded results in practice. The foundations of the latter were laid between 1787 and 1803.[10]

SUPREMACY OF THE CONSTITUTION

In the American solution to this age-old problem of making government both responsive and responsible (that is, of giving it the power

[10] 1803 was the date of the decision in *Marbury* v. *Madison.* See p. 255.

to serve, but denying it the power to dominate), the distinctive feature is the special role assigned to the Constitution. Whereas the English Revolution of the seventeenth century left Parliament supreme, the American Revolution resulted in the supremacy of the Constitution. How was this ensured? Various measures have been employed to guarantee that the Constitution would occupy the paramount position in the American system. Its drafting was undertaken by a special convention of delegates, presided over by George Washington. The adoption of the finished product was referred to the states, in all of which, except Rhode Island, delegates were elected to special state conventions which debated and voted on the issue of ratification. Ever since it went into effect, the Constitution has possessed the unique status which its contents intended it to have. The preamble announces unequivocally that "We, the people . . . do ordain and establish this Constitution," thereby affirming that the government is founded upon popular will. While it is the people who create the Constitution, it is the Constitution that creates the institutions whereby government is conducted. All of these—the Congress, President, and Supreme Court, as well as the state constitutions and their officials—are subordinate to the Constitution of the United States, to laws that conform to it, and to treaties made under its authority, which together comprise "the supreme law of the land."[11]

Besides being asserted, the supremacy of the Constitution must be enforced. How is this accomplished? In the first place, by the requirement that all governmental officials—federal, state, and local, elected and appointed—take an oath or affirmation to support the Constitution. Second, by the provision of judicial procedures and penalties, including impeachment, in case any official betrays the people's trust. Third, by the institution of a special system, distinct from the ordinary process of legislation, for amending the Constitution's written text. Further, for good measure there is a fourth method—the judicial review of legislation. Under it, any statute enacted by the legislature and approved by the chief executive or repassed over his veto may be challenged on the ground of unconstitutionality. A case will then be heard in the courts, where it is the judiciary who determine whether the contested statute is to be obeyed as law or regarded as null and void.

THE PRACTICE OF JUDICIAL REVIEW

The system of judicial review of legislation, involving as it does the two points that statutes must conform to the Constitution and that the

---

[11] *Constitution of the United States,* Article VI.

judges will decide whether they do conform or not, is nowhere explicitly mentioned in the Constitution.[12] In a partial[13] sense, however, the practice was known in the period before 1776, and certain of the Founding Fathers assumed that it would be employed under the new Constitution.[14] It was, therefore, left to the judges to pick an occasion for asserting this power, if they were so minded, and exercising it successfully, if they were able. Their occasion was the case of *Marbury* v. *Madison*, decided in 1803. Chief Justice Marshall there used a relatively minor incident as an opportunity for proclaiming the momentous power of judicial disallowance of legislation enacted by a coordinate branch of the same government. His words deserve to be quoted:

It is a proposition too plain to be contested, that the Constitution controls any legislative Act repugnant to it; or, that the legislature may alter the constitution by an ordinary Act. Between these alternatives there is no middle ground. The constitution is either a superior paramount law, unchangeable by ordinary means, or it is on a level with ordinary legislative Acts, and, like other Acts, is alterable when the legislature shall please to alter it. If the former part of the alternative be true, then a legislative Act contrary to the constitution is not law; if the latter part be true, then written constitutions are absurd attempts, on the part of the people, to limit a power in its own nature illimitable. Certainly all those who have framed written constitutions contemplate them as forming the fundamental and paramount law of the nation, and consequently the theory of every such government must be that an Act of the legislature repugnant to the constitution is void. . . . It is emphatically the province and duty of the judicial department to say what the law is. Those who apply the rule to particular cases must of necessity expound and interpret that rule. If two laws conflict with each other, the courts must decide on the operation of each.[15]

THE RULE OF LAW

The cumulative effect of this reasoning and these principles is impressive. Added together, they form a special derivation from the

[12]However, the point that laws should conform to the Constitution can be inferred from the wording of Article VI: "This Constitution, and the laws of the United States *which shall be made in pursuance thereof,* . . . shall be the supreme law of the land." My italics.

[13]Prior to independence a colonial statute could be disallowed by the Privy Council if it contravened the colony's charter or an act of the British Parliament. In such instances, an agency of a legally superior government was supervising the legislation of a government legally inferior—as when the United States Supreme Court now reviews a state law.

[14]For example, Alexander Hamilton in *The Federalist,* No. 78.

[15]*Marbury* v. *Madison,* 1 Cranch 137 (1803).

broader principle summed up in the phrase which has become symbolic, "the rule of law," and, because the offspring of the same parents are related to one another, an affinity also exists between Marshall's logic and other specific points deducible from the same general source. Some of these points are the following:

1. Governments shall exercise their powers in conformity with known laws enacted through a regular procedure
2. No laws be passed to convert into offenses actions which were lawful at the time when performed
3. No one may be convicted on any charge save after a fair trial in open court
4. The judiciary, when applying the generalities of the law to particular cases, must be independent of external pressure and control

Such maxims, while arguable on theoretical grounds, are chiefly derived from hard facts and bitter experience. Each was formulated as an ideal contrasting with the proven practices of many governments in the past and present. When a state does not enthrone the rule of law, the governed have no adequate protection against the whim and caprice of those in power. Tyranny, despotism, or dictatorship exists when a government makes and unmakes the law without permitting public criticism or challenge; when it imprisons an individual without public hearing and an equal opportunity for defense; when judges decide cases under the intimidating shadow of executive power; and when laws are enforced arbitrarily, that is, so as to discriminate on grounds of political or personal favoritism between citizens who deserve like treatment.

The Constitution which the state of Massachusetts adopted in 1776 contained the hope "that it may be a government of laws and not of men." This antithesis, of course, cannot be taken too literally. No legal system can operate with automatic, impersonal, machinelike precision. Laws, unlike men, are not self-made. Still less are they self-enforcing. It is men who must draft, enact, interpret, and apply the law. A human—indeed, a humane—discretion must scale down the broad classification to the narrow particulars. But though the Massachusetts statement is a rhetorical exaggeration, the contrast between a government of laws and a government of men serves to emphasize an important distinction. A state may be of a kind which acknowledges and observes certain restraints upon its activities. Or it may flout and defy all efforts at restraint. In the former case, the government's power is bridled and harnessed. In the latter, the powers of government are absolute, and therefore uncontrollable.

CONFORMANCE OF LAW TO CUSTOM, NATURE, OR UTILITY

The attempt to impose restraints upon government through the medium of the law manifests itself in different ways and has evoked a number of principles, each with attendant merits and difficulties. One example is the concept that law is the product of immemorial custom. Just as the activity of millions of small coelenterates eventually surrounds an island with a coral reef, so the acts of millions of human beings, repeated in patterns which become habitual, construct a ring of custom around a community and its government. Custom is then thought of as a barrier confining the operations and powers of officials within limits they may not overstep, and law is merely the collection of practices that custom has confirmed. Discover the usages of the past, and you find the law of the present. This done, the duty of government becomes the simple one of preserving unbroken the links that connect the chain of custom. Such a view of the relation between law and government is admirable if its purpose is to maintain stability and continuity in a static or imperceptibly changing society. It accords ill with the problems of government under circumstances of rapid flux when experimentation and flexibility are more at a premium than traditionalism.

Another device for subordinating the state to the restraints of law is the belief, referred to earlier, in a law of nature or reason. Once the preliminary assumption is accepted that such a law exists—which is itself a matter of faith rather than reason—various consequences can be readily deduced—for instance, that nature embodies principles which are in themselves rational and can be understood by reason, that these are universal in scope and eternal in duration, that the state governs well when it assists men in conforming to natural law, and that acts which violate such law are therefore invalid. The "higher law" theory here outlined, like the doctrine which derives law from custom, is appropriately adapted to a certain goal. By appealing to a higher law (that is, higher than that proclaimed by the state) men may justify resistance to authority or outright revolution, since it is always psychologically necessary for people who resist or rebel to make their opponents, and not themselves, appear in the wrong. Alternatively, the higher law doctrine suits the needs of other institutions which fear the state or are its rivals, since these can affirm that men do not live by politics alone and that in nature's house there are many mansions. For such reasons, both churches and business organizations have heavily subscribed to the natural law philosophy.

But this same philosophy abounds with unsolved problems. For who is to say which principles are natural or what is reason's law? When different interpretations are offered, whose shall be adjudged correct? Because of these uncertainties the net practical effects of appealing to natural law doctrines are often unfortunate. One outcome is for men to flee from one type of authority, that of the state and its laws, and seek refuge in the arms of another, for example, that of the priest, pastor, or businessman. The law of nature is then respectively translated into the law of nature's God, as clerical authority affirms it, or the natural laws of economics as some economist expounds them. Alternatively, if men shrink from substituting new authoritarianism for old, they will escape into the skepticism which rejects every interpretation of natural law on the ground that anybody's guess may be right and none can be definitely proven. In this case there is a flight from reason; decisions are reached through force; and the more powerful proclaim themselves the rightful.

A third, celebrated formula for using law to place restraints on government is the one coined by Jeremy Bentham and popularized into a slogan by the Utilitarians—the notion that governments must promote the greatest happiness of the greatest number. The Utilitarians were the British reformers of the nineteenth century, who, seeking to modernize their political machinery and legal code, applied to each established law and institution the test, What is its utility? Whatever statute or executive act helped to increase the sum total of happiness in the community was considered good. Whatever diminished that stock of happiness must be removed or reformed. A government merited support or opposition according to how it influenced happiness. Such a yardstick subjects the state to a different standard. To appraise a government's action by its degree of conformity to custom or nature means referring to the source of authority. To test an act by its relation to happiness means studying its effects and comparing one set of results with another. In spirit at least, this latter approach is experimental and scientific. Applied in practice, however, Bentham's formula fails to be as scientific as one would wish, because it is impossible to measure a quantity of happiness. People will therefore wrangle endlessly about whether a particular governmental action, compared with possible untried alternatives, produces more happiness or less.

CONSTITUTIONS AND CONSTITUTIONALISM

Besides these specific methods of restraining government by law, there is the more general argument that the state will not tyrannize over its citizens if it is imbued with respect for constitutionalism. What is meant by this? A distinction should be made between "constitutionalism" and "constitution." A constitution is the basic design of the structure and powers of the state and the rights and duties of its citizens. In that sense there is a constitution in every state which has a settled form and an established government—in the United States, Canada, and Britain, as well as in Nazi Germany, Franco Spain, and Stalin's Russia—and to say that a state possesses a constitution implies nothing about its democratic or dictatorial character. "Constitutionalism," however, is a term which does have definite implications. It is bound up with the notion of the rule of law. It embraces the idea that a government should not be permitted to do anything its officials please, but should conduct itself according to equitable and agreed procedures. The purpose of this restriction on its freedom of action is of course to safeguard a fundamental area of freedom for its citizens. For tyranny is most probable where power is total.

Clear though it is that constitutionalism is incompatible with dictatorship, and that political freedom requires some curbs on power, the nature of these limits calls for more discussion. It is one thing to harness a horse and another to hobble it. It is one thing to control a government, and another to cripple it. The difference may be one of degree or emphasis. But it is all-important. It stems from contrasted attitudes toward power. Some thinkers are so preoccupied with the abuses of power that their interpretation of constitutionalism is a series of negatives. Their rule of law degenerates into a bundle of prohibitions. A government must be prevented from doing this, that, and the other. To devise checks, controls, restraints, and limitations becomes the essence of constitutionalism and the prime guarantee of human freedom. But is it really necessary to lean so far backwards? May not this overattention to abuses defeat its own purpose? Since government is indispensable, and since no one can govern without power, it ought to be evident that constitutionalism should first be concerned with how power must be used and then, second, with how it may be abused. The state should be envisaged as a canal through which political power may flow, releasing its energy for the benefit of mankind, rather than as a dam to hold it back. After all, the basic task in any philosophy of government is to figure out what the state must do, not what it should be prohibited from doing. Nor is it to be forgotten that, while tyrannical governments destroy freedom, other governments may enlarge it. Many of the functions which the modern state undertakes are designed to make opportunities more nearly equal for everybody and to protect weaker individuals from the rapacity of the strong.

But there is a still more basic objection to those who develop their photograph of constitutionalism in the negative and neglect to print it in positive colors. If constitutionalism is approved on the ground that it causes restraints upon government, the inquiry has to be thrown one stage further back. Constitutionalism is itself the result of other factors which are its causes. What are these? Essentially, as can be demonstrated, their character is political. This is an assertion which has the effect of switching the discussion onto another track. Hitherto in this chapter the problem of making government accountable to the governed has been viewed in a predominantly legal light—in terms of the rule of law, of legal curbs upon power, of constitutionalism—so that political freedom appears as the consequence of a certain legal situation. But this is an illusion, for the image has been turned upside down. Although there is always some interaction between law and politics, it is primarily politics that controls and determines law and not law that controls and determines politics. It is not any rule of law or respect for constitutionalism that gives birth to a politically free society, but rather the politics of freedom that creates the sanction for constitutionalism and law. What has been called "the firmament of law"[16] is not self-supporting. It is propped up on political pillars. Without them it would topple.

THE POLITICAL ROOTS OF THE AMERICAN CONSTITUTIONAL SYSTEM

To understand this better, let us take a closer look at the government of the United States. The Constitution stands at the center and is the chief symbol of the American form of government. Because the Constitution is a supreme law, because it contains a list of judicially enforceable rights, and because of the practice of judicial review of legislation, it has become customary in many quarters to think of the Constitution as a lawyers' document to be construed in legal fashion.[17] But this is to overlook the political context which ascribes to law its significance and to judges their status. The ultimate power under the Constitution is lodged, not with the Supreme Court, but with the people. It is "We, the people" who "ordain and establish" the Constitution. It is the people's elected representatives who amend it and may express disapproval of a Supreme Court decision by amendment, making it inapplicable to future cases.[18] It is the political branches of

[16]By Robert M. MacIver in *The Web of Government* (New York: The Macmillan Company, 1947), Chap. 4.

[17]A cynic has observed that "a government of laws, not of men" becomes a government of lawyers, not of men.

[18]There are several instances of amendments that reversed decisions of the Supreme Court. To wit, the Eleventh, which recorded the indignation of the states at *Chisholm* v. *Georgia;* the Thirteenth, Fourteenth, and Fifteenth, which repudiated the principles

the government, the President and the Senate, which nominate and confirm appointees to the Court and, by choosing its personnel, influence the trend of future decisions. Where the rule of law exists, it is because a political will wants to have it so.

This point is reinforced by a further reflection. As every practicing politician knows and any student of government soon discovers, there are many essential features of the American system of government that cannot be learned from a reading of the Constitution. The Constitution is a concise, compact document, its brevity being one of its many merits. On few issues does it elaborate in any detail, and these are mostly concerned with electoral machinery or the procedure for a presidential veto of legislation. For the rest, as a Constitution should be, it is broad in scope and general in its terms. Since the addition of the Bill of Rights (the first ten amendments) in 1791, the text has been changed only fifteen times in a century and three-quarters. But the nation over whose growth to greatness the Constitution has presided has altered almost beyond recognition. From a community of four million people living in thirteen states along the Atlantic seaboard with an agrarian economy and a precarious military position, this Union has expanded to more than two hundred millions spread across fifty states from the Atlantic far into the Pacific and from the Arctic Circle to the Tropic of Cancer, exhibiting the world's most highly developed industrial technology and living standards, administering distant territories and possessions, and wielding the mightiest single contemporary aggregate of military strength. Of all these changes there is scarcely a trace or record in the written text of the Constitution. But such social transformations cannot fail to have their effects upon the basic design of the powers and structure of government and the rights and duties of citizens—to repeat the definition of a constitution suggested earlier.[19] It stands to reason therefore that these effects have been registered in other ways than by the formal method of constitutional amendment. What are they?

The first is by legislative enactment. Much of the output of Congress, admittedly, is of no fundamental importance. Legislation runs the whole gamut from private bills which concern a particular person or mere municipal ordinances for the District of Columbia to the weightiest measures affecting national and international prosperity and security. But although opinions will differ in certain cases, some statutes, as judged by their subject matter and content, clearly occupy

---

of the Dred Scott case; and the Sixteenth, which overthrew the opinion of the Court concerning federal inability to levy income tax.

[19]See p. 259.

a crucial position in the governmental process. Laws, for example, which organize the federal district and appellate courts, which establish such agencies as the Defense Department or the Interstate Commerce Commission, which provide freedom from want through a program of social security, which regulate the franchise or the conduct of elections, these and others like them deal with matters no less fundamental than some sections of the Constitution itself. The continuous labors of over ninety Congresses have done much to shape the primary patterns of American government.

The same may be said of the work of the Supreme Court. Because the Founding Fathers were writing a Constitution rather than a statute, they wisely drafted many a critical clause in language so broad as to permit diversity of future definition and detail. In innumerable instances it has been left to the Court to supply the guiding principles for Congress and the executive branch to follow. Take the federal powers over interstate commerce and general welfare.[20] The terse wording of the clauses in which these are described has lent itself to wide possibilities, as may be seen from the questions that the Supreme Court at some time or other has decided. Does the power to regulate interstate commerce permit the federal government to prohibit certain commodities outright (for example, impure foods, unsafe drugs, or pornographic publications); or certain business practices, such as competitive methods that are specified as unfair; or certain forms of corporate organization, such as trusts and monopolies? Does the definition of commerce include the channels of transportation (such as navigable waterways, highways, railroads, and airlines) and other means of communication like the telephone, telegraph, television, and radio? Does commerce mean only the exchange of a finished article, or does it extend backward to cover manufacturing and forward to include retail prices? From the kind of answer given to these questions there follows, in accordion fashion, either a sharp contraction or a huge enlargement of federal authority with its consequent effect upon the relation of government to business. The same has happened with other critical clauses of the Constitution. By interpretations of such clauses as those which deal with general welfare, due process of law, equal protection of the laws, or freedom of speech, the Court is virtually engaged in amending the basic law by giving more precision to

---

[20]In its list of subjects on which Congress may legislate, Article I, section 8 of the Constitution includes the powers "to regulate commerce . . . among the several States" and "to lay and collect taxes . . . and provide for the common defense and general welfare of the United States."

its generalities. Judge-made definitions[21] have thus added essential portions to the foundation work of the Constitution.

Nor is this all. Many of the fundamental facts of the American system of government can be explained only in political, not in legal, terms. Some sections of the Constitution have not been applied in practice because political considerations did not permit their enforcement. Thus the Fourteenth Amendment declares, in section 2, that if a state denies voting rights to any of its citizens, the congressional representation to which its population entitles that state shall be proportionately reduced. Until 1958, no effect was given to that provision because, had it been properly enforced, both major parties and many states, northern as well as southern, would have suffered a loss of representation. By "gentlemen's agreement," therefore, the Constitution was tacitly ignored. At long last, however, the Civil Rights Laws of 1957 and 1964 attempted to cope with this problem. The Commission created by the Act of 1957 probed into districts where Negroes were systematically prevented from registering to vote and initiated action in the courts against the responsible local authorities. The same point holds true for another politically sensitive matter—the apportionment of electoral districts, whether of the House of Representatives or of the state legislatures. For allotting representation in the branch of the legislature which is designed to represent the public on the basis of population, the federal Constitution and those of many states demand a reapportionment every ten years (that is, after the census). But it is left to the states to redraw the boundaries—a responsibility in which many have notably defaulted. Since the rural areas several decades ago contained a larger percentage of the whole population than now, they received their due share of the seats, and their representatives in the 1950's and 1960's were generally reluctant to surrender seats to the large cities. In fact, the underrepresentation of the big metropolitan regions has continued in flagrant violation of constitutional provisions because the political branch of the government (the legislature), which should have modernized itself, neglected to do so. In this situation it was the Supreme Court of the United States which had the courage to "enter the political thicket."[22] Taking a series of cases on this subject, the Court extended the "equal protection" clause of the Fourteenth Amendment to cover the principle that one vote should have one

[21]Many doctrines have been enunciated by the Court that, until modified by a later majority of judges, have controlled the legislative and executive branches—for example, the doctrines of "original package," "business affected with a public interest," "the flow of commerce," "clear and present danger," and so forth.

[22]Against the advice of Justice Frankfurter, who used this phrase in a dissenting opinion. The Supreme Court has also ruled that state senates should be truly representative.

value—which manifestly did not occur when electoral districts were grossly unequal in population.[23]

This truth becomes yet plainer when one reflects upon other features of American government which have developed in political practice and of which the Constitution remains entirely innocent. Many examples of this can be cited; but there is none more revealing than the rise and organization of political parties. The party system which grew and matured in the nineteenth century was antithetical to the ideals of the men who drafted the United States Constitution. Thus the institutions they constructed did not anticipate the emergence of parties, were not designed to admit them, and have not always dovetailed with them in a harmonious fit. What is more, James Madison and other leading spirits of his generation would have regarded government by parties as an evil since they habitually described their eighteenth century equivalents by the unfavorable term, "factions." Modern democracy, however, has taken the parties into the inner sanctum of power, and its political process is nowadays unthinkable without them. Voting for a president by means of a college of electors; the organization, procedures, and output of Congress; cooperation or friction between chief executive and legislature; the people's choice of policies and personalities; none of these would be as they are if parties did not profoundly influence the result. No small slice of American government is composed of political customs whose content is as important, whose character as enduring, as what is written in the Constitution.

All this suggests the need for a realistic approach to the problem of explaining constitutions and what they stand for. The basic pattern of government in the United States can be compared to a broad river created by four streams flowing together. First is the document entitled the Constitution. A second is made up of certain legislative enactments. A third consists of judicial opinions. The fourth is political custom. If a name is needed to describe the sum total, a convenient term is "the constitutional system." It is this that underpins the entire structure of government, deriving its strength from the bedrock of political power rather than the sands of legal formulas.

THE POLITICS OF THE BRITISH CONSTITUTION

If more evidence is needed to sustain this view, it can be furnished from the case of Britain. To many writers on politics the British form

---

[23]Likewise, in the controversy about integrating the public schools and universities, it has been evident that the Constitution is only as effective in practice as the political will behind it.

of government appears a paradox, especially when compared with that of the United States. Some striking differences exist between the American and British constitutional systems. In Britain there is no document analogous to the United States Constitution. Parliament, unlike Congress, is empowered to make any kind of law it chooses. The courts have no authority to nullify legislation. From the purely legal standpoint, therefore, it is impossible in Britain to specify which rules, procedures, and institutions are part of the constitution and which are not; and a constitutional lawyer, reasoning solely from legal assumptions, can never satisfactorily explain the nature of the constitution and its sanctions. Much nonsense has consequently been written about Britain by those who, starting with false premises, arrive at wrong conclusions. Thus Tocqueville asserted that because of the legal supremacy of Parliament, which may change the constitution at any time by simple legislative act, there is in reality no constitution at all.[24] An odd argument this one, since it involves defining a constitution so narrowly and restricting it to those states where the power of the legislature is limited by a superior law.

Equally queer was the reasoning of A. V. Dicey, the English jurist, who wrote a classic book on *The Law of the Constitution*.[25] Dicey there distinguished between what he called the law of the constitution and its conventions (customs). The former consists of rules that the courts will recognize and enforce, the latter of rules that are binding in political usage. Both kinds of rules, legal and political, are, as Dicey observes, habitually obeyed and occasionally breached. What is the explanation? A constitutional lawyer easily understands why legal rules are observed. The courts are there to enforce them. But what is it that secures respect for political rules and why should these be obeyed? To Dicey this is a major difficulty. And how characteristic his answer! Political rules, in his opinion, are followed because, if they were not, some breach of law would be included among the consequences[26]—which brings him back to the courts and to a legalistic interpretation of the constitution.

As a general statement, that is an error. It is true of some political customs, but inapplicable to many others. It does not apply, for instance, to various well-established rules which are essential to Britain's cabinet type of government: that the Crown must assent to all bills

---

[24]Alexis de Tocqueville, *Democracy in America*, Part I, trans. Henry Reeve (New York: J. & H. G. Langley, 1841), Chap. 6, p. 103.

[25]First published in 1885, this work went through eight editions in thirty years and has been reprinted many times since its author's death.

[26]*Law of the Constitution*, 8th ed. (London: Macmillan & Co., Ltd., 1931), Chap. 15, pp. 441 ff.

passed by Parliament, and grant a dissolution when requested by the prime minister; that the prime minister and the majority of the cabinet should be members of the House of Commons; and that all ministers should belong to one of Parliament's two Houses. If these rules were violated, as some have been, there would be a serious departure from settled political practice, but no offense punishable in a court of law.

The failure of Dicey's explanation does not mean that the British constitution is inexplicable. It indicates that the constitution is primarily a political instrument, and not a legal charter. What the British refer to as their constitution is simply a way of summarizing the popular consensus about the principles to which their government should conform and the institutions with which to make them effective. The consensus is political in character because it embodies the will of an overwhelming majority in favor of a particular governmental system and their determination to preserve its basic features. This will, of course, find varied forms of expression. One way is for Parliament to enact a statute, or for the courts to render a decision acceptable to Parliament, in which case a political will is dressed in the outer raiments of law. Another way is to leave it to usage to build a system of rules, creating the expectation that what was done under like circumstances in the past will ordinarily be followed in the present. Each method has merits of its own. To write a political agreement into legal form normally results in greater precision and definiteness and thereby reduces the area of controversy. To leave decisions to the formulation of custom may permit a change, when desirable, to be speedily accomplished without the need for overcoming legal impediments.

THE AMERICAN AND BRITISH SYSTEMS COMPARED

A comparison of the two constitutional systems, those of the United States and Britain, will now make it possible to view the whole question of constitutions in true perspective. Misunderstanding has been responsible for a number of false contrasts and exaggerated distinctions. Thus the American Constitution has been described as a written one; the British, as unwritten. If these words are taken literally, they are incorrect. If figuratively, their meaning is anybody's guess. The truth is that both constitutional systems include portions that have been committed to writing and portions that have not. Statutes and judicial decisions, as well as the document we call the Constitution of the United States, are put in written form—as if the mere form were the decisive factor in determining the character of a constitution! That certain topics receive written statement, while others are left to informal understanding, is of itself a somewhat trivial difference. What surely matters more is the choice of the content that receives expression in one medium or in the other.

Another contrast calls the British system flexible, the American rigid. The point at issue here is not trivial. It concerns the ease or difficulty of the method by which the constitution is changed in each of the two countries. The belief, however, in the flexibility of the one vis-à-vis the rigidity of the other is a glaring example of fallacious inferences, as an analysis of the reasoning will show. The British constitution, it is argued, consists of two parts—law and custom. The law may be changed at any time by ordinary Act of Parliament. Custom, too, may be altered by statute, or by the simple device of breaking away from precedent. In either case, a procedural green light facilitates change. The American constitution, however, consists of the document drafted in 1787 and amended only twenty-five times since then. The amending process, enshrined in the Constitution itself, presents a formidable obstacle to innovation.

The errors and omissions in this argument are numerous. For one thing it rests upon a myopic view of the American Constitution, excluding from sight the statutes, judicial opinions, and political usages, which in a broader, but truer, sense are integral parts of the constitutional system. It further assumes that amendments to the Constitution of the United States can be obtained only with the greatest difficulty; that Parliament will dare in political reality to proceed as far as its legal powers extend; and that rules of custom are more readily modified than rules of law. But all this is nonsense. When the people of the United States after a dozen years of nationwide prohibition decided that the experiment was unworkable, they adopted the Twenty-first Amendment with remarkable ease and in record time. On the other hand, the tradition that no president should serve more than two terms was maintained for a century and a half with a rigidity which only the grim menace of Hitler and the demonstrated greatness of Franklin D. Roosevelt could shatter.[27] As for the use by Parliament of its theoretically unlimited authority, it will be shown later that obstacles and limitations do exist—but of a political, rather than a juridical, nature.

This does not mean that on the subject of rigidity or flexibility the two constitutional systems are indistinguishable. There are some genuine distinctions to be drawn, but the reasons for them have been

[27]What was a rule of custom became a rule of the Constitution by the adoption of the Twenty-second Amendment.

wrongly stated. Any portion of a constitutional system, whether legal or customary, is likely to be rigid if expressed in minute detail and supported by an organized sentiment. Conversely, any provision, legal or customary, can be flexible if its terms are vague or general and if sentiment in its favor is lukewarm or disorganized.

Some examples will illustrate these points. One of the most rigid features of the American Constitution is the clause prescribing a four-year term for the president and an election for a new term in every fourth year. Never yet have the American people deviated from the requirement of conducting the presidential election at identical and regular intervals. In 1864 when civil war was still being waged, and again in 1944 when the nation was locked in mortal conflict with deadly adversaries, the election was not postponed but took place at its appointed hour. Likewise in the gloomy years from 1930 to 1932 when the economy was paralyzed by depression, the people had to wait their opportunity to give their verdict on the stewardship of President Hoover and to vote for a new man and a New Deal. Only by amendment to the Constitution can a president's term be shortened or lengthened and a special election be held. Rigidity on this point is mainly due to the exactitude with which the Constitution expresses itself. On the other hand, where the wording is general and imprecise, the same Constitution (though "written"!) can prove conveniently flexible. Look, for instance, at the interstate commerce clause, whose text has never once been amended. This clause has proved adaptable, however, to vastly different interpretations that reflect the changing will of the majority of voters, of congressmen, and of Supreme Court judges.

The same story can be told about the rules that are the product of political custom. As was mentioned earlier, the rise of parties is a subject on which the Constitution is entirely silent. Yet its operation has been profoundly influenced by them. For purposes of contrast let us note two examples. The president of the United States is not elected directly by the people. He is chosen by members of an electoral college whom the people in their respective states elect for that specific function. When people wish to vote for their party's candidate, they vote in fact for others of the same party who will subsequently cast their ballots in the electoral college for the presidential candidate. Nothing in federal[28] law compels a member of the electoral college to cast his vote for the party nominee. In political obligation, however, he is forced to do this. The member of the college performs this one duty under a rigid compulsion, whereupon his office immedi-

[28]The laws of some states, however, place certain restrictions on presidential electors.

ately terminates. How different is the system of voting in the two houses of Congress! Nearly every senator and representative is elected under a party label and continues during his term of two or six years to be a party member. But he does not consider himself, and is not considered by his constituents, under obligation to vote with the majority of his party on every issue or to support every measure that a president of his own party proposes. Indeed, on many a legislative division, a minority of Republicans will be found voting with the majority of Democrats, and vice versa. What this means is that the party system requires absolute discipline on the one specific matter of getting its candidate into the White House, since control of the presidency is deemed vital to the power of the party. The parties do not yet, however, regard the enactment of legislation or the acceptance of a president's program as equally vital. They therefore tolerate some independence in the halls of Congress. Thus rules of custom, it appears, like rules of law, may be rigid or flexible according to the precision with which they are formulated and the force of opinion that backs them.

THE FRENCH CASE, AS A CONTRAST

A still broader comparison provides conclusive proof of the point that control over the government rests ultimately on political, not on legal, sanctions. In the United Kingdom and the United States the constitutions have stood the test of time, and they do work. The reason is that behind them lies the consensus of a community whose union outweighs its divisions. But observe what happens when the picture is reversed. When disunities transcend agreement, not only is it impossible to establish constitutionalism but a constitution itself cannot properly function. Where the needed political underpinnings are absent, the legal superstructure will sag and bend out of alignment.

A pertinent example is the experience of France. Since the outbreak of the Revolution in 1789, that country has tried no less than fourteen[29] constitutional regimes. Some were quite short-lived. The longest, that of the Third Republic, lasted from 1875 to 1940, breaking up under the blows of a military collapse. The average duration for a constitution, through the Fourth Republic, has been thirteen years. The reasons for this state of affairs do not lie primarily in the nature of the governmental framework which the French have attempted to operate. As is clear from the foregoing figures, France has run the

---

[29]I exclude the Vichy regime of 1940–44, since that was a puppet government set up under German military occupation.

gamut of constitutional experiments and could by now have found one type to suit its needs. But none of the institutional patterns adopted thus far has succeeded in gaining the support of enough people so that it could endure and evolve. This has been equally true of presidential supremacy, legislative supremacy, and the cabinet system. Since de Gaulle has ceased to be president of France, it remains to be seen whether the constitution which he contrived will be able to outlast him. The institutions of the Fifth Republic cohered for a decade around the political fact of the ascendancy of one autocratic personality. Can the same structure continue with political power again diffused? It is probable that French politics will return from its recent Bonapartism to the earlier multipartyism, although with a smaller number of groupings than before.

During the lifetime of the Third and Fourth Republics, it was evident to anyone that the root cause of the French political malaise lay at a deeper level than the structure of government. Some, with greater realism, were disposed to attribute the blame to the party system, whose turbulence and inner discords made crisis endemic and agreement abnormal. But the party system itself was an effect, even more than a cause. Its own chaotic character was symptomatic of a more fundamental malady. This consisted in the cleavages within French society, whose number and crisscrossing made widespread and long-term combinations impossible. The French Revolution, when it did occur, not only came later than the English, but left scars that time has not yet effaced. The representatives of the old order were weakened, but not crushed. Aristocrats, and others of authoritarian bent, despised the unglamorous republic and its talkative democracy. The army leaders, bred in discipline, saw politics as anarchy. Patriotic as Frenchmen, they were often disloyal to the regime they were supposed to defend. The church, identified with the traditional order, found in the secular state a disturbing competitor and in the accompanying rationalistic philosophies a challenge to its dogma. The economic transformation, which industrialism required, was not as effectively absorbed by the French as by the Americans, British, Germans, and Japanese. Most Frenchmen do not take readily to large-scale organization. Basically individualistic, they like the little enterprise, be it in farming, commerce, or manufacturing; and they are craftsmen first, and mass-producers second. When forced into a massive organization, their individualism renders them impotent and mutually discordant.[30] Hence,

[30]There were increasing signs, however, in the 1960's that certain French business firms were adapting successfully to the requirements of organization on a larger scale. The underlying causes lay in the economics of the new technology (especially in electronics, aircraft, and automobiles) and the stimulus provided by the policies and poten-

by reaction and resignation, they accept an authoritarian system—witness the army, church, and empire. Large-scale democratic organization they have not yet devised. In France, therefore, the majorities that are needed, not only for stable government but also for a constitutional consensus, are lacking. Negative majorities—that is, a vote against something—are always forthcoming.[31] Positive majorities in favor of something definite are hard to find. Under these conditions, therefore, the competitive factors outweigh the cooperative. Interests, pressure groups, organizations, and parties struggle among themselves—but without the wider harmonies that keep divisiveness in check. Again, one concludes that it is politics which will determine the constitution, the restraints of law, the orderly alternation in power of changing majorities, and all the rest. In the political process reposes man's governmental salvation—or damnation.

THE KEY TO FREEDOM

What is the political method whereby the people can control the powers they grant? How can a populace which reposes trust in its officials be sure that they will not overstep the limits of their authority? A clue is suggested by the events discussed in Chapters 6 and 7. The efforts of medieval churchmen and modern businessmen to curb the power of the state produced competing institutions which rivaled the state in the interests they mobilized and the loyalty they exacted. The peculiar significance of those ventures lay in the attempt to construct within society, but outside the political framework, an association capable of resisting the state. When dualism led to discord, and discord to conflict, the unity of the social order was eventually reaffirmed under the aegis of the political order. The triumphant assertion, however, of the primacy of the state over the rest of society could permit a tyrannical abuse of power, if no corrective existed. The secret of the new solution is to limit political power not from outside, but from within; to make the state safe for its citizens not by an external but by an inner check.

The method by which this is done is ingenious. It consists of an argument in various stages. Stage one asserts that the state belongs to all its members, whether they are of the government or of the governed. This is a rejection of the authoritarian, elitist view that the rulers are the state and that the people are subjects who belong to

---

tialities of the Common Market.

[31]When the Constitution of the Fourth Republic was adopted in 1946, only a minority of the registered electorate voted for it. Those who voted against it, plus the large number who abstained, formed a majority.

them. The contrary belief is contained in the two famous terms, "republic"[32] and "commonwealth." Both have essentially the same meaning that the state is possessed by the public who own it as wealth shared in common. The second stage is a corollary of the first. If the state is the property of the whole people, including both government and governed, a distinction exists between the state and its government. The government is not identical with the state. It consists of a few chosen from the whole people who act in the name of the state and on its behalf and for a while dispose of its authority. The implication is that the same state can have a succession of different governments. These may change while the state continues.

But how can the government change and one group of rulers take the place of another? By a device that is perhaps the most notable of modern contributions to the art of politics, the organized party system. In itself, the existence of parties is not distinctively new. Their genealogy can be traced across the centuries. A single theme unites the attacks of Thucydides[33] upon Pericles in Athens in the fifth century B.C. and the criticism of modern governments by leaders of the opposition. What is novel, however, is the place that parties have come to occupy in the political process and the attitude that now prevails toward them. Not long ago the organization of parties was viewed with disfavor. A party was regarded as a menace to the unity of the state. Because men had banded together in resistance to despotic kings, a party was associated with the taint of treason. Because schisms had split the church, the whiff of heresy clung to parties. The name of faction, by which a party was commonly described, possessed unsavory connotations. Hence it was not only because of his anxieties for a Union still in its infancy but also because he reflected the dominant thought of his time that Washington in the Farewell Address uttered this solemn warning:

I have already intimated to you the danger of parties in the State, with particular reference to the founding of them on geographical discrimination. Let me now take a more comprehensive view, and warn you in the most solemn manner against the baneful effects of the spirit of party, generally. This spirit . . . exists under different shapes in all governments, more or less stifled, controlled, or repressed; but in those of the popular form it is seen in its greatest rankness, and is truly their worst enemy. The alternate domination of one faction over another, sharpened by the spirit of revenge, natural to party dissension, which in different ages and countries has perpetrated the most horrid enormities, is itself a frightful despotism. But this leads at length

[32]From the Latin *res publica*, "a public possession."
[33]Not the historian of that name, but a political leader, the son of Melesias.

to a more formal and permanent despotism. The disorders and miseries which result gradually incline the minds of men to seek security and repose in the absolute power of an individual. . . . There is an opinion, that parties in free countries are useful checks upon the administration of the Government, and serve to keep alive the spirit of liberty. This within certain limits is probably true, and in governments of a monarchical cast, patriotism may look with indulgence, if not with favor, upon the spirit of party. But in those of the popular character, in governments purely elective, it is a spirit not to be encouraged.

Since Washington's day political developments in democratic countries have produced a complete about-face on the subject of parties and their value. While nobody would deny that a system of government by alternating parties contains imperfections and invites risks, a superior method of ensuring political freedom has yet to be discovered. So strongly is this opinion held throughout a large portion of the contemporary world that the existence of more than one party is nowadays considered one of the essential criteria to distinguish a regime of liberty from one of dictatorship. For wherever there is an opportunity of choice, there is some freedom. Where no choice exists, there is coercion. Hence when the nature of the state is appraised, an all-important test is whether more than one party is tolerated. When the connection between party politics and the principle of freedom is studied, the difference between a two-party and a multiparty system appears far less significant than the gulf between one-party government and any system permitting more than one. Indeed if language has any meaning, the term "one-party system" is a misnomer. By definition, a party is a part of the whole and therefore implies the presence of an alternative and an opposition. To speak of the one-party state is to employ a contradiction in terms. Such a state, whether Fascist or Communist, whether its capital is Moscow or Madrid, Peking or Lisbon, exhibits a monopoly of power. Its proper name is dictatorship.

THE REQUIREMENT OF TWO OR MORE PARTIES

A genuine party system, containing two or more parties, is a major step in the attainment of political maturity. Historically the emergence of the modern party has accompanied the growth of the modern electorate. Indeed, it was the latter that made the former possible. As the right to vote was extended throughout the nineteenth century, party organizations, which previously had been mainly based upon legislative cliques, undertook to attract and mobilize the ever-increasing electorate. Parties then acquired their new character. They became mass organizations, linking together a large body of citizens with their representatives in the legislature; they developed institutions of their own, and, to fight and win elections, they besought financial contributions. In this way the parties responded to a genuinely felt need. Without them, the millions who composed the new electorate would have become a disorganized crowd, unable to formulate their aims or debate the vast issues they confronted. By means of parties, the voters obtained a medium which, to state it in no stronger terms, afforded a chance for coherent action and, hopefully, responsible policies.

Nothing in the entire conception of the party system is as crucial as the requirement that there be more parties than one. It is this condition that sanctions the right of criticism and opposition as a legitimate and necessary element in the political process. The government of Britain symbolizes this situation with a unique terminology. There the ministry is officially styled Her Majesty's Government. In like manner the minority party is Her Majesty's Opposition—its loyal duty being to oppose in the name of the Crown what the majority is loyally doing in the name of the Crown. The result of this remarkable concept is that resistance to constituted authority—so long as it confines itself to words, not deeds—is brought within the scope and shelter of the constitutional order. No longer is it necessary for men who seek a change of government to launch a revolution. No longer does the prevention of political tyranny depend upon the construction outside the state of institutions capable of opposing it. Through a two- or multiparty system the means of curbing an overpowerful government is a built-in fixture of the political order. The party (or parties) that fills the role of opposition supplies the modern equivalent and takes the place of the captains of industry and finance in the era of unregulated capitalism or the popes and cardinals of a still earlier age. But the relation of the state to society, and the nature of the state itself, are vitally different when that which prevents abuse of power derives from inside the political order, not outside. Freedom is not primarily the legal concept which jurists depict. Nor is it, as Robert M. MacIver holds, solely the consequence of a pluralistic[34] society. In the modern state freedom is basically political. It permits and is then perpetuated by a two- or many-party system.

THE INS AND THE OUTS

Saying this, however, does not exhaust the complexity of the rela-

[34]For the meaning of this term, see Chap. 6, pp. 148–50. See MacIver's *The Web of Government* (New York: The Macmillan Company, 1951), Chaps. 8, 13.

tion between a party that governs and one that opposes. The peculiarity of this relationship is that the party in power does not eliminate those opposed to it, and the latter, while opposing, obey the declared will of the majority. Each side recognizes that it is a member of a system requiring, as a permanent feature, the existence of an opponent. Each accepts the principle of "live and let live" in the knowledge that the system allows to each in turn and in time its fair share of power. This means, of course, that parties which are thus prepared to alternate in office do not disagree on everything. On certain points there must be a consensus that overrides their differences on other matters. It is evident from what has already been said, that the agreement must extend to the basic features of the system to which they belong. This, however, is only another way of describing the constitution, which, as was noted earlier in this chapter, must be understood as a political instrument. The contents of the constitution include those principles and procedures about which the parties are in the main agreed. Conversely, the parties give their general support to the constitutional system which embodies some of their wishes and guarantees each its place. A revolutionary party is, of course, one that wholly rejects these fundamentals and operates from outside or inside the constitutional system in order to destroy it.

More proof of the way in which parties, otherwise opposed to each other, are prepared to sink their differences can be discovered in the field of foreign policy. The conduct of external relations is an activity of government that puts a premium on the maximum display of internal unity. When it represents the state in international affairs, a government is ordinarily able to appeal to the solidarity of common interest and loyalty that welds a group together. A bipartisan foreign policy, therefore, is more likely to lie within the realm of the practical than a bipartisan policy on domestic issues. Evidence for this can be observed in time of peace. But it is plainest of all in wartime, when a country is engaged in a life-and-death struggle against a major opponent. Then the survival of the state and the independence of its people are at stake, so that their motivation for strength through unity is greatest. On the other hand, when a government plunges into a war which millions of its citizens do not regard as their country's vital interest, and if such an involvement postpones or prevents the solution of urgent domestic problems, people will be divided into bitter partisans over the merits of the war itself. This was exactly what President Johnson discovered in the course of his ill-conceived and disastrous military adventure in South Vietnam.

Some further reflections are invited by the character of the party system. The preceding paragraphs have shown that it is the nature of parties, where two or more coexist, to work within the same constitution, yet to be rivals in the contest for political power. Expressed differently, this means that parties cooperate on some matters and compete over others—which is precisely the crux of the problem discussed in the second chapter of this book. There it was stated that human beings and the groups they form are thrown into social relationships by the contrasted, yet complementary, influences of cooperation and competition. The relation between parties and the constitution, and the manner in which government and opposition reciprocally contribute to freedom and to constitutionalism, afford an example of competition within a framework of cooperation. The forces which operate at the core of the political process are the same that explain the formation of groups and the development of society itself.

Moreover, as may be inferred from the discussion in Chapter 3, the possibility of cooperating and yet competing within the same framework is linked politically with certain requirements as to means and ends. The former can be stated negatively. If people are to coexist through the medium of constitutionalism, they must abandon the resort to violence. Otherwise, might prevails—whether this be the majority crushing a minority or a resolute and disciplined minority intimidating an apathetic, unorganized majority. In the late 1960's many countries rediscovered, amid domestic turmoil, a truth which had been forgotten since the thirties, that violence employed by any side begets its counterviolence. Once this happens, a community is drawn into a spiraling sequence of conspiratorial coercion, mob reaction, and police repression.

But to prevent recourse to violence, a positive requirement must be satisfied. All individuals and groups in the society must be treated according to a common standard of justice in the sense that their basic substantive rights are respected and enforced. Wherever people feel that they are denied justice and that the system of government is not responsive to their legitimate claims, they will be disposed to attack it with violence; that is, they will resort to extraconstitutional means. In that case, the law and the order which the public authority seeks to maintain are imposed by those who enjoy their benefits upon those who do not. Society will avoid disorders only when the order which the power of the state underpins by force is recognized as universally just—or as capable of achieving justice through flexible adaptation.

FLAWS IN THE "IRON LAW" OF OLIGARCHY

To the view presented here, an objection has been raised which, if valid, strikes at the root of the argument. As against authoritarian doctrines which subject the governed to a ruling elite, the principle of freedom proclaims that the governed must and can control their rulers. For this to be realized in practice, the many have to be able to control the few. But can they? An emphatic answer denies that they can. There is an influential school of writers which holds that any social activity requires organization; that organization evokes leadership; that leaders must be in command over their followers; that so it has always been and ever shall be. Two Swiss are notable among the modern founders of this school.[35] One of these, Vilfredo Pareto, is author of the saying: "In fact, with or without universal suffrage, it is always an oligarchy which governs, and which knows how to give whatever expression it likes to the 'popular will'." The other, Roberto Michels, formulated what he called "the iron law of oligarchy." Its central assertion is that in every human association power gravitates by an inevitable tendency into the hands of a few. By the force they wield, the fear they instill, the prestige they possess, and the propaganda they spread, the superior few outwit and overawe the mass. "Majority rule," "responsibility to the people," "popular sovereignty," these and like phrases are samples of the illusions which cunning rulers pour into the minds of their unwitting dupes.

This point of view is backed by enough evidence and wears enough plausibility to have gained many adherents. Nobody would deny that human institutions of every type abound with examples of oligarchical rule. Scan the records of churches, clerical orders, armies, navies, universities, business corporations, trade unions, governments, political parties, civil services—this list is by no means exhaustive—and the same story of controlling cliques, power monopolies, and autocratic bossism can be illustrated in almost identical terms. The social history of the human race includes several upheavals against tyrannical authority which were designed to set men free, but did not always turn out as planned. The Gospel of Jesus was a challenge to the might of Rome. Its teaching was pacifist and equalitarian; its ultimate political ideal, anarchic. But in a later century the church became wedded to power and then showed itself ready to do what seemed necessary for maintaining its power. The French Revolution was initially dedicated to the principles of liberty, equality, and fraternity. Yet its attempts to usher in a new birth of freedom delivered the military autocrat Napoleon. The Bolshevik Revolution was once greeted with the plaudits of many an

---

[35] A contemporary writer of the same outlook is James Burnham. See his *Managerial Revolution* (Bloomington: Indiana University Press, 1960) and other works.

idealist who hailed it as a landmark in the liberation of man. But Stalin's relentless rule forged the fetters of a new despotism.

What does all this add up to? That the larger part of the government of mankind has been oligarchic? That many a movement conceived in freedom has degenerated into its opposite? This much is true and cannot be gainsaid. When Michels spoke, however, of an iron law, he was asserting its universal applicability. In one sweeping formula he sought to summarize the whole range of mankind's experience in constructing institutions to serve their needs. But this effort, as all such, could not avoid the pitfalls of error, exclusion, and exaggeration. It is not true that all species of organization, political and other, have been and inevitably must be oligarchic. Apart from two exceptions—the military and the civil service, both of which are everywhere built on the hierarchical pattern from the top downwards—every kind of institution offers some instances of genuine control by the mass of the membership. As far as the state is concerned, it is perhaps not surprising that Pareto and Michels should have been ill-acquainted with the democratic achievement of the Anglo-Saxon peoples. But how could they make so little allowance for the traditions of their native Switzerland? One may grant that democratic governments are themselves imperfect and do not yet fully attain the high standards of their own ideal. Nevertheless, to dismiss as a sham and a delusion the record of what has been accomplished in countries, great and small, like the United States, Britain, Switzerland, Norway, and New Zealand, does violence to realism.

The fact that in any community power tends to gravitate to a few and that authority is ordinarily exercised by a minority does not refute the possibility or genuineness of democracy. What makes the vital difference between dictatorship and freedom, between responsible and irresponsible power, is the method whereby authority is acquired, the conditions under which it is wielded, and the manner in which it is forfeited. The nature of power is changed—not merely its external apparatus, but its inner character—when its holders must run the gauntlet of periodic elections and respond to the charges and criticisms of a free press. Nor are such phrases as majority rule and popular control empty of all meaning. A system that invites its citizens to believe in these principles often ends by bringing the beliefs to life, for people will demand of their government that it pay more than lip service to its professions. Moreover, there is the corrosive effect upon the iron law of oligarchy of a two- or multiparty system. It is not so difficult for a Fascist or Communist party in a one-party state—or any monopoly for that matter—to be authoritarian. But where a choice exists, the knowledge that people may select an alternative is itself a check against oligarchy. A party's rival is likely to create trouble for a controlling clique by encouraging its followers to rebel against their leadership, and such revolts, outside of a police state, are not so easy to suppress. Those who formulated this iron law did not pay enough attention to the mutual interaction of competing organizations. For nothing does so much to make men free as a chance to choose.

CIVIL LIBERTIES

Where the opportunity exists to choose between two or more parties and to oppose a government within a constitutional framework, certain related liberties are found which negate or mitigate the strength of oligarchy. The state can be subordinated to popular control, instead of the people being subservient to the state, when freedom of association and the right to criticize are preserved inviolate. Without freedom of association men could not organize a group of like-minded individuals as an alternative to those in power. Without the right to criticize, genuine debate of public issues, such as those analyzed here, could never be conducted. These rights are in turn buttressed by the accompanying freedoms which prevent enslavement of one's person or one's mind. Freedom from arbitrary arrest and secret trial, from seizure of one's belongings or cruel and unusual punishments, these and the like protect the liberty of the person. Equally important are the particular rights that add up to liberty of thought in general, the right of access to information and to publish without censorship, the right to read whatever one wishes, and the right of free speech.

For those who cherish the values of a free society such rights are as indispensable as the air they breathe. The reasons for them are written in clear type in the annals of every police state, old and new, and in the long uneven record of men's intellectual progress. There would be no Bill of Rights in the United States today or its equivalent in any other democracy if dissident minorities and individuals had not clashed with past wielders of power in the name of truths they held to be self-evident. There would be none of our modern achievements in pure and applied science, no betterment in our methods of living together in organized society, if some of our ancestors had not been willing at times to express unconventional ideas or challenge the established mores. The memory of Socrates before his Athenian accusers; of Jesus before Pilate; of the library at Alexandria, whose books the Arabs destroyed; of Roger Bacon, Copernicus, Galileo, and Darwin, whose scientific method demolished untruths sanctioned by the religious orthodoxy of their time; of Spinoza excommunicated by his synagogue; of beliefs in sorcery and burning of "witches"; of propa-

ganda and persecution as practiced by Joseph Stalin, Joseph Goebbels, and the Japanese thought controllers before 1945—these are
salutary warnings to prove that it is not the punishment of men that
guarantees which ideas shall perish and which prevail.

But though political liberty depends on these accompanying freedoms, it is no simple task to dovetail them in the structure of the
state. If a passion for order, pushed too far, can degenerate into
authoritarianism, so can a zeal for liberty become license by excess.
All rights involve responsibilities, and there is no right exercised
within society that is absolute and admits no exception. Even the
right to life itself can be forfeit in those states whose criminal code
provides for capital punishment and whose defense policy includes
conscription. The same applies to freedom of speech. On the principle that my right to swing my arm ends where the other fellow's
nose begins, the right of free speech must similarly avoid infringe-
ment of the rights of others. Hence it is appropriate to have laws
against libel and slander, against obscene publications, and against
incitement to violence.

Added to the difficulty of definition is that of enforcement. The
rights of a citizen may be invaded by other citizens or by his government. They may therefore require protection by the government or against it. Rights produce their impact upon government,
as does government upon rights, through the medium of institutions
or agencies. How vigilantly these operate, how they are staffed,
what precedents they develop, to what pressures they bow—this
can make all the difference between paying lip service to freedom
and practicing it. Traditionally, the branch of government that has
encroached the most on civil rights has been the one whose opportunity is greatest—the executive. That was so under the regimes of
absolute monarchy, and continues to be true of the modern dictatorship. Naturally, since the executive administers the law and has
military force, police, and prisons at its disposal, threats to liberty
will always come from this source if such powers be abused.

For that reason, in countries where civil liberties have nurtured
political freedom, the other branches—the legislature and judiciary
—have often been called upon to champion the rights of citizens
against executive invasion. But institutional history may so vary
from one state to another as to place a different emphasis on the
respective roles of legislators and judges. In the United States,
where the hierarchy of law subordinates a statute to the Constitution, where the Constitution contains a Bill of Rights, and where it
is the judges who say what the Constitution is,[36] the courts have

---

[36]This is the observation of the late Charles Evans Hughes, former chief justice.

become the inner citadel in which the defense of civil liberties is conducted. Political factors, moreover, reinforce this arrangement. The courts—and more particularly the federal judiciary headed by the Supreme Court—have a deservedly high reputation among the American people for dignity, impartiality, and scrupulousness. The same reputation is not enjoyed by Congress and the legislatures of the states. The legislative branch in general has shown considerably less zeal to uphold civil rights than the judicial, and not infrequently it endangers them. What holds true in one democracy, however, does not necessarily obtain in all. In Britain, on the whole, the boot is on the other foot. There the judges are accorded high social prestige and are respected for their integrity and learning. But the court system is so complex, its costs are so high, and its delays so notorious, that few persons in fact can obtain the substance of justice when a wrong needs to be righted. Parliament, on the other hand, has earned the respect of the British public, not the least for its continued championing of popular liberties against encroachment from any source. A question raised by a member in the House of Commons is more likely than litigation to bring prompt and proper redress.

Finally, there is the problem of determining the ultimate sanction which guarantees that civil rights will be operative. Though it is valuable to have basic rights spelled out in classic formulas and constitutional definitions, those are not self-enforcing. Many a constitution has been drafted to include the finest sounding liberties which in practice were not worth the paper on which they were written. Nor does the secret of the defense of rights lie solely in such institutions as courts and legislatures, indispensable though these be. Again it is necessary to remember that institutions, like rights, will vary in effectiveness, that courts may function under the shadow of intimidation, and legislatures may be maintained as a convenient fiction. The truth is that institutions are strong to the extent that a large enough section of the public feels keenly enough to have them so. Exactly the same applies to civil liberties. If enough people are sufficiently determined to preserve and exercise their rights, those rights will be exercised and preserved, and the institutions will then be found to do the job. But where that determination is lacking, no court, no congress, no parliament can fill the gap. The ultimate sanction, therefore, of all civil liberties resides in the same source that creates the constitution initially and renders it effective—the political will of the people. Freedom in any society is what the people earn and guard for themselves.

10

–1– Concentration of Power Versus Dispersion of Powers

POWER, FUNCTIONS, AND INSTITUTIONS

The difficulties surrounding the problem of authority are not limited to the controversy over its source that was discussed in the two preceding chapters. Regardless of how authority originates—whether from the government that wields it or the people who entrust it to the government—there still remains the question of its organization and use. As the electric energy generated at a dam is released and distributed through a complicated network of transmission lines, so the current of political power is conducted from its source to the various points and outlets where the tasks of government are carried on. The machinery for doing this consists of an elaborate structure of institutions and procedural arrangements, whose design may conform to one of a number of patterns. The choice of the pattern creates the issue.

For understanding the nature of the issue, two points that emerged in earlier chapters are relevant—first, that people have certain needs which they want the state to satisfy, and, second, that power seeks recognition as authority. In an important respect the two factors converge since they have a common bearing upon an identical problem. Both the provision of services by the state and the organization of authority have the like effect of stimulating the growth of institutions. Law enactment, for instance, produces a law-making body—the legislature; the establishment of justice evokes a system of courts; the mail is administered through the post office, and so on. Similar consequences follow from the mobilization of power. For the latter also operates through institutions in order to obtain its results. The Roman Senate and the later emperorship; the British monarchy, Parliament, and cabinet; the American Congress, presidency, and Supreme Court; the Japanese shogunate; the Nazi Führer and the Italian Duce; the Presidium of the Central Committee of the Communist party in the Soviet Union; these are examples of institutions whereby the political power generated within society is canalized and exercised.

The machinery of government thus varies in design according to the needs of its consumers or the plans of its engineers. The framework which fits a period of prosperity and full employment may be ill-adapted to a time of economic stringency. The structure that suits the more leisured tempo of peace may have to be streamlined amid the urgencies of war. If those in power desire to act with a minimum of delay and forestall a challenge to their supremacy, they will weaken or destroy whatever institution can be a rallying point for opposition. This will involve the concentration of authority to facilitate decisions, together with an unimpeded line of communication from the authority which decides to the subordinates who execute. But if the overriding aim of constitution builders is to put a brake upon the government, restrict its functions to a minimum, and prevent abuse of power, then institutions will be constructed upon different principles. In any case, and irrespective of the kind of government, the ever-present problems are to devise machinery appropriate to whatever functions men expect from their state and to see that political power and governmental institutions are meshed together. For those institutions are strong in fact which serve the citizens' needs and faithfully reflect the realities of power. But woe betide an institution that retains the shell of authority from which the kernel of power has departed! Where revolutions occur, that is, where one form of political power is substituted for another, there is generally some change in the functions of government and always an overhaul of its institutions.

CENTRALISM OR LOCALISM, SEPARATION OF POWERS OR INTEGRATION?

There are two angles from which the concentration or dispersion of authority needs to be viewed. One kind of power relationship exists between a central government possessing jurisdiction over the entire territory of the state, and the various localities into which the whole is subdivided. In some states local government is merely an extension of the center, and local officials resemble the fingers at the end of a long arm controlled by a single brain. In other states local governments enjoy varying degrees of autonomy and independence of central direction. A second power circuit arises from the relations between the various governmental agencies constituted on the same level. It is possible to have one focal institution or office, to which the rest are inferior. Or powers may be distributed among several coordinate branches so designed as to maintain an equilibrium. The choice between strength at the center and strength in the localities is the difference between centralization and decentralization; the alternatives of having one integrating agency or several which are coordinate is the contrast between integration of powers and their separation.

These contrasts must be carefully distinguished. The government of the United States combines a separation of powers with decentralization. But in Switzerland decentralization is combined with integration. In the case of France, power is not only centralized, but also integrated at the center. In Costa Rica, however, a separation of powers is associated with centralism.[1] How these different combinations occur and what results they yield forms the subject matter of the present chapter.

THE CONTRAST BETWEEN ATHENS AND ROME

The fact that such questions are not confined to contemporary states, but were raised in bygone centuries, is proof enough—were proof required—that they comprise an issue basic to governments everywhere. The politics of antiquity provide in this respect a preview for many a modern controversy. There was a period in Athenian history when the city was governed by a dictatorial ruler, Peisistratus, in whose hands all power was gathered. After his system broke down under his sons, a major stride was taken toward achieving popular self-government through the assembly of citizens. Its authority was limited, however, in certain respects by the veto of a court, the Areopagus, which represented oligarchical, rather than democratic, influences. A more fully democratic system was instituted in the middle of the fifth century B.C., when the Areopagus was stripped of many functions and the power to declare legislation enacted by the people unconstitutional was transferred to the ordinary law courts where mass juries formed a cross-sample of the citizen-body. Thus a decision approved by a majority of the Assembly could be taken on appeal to the majority of a jury—an appeal presumably from the people drunk to the people sober. With this single exception—that the people serving as a jury could be a check upon the people serving as legislators—the structure of Athenian government was tightly consolidated under the authority of the Assembly.

[1] All four countries cited here, it will be noted, are democracies. Presumably, therefore, democracy may coexist with any of these four patterns.

The Roman experience offers an instructive comparison with the Athenian.[2] The Romans, too, retained a vivid memory of a past spent under the despotic rule of a king named Tarquin the Haughty. After he was driven into exile, so intense was the feeling against the title of *Rex* (king) and any type of one-man rule, that the Roman constitution evolved with a pattern in which authority was elaborately subdivided and distributed. Instead of one popular assembly, there were several with different functions and powers. Instead of one consul (the most important of the annually elected officials) there were two, who had equal status and could check each other's actions. And as if this were not enough, for protection of the plebeians from the upper class (the patricians), ten tribunes were instituted with power to veto a consul or any lesser official. Hovering between the assemblies and the magistracies was the Senate combining enormous influence in practice with slender legal authority. Under such a system it is small wonder that when the Romans faced a military crisis, their constitution allowed for an emergency office which could produce a temporary integration of powers. This was the office of the *dictator,* who for a six months' period was granted supreme command over the army and could virtually dominate the civil government through martial law.

Such institutions proved inadequate to govern the extensive empire that Rome acquired. Neither the annually elected officials nor the assemblies nor the Senate itself could maintain the necessary continuity of policy or keep a rein on distant commanders in the field. A repetition of civil turmoil led to the drastic expedient of converting a republic into an empire under an emperor. The wheel thus turned full circle; and after its lack of success with dispersion of powers, Rome went to the extreme limits of integration.

Over the companion issue of centralism versus issue of decentralism the experience of the Greek states also contrasted with that of Rome. A city-state was ordinarily so small and compact in area that problems of internal decentralization were scarcely pressing. Larger states, like Athens, might contain smaller units (the *demes*) for purposes that were tantamount to local government. But such units were strictly subordinate to central jurisdiction. Indeed, it was this heavy emphasis on centralism that contributed to the ultimate downfall of the city-state system, since the Greeks were unable to invent a workable method of consolidating their small states into larger and stronger units.[3] To this problem, however, the Romans did find a solution. The vexed issue of how the central government should control the governors of imperial

[2]This paragraph summarizes the results of a constitutional development spread over three centuries.

[3]See Chap. 12, pp. 343 ff.

provinces was settled, as has been seen, by the emergence of an emperorship which swallowed up the divided institutions of the republic. But along with integration at the center, the emperors made it their policy to promote a measure of autonomy (or local self-government) in the cities of their empire. While fundamental questions of foreign relations, military security, and to some extent finance, were reserved for the jurisdiction of Rome and its proconsuls within the province, on a wide variety of other matters local diversity and discretion were tolerated. The grant of special privileges of home rule to the *municipia* was one of Rome's outstanding accomplishments and partially explains the long duration of its empire.

THE MEDIEVAL DISPERSION OF POWERS

The Roman way of combining some measure of decentralization with strong integration at the center was abandoned in the centuries which followed that empire's collapse. Though municipal autonomy was permitted and encouraged, the rule of Rome, at the times when the empire was firmly knit, tilted the balance to the side of central supremacy. The medieval world, however, developed a social and political organization in which the scales dipped heavily on the other side. Decentralization was the chief characteristic of that period, despite its theory of universal unity. Indeed, few facts impress the student of medieval government more forcibly than the contrast between the strength of localism and the weakness (sometimes the impotence) at the center. To this end some of the weightiest forces in medieval society jointly contributed. The principal resource in the feudal economy was land, whose ownership and tenure were closely linked with the character of feudalism. Much of the land was parceled out in large-sized estates which were assigned as the property of a nobleman. The labor of production was carried by tenants who occupied the lord's land, paying their rent in services and kind. In rural England under the manorial system[4] these formed a community that was largely, though not completely, self-sufficient. All tenants owed allegiance to the lord, while he owed them protection. For the nobility, besides being landowners, were also a political and military elite. The lord extended his influence to protect the vassals dependent on him. If able to bear arms, he was expected to don the heavy suit of mail, which only the wealthy could possess and which made the armored knight on his mount the heavy tank of the medieval battlefield. Since

---

[4] For a detailed study, see E. Lipson, *The Economic History of England,* Vol. 1 (London: Adam and Charles Black, Limited, 1937), Chaps. 1-2.

the nobility occupied a strategic role in the administration of justice and in the mustering and supply of armies, since good highways were infrequent or nonexistent, and since the economy was organized around tightly knit local units, the political structure consisted less of a state than of a collection of estates. Consequently, in the struggle between king and nobles—the key conflict of medieval politics[5]—the decentralized fragments were normally more powerful than the institution which represented centralism. And as for the government that did exist at the center, the king, though he bulked largest, was by no means omnipotent. Wherever any council or parliament or estates-general was organized, even though its functions might be mainly consultative and its structure rudimentary, such a body was likely to limit the king, since in it the nobility were the mainstay. Furthermore, the presence of the church, in the Middle Ages virtually a state within the state, posed another obstacle to an ambitious monarch.

SOVEREIGNTY AND ABSOLUTISM IN THE NATION-STATE

When the changeover occurred from the medieval system to the nation-state, and from a feudal to a mercantilist economy, the attempt was made both in theory and practice to construct the government upon opposite principles. In place of localism, the accent was put upon centralization, drawing its breath of life from the new sentiment of nationality. To achieve this, it was, of course, necessary for the king to triumph over the aristocracy, a feat which was accomplished in every state that succeeded in making the transition from medievalism. But royal supremacy over the nobles brought an additional consequence besides centralization. The power that redounded to the king at the center was there concentrated in his office. Monarchy became the magnet, attracting local loyalties to the capital and the court, and overriding the separatist tendencies of competing institutions. With centralization, therefore, came integration. From both of these the king was the gainer. In theoretical terms these facts were synthesized in the new doctrine of "sovereignty."[6] The consolidation of power, which this term signified, meant the recognition of one supreme will, paramount over other central agencies and local particularisms. The identification of the symbol of sovereignty with the office of monarchy was easily brought about. The king was "the sovereign" personified. What could be more simple?

[5] See Chap. 9, pp. 247 ff.
[6] See Chap. 6, p. 171.

Thus was inaugurated in Europe a period in which monarchy attained its zenith, accumulating so much power as to merit the description "absolute." Never was this absolutism more fittingly epitomized than by Louis XIV of France, the Sun King, in his remark: "L'Etat, c'est moi," a comment whose boast of personal preeminence exceeds even the claim of Adolf Hitler, "For twenty-four hours I was the supreme court of Germany," or the statement, "I am the law," attributed to a sometime mayor of Jersey City.

But as often occurs in politics, a tendency that is originally justified in response to public need can breed faults of its own with lapse of time. Exaltation of the monarch, who served as a foil to the obnoxious nobility, outlasted its usefulness when the power of the nobles was reduced or when a corrupt and incompetent prince sat on the throne. In various countries, therefore, resistance developed to royal absolutism and to the identification of sovereignty with monarchy. It was this opposition which culminated in the series of three revolutions out of which the modern democratic state was born. What bearing did these revolutions have upon the age-old issue of concentration versus dispersion of power?

PARLIAMENTARY SUPREMACY IN BRITAIN

Because the British Revolution, which opened in 1640 and finished in 1688, was the earliest, and thus provided an example for others to copy or alter, it will be discussed first. It was from the membership of the House of Commons and within its chamber that much of the protest against the autocracy of Charles I was voiced. Parliament, therefore, spearheaded the rebellion against the king. But to fight Charles and his supporters an army was needed. The occasion produced an Oliver Cromwell who organized the "New Model Army" on the parliamentary side. When the battle was fought, however, and Charles had been sent to his execution, Parliament found itself the servant of a new master who preferred to govern without assistance from the legislature. Not until after the death of Cromwell, the restoration of the Stuarts, and their final expulsion in 1688, was the supremacy of Parliament over the Crown irrevocably established. What was thus politically accomplished duly received formal legal recognition. The sovereignty that once belonged to the monarch was transferred to Parliament, which thereby became the omnipotent lawmaker. Integration, therefore, continued to be the keynote of the British political system, but with the important difference that the supreme institution was henceforth a legislature and not a king. The supporting theory was stated by Locke: "In a constituted commonwealth standing upon its own basis and acting according to its own nature—that is, acting for the preservation of the community, there can be but one supreme power, which is the legislative, to which all the rest are and must be subordinate. . . ."[7]

Nor was the supremacy of the legislature diminished in 1700 when permanence of tenure was granted by Act of Parliament to the judiciary. During the constitutional struggles of the mid-seventeenth century, the position of the judges vis-à-vis king and Parliament was much debated. Against a royalist like Bacon, who contended that judges were "lions *under* the throne," Chief Justice Coke argued for judicial review of the constitutionality of parliamentary acts and royal actions. To him the principles of the common law imposed a restraint upon both and it was for the judiciary to expound those principles. The result of Parliament's successful rebellion against the monarchy was that the legislature insisted upon the subordination of judges to itself, but approved their independence of the executive. Judges were not to be intimidated by the Crown or its representatives or be subjected to any pressure in deciding individual cases. On the other hand, they were to accept as definitive the law which Parliament enunciated and they were never to invoke any other or higher law. To these arrangements Britain has steadily adhered, even since the time when the political power of the cabinet absorbed the legal authority of Parliament.[8]

THE FRENCH PATTERN OF UNIFIED POWER

The French Revolution, though it postdated the American, can be discussed next, because in this respect the pattern of its institutions resembled the British. Through the many stages of France's revolutionary agony runs one persistent theme—the concentration of all power in a single supreme body. Whether that were the Convention or the Directory made little difference from the standpoint of integration. The new rulers of France were conducting revolution, the temper and tempo of which do not brook opposition, delays, or checks and balances. One critical difference did exist, however, between the British and French situations. The European repercussions of France's revolution brought on that country the threat of invasion and before long its domestic upheaval embroiled the nation in foreign war. Whereas Britain's revolution produced a civil war and required an autocrat to bring Parliament to victory, the revolution in France,

---

[7] *Second Treatise of Civil Government,* Chap. 13, Sec. 149.
[8] See pp. 250–51.

which lacked the advantages of an island, led to prolonged and deadly conflict with her neighbors and discovered the military genius of Bonaparte. His dictatorship, however, was imposed for longer on the French than that of Cromwell on the British, first because the survival of the nation was more imperiled by foreign than civil war, and then because of Napoleon's far-reaching ambitions. So deeply was the mark of Napoleonic statecraft imprinted on the government of France that when his empire was replaced by constitutional monarchy, and that in turn by a democratic republic (1875–1940), the principles of integration and centralization remained as his permanent legacy. Both of the constitutions with which France has thus far experimented since 1945, despite their differences in spirit and structure, have been similar in this respect. The Fourth Republic embodied the principle and practice of legislative predominance. Its regime was a *gouvernement d'assemblée*. Equally strongly, and by reaction against the executive weakness of the Fourth, the Fifth Republic—the creation of General de Gaulle—reverted directly to the Bonapartist type in its aims and its administration alike. The nucleus of power became the presidency. Animated by the *mystique* of a France revivified, de Gaulle ruled his country with a mixture of personal prestige and popular referenda. Others were permitted to talk, but he alone decided.[9]

From this it can be inferred that when the French have set themselves the task of constructing a framework of government, they have followed the course laid down for them by Rousseau rather than by Montesquieu. Montesquieu, however, was not without influence. Less heeded by his own countrymen, his ideas helped to shape the government of the new republic of the United States.

SEPARATION OF POWERS IN THE UNITED STATES

The American Revolution resembled the British and French in being directed against authority uncontrollable by the governed. Moreover, in practically all the constitutions which the states adopted within the first decade of independence, and in the machinery set up by the Articles of Confederation, clear provision was made for legislative supremacy. That the legislature should have been designated for this role is understandable in the light of the part played by the colonial assemblies in resisting British authority. "Thus in a typical revolutionary manner," writes William Anderson, "all powers of government were brought for the time under a single control, that of the

[9]It is still too early to say whether this pattern will continue under President Pompidou.

convention or congress in each state. Perhaps in no other way could the quick and decisive measures have been taken that were needed to sever the bonds with Great Britain. Surely it was no time for a separation of powers and checks and balances in government."[10]

A short experience, however, with legislative predominance convinced the leading spirits of the generation that concentration of power in any one institution is fraught with abuse. Consequently, it was Jefferson who wrote thus about the first constitution of Virginia: "All the powers of government, legislative, executive, and judiciary, result to the legislative body. The concentrating these in the same hands is precisely the definition of despotic government. It will be no alleviation that these powers will be exercised by a plurality of hands, and not by a single one. One hundred and seventy-three despots would surely be as oppressive as one."[11] The same point was observed by Madison, who issued this warning: "The legislative department is everywhere extending the sphere of its activity, and drawing all power into its impetuous vortex. . . . They [the founders of our republic] seem never to have recollected the danger from legislative usurpations, which by assembling all power in the same hands, must lead to the same tyranny as is threatened by executive usurpations."[12]

If concentration of power was the evil to be avoided, was there, besides executive or legislative omnipotence, some third possibility? The answer was provided by the introduction of what has come to be called the separation of powers. The republic of the United States has followed the model of the republic of Rome in the respect that its institutions have been intentionally constructed with the idea of dispersing authority. Let us see how this came about and what the results have been.

Prior to its adoption as the architectural design of American governmental machinery, the doctrine of separation of powers had evolved in long, slow sequence. Its origins may be traced to Aristotle, if not indeed to earlier writers. In the *Politics* is found an analysis of three "parts," or branches, of government—the deliberative, executive, and judicial.[13] Aristotle confines himself to a description of their personnel, organization, and functions, and is content to leave his account at that. The modern phase of the doctrine opens in seventeenth century England and forms an aspect of the philosophical inquiry into the fundamentals of politics that the Puritan revolution stimulated.

[10]*American Government* (New York: Holt, Rinehart & Winston, Inc., 1938), pp. 39-40.

[11]*Notes on the State of Virginia,* Query XIII.

[12]*The Federalist,* No. 48.

[13]Book IV, Chaps. 14-16.

Locke's *Treatise* distinguished between three powers which exist in every commonwealth. These he called legislative, executive, and federative—the last-named being equivalent to the conduct of foreign relations.[14] The executive and federative powers, he pointed out, "are always almost united," and to this union he expressed no objection. But it was otherwise with the relation of the executive power to the legislative. The latter "in well-ordered commonwealths, where the good of the whole is so considered as it ought," is placed in the hands of an assembly that convenes at intervals. But since the administration and enforcement of law is a continuous task, a power distinct from the legislative must remain "always in being." In practice, therefore, "the legislative and executive power come often to be separated." In principle, however, there is also a good reason why this should be so "because it may be too great temptation to human frailty, apt to grasp at power, for the same persons who have the power of making laws to have also in their hands the power to execute them."

THE IDEAS OF MONTESQUIEU

It was the suggestion contained in this last sentence that formed the theme in the next development of the doctrine. The French writer Montesquieu visited England in the middle of the eighteenth century and compared favorably the independence of the judges and the strength of Parliament with the subordination of the judiciary to the French monarchy and the virtual extinction of the Estates-General. Not foreseeing the rise of the cabinet system in Britain, and wanting to substitute political liberty for royal absolutism in France, Montesquieu advocated the separation of powers as a device to make government safe for the governed. The division of powers that he envisaged was similar to Locke's conception. But in his insistence that they must be entrusted respectively to different personnel he went considerably beyond his predecessor.

In every government there are three sorts of power: the legislative; the executive in respect to things dependent on the law of nations; and the executive in regard to matters that depend on the civil law. By virtue of the first, the prince or magistrate enacts temporary or perpetual laws, and amends or abrogates those that have already been enacted. By the second, he makes peace or war, sends or receives embassies, establishes the public security, and provides against invasions. By the third, he punishes criminals, or determines the disputes that arise between individuals. The latter we shall call the judiciary power, and the other simply the executive power of the state. . . . When the legislative and executive powers are united in the same person, or in the same

[14]*Second Treatise of Civil Government,* Chap. 12, Secs. 143-48.

body of magistrates, there can be no liberty; because apprehensions may arise, lest the same monarch or senate should enact tyrannical laws, to execute them in a tyrannical manner. Again, there is no liberty, if the judiciary power be not separated from the legislative and executive. Were it joined with the legislative, the life and liberty of the subject would be exposed to arbitrary control; for the judge would be then the legislator. Were it joined to the executive power, the judge might behave with violence and oppression. There would be an end of everything were the same man or the same body, whether of the nobles or of the people, to exercise those three powers, that of enacting laws, that of executing the public resolutions, and of trying the causes of individuals.[15]

While the framers of the American Constitution were profoundly influenced by Montesquieu's argument,[16] their own political experience reinforced the persuasiveness of his theory. For the governmental system with which they had the longest and closest acquaintance —that of the colonial period—embodied a species of separation. Prior to 1776 the executive branch under its governor was distinct from the legislature, and controversies between them were rampant in the two decades that led to independence. With the principle of judicial review, at least when applied to an inferior legislative body, the statesmen of that day were equally familiar, since the constitutionality of colonial enactments could be challenged before a British court, the Judicial Committee of the Privy Council.[17] History, therefore, joined hands with philosophy in writing a separation of powers into the federal Constitution.

DESIGN OF THE AMERICAN CONSTITUTION

To be more precise, however, the separation of powers was not explicitly stated in the Constitution. For an exposition of the principle one must turn to such a constitution as that of Massachusetts, which affirms: "In the government of this commonwealth, the legislative department shall never exercise the executive and judicial powers, or either of them; the executive shall never exercise the legislative and judicial powers, or either of them; the judicial shall never exercise the legislative and executive powers, or either of them; to the end that it may be a government of laws and not of men."[18] In the United States

[15]*Spirit of the Laws*, XI, 6, ed. Franz Neumann, trans. Thomas Nugent (New York: Hafner Publishing Co., Inc., 1949), pp. 151-52.

[16]Note Madison's remark in *The Federalist*, No. 47: "The oracle who is always consulted and cited on this subject is the celebrated Montesquieu."

[17]See Chap. 9, p. 255.

[18]Preamble to the Massachusetts Constitution, Sec. 30.

Constitution the principle is implied rather than asserted. Hence a need arises to understand what kind of separation is intended and what is not. Clarity, however, is obscured by the traditional use of the ambiguous term "powers." The meaning of the doctrine can be better analyzed if one drops the reference to powers and distinguishes instead between "branches" of government and their "functions." A branch is an organization of agencies with their personnel. The services they undertake are their functions.

If this distinction is borne in mind, the doctrine can be redefined and its logic expressed in the following manner. The activities of government group themselves into three divisions. That these divisions exist is a fact which observation may verify, for they arise not from preconceived theory but from the character of the functions. It is one thing to legislate, another to administer, a third to judge. Such is the nature of the governmental process, as one finds it. How can these three activities be embodied in the institutions of the state? If separation is the guiding aim, that can be achieved by establishing in the government three branches composed of separate personnel. Assign to one of these the whole task of lawmaking; to a second, the entire function of administration; to a third, the full judicial process. Thus by creating a division of branches to correspond with the division of functions one may transfer separation from the realm of theory into the structure of political fact.

To what extent were these principles incorporated into the federal government of the United States? The Constitution completely achieved the formation of three branches, each distinct in personnel. Expressly, it prevents any legislator from simultaneously holding either an executive or a judicial office.[19] Simultaneous tenure of two such offices as those of administrator and judge is not explicitly forbidden. But on this score the text could afford to be silent because judicial independence of the executive, secured in England in 1700, had already entered into the American tradition and, being no longer controversial, did not require statement in writing. The question whether a senator or representative could administer an agency was controversial. Therefore the solution had to be recorded in black and white.

The threefold division of functions, however, was not designed to correspond with the organization of the three branches. Instead of assigning each function in its entirety to one branch, the Constitution adopted a pattern of distribution. The lion's share of a function was apportioned to one branch, but smaller slices were given to each of

[19] *Constitution of the United States*, Art. 1, Sec. 6.

the other branches. In the field of legislation, for example, the bulk of the lawmaking power was placed in the Congress. But the president received his share in the powers to recommend measures, to summon Congress in special session, and to veto their bills. The Supreme Court, likewise, by exercising the power of judicial review, asserted its claim to a portion of the legislative function. Similarly with the judicial process, although most of this is undertaken by the courts, Congress acts in a judicial capacity in cases of impeachment where the House is empowered to prosecute and the Senate sits in judgment. The president, too, can intervene in the business of the courts through his power of pardon for all offenses except treason.

Hence the term "separation of powers" oversimplifies a complex set of facts. Though many have misunderstood the doctrine, the leading lights at the Philadelphia convention did not deceive themselves about what they were doing.[20] Because portions of each function were distributed among agencies of different personnel, the "separation of powers" was intended to result in a system of checks and balances. Ordinarily, unless the members of the three branches saw eye to eye and cooperated harmoniously, none of the principal functions of government could be adequately performed. Conversely, a branch or pair of branches which sought to overstep their constitutional authority could be restrained by the refusal of a third to connive.

TRADITION VERSUS MODERN DYNAMICS

It was only to be expected that an institutional framework which emerged from the political upheavals of the seventeenth and eighteenth centuries must undergo later adaption. As the age of Jefferson, Napoleon, and Nelson receded into history, Western societies faced fresh problems, or new forms of old problems. An industrial revolution, geared to a novel technology which harnessed unprecedented quantities of energy for men's productive enterprise, upset the equilibrium of primarily agrarian economies. The extension of occidental influence around the world, first under European and then under American leadership; the ambitions of new states, such as Germany and Japan; the impact of two global wars; the revolutions in Russia and China; the growth of a mass franchise and demands for social reform; changes like these were bound to impose a strain upon structures designed originally for different loads.

Two other factors were responsible, however, for more immediate effects upon the relation between legislature, executive, and judiciary.

[20]For example, Madison in *The Federalist*, Nos. 47–48.

These were the increase in the functions of government and the rise of organized parties with a mass following. As the state enlarged its activities, it was inevitable that the burden on all branches should increase. Lawmaking bodies had to debate new issues of public policy, discuss fresh objects of expenditure and modes of revenue, and provide more grants of statutory authority. The courts found their dockets crowded as they were called upon to interpret legislation and review administrative acts. But the greatest expansion occurred in the executive branch, for there lay the responsibility of translating policy into practice. Every new service which the voters thrust upon the state, every additional power which the government sought, redounded to the advantage of the executive. New programs brought more agencies into being, thus multiplying the number of civil servants. Huge sums of public money were theirs to disburse. Broad legal powers were entrusted to their discretion. In their files and records a treasure house of specialized information was garnered. The administrator's status was converted from that of amateur to professional. He became an expert in the art of managing the relations between men.

These changes resulted in shifting the foundations on which the doctrine of the separation of powers was built. Locke had conceived of the relation between the three powers in terms of legislative supremacy. Montesquieu and Madison preferred to see an equilibrium between three coordinate branches. Despite such differences, however, all of them joined in opposing executive predominance, which they associated with royal absolutism. But though no longer linked with monarchy, executive predominance or something close to it has become customary in the twentieth century. This is to be explained not only by the contrast between the small number who compose a legislature or a judiciary on the one hand, and the huge staffs engaged in administration on the other, but by some further advantages which the latter possess. The strength of a judiciary, for example, lies in the mastery of the content of law—a mastery that requires skilled and trained practitioners and familiarity with elaborate forms. On these counts the civil service based on the merit system of appointment and promotion—that great governmental invention of the late nineteenth century—has nothing to yield to the judges! The complexity of public administration, its large-scale character, its technical content and intricate procedures, its opportunities for career service and the system of recruitment and promotion by merit, these have made public employment a profession comparable to the practice of law. Neither one is more or less scientific than the other, and each is as much of a mystery to the uninitiated.

The role of the legislator, however, has not become as professionalized. Because he comes to his office by public election, his masters are the majority of his constituents; and since some of these may switch favorites, he cannot be sure of steady employment. Though his legislative service, if continued long enough, acquaints him with governmental problems, his relation to civil servants is that of amateur to expert. While they depend on him for political backing, legal authority, and financial resources, he is in need of their technical know-how. He may supervise them, conduct inquiries, watch, and castigate. But in the final analysis, if the state is what its functions are, a government becomes what its functionaries do. It is the administrator who makes or mars the policy. Power, in daily practice, resides in the hands that execute and enforce. Small wonder, therefore, that much modern government has come to be realistically described as bureaucracy,[21] or rule by the bureaus.

There is still another respect in which modern developments have upset the original concept of the separation of powers. Besides changing the relation of the three branches, the needs of modern government have also blurred the distinctions between the three functions. Administration and adjudication, for instance, no longer seem as different as they may have once appeared. Both judges and administrators apply broad rules of law to individual cases, each possessing within limits some discretion in fitting the particular facts under the general principle. Bureaus and courts are alike engaged in the same task of law enforcement,[22] the essential difference being that the former take the initiative in administering law whereas the latter wait until a dispute arises and one party seeks a judicial settlement. Nor is the function of lawmaking as dissimilar from that of law enforcing as it was once thought to be. Owing to the intricacy of modern social problems, the formulation of general principles and the administration of concrete facts are no longer clear-cut or sharply separable. Many intermediate steps must be taken before broad rules are narrowed down to the particular circumstance. A realistic way to visualize the process of government is to think of a series of concentric circles. Each circle represents a field of choice among a number of possible policies. When one of these is adopted, the next smaller circle provides for a new choice—limited and bounded, of course, by the previous decision—and so on. Most legislation nowadays has to be supplemented by a series of rules, regulations, or orders, which spell out the generalities of a statute in finer detail. Certainly at the higher

---

[21]Like the term "politician," bureaucracy has acquired some unfavorable connotations. But it can be used neutrally and descriptively, as above.

[22]Courts in earlier periods performed many administrative services, and still perform some.

levels of any executive department, the work of officials is primarily concerned with matters of policy, on which subject they render advice to members of the legislature and give instructions to their official subordinates. Between a people adopting a constitution and a mail-man delivering a letter to the correct address, there are rings within rings of diminishing fields of choice and ever-narrowing decisions. The molds have broken in which the thoughts of Locke, Montesquieu, and Madison were cast, and their contents have spilled together.[23]

EFFECT OF POLITICAL PARTIES ON INSTITUTIONS

The rise of the executive branch to preeminence, however, and the blurring of the traditional division of functions are not due solely to the increase of governmental activities. Besides the organization of the career civil service a second great innovation of the nineteenth century was the new kind of party system with its mass following. Political parties had no place in the calculations of those who espoused the doctrine of the separation of powers,[24] an omission which, though regrettable, is not altogether surprising for a period when parties were despised as factions. But their impact on the separation of powers was bound to be felt after the extension of the franchise had encouraged the electorate to mobilize under the banner of parties and thus compete for control of the state. Being a newcomer to the political scene, the mass party lacked restraining inhibitions about the sacrosanctity of separation. Avid for power, it was less scrupulous about the nicety of distinctions between powers. It would not willingly exempt any segment of authority from its grasp. What constitution framers had divided into three and put asunder, the party was prepared to reunite.

Thus it was that in mid-nineteenth century America, from the time of Jackson roughly to Cleveland, the parties made their onslaught upon the institutions of government. They regarded jobs in public offices as the spoils of political warfare, to be looted after an electoral victory. The patronage thus obtained was used to grease the party machine. But simultaneously it filled the civil service with partisan employees of uncertain tenure and dubious qualifications. Almost the same treatment was accorded to the judiciary. Control of the courts

[23] A familiar example of this is the so-called regulatory agency (for example, the Interstate Commerce Commission or Federal Trade Commission). Under an Act of Congress these issue rules, enforce them, and serve as tribunals to hear disputes and complaints. Their work, exemplifying the unity of the governmental process, marks a fusion of powers rather than a separation.

[24] See Chap. 9, pp. 264, 272–73.

was necessary to the party because of the key role they played in law enforcement plus their power of judicial review. Where judges came to the bench by election, as in many state and local governments, the parties determined the selection of candidates and ensured the support of the voters. Otherwise, if judicial office was filled by appointment, the party could influence the chief executive who made the nomination and the senate that confirmed. The capture of the legislature, and of elective posts in the executive branch, was achieved through the electoral system, where the parties maintained a firm grip on nominating procedures and methods of balloting. The extreme point in this series of developments was reached when, like an octopus extending its tentacles, the party fell under the domination of a boss. Often without holding any public office himself, a boss was able by his unchallenged mastery of the party machine to achieve a concentration of power which violated the fundamental concepts of American democracy.

The popular reaction, however, to the scandals, which in this instance, as always, accompanied excessive power, ushered in a trend of reforms, designed to purify the processes of government and restore to the people their birthright of political authority. Slowly, but surely and inexorably, the evil of bossism, entrenched in so many sectors of American public life, has been attacked and, if not completely eradicated, at least reduced to smaller and safer proportions. Slowly but surely, around two institutions, the civil service and the courts, a *cordon sanitaire* of political neutrality has been drawn. Since law must be applied by both bodies with fairness and honesty, there is no room for spoilsmen in the bureau or partisans on the bench. Administrators and judges, therefore, must be kept independent of party pressure—in one case through security of tenure and appointment by merit, in the other by nonpartisan election or selection.

While dikes and dams were thus erected to hold back the floodwaters of party power, alternative channels had to be provided in which the new pressures could usefully and legitimately flow. Since parties inevitably brought politics in their train, any place in the governmental system which fitted one was appropriate for the other. Plainly then, the correct fields for parties to penetrate and occupy were the legislature and the elective offices of the executive branch. These areas were rightfully theirs. Nobody[25] would want to see the parties ejected from the institutions that represent and translate the preferences of the voting public on broad issues of economic and social

[25]Exceptions are the states of Nebraska and Minnesota, whose constitutions require nonpartisan elections of members of the legislature.

policy. But that being so, if it were permissible for the parties to capture the presidency and governorships and to organize majority and minority caucuses in Congress and the state legislatures, the structural separation of the executive and legislative branches was certain to be modified by the party tie. Though discipline within the party may not always be strong, though there may be opposition to the leadership of the chief executive, nevertheless a common interest of a sort—even if it is no more than the desire to keep their side in power—unites all those who bear the same label. At least they know that, unless they hang together, they are more likely to hang separately!

GOVERNMENT BY PARTY AND CIVIL SERVICE

Thus a study of the party system and its consequences suggests that modern government can be viewed in a fresh way. In the eighteenth century an elaborate attempt was made to explain government in terms of three powers with their corresponding branches. The nineteenth century, under the stimulus of expansion both in the electorate and in state activities, witnessed the formation of two potent institutions—the political party and the civil service based on the merit system. When these were superimposed on the existing trio of branches, the junction of two such newcomers with the three older bodies produced at the outset much friction and disturbance because the older institutional framework had to accommodate itself to the intruders. In the twentieth century the governmental process has consisted increasingly of a partnership between party and civil service. Between them they have harnessed administrative techniques to political strength, and it is in their hands that effective power lies. Most of the work of the modern state is accomplished by party and civil service together.

NEW ROLE OF THE AMERICAN PRESIDENCY AND GOVERNORSHIP

In the American system the clearest evidence of the joint impact of party and civil service is revealed in the modern status of most presidents and governors. When the potentialities of each office are fully developed, the man who fills them ceases to be, in any narrow or restrictive sense, a chief executive. He becomes, in addition, a party leader, chief legislator,[26] and general mobilizer of public opinion. This

[26]This is a phrase used by Howard L. McBain in *The Living Constitution* (New York: The Macmillan Company, 1937), Chap. IV.

is an accurate description of the role played by outstanding presidents of this century, such as Wilson and the two Roosevelts, and by successful governors, like the elder LaFollette of Wisconsin, Smith and Lehman of New York, and Warren of California. The leadership provided by these men has been dual, since it has embraced both the legislative and executive branches. To them may be applied, not inappropriately, the words that Walter Bagehot used to describe the British cabinet in the mid-nineteenth century: "a *hyphen* which joins, a *buckle* which fastens, the legislative part of the state to the executive part of the state."[27]

Various circumstances have combined to thrust the chief executive, whether of a state or of the United States, into a more prominent role. A new dynamism was infused into politics by the readjustment to a continent-wide expansion, a rapid industrialization, and the absorption of immigrants. With the mounting demands of underprivileged people, both actual voters and potential, for a more secure status, the governments of states and nation assumed increasing responsibilities. As a consequence, people who had some common interest to promote formed pressure groups to influence legislative action. Issues of public policy were aired in public debate. Party organizations had to decide what course of action to endorse—or inaction, since dodging or straddling an issue was itself a decision. Inevitably such a situation created the need and opportunity for some person or agency to take the initiative and give a lead. It was possible for that leadership to emanate from within the legislature, but difficult, because in a bicameral body there were usually several members in each house with independent influence who competed for the limelight. A tactical advantage thus lay with the chief executive, since in the White House or the governor's mansion there could be only one occupant and, if he chose to dive into the center of the fray, he could immediately command an audience and something of a following. For this, the constitutional powers of his office provided a springboard. The president, and many of the governors, had a direct entry into the legislative field through their powers to send messages, recommend measures, summon special sessions, and veto bills. In addition, however, they could harness other techniques to supplement their political strategy. By the use of patronage, jobs could be traded for votes.[28] By effective appeals to the voters through the spoken word, press, radio, and television, chief executives have been able to dramatize their programs and compel

[27] *The English Constitution,* World's Classics edition (London: Oxford University Press, 1928), p. 12. Italics in original.

[28] This technique was formerly more effective than it is nowadays because of the extension of civil service protection to large numbers of government jobs.

consideration of their views. In this way, the presidency and governorship became the focal offices in national and state politics whereby the force of public opinion and the power of the party system have been funneled into the structure of the Constitution.

CABINET DOMINANCE IN BRITAIN

The analogy with the contemporary development of British institutions is instructive. It is one of the ironies of political science that Montesquieu based his support of the doctrine of separation of powers in large part upon his study of the British system, wherein he believed it to be embodied. He omitted to notice, or failed to consider significant, the rise of the cabinet in the reigns of George I and II, and the emergence under Sir Robert Walpole of the prime minister as the cabinet's presiding officer. It is precisely the cabinet, however, that has become the distinctive agency of British government, and has made the fusion,[29] rather than separation, of powers its focal principle. In the course of two and a half centuries the cabinet has evolved by stages, owing its modern preeminence to precisely the same factors as have modified the American system—on the one hand, the extension of the suffrage and of governmental functions, and on the other, the organization of the party and the civil service.

The stages through which the cabinet has passed are briefly these: The first phase lasted from the accession of George I in 1714 to shortly after the close of the Napoleonic Wars in 1815. During that period the cabinet successfully emancipated itself from royal domination. In so doing it was aided by the lucky circumstance that the first two Georges, being German immigrants from Hanover, were ill-acquainted with the English language and British politics. They, therefore, discontinued the practice of presiding in person at cabinet meetings and left this duty to a leading minister, who was designated prime minister. In the absence of the monarch it was easier and relatively safer for the ministers to oppose his wishes and strengthen one another by assuming collective responsibility for decisions. When George III, being English-born, sought to revive the royal power, the total failure of his policies in 1776 and the illness to which he fell victim in the later years of his reign enabled the cabinet to reassert its supremacy over the Crown.

The second stage opened with the beginnings of parliamentary and electoral reform in the early 1830's. In the middle decades of that

---

[29]The only exception to this statement is that the judiciary, though subordinate to Parliament, is independent of the executive.

century the extension of the franchise encouraged the growth of a party structure among the voters, whose allegiance, particularly when newly enfranchised, the parties were eager to capture. Increasingly, therefore, candidates were elected to Parliament because of their affiliation with a party and support for its program. This was a process, however, which took time to consummate because economic and social conditions were fluid and the size of the population and the electorate was expanding. Hence, although party discipline was crystallizing within the legislature, there were still minority blocs and a number of independents whose political fluctuations could determine the rise and fall of governments. Cabinets in this period, therefore, were dependent upon the House of Commons and it was there that they could be made and unmade.

The third stage commenced around 1884, when the adult male franchise was obtained. The consequent increase of the electorate made stronger party organization both desirable and imperative. The heavier expense of canvassing and campaigning in a larger constituency led to the dependence of local candidates upon central endorsement and assistance. Since the central organization of the party was controlled by its parliamentary leaders, they had the wherewithal to determine the votes of the parliamentary rank and file. As the two-party system became more firmly established, and the number of independents in the legislature dwindled into insignificance, the majority and minority in Parliament were predetermined by the effectiveness of party discipline. Only in the rare and unlikely event of a split within the major party, or during the temporary existence of a three-party system[30] can Parliament nowadays reassert its power to make the cabinet. The rule in modern times has been that the people determine at the polls which party shall have a legislative majority, and the party leaders determine the composition of the cabinet. A mid-twentieth century British Parliament records the popular decision in much the same way as the electoral college ratifies the American people's choice of a president.

Nor is this all. The cabinet's functions are not limited to the legislative sphere. They extend to the executive branch by virtue of the fact that members of the cabinet are ministers of the Crown. Severally, they are responsible for administering the various departments of state. Collectively, they must weave together the countless strands of administration and decide the broadest issues of national policy. To accomplish this they have at their command the skill and resources of

---

[30]As occurred in Britain in the 1920's, when the Liberals were declining and Labor were gaining strength.

the civil service which staffs the agencies that ministers direct. The role, therefore, of the cabinet is essentially dual. In that body resides the ultimate responsibility of leadership in the legislative and executive spheres alike. The cabinet has proven itself the convenient and flexible, although currently overworked, institution where the potencies of party and civil service are fused.

Within the cabinent, too, the office of the first, or prime, minister has acquired a significance that suggests many analogies with the presidency. British cabinets do not all function in the same way, any more than all administrations do in the United States. Granted that the institutions carry with them in both cases an important minimum of constitutional authority, this will be supplemented in varying degrees by the political strength of the individual president or premier, by his own personal magnetism or lack of it, by his energy or passivity. Who presides makes a difference, and both offices have their political history of alternative strength and weakness. A cabinet containing many powerful politicians and strong personalities may need, as its chairman, a moderate conciliator—a Campbell-Bannerman or Attlee. At other times, dynamic qualities will come to the fore, the nation can be bound by one man's spell, and the cabinet (not without some resistance) follows where he leads. Disraeli and Gladstone, Lloyd George and Churchill, mark the high peaks where the premier is as preeminent and alone as the greatest of presidents.

A century and a half ago the American and British systems were poles apart in important respects. Moving by different routes, the two democracies have lately been converging upon the same destination. This does not mean, of course, that the distinctions have been obliterated. There is still an important contrast between a leadership exercised within the legislature and one exerted from outside. There are divergences due to dissimilar electoral patterns, since in the United States it is possible for the party opposed to a president or governor to have the majority in one house or even in both. Furthermore, the relatively disciplined character of the British parties makes parliamentary action much more predictable than the actions of American legislatures. Nevertheless, it is true that the similarities between the two systems are now at least as significant as their differences, and at certain periods—still admittedly the exception rather than the rule—they function alike. President Franklin D. Roosevelt's relations with Congress in the first three months of his first term strongly resembled a prime minister's relation to the House of Commons. Conversely, during the war years from 1940 to 1944, Prime Minister Churchill's relation to the House—which he attended infrequently and where he spoke only on major occasions—was not unlike the contact between Congress and the president. Affected by the operation of the same influences, both systems have changed, and it is arguable that they may now be approaching a common denominator.

THE LEGISLATURE AND THE COURTS

At this point, however, a word of caution is necessary if misunderstanding is to be avoided. To say that the party and civil service have been superimposed upon the organization of the three branches does not mean that the latter have been replaced or obliterated. Likewise, the argument that presidents and governors have risen to a new peak of power, or that the cabinet has become preeminent over Crown and Parliament, does not imply that legislatures and courts are nullities and no longer perform a useful function. It is true that there has been a change in relative power. It is not true to state that institutions, which are now less influential than they once were, have been placed in the discard.

Courts of law continue to be indispensable bulwarks of personal freedom, since they offer a tribunal where citizens who are involved in a dispute or who have a case against their government may sue for justice. To this end it is essential that courts be immune from outside pressure, that they prevent an arbitrary use of executive power, and that, under the American system, they prohibit violations of the Constitution by a legislative majority. If courts be guardians of personal freedom, it is the legislature that safeguards political freedom. In countries which recognize that there is a proper place in the governmental process for discussion, criticism, and opposition, the interplay of rival parties is deemed valuable and constructive. The institution designed for this purpose is, of course, the legislature. Here the parties meet and are tested in public debate as it is intended they should. Here alternative policies are proposed and analyzed and popular grievances are ventilated. The party and the civil service could wield power and perform their jobs without the presence of a judiciary and legislature. But their regime would not be one of liberty; and if efficient at the outset, it would, if history is a safe guide, end in corruption.

Ultimately, therefore, it is on the legislature that political freedom depends, since it is here that government and the opposition to government are both rightfully represented. The legislature constitutes the public forum where the power of leadership confronts the power of criticism. Not a little is at stake, therefore, in the manner wherewith the legislature discharges its responsibilities. If the legislature does not merit the people's respect, if it succumbs to the pressure of special interests, if it fails to strike a balance between the roles of a rubber stamp and a negative obstructionist, then it does democracy no service, since it forfeits its claim to be the unique institution differentiating democracy from dictatorship.

THE POWER PATTERN OF DICTATORSHIP

Unfortunately the evidence on this point is not taken only from the pages of the past. Modern dictatorships—Nazi, Fascist, and Communist—supply corroborative testimony. There, too, the executive branch has acquired enormous new power and the work of government is carried on through the twin media of party and civil service. But these institutions, though employed by democracy and dictatorship alike, differ radically in the two political contexts. The spirit and status of a party are completely changed when only one has the legal right to exist and therefore possesses a monopoly. Likewise a civil service, organized to serve a one-party state, must itself share a partisan loyalty and does not dare maintain the political neutrality that is expected when two or more parties may alternate in office.

A dictatorship, furthermore, goes to extreme lengths in subjecting other branches to the domination of the executive. The courts may not, in any case that has political relevance, give a decision contrary to the will of the party leadership. Judges must be mice under the throne. So too with the legislature, which in a dictatorship is a superfluous and dangerous institution since it could be a rallying point for opposition. Dictators, it is true, permit the outward form of a legislative body to survive. But it is hollow shell, with the kernel removed. By packing it with party stalwarts, convoking it at long intervals, and controlling its agenda and procedure, the dictator turns it into a receptive sounding board for his own and his party's propaganda. Such was the fate that befell the Italian Parliament after 1925 and the German Reichstag after 1933, and the history of the Soviets in Russia has been similar. That system of councils or representative assemblies was constructed in 1917 by the revolutionary movement both as an instrument of opposition to tsarism and as a nucleus for a new government. But because they were representative and elected bodies, the Soviets contained within themselves a seed of democracy which Stalin did not permit to grow. Under his rule, therefore, the Soviets were reduced to a nullity. Any possibility of their independence was throttled by the stranglehold that the Communist party secured over them.

As examples of concentration of power, pushed to its utmost, the following may be grouped: the autocracy of the Russian tsars prior to

1905, the dictatorship of Stalin as boss of the Communist party in the USSR, the Hitlerite regime in Germany, Mussolini's Fascist system in Italy, and the oligarchy of militarists, bureaucrats, and businessmen who controlled Japan from 1931 to 1945. Elsewhere too, in recent decades, there have been plentiful examples of individuals who have aggrandized themselves at the expense of their rivals, crushing their opposition with force. Nor have such dictators been only military men or Communists; nor have they arisen only in older states where this system was traditional. The Ghanaians won their independence from the colonial control of Great Britain. But Kwame Nkrumah proceeded to imprison his political opponents, to dismiss judges whose decisions he did not like, to censor the press, and to conduct a campaign of personal glorification, until retribution caught up with him. In the Republic of Haiti, a former doctor maintained a brutal tyranny over a people who are mostly backward, poor, and illiterate. Whatever changes have occurred in recent decades in such governments as the American and British are meek and mild indeed in comparison with those cases.

To conclude this chapter, two quotations will serve. Said James Madison: "The accumulation of all powers, legislative, executive, and judiciary, in the same hands, whether of one, a few, or many, and whether hereditary, self-appointed, or elective, may justly be pronounced the very definition of tyranny."[31] The head of the government of a newly independent state described himself thus: "I am the boss and anyone who does not know that is a fool. I decide everything without consulting anybody and that is how things will be done in Malawi. Anyone who does not like that can get out."[32]

---

[31] *The Federalist, No. 47.*

[32] A quotation from Dr. H. Kamuzu Banda, prime minister of Malawi (formerly Nyasaland). *New York Times,* September 20, 1964.

11

FOURTH ISSUE:

–2– Localism, Centralism, and Federalism

AREAS AND GOVERNMENT

Some of the same causes that have impelled the party and the civil service in the modern state to remold the relations between the three traditional branches have also affected profoundly the choice between a concentration of power in one place and its decentralization. There are additional factors, too, such as the revolution in transport and communications, which bear specially on this problem. It is the purpose of this chapter to continue the discussion of the issue presented in the previous one in order to see to what extent and by what means the powers and functions of central and local governments have lately been redistributed.

No modern government, not even the smallest, can transact all its affairs in one place. Because the territorial range of the state must be coextensive with that of society, wherever there are social relationships between individuals, situations will develop which call for governmental regulation on the spot. Thus any modern political system, whatever its nature, must provide for local administration. Two questions then inevitably arise: What functions are to be assigned to which level? Which authorities are or should be preponderant, the central or the local?

The issue posed by such questions has several ramifications that are fundamental to statecraft. Ever since governments began to be organized upon a territorial basis, their structure has necessarily been influenced by considerations of area. The state is conditioned by geography as well as by history. Its operations extend continuously over space and over time. Hence the problem has arisen—and always will arise—of relating its functions, institutions, and jurisdiction to the area that has to be served. This is no easy puzzle to solve because the boundaries which would be the fittest from the standpoint of any one governmental activity are seldom identical with those which are appropriate from another. A large-sized city will obtain its water supply from one place; its electricity and other forms of power may come from a second; its sewage will, or should, be disposed of in a third. The plan of a transportation system connecting the various districts of a city and linking it with adjacent dormitory suburbs, will assume one shape, but the organization of districts for school construction or the prevention of air pollution or crime may require yet other contours. Food for the urban population will be drawn from nearby farms, and also from distant flour mills, stockyards, fruit orchards, and fishing grounds. The livelihood of the city dweller, who must find employment in a factory, business office, or retail store, depends on the intricate relationships of complex economic mechanisms whose boundaries are sometimes national, sometimes international, in extent. Finally, military defense, which in the Middle Ages was provided by the thick stone wall that circled the city's perimeter, is today secured by bases or satellites which circle the globe. In short, each function of government, envisaged geographically, projects itself on a map corresponding to its own needs; and if the maps were superimposed, no two would coincide.

That being so, how is the structure of the state best adapted to interests and services which spread themselves so differently in space? The answer is a common-sense solution. Since it would be impossible to organize separate governmental systems with different areas for each function, and since identical areas would be unworkable, a compromise has to be adopted. This consists in drawing a distinction between needs or problems of general concern, and those whose range is essentially limited. Hence the familiar division between a central agency and units of more circumscribed jurisdiction.

THE COMMUNITY OF INTEREST

Besides this argument of convenience, the case for separating local from central authorities is reinforced by further political considerations. It is undeniable that proximity creates a community of interests. People who live in the same neighborhood have many ties with one another. They are equally concerned about sanitation and public health, about water and similar essentials, about transportation to and from their work, about shopping and recreational facilities. What is more, the inhabitants of the same area are in constant contact. They meet face to face and communicate directly. Their daily activities bring them together; their children go to the same school or playground; they find most of their friends among those who live within easy reach. In circumstances such as these, many elements which are basic to the community are present, for a community consists in that sense of solidarity which springs from common interests and shared experience.

But it is also politically possible for that feeling of oneness to extend beyond the small area of face-to-face relationships, provided that common interests exist and similar experiences are shared. The latter may assume a variety of forms. Men can be united, for instance, by the problems of growing and selling the same crop, as the Old South paid homage to "King Cotton," or Canadian prairie farmers to wheat, or Sao Paulo *fazendeiros* to coffee. Membership in the same religious faith may serve as a bond between persons, such as with Catholics, Jews, or Moslems who are scattered among different localities, or nations, or even continents. So may people be drawn together who speak the same language, or have similar systems of government, or acknowledge one cultural tradition. However, all such wider unions— or extended communities, as they may be called—are reinforced politically when the territory they occupy forms a physical continuum. What gave the Old South its strength and made secession, even at the risk of civil war, seem practicable was the compactness of the Cotton Kingdom. What consolidates the French-speaking Canadians, besides their church, is their concentration and dominance in the Province of Quebec. An extended community is always stronger when its members are contiguous than when they are dispersed. For like reasons, because proximity makes organization easier, a concentrated minority is generally more effective than a scattered minority of the same size. If this was not so, it would be impossible to explain such political phenomena as the separation of Ulster from Eire, Norway from Sweden, Pakistan from India, Israel from the Arab states.[1] "Decentralization," "local autonomy," "states' rights"—such terms and all that they imply are grounded in the fact that proximity makes a difference to politics.

---

[1] However, the geographical concentration of the minority, though a vital factor in all these cases, is not the sole explanation of such splits. Sometimes the resistance which the local minority offers to the majority is fortified by a potent group outside. Thus the support of Protestant Britain was indispensable to Ulster; that of the Moslem peoples in the Middle East, to Pakistan; that of American and British Jewry, to Israel.

BOUNDARIES AND PSYCHOLOGY

Moreover, a political boundary itself contributes to a sense of solidarity. To assume that a community of interests is a result, transferred to politics, of causes which always originate in other social groupings, would be erroneous. Among the most important of the experiences which can unite a group is that they share the same unit of government. The structure of the state has no less intimate an effect upon the organization of society than has that of society upon the state. When territorial areas are delimited so that jurisdictions and services may be clearly distributed, symbolic associations tend to cluster around the selfsame boundaries. Cooperative sentiments of pride and loyalty, competitive attitudes of jealous rivalry, attach themselves readily to spatial units. Thus it is that cities, big and small, can evoke a city-centered patriotism of their inhabitants. People may then become very conscious of their identity as Londoners, Parisians, New Yorkers, Bostonians. Or they may identify themselves with some wider, yet politically articulated, areas. A county, perhaps, or a province, or a state within a union will acquire an individual character. Witness the traditions and folklore of the Vermonter, the Texan, the Bernese, the Gascon, the Castilian, the Yorkshireman. Or again the area may broaden out into regional dimensions, as long as it is endowed with recognizable features, real or supposed; for example, New England, Dixie, the Border Country, the Highlands, the Midi, the Sertao,[2] the Outback.[3]

It is the purpose of boundaries to divide. Physical separation lends itself to psychological alienation. All who are on "your" side of the line belong to "your" group; those beyond it do not. This feeling is heightened by the opposition that often arises mutually between different communities. A pair of cities may develop a strong rivalry, as in the cases of San Francisco and Los Angeles, Toronto and Montreal, Sydney and Melbourne, Madrid and Barcelona. So may a pair of counties, like Yorkshire and Lancashire in England; or two cantons, such as Bern and Zurich; or two provinces, like Ontario and Quebec; or two sections, like the North and the South, develop strong rivalry. It is precisely because of the psychological significance which attaches to boundary lines that common speech confers a symbolic meaning, of deeper import than their literal one, on such terms as "crossing the

[2]The arid area of northeastern Brazil.
[3]The interior of Australia.

Rubicon,"[4] "beyond the Pale,"[5] "the Chinese Wall," "the Mason-Dixon Line," and "the Iron Curtain."[6]

LOCAL LIBERTIES VERSUS CENTRALIZED DICTATORSHIP

Local loyalties, regional rivalries, separatist sentiments—these, where they exist in force, are barriers to unity and therefore to centralization. But there is a further factor, sometimes working in conjunction with these influences and sometimes operating independently, which also produces a decentralizing effect. It is the fear that power is always susceptible to abuse, and that any accumulation of power which is not counterbalanced by an independent power can become dangerous. This is the core of the argument against monism, since the net result of ecclesiastical or business autonomy was to create social groups largely exempt from the control of the state and therefore capable of resisting or obstructing it. This is equally the logic of the separation of powers, since there can be no omnipotent state to fear if the institutional structure of the government is dispersed in the form of coordinate branches. Likewise, this is the rationale of a preference for federalism and for "local liberties," the assumption being that Leviathan's grip is weaker when its skeleton is loose-jointed. Local or state governments, on this theory, can to some extent be made independent of the center, so that they may provide focuses of resistance if tyranny should ever be established there.

The nature of such tyrannies has been too vividly exemplified in modern times to leave any doubts as to their character. Modern dictatorships are a product of aggressions, attaining control by the use of violence. Because their regimes are founded primarily on force, and not on right, they continue, even after they have come to power, to feel insecure, and hence they continue to display aggressiveness. This they vent against their opponents and against any institutions where opposition can rally. It is obvious that, if the government at the center is dictatorial, men may turn to local parties as a medium for criticism and to local government as a vehicle for organization. To prevent this happening is important to the modern

[4]This river formed the boundary line between Italy proper and the province of Cisalpine Gaul. Caesar, in 50 B.C., led his army south across it, which the governor of a province was forbidden to do. Thereby he declared war on the central authorities of Rome.

[5]When English power was expanding in the Middle Ages, the area where English law and jurisdiction prevailed (for example, in France, Scotland, or Ireland) was called the Pale. Those outside it were not subject to England.

[6]Compare the expression that describes the gulf between social and economic classes in an urban community, "the other side of the tracks."

dictatorship which never feels safe if its control is not total. Hence it is characteristic of the authoritarian regime to eliminate any traces of local autonomy and to subordinate all local authorities to the central will.

That autocracy is unlikely to permit decentralization is exemplified equally in both extremes of right and left. Before Mussolini's supremacy was established in Italy, a system of local self-government was in operation which, despite all its shortcomings, allowed for manifestations of local sentiment. This was particularly so in the regions of Tuscany and Lombardy, where so many famous cities flourished, where great men had lived and worked, and where historic events were cradled. The quality, however, which a dictator prizes in his fellow citizens is that of dependence, not independence. The Municipal Council of Milan, for instance, had been controlled by Mussolini's political opponents, the Socialists, and he would not permit this. Hence he abolished the locally elected councillors and substituted for them an official appointed from, and responsible to, the center—the *Podestà*. The same method of organization commended itself to Adolf Hitler, an authoritarian centralist by temperament and conviction. In the German Empire which Bismarck made by blood and iron, and in the Weimar Republic, which the moderate left and center parties created after World War I, the structure of the state followed a federal pattern. But Hitler would have none of it. As he consolidated his power after the summer of 1934, he proceeded to abolish the Lands (or states) which had composed the federal system. Then, applying the *Führerprinzip*, he organized the German government from the top downwards, appointing in each region and district a hierarchy of officials *(Gauleiters* and others) whose power derived from his.[7]

The Communist dictatorship in the Soviet Union, as Stalin practiced it until his death, conformed to the same tendency. In semblance, at least, a federal structure was adopted which diverged outwardly from the centralization of the Romanoffs. Moreover, in reaction against the tsarist policy of "Russification"—a requirement of cultural uniformity imposed on the Poles and other minorities—the Bolsheviks initially sponsored a program of cultural diversity. But circumstances conspired to suppress these decentralizing influences.[8] In the economic sphere a centralizing factor of great importance was the series of plans, prepared and directed in Moscow, and encompassing the entire

---

[7]It should be noted that in the Italian Fascist and German Nazi cases, this excessive centralism represented in part a reaction to the lateness of both countries in achieving national unification. See Chap. 12, pp. 364–65.

[8]Soviet publicists themselves recognized this aspect of the facts by describing their system as "democratic centralism." Centralism it certainly is; democratic it certainly is not.

Soviet Union. To these national plans the policies of the component "republics" and "autonomous states" were subordinated. At the same time, in the political sphere, the monopoly of power by a single party prevented that interplay between the union and its components which is so characteristic of federal politics. In the face of the discipline of the Communist party and its hierarchical command, no unit of government was able to deviate from the central line. Finally there was the incalculable force of Stalin's personality, which did not brook opposition and would not see authority delegated. A Georgian from the Caucasus, Stalin had made himself supreme over all the Russians, and, like many a leader who emerges from a minority group on the border, he evolved into the supercentralist.

THE SPECIAL CASE OF YUGOSLAVIA

The exception among Communist regimes is the unusual case of Yugoslavia, and it is worth examining. When the Communist regime proceeded to govern Yugoslavia after the defeat of the Nazi invaders, Tito first sought his inspiration in Moscow and imitated many features of the Stalinist model. Stalinism broke down in practice, however, for reasons that were both economic and political. With their diversity of cultures, languages, and religions, the Yugoslavs did not take readily to the heavy-handed centralism which Stalin's methods demanded. Industrial production did not revive in the way that was expected, and the attempts at enforced collectivization of the peasants were a catastrophic failure. Politically, this proud and independent people resented the domineering attitudes of Russian "advisors" in Belgrade. In 1948—at a time when three-quarters of his foreign trade was directed East and the Red Army was on the Romanian border less than a hundred miles from Belgrade—Tito had the courage to dismiss the Russians and break with Stalin. The Georgian despot declared that he would bend his little finger, and Tito would fall. But in this instance he had not correctly assessed either the man or the situation.

Since then, and aided by the United States after 1950, the Yugoslavs have experimented along their own lines. What they have thus far developed is something different. It is not the same as the Communist systems to the east of them, nor does it resemble the practices of North America or Western Europe. In eclectic fashion, they are pioneering a mixed political economy whose blend is original. To understand and appraise it, one should distinguish the intention, the results to date, and some of its internal contradictions.

The essential feature of the contemporary Yugoslav experiment is the insistence that every social activity—be it a factory, hotel, orchestra, or housing development—should belong collectively to, and be managed by, the persons who work in it. This is the principle of ownership and control by the producers of a commodity or service, which is how socialism is interpreted in Yugoslavia.[9] In order to convert this principle from theory to reality, the Yugoslavs conclude that their system requires the maximum of decentralization. Popular ownership and operation would be more genuine if the local community —not the central government—were directly in charge. Consequently, the constitution adopted in 1963 incorporated a plan built, somewhat like the Swiss, from the local level up.

In any system it is difficult to make practice conform to principle. What is the situation in Yugoslavia? Do the realities match the theory? The answer, as might be expected, is that the match is only partial. The Yugoslavs are experimenting with something which would be difficult anywhere and is thoroughly novel in the light of their own past traditions. To encourage the citizens of a local area, or the members of a particular enterprise, to share personal responsibility for policies and to supervise their administration intelligently and conscientiously is a tremendous task in civic education. The public has to be well informed, and the directors of particular enterprises require training and experience. Yugoslavia was deficient in both respects, and mistakes have consequently been made. But making mistakes, and learning to draw the right lessons from them, are aspects of the process of self-government. At any rate, the country is facing the implications of transforming groups of subjects into communities of citizens.

Besides the problems of converting theory into practice, the system which has evolved thus far contains its inherent contradictions. There are factors of a political nature that militate against some of the intentions previously described. Although the avowed aim of the regime is to decentralize and rely on local initiative, some centralized planning continues. Nor is this avoidable. In various aspects of its social and economic development, Yugoslavia has a long way to go before it catches up with the countries of high living standards. The responsibility for adopting measures to strengthen the country as a whole has necessarily fallen on the government at the center. At the same time, internal conditions have varied considerably because of the contrasting legacies which Yugoslavia inherited from the Hapsburg and Ottoman Empires and the destruction of different areas in two world wars. Slovenia and Croatia, for example, are considerably more advanced than Macedonia and Montenegro. But to achieve an internal redistribution and to utilize the resources of the more developed regions for

[9]As distinguished from its interpretation in Russia, where the owner is the state.

the benefit of the less developed requires central power, central planning, and central budgeting. Under these circumstances, the desire for control of economic enterprises at the local level may not be readily reconciled with the priorities and programs which the national government seeks to establish.

A similar contradiction has permeated the politics of the system. It has been normal for Communist parties to be centrally disciplined and to be directed from the top. Also, in the practice of many Communist regimes, Marxist theories notwithstanding, the subjective cult of an individual personality has loomed larger than objective laws of historical development. How does this fit in with the laudable emphasis on community initiative, flexible experimentation, and local responsibility? The answer is that the Yugoslav system is neither one thing nor the other. The contemporary regime is evidently in the course of transition and therefore exhibits opposite tendencies. Both within the Communist party and outside, there are spokesmen advocating alternative lines of future development. For a quarter of a century, one man and one party have been politically preeminent. Tito emerged the victor in a war which was civil as well as foreign, and, after it was over, he conducted a genuine revolution. During those periods and when Stalin was seeking his destruction, his government did not deal gently with opposition. But once his power was consolidated and his position became secure, his rule underwent a subtle evolution. He gained a wide respect and popularity for the valid reasons that he stood up to both Hitler and Stalin, preserved his country's independence, and has done more than anybody else to unify it. In addition, as a Croat, he is sensitive to the internal diversities of so complex a society and has been well aware that centralized uniformity or domination by a single group would be inconsistent with Yugoslav realities.[10] Hence he has both permitted and encouraged the policy of decentralization.

Under these conditions, the Communist party has also modified itself. To express its distaste for a centralized monolith of the Stalinist type, it changed its name from party to league. Within its ranks, distinct groups evolved in the 1960's arguing—even in public—for different policies. Some contended that the Communists should retain their monopoly of continuing as the unifying, directing force in the government, the economy, and society at large. Others believed that they should withdraw from positions of control and increasingly share their power, in order to function as a source of ideas, enthusiasm, and

---

[10] I once heard a Yugoslav scholar say: "Yugoslavia is a country with six republics, five cultures, four languages, three religions, two alphabets, and one party."

criticism. Tito himself responded to these discussions in a manner which was not only extraordinarily flexible for a man in his seventies, but also indicated a statesmanlike resolve to safeguard the future. When he ousted Rankovic and his entourage, he stopped a tendency which could have taken Yugoslavia back to the Stalinist model of an authoritarian police state. Then, after the Soviet occupation of Czechoslovakia, he reorganized the personnel and structure of the Communist party by bringing many of the younger generation into the top councils of leadership. Among this pragmatic, independent-minded people something original is being created. If it succeeds, this could become a new form of society associated with a unique species of politics—blending some elements of Marxism, the Scandinavian cooperatives, and Swiss localism.

FREEDOM AT, OR FROM, THE CENTER?

Like Switzerland, Yugoslavia is an exception to many generalizations. Centralism is so common wherever a single party or personality predominates that one wonders whether this combination expresses a natural affinity. Conversely, one asks whether centralism and liberty are compatible. Some indeed argue that political liberty positively requires a substantial measure of decentralization. The theme has been developed by both statesmen and scholars that local self-government spells local liberties, which, when added, make up the sum of national liberty. Historically there is some evidence to support this view. In the case of England, for example, undeniably the grant of corporate privileges to London and lesser cities and the growth of a rural administration in which the country gentry (as distinct from the higher nobility) played a major role were factors which encouraged a sturdy spirit of resistance to anything that smacked of oppression from the center. Moreover, it is true that in the arena of local politics and administration many persons discovered a preparatory training ground where they were initiated into the art of government before deploying the experience thus gained in the national sphere. These are considerations too important to be overlooked.

But in a broader perspective one notes that sin is no monopoly of the center and virtue no monopoly of the localities. Examples of despotism emanating from the center can be matched by as many cases of local dictatorship."There are village tyrants as well as village Hampdens."[11] People have often sought the aid of a distant protector to

---

[11]Justice Jackson, in *West Virginia State Board of Education* v. *Barnette*, 319 U.S. 624 (1943). Gray in his "Elegy Written in a Country Churchyard" spoke of: "Some village

defend them from a nearby oppressor. The local bully—whether land-owner, ecclesiastical potentate, captain of industry, or political boss—cannot in all cases be opposed by the people of the locality where he dominates. If they are to be freed, he must be overawed by some greater power from outside. In short, dictatorship can reign at the center; but so can freedom. There can be local tyrannies; or, alterna-tively, local liberties. Local independence may defy a central dictator; and freedom, centrally organized, can defeat a local autocrat. Political chemistry is a rich amalgam of the same basic elements in diverse formulas which are combined in new compounds.

UNITARY AND FEDERAL STATES

Though it is true that modern dictatorships prefer a centralized structure of government, it does not follow that all contemporary democratic states have decentralized systems or are decentralized to the same degree. The fact is that wide differences exist and are ex-pressed in contrasted institutional patterns. The most familiar of these is the distinction between a unitary state and a federal one. In the former the government is organized on two levels only—national and local, the latter comprising both urban and rural authorities. A federal state has three levels instead of two, since between the national gov-ernment and the local ones is placed an intermediate layer, desig-nated as states in the United States or Australia, as provinces in Canada, or as cantons in Switzerland. Intergovernmental relationships are therefore much more complex in federal systems than the unitary. In the latter, only central-local and interlocal relations need be consid-ered. But under a federal union there are not only federal-state, feder-al-local, state-local, and federal-state-local relationships, but also interstate and interlocal. Hence, the problem of delimiting jurisdic-tions and then of meshing them together in a smooth-running ma-chine is vastly more intricate. Federal systems therefore are normally more "jurisdiction-minded," more legalistic, and slower moving than the unitary.

But still another caution is required, lest these generalizations become oversimple and thus inaccurate. Even when federal and uni-tary states are distinguished, it must be remembered that differences occur within the selfsame category. The unitary state may be as highly centralized as France or New Zealand; or centralized, but to a slightly less degree, like Britain. The federal system can embody the amount of decentralization which is found in the United States or Switzerland.

Hampden that . . . the little tyrant of his fields withstood."

Alternatively, the blend, while remaining genuinely federal, may include more centralizing features, as is the case in Canada.

CENTRALIZATION IN BRITAIN

A review of some contrasted types will make these points clearer. Great Britain can be taken as an instance of an unquestionably democratic state which has been both unitary and centralized. How important in that country are the local governments and what functions do they perform? Being the product of ancient traditions and continuous adaptation to changing social patterns, the design of British local government is neither uniform, simple, nor entirely logical. Its outline, as a compromise between the practicable and desirable, between old and new, is not wholly self-consistent or clear cut. But certain features stand out prominently and endow the system with its general character. One of these is the differentiation between urban and rural units —the former being classed as country boroughs or boroughs, the latter as counties. A second dominant trait is the dependence of the great majority of local governments on financial aid from the center, and their complete subordination in matters of legal authority. A third factor of importance is the method by which functions are distributed between the two levels. Let us see what bearing this has on the dispersion or concentration of power in the British system.

Even when the structure of the state is specifically designed to avoid excessive centralization, it is never easy to determine the best allocation of powers. In Britain the decisions about what functions "belong" respectively to the national or local level have been influenced by such considerations as social convenience, political pressure, fiscal resources, and historical tradition. In certain cases a dividing line between local and national concerns can be drawn without too much difficulty. Maintaining a fire brigade, for example, or providing public transport for an urban population inside municipal limits is clearly appropriate to local authority. On the other hand, the organization of a police force to protect both persons and property— a function which could be either central or local—has remained under local control,[12] largely through a series of historical circumstances hardening into tradition. The social and economic changes of the last century have, of course, evoked a national concern in many matters where the original emphasis was primarily local. In a complex of con-

---

[12]The nature of modern crime detection, however, and the problems of apprehending criminals have enlarged the activities of Scotland Yard as a nationwide police service. In addition, through its grants to local bodies, the Home Office prescribes some general standards to which the local police must conform.

tributing factors, the root cause can be traced to the expansion of industry with its consequent stimulus to population growth and urban concentration. Britain nowadays has about 27 per cent of the population of the United States in an area about equal to the state of Oregon. Even within that small space, a high proportion of the people are densely congested in and around London, in the "Black Country" of the Midlands, the Industrial North, and the "waist" of Scotland. The larger cities have further increased in size. Their suburbs and satellites have sprawled into the nearby countryside. Their economic urgencies and opportunities, acting as a magnet, have drawn the rural economy into their orbit. The culture of the capital, transmitted by newspapers,[13] magazines, books, radio and television, continues to pervade the village. The automobile—that "magic carpet" of the modern family—brings urban tourists, sightseers, and holidaymakers to "Ye Olde Tea Shoppe" and the parish church. Equally, it permits Farmer Giles to take his wife and children for an outing so that they may savor the throngs, hubbub, and sooty air of city streets.

Economics, congestion, and mobility have necessitated many readjustments in central-local relations. Programs of public assistance to the poor, for example, were once regarded as a local responsibility. But when the realization dawned that poverty (especially if associated with inadequate education or prolonged unemployment) was mainly a consequence of nationwide economic circumstances, when furthermore the areas hardest hit by a business depression were unable to offer sufficient public relief to needy families out of local resources, the conclusion was inescapable that the responsibility for assistance must be spread over the entire community. In this way, and for these or similar reasons, many a governmental service has literally been "nationalized." Some functions have been wholly transferred from local to national jurisdiction. In other instances a partnership has evolved whereby national and local governments cooperate in a specific activity (for example, education, health, housing).

Under such a system the partners are not, and never can be, equal. A government which represents the whole is inevitably more powerful than those which represent the parts, irrespective of whether it deals with the parts severally or collectively. The realities of their relationship, as these exist in political power and financial resources, are faithfully mirrored in the law of the United Kingdom. Only one institution in Britain has the legal authority to decide how to distribute governmental functions between the center and the localities, and

[13]Britain's small territorial expanse, and the integration of the railways that radiate from London, permits the London morning newspapers to circulate throughout the country.

when to add or take away. That institution is necessarily the supreme lawmaking body, Parliament. At law, every local government is subject to the Parliament, which created most of them, can reorganize any of them, and has clothed them all with their legal authority and defined their areas and powers. In this sense, because of the legal omnipotence of Parliament, the form of the British system is highly centralized. Moreover, the difficulty of financing the social services has reinforced the centralizing principles of constitutional law. The increase in governmental functions has been felt at both levels, local as well as national. But many of the newer local activities cost more than local resources can afford, particularly in the less wealthy areas where the need for governmental aid is so much greater. With most sources of taxation engrossed by the national treasury, there is a limit to the revenues of local bodies, which must thus depend on annual grants from the center. These are given subject to conditions about programs and standards determined in Westminster and Whitehall.

Nevertheless, despite the potency of centralizing pressures, the practices of Britain continue to be more decentralized than its formulas would indicate. Historically, the tradition of local self-government has maintained an unbroken continuity. Though fewer voters are interested in local affairs than national, local politics are often vigorously conducted and the locally elected councils, which appoint their own officials and disburse large sums of money, are far from negligible. Also, for those who have political talent and ambitions, local government provides a valuable training ground for acquiring experience, as the careers of Joseph Chamberlain in the nineteenth century and Herbert Morrison in the twentieth bear witness.

In the 1970's it is probable that the trends toward centralization will be checked and that more vitality will be infused into the local authorities which, in the geographical sense at least, are closer to the people they serve. Throughout the United Kingdom the feeling was growing in the 1960's that too much power had gravitated to London. Understandably, this sentiment was most strongly felt in the regions most distant from the country's capital. Since these happened to be areas of Celtic, rather than Anglo-Saxon, culture (Wales, Scotland, and Northern Ireland), their grounds for resisting the rule of London were deeper than those of mere physical separation. Not only could they appeal to their past historical identities, but in the present their grievances were aggravated by the knowledge that the most prosperous portion of the United Kingdom was its southeast corner; whereas, the economic development of the far north and the far west were backward in comparison. These facts in part explain the resurgence of Welsh and Scottish nationalism in the 1960's as a political phenomenon with which the two major parties and the central government were forced to reckon.[14]

AMERICAN FEDERALISM, THE START OF AN INVENTION

Much more decentralized, however, both in form and fact is the government of the United States. In this respect, as when following Montesquieu and separating the three branches, the framers of the Constitution displayed their preference for a dispersion of powers. Their accomplishment was the novel and ingenious one of federal union, which has undoubtedly been the most distinctive, enduring, and influential contribution of America to the art of government. In what did the novelty consist? Prior to 1776 the thirteen colonies were bound to Britain, severally and separately. In no way were they linked together. But to declare independence, to fight and win a war, and to build a new nation, required union. The first framework designed for this purpose and proposed to the states by the Continental Congress was experimental, and its construction was imperfect. Under the aegis of the Articles of Confederation a government was organized for the United States. When faced, however, with the urgent problems of postwar development, its powerlessness was quickly revealed. The Congress resembled not so much a legislature as a conference of ambassadors, acting under the instructions of the governments they represented. Its most important decisions required a majority of at least nine states; and the Articles themselves could not be amended without unanimity. The central authority was weak in its executive arm and altogether devoid of a judicial branch. For revenues and for troops it depended upon what the states contributed from their resources.

Only a few years of experience with such a system were needed to demonstrate its inadequacies. The Congress lacked the authority to weld the states into a unity, to mitigate their commercial rivalries, to establish a sound currency, to remove the causes of domestic disorders,[15] and to foster American interests abroad. The delegates to the Philadelphia Convention of 1787 were sent, therefore, by the states for the purpose of revising the Confederation. Fortunately they went beyond their instructions and drafted the Constitution of a federal union. As Hamilton saw it, the Articles had failed to meet the need of the United States because the parts predominated over the whole.

[14]The broader implications of this phenomenon, as it relates to the revolutionary changes in modern society, are discussed at the end of this chapter. See pp. 336 ff.

[15]Such as Shays' Rebellion in 1786.

The principal weakness that he diagnosed was the dependence of the government at the center on those of the states which acted as intermediaries between it and the individual citizen.[16] It was precisely this defect that the Constitution removed, thereby inaugurating a more perfect union. The new central government was endowed with a Congress, whose powers are genuinely legislative; an executive, with adequate means of enforcement; and a judiciary, with authority to preserve an equilibrium between the whole and the parts and to uphold the supremacy of the Constitution. The federal powers include that of levying taxes. Above all, the federal government derives its support and mandate directly from the people as voters, and carries its services directly to them as individuals.

When George Washington was inaugurated president of the United States, something else was inaugurated with him. This was the principle of a new and stronger type of federal union, the like of which was unknown in earlier history and was unfamiliar to the generation that witnessed its birth. Leagues were no novelty, nor were confederations. But all of them, and the Articles of Confederation, were alike in the essential feature that real power lay with the parts, and the institutions at the center provided machinery for cooperation rather than for government. The feature which distinguished a federal union from leagues, confederations, and unitary states is that everyone in it is subject to and is served by three levels of government. This is because every parcel of land in the fifty states falls under three jurisdictions—federal, state, and local.[17] What further distinguishes a federal union from leagues and confederations is that in the former the law and procedure of the constitution make it impossible for the federal government to abolish the member states or for them to eliminate the federal government. The reason is that the governments at both higher levels are derived directly from the people, and the constitution not only creates a national authority, but guarantees to the states their permanent position within the federal union. Thus, in an opinion[18] rendered after the Civil War, Chief Justice Chase described the American system as "an indestructible union composed of indestructible states." By the first part of this phrase he meant that the states could not break up the union or the federal authority which unifies it; by the latter, that the federal government may not destroy the states and replace them with a unitary state.

[16] *The Federalist*, No. 15.

[17] Except for the District of Columbia, which comes solely under federal jurisdiction. Its residents do not control the city government of Washington, which is directly supervised by Congress.

[18] *Texas* v. *White*, 7 Wallas 725 (1868).

VARIATIONS ON THE FEDERAL THEME

Once the example of the United States had demonstrated that a federal union could work successfully, a precedent was established which others whose situations were similar could follow. Thus in 1847 the Swiss Confederation was convulsed by an attempt of seven Catholic cantons to secede. The Protestant majority crushed the secessionists (the *Sonderbund)* in a civil war of short duration. Next year the victors rewrote their constitution and created a federal union closely patterned on the United States. For the first[19] time since 1291, when the confederation was launched in a mutual defense pact between the cantons of Uri, Schwyz, and Unterwalden, the Swiss organized a genuine central government, which has now lasted for twelve decades.

It is interesting to speculate whether the Swiss would have copied the American model so faithfully if the Civil War had already broken out in the United States. But a possible clue is provided by what happened in Canada in the middle of the 1860's. A Canadian federal union was brought into being by the combined forces of three powerful reasons. An economic depression had struck the maritime settlements of Nova Scotia, New Brunswick, and Prince Edward Island, which sought to achieve recovery through a wider political framework. A unitary government had proved unworkable for the French and English inhabitants of Quebec and Ontario. Cool relations with the United States[20] and a determination to hold the West for Canada enforced the argument for a national authority. Federal union seemed the obvious solution, since it would permit the incorporation of the Atlantic seaboard with the upper St. Lawrence region, the separation of Quebec from Ontario, and the eventual inclusion of western territories when adequately peopled. But the recent experience of the near-dissolution of the American union in the Civil War led British and Canadian statesmen to the conclusion that the central government of Canada must possess more powers than belonged to its counterpart in the United States. Thus, whereas the federal government of the United States was organized on the principle that its powers are delegated to it by the Constitution while the states retain the residue, the Canadians reversed the distribution by delegating powers to the provinces and reserving the rest for the Dominion.[21] In Canada, more-

[19]A partial exception is the unitary state that Napoleon imposed on the Swiss shortly after conquering them. This was accepted, however, only under foreign duress and proved so unworkable that Napoleon himself aided the Swiss in restoring confederation.

[20]These were due to the British government's unfriendliness to the North during the Civil War, and to intimations of possible expansion by the United States in the north and northwest.

[21]On this point compare the Tenth Amendment to the Constitution of the United

over, the national government (in effect, the cabinet) has authority to veto the legislation enacted by a province, an ultimate weapon clearly intended to bolster national supremacy. With or without this last power, however, the Canadian case demonstrated another important discovery: to wit, that it was possible to fuse the American and British institutional patterns by combining federal union with the cabinet system. Concentration of powers, or integration, at the center along with dispersion of powers, or decentralization, in the field of Dominion-provincial relations—that is the Canadian compromise. It provides a solution to this issue which is also workable elsewhere, in the South Pacific as well as in North America. Thus, when the Australian states federated to form their present commonwealth in 1900, the same pattern was followed in the sense that federal-state relations were modeled on those of the United States while the British preference for a fusion of legislative and executive powers was continued in the cabinet.

CENTRALIZATION IN AMERICAN GOVERNMENT

The great merit of a federal union is its flexible capacity to extend a single jurisdiction over a bigger area and more people and to allow at the same time for diversity and decentralization. But federalism, like all systems that succeed, has not, and could not have, remained the same as in 1789. In the United States, for example, it has had to keep pace with the expansion in numbers and power of the American nation. Federalism in this country has presided over, and responded to, the industrialization of the American economy and its social after-effects; the migration of tens of millions from Europe who filled a continent with farms and cities, like water trickling through irrigation channels; participation in two world wars; the growth of a national loyalty; and acceptance of international responsibilities. Events such as these have led to the changes which one author called "the new centralization," and another "the rise of a new federalism."[22] The immediate cause of modifications in the federal structure has been the assumption by governments of various new functions, described in Chapter 7.[23] This trend has been felt at all three levels with the result that federal, state, and local authorities have undertaken in the twen-

---

States with the British North America Act, 1867, Secs. 91–93. The Swiss copied the American pattern in their Federal Constitution, Article 3, as did the Australians later, Commonwealth of Australia Constitution Act, Secs. 51, 52, 107.

[22]These are the titles of books by George C. S. Benson and Jane Perry Clark, respectively.

[23]See pp. 198 ff.

tieth century far more activities than ever before. The amount and rate of growth, however, have differed from one level to another, so that the equilibrium formerly existing between the three has altered.

It is an important but inadequately known fact that until recent decades more than half of the American system of government was local in character. Prior to the outbreak of World War I local revenues and expenditures exceeded the total revenues and expenditures of the federal and all state governments combined.[24] Even as late as 1932 local revenues and expenditures stood at higher figures than those of the other forty-nine governments. What happened thereafter was a spectacular extension of federal activity. On the domestic front this was occasioned by the economic depression of the early 1930's and the political demands for security, relief, and social services to which it gave rise. According to the traditional pattern whereby powers were distributed under the federal system, it was with the local governments that the first responsibility lay for taking remedial measures. Their financial resources, however, were inadequate for meeting their legal and political obligations. Consequently, the cities and counties turned elsewhere for aid. First, to their state legislatures, which provided what help they could, but in most cases were themselves too weak financially to underwrite the whole bill. Eventually, it was the federal government alone, in President Roosevelt's New Deal, which mobilized the resources of a nation to alleviate a catastrophe of national dimensions.

The result of six years (1932–38) of legislative debate, electoral decision, and judicial review was a federal commitment to such policies as the regulation of agriculture along with subsidies for farm products, unemployment relief, public works, and social security, the generation and sale of hydroelectric power, fixing maximum hours and minimum wages in industry, control of the securities market and insurance of bank deposits, and more besides. For certain of these programs, limited precedents had been established earlier. In other instances federal intervention was entirely new. In every case, however, the scope of the federal undertakings was unprecedented for peacetime. Nor, throughout the entire period of President Roosevelt's leadership, was any amendment made to the written text of the fundamental law, save one[25] which, ironically enough, diminished federal authority by restoring to the states the power to regulate or prohibit the sale and consumption of alcoholic beverages. Central jurisdiction was extended by the simple device—simplification being helped by

---

[24]Consult on this point the figures in Table IV, p. 328.

[25]The Twenty-first Amendment, repealing the Eighteenth.

Table IV*

PUBLIC FINANCES AND PUBLIC EMPLOYEES IN THE AMERICAN FEDERAL SYSTEM, 1902–1968

	Government revenues (000,000's omitted)			Government expenditures (000,000's omitted)			Government employees (000's omitted)		
	Federal	State	Local	Federal	State	Local	Federal	State	Local
1902	653	183	858	565	136	959	—	—	—
1913	962	360	1,658	958	297	1,960	—	—	—
1932	2,634	2,274	5,381	4,034	2,028	6,375	—	—	—
1938	7,226	4,612	5,646	7,687	3,082	6,906	—	—	—
1944	51,399	6,714	6,665	99,448	3,319	7,180	3,365	—	—
1950	43,527	11,480	11,673	42,429	10,864	17,041	2,117	1,057	3,228
1956	81,294	18,903	19,453	72,644	15,148	28,004	2,410	1,268	4,007
1962	106,441	30,115	31,506	105,693	25,495	45,053	2,539	1,680	5,169
1968	153,676	68,460	70,171	178,862	66,254	72,357	2,984	2,495	6,884

° SOURCE: Historical Statistics on Government Finances and Employment: Census of Governments, 1962. Blanks indicate that the data are not available for these years. Grants from one level to another are included, as expenditures, at the level that spends the money; and, as revenue, at the level that collects it. Trust fund data are also included. On this general subject the reader should consult Frederick C. Mosher and Orville F. Poland, *The Costs of American Government* (New York: Dodd, Mead & Co., 1964), to whom I am indebted for advice in preparing this table.

the effect of the presidential election of 1936 on some judges of the Supreme Court—of elastic interpretations of the interstate commerce and general welfare clauses and such a liberal use of the Marshallian doctrine of "implied powers"[26] that little meaning now attaches to the Tenth Amendment.

Equally important from the standpoint of the operation of federalism were some political and administrative techniques adopted more systematically than before. The New Deal inaugurated and bequeathed as its permanent legacy a new era in intergovernmental relations. The older federal system has been compared to a three-layer cake. There was some thin icing to the horizontal layers, but little else. Most of the work of government was conducted at one level with little or no reference to either of the others. The states, it is true, exercised some controls over the localities within their midst. But federal-state relations were few and loose, while federal-local relations were nonexistent. After the New Deal, the situation changed almost beyond recognition. Federal-state relations became ampler and closer. Federal-local relations have been established. Federal-state-local cooperation is now frequent. Much of this is due to the more generous use of a device employed sparingly before the 1930's—the conditional grant-in-aid. For running the new model federal machine the fuel and lubricant are the financial grants which a government of wider jurisdiction and broader taxing powers allocates—on conditions—to smaller governmental units. Thus, today's three-layer cake is cut and consumed in vertical slices. Various functions (for example, social security or the regulation of agriculture) are nowadays performed by the governments of all three levels acting in unison.

The root cause underlying these readjustments can now be understood. When government is decentralized, functions must be assigned to the level at which they are most appropriately conducted. How is this "appropriateness" to be gauged? The problem is to work out a relation between four factors—people, areas, fiscal resources, and governmental services. The ideal would be to create for any governmental service an area whose residents possess the fiscal resources to maintain it. Most of the modern modifications of federalism are due to the emergence of social needs for which the political boundaries drawn in an earlier, preindustrial, society are inadequate. If business corporations and trade unions become big, developing a nationwide organization and producing goods that move across state lines, labor relations can no longer remain within the jurisdiction of the states. If

[26]Formulated in the opinion of the Court in *McCulloch* v. *Maryland*, 4 Wheat. 316 (1819).

a huge metropolis like New York City requires a daily supply of fresh milk of certified quality to be sold at a price that will remunerate producers, processors, and distributors, a governmental solution has to be reached by agreement between the authorities of the city, of the several states whose farms supply the milk, and of the federal government which supervises interstate compacts and regulates farm production. If the automobile and the factory together pollute the air we breathe, if industrial waste or domestic sewage contaminate a lake or river or ocean shore, the remedies and the prevention normally require not only strong governmental power but the mutually reinforcing efforts of several political jurisdictions. If welfare recipients choose, as they have every right to do, to move from an impoverished to a more prosperous region and then become a charge on the latter's budget, the problem of providing them with assistance, training, and employment is presumably national and not merely state or local. If a river valley in a backward region, like that of the Tennessee, suffers from periodic floods and chronic soil erosion, only an authority that is wider and wealthier than the states and localities concerned can raise their economic and social conditions nearer to the national average. In the modern world, especially in a relatively young country, population is often mobile. New industries can choose the most advantageous among a variety of sites. Cities attract more people and their suburbs expand into the countryside. The social order, the economy, and its human material, are flexible and dynamic. But political boundaries tend to become rigid. A jurisdictional line, once drawn on a map, is likely to be indelible. To eliminate a county or city is almost impossible. To abolish a state is unthinkable. The structure retains its decentralized form. Powers continue in theory to be distributed as constitutional law would have them. But the transformation of our social system and the conditions of modern government have been remolding their relationships.

EVOLUTION OF OTHER FEDERAL SYSTEMS

In essentials, the same story is repeated in other federal systems. There too, the economic and social results of industrialism created conditions whose remedy or regulation could no longer be subsumed under earlier ideas concerning which powers fit best at which level. Alike in Switzerland, Canada, and Australia, the amendments to the text of the constitution, the construction of new machinery for cooperation between units of government, and the increase in the functions to which two or more levels contribute, all these changes bear impressive witness to the dynamics of a modern and maturer federalism.[27] Being democracies, these countries have been politically responsive to the needs of their citizens who sought a measure of social security, stable and full employment, the moderation of industrial strife, and the provision by the state of certain enterprises which were suited to public monopoly.

But the old forms have not been flexed to their new shapes without difficulty. In its traditional structure, federalism embodied rigidities whose softening took effort and ingenuity. Apart from the geographical delimiting of jurisdictions and the legal divison of responsibility for specific services, the crucial questions have revolved around finance. It is senseless for a constitution to assign particular functions to this level of government or that and then to deny the fiscal means of paying for them. But this, or something like it, has been the history of federalism in the twentieth century. Remember that many of the modern federal systems were devised at a time when the volume of governmental activities was still relatively small and inexpensive, and was expected by their founders to remain so. Taxes were mainly of the indirect variety; and that major revenue gatherer of today, the income tax, was unheard of or was very new. The financial crisis provoked by the economic depression of the early 1930's produced great strain in federal unions, some of whose component units became, in fact, insolvent. Costly functions, such as social services, devolved upon the national level of government, which could only defray them if it commandeered the most lucrative sources of revenue. Moreover, within each union were poorer members that could not match the standards of the richer unless aided by grants from the center. New York, Zurich, Ontario, and New South Wales could afford what South Dakota, Graubunden, Nova Scotia, and Western Australia could not. Hence, by various schemes and devices—different in detail, but similar in principle—the central governments have both undertaken more functions and also have acted as equalizers between regions and as redistributors of the national income.

If the federal systems established before World War I have been driven to modify their traditional designs in the direction of greater centralization, a fortiori their imitators since World War II have found it difficult to achieve a stable balance between the centripetal and centrifugal forces operating in their communities. This holds true particularly of underdeveloped countries when their governments and peoples become committed to growth and innovation. One has only to

[27]On this subject, two noteworthy books are: K. C. Wheare, *Federal Government*, 3rd ed. (New York: Oxford University Press, Inc., 1953), and *Federalism, Mature and Emergent*, ed. Arthur W. Macmahon (Garden City, N. Y.: Doubleday & Company, Inc., 1955).

read the constitutions of the newer federal states—India, for example —to realize how great is the scope of their central authority if it extends its programs as far as its powers and resources permit. In practice, however, when the structure of government has to be adapted both to the decentralizing needs of religious, linguistic, and cultural differences and to the centralizing pressures of economic planning and development, it is no wonder that tension occurs in the relations between New Delhi and the capitals of India's component states. Elsewhere—most tragically of all in Nigeria—such inherent contradictions have already led to the breakdown of the federal experiment and the dissolution of that society in the throes of civil war. Though it may be sanctioned by legal formulas, a dispersion of functions and jurisdictions will not be worth the paper it is written on unless the constitutional pattern accords with a substratum of social reality. For nothing political could be more futile, or potentially more perilous, than a formal structure that the facts of life belie.

THE EXPERIENCE OF BRAZIL

This general comment can be illustrated from the experience of one country, Brazil, which thus far has twice experimented with constitutionalism, a federal regime, and a limited form of democracy. After becoming a republic in 1889, the Brazilians modeled their constitution on that of the United States and attempted a dispersion of powers and their separation. Indeed, there was good ground for hoping that the balance between union and diversity which federalism requires was well adapted to the Brazilian reality. In the huge area that appears on our maps as the Estados Unidos do Brasil—much of it in Mato Grosso, Amazonas, and Pará, still uncharted and unoccupied—there are contrasts enough to satisfy the most meticulous devotee of a pluralist society. The history, folklore, and contemporary attitudes of Brazil are replete with the distinctive characteristics of provinces, cities and occupations. The picture which the country presents is not one of uniformity, but of a diversified social base; and its politics too conformed to this character. The two largest states, Sao Paulo and Minas Gerais, jointly took the lead and alternated in the control of the presidency.

But this equilibrium was too delicately poised to withstand the centralizing forces which have transformed society and politics in the twentieth century. When the worldwide depression struck Brazil in 1930, the political system collapsed along with the economy. Vargas then emerged as a strong man, discarded the constitution, and imported from Italy a new regime *(Estado Novo)* of Fascist style. His power lasted until the end of World War II, when, like most Fascist dictators, he fell. Accordingly in 1946 the Brazilians redrafted their constitution and resumed their interrupted experiment in federalism, constitutionalism, and the beginnings of democracy. This second attempt lasted for almost two decades, but broke down in April, 1964. What happened, and why?

The essence of the answer can be summarized in three points. First, the principles of a federal system appeared as an alien import and were never fully incorporated with the inherited tradition. In adapting itself to modernity, Brazil has suffered the disadvantage that its Portuguese past cannot help it in the present. Therefore, Brazilians have to search outside for other models to emulate. But whatever they introduce—be it American federalism, the British parliamentary system, Italian fascism, or communism in either the Russian or Chinese variety—is vulnerable on the ground that it is foreign. Second, although federalism accords properly with the size of Brazil and its social diversity, the component units, or states, are too unequal. The majority are still so backward and lacking in financial resources that they are unable to support the services which a modern government must provide. The states which do have the means and wherewithal are Sao Paulo, Guanabara (the city of Rio), Minas Gerais, and Rio Grande do Sul. But of these, the one state of Sao Paulo, embracing in the city of the same name the economic capital of South America, far exceeds the rest in population, capacity, and power. With 18 per cent of the country's population, the state of Sao Paulo alone accounts for one-third of the national income, supplies 45 per cent of the revenues collected by the union, and produces 55 per cent of the industrial wealth. Its state government collects 46 per cent of the total revenue of all states combined; and its local authorities take in 47 per cent of all local revenues in the country. Under these conditions, the balance between the center and the parts which federalism presupposes is utterly lacking, and the great majority of the states inevitably depend on the grants they receive from the union.

Finally, this centralizing tendency is reinforced by the requirements and results of a rapid industrial development. All society was convulsed by the changes that industrialization set in motion. But the other needed revolutions—agrarian, social, and political—did not keep pace with the industrial, or were deliberately arrested by the prevailing oligarchy which did not wish to lose its privileges and share them with a larger number. Poorly managed by successive presidents and congresses, the Brazilian economy floundered in a chronic position of internal inflation and external insolvency. Matters came to a head in March and April, 1964, when President Goulart advocated a series of economic and political changes that were enthusiastically supported by the Left. This was the signal for the Right to mobilize. A combination of the propertied interests, the governors of the leading states, and most of the army commanders toppled the President from office, installed a retired marshal in his place, empowered him to govern by decree, postponed elections, and deprived their opponents, including two ex-presidents, of their civil rights. By the end of the sixties, this military regime, oriented towards the Right and strongly centralist, was still firmly in control of the country and was, if anything, tightening rather than loosening its grip on the political and economic system. The moral is plain. The balance and moderation that a federal system requires cannot withstand the stresses of rapid economic change in an underdeveloped society with an unstable government.

THE NATIONAL ENFORCEMENT OF EQUALITY

The centralizing pressures, however, have not flowed only from economic causes. For a dramatic example of this truth one may cite the recent school integration controversy in the United States. This demonstrates that the civil rights of the individual frequently require national guarantees against local infringements. The problem of winning acceptance for the principle that children of different races may be educated together is especially relevant to the issue now under discussion. Both aspects of the choice between concentration and dispersion of powers have come to the fore in the conflicts that erupted in many areas. Through the tortuous episodes of this struggle to enforce equality under law, all three branches of government at all three levels were compelled to participate and did so. The record illustrates what can happen when the political process uses government as a catalyst to speed a social revolution. Under a system where powers are dispersed, built-in structural cleavages facilitate the tactics of obstruction. Significantly enough, the leadership came, and had to come, from the center. There, it was the Supreme Court that took the initiative, pronouncing the general principle of equality and instructing the federal district courts to apply it in local areas. Congress originally gave the Court no help, being paralyzed by the capacity of southerners to filibuster in the Senate and by their control of key committee chairmanships through seniority. Eventually, however, the national pressure of majority opinion squeezed out of Congress the two Civil Rights Acts of 1957 and 1964. Successive presidents have grappled with the problem of enforcement, although it was clear that neither Eisenhower nor Kennedy relished what he had to do. At the local level and in the capitals of the states concerned—more particularly Arkansas, Alabama, Mississippi, Louisiana, and Virginia—opinions were divided. There were moderates who believed that some integration had to be accepted; and others argued in favor of obeying the law, however distasteful its terms. But generally the extremists prevailed, and they pushed the legislators and governors into impossible defiance of the United States. One will not forget, in this connection, the postures of Governors Faubus of Arkansas, Barnett of Mississippi, and Wallace of Alabama.

As far as these events concern the issue of concentration or dispersion, two major conclusions emerge. One is that a system of divided jurisdictions permits the passing of ticklish responsibilities from one agency to another. By default of the other branches, it was the judiciary which exercised leadership and statesmanship and which, in the course of interpreting the law, was in reality helping both to make and enforce it. The other result of significance has been the strengthening of central power. Even the Eisenhower administration, which by policy and conviction favored less government in general and less central government in particular, was compelled by political pressures to impose the authority of the nation upon the affairs of a school board. The old and long-accepted principle that school education was strictly a local, or at most a state, concern gave way before the greater principle that fundamental human rights (for example, the dignity of the individual that flows from equal treatment) form a national obligation. Local discrimination had to be abolished in this case by central authority.

THE MILITARY IMPACT ON FEDERALISM

Besides these developments on the domestic front, the tendency to centralize has been reinforced by what has happened on the international front. The two world wars of the twentieth century were such that no major power could remain outside the struggle. On a federal government the effect of participation in an all-out conflict for survival is indeed drastic. War is always a great centralizer. It increases the control of the state over society, since protection and security become the nation's paramount concern and these are preeminently the responsibility of the state. In addition it concentrates in the capital city the authority to plan, decide, and execute in order to promote a speedy and unified direction of military operations. These statements can be proven by the evidence contained in the nation's budget. In 1916 the expenditures of the federal government amounted to $734,-000,000. By 1919 the figure had risen to $18,515,000,000. With the "return to normalcy" under President Harding by 1922 that amount was cut back to $3,373,000,000. The same story was repeated in World War II. In 1940 federal expenditures stood at $8,998,000,000. The effort to defeat Germany and Japan cost the United States, in 1945 alone, the unprecedented sum of $100,405,000,000, of which over $80,000,000,000 represent appropriations for the War and Navy Departments. Victory over the Fascist powers was again reflected in a reduction of expenditures, especially for the military services. Thus in 1948 federal expenditures amounted to under $34,000,000,000. After that year, however, the strained relations with the Soviet Union and the outbreak in 1950 of Communist aggression in Korea sent the federal budget soaring once more to the higher altitudes of public finance. In 1952 federal outlays approximated $80,000,000,000, of which some four-fifths was directly attributable to the obligations incurred in past wars, the cost of operations in Korea, aid to friendly foreign governments, and military preparedness as insurance against a third world war. In 1968 federal expenditures reached a total of $178,862,000,000. Of this amount, as much as $79,000,000,000 was spent by the Department of Defense alone—in addition to war-related expenditures of other agencies—and $30,000,000,000 of that sum (that is, $3,500,000 in every single hour) was the financial price of the insane involvement in Vietnam.

When the activities of a modern state are focused on military tasks, irrespective of whether the political system be democratic or autocratic, the framework of its institutions will be skewed to the performance of this primary function and the mobilization of the requisite power. Because of the military need for coordinated planning, unified command, continuous vigilance, and instant action, a system which is preoccupied with its own defense is unlikely to maintain either checks and balances between branches of government or the powers of state governments vis-à-vis the nation. Separation and dispersion are difficult policies to practice in a world that is scarred by the wars of the past and scared about those of the future.

THE REVOLT OF THE INDIVIDUAL

When the major trends and dominant influences of the twentieth century in politics, economics, and technology are considered in unison, it would appear that ours is indeed an era of integration and centralization. Many of the great driving forces in modern society combine in this direction—the political demand for equal rights and greater equality of conditions, the extension of the market and standardization of products, the quest for social security and economic stability, the continuous reiteration of identical messages in the press, radio, and television. True enough—and the evidence is all around us in whatever direction we turn.

But in recent years—more precisely, in the late sixties—a contrary tendency has begun to manifest itself. This has consisted in a rising opposition to various dominant traits of our contemporary society, to its professed values, as well as to its structure and the style of its operation. Since the political system is completely enmeshed in the social order, those who reject the leading characteristics of society have directly attacked the leaders of its government, seeing in them the focus of the power which maintains the whole. This swelling chorus of protest, large enough now to have taken on the dimensions of a political force, is not simple in its origins nor single minded in aim. Its assault has been levied on certain elements which are traditional as well as on others of recent date. Most significant of all, it is worldwide in scope and thus is not confined to any one species of political system or culture. Its effects have been felt already in communities as varied as the U.S.A. and the USSR, Great Britain and France, Yugoslavia and Czechoslovakia, West Germany and Canada, Mexico and Japan.

The nature of this movement[28] can perhaps be deciphered by noting what are the objects of its attack. Certain of its targets are generalized conditions or trends; for example, depersonalization, materialism, established authority, centralization, "the system." Others are somewhat more specific and concrete—the war in Vietnam, racial or cultural discrimination in housing, education, or employment, authoritarian and old-fashioned regimes in universities and schools. Much of this is inspired by an underlying common attitude, the conviction that our present social system has grown too cumbrous and complex and too intricate in organization and procedures. The effect on countless individuals has been to produce a sense of helplessness and incomprehension. Many have the feeling that they are lost—caught within the toils of a social mechanism which, in their experience, becomes ever more distant, impersonal and routinized.

The topic which has formed the subject of this chapter—the relationship between central and local authorities and the distribution of powers between them—supplies abundant examples which fortify that feeling. Most modern states have been conspicuously less successful in the sphere of local government than at the center, and nowadays the network of local jurisdictions is even less adequate than

---

[28]The term "movement" should be interpreted here with care. Some of the protest has been organized along similar lines, but much has been a spontaneous outpouring of discontent.

previously for the solution of our social problems. The transformation of the physical environment alone has created new conditions affecting the life of the individual and extending over areas for which the inherited boundaries of governments are obsolete. Man is endangering the future of his species by the damage he is doing to his habitat —the pollution and poisoning of air and water, the rape and ravage of the land. Millions are victims of a social disorganization, so apparent in all of the largest metropolitan centers which reverberate with noise and are choked with traffic and crowds.

Over and above these general conditions from which all of us suffer, there are the special grievances of persons who are situated on the outer fringe of a community or at the base of its hierarchy. Such are the poor, the young, and any minorities identified by race, religion, or language. Together, therefore, these react against what they designate collectively as the system. Frustration turns to rage and rage to violence when remedies come not at all or come with glacial slowness, and the resort to violence is then triggered by the instant communication which the mass media supply. The television screen, in particular, brings to the eyes of the underprivileged the daily images of an affluence they do not share, at the same time as it reports with vivid and contagious accuracy the explosive outbursts of any corner of the world. Hence, although the occasion, dimensions, and immediate protest may vary, the same thread connects a Watts and Londonderry, Mexico City and Tokyo, Columbia University and the Sorbonne. Hence, too, the reassertion of cultural identities which differentiate a person from the majority or redefine his remoteness from the centers of power. This takes the form of nationalism, particularism, or separatism among Scots, Welsh, and Bretons; among French-speaking Canadians; among Croats and Slovaks; among Tartars and Kurds, Black Panthers and white Rhodesians. For full measure, add in the ethical revulsion at any injustices which continue in our midst and which are ignored or condoned by too many of those who have the power but lack the wish to alter them. Established authority is always endangered when its moral claim is challenged. Once people reject its legitimacy, the process has started in which authority will be reduced to power and power will then revert to force.[29]

[29]See Chap. 3, pp. 81–85.

12

FIFTH ISSUE:

–1– The Size of States and the Relations Between Them

TERRITORIAL BASIS OF THE STATE

The subject of the preceding chapter carried the discussion across the final threshold—the effect upon government of the size of the area it controls. This is the last of the five classic issues that give the state its character and politics its problems. Many questions are wrapped up in this issue. How large is the most desirable and practicable unit of government? Can a state be too small or too big to function effectively? What is the community which the state organizes? What loyalty inspires the people inside the same political boundaries to feel that they belong together? Must a state have a piece of territory which it can guard as its own? Is there any other basis, besides the territorial, for organizing a state? When many states coexist, what are the relations between them? What is the meaning of international politics, international law, and international organization, and is there anything that can be called international government?

It is the universal rule nowadays that for a state to exist and be recognized as such by others there must be an area within defined boundaries over which it exercises jurisdiction. Unless this condition is met, there is no state. Some modern examples will illustrate the point. Until 1860 the papacy ruled a belt of land in the center of Italy running from the west coast to the east. When Italy was unified in 1860–61, the new kingdom absorbed the Papal States. The pope retained only the city of Rome, and this too he lost in 1870. In that year the papacy ceased to be a state, although it did not cease to have political influence. Half a century later, Mussolini and the pope reached an agreement (the Lateran Treaty of 1929) about church-state relations. Under its terms a Vatican State was constituted, covering 109 acres in the heart of Rome, which has received ambassadors from foreign powers and has sent nuncios to their capitals. Because of its temporal jurisdiction over this pocket handkerchief of territory, the papacy was again recognized as a state. Another case in point is the history of Poland. That kingdom, formerly a great power in eastern Europe, was obliterated and partitioned in 1772, 1793, and 1795 by the joint action of Russia, Prussia, and Austria. No Polish state existed until one was reestablished in 1919. That state lasted two decades, but again disappeared in 1939 by partition between Germany and the Soviet Union. With the German defeat in 1945 the state of Poland arose once more from the ashes and has been admitted to the United Nations though its boundaries had not, by 1969, been approved by the western powers. A third illustration of the fact that territory is a prerequisite of the modern state is provided by Israel. The Jewish religion and culture have survived the dispersion of Jews around the world and their persecution for centuries by people of other religions and cultures. There was no Jewish state, however, until 1949 when the partition of Palestine was internationally sanctioned by the United Nations and the new state of Israel earned its right to exist by repelling the armed attacks of Arab and Egyptian forces.

What matters, then, is that a state must have some territory to call its own. How much is immaterial. Consequently, states come in all shapes and sizes. At present, the biggest in territorial extent is the Soviet Union, which embraces one-sixth of the land surface of the globe. Luxembourg, however, is also a state and a member of the United Nations although its area is only 999 square miles—smaller than that of Rhode Island. China contains a population which is estimated around 760,000,000. At the other extreme lies Iceland, an independent republic since 1944 and a member of the United Nations —but with a population of only 200,000. The contours and contents of the states vary as they are rough-hewn by the vicissitudes of history, geography, and war.

KINSHIP THE EARLIER BASIS

The truth that the possession of territory is necessary for a modern state invites the initial question whether this has always been so. Is it possible to erect a government upon some other foundation than area? The answer, of course, is yes. In an earlier stage of social development government was generally based upon kinship rather than territory. A political relationship between men was derived from their physical relationship due to common heredity. Authority was thus a by-product of ancestry. Frequently the unit of political organization has been created by the collection of families into larger groupings of tribes or clans. Historical research on this point is confirmed by linguistic evidence. The vocabulary of politics, ancient and modern, contains many terms whose roots come from words that connote human procreation and birth. The Greek *phule,* meaning "tribe," derives from the verb *phuein* (to "bring forth" or "beget") and has the same etymology as "physique." The subdivision of the *phule* called the *phratria* (that is, fraternity or brotherhood) was a clan composed of kinsmen and was used in Athens for political as well as religious functions. Likewise the *genos,* or "clan," is formed from a root that means "to be born," as is the identical Latin word *gens,* which has yielded the terms "genocide" and "gentile."[1] "Nation," in Latin *natio,* is taken from the verb *nasci,* "to be born," which has also given us "nature" and "nativity."

Two conditions could make kinship a possible or appropriate basis for governmental organization. First, the size of the group must not be too large. The bigger it becomes, the remoter the physical connection must be, until eventually a belief in a common ancestry is more fiction than fact.[2] The state has often resembled the family writ larger. But there are certain inherent limits to the elasticity of the family concept. To enlarge it indefinitely is to cease to take it seriously. Second, besides its appropriateness to a small group, kinship could serve a useful purpose for people who were nomadic. If military or economic reasons compelled men to move, on what better principle could they unite? For working or warring[3] together the kin group was a convenient, ready-made association.

It is understandable, therefore, that, when these conditions no longer applied, political organization would seek some alternative foundation. Men who gave up the life of the gypsy for that of the peasant found in territory an obvious substitute for kinship. The state was then organized around the fact that people were neighbors rather than kinsmen. The land under them became more relevant politically than the genes inside them. The transition from one principle to the

[1]Also "gentle" and "gentleman"—though any resemblance between these and politics is purely coincidental.

[2]The political mythology of the Greeks, whose name for themselves was Hellenes, contained the belief that they were all descended from one ancestor, Hellen, just as the ancient Hebrews assumed a common descent from Abraham.

[3]Shakespeare gives a reverse twist to this ancient principle when he makes Henry V say to his army in the eve-of-Agincourt speech:
> We few, we happy few, we band of brothers;
> For he to-day that sheds his blood with me
> Shall be my brother; be he ne'er so vile
> This day shall gentle his condition.

Henry V, Act 4, Sc. 3, 60–63

other is familiar in the early history of many peoples.[4] In some instances even the exact events and time of the substitution are known.[5] Few political changes have wrought so revolutionary a transformation as this. Previously, when the state was an extension of the kin group, there was an immediate link between person and person through kinship. When territory took the place of kin, one person was linked with another by their common relation to land which acted as the intermediary between them. A new factor was thus introduced into the political equation, raising a host of derivative problems. Since land had become the foundation of government, its ownership and distribution brought political results. Political status depended on whether men were owners or tenants or serfs. Control of the land meant control of the men upon it. Property, rank, wealth, and power found in land their common denominator.

THE OPTIMUM AREA FOR THE STATE

Among the most perplexing of the new problems was that of the shape and size of the land area over which the jurisdiction of the state could extend. The kin group, for obvious reasons, did not admit indefinite extension. If a political association based on kinship sought to incorporate persons of different stock, some formula or fiction such as "adoption" had to be invented. A state set up on a territorial basis confronted no such difficulties. Conceivably it might expand by accumulating more segments of land and thus acquiring control over those who resided thereon. But there were obstacles which prevented an indefinite enlargement of terrain. If the area exceeded a certain limit, could its military defense be ensured? Could it be administered from one center? Would its inhabitants feel a sense of union? What would be its relations with other states similarly organized? These relations could be friendly or hostile, or neutral and indifferent. Their character would be determined in each case by size as well as propinquity, by community of interests or conflict. By necessity, the pygmy must tolerate the giant. The latter also could be tolerant, if so minded —but only by grace. A small or medium state, placed between two large ones, could serve as a buffer, keeping them apart. Its survival would depend on balancing one side against the other, on being cor-

---

[4]Thus the Romans, whose original popular assembly was the *comitia curiata* (based on the *curia*, a kin group), set up alongside of it the later *comitia tributa*, an assembly based upon a territorial unit, the *tribus.*

[5]For example, in Athens the constitutional reforms of Cleisthenes in 510 B.C. replaced the *genos* (a kin group) by the *deme* (a local subdivision) as a unit for governmental purposes.

rectly polite to both but intimate with neither (witness Uruguay or Switzerland).

Since a state, like an individual, can never be "an *iland,* intire of it selfe,"[6] its destiny is always involved with that of others. As a matter of fact, in their external affairs all states seek two objectives which are permanent and do not vary. These are safety, in the physical or military sense, and prosperity, in the material or economic sense. Governments must insure themselves against attack in order to survive. They attempt to raise their living standards by exports and imports. These aims do not alter. But the means of attaining them do. In one era safety and prosperity will be best promoted by certain methods and techniques, and by a different set at a later age. The unit of government in vogue at any given time is the one which seems, under the conditions prevailing, best adapted to the two goals. But when people no longer feel safe or prosper under its aegis, they turn to some other unit which appears to hold out greater hope.

It is in this way that one can analyze and understand the various units of government which men have employed successively. It is these twin permanent objectives of foreign policy that give continuous meaning to the continuing debate over the optimum unit of government and the appropriate size of the state. During the course of twenty-eight centuries the Western world has experimented with three solutions to this problem and is currently groping for a fourth. In chronological order these have been the city-state, empire-state, and nation-state; and perhaps, though it is still incomplete, the region-state. Ultimately, there is the possibility of having a world-state. But that ideal is still—alas!—remote from today's practicalities. What light is thrown on the nature of government by each of these attempts and aspirations?

THE GREEK POLIS

The city-state (or *polis*) was the characteristic unit of political organization in the Mediterranean region from about the ninth to the third century B.C. Typically it consisted of a central urban nucleus and an adjacent rural area. Food production in the one supplemented commerce, government, the arts, and military defense in the other. Its population, like its area, was small—anything over 100,000 being abnormal. The reasons for a state on this scale are best explained by the obstacles of geography, scarcity of agricultural land, and difficulties of communication. Practically everywhere in Greece, in central and

[6]See p. 34.

southern Italy, in Sicily, along the coastline of modern Turkey, and throughout the islands of the Aegean, the interior was rugged, broken, and mountainous. Land forms created barriers, rather than a passage, and offered plentiful opportunities for roadblocks and ambush. But the sea was a highway, and an open one as long as piracy was suppressed. Most settlements were located, therefore, on the coast, wherever there was a usable harbor; or at some defensible strongpoint, slightly inland but connected with a nearby port (for example, Athens and Peiraeus, Rome and Ostia).[7] These were conditions that imposed fairly definite limits on the size of the state, the primary considerations being that its inhabitants must receive physical protection and should not exceed their food supply.

But it was impossible continuously to preserve a stable equilibrium. That ideal was precluded by the growth of population because of a high birth rate—even though offset by a high death rate. When the state could no longer contain its numbers, what outlets were available? One solution was for a section of the citizen-body to depart and found a new settlement, a colony or "home away from home" (*apoikia*) as the Greeks called it. A second venture was to indulge in widespread commerce and search for distant markets and sources of food. Athens and Corinth were examples of states which did both, and became commercial and colonizing powers. This policy, if successful, might bring prosperity, power, and even luxury. But it involved far-off commitments with long sea lanes to guard and the risk of starvation if those lanes were cut. The third possibility was to expand by warfare and appropriate the resources of another community. To this practice, states were led by population pressure[8] and commercial rivalries, and also by political ambitions.

ANARCHY AND IMPERIALISM IN CLASSICAL GREECE

The combined effect of military insecurity and inadequate economic resources impelled the city-states to experiment with wider unions. Various methods of enlarging the scope of political organization were accordingly tried. One way was to establish a league of states. This could ostensibly cluster around a common shrine, as the Amphictyonic League joined in the worship of Apollo. Or it could be frankly constituted for defense with some powerful member for its nucleus, like the Boeotian League over which Thebes presided. In

[7]From this standpoint Sparta and Thebes were exceptional, since they were inland cities that succeeded in making history.

[8]Plato ascribed the cause of war to the need of a growing population for more land to supply the necessary food. *Republic*, ii, 373.

these leagues lay the rudiments of federalism. But the structures never developed sufficient firmness and were weakened or destroyed by rivalries within or blows from without. Another way of broadening the unit of government was for some unusually powerful state to carve an empire for itself, signing up as allies the smaller fry who accepted protection and imposing its domination on whoever resisted. Virtually all big states tried in turn to achieve this leadership (the Greeks called it *hegemony*), as opportunity seemed for the moment to smile in their direction. First it was Sparta, then Athens, next Sparta again, then Thebes, and finally Athens once more. None of these efforts succeeded. All collapsed, because even the mightiest states could not forever prevent their unwilling subjects from trying to throw off the yoke, and because the aggrandizement of one superstate conjured up a coalition of rivals. Thus it was Athens that led the opposition to Sparta. Then, when Athenian leadership menaced the autonomy of others, a powerful alliance of Sparta, Corinth, and Thebes was arrayed against her and Greece was torn asunder in the long agony of the Peloponnesian War (431–404 B.C.). With Sparta again predominant, Athens and Thebes joined to restrain her; but when their success was followed by Theban supremacy, Sparta and Athens sided together. The balance of power, as practiced in modern times by giants, was no mystery to those Lilliputians.

The worst of this situation from the standpoint of the Greeks was that their jealousies and divisions left them a tempting prey to the powers on their periphery. Their traditional foes were the Persians. The Greeks came in conflict with them when the Persian empire, which Cyrus founded, sought in its westward expansion to engulf the Greek settlements along the coast of Asia Minor and these settlements were reinforced by the Greeks farther west (for example, by Sparta). The Persians thereupon decided to strike at the heart of the Hellenic world. The expedition they launched in 490 B.C. was repulsed by the Athenians at Marathon. A decade later came the major invasion by strong sea and land forces commanded in person by Xerxes the Great. His offensive power was broken in the series of valiant encounters that made the names of Thermopylae, Salamis, and Plataea immortal. On this occasion the city-states under the joint leadership of Sparta and Athens reached their high point of unity. But as the danger receded, their solidarity melted and Persian diplomacy and military power were able again to take advantage of Greek discord. The same tactics were employed with complete success a century and a half later by the astute and unscrupulous Macedonian king, Philip the Great. By the alternate use of strength and cajolery he insinuated himself into the chaotic politics of the Greek world. Systematically he extended his influence until, when Athens was finally bestirred by the oratory of Demosthenes (that is, the "Philippics") to rally a coalition against him, the hour was too late. The autonomy of the city-state was extinguished in the battle of Chaeronea (338 B.C.). When Alexander took over his father's legacy, he confirmed the position of the Greek states as a dependency of Macedonian power.

Considering the fact that the loss of Greek liberties was directly due to an inability to combine in a larger political union, one is astonished that the political philosophies of the two most eminent Greek thinkers are scaled to fit the small dimensions of the *polis*. Though they were familiar with larger formations (for example, the kingdoms of Persia, Egypt, and Macedon), Plato and Aristotle wrote a theory of government that treated the *polis* as ideal for size.[9] Well aware of the economic and military reasons for its limited territory and population, they provided also a philosophical justification. Unity, they argued, is the greatest political good. A people will feel united only if they have a sense of belonging together. This they will lack if they are too many, for they will then lose the spirit of a single community. What is too large cannot be understood, since it passes the limits of man's comprehension and is therefore no longer orderly or rational. A community, moreoover, must be self-sufficient. If too small to maintain itself (for example, a family or a village), it must be absorbed into a greater whole. But if too large, its interests become involved in the well-being and goodwill of others so that it ceases to be strictly autonomous. Hence the Aristotelian conclusion that the upper limit in size for an ideal state is a citizen-body of adult males who can be assembled in one spot at one time and hear the voice of one speaker.

The most interesting aspect of this theory is its startling deviation from so many facts of Greek history and its utter impracticality for the times when it was written. If the Platonic-Aristotelian doctrine was formulated on the right lines, then most of the city-state politics known to us proceeded on wrong lines. Nor could the philosophers plead that their speculations were dated to an early stage in the development of the *polis*, for Plato flourished in the first half of the fourth century B.C. and Aristotle in the second half. Indeed, when Aristotle wrote the *Politics*, the military conquests of his pupil Alexander had once and for all destroyed the independence of the unit of government about which the master, with his eyes in blinkers, continued to philosophize. What is described and evaluated in the *Politics* is an institution, the *polis*, which was already receding into history because

---

[9]In Aristotle's case this is still more extraordinary in view of his connection with Macedon. His father had served as physician to Philip and he himself was tutor to Alexander.

it could no longer ensure physical security and material prosperity. In this instance at least, philosophy's function was to write the postscript to the end of an epoch, thereby for once exemplifying Hegel's remark that "the owl of Minerva takes its flight only when the shades of night are gathering."[10]

THE ROMAN PEACE

But in the movement of history the night that closes one era is followed by the dawn of another. The inability of Alexander's successors to hold his conquests intact, and the rivalries of the kingdoms into which his empire was subdivided made the central and eastern Mediterranean a scene for conflict. It was therefore left to the West to produce a power which could accomplish what all others had failed to do—the military subjugation and political consolidation of the Mediterranean world. Such in fact was the achievement of Rome. The means employed by this doyen of empire builders deserve a scrutiny, not merely for antiquarian interest, but because their effects are still felt today.

The Romans had one method for founding an empire, another for governing it. New possessions, or provinces, they acquired by a blend of military might and judicious bribery. Their soldiering became renowned for its qualities of sturdy courage and dogged tenacity, and the legions, when commanded by a Scipio, Sulla, or Caesar, were invincible. In their initial engagements they were likely as not to suffer defeat. But once they had reorganized and discovered a competent general, they demonstrated their knack of always winning the last battle. To their subjects the conquerors presented the gift on which they prided themselves most, the Roman peace *(pax Romana)*. But this "peace," though eventually it brought order, security, and the reign of law, could be a brutal experience whenever its victim was a formidable opponent or a rebellious former subject. The Roman was a pitiless foe when he played for the high stakes of empire. Nearby rivals like Alba, Veii, and Capua were crushed or destroyed. Carthage was razed to the ground. Corinth was sacked and blotted off the map. Even the famed clemency of Caesar did not spare from death the brave leader of the Gallic uprising, Vercingetorix. The majestic formulas of the Roman law were grounded in a politics of frightfulness *(Schrecklichkeit)* which even a Nazi could admire.

To govern the empire they had gained, however, the Romans used

[10]This is the closing sentence in the last paragraph but one of the Preface to his *Philosophy of Right* (1820).

other techniques. Two of these, the development of the *jus gentium* and the gradual extension of the imperial citizenship, were described earlier.[11] But some of their other practices should be mentioned here. Once they had cowed a people into submission, they proceeded by degrees to raise them to partnership within the empire. The process was slow. For, whether they constructed a road or an aqueduct, a legal code or a civilization, the Romans built for eternity and were not disposed to hurry. Adroitly they would win over the potential leaders of a conquered community (those, that is, who had not been sold into slavery or massacred) by conferring favors on men of wealth and the heads of influential families. These then became the clients *(clientes)* of Rome. In return for their privileges, instead of becoming the instigators of local revolt, they cooperated with the imperial authority.[12] Thus with the grant of citizenship, the Latins, the Italians, and eventually the inhabitants of the provinces, found themselves sharing the benefits of the empire as a common enterprise. Why then rebel when the Roman masters had abandoned their exclusiveness and from every province the roads of opportunity could lead to the city on the Tiber?

Besides peace, law, and citizenship, the Romans scattered the seeds of their civilization among the peoples within their jurisdiction. Throughout the provinces by deliberate policy they planted centers from which their culture might spread. For this purpose, the chosen medium was the city—whether this were of ancient foundation and incorporated by Rome as a municipality, or some new colony of Roman émigrés, or an army camp on the frontier where the legions kept vigil against the "unpacified" and "uncivilized" peoples beyond. Here one might find the schools that taught provincial children the Latin tongue; the central-heated villas of the Roman administrators; their baths; yes, and their circuses. Rich dividends were yielded by this policy of Romanization. Not only did people far afield become assimilated in their thoughts and ways to the pattern of Rome (witness the Latin culture shared in common to this day by France, Italy, and Spain), but talented individuals from the provinces were drawn to the capital or applied their abilities in her service.

Especially was this so in the field of literature. Already, in the closing decades of the republic (from 79 to 49 B.C.), some of the most gifted figures hailed from Italian cities outside of Rome. Thus Cicero, whose spoken and written words converted the cumbrous Latin language into a vehicle for flowing prose, was a native of Arpinum, and the exquisite lyric poet Catullus was born near Verona. In the Augus-

[11]See Chap. 5, pp. 122–24.

[12]This is similar to the policy successfully followed for many decades by the British in India.

tan age, it was Italy that gave Rome her Virgil and Horace, as well as two other poets, Ovid and Propertius, and, among prose writers, the historian Livy. During the Silver Age in the second half of the first century A.D., an eminent group of Roman literati were Spanish born —the two Senecas, the rhetorician and critic Quintilian, and the verse writers Lucan and Martial. In the following two centuries it was North Africa that contributed much of the greatest talent, as the names of Apuleius and Tertullian indicate. Truly the provincials were apt pupils and their sons repaid the debt to Rome in full!

But this process of cultural assimilation, remarkable though it was, succeeded only in the western portion of Rome's dominions. The Latin language and literature were capable of dominating France, Spain, Italy, and North Africa. But they could not oust the Greek tongue from its ascendancy in the eastern Mediterranean. Politically and militarily one, the empire was cut culturally in twain, with the Adriatic serving as the geographical boundary. It was understandable, therefore, that the structure of government would eventually conform to the facts of social division. The Emperor Diocletian was accordingly responsible (in 286 A.D.) for slicing the empire into two halves and assigning the administration of one half to a colleague. The unity of the whole was later restored by Constantine, who also moved the capital from Rome to the city of Byzantium, which he renamed Constantinople (330 A.D.). But the empire once more fell apart at the seams and was partitioned between the sons of Theodosius, after their father's death in 395 A.D.

LIMITS OF THE ROMAN EMPIRE

The truth was that onward from the third century A.D. the huge sprawling mass of the Roman Empire could only with the greatest difficulty and by an exceptional man be ruled from one center. This was due to a mixture of circumstances and accumulation of changes taking place both inside the boundaries of the empire and beyond. As Rome added to her possessions and laboriously cemented the political mosaic of the Mediterranean world, the question was inevitably posed: Where should this expansion stop? With every new acquisition Rome lengthened the frontier she had to defend and the lines of communication from the capital to the perimeter. A permanent military establishment was required, as legions must be stationed at the chief danger points, and their loyalty and that of their commanders created anxiety for no few emperors. Besides, the incorporation of more peoples with alien ways imposed further strain on the absorptive capacity of the Graeco-Roman civilization. Where would the Roman Eagle find the limit of its cruising radius?

The limits were set at the two extreme points where the force which

Rome could exert was at last matched by the defensive strength of another people with a resistant culture. One place where this occurred was in Germany. With the conquest of Gaul (that is, France) completed, the Romans fanned out across the Rhine, hoping at one time to make the Elbe their frontier. But the hostility of leading German tribes, aided militarily by the thick cover of their forests, was climaxed in the year 9 A.D. when they ambushed and decimated an army of three legions. Augustus, the emperor, accepted this verdict and drew back his frontier to the Rhine. The other point at which distance weakened the striking power of Rome was in the East where the civilization of Greece confronted that of Asia. For many centuries the control of the interior highlands of Turkey, of the Arabian desert and the river valleys of the Tigris and Euphrates was hotly contested by rival oriental monarchies and by occidental invaders. Here in this embattled region, the cockpit then as now of East-West relations, the Romans retrod the paths and refought the issues of the Trojan War, the Graeco-Persian Wars, and the campaigns of Alexander. But the legionary, superb infantryman though he was, could not so readily dominate a terrain whose aridity forced men to be mobile and placed a premium on the camel or the horse. When the army of Crassus was cut to shreds by the Parthians[13] at Carrhae (53 B.C.), it was cavalry that won the day. Sometimes with success, but more often not, the emperors sought to plant the Eagle on the Euphrates, making it the Rhine of the East. Even when the limit was attained, however, the Romans were never able to recreate the union of occident and orient of which for a brief moment Alexander the Great had seen and left a vision. Albeit a titanic achievement, the empire of Rome was not universal. Before the opposition of Germans and Parthians its expansion halted.

Then came the time when the power that Rome could direct outward was exceeded by the pressures upon her from north and east. The reasons for her decline and fall have long been a topic of debate and speculation among historians, many of whom have searched for a single root cause in the general complex of disintegration. To Christian theologians the humbling of Rome was a sign of the wrath of God for the sins of the city. To Gibbon it appeared that Christianity was itself responsible, for by glorifying meekness and pacifism, it was supposed to have weakened the martial nerve of the population. Economists have pointed to the evidence of economic decay—to the decreasing fertility of the soil, especially in Italy; to the impoverishment of the citizen farmers and to the chronic shortage of precious

[13]The "Parthian shot" was their celebrated trick of feigning retreat and, when the enemy gave chase, turning around on horseback and firing a last murderous volley into their pursuers.

metals and ensuing monetary crises; to the huge corps of imperial civil servants and the fiscal difficulties of the exchequer. Add for good measure the political turmoil created by the ambitions of rival generals, who competed for the succession to the emperorship, and the insecurity and loss of life and treasure when the control of an empire hung periodically on the decision of civil war. So far had internal dry rot proceeded that when the empire's outer shell was finally cracked in the West (410 A.D.), the inside substance softly crumbled before the hammer blows of Goth and Visigoth and Vandal. Like the city-state of the fourth century B.C. Rome could no longer provide for its citizens those two essentials of government—security and prosperity. Therefore it had to fall.

THE MEDIEVAL DREAM OF UNIVERSAL ORDER

Politics is often molded by the survival of a memory. Few examples of this truth are as striking as the almost legendary spell that the name of Rome has never ceased to shed. Long after its collapse in the West, the empire continued to be an influence in politics because of the remembered fact that it had once existed. The feat of uniting the Mediterranean world, of which Rome proved itself capable, inspired a series of would-be imitators; and autocratic rulers with the title of tsar or kaiser have proudly taken the name of Caesar.

The first attempt was launched by Charlemagne in 800 A.D. Two circumstances had occurred in the three preceding centuries to make his venture feasible and justifiable. First, the "barbarians" from the north, falling heirs to the legacy of Graeco-Roman civilization, slowly imbibed its characteristics. As the Romans before them were educated by the Greeks they conquered, so the victorious Franks, Goths, and Lombards became Christianized and partly Romanized, and such cultural assimilation made easier politically the revival of a single empire. A second factor was the stimulus of a new pressure from outside. This was the militant growth of the power of Islam, which rose out of the Arabian desert and turned the flank of Europe by its lightning spread across North Africa. As André Maurois has written: "Mahomet died in 632; by 635, the Moslem armies were at Damascus, in 641 at Alexandria, in 713 at Toledo. In 725 the Arabs pushed up the Rhone Valley as far as Autun. These new conquerors could not be assimilated as the Germans had been. The Franks had admired Rome and adopted Christianity; the Moslems remained faithful to their own ways and religion. At the beginning of the eighth century, they were virtually masters of the Mediterranean.

They occupied the whole of Spain, and a portion of southern France."[14]

The popes of the eighth century were preoccupied with the fear that the Crescent might supplant the Cross. No less concerned were the kings of the Franks, whose dominions were menaced by the advance of the Saracens. An additional reason impelled the eighth century popes to bid for French support. From their north Italian base in the Po Valley the Lombards were spreading south and threatened to take Rome. The Franks, in the rear of the Lombards, were natural allies for the papacy. First to Charles the Hammer, and later to Charlemagne, the pope appealed for protection. When Charlemagne by the close of the eighth century had established his supremacy in Western Europe, he struck a mutually advantageous bargain with the Pope. Using his temporal power to bolster the church, in St. Peter's on Christmas day, 800 A.D. he received from Pope Leo III the title, "Emperor of the Romans."

But words and ceremonies, though in politics they have symbolic value, cannot alone perpetuate the realities of empire. His successors were unable to maintain the unity of the territories that Charlemagne had knit together. In 843 his three grandsons divided their patrimony. One obtained the eastern section, comprising portions of Germany. A second received in the west a large slice of France. To the third, Lothair, was given a middle kingdom, following the direction of the Rhine and extending from north Italy to the North Sea. Much of the subsequent history of Europe is related to that division: the separate political development of the French to the west of the Rhine and the Germans to the east, and the struggle between them for the control of the middle kingdom. Once again, however, the idea of a single empire outlived the disappearance of the fact. This time it moved east, cropping up among the Germans, whose efficient ruler Otto the Great was crowned emperor by the pope in 962. Henceforth, for what it was worth, the title of emperor and the claim to universal empire remained with the Germans. Thus was the stage set for the turbulent medieval politics of a German-based empire and an Italian-based papacy.

To the problems of the size of the state, with which this chapter deals, the Middle Ages contributed an ambitious dream imperfectly realized. The governing concept of the period was that of a universal society permeated with the Christian spirit. Lacking, however, were the means of making the dream come true. The medieval structure,

[14] *Histoire de la France*, Vol. I (New York: Éditions de la Maison Française, 1947), p. 41 (my translation).

described earlier,[15] was a dual one, with church and state organized to take care of men's spiritual and bodily needs respectively. On the temporal side, the universal society was a pretentious fiction to which the facts bore no resemblance. Because of the feudal system, localism was the order of the day.[16] Kingdoms were mostly patchwork quilts, where much depended on the personality of the reigning king. Central authority was frequently defied; with difficulty imposed. The Holy Roman Empire embraced a group of German principalities. But its writ did not run in France or Spain, in England or Lombardy. After the collapse of Rome and the turmoil of the Teutonic invasions, the state had suffered fragmentation, and its essential functions were as often as not decentralized. Rather than be without shelter amid the perils of a world in flux, men tried to rebuild security and prosperity in small oases of local order.

On the ecclesiastical side, the dream came a few steps nearer to fulfillment. The Roman Church had a centralized authority, a single canon law, a common ritual and theology. As a citizen of Rome in any province could formerly appeal his case to Caesar, so in matters pertaining to salvation—and they were many—a Christian could make appeal to the pontiff, who jealously guarded the principle of uniformity. Stern punishment was meted out to heretics. The Albigenses in the southwest of France and the Waldenses in the southeast, who deviated from the Latin rite and challenged Roman authority in the late twelfth and early thirteenth centuries, were fiercely attacked and all but exterminated.[17] Nor was the church loath to invoke for this purpose the military forces of the temporal sword. Whoever indeed paid more attention to realities than forms could argue that the imperial mantle had fallen on the shoulders of the pope, not on those of the Holy Roman emperor.[18] Certainly many a clergyman, in order to associate his church with the symbols of Roman power, talked and acted as if the most important place in the Christian world were not Jerusalem or Bethlehem, but Rome.

[15]See Chap. 6, pp. 161 ff.

[16]See Chap. 10, pp. 287–88.

[17]It was at this time and in this connection that the papacy inaugurated the Inquisition which was responsible for infamous cruelties in the name of religious orthodoxy.

[18]In a later century such a hostile critic as Thomas Hobbes wrote in the *Leviathan:* "And if a man consider the originall of this great Ecclesiasticall Dominion, he will easily perceive, that the Papacy, is no other, than the *Ghost* of the deceased *Romane Empire*, sitting crowned upon the grave thereof." Part IV, Chap. 47 (Everyman's Library), p. 381. Italics in original.

THE CRACKS IN MEDIEVAL UNITY

Yet there precisely was the rub! One reason for such talk and action was the geographical fact that Rome lay in the West, whereas the Holy Land belonged to the East. The split of the Roman Empire into two halves, divided by language and having separate administrative capitals in Rome and Constantinople, outlived the social and military breakdown of the western half. In the east a Byzantine empire based in Constantinople continued in existence. Associated with it was the eastern church, employing a Greek rite, and further differing from the western church in being a department, rather than a partner, of the state. Situated closer than Rome to Islam, the eastern church and empire were harder pressed by the upsurge of oriental power. In 637 Jerusalem passed into the hands of the Moslems, though Christian pilgrims were still admitted to the holy places. But in 1071 the Turks of the Seljuk dynasty captured the city from their Islamic rivals and forbade entry to Christians—a decision which the Byzantine Empire was too enfeebled to alter.

Then was initiated that series of dramatic events which, more than anything else, reveals in its true light and perspective the medieval assumption of a universal society. These were the Crusades. No less than seven were launched in the period between 1096 and 1270. The Turkish policy of sealing off Jerusalem provided a pretext and an occasion. To drive the infidel from the Holy City and recapture it for Christendom was the mission preached by Peter the Hermit, evangelist of the First Crusade (1096–1100). But the motives and objectives were in fact as mixed as the participants. The various French kings who gave their blessing to the enterprise saw an opportunity to extend their influence in the East and there found a Latin kingdom. North Italian merchants, in cities like Venice, welcomed a chance of creating or reviving a trade with the Levant to which Turks and Saracens offered so serious an obstruction. A motley assortment of religious zealots, adventurers, fortune seekers, footloose knights, and romantics were lured by the glittering prospect of excitement, mystery, and plunder. The papacy itself was influenced by three-sided calculations. Under the banner of the Cross, raised by the Church Militant, the unity of Western Europe could be consolidated. A display of occidental strength on the continent of Asia would check the onrush of Islam by penetrating its own domain. Furthermore, the superiority of Rome over Constantinople, of the Latin rite over the Greek rite church, would be triumphantly asserted if the Christians of the West accomplished what those of the East could not. That this thought was by no means last or least among papal hopes seems clear from the evidence. Certain of the Crusades were as evidently directed against the Byzantine power as against that of the Seljuks, and the fourth in the series (1202–1204) actually resulted in the temporary establishment of a Latin kingdom in Constantinople!

Perhaps the most remarkable aspect of these expeditions is that so many were sent and that they were prolonged for nearly two centuries. This can prove only one thing—that those who launched and led the Crusades were convinced of their political value. Despite all the difficulties in that period of transporting an army from Western Europe to Palestine and supplying it in the field at such a distance from its home base, despite reverses and failures,[19] the organization of Crusades developed into a medieval habit. They must, therefore, have produced a profit which nowhere appears on the military balance sheet of gain and loss. Nor is that profit hard to discover. It was the kind of gamble which is expressed in the maxim that a divided community should prosecute a vigorous foreign policy. It would be exaggerating to call the Western Europe of that time a happy band of brothers, and the unity to which the papacy aspired had to be created through subjective loyalties as well as structured institutions. The papacy hoped this inner consolidation could be achieved by attacking an outer enemy; by hostility, not only to Islam, but also the eastern church; by a policy of clenching both fists and brandishing both swords, not of turning the other cheek. The medieval Christian society, in short, was not fully unified and was never universal. Christendom itself was split and against it was arrayed the militancy of a rival faith and culture.

Even a series of Crusades, however, could not cement the cracks in the West's foundation walls or prevent new fissures from opening up. For the reasons mentioned in earlier chapters,[20] the structure of the feudal economy and church-state dualism began to sag in the fourteenth century and broke in the fifteenth. The theories of Thomas Aquinas were predicated upon an ideal of universality and a social hierarchy reinforced by rural conservatism. But between Thomist doctrine and political and economic actualities the gap grew ever wider, until one bore as little relation to the other as the Aristotelian *polis* did to the results of Macedonian statecraft. The same fundamental causes which had brought first the city-state and then the Roman Empire to its downfall were operating again in the fourteenth and fifteenth centuries. The unit of government, which men had earlier contrived to

[19]For instance, the First Crusade did succeed in taking Jerusalem (1100). But in 1187 the city once more fell into Moslem hands. Recovered in the Fifth Crusade (1228–29), it passed again to the Turks in 1239.

[20]See Chap. 6, p. 166, Chap. 7, pp. 178–79.

yield them the necessary minimum of security and prosperity, was no longer adequate for its functions. Because of conflicts among the feudal nobility, the rise of urban centers which desired a wider extension of commerce, and the schism and corruption in the papacy followed by the Protestant Reformation, a new territorial unit had to be organized wherein people could once more feel themselves safe and could work to be prosperous. Nor should one overlook the effects of the invention of gunpowder. Applied to the art of war, it blew the knight in armor to bits, thus lowering the political status associated with his military importance. Shakespeare has a reference to this when he describes "a certain lord, neat, and trimly dress'd," who enraged the battle-weary Hotspur with his foppish manner and elegant chitchat:

> And that it was a great pity, so it was,
> This villanous saltpetre should be digg'd
> Out of the bowels of the harmless earth,
> Which many a good tall fellow had destroy'd
> So cowardly; and but for these vile guns,
> He would himself have been a soldier.[21]

Similarly the vanished world of the medieval knight-errant and its illusions form the subject of Cervantes' satire in *Don Quixote*. The windmills at which the superannuated knight tilted were cannons and commerce. Under such sponsors Western Europe witnessed the start of its third experiment in the search for the state of ideal magnitude.

BIRTH OF THE NATION-STATE

This third attempt, the nation-state, marked a new departure in two ways. Since the medieval system combined an ideal of universalism with the realities of localism, its successor had to differentiate itself by rejecting both those characteristics. The result was a focus on the nation. The nation spelled a reaction both against the universal order at one extreme, and the local emphasis at the other. Since the new unit was to be the nation, the new unity must be national. The nation would now impose its unity on the localities, while simultaneously defying the larger, external unities of papacy and empire. Consequently, the nation-state would differ from its predecessors—city-state and empire-state—by reason of its intermediate size. Its area was designed to be larger than the city-state, but smaller than the empire-state of the Roman and medieval pattern. Thus did its architects hope to avoid the extremes of a unit which was too little or too large. The

[21] *Henry IV*, First Part, Act I, Sc. 3, ll. 59–64.

new arrangement had the appearance of a compromise. Perhaps this time Europe would strike the happy medium. Here at least was one angle from which the nation-state could be seen and judged.

But something as complex as the nation-state presents many angles. Viewed in time, the nation-state flourished as the dominant unit of government for almost four and a half centuries. Such a statement, of course, contains an element of the arbitrary. One cannot assign precise dates to the beginning or end of a political category, which takes unconscionably long to be delivered or die. Nevertheless, it is not unreasonable to place the official birthdate of the nation-state in the later decades of the fifteenth century. In 1469, the year of Machiavelli's birth, a marriage between Ferdinand of Aragon and Isabella of Castile sealed the union, and inaugurated the sixteenth century greatness of Spain. Martin Luther was born in 1483, and with him a generation which was to commit the irrevocable acts of the Reformation. Two years later, after his victory at Bosworth Field, Henry VII ascended the throne of England. Himself a Lancastrian, he married Elizabeth of York in 1486, thereby founding the strong Tudor dynasty and healing the feud between rival aristocratic clans which had brought upon England the long travail of the Wars of the Roses.[22] And when did the death throes of the nation-state commence? Probably in 1914,[23] though it is still too early for death to be officially certified.

Viewed in space, the nation-state illustrates a singular combination of politics with geography. All those that were organized earliest and rose to prominence in the sixteenth and seventeenth centuries— Spain, Portugal, England, France, and the Netherlands—were situated on the coast with direct access to the Atlantic. Interestingly enough, however, the initial reasons for the influence of the seaboard states of the West lay in the East. In 1453 the Turks succeeded in a centuriesold dream by the capture of Constantinople and extinction of the Byzantine Empire. Thereupon, with complete strategic command of the Mediterranean's Asiatic fringe, they were able to consummate the policy already applied in Jerusalem and elsewhere. Europeans were denied access to the region under Turkish-Arabian control. The caravan routes which for over a millennium had given the West its most direct approach to the trade of the East were cut and blocked. A crippling economic blow was dealt to such commercial states as Venice, of whom Wordsworth was later to write:

> Once did she hold the gorgeous East in fee;
> And was the safeguard of the West.

[22]See Chap. 9, pp. 247 ff.
[23]See Chap. 13, pp. 376 ff.

Between Europe and India, Islam had stretched its crescent of steel and cordon of sand.

To this challenge the Europeans replied with a search for alternative routes that would bring them around to the rear of the obstructive Moslems. The Portuguese prince, Henry the Navigator, sent out a series of expeditions to chart a course round Africa. Financed by Isabella in 1492 the Genoese captain Columbus sailed west and found what he thought were the Indies.[24] Thus was a New World opened up to compensate for the loss of the Old, and soon the spoils of Mexico and Peru were replacing the treasure of the East. The effect of this geographical reorientation was to give to the English Channel and the Straits of Gibraltar the significance formerly possessed by the Dardanelles and the Isthmus of Suez. The routes linking Europe to the rest of the world no longer pointed east, but south and west. The great inland sea, the Mediterranean, ceased to be the main artery for traffic. It became instead a side road, for the Oceanic Age had begun. Through centuries past, the calculations of political and military strength had been primarily computed in terms of land power, since the landlocked Mediterranean could be commanded by armies as the Romans, who were certainly no sailors, had demonstrated. Now, however, it was the sea which figured with equal, or in some cases greater, prominence. The peoples who bordered on the Atlantic began to think of the coast as their front door and, when that door was opened, the corridors of a stale diplomacy were freshened with briny breezes. Upon the wave of sea power the nation-state floated to its destiny. What started, though, as an Atlantic phenomenon did not remain a preserve of the western seaboard. Not the least remarkable aspect of the nation-state has been its capacity to spread. The city-states, after all, were never able to extend over much more than the coastal fringe and islands of the Mediterranean. Even the empire-state and medieval Christendom were stopped in their advance. But the nation-state has left no portion of the world uncovered. As seven decades of the twentieth century are completed, virtually the whole of the continents of Asia and South America has been subdivided into nation-states. The only continent in which significant areas continue under colonial rule is Africa. But there, too, the ultimate result is only a matter of time. No unit of government previously known to history has achieved so comprehensive a coverage.

[24]Besides Columbus, the leading men who pioneered the ways to the future were Vasco da Gama, discoverer of the route around the Cape of Good Hope; Pedro Alvares Cabral, who found South America and landed in Brazil; Amerigo Vespucci, who gave his name to America; and Fernao de Magalhaes, after whom the Straits of Magellan are called.

There are three explanations for this fact. The chief characteristic of sea power is its mobility, which facilitated the spread of Western European influence in Asia and the Americas. Second, the Europeans, when they came into contact with non-Europeans, were the possessors of demonstrably superior technical skills in many fields. Hence the understandable impulse of non-Europeans to borrow from Europe not only its techniques but also its political system. The third reason is perhaps more subtle. The nation-state seems to operate with a contagious magic on those beyond its borders. The pressure that one people organized around the principle of nationality exerts upon another has often stimulated a rival growth of national feelings. Thus the attempts of English kings to extend their grip on France and secure its throne assisted the birth of French nationhood, of which Joan of Arc in the years 1429–31 supplied a flaming symbol. The might of Spain in the sixteenth century was challenged by English seamen in duels which ranged across the Atlantic and the Caribbean and even reached into the Pacific. When the Spanish Armada was defeated in 1588, Elizabeth's England experienced that outburst of national *élan* to which Shakespeare's *Histories* are testimony. The protracted hostilities of Poland and Russia developed in both an ardent patriotism. Napoleonic conquest set spurs to Prussian reorganization and speeded the pan-German aspirations on which Bismarck later rode to power. Austrian resistance to Italian unification boomeranged against the Hapsburgs by giving Mazzini and Cavour a target to attack. Similar events occurred the world over. British rule in India eventually provoked an Indian national sentiment. The action of the United States in forcing Japan to open itself to contact with the world (1853–54) aroused a rapid reaction in the overthrow of the shogunate, industrialization of the economy, and the aggressive nationalism that reached its climax in 1941. Likewise Japan's own endeavor to subjugate the mainland, coming on top of successive encroachments by European powers, added new motive and momentum to China's revolution.

COMPONENTS OF NATIONALITY

These facts raise queries which require explaining. What is there in the components of the nation-state that has both made it an article for export and encouraged the domestic manufacture of a competing product? What makes a community a nation? What makes a nation organize a state? Above all, what is a nation?

A unit of government tends to inspire and reflect a certain feeling among its citizens. If the state is adequate in providing security and prosperity, the feeling will be one of positive loyalty and willing allegiance. This is the subjective side of government, so-called because it includes the emotions and attitudes, the hopes and hates and sympathies, for which men find fulfillment in the political process. Every kind of state, in order to survive, must breed an appropriate patriotism as the counterpart to its institutions. The city-state had to glorify its own achievements, so that a man might take pride in being Athenian or Spartan. The empire-state had to inculcate a loyalty to Rome, as the medieval society sought to unify mankind through acceptance of the Christian creed. The same has been true of nation-states. The subjective element in this case is the feeling of nationality, which gives a group of human beings the sense of belonging together. When people feel this way, that is, when they unite around a national symbol, they think, live, and act—and, if necessary, die in warfare—not as Athenians, Romans, or Christians, but as Americans, Russians or Germans.

BUILDING THE AMERICAN NATION

How do such sentiments arise? What are the conditions of nationhood? From what has just been said, it follows that, if a nation must have a sense of belonging together, anything shared in common may help to weld people into a nation. Conversely, anything that divides them weakens the union. Hence the foundations of nationality are embedded in the structure of society. Any of the various associations, through which men combine or compete in their economic, religious, cultural, and other activities, can become politically significant because of its effect upon national unity or division. This truth will be evident from some examples. The slavery issue precipitated a crisis on which the American nation almost broke. "A house divided against itself cannot stand," said Lincoln quoting the Scriptures. "I believe this government," he went on, "cannot endure permanently, half slave and half free. I do not expect the Union to be dissolved,—I do not expect the house to fall; but I do expect it will cease to be divided. It will become all one thing, or all the other."[25] In that instance a social cleavage culminated in a civil war because of the powerful interests and passionate feelings arrayed on the two sides, and their near-equality of strength.

Another American case can be cited, however, which also involved the fundamentals of the social system, but was differently settled because a huge majority confronted a small minority. In 1846 the Mormons trekked to the western wilderness to found their own

[25]From the speech at Springfield, Illinois, on his nomination to the United States Senate, June 17, 1858.

community under the dictates of their church. Yet their Promised Land could not escape the pursuit of the society they had left. When the hour arrived for Utah to be organized as a state, Congress would not confer statehood until the Mormon church abandoned polygamy. That raises an interesting point. The Constitution certainly gives Congress exclusive authority over the admission of new states. But on the question of the family and its place in the social order, the document is silent. Nevertheless the members of Congress felt that the Constitution assumes, though it does not specify, a marital orthodoxy which frowns on one man having more than one wife simultaneously. This government could not endure permanently, part monogamous and part polygamous. It had to become all one thing, or all the other.

Among the social ties that contribute to national unity, it is customary to include such factors as a common language, common religion, and common race. People who speak the same tongue, worship in the same way, and belong physically to the same branch of mankind, clearly possess important points of resemblance and avoid some potential causes of misunderstanding. One of the marvels in the history of the United States has been the ability to absorb millions of immigrants from many lands and mold their children and grandchildren to a new design. Out of the "melting pot" has flowed the material of an American nationality. What made this possible? Much of the credit belongs to provisions of the Constitution that tolerate the practice of any religion, guarantee to individuals the same fundamental rights, and allow for the naturalization and enfranchisement of aliens. These principles were reinforced by the opportunites of an expanding economy and the conformist tendencies of the public schools which have taught one language and imparted the same basic beliefs to the younger generation.

That is not to say that such a phenomenon as the creation of a new nationality for 200,000,000 people could be accomplished without friction and end in complete assimilation. When Catholics arrived from Ireland in great numbers during the 1840's and after, some Protestants voiced and organized an opposition. When Italian and Slavic immigration increased in the decades between the Civil War and World War I, qualms were felt by anxious Anglo-Saxons.[26] Divided by religion, Americans have been united by the English language, which for reasons of economic and social necessity became the common medium of expression. Most difficult of all, however, has been the absorption of America's oldest minority, the Negroes,[27] who have

---

[26]This problem forms a central theme in André Siegfried's *America Comes of Age* (London and Toronto: Jonathan Cape Limited, 1927).

[27]See Gunnar Myrdal, *The American Dilemma* (New York: Harper & Row, Pub-

been the victims of more persistent discrimination than any other group. In their case the single item of racial difference has outweighed all of the human and cultural similarities—including the fact that they are English-speaking Christians.

NATIONHOOD IN THE BRITISH COMMONWEALTH

The American problem of transforming immigrants into nationals may be compared with the experience of countries in the British Commonwealth. Australia and New Zealand escaped many of the difficulties of the United States because more than 95 per cent of their European population was drawn from the British Isles. In Australia the Aborigines were too few and too weak to withstand the onset of the newcomers. The sturdy New Zealand Maoris were a match for the colonists in the early days of settlement; but since the 1870's they have been outnumbered, although relations between the races are formally equal. Both countries, of course, while they enjoy the advantages of homogeneity, suffer from its defects since their culture is inevitably lacking in richness and diversity. That this same diversity, however, may spell division, and impede the building of a nation, is the lesson supplied by Canada and South Africa. Though the population of Canada is one-tenth of that of the United States, Canadianism is a less potent sentiment than Americanism. The reason is that Canada is an addition of two cultures which have not amalgamated. Canadians are divided by language as well as by religion, and the linguistic boundaries largely coincide with the religious.[28] So do the boundary lines of economics, for in industry and commerce it is the English-speaking Protestants who predominate. Furthermore, the geographical concentration of the French-Canadians enhances their group consciousness and physical separation always assists a feeling of political separateness. American and Canadian history alike confirm the generalization that the most dangerous way in which a nation can be internally subdivided is into two parts, territorially distinct. It was the sectional basis of North-South rivalry which strengthened the secessionist tendencies of the cotton economy, the plantation system, and the slaveocracy, thus making the Confederacy seem practicable. Likewise, it is the solidarity of Quebec, a residue of France's *ancien régime* reinforced by a tenacious church with long memories, which

---

lishers, 1944).

[28]A bridge between the British and the French is provided by the small minority of English-speaking Irish Catholics, whose religion draws them to one side while language attracts them to the other.

interacts with the reluctance of English-speaking Canadians to absorb the French culture, and these barriers together retard the achievement of a truly united Canada. As the motto *e pluribus unum* indicates, and odd though this may seem, it is sometimes easier for many to become one, than for two!

If the United States is more unified than Canada, Canada is more united than South Africa. The bitter discords of the nineteenth century have left in that unhappy country a legacy of frustration and antagonisms. As in Canada, the European population is divided by religion, language, and economics, along lines that coincide in each case and therefore accentuate the differences. What then maintains their fragile union? One factor is that the speakers of Afrikaans and English, though the former are mainly rural and the latter mainly urban, are relatively interspersed. More important, however, is the pressure on both European groups to combine in the face of an African majority outnumbering them by four to one. The color bar thus counts in the balance for more than everything else put together. Even so, it is dubious whether one can talk accurately about a South African nation. The most one dare assert is that such unity as exists is for whites only and that its cement is fear.

THE PROBLEM IN EUROPE

1. The Effects of Cultural Division. Among the nation-states of Europe the problems of race relations are virtually nonexistent. But religion and language and the other aspects of culture have served as cutting teeth to shape the pieces of a continental jigsaw puzzle. The continent contains three principal cultures—Latin, Germanic, and Slavic. With the exceptions of Switzerland and Belgium (the latter being a less successful union than the fomer) no nation-state has been compounded of Latin and Germanic elements. Similarly, in east-central Europe no nationality has ever been formed out of a Latin-Slavic blend, save in the case of Poland and possibly Yugoslavia. For, though the Poles are a Slavic people, their church has retained a link with Rome; and in Yugoslavia the Croats are Latinized and Catholic, while the Serbs are Slavs and follow the Greek rite. A fusion of Germanic and Slavic people into one nation has been even harder to accomplish. The only state which had both the chance and motive to do this, namely Austria, was unequal to its opportunity. The Austrians organized their government upon the principle of German ascendancy, and, in contrast with the Roman policy, admitted none but the Hungarian Magyars to the charmed circles of influence. Slavs were not welcomed as partners in the citadels of power.

The case of Austria is particularly interesting for the light it throws on certain problems of the nation-state in Europe. The Hapsburg Empire in east-central Europe originated and continued for many centuries because it appeared to serve a useful purpose. It kept the Ottoman Empire out of central Europe. The Slavs were the subject of a squeeze and, to the extent that they could act for themselves, might choose between a Hapsburg emperor or a Turkish sultan. Both alternatives left much to be desired. The odds were by no means always in the favor of Austria, whose political stupidities were a fair match for Turkish cruelties. Indeed the Balkan Christians of the eastern Orthodox church were at times more tolerantly treated by the caliphate than by the papacy. But to those who thought and felt in terms of a conflict between Europe and Asia, Austria could at least claim to be Europe's champion. Even so, the appeal of Vienna to the Slavs fluctuated in inverse ratio with Turkish strength. When Ottoman power was expanding, Vienna might seem the lesser evil. But when the Turks were in a decline, as in the nineteenth century, the Austrian empire lost its *raison d'être,* and the Balkan peoples were disposed to say: "A plague on both your houses!" Then came the opportunity that Austria missed. If she were to avoid a series of wars of independence, she must unite her multinational empire around a comprehensive loyalty and, as Rome had done, turn subjects into partners. This would involve either decentralization of government from Vienna and the grant of more power to Hungarians, Czechs, and other peoples, or a sharing of authority at the center. The former solution was applied only to Hungary. The latter, which meant, of course, a representative legislature and the abandonment of autocracy, implied also the sacrifice of German leadership. To Metternich and his successors, the full consequences of both policies were unthinkable. Hence, amid the babel of national aspirations which its domination provoked, the Austrian autocracy waltzed in step with Johann Strauss to its own destruction.

The dilemma of the Austrians, caught between their desire for German superiority and the demands of a multinational population for equality, can be seen from another perspective, that of the national consolidation of two neighbors: Germany and Italy. At first glance it is puzzling that these countries were not unified until some four centuries later than Spain, France, and England, and that their unification, when it finally occurred, took place in the same decade (1860–71). The reasons can be discovered, however, in the policies of Austria and the papacy and the relationship between them, the roots of which reach back to the Middle Ages. The attempt to organize western Christendom under the Holy Roman Empire and the papacy was formulated in terms of a universal society. In fact, however, the papacy was based upon Italy, a portion of which the popes governed as temporal sovereigns, while the empire acquired a German base. Even when pope and emperor cooperated, it was not in either's interest to permit the other to consolidate his jurisdiction over Germany or Italy respectively. If Italy remained divided, the pope's position was more precarious and he was less able to dominate the emperor. If the empire was a loose and tenuous union, the emperor was less likely to control the pope. Each must therefore support a balance of powers, and prevent a concentration of power, in the other's terrain.

As the Reformation sapped the foundations of Catholicism by breaking the unity of western Christendom, so the emergence of the nation-state presented a challenge to the empire by negating its claims to universalism. Not until the conclusion of the Thirty Years' War (1648) were the division of western Christendom and the system of nation-states accepted as irrevocable features of Europe's political order. Both papacy and empire in the eighteenth century steered against the prevailing wind and current with just enough power to keep at a standstill. But in the century that followed, the dominant forces within society were those of industrialism, laissez-faire economics, liberal democracy, and a latter-day nationalism which, because belated, was all the more intense. Against all these movements empire and papacy set themselves in opposition; and, being on the defensive and compelled to retreat, found themselves allies in a last-ditch resistance.

Neither Germany nor Italy could be unified except by defying both the Hapsburgs and the pope. Metternich had condemned the union of all Germans in a single state as "an infamous object." Those who thought in pan-German terms hoped to include Austria in a German state, but wanted to exclude her non-German subjects. For her part, Austria was unwilling to pay for admission into an all-German state the price of losing her empire; and until the middle of the nineteenth century, while unwilling to unify Germany herself, she was strong enough to prevent anybody else from doing so. A similar situation existed in Italy, of which Austria controlled the northeast. To unify Italy meant the defeat and expulsion of the Austrians. Metternich had declared that Italy was only a geographical expression and he intended to keep it so. The other obvious loser in any Italian unification was the papacy, which would have to surrender its temporal rule over the center of the peninsula. Consequently, when the Kingdom of Italy was established in 1860, and when Bismarck's Prussia (Protestant-led) organized the German Reich in 1871, it was nationalism in both cases which triumphed over a multinational empire and a supranational church.

2. The Religious Cleavage. If it has proven difficult in Europe to create a nationality out of mixed cultures, it has been no less difficult with mixed religions. The most successful nation-states have been those containing a big majority of either Protestants or Catholics. The oldest powerful nation-states are witnesses to this truth. In Britain the Protestant Reformation triumphed—and though England could amalgamate with Wales and Scotland, she was never able to absorb the Catholic portion of Ireland. In France and Spain the Catholic Counter-Reformation triumphed. Thus in all three countries nationalism in its early phase was associated with religious intolerance. Only in exceptional cases and under great difficulty has a nation been formed with a blend of Protestants and Catholics in relatively equal strength. On this point the example of Switzerland is instructive. Because of the work of Zwingli in Zurich and Calvin in Geneva, portions of Switzerland became a Protestant stronghold. Because, however, of its geographical proximity to France, Austria, south Germany, and north Italy, the Swiss were strategically important to the papacy and the Jesuit order attempted to recapture their allegiance. In 1847 a minority of Catholic cantons seceded—without success; hence, in 1848 the Protestant majority wrote the new federal constitution— which incidentally banned the Jesuits from Switzerland.[29] But though religion has split the Swiss, and though they are divided by language into French, German, and Italian sections, they are helped in holding together by the fact that the religious and linguistic divisions cut across each other. While Geneva is French-speaking and Calvinist, Neuchatel and Fribourg are French-speaking and Catholic. Whereas Bern and Zurich are German-speaking and Protestant, Luzern and Glarus and Schwyz are German-speaking and Catholic. In this respect the Swiss are more fortunate than the Canadians.

Even this fact, however, would not account for the miracle of Swiss nationhood if there were not also an additional reason. Instead of preferring incorporation into France, Germany, Austria, or Italy, the Swiss have chosen to become Swiss because of their reaction to the pressures of surrounding big powers and because of a geography which made defense and independence militarily practicable. Furthermore, the survival of their state has been guaranteed by the consistent integrity of their policy of permanent neutrality. The Swiss, therefore, illustrate a point discussed earlier, that a nationality is often a response to a pressure exerted from without. But they illustrate something else. When one is analyzing the nation-state, it is appropriate to ask whether the nation helps create the state or the state helps

[29] *Constitution of the Swiss Confederation*, Article 51.

create the nation. The answer is that examples occur of both, which proves that, while a nation may be molded out of social factors, it can also originate in politics. Switzerland is an example of a state being organized first, and a national sentiment developing second. So is the United States, where the foundation of a federal government in large part preceded and then promoted the ripening of an American nationality. In other words, to live under the same system of government and the tradition which it acquires with the lapse of time stimulates a popular sense of belonging together. Thus it is not only the English language, the monogamous family, and the abolition of slavery that have contributed to an American nation, but also the common pride and respect inspired by the Declaration and the Constitution and by such names as Franklin, Washington, Jefferson, and Lincoln.

Conversely, a group that already feels a national unity because of a common language, literature, and religion may eventually develop such cohesive political force as to found a state. Witness the modern instances of Poland, Czechoslovakia, and Israel. This is especially likely to happen to a minority group governed by a repressive majority of different language or religion. Where an intolerant majority monopolizes the government, the minority, unable to take part in politics on an equal basis, clings to other associations than the state, seeking thereby a medium for its own representation. Often this role has been assumed by religion which supplied a structure and a voice for a group that felt itself suppressed. Thus the Catholic church traditionally assisted the nationalism of the Poles and their resistance to the tsarist program of Russification. The same church provided the Irish with a vehicle of opposion to the British and has been the mainstay of the French-Canadians. Jewish synagogues, transmitting the *Torah* from one generation to the next, kept a Hebraic culture alive among a people sorely persecuted in their dispersion. On the island of Cyprus the Greek church led the agitation against British colonial rule and has espoused the demands for union with Greece. So in Burma the Buddhist priesthood, at odds with Britain on educational policy, lent its support to the independence movement. Similarly on the South African veld the Dutch Reformed church has fostered the fierce nationalism of the Afrikaner extremists.

NATIONALISM AND THE ARTS

As a substitute for religion, or to supplement it, an emergent nationalism, excluded from the government of the state, may find its outlet in the arts (especially music and literature) and in higher education. Thus nationalistic Poles have sung their folk songs and made the most of Chopin. The Czech renaissance was expressed musically by Smetana and Dvorak. The "blood and iron" of Bismarck's Reich was rendered into appropriate music by the pompous Wagner, who was understandably a favorite of Hitler. The significance to nationalism of the arts lies in their appeal to the intelligentsia, who have been the prime movers in many modern national uprisings. This further explains the interest of nationalists in education, in fostering their own language, and in organizing institutions of higher learning. Hence the importance of Charles University in Prague to the Czechs; of the Hebrew University to the Zionists; of the University of Cairo to the Egyptians. Hence the well-known phenomenon of an ardent nationalism and political activity on its behalf among the university students of so many lands. Hence the insistence of nation builders on reviving their ancestral tongue—as Hebrew became again a living language in Palestine, and as the government of Eire officially adopted Erse while Irish literati like Shaw, Joyce, O'Faolain, and Yeats were writing in matchless English!

The interaction that occurs so often between national feeling and cultural achievement is important and significant. The foundations of the state may be embedded in the material needs of safety and prosperity. But while it is essential that these needs be satisfied, they do not alone complete the development of man or fulfill his every aspiration. Political organization, which serves our creature comforts and is the guardian of life itself, can also minister to the spirit. When a governmental system imbues a people collectively with self-respect and strength, the most gifted individuals in the group may be stimulated by the surrounding *élan* to creative production in literature, philosophy, the sciences, and the arts. Thus it is that great luminaries have often shone with intellectual and aesthetic brilliance in the very century when a people attained politically "their finest hour." It was hardly an accident that the most glorious period of Athenian culture was contemporaneous with the rise of Athenian power to its zenith after the heroic combat against the Persians; that the golden age in Roman literature coincided with the establishment of the Augustan peace; that the thirteenth century, which witnessed so fine a flowering of medieval genius, saw the papacy at the height of its ascendancy under Innocent III and his successors; that intellect and the arts flourished so brilliantly in seventeenth century Holland, when the Dutch nation, self-liberated from Spanish rule, was riding the crest of financial and maritime leadership; and that the reigns of Elizabeth I and Victoria, which represent the high-water marks of Britain's political influence, presided over some of the most notable of her achievements of the mind. With each unit of government, therefore—city-state, empire-state, and nation-state—examples can be found of a correlation between political success and cultural greatness.[30]

That the love of one's country has often provided an inspirational focus for rare creative work is evidence of the capacity of the nation-state to serve humanity well. Countless are the poets, writers, musicians, painters, scientists, and scholars who have been stirred by national pride to activity of intellectual or imaginative eminence. Such an emotion has offered to many a sensitive spirit an attraction that is not to be equated with the crudities of jingoism. On that note of appreciation, before the analysis turns to the pathology of nationalism and the decline of nation-states, let this chapter end.

[30]The two are not always correlated, however; for example, the Italian Renaissance, despite Machiavelli's pleadings, did not produce a political record that matched the artistic output.

13

FIFTH ISSUE:

–2– Nation-States and International Order

THE CRISIS OF THE NATION-STATE

No unit of government ever conformed consistently to its own ideal. The system of classical Greece, with its principle of autonomy for each urban-rural cluster, negated the possibility of wider union either through a free combination of states or through imperial subjection to one. Efforts of the former kind were not long enduring and efforts of the latter, though repeatedly made, provoked opposition and war. Rome, which commenced its political history as a city-state like the rest, was the one which enjoyed spectacular success in the policy of imperial conquest, thereby eliminating the city-state as an independent entity and substituting for it the new unit of a widespread empire. But even Rome could not command the world,[1] and the unity and peace which were her ideals arrived at their bounds to the north and east. A similar story was repeated in the Middle Ages, when the dream of a universal order was pursued by papacy and Holy Roman Empire alike. In practice, however, neither in the secular sphere nor the spiritual was universality achieved. Each of these three experiments was an endeavor to provide a structure within which men could build their welfare in safety. Each lasted for as long as it was able to fulfill that need, and collapsed when it could do so no longer.

In this respect, the history of the nation-state repeats that of its predecessors. The nation-state emerged at a time when it was more capable than the medieval system of supplying humanity with security and well-being. But this unit of government, like the rest, has failed

---

[1] The concept of expansion from a city to the world (*ab urbe ad orbem*) was a rhetorical flourish, never a political reality.

to apply its own ideal, with the result that it is now decaying or even dying. Our contemporary world is in the throes of transition from the out-moded nation-state to some new unit. Thus, seen in historical perspective, the age in which we live is comparable to the readjustment that occurred between the breakdown of the *polis* and the rise of the Roman Empire, or between the fall of Rome and the emergence of the medieval order, or between the collapse of the latter and the founding of the nation-state. Once again, an attempt is being made to discover the territorial unit best adapted under twentieth century conditions to furnish men with their basic political needs. Since modern internationalism, however, is a reaction to the declining adequacy of nationalism, the threads of the discussion must be picked up where the last chapter left off. What failings has the nation-state revealed? Is any more workable alternative in sight?

Despite the strivings of states to build nations and of nations to organize states, no perfect correspondence has been achieved between nationality and statehood. The world still exhibits instances of people united by a common culture, language, and religion who are striving toward a national consciousness and seeking to formalize it in a state of their own. Conversely, there are cases of states which continue to include in their jurisdiction a subject people who are unincorporated in the national body politic. In some countries those subjects are a minority; in others—South Africa, for example—they are the majority. Also there are numerous states, some of them very new, which are peopled by inhabitants, but not by a nation. These are facts that require explanation. If the nation-state was in vogue and set the fashion for over four centuries, why has there been so imperfect a correlation between statehood and nationality?

IMPERIALISM AND SEA POWER

The answer—which is a product partly of historical timing and partly of economic and military factors combining in a political result —is most revealing. It must not be forgotten that, when the nation-state was born, simultaneously into the world came its twin—sea-powered imperialism. How inseparably these were connected is plainly written in the annals of Spain, Portugal, England, France, and the Netherlands. Of course, the practice of imperialism, which can be defined as the forcible subjection of a community to alien rule, was no novelty. Nor was the employment of sea power, as the Athenians, Phoenicians, Norsemen, and Venetians may bear witness. What was new, however, was the expansion of political power upon an oceanic scale. The discovery that the earth was round and could be circumnavigated was quickly put to a use that challenged comparison with Rome. The peoples of Western Europe first mapped the world; then with gunpowder and galleons they partitioned it.

The result was a succession of struggles for maritime supremacy, colonial acquisition, and the wealth to be gained thereby. The first pair of competitors were Spain and Portugal. Between their claims Pope Alexander VI arbitrated in 1493, so that by his award and the Treaty of Tordesillas in 1494 the ownership of the non-European world was divided. To Spain was assigned the exclusive possession of all that lay more than 1,110 miles to the west of Cape Verde; to Portugal, all that lay east. Such an award was no more acceptable to Catholic France than to Protestant England, both of which had ambitions of their own. When the might of Spain was humbled by the English victory over the Armada and the Dutch had fought successfully for independence, the Atlantic seaways were open to a new round of contestants. Neither France nor England could take full advantage of its opportunity until internal disunion was overcome. This was achieved in the seventeenth century by the triumph of Catholicism and absolute monarchy in one country, of Protestantism and Parliament in the other. Then the two powers were ready to inaugurate their second Hundred Years' War over wider battlefields on sea and land. The epoch that opened with England's resistance under Marlborough[2] to the aims of Louis XIV closed with Napoleon's downfall at Waterloo. In between occurred the colonial rivalry, extending long and far, wherein France during the Seven Years' War (1756–63) bowed to the British in India and North America, but secured a partial revenge by aiding the United States in the War of Independence. To the latter setback Britain responded resiliently, first, by speeding up the technological revolution of her industries in the struggle against Napoleon and later by reorganizing her empire on the principle of self-government for the component parts as they matured.[3] Thus, with her nearest military rivals worsted or enfeebled, Britain preempted the nineteenth century.

Secure in the assets of a factory system whose productivity then led the world, and of a navy and merchant marine predominant in every ocean, the peoples of a small island off the coast of Europe constructed and commanded an empire which by 1914 covered one-fourth of the land surface of the globe and one-fourth of its population. In this climactic episode, sea power, the progenitor of the

---

[2]John Churchill, first Duke of Marlborough, victor of the battles of Blenheim (1704) and Ramillies (1706) was the ancestor of Winston Churchill.

[3]This principle was first officially recommended for Canada in Lord Durham's Report (1839) and applied in that country in 1846–47.

nation-state, had reached the ultimate. To make it all possible, the varied talents of an ebullient age contributed their quotas—Victoria, the queenly symbol; Palmerston, the swashbuckling spirit; Disraeli, the imagination and brains; the City of London, the financial sinews; Kipling, the ballads; and Gladstone, the outraged liberal conscience in self-rebuke for the sins it did not prevent.

CONTRADICTIONS OF SOVEREIGNTY

The success of imperialism, however, and its duration for four centuries, involved the nation-state in a fundamental inconsistency. Depending on the angle from which it is viewed, this unit of government can be considered the opposite of either localism or internationalism. Both of the latter were characteristic of the medieval period, one receiving theoretical[4] lip service and the other reflecting more accurately the realities of social organization. Since the nation-state marked a rejection of the system immediately preceding, neither local nor international influence was tolerable to its architects. The centralizing tendency of the nation-state, drawing powers and functions from the localities to the capital, was described in a previous chapter.[5] Now is the place to discuss the international relations of nationalism.

As in other respects, the doctrine that was the maid-of-all-work for the nation-state—the theory of sovereignty—here, too, was enlisted into service. Sovereignty was construed to mean that the government of the nation-state, supreme within its own jurisdiction over local bodies and churches, acknowledged no political or legal superior beyond its territorial boundaries. "My dogs," as Queen Elizabeth I of England once phrased it, "shall wear no collars but mine own." Authority, allegiance, and law were to be the exclusive monopoly of the nation-state, and as such, were not articles for import across national frontiers. Were they, however, articles for export? There precisely lay the inconsistency. The nation-state, whatever its professions, acted on a double standard. Both in external and internal affairs it claimed to be a law unto itself. Limitations upon its freedom of action diminished its sovereignty and consequently were inadmissible. But, though unwilling to submit to control from outside, it professed to see no wrong in subjecting others to its own will. The practice of imperialism violated the principle of sovereignty by denying to others the very freedom on which the nationalist insisted. In effect, throughout the entire era of the nation-state, there never was a time when the political ordering

---

[4]Except in the ecclesiastical sphere, where the international power of the church was more than theoretical.

[5]See Chap 10, pp. 288–91.

of mankind conformed consistently to the idea of having a number of separate units of government, each self-contained. Imperialism meant a division of the human race into elite peoples who ruled, and whose nationality could find outlets for expression, and subject peoples whose national aspirations were suppressed. Hence imperialism negated the first premise from which the nation-state proceeded. Therefore it is no accident that the twins, which were born together and have lived in perennial incompatibility, in this century are dying together.

This combination of nationalism with imperialism and the ensuing dilemma produced an economic counterpart. During the sixteenth, seventeenth, and eighteenth centuries—that is, before the philosophy of laissez-faire became prevalent—prosperity was sought by methods that applied political concepts to economics. The politics of nationalism were matched by the economics of nationalism, which was the essence of the mercantile system.[6] Correspondingly, political imperialism was yoked to economic imperialism. Colonies, considered the "possessions" of the imperial power, were organized to supply it with raw materials and precious metals, as they were also to import its manufactures and carry their commerce in its ships. This is not to deny that additional motives influenced the settlement or acquisition of colonies. The desire of dissident minorities to emigrate; the strategic quest for bases, ports of call, and defensible frontiers; the work of missionaries who preached the Christian gospel—many a magnet, besides trade, attracted nations to plant their flag on distant shores. But that the single most important factor in empire building was the economic can hardly be denied. Through imperialism the nation-state could grow more prosperous—or so it was hoped.

From the standpoint of security an empire might be judged as much a liability as an asset. True, the treasure that some colonies yielded could be used to build more warships and pay more troops that would both defend the mother country and keep subjects more surely in subjection. But colonies situated across the oceans were remote and exposed. They might prove hard to defend against an invading rival or to hold against a rebellion. Furthermore, when the imperial power was itself in danger of attack on its home terrain, less force could be spared for garrisons abroad. By spreading its resources thin, the imperialist nation-state held out many hostages to fortune. It was therefore vulnerable to either amputation at the extremities or attack at the heart. The latter alternative was, of course, the primary concern of nation-statesmen, since colonies were of no avail if the motherland

[6]See Chap. 7, pp. 178–79.

were insecure. Hence in every case the organization of the nation-state passed through a phase of expansion and consolidation wherein the purpose was to arrive, if possible, at a defensible frontier. Let us observe what happened and the consequences.

The United Kingdom, as Great Britain is officially called, was created in a series of absorptions and additions. England, itself a fusion of smaller and previously separate kingdoms, provided the nucleus for a larger union. Amalgamation with Wales was achieved by conquest in 1284. Scotland and Ireland, being larger than Wales and less easily accessible, presented more formidable problems. But their independence posed a threat to England since a continental enemy like France could form an alliance with the Scots or Irish and threaten England from the flank or rear. An island has an obvious frontier in its coastline. The union of England and Scotland, facilitated by triumph of Protestantism both north and south of the border, was formally effected in 1707. "John Bull's other island,"[7] whose proximity made it strategically vital, could be conquered, but largely because of religious differences could not be absorbed. All that remained thereafter was for Britain to control the seas around her coasts and prevent any one power from dominating the European mainland. If this was done, her security was assured. The same problem confronted the continental nation-states, but with an important difference. They had a land as well as a sea frontier to defend. Besides navies, therefore, they had to maintain standing armies which affected their internal politics, tending to reinforce the authoritarian structure of their government. Armies, more easily than navies, could reach the heart of an enemy state. Napoleon was able to cross the Pyrenees but not the Channel, and Frenchmen and Germans have been moving in and out of each other's territories for centuries.

The military conditions which geography imposes go far toward explaining why it was Britain, and not any of her rivals, that emerged in the nineteenth century as the highest-ranking power. But in that century new factors intervened which in the short run enhanced the might of Britain, yet in the long run contributed both to her decline and to that of the nation-state system. The intruding element was the technology of industrialism and the economic potentialities thus unleashed. Its immediate effect was to create a productive capacity that exceeded the needs and the resources of the nation-state. Britain had always engaged in foreign trade. But now in volume and extent this trade grew to unprecedented proportions. The terrain that the nation occupied did not yield all the raw materials that manufacturers re-

[7]The title of a play set in Ireland by G. B. Shaw.

quired. Nor did its population offer a market sufficient to consume their output. More than before, the prosperity of peoples became interdependent.[8] If somewhere in the world there occurred a curtailment of production or a decline of purchasing power, a fall in the prevailing price of a commodity or its replacement by a substitute, other economies thousands of miles away were intimately affected.

ANARCHY AMONG NATIONS

The nation-state was now hopelessly caught in a tangle of contradictions. As if it was not already difficult enough to make the boundaries of state and nation coextensive, it now became abundantly plain that the territorial unit chosen for military purposes was completely at variance with the area appropriate to economics. Protection was organized to run along national lines; prosperity, to run across them. The task of organizing a unit wherein the needs of nationality, security, and prosperity would coincide harmoniously was well-nigh impossible, and the situation was rendered more chaotic by the competition between states for the same objectives. An area which a state considered strategically necessary for its own protection might be inhabited by people whom its neighbor regarded as belonging to its own nationality. Valuable economic resources that lay in the borderland between two states would be sought by both. Thus Alsace-Lorraine, the Low Countries, the Brenner Pass and the Trentino, Bohemia, the Polish Corridor, Suez, and Panama, all these and others became focuses for international rivalries and scenes of conflict.

Under such circumstances, it is not surprising that the nation-state became less and less capable of providing for the minimal needs of protection and order. Even at its best, though it maintained order within its own territory and minimized, without eliminating, the possibility of civil war, it could not guarantee that international relations would be peacefully conducted. The very doctrine of sovereignty meant juxtaposing internal stability with external anarchy. In all essentials, therefore, the history of the nation-state merely repeated (with a change of scale, because the unit was larger) the earlier experience of the city-state. International relations were like inter-*polis* relations, and the old drama was reenacted in modern dress. Nation-states, like city-states before them, were small, medium-sized, or big. If small, their only chance of survival was to accept protection from the biggest power nearby, or, if they lay between rival powers, to announce their neutrality and trust it would be respected. Medium-sized states could also serve as buffers to keep their larger neighbors

[8]The British adoption of free trade in the 1840's was a frank recognition of this fact.

from one another's throats. They might, however, be induced to enter into systems of alliances since their support of opposition could have some effect on the balance of power. Their riskiest policy, of course, was to be afflicted with delusions of grandeur and dress in big power costume without having the chest to fill it, as was true of Italy.

The major states themselves took up the script where Athens, Corinth, Sparta, and Thebes left off. Each in turn strove for leadership. Each was destined to strut and fret its hour upon the stage—Spain, Austria, France, Britain, and Germany. All had their periods of ascendancy. None could perpetuate its domination, because new challengers arose against every champion. The net result was that throughout more than four centuries the nation-state system was incapable of securing a lasting peace. Major convulsions recurred with frightening regularity—the Thirty Years' War (1618–48), the War of the League of Augsburg (1688–97), the War of the Spanish Succession (1701–13), the Wars of the French Revolution (1793–1815), World War I (1914–18), and World War II (1939–45). These were interspersed with more limited conflicts, so that scarcely a decade went by without an outbreak of hostilities somewhere. Indeed, the history of any important country contains testimony to prove that the establishment of a nation-state gives no assurance that its citizens will escape the horrors of war. For example, during the period that has elapsed since 1776, the United States has engaged in four major wars (1776–83, 1861–65, 1917–18, 1941–45) and five minor ones[9] (1812–15, 1846–48, 1896, 1950–53, 1965–?) so that our peace has been broken on an average every twenty–one years.

THE CONSOLIDATION OF LAND MASSES

The perennial anarchy of the nation-state system and the discordance between national politics and international economics were not the only reasons for the ending of an era. Another factor was the declining effectiveness of sea power. By the end of the nineteenth century the peoples on the Atlantic seaboard of Europe were losing the monopoly of advantages that had so long been theirs. It was to the east of them and to the west that fresh opportunities for expansion were being discovered. The new goal was to consolidate the continental land masses under the jurisdiction of a single state. Three attempts of this kind were made. The first was launched by Germany. The marriage of the Prussian army with the industries of the Ruhr and

[9]This distinction means that victory in a major war requires the mobilization of a people's entire resources in order to survive, while a minor war requires only a limited effort and does not involve a danger to survival.

Rhineland created a formidable power in the north-center of Europe. From this base, with a strategy formulated in terms of land domination, the efficient and ruthless German *Reich* set out to unify the continent. Twice its leaders tried this in wars they instigated. Twice their efforts were beaten, but at a dreadful cost. Since Germany with its central position enjoyed the advantage of interior lines, she could be defeated only by encirclement. Thus the Atlantic nations perforce were allied with Russia in World War I and again in World War II. Even the western front could not be maintained by Britain and France alone, who in both wars, and particularly in the second, depended on American participation to push back the common foe. Europe's loss of power after 1945 was the price paid by an entire continent for the necessity of curbing the ambitions of the Germans.

The other two attempts have had different results. From its birthplace on the Atlantic seaboard the United States expanded westward to the Pacific, spreading the Constitution and applying the principles of representative government over an area three million miles square. Simultaneously, tsarist Russia fanned out eastward along the northern part of Asia, incorporating Siberia in its dominion and crossing the Bering Strait into Alaska. The phenomenon of states which spanned continents was noted by Tocqueville, who in 1835 made this prophetic comment:

There are, at the present time, two great nations in the world which seem to tend toward the same end, although they started from different points: I allude to the Russians and the Americans. Both of them have grown up unnoticed; and while the attention of mankind was directed elsewhere, they have suddenly assumed a most prominent place among the nations; and the world learned their existence and their greatness at almost the same time. All other nations seem to have nearly reached their natural limits, and only to be charged with the maintenance of their power; but these are still in the act of growth; all the others are stopped, or continue to advance with extreme difficulty; these are proceeding with ease and with celerity along a path to which the human eye can assign no term. The American struggles against the natural obstacles which oppose him; the adversaries of the Russian are men; the former combats the wilderness and savage life; the latter, civilization with all its weapons and its arts: the conquests of the one are therefore gained by the plowshare; those of the other by the sword. The Anglo-American relies upon personal interest to accomplish his ends, and gives free scope to the unguided exertions and common sense of the citizens; the Russian centers all the authority of society in a single arm: the principal instrument of the former is freedom; of the latter servitude. Their starting point is different, and their courses are not the same; yet each of them seems to be marked out by the will of Heaven to sway the destinies of half the globe.[10]

[10]Alexis de Tocqueville, *Democracy in America,* Part I, trans. Henry Reeve (New York:

By the time the United States and Russia had attained a territorial size that dwarfed the nation-states of Western Europe, the same technology which had already outmoded the economics of nationalism shattered its military defenses. If the nation-state floated into history on the wave of sea power, it sank under assault from the air. Blériot flew across the English Channel in 1909. Alcock and Brown made the first transatlantic flight in 1919. Applied on only a limited scale in World War I, air power was a decisive factor in the strategy of World War II. When the Nazis in 1941 defied the British control of the sea and captured the island of Crete from the air, they rang down the curtain on an epoch. Four years later, when the Japanese surrendered their islands after being the victims of two atomic bombs, they acknowledged realistically that the old politics must conform to the new physics. The foundations of the state have been resited and are being rebuilt—above in the stratosphere and in outer space.

COLLECTIVE INSECURITY

There is abundant evidence to confirm the fact that the nation-state is no longer able to provide protection and prosperity within its own borders. In the first half of the twentieth century two wars occurred whose worldwide scale of operations was without precedent. Together they demonstrated that the anarchy of the nation-state system breeds an insecurity that is contagious and allows few to isolate themselves from its effects. The fears, suspicions, and distrust of nation for nation cause each to maintain whatever armaments it can afford, and their costliness is a drain upon economies that otherwise could make more progress in the arts of peace. For other than military reasons, these same economies have become interdependent, which renders them vulnerable to worldwide movements over which no single nation has control. To this truth the depression of the early 1930's bore witness. As a plague that sweeps across political frontiers, the same malady struck at one country after another, producing the same symptoms: falling prices, lowered purchasing power, rising unemployment, reduced revenues from taxation, unbalanced budgets, bankruptcies, bank failures, and default on debts. Prosperity, as well as peace, had become indivisible.

This worldwide succession of events in a thirty-year period—war, depression, and war again—offered the clearest proof that an international society was emerging for which the nation-state was an unsuitable unit of government. Not only in trade and commerce, but in

---

J. & H. G. Langley, 1841), Chap. 18, pp. 470–71.

cultural contacts and the movement of ideas, communication between peoples had become easier and more rapid. As in the fifteenth and sixteenth centuries a national order could not predominate unless the localism of the medieval system was abandoned, so in the twentieth century an international order could not prevail if politics were conducted through national channels. For paradoxically the determination to build security within the borders of the nation-state contributed to everybody's insecurity. States were behaving severally like individuals who place their reliance on self-protection and carry weapons on their person instead of resorting to public agencies such as police and courts. That system, as imagined by Hobbes or as practiced under frontier conditions, produces only general disorder, which is precisely what happened in the world of nation-states. The efforts of each to build its own protection intranationally ultimately brought little protection to anybody. What is more, the particularism of nation-states defeated any possibility of a political development from the protection of each to an order embracing all. International politics had thus reached an impasse that illustrates the general problem of human association discussed in Chapter 2. Instead of achieving a balance between cooperation and competition, the relations between states were characterized by too much of the latter and too little of the former. All states were suffering from the harmful effects of an excess of competition pursued in self-centered isolation. They were insufficiently aware of the fact that the objectives which all had sought separately could be better achieved if all cooperated collectively. Somehow a method had to be devised of securing protection through order and of infusing the latter with a concept of justice. In short, the need to reorder the relations between states was similar in principle to the problem of harmonizing associations within the state. The jurisdiction of government had to become more nearly coextensive with the ambit of society.

THE REMEDIES OF INTERNATIONAL LAW

What steps have been taken in this direction? Among the constructive efforts to mitigate the imperialism of the strong and remedy the general anarchy of interstate relations, the developments in international law, international arbitration and adjudication, and international organization have become cumulatively significant. While each of these, it is true, has received its most vigorous extension during the present century, their roots can be traced back in one form or another to earlier periods. For instance, the attempt to formulate and systematize the rules of international law was begun only a short while after the establishment of the nation-state. It was in 1625 that Grotius published his treatise *De Jure Belli ac Pacis* ("On the Law of War and Peace"), which is ordinarily considered the foundation of the modern writings in this field. Moreover, the need that prompted some outstanding minds to turn their attention to this subject is indicated by the type of country of which they were nationals. Grotius[11] himself was Dutch, as was one of his eminent successors Van Bynkershoek. Pufendorf worked in the service of Sweden, Brandenburg, and German universities at a time when there was no formidable *Reich,* and the term "Germany" was merely a cultural expression; and Vattel came from the little state of Switzerland, which, situated between big and belligerent powers, had already adopted its nonaggressive policy of permanent neutrality. Thus the classic early contributions to international law were penned, appropriately enough, by representatives of small, weak states that wanted the protection of law because they were inadequately supplied with the protection of force. How deep was their concern to retrieve a modicum of security from the anarchy of the nation-state system is further revealed by the emphasis of the leading seventeenth and eighteenth century treatises, much of whose content is devoted to outlining principles which might regulate the conduct of war and mitigate its ferocity and might insulate neutrals from some of its effects.

The formulation of international law—that is, of rules of conduct for states to observe in their dealings with one another—has now proceeded for over three and a quarter centuries. There has, of course, been much disagreement concerning the substance of these rules, because the governments of different states have had different views of their respective interests and advantages and, if a law of nations is drafted, it must somehow reconcile the competing, particular national interests into a cooperative, general international order. The task is rendered more complex by the diversity of sources from which the content of international law derives. Included in these are the customary practices that states have habitually followed in their external relations; the substance of treaties, both bilateral and multilateral, to which the constituted authorities have put their signatures; principles of justice, as expressed in ethical philosophy; the opinions of courts, whether national or supranational, when they pass judgment on international matters; and the systematic treatises of learned jurists, who have followed the trail that Grotius blazed.

Despite these manifold complications, it is well within the scope of human ingenuity to devise a satisfactory body of rules that could en-

---

[11]This was his Latinized pen name for his Dutch name, de Groot.

sure a place in the sun for all peoples of the world and eliminate the excesses of competitive hostility. But law, when framed, requires a framework of institutions in which to operate. For rules will sometimes be violated; and, if so, they must receive enforcement—or they will be disregarded with impunity and will then cease to have any utility as rules. Hence the same problem that existed originally in the foundation of the state is repeated—identically in principle, although differently in scale—in the construction of order among states. Merely to rest content with the writing of law is insufficient because, as Hobbes observed long ago: "Covenants being but words, and breath, have no force to oblige, contain, or protect any man, but what it has from the publique Sword."[12] The same truth is understood in every city that places signs on the highway warning the motorist: "Traffic Laws Enforced." A committee of competent international jurists could codify an equitable set of rules of international conduct. But how are such rules to acquire official recognition, public acceptance, and authoritative enforcement? Without international government, international law is left hanging, as it were, in the air.

THE GROWTH OF INTERNATIONAL INSTITUTIONS

Hitherto no international government has been created to supersede or bridle the nation-states. But what may be its embryo is growing. Already before World War I some specialized agencies had been set up by agreement between governments to administer particular services. Examples of this are the Universal Postal Union and the International Red Cross. Such bodies have suggested the possibility that, just as the growth of the nation-state promoted and was aided by the centralized administration of services (for example, highways, courts, and defense), so might a superstate develop from the internationalization of governmental functions. Moreover, since mankind's greatest man-made scourge—warfare—is due in part to a failure to settle disputes by peaceful means, and since the settlement of disputes is aided by the existence of institutions and procedures, a number of experiments of this kind have been initiated. In the attempts of states to devise methods of resolving controversies without resort to war, a long progression leads from direct diplomacy between the parties concerned through the intermediate steps of good offices, mediation, conciliation, and arbitration, to the goal of adjudication by an independent tribunal. What takes place in such a process, if and when it is completed, is that the disputants finally invoke a third party to

[12]*Leviathan,* Chap. 18.

render a decision, and it is that third party's interest to see both that justice is done and that the general framework of order is undisturbed by violence. In other words, to refer again to the Herodotean story about the kingdom of Media,[13] the modern problem has been to produce an international Deioces, at whose tribunal just rules would be impartially applied. Prior to 1914 this need was acutely felt. Some states were already employing the system of arbitration to settle disputes that arose between themselves. This happened especially in the relations of the United States and Great Britain, which between the end of the American Civil War and the outbreak of World War I reached agreement in five disputes through a series of notable arbitrations. In fact, the demonstrable usefulness of this technique prompted the signing of an international convention at the Second Hague Peace Conference of 1907, whereby the procedures of arbitration and a panel of arbitrators were made available to states that wanted to use them.

The outbreak of World War I, the German government's violation of its treaty obligations, the long grimness of the conflict and its bloody slaughter so shocked the conscience of civilized humanity as to bring about a climate of opinion in which Woodrow Wilson, and other men similarly inspired, could work. The result was the establishment in the years 1919–21 of a trio of institutions dedicated to noble conceptions. The International Labor Organization, representing governments, employers, and labor, set out to raise progressively the minimum level of working conditions throughout the world, so that states which improved the lot of their workers and thereby raised their own costs of production would be less at a disadvantage in competition with sweatshop countries. The Permanent Court of International Justice, with a bench of judges drawn from the principal legal systems of the world, was established as a judicial body to give advisory opinions on points of international law and to try any case that disputing states would submit to its jurisdiction. Most comprehensive in scope, however, and most ambitious in aim was the League of Nations whose avowed objective was to prevent future wars and provide a regular international forum where states would debate, and supposedly settle, their differences.

Such institutions did not create an international government or superstate. But they constituted a step forward in both principle and practice. The International Labor Organization was novel because from every member-state it included representatives not only of the government but also of employers' groups and of trade unions, which

[13]See Chap. 3, pp. 66–67.

signified some recognition of the emerging international society in its economic aspect. The Court, as its name implied, was meant to be more than a tribunal for arbitration. Its authority to render decisions, however, was limited by the willingness of states to accept its jurisdiction. In fact, many of the states which ratified the Court's Statute (or constitution) reserved certain classes of disputes concerning which they would give no general prior undertaking to "go to court." In any case, if a decision were rendered, who would enforce it upon the losing state? For as has been noted earlier, while power seeks translation into authority, authority, to be effective, must be backed reciprocally by power. Where then did power lie under the Peace of Versailles?

THE LEAGUE OF NATIONS

In an ultimate sense this was the gap in the system that the League of Nations was supposed to fill. The League was the product of some eminently sound reasoning. Before 1914, it was pointed out, the methods employed for restraining the excesses of competition among states relied on direct diplomacy, the formulation of rules of international law, and the development of arbitration. Each of these was useful in itself. But even added together, they were inadequate. By direct diplomacy the negotiating states might reach agreement. But it might be an agreement to sacrifice or victimize a third state (as when Poland disappeared under partition). Law and arbitration were necessary. But not all controversies that lead to war are justiciable, that is, appropriate for settlement in a court according to rules of law. Many disputes involve conflicts of interest, where choices must be taken between alternative policies and the values or ideals they embody. Consider, for instance, the heavy cost of armaments and the militarization of youth which occur when governments are mutually hostile or suspicious. No rules of law, no panel of arbitrators, no bench of judges, could decide on the wisdom of disarmament or the appropriateness of various levels of armament. Thus there were issues—vital issues, in the sense that they related to the lives of men and states—that called for determination by political means. What Wilson and the other architects of the League were hoping was that regular public discussion in the continous conferences of the League would lead to an atmosphere of trust and good will and make cooperation possible for an international order.

At its best, therefore, the League was a convenient instrument for cooperation, available to those who felt a need to cooperate. It offered admirable facilities for discussion, negotiation, and compromise. It could proceed to a vote and make recommendations to the governments of member-states. There, however, its effectiveness ceased. Power within the League still remained with the parts; it was not transferred to the whole. The League lacked authority to take decisions because it did not possess its own means of enforcement. As was proven in the critical cases of Japan's aggression against China and Italy's aggression against Ethiopia, a resolution of the League could not be put into practice unless national governments placed their forces at the League's disposal; and this meant, when the aggressor was itself a major power, that other major powers must take up the cudgels on the League's behalf and their own. The big nations, however, did not yet feel a sufficient community of interest to intervene jointly in restraining one of their number that ran amuck. The League was paralyzed by the coolness between Britain and France, the nationalistic violence of Italy and Japan, the renewal of German aggressiveness, the disorganization of China, the mutal antipathy between the Soviet Union and the non-Communist world, and the nonmembership of the United States. What is more, the meetings of the League were attended only by delegates of governments, who functioned as a conference of ambassadors. The opposition parties, within those nation-states where they existed, had no mouthpiece at Geneva, and the deliberations of the League were not broadly representative of peoples. Of course, for this weakness in the League's structure the peoples of mankind had only themselves to blame, since their loyalties and allegiances were still overwhelmingly national. Until they could acquire a sense of international kinship, the looseness of international machinery accurately corresponded to the political divisions of the human race.

This continuation of old attitudes that no longer chimed with newer realities found its confusing way into the Versailles Treaty. President Wilson had correctly diagnosed the military and political needs of his age when he called for an association of states to make security collective. There spoke the internationalist. But at the same time he inconsistently espoused the doctrine of national self-determination, approving the dismemberment of the Austro-Hungarian Empire and the multiplication of states in central and eastern Europe. There acted the nationalist. International organization was then supposed somehow to unite a larger number of smaller nation-states than had existed before. That faith was wrecked by two miscalculations. The political error was the unawareness that a nationalism, which is highly sensitive because it is new, is generally reluctant to accept any external restraints, including even those that emanate from an international source. The economic fault lay in the opportunities thus provided for economic nationalism. More miles of political frontiers meant so many extra miles of customs barriers—a truth that was driven home in the early 1930's, when states the world over reacted against the depression and the shrinkage of international trade with foolish attempts to insulate and isolate their economies.

THE UNITED NATIONS

At the end of World War II mankind was offered its second chance within the span of a generation. The problem confronting the victors in 1945 was even more urgent than that which existed in 1918 because prosperity and security were far more seriously jeopardized. Not only were the economies of many countries disorganized and damaged, but the long-range bomber loaded with an atomic cargo and flying at jet-propelled speeds constituted a greater menace to life than any destructive weapon previously used by man. To organize a general economic recovery and police the world against future acts of aggression would require global solutions. So during the years 1944–46, a number of new international bodies were established. All but one of these are specialized agencies in the sense that their work in each case is limited to a particular function or service whose program and problems are often highly technical in content.[14] The exception is the United Nations, which, as the successor to the League, took over the general responsibility of promoting cooperation between states and keeping them at peace.

Any sure judgment about this institution, which has existed for less than three decades, is premature. But some observations may be attempted. A comparison of the League Covenant with the United Nations Charter shows that the latter was intended not to repeat its predecessor but to improve on its defects. Though it embraces a wide range of international problems from declarations of human rights to control of atomic weapons, the United Nations organization has been influenced from the start by more realism and fewer illusions than was the case with its predecessor. The League did not measure up to its great ordeals in the 1930's because it had no bullets to secure obedience to its ballots. Consequently, when the Charter was drafted, great attention was paid to provisions for enforcement, and the Security Council became the hard core of the new organization.

Its strength was quickly put to the test. Almost from birth, and

[14]Examples are the International Monetary Fund; the International Bank for Reconstruction and Development; the Food and Agriculture Organization; the World Health Organization; and the United Nations Educational, Scientific, and Cultural Organization.

before the bone structure had hardened, the United Nations was forced to take arms against a sea of troubles. A number of major assumptions that had run current in 1945 were then found wanting. In the first place the British economy was discovered to have suffered a more severe strain than most people had imagined. Hence the nation, which in 1938 had accounted for one-fifth of the world's trade, was unable to recover its prewar position and was too impoverished to shoulder all the commitments that it formerly undertook. Second, the expectation that Chiang Kai-shek and the Kuomintang would retain their position in China and guide its postwar reorganization was not fulfilled. Their replacement by a Communist regime brought nearly one-quarter of the human race under Communist control at one stroke, thereby changing the balance of power in Asia with profound consequences for relations between East and West. Third, the belief that Western states, after defeating Japan, would be able to maintain their former empires over nonwhite peoples was unrealistic. The Dutch lost the East Indies, which were converted into the state of Indonesia. The French, defeated at Dienbienphu, were forced out of Indochina, which was then subdivided into a group of new states. In Africa they granted independence to their colonies and to Tunis; and eventually, after a long and unsuccessful struggle, left Algeria to the Algerians—that is, to the Muslim majority. The Belgians, who did little to prepare the Congo for self-government, suddenly reversed their intention to hold on and abandoned the region to its own devices. As for the British Empire, the mightiest of them all, liquidation proceeded continuously and inexorably. Beginning in 1948 with the independence of India, the ritual of withdrawal was repeated throughout Asia and most of Africa, until the areas remaining under London's control by the end of 1969 were a scattered assortment of small possessions, many being economic liabilities, and of a few ports and islands strung along the routes to vanished glories.

Elsewhere too, the sometime dominance of occidental peoples has evoked a reaction of angry outburst and violent challenge. Premier Mossadegh of Iran led the way by taking over the properties of the Anglo-Iranian Oil Company. Colonel Nasser repeated this coup in Egypt by nationalizing the Suez Canal, after which he set about fomenting movements throughout the Arab world to expel the influences of the West. Indeed on every continent, the opposition to colonialism has become one of the most active political forces of our time. The words and deeds of 1776 have been much imitated and oft repeated—sometimes with a sound that rings true, sometimes with a false note—in Accra, Cairo, Djakarta, New Delhi, and other capitals. Nor can their influence be successfully resisted. In the eighth decade of the twentieth century, uneasy sways the head that once did sway an empire.[15]

As the old-style empires have been disappearing from the map, the cumulative results of the transformation are visible in the expanding membership of the United Nations. What began in 1945 as an organization of 51 states had grown by the end of 1969 to a membership of 126. Even so, although such figures amount to a revolution in international politics, the number of member-states is somewhat less significant than the population they contain. Judged from the latter standpoint, the United Nations continues to exhibit two major gaps. The two parts of Germany, divided since 1945, do not belong in the organization because the erstwhile allies of World War II have never agreed about their unification or permanent separation. More momentous in human terms is the exclusion of Communist China, whose government controls one-quarter of the human race. It is a fiction to maintain that China is represented in the United Nations by the party that lost the civil war and now rules only over Taiwan and a few small islands. Far from being peace-loving, the Peking regime has demonstrated that it is both aggressive and dangerous—in Korea, Vietnam, Tibet, India, and along its border with the Soviet Union. Hence, the argument for seating it in the United Nations rests on the belief that exclusion makes it even more dangerous and isolation more fanatical.

THE EAST-WEST SPLIT

As practiced both in the United Nations and outside, world politics was primarily influenced for a decade and a half after 1946 by the opposition between the Communist governments and the Western domocracies. The United Nations had been predicated on the hopeful assumption that the coalition of states which won the war against fascism would continue to act with a substantial degree of harmony. Nor could one otherwise justify the right of the five principal states in the Security Council to exercise a veto, since, if they failed to cooperate, the United Nations would be doomed to deadlock. But as long as Stalin lived, not only cooperation, but even a tolerable coexistence, was out of the question. For at least a decade the major activities of the United Nations—diplomatic, technical, and peacekeeping—

---

[15]The second edition of this book, published in 1960, contained this prediction (p. 394): "Indeed, if one projects into the future the trends of the last twelve years, it seems certain that the French cannot maintain their hold on Algeria, that a handful of British planters cannot monopolize the Kenya highlands, and that the Afrikaner Nationalists cannot perpetuate the privileges of Europeans in South Africa." Two of those predictions have come true. The third will take longer.

were gravely hampered by the formation of two potent and antagonistic blocs: one led by the United States, the other by the Soviet Union. In June, 1950, when North Korea attacked South Korea, it proved possible for the Security Council to authorize collective aid to the South only for the reason that the Soviet delegate had walked out[16] six months earlier and was not then occupying his seat.

In 1956, at the time of the Suez affair,[17] the United Nations emerged as the effective agent for ending hostilities in Egypt, inducing Britain, France, and Israel to withdraw their armies, and subsequently policing the Gaza Strip and the Gulf of Akaba. The political reasons for this achievement invite reflection. In the first place, the majority opinion throughout the world sided with Egypt. Although Britain, France, and Israel had the military means to make their will prevail, a political fact—the concerted pressure of international opinion—compelled them to pull their armies back. The second, and conclusive, fact was the agreement of the United States and the Soviet Union, both of whose governments at that time were unwilling to court the displeasure of the Arabs. But it is equally significant that, simultaneously with the events at Suez, the Soviet Union sent the Red Army into action in the streets of Budapest in order to reinstall the Communist government which had fallen from power through a popular uprising. Action by the United Nations against the Soviet Union, however, was not possible because of the widespread fear of initiating measures that could lead directly to a third world war between the superpowers.

Since then, there have been other occasions when the United Nations has been charged with peace-keeping responsibilities—which means that various countries contributed contingents to serve under its flag and maintain order in areas where there was serious danger of a major war erupting. This necessary, but unwelcome, service was performed in both the Congo and Cyprus, despite the objections of the Soviet Union and France, which refused to pay a share of the expenses. Indeed, the United Nations undertook those particular functions on the basis of votes in the General Assembly, where, unlike the Security Council, the veto of the five principal members does not apply. However, it was shown in May, 1967, that the opposition of the government of the country in which the United Nations places its forces can constitute a veto of its own. When Nasser demanded that

[16]Over the issue of the Council's refusal to place a representative of Peking in China's seat.

[17]In October, 1956, Israel sent its army to occupy the Gaza Strip from which Egypt was mounting commando raids against Israeli settlements. The British and French sent in their forces to retake the Suez Canal, which Nasser had nationalized earlier.

the United Nations withdraw its peace-keeping units from the Gaza Strip and from Sharm-el-Sheik at the entrance to the Red Sea, the Secretary-General agreed. The consequences were immediate. Egypt began closing the Gulf of Akaba to Israeli shipping. Then the six-day war erupted in which Israel crushed the combined forces of Egypt, Jordan, and Syria.

INTERNATIONAL RELATIONS IN A DOUBLE-STANDARD WORLD

Although some form of rivalry between major powers is normal and to be expected, the raw material for conflict lies ready at hand in the inequality of conditions that divide vast sections of the human race. Most of mankind—throughout Asia, Africa, and South and Central America—are chronically undernourished and suffer periodic starvation. They are illiterate, miserably housed, and poorly clad. Victims of endemic disease, they die before they are middle-aged, and sunk in poverty, they lack any possessions except the most rudimentary.[18] Probably the great majority of people have always fared this way—or at least have so fared throughout the few millennia over which historical records extend. It is impossible for a double-standard world to be a contented one, and inequality, as Aristotle noted, has ever been a fertile source of revolution. But, though social upheavals have not been wanting in the past, their effects when they occurred were less widespread and less interconnected than those that characterize our epoch. Until a few centuries ago, large segments of humanity and entire civilizations endured in comparative isolation from one another. A change of dynasty in China stirred not a ripple in Europe. The death of a Russian autocrat caused little concern to any beyond the borders of Muscovy. Discussions and decisions on the banks of the Potomac or the Thames did not make the whole welkin ring. The supply and control of oil, iron ore, and uranium were not matters of global life or death.

We have succeeded in changing all that. For our woe or weal, we have

[18]Statistical evidence for these generalizations is overwhelming. In 1960, Dr. B. R. Sen, the director general of the United Nations Food and Agriculture Organization, stated that more than half of the world's population suffered from varying degrees of undernourishment and malnutrition. (*New York Times,* Sept. 11, 1960.) In 1967 the annual gross national product per capita, calculated in U.S. dollars, was 3560 in the United States, 1810 in the United Kingdom, 890 in the Soviet Union, 270 in Colombia and Peru, 230 in Algeria and Ghana, 90 in India and Kenya, 70 in Indonesia and Tanzania. (Reported in the *Sunday Times,* [London], Jan. 28, 1969, from Overseas Institute of Canada.) In the same year the world's population was estimated to include, among those over age 15, some 740,000,000 who could not read or write. (*The Economist,* [London], April 29, 1967.) By 1968, because of the absolute increase in population, that figure was estimated by UNESCO to have risen to 810,000,000. (*Times* [London], Sept. 8, 1969.)

made of all the world a single stage where the drama of man's fate is enacted in scenes that shift rapidly from place to place, but form part of one plot. What distinguishes our age from those that have gone before, and complicates the solution of its problems, is the extension of the community of interests to an area as wide as the world, the greater spread of information, and the deeper awareness by millions of their common lot. The huddled masses of humanity not only yearn to breathe free; they also crave a share in things they have never enjoyed. The demand for economic development, to be achieved rapidly, has become the item of first priority in countries with a backward technology and a traditional social system. Such circumstances make a spawning ground for political movements of many kinds. People who resent their under-privileged status, but who are politically unsophisticated, will readily listen to promises and follow a prophet. They may be fortunate in re-ceiving wise counsel and discovering a government that has their inter-ests at heart. Or they may fall dupes to false propaganda and power-seeking politicians. Or again, they may be checked by the stub-born opposition of those who do not accept as legitimate the claims of the masses to more equal treatment. Out of this milieu spring personal-ity types as diverse as Gandhi, Nehru, Lenin, Stalin, Tito, Chiang, Rhee, Mao, Atatürk, Nasser, Nkrumah, Malan, Castro, and Perón. Out of it come regimes that may be fascist, communist, nationalist, militarist, ra-cist, theocratic, or democratic. When the lid is off and once the genie is out of the bottle, there is no telling what shape it will assume.

At the time when the Charter of the United Nations was written, many statesmen recognized that colonial aspirations for independence and the general desire of people in underdeveloped areas for higher living standards are a constant source of friction and hence a possible cause of war. For this reason the structure included among its princi-pal organs a Trusteeship Council and an Economic and Social Council. The function of the former has been to safeguard the interests of weaker peoples, whose government is entrusted by the United Na-tions to another state. The latter's objective is to diminish the gap that separates the technologically advanced communities from the back-ward. Despite inadequate budgets which have severely limited the programs, much significant aid has been rendered to underdeveloped countries by the Technical Assistance Administration of the United Nations and by its specialized agencies. Besides the granting of loans, this help consists in gathering and publishing information, disseminat-ing scientific knowledge, and recruiting teams of experts and in-dividual technicians who are sent to cooperate with countries that request assistance. The details of such programs, like the work of any national government, are for the most part concrete, practical, and specialized; for instance, the authorization of a loan to construct a steel mill, the launching of reforestation schemes, development of fisheries, eradication of malaria, control of narcotics, reduction of illiteracy, safety for civil aviation, reorganization of a revenue system, and so on.

PROBLEMS OF INTERNATIONAL COOPERATION

Activities of this character, although constructive, do not lack their quota of difficulties. International agencies always have inadequate budgets. The poorer countries, which need help, have little to give. Richer ones, which must contribute a high proportion of the total, may feel that they are already paying enough.[19] They may then oppose a budgetary increase since they are the donors, not the recipients, of aid. Competent personnel are hard to recruit, because many individuals can see better career opportunities in their own national civil service or because governments are sometimes disinclined to make their best men available to an international agency. Agreement about programs may not be so difficult to elicit when the subject matter, as in the case of food or health, is of universal interest and has a direct connection with life. But in an agency like the ILO, which treads the thorny path of employer-employee relations, or one such as UNESCO, which seeks to combat ignorance and enrich humanity with the treasures of the mind, the conflict between competitive interests or opposed philosophies is a hindrance to positive action.

What accentuates these problems is the touchiness of national governments whenever an issue is raised that they deem vital. Where a great power is involved, other states are reluctant to outvote, and dare not coerce it. But even small states produce governments and leaders who can be violently stubborn and self-willed in what seems to them their national interest. In particular, the rulers of countries that have recently emerged from a dependent or colonial status are torn two ways in their external policies. Without aid from outside—loans, investment, goods, and technicians—they cannot develop their econo-

---

[19]In fact, however, they are not paying nearly enough—whether in bilateral aid programs or in contributions to the international agencies. During the 1960's, while living standards rose in most parts of the world, the growth rate of the "haves" surpassed that of the "have-nots" by 50 per cent, so that the gulf between rich and poor peoples has further widened. (In 1966, this rate averaged 2.4 per cent in the underdeveloped countries, as compared with 3.6 per cent in the advanced. *Washington Post,* April 10, 1967, commenting on a report of the U.S. Agency for International Development.) The developed countries had promised to devote 1 per cent of their gross national product to aid. Actually the percentage declined from 0.87 per cent in 1961 to 0.62 per cent in 1967. *(Times* [London], Feb. 1, 1968.)

mies and raise their living standards to the level they desire. But aid will normally be accompanied by some list of conditions, some attachment of strings, which then is interpreted in the guise of "foreign control"—especially when the aid is received from one government instead of from an international source. Those who were recently subject to another power will chafe at new restraints, even when their source is an international agency. Furthermore, men who can consistently espouse idealism in opposition, find themselves making concessions to expediency when in office.

The crux of the problem can be simply stated. All over the world there are people who are dependent in economics and technology but in politics feel strongly about independence. That paradox is perhaps explicable in terms of the time lag which has occurred in the spread of the nation-state. This unit of government, as we have seen, originated in Western Europe in the fifteenth and sixteenth centuries. Its force was not fully felt in Eastern Europe until some time later. Among colonial peoples the first effective blow for national independence was struck in 1776 in North America, and Latin America followed suit almost five decades afterwards. Not until the closing decades of the nineteenth century did the force of nationalism begin to explode in Asia, with results that have been manifest in recent decades. Last on the list came Africa, where much writing is already visible on the wall, but more has yet to be written.

It is a truly formidable task, therefore, to construct an international order out of such discordant elements. The mansion of peace and prosperity has to be built with bricks of different materials and varying in size and shape. The edifice must include states like Britain and France, which once were leading powers and which continue to count, but have lost much of their strength; states which stand today in the forefront, like the United States and the Soviet Union; states that are the homes of proud and ancient civilizations and will once again be mighty when their potentialities are unleashed, like India and China; states which give few thanks to the past, but consider themselves, as does Brazil, "lands of the future"; states that have made their bid for imperial hegemony and failed, such as Germany and Japan, and have recovered economic strength while lacking political power; decadent states, as Spain; medium-sized states—some developing peaceably, others aggressively in wish or deed; others again of which little need be said except that they exist; and finally the small fry—buffer states, like Belgium, Austria or Uruguay; honest neutrals of the Swiss model; client-states like Albania, Liberia, Jordan, Paraguay, and Bulgaria; courageous new creations, like Israel; and such anomalies as Iceland, Panama, Luxembourg or Botswana. Finally, among the more recent additions to the list are some of which one must say in candor that they are only states by fiction, governments by courtesy, and nations in the imagination. Yet they are clothed in the panoply of juridical attributes which states accord to each new member admitted to the club. If statesmanship be an art, as is sometimes said, what artist ever worked with so intractable a medium?

There exist then certain basic conditions, some of which serve to encourage, others to delay, the formation of an international community. First is the fact that no nation-state today is adequate to provide within its own boundaries all that is required to be safe and prosperous. Second is the inequality of living standards, provoking the resentment and envy of the underprivileged. Third is the survival of strongly held nationalist sentiments, not the least among those to whom nationhood arrived late. Fourth is the mutual antagonism of political systems, which have derived from different historical traditions and which represent contrasted forms of social, economic, and governmental organization.

For those who believe in the ideal of human brotherhood and wish to forestall the holocaust of a thermonuclear war, the continuation of power politics on a global scale is as sobering as the divisions within the United Nations are disillusioning. Though it has acted constructively and positively in several disputes, all too frequently the United Nations is reduced to a body which can only debate, declare and deplore. On most major issues it has been so rent by internal hostilities that it lacks the capacity to decide and enforce. Speakers in the Security Council and the Assembly are often talking to their home audiences and have scant prospect of influencing their principal antagonists. Nevertheless, even in this restricted role, this institution performs an indispensable function. It remains the one association that houses the divided fragments of most of humanity. It is the closest we have yet come to constituting a forum for the conscience of mankind. Its freedom of debate impels all governments to reply in public to the worst criticisms, whether merited or false, that foes can hurl. Its existence and its survival in each passing year represent an advance toward the ultimate goal of "the Parliament of Man, the Federation of the world."[20]

REGION-STATES IN THE MAKING?

But the realization that the world politically is not yet one in heart and spirit has persuaded some that prosperity and security may per-

20The words are Tennyson's, from the poem "Locksley Hall."

haps be organized in a manner intermediate between the nation-state, which is outmoded, and a global state, which mankind is still too divided to accept. There are signs that a new, and possibly workable, unit of government is already evolving. The peoples who live around the coasts of the Atlantic have begun experimenting with a variety of novel and imaginative unions. On the mainland of western Europe one finds such projects as the Council of Europe, the European Community, and the European Free Trade Association. Linking the two sides of the ocean are the programs of the Organization for Economic Cooperation and Development[21] and the diplomatic and military agreements of the North Atlantic Treaty Organization. These schemes envisage the enlargement of the area of military, political, technical, and economic cooperation and the patient building of the appropriate machinery by peoples who belong in the main to the same civilization. Indeed, when one reflects on the divisions that have marked the history of Europe for centuries, when one considers the physical and psychological gulfs that have separated the peoples of the New World from the Old, what was accomplished in two decades is truly remarkable.

Among the positive gains already recorded are the recovery of the Western European economies; their steps towards integration in such essential matters as coal and steel, atomic energy for peaceful uses, and tariff policies; the introduction of coordinated peacetime planning for military defense; the regular practice of close consultation and informal discussions between their heads of government, foreign secretaries, and leaders of opposition parties; and finally, the growing realization that their interests are intertwined. Most importantly, the United States and Canada jointly helped to underwrite and stimulate the union, declaring a common interest with Western Europe in the vital concerns of safety and prosperity. If these relationships continue, an ocean will become, not a barrier that separates, but a highway that unites. As was the Mediterranean to the *pax Romana*, so may the Atlantic prove to be the "inland sea" of the Western civilization. Nothing in this, however, is certain; nothing is inevitable. Whereas the decade of the 1950's witnessed an accelerating movement in the direction of regional integration of nation-states, during the sixties that movement was slowed down. In some spheres it was even halted by a resurgent nationalism, which was most evident in France and was stimulated by de Gaulle—although this phenomenon was by no means confined to him or restricted to his country.

Nor is this pattern which has been thus evolving in the Atlantic

[21]This now includes Japan.

region the only instance of its kind. Something similar in its general aim, though different in principles and method, has been established in Eastern Europe by the Soviet Union. There, the military relationships were formalized in the Warsaw Pact (1955), as were economic relations in the Council for Mutual Economic Assistance (1959). Both resemble their Western prototypes in seeking to encompass a greater range of territory and population within a common system. The economic organization in this case has been guided by concepts of centralized state planning. The military arrangements are largely inspired by past memories and future fears of German invasion and occupation. Underlying the forms, however, the stark reality has consisted in Soviet power imposed to further Soviet interests. The glaring proof of this lies in the fact that on two occasions (Hungary in 1956 and Czechoslovakia in 1968) the Soviet Union employed its military power to install persons amenable to its wishes in charge of governments which it plainly envisaged as satellites.

Elsewhere in the world—in Asia, Africa, and Latin America—regional entities have been drafted on the European model. So far, these exist mainly on paper, and without conspicuous success in practice. When the member-states themselves are unstable and their governments ill organized, how can their multiplication into a larger unit avoid the same weaknesses? The most that can be said is that in various of the subregions of these continents, some of the same reasons and occasions already exist for ultimate integration as may be found in Western Europe—that is, the need to encourage economic growth by diversification in wider markets, the advantage of geographical contiguity, the memory of a shared past, and elements of a common culture in the present. But such potentialities cannot be realized until some traditional customs and institutions have been radically changed and a political will to unite becomes paramount.

If, however, one can extrapolate the developments since 1947 without flying in fancy too far ahead of the facts, at least the possibility exists for developing a new and wider unit of government. To distinguish it from a nation-state or world-state, we might call it the "region-state." Through the nascent region-state, some portions of mankind may perhaps construct their political defenses against economic blizzard and nuclear-rocket annihilation. How urgent is the need can be gauged by projecting into the future two contemporary facts. One is the worldwide rise in population, which is now increasing so rapidly that its implications and effects have been termed "explosive" by demographic experts.[22] The reduction of the death rate,

---

[22]It took tens of thousands of years for the human population of the world to reach

improvement of health, and material gains from industrialism will do for Asia, Africa, and Latin America what they have already done for Western Europe and North America. There will be millions of more people to feed in each coming decade—to feed, let alone to be prosperous. If the "Malthusian checks" of povery and war are no longer acceptable, wider political unions and more enlightened policies will be required to augment the supply of food and provide industrial goods. The second inescapable fact is the technology that today enables mankind to place satellites in orbit around the earth or to propel them free from the gravity of our planet. Already, human beings have walked on the moon, and doubtless within a few years they will be landing on the less remote planets of the solar system. Now that we have entered the age of outer space, conventional airpower has been superseded by a still more formidable weapon. Where then will mankind locate its military defense tomorrow? Humanity arrived at the moon long before it was capable of organizing peace on planet Earth. Surely it is self-evident that the nation-state, a unit of government that evolved under the special conditions of the sixteenth and seventeenth centuries, is utterly inadequate to care for mankind's needs under the altered conditions of the twentieth. The new, expanding population, the new technology, the new weapons, point to one political conclusion: a new unit of government.

CONTOURS AND CONTENTS OF REGION-STATES

Yet a word of caution is necessary, lest hopes again be raised too high and be dashed more cruelly to the ground. A region-state will present problems of organization fully as complex as its predecessor. If it was difficult to delimit the boundaries of the nation, it will be no less hard to define those of the region. An example is the fact that the North Atlantic Treaty Organization already reaches as far afield as Greece and Turkey. Some states, moreover, have interests—geographically and economically—in more than one region. Thus the United States belongs to the North Atlantic Treaty Organization as well as to the Organization of American States and has a major stake in the affairs of the Pacific, where it has contractual commitments with Aus-

---

one billion in 1830. It took only 100 years more for that figure to double, and only 30 years after that, 1930–60, for the total to rise to three billions. By 2000 A.D., the figure is estimated to become six billions. Meanwhile, in many of the underdeveloped areas, the rate of population increase is outstripping that of food supply. The implications are obvious. The control of population is one of the most important problems facing humanity. Governments and churches which oppose making the means of control available are contributing directly to poverty, misery, and war.

tralia, New Zealand, the Philippines, and Japan. Nor should anyone assume that wars between region-states are impossible. The region-state can justify itself for the time being only if it provides a broader framework for enhancing the economic well-being of all its members, and if each region-state presents such a picture of strength to a possible antagonist that nobody will run the risk of initiating a third general war from which none can conceivably come out unscathed. Nor should it be forgotten that some of the same factors which impede the task of international organization can also be obstacles to the formation of region-states. To create the latter, a union may be required between a superpower and a group of medium-sized and smaller countries. But nationalism and differences of living standards may provoke a rift in that relationship, and the superpower may even aggravate the difficulties of leadership by demonstrating that might is not always correlated with wisdom. This can be illustrated from the experience of both the United States and the Soviet Union.

Since 1947, the United States has served as the nucleus to a large and loosely structured coalition of states which included virtually all of the world's most advanced communities and many of the most backward. Out of their rich resources, financial strength, and great productive capacity, the American people rendered economic and military assistance to numerous governments in the hope that such aid would increase their means of resistance to armed aggression from without and political upheaval from within.

The results of this program have been as varied as the characters of the recipients. In a country where the government is honestly organized and the people in general are hard-working and self-disciplined, the American contribution has been notably successful. There are countries, however, in which corrupt cliques and incompetent governments have misused or squandered much of the aid that was granted. In those cases it is only natural that the donors should feel disposed to attach conditions that the recipients must fulfill. But when that is done, the nationalistic pride of the latter is likely to be outraged and they will voice angry protests that their "sovereignty" is being invaded. The American public sees a portion of its tax dollar appropriated to finance the foreign aid programs which, while they help other countries, simultaneously promote the interests of the United States. That such efforts sometimes provoke resentment rather than thanks is often a matter of surprise to those who provide the money. But it is not a normal human trait—in the relations between groups, any more than in the relations of individuals—for the stronger, wealthier, and luckier to meet with gratidude and affection, or for the dependent to like their position. Moreover, in numerous instances those dependent on us happen to be privileged oligarchies within their own society, which have no intention of sharing power and its perquisites with their own have-nots. Consequently, the weapons which the United States has placed at the disposal of such oligarchies have sometimes been employed in internal contests for power—with the obvious result of fostering the anti-Americanism of the victims. No mistake of American foreign policy, however, was ever as egregious as that committed in Vietnam. There, without any declaration of war by Congress, President Johnson interposed more than a half a million young Americans into the middle of a civil war which had no close and demonstrable bearing on this country's vital interests. The result was to raise doubts all round the world concerning the wisdom of Washington's leadership and to bring condemnation on our heads for the sheer indiscriminate destructiveness which our weapons inflicted on a primitive Asian society.

DIVISIONS WITHIN EAST AND WEST

Meanwhile, in another part of the international jungle another superpower has found itself unable to control the course of events. Almost without exception,[23] the countries under Communist rule are underdeveloped socially, economically, and politically. During Stalin's lifetime, the relations of the Soviet Union with other "dictatorships of the proletariat" were far from harmonious. The imposition of Moscow-directed programs, the requirements of orthodoxy in word and deed, and the doctrinaire application of uniform principles to diverse situations generated much discontent even within parties as strongly disciplined as the Communists are wont to construct. For a decade after 1945 a spectacle frequently witnessed in one Eastern European country after another was the "discovery" of treasonable plots within the party hierarchy, and the vilification, imprisonment, or execution of men until recently idolized as Communist heroes. Much of this was due to the subordination of other peoples' interests to that of the Russians and to the understandable reaction of various Communist leaders in satellite states who preferred to espouse and represent the feelings of their fellow nationals. In Yugoslavia, the man who was master of his domestic situation dared to flout the Kremlin by giving first priority to what he considered the interests of his own country. Similarly, after Stalin's death, the suppressed resentment of other peoples in Eastern Europe came to the surface, as manifested by riots in

[23]From the standpoint of living standards and general development, the two most advanced areas under Communist rule, at the time when they were sucked into the Soviet orbit, were the Bohemian portion of Czechoslovakia and East Germany.

East Germany, defiance in Poland, and outright revolt in Hungary, which the Russians crushed with force. Since then, the same practices have been repeated by the other great power of the Communist world. The Chinese, who had placed their grip on the mountain fastnesses of Tibet, found a full-scale rebellion on their hands in the spring of 1959. This they dealt with by the full deployment of their military power. Here indeed was evidence that the two revolutionary governments of Europe and Asia which declaimed against the old imperialism were themselves founding new ones. The superpowers of Eastern Europe and eastern Asia, because of their methods, have acquired the flavor, respectively, of an *imperium Sovieticum* and an *imperium Sinicum.*

The reference to these as two superpowers, not one, suggests a further reflection on trends that were increasingly apparent in the 1960's in both the Communist sphere and the Atlantic community. During the decade from 1947 to 1957 the course of world politics was largely dominated by the formation of two powerful blocs and by their mutual hostility. Since that time, however, two unmistakable changes have occurred. Relations between the United States and the Soviet Union have become less antagonistic, and limited agreements on a variety of matters (for example, cultural exchanges and the banning of nuclear explosions in the atmosphere) became politically possible. Such dangerous confrontations as developed over the construction of the Berlin Wall in 1961 and the installation of Soviet missiles in Cuba in 1962 were disposed of by diplomatic means without a shot fired—although guns and missiles were ready. Simultaneously, inside both blocs cracks appeared which, though small at first, widened visibly with each passing year. In the Atlantic region, an alliance had come into being because of the dependence of Western Europe on the United States for economic aid and military protection against the Soviet Union. But once the recovery of the West European economies was accomplished, and when milder relations started thawing the ice of the cold war, it could be expected that European statesmen would reassert themselves and, whether justified or not, would draft some declaration of independence of their own. Such notions were not loudly voiced in Germany, since the people of that country, divided and devoid of nuclear weapons, depended still on America. But in France, the union of Gallic pride and Gaullist personality resulted in a new nationalism expressing itself in European terms as distinct from the broader embrace of the Atlantic region. Thus, in all spheres that were crucial—economic, military, and political—the question posed to the peoples of the West was this: Shall our civilization sustain two power blocs or one? Shall the Atlantic Ocean be our inland sea or a frontier between us?

For other reasons that converged towards the same result, the one-time Communist monolith was breaking into two. The Soviet Union had started a program of economic and technical assistance for China. But disagreements over policy and principles of organization led to its abrupt ending and to the sudden recall of Soviet specialists and advisors. The Chinese then decided not only "to go it alone," but also, wherever possible, to make difficulties for the Russians. Before long, with strident clarity, Peking was challenging Moscow everywhere for the leadership of the Communist world, and Communist parties throughout Europe, Asia, Africa, and Latin America were asked to take sides and choose between two lines. The détente between Moscow and Washington was interpreted, in China, not as a contribution to peace, but as treason to the Communist revolution. To Westerners, the dissension between Communist regimes appeared as yet one more scrap of evidence to show that revolutions do not rebuild human nature and that new social systems, organized politically in separate states, will continue the traditional rivalries for power and profit much like the older systems they denounce. The Russians, guarding the results of a revolution achieved a half century earlier, had something to conserve. The Chinese, being rich only in numbers and in the tenacity of their civilization, could even contemplate without horror the prospects of a thermonuclear war in which the more advanced technologies were likely to annihilate each other and the fragments of the world would be left to the more primitive.

Moreover, while Moscow experienced this pressure from the one state that could challenge it for the leadership of world communism, in Eastern Europe too the evidence was mounting that Russia could not automatically count on having everything its own way. As the economic recovery and increasing sense of security in Western Europe prompted the French government to raise its voice in opposition to Washington, so the relaxation of tensions and the gradual rise in living standards permitted the leaders of former satellites the luxury of self-assertion. Yugoslavia had cut loose from Russia and had not been destroyed. Indeed, it had gained in prestige, and its economy was on the upgrade. The example was contagious, and Russia found within its immediate sphere of influence that it must consider opinions and seek support. This need was apparent at the time when Khrushchev was ousted, and the new rulers in the Kremlin were placed in the position of having to explain and justify their actions to the heads of other Communist parties. A "public opinion" of the Communist sphere had emerged to which even the strongest had to pay attention—as was not the case in Stalin's time.

This growing flexibility in the relations between blocs and within them had unexpected by-products. When Yugoslavia announced its independence of Russia, it needed American help to survive. Likewise, when Castro embarked on a policy of outright hostility to the United States, he needed help from the Soviet Union. Cuba has been the same thorn in our flesh as Yugoslavia was for so long to the Russians. But when the Sino-Soviet antagonism commenced, it became possible for so weak a state as Albania, situated geographically in the Russian sphere of influence, to express its independence of Moscow by turning for support, not to Washington, but to Peking. Thus the rise and organization of separate power centers provided greater room for maneuver and increases both the number of potential region-states and the complexity of relations between them. An immediate result of this direct, and potentially mortal, conflict between China and Russia was that the former veered further to the left in its attempted, but abortive, cultural revolution, while the latter shifted course to the right. Preoccupied, if not obsessed with the Chinese challenge, Brezhnev and Kosygin revived the repression of dissident intellectuals in their own country and sent troops into Czechoslovakia to overthrow a regime of liberalizing Communists.

Like any long-established system, nationalism dies hard. The erection of a superstate, particularly when it is committed to a systematic ideology, has overtones of civil war besides being a struggle between governments for leadership. Old sentiments and old ideas continue to exert their force in the present, and sometimes most fiercely so among those to whom they have come late. No nationalism is as prickly and sensitive as a new one. Hence, while humanity should be establishing a small number of larger states, it is in fact recognizing (and sanctifying by admission to the United Nations) a larger number of small ones. For the most part these are economically backward, politically immature, and militarily weak. As the Greek *polis* committed suicide in the fourth century B.C. by splitting more than it coalesced, so today we are witnessing the *reductio ad absurdum* of the nation-state. The old empires are liquidated and the fragmentation is occurring faster than the reverse process of merging. Region-states may be in the making. They could help in organizing the larger areas in which men may find their safety and prosperity. But in any case, region-states alone will not be enough. They, too, have to learn to live together within one world for which a truly global organization is required. Such problems as the population explosion (with all its implications of a death explosion also), the gulf between haves and have-nots, and the control of nuclear weapons, are of universal concern. They affect all humanity. Hence, the region-states, too, if indeed they do succeed in becoming organized, will need ultimately to come to rest within the same tent.

If they do not, they are certain to start in motion a train of rivalry which could lead to the destruction of the human species on planet Earth.

The conclusion, then, would appear self-evident. Man's inventiveness must succeed in consolidating both the world and its regions simultaneously, and he must give priority to cooperation over competition.

14

The Dynamics of
Political Change

THE UNITY OF THE POLITICAL PROCESS

When a surgeon operates on the human body, he must sew his patient together and see that the severed tissue reunites. When a psychiatrist unravels the tangled complexes of the unconscious mind, he must reknit the threads of personality to a changed design. The same obligation befalls a political scientist who subjects the social order to his analysis. Dissection of a whole into its parts contributes to clarity of understanding. But unless the parts are reassembled, what is thus obtained is an understanding of isolated fragments, not of the related pieces of a unity. The purpose of this chapter, therefore, is to stitch up the seams and observe the significance of the resulting pattern.

The discussion of the ten preceding chapters may be summarized in a few sentences. Politics is the process by which a community confronts a series of great issues and makes a decision on each. Nowadays the institution under whose auspices this is done is almost universally the state, though there have been occasions when the same role was performed by religious, kinship, or economic groups. Government is the name for the machinery and methods used by the state in carrying out its functions. In every political situation, in each kind of state, and under all forms of government, the same basic issues are perennially present and all must receive a solution. Since every issue admits of more than one choice, states and their governments differ in the various choices they embody and in the manner of combining them.

This way of looking at politics offers some insights into certain of its fundamental characteristics whose significance would otherwise be missed. Too many political analyses suffer from the fault of reducing the subject to terms and categories which are primarily static. That is an unfortunate by-product of an attempt that is laudable in itself—the effort at logical exposition. Logic aims at concepts and propositions which are, as far as possible, clear-cut, unambiguous, firm in outline, and mutually exclusive. But the actual content of politics—as distinct from theories about it—is fluid and mobile. It is therefore difficult, and can even be inaccurate, rigidly to impose a logical framework upon a shifting material. A political philosophy that satisfies the tests of a logical system conceptually often fails at the no less rigorous task of explaining political phenomena as they have been, as they now are, and as they may yet be. A political analysis which is to be successful must meet two criteria. It should designate the underlying problems that are the invariable constants and indicate the variable ways of resolving them.

The reasons for these requirements, and for the two being jointly necessary, are implicit in the treatment attempted throughout this book. To argue that the political process is composed of constant factors is to recognize the similarity between situations greatly separated in time and place. If it is meaningful to speak of the existence of politics, state, and government in Greece of the fifth century B.C., in Rome of the first century A.D., in the age of Thomas Aquinas, in the revolutionary century from 1688 to 1789, or in the world of Roosevelt, Churchill, Stalin, and Hitler, then there should be some unifying threads which, despite the manifold differences, persist unbroken. Presumably the problems that confronted Pericles or Augustus, Louis IX or Louis XIV, Lincoln or Nehru, bore some resemblance to one another and may be appropriately grouped as aspects of man's incessant striving to control and reorder his environment. It was a stroke of fancy to conceive of the Connecticut Yankee at the Court of King Arthur. But a Pericles in the White House would have found himself as much in his element as a Roosevelt in the Athenian Assembly. The issues that both statesmen faced and the skills they practiced were sufficiently alike for their abilities to be transferable. Likewise a Clodius with his gang fights in the streets of Rome could have changed places readily with a Capone and his Chicago gang. As a stream of history flows uninterruptedly from prehistoric times to the present without regard for our divisions into periods, so there is a stream of politics that rises at a source concealed in the forests of man's primeval past and follows its single course down to the rapids and whirlpools of our own troubled age.

PERMANENT PROBLEMS, CHANGING SOLUTIONS

Though its flow be continuous, a stream will change direction. Its main channel of movement can shift. Its current may be fast for a while or sluggish. Similar is the action of politics. For its continuity represents the unity of energy, not of mass. It is a unity of flux and movement. It extends over time, not over space. Throughout its process runs a rhythm that is ceaselessly changing because it is patterned from issues whose solutions change. In the opportunity of choice that each issue confers lies the springs of political dynamics.

How are such changes manifested? Many examples have been noted in this work, of the human tendency to tack and turn like yachtsmen taking advantage of the wind. The history of politics reveals an expanse of creative activity which allows wide room for inventiveness and resource. After making what progress they can in one direction, men veer around and strain toward another point. Thus the monistic city-state of Greece and Rome was replaced by the Christian experiment in church-state dualism. This in turn gave way to the monism of nation-state sovereignty, which was later followed by the attempt to separate the economic order from politics. The unit of government has likewise passed through a succession of forms. City-state, empire-state, and nation-state have all been tried and tested. Each yielded what benefits it could and then succumbed to conditions for which it had ceased to be appropriate. So too with the other great issues. Mankind perennially explores new ways of meeting old problems, as the United States in 1787 pioneered with the structure of federalism; or they revive under different circumstances a system used centuries before, as the American Republic designed its institutions with a separation of powers similar to what the Roman Republic once employed.

INTERACTION BETWEEN THE GREAT ISSUES

There is, however, another aspect of the process of political change whose operation is more intricate than what has so far been described. If it is correct to suppose that politics forms a single compound that can be analyzed into five basic elements, it would seem to follow that when one component undergoes a major alteration, the remainder are likely to feel its effects. This probability raises a fundamental question. When people turn to a different solution of one of the great issues, are there any consequent changes which that decision tends to produce among the rest? Does the evidence of history, subjected to this analysis, suggest that specific solutions of the respective issues ordinarily accompany each other in pairs or groups? If so, one could indicate which alternatives are mutually compatible, and which are not—and that would constitute a valuable guide for interpretation of the past and prediction of the future. On the other hand, it may be found that no relation—positive or negative—can be traced between some pairs of issues, in which case a choice among one set of alternatives would be unconnected with, and thus irrelevant to, a choice among another set. There is only one way of finding out whether this is the case. Every issue must be discussed in its relation to each of the others, so that any pattern in which their solutions tend to combine will be detected.

1. The Relations of Privilege or Equality to Other Choices. Consider first the choice between regimes of privilege and equality. What correlation is there between either of these and the manner in which other issues are solved? Does a swing from privilege to equality, or vice versa, lead to corresponding reversals in the treatment of other issues? Wherever a few privileged persons are in a position of superiority over a much larger number, the dominant oligarchy will use all means that enable them to stay on the top of the heap. Necessarily, the favored few must possess political power and therewith must control the state—or they would eventually be ousted from influence by those who do. Does this mean, however, that when an elite monopolizes the government, the entire society is subordinated to the state in monistic fashion? Or is it possible for privilege to be associated with pluralism, in which case, though politics would be reserved for the few, the functions of the state vis-à-vis other associations would somewhere be limited?

The historical answer is that the principle of oligarchy, as such, does not necessitate either a pluralist or monistic policy by the state toward society. Oligarchies have in fact been indifferently associated with one or the other. Thus in the medieval period, when the state was controlled by an oligarchy of nobles and the church by an oligarchy of priests, the prevalent theory of the state was steadfastly opposed to monism. Where a conquering people have taken over the government of the conquered, the victors have sometimes been content to restrict their authority to a few essentials (for example, finance, police, and military affairs), leaving their subjects free from state intervention otherwise. Such, in general, was the character of British rule in India. By contrast the tsarist autocracy in Russia during the eighteenth and nineteenth centuries contrived a complete subordination of society to the state. Similar in spirit have been the modern one-party dictatorships—whether Fascist, Nazi, or Communist—whose efforts to make the functions of the state coextensive with social activity have become a byword.

What happens when a regime of privilege is replaced by one of equalitarianism? Does the latter have a closer affinity with monism or pluralism? The evidence indicates that a sizable extension of the citizen-body is likely to be accompanied by an extension of the functions of the state, though there may be a time lag before the latter takes full effect. The period that can throw most light on this problem is the century from 1840 to 1940. During that time the spread of democracy culminated in many states with the achievement of universal suffrage, and with this was associated a tremendous increase in the functions of their governments. Was this combination of events a coincidence or a case of cause and effect? Without much doubt it was the latter. Generally, the impetus behind the movement to extend the franchise came from a desire to remedy specific ills by political action. Some of these ills were due to differentiations of humanity into classes which determined the breadth of opportunity available to their members. Other ills, however, were of economic origin and stemmed from the union of industrialism with urbanism. Political equality, signalized by the ballot, was desired as a means to social and economic betterment, and the state was then employed as the instrument of equalization. Hence as new voters were enrolled, political parties formulated programs to represent their interests, and these were eventually translated into legislative and administrative form. Being composed of people who were poorer and underprivileged, the recently enfranchised electorate were disposed to invoke the powers of the state since other institutions of society relegated them to an inferior position.

The choice between privilege and equality can be precisely correlated with the next pair of alternatives: irresponsible or controllable government. A system dedicated to the exaltation of a privileged few dares not submit to any genuine procedure of control by the governed. The texture of privilege is shot through with the dye of authoritarianism, for in no other way can a minority obtain and enforce the submission of the majority. No less true is the converse. Wherever equalitarianism is substituted for privilege, the governed develop institutional means of keeping the power of their officials within bounds. Equalitarianism is no more compatible with authoritarianism than is privilege with accountability.

When one turns, however, to the choice between the unity or dispersion of power, no definite correlation can be noted with either oligarchical or majority government. A few examples will make this plain. In the Middle Ages, when politics was certainly reserved for the few, the structure of authority was loose-knit and powers were highly dispersed. The church struggled with the state. The localities resisted the center. The nobility defied the king. On the other hand, various modern oligarchies, especially those of Nazi Germany and

Fascist Italy, have been centralized and integrated to the nth degree. The same contrasts may be observed among equalitarian systems. Whereas government in the United States was constructed according to the principles of federal decentralization and the separation of branches, the British system has evolved into the predominance of central over local authority and of the cabinet over the other institutions at the center.

The same can be said concerning the size of the state and its possible effect upon the enlargement or contraction of citizenship. A comparison of ancient city-states with modern nations confirms the view that either oligarchy or its opposite can flourish indifferently in states of Lilliputian or mammoth size. This conclusion is further reinforced if the suggestion offered in the previous chapter should prove correct, namely that a new governmental unit—the region-state—is nowadays being founded. Here again, within units of comparable scale, the same contrast may be observed of a privileged Communist party hierarchy in the Eastern bloc and a significant approximation to political equalitarianism in the Atlantic[1] community. The size of the political unit, therefore, has no direct bearing on the internal distribution of rights and influence.

2. *The Accompaniments to Monism and Pluralism.* The same method of analysis must be applied to the second of the great issues. The preference for a state of limited or comprehensive functions has been discussed in relation to the alternatives of privilege or equality. How are the other choices affected by the adoption of either pluralism or monism? The answer will appear after a look at some contrasted examples. Medieval society was emphatically pluralist, alike in principle and practice. The same society exhibited a government both in church and state that was not responsible to the governed. Pluralism by itself, therefore, is no certain guarantor of freedom. On the other hand, as nineteenth century America will demonstrate, pluralism and freedom can readily be mixed in one compound. The same can be told of experiments in monism. There are classic instances of a monistic state combined with a controllable government. Such was the Athenian *polis* in the heyday of its glory. Such is contemporary Britain, where a parliamentary majority may legally do anything, but is ordinarily circumspect in using its theoretical powers. Such, too, is contemporary New Zealand, where the state is all-powerful within society, yet the government is emphatically subject to popular control. But monism can also be harmonious with dictatorship. Indeed, the most notorious dictatorships of this century are noted for their deter-

---

[1]Spain, Portugal and Greece are the principal exceptions to this statement.

mination to make state and society indistinguishable. One could haz-
ard the hypothesis that, because the modern dictatorship arises for
military or economic reasons or from a desire to accomplish rapidly
some cultural revolution (for example, Kemalist Turkey), it is now less
likely than in the past that an authoritarian regime can be safely
pluralist. For beyond the line where the boundaries of state action are
drawn, opposition may develop against those in power.

The other aspect of power, its unity or dispersion, has a more obvious connection with monism and pluralism, respectively. There is an
understandable tendency for a monistic state to construct authority
according to a centralized and integrated plan. Where a state assumes
the responsibility for the overall coordination of other associations and
their activities, it is less practicable to have a governmental structure
in which the branches are too independent and the localities too
autonomous. Traditionally, therefore, a monistic state like Britain has
its powers both centralized and integrated.[2] In a pluralist state, on the
other hand, both separation of branches and devolution from the center are suited to the prevailing character of a government whose functions are limited. Where the activities to be conducted are fewer, the
chances of overlap, duplication, or conflict between agencies and
their programs are fewer. Hence there is less demand for a unified
focus of power. Moreover, as American experience in the twentieth
century testifies, a government of restricted scope that is impelled by
economic and military necessity to expand its activities must simultaneously modify its previously accepted canons of separate branches
and federal-state dualism. Today in the United States there is more
evidence than fifty years ago of unification among branches and levels
of government, precisely because more is done by every branch of
government at every level and these additional activities would collide unless they were somehow coordinated.

Whether the size of the state influences the functions it undertakes
is more difficult to determine. History suggests on this point some
tentative hypotheses, but no conclusive verdict, as a review of the
evidence will show. The classic case of a state whose expansion covered a huge area and contained a large population is the Roman Empire. Rome was successful in organizing an administrative apparatus,
legal code, and military machine to unify its diverse and scattered
provinces. It was much less successful in uniting the peoples of its
empire with a common emotional bond. By deliberate policy, efforts

[2]This tradition is now being reexamined by a royal commission. Its inquiry is the
response to the political challenge of Scottish and Welsh nationalists and the pleas of
those in England, too, who argue for the devolution of powers from London to regional
bodies broader than the existing urban and rural authorities.

were made to employ religion for this purpose. But when little head-way was made with the official ritual of the Olympian deities, or the worship of Mithra, or the deification of emperors, Constantine turned to the Christian faith to inspire a unity of sentiment that was other-wise lacking. The effect of his action, however, was to substitute dual-ism for monism, and thereby to reduce the scope of state activity. Hence the problem of extending the size of the state outwards was solved only by diminishing the sphere where the state could operate inwards.

Similar in a sense has been the experience of the United States. The process of peopling a continent from the Atlantic to the Pacific, from the forty-ninth parallel to the Rio Grande, was accompanied by the organization of society along pluralist lines. The circumstances under which the state expanded its territory and population in North America were ill-suited to a monistic view of the role of government in society. Elsewhere, however, there have been instances to the con-trary. The growth of European Russia was associated with the estab-lishment of a powerful state which embraced and absorbed the entire social order. Later, when tsarist power spread across central Asia to the Pacific, the same all-pervasive state controlled and directed the expansion. The change in scale never resulted in modifying the mon-ism of the Russian *vlast*.[3] However, in drawing this contrast between the United States and Russia, one should remember that the expansion of the United States, though it encountered opposition, did not face a hostile neighbor of equal force on the same continent. The consoli-dation of the Muscovite state, on the other hand, was achieved in the teeth of prolonged and repeated warfare against nearby powers (Po-land, Sweden, Prussia, Turkey, and so forth), and the military stamp left an ineradicable imprint on Russian government in the form of complete state domination of society, which the Communists have continued with their more thoroughgoing methods.

If large states then can be either monistic or pluralist, what about small ones? There is some evidence to justify our supposing that, as the size of the unit of government decreases, the number of functions performed by the state in society increases. At any rate, the smallest territorial unit in the history of the West, the Greek *polis*, was charac-terized by comprehensive state control. So little was that control ques-tioned that Plato and Aristotle do not even include in their political theory a discussion of the possible or desirable limits of state activity. Nor is it hard to understand why monism should bring advantages to

---

[3]A word, not precisely translatable into English, meaning governmental power viewed in its totality. It corresponds fairly closely to the Roman concept of the *imperium*.

the smaller units. Where a state is composed of a small population in a small area, it is simple, effective, and inexpensive to organize the activities of society under one institution only. In such a community many, if not most, of the inhabitants can have direct face-to-face contact. If separate institutions are created for governmental, religious, economic, and other purposes, their members are likely to be the same persons reassembled in different guises. In a little state pluralism would seem superfluous; only in larger units can it be defended.

3. How the Remaining Issues Combine. The third great issue, in which men must choose between dictatorial or responsible government, was considered above in its relation to the extensiveness of citizenship and of governmental functions. But how do the rival conceptions of the source that validates authority affect the problem of whether powers are better unified or dispersed? Between these pairs of alternatives there seems no positive correlation. The United States and Britain are countries in whose political systems the authority of officials is derived from the will of the governed. Yet the structure of power is highly dispersed on the American side of the Atlantic and highly unified on the British. Apparently, therefore, it is not directly relevant to the politics of freedom to inquire whether the mechanics of government conform to the one design or the other. The same alternatives may be found in regimes of authoritarianism. In the medieval period the mass of the populace was expected to obey the established authorities and not to question them. Nevertheless, those authorities were subdivided into numerous fragments. In the modern dictatorship unswerving obedience to officialdom is the duty of the masses. But authority in this case (except for Yugoslavia) is solidly compacted together, and the colossus that doth bestride the state reveals on its surface no seams or fissures.

Whether the size of the state has any connection with authoritarianism or its opposite is the next question. At first glance, size appears immaterial since governments of small, medium, and huge states have belonged to either variety, some being controllable and others irresponsible. Sparta, Spain, Germany, and the Soviet Union are examples of one kind. Athens, Switzerland, Britain, and the United States illustrate the opposite. Mere size, however, is not the only factor to be considered here. In a world that contains many states, size is relative. A state may be weak or powerful, safe or insecure, according to the kind of neighbors it has and their friendliness or hostility. Irrespective of size, any state that feels itself threatened or that harbors aggressive intentions will emphasize the need for military organization, and the tendency of the latter is generally to influence the character of the government in an authoritarian direction. The so-called "garrison state,"[4] applying to government the discipline of a barracks, can often[5] be explained in terms of relations between states and not as the phenomenon of a single state standing in isolation.

Finally, to complete the circle of correlations, two issues remain whose effects on each other must be discussed. Can any connection be traced between the size of the state and a preference for a dispersed or unified structure of power? To answer such a question one must recall[6] that relations between levels of government are not the same as those between the branches that function at the same level. The problem of centralization is not identical with that of integration, and the size of the state bears more immediately upon the former than on the latter. It needs little elaboration to show that, the smaller the state, the less the likelihood of decentralization.[7] Indeed, in the city-state virtually all government is conducted at one center. Conversely, as population and territory increase, the sheer growth in size creates complexities and adds to the difficulty of communications. Regional diversities are likely to become pronounced. Differences of soil, climate and resources will lead to divergent economic interests. Expansion may be accompanied by the absorption of mixed cultures with hankerings for autonomy. Separatist tendencies will be a by-product of bigness; as witness the attitudes of the Old South to the United States, of the Ukraine to Russia, of Western Australia to the Australian Commonwealth, of Manchuria to China. No matter what the internal character of its government may be in other respects, any large state must permit a measure of decentralization. Neither Washington nor Moscow,[8] neither Brasilia nor Ottawa, can undertake the entire government of the sprawling territories under its general jurisdiction. Understandably, therefore, federalism is found in some of the world's largest states.

As contrasted with the problem of centralization, the choice between integrating and dispersing the structure of governmental power is not so obviously linked with the factor of size. States with tightly integrated institutions have run the gamut of size, from diminutive to huge. It is questionable, however, whether the same can be said about

[4] A phrase of Harold D. Lasswell.

[5] Not always, of course. Some garrison states are such because a conquering elite is holding down a larger subject population, for example, Sparta.

[6] See Chap. 10, pp. 284–85.

[7] The exceptional case of Switzerland is due to the mountainous geography and cultural dissimilarities.

[8] The genuineness of federalism in the Soviet Union is vitiated by the power monopoly of the Communist party, which insists on political centralism. Administrative decentralization, however, is necessitated by the physical extensiveness of the Soviet Union.

the separation of branches and its application to states of different magnitude. Two famous instances of governments deliberately embodying the principle of separation are the republics of Rome and the United States. But it was the tragedy of the Roman Republic, and also a fundamental reason why the century from 133 B.C. to 31 B.C. suffered from prolonged constitutional crisis and spasmodic civil war, that the checks and balances between the branches of the Roman government were unsuited to the territorial expansion of Rome's imperial power. When the Senate clashed with the consuls, and the home authorities conflicted with a proconsul in an outlying province, civil turmoil and military weakness were the result. Hence, in order that an empire might be governed, the emperorship arose to integrate the powers at the center.

How does this apply to the United States? Has the expansion of the American Republic imposed any strain on the traditional separation of government into three branches? Undoubtedly it has. The adjustments required by the depression of the early 1930's certainly evoked the need for closer cooperation between presidency, Congress, and Supreme Court. Still more acute have been the tensions arising in the aftermath of World War II. The assumption by the United States of a position of international leadership made it necessary to pursue long-range policies and shoulder long-term commitments in conjunction with other governments. For this purpose not only harmony between the president and the Congress, but also agreement between the major parties, was required. The results were substantially good until the bipartisan foreign policy foundered in 1949 and 1950 on the issues of China and Korea. Simultaneously a new problem was precipitated to the forefront of American politics. The dissension between President Truman and General MacArthur, climaxed by the latter's dismissal, involved more than the supremacy of civil over military authority. For the first time the American Republic faced the same question that Rome confronted in the case of Sulla or Caesar, and Britain in the case of Clive or Hastings in India: How does the home government control a strong and imperious commander in a distant theater? To solve this problem, the Republic of Rome gave way to an Empire; the balance between royal prerogative and parliamentary power in Britain was superseded by the rise of an all-powerful cabinet. Whether some comparable change will occur in the structure of American government remains to be seen.

At any rate, it is reasonable to expect a change and desirable to have this happen. The government of a democracy rests on the assumption that those who represent the majority should hold office and should be continuously and publicly confronted by their critics. This is a good system because it has the merit of focusing responsibility for action on one side, for dissent on the other. However, while it is essential in democratic politics always to have two or more organized parties, it is of dubious wisdom to divide between them simultaneously the authority for actually taking decisions. Because of the different electoral procedures and length of terms of the president and the two Houses of Congress, it is possible for one party to run the executive branch while the other controls the legislature. Indeed, this situation occurred during President Eisenhower's second term, and again at the beginning of President Nixon's. Such a division, which can aggravate conflict of policy and divergence of outlook, may cause harm in domestic matters because it is likely to lead to either inaction or unsatisfactory compromise. In foreign affairs, too, the consequences can sometimes be harmful. They may even be fatal to the national interest.[9]

For it is not right to say, as a fact or as a wish, that politics ends at the water's edge. It does not, and in certain cases it should not. Many crucial problems of our time overleap national boundaries. Some of the issues on whose future solution our civilization depends cannot be settled within the confines of the present-day nation. They require negotiation between the governments of many states. On these matters there is frequently as much room for legitimate disagreement between equally loyal and dedicated citizens as there is on problems strictly internal in scope. In countries that have vast commitments in the world beyond their borders, the political parties, to the extent that they differ in philosophy, may appropriately stand opposed on both the strategy and tactics of foreign relations. For that reason, the machinery of government can be seriously clogged, if political rivals control its different branches. A strong case exists for unity of decision and fusion of responsibility between the legislative and the executive, especially in the conduct of diplomacy. But equally strong is the need for vigilant and constructive criticism by an informed opposition, which has a continuous incentive and responsibility to expose the majority's mistakes.

APPLICATIONS OF THE GREAT ISSUES

This analysis may suggest some ways of applying the techniques used in this book. In the introductory chapter, I expressed the hope that the political process can be more clearly understood if its com-

[9]On the other hand, it must be remembered that, when President Johnson plunged the country into full-scale war in Vietnam, the most outspoken opposition came from men of courage and intelligence in his own party—notably led by Senator Fulbright.

plexities are unraveled in terms of its component issues. Politics has been presented as an arena of controversy about permanent problems which permit alternative solutions. This conception allows for various applications, which can now be discussed. Thus, the Great Issues can be used in the classification of states, in comparing the political characteristics of broad historical periods, in comprehending the rival systems of the modern world, and in explaining the distinctive features of contemporary politics. Let us review these themes.

THE CLASSIFICATION OF STATES

From the earliest speculations by students of politics to the most recent, the problem of classifying the forms of government has occupied a prominent place. Nor is it difficult to see why attention has been paid to this·topic. When states of different character are examined and compared, they can be better understood if they are grouped according to their resemblances or distinguished by their contrasts. This involves the problem of classification. Is it possible for the political scientist to classify states in somewhat the same way that the zoologist, botanist, or geologist arranges animals, vegetables, and minerals by genus and species? Some system of classification is implicit, as a matter of fact, in the vocabulary that is ordinarily used to describe the various forms of government. If we speak of the United States, Britain, and Switzerland as democracies, we must have in mind some overriding similarities in their politics and institutions which warrant a common definition. Correspondingly, when states are referred to as Fascist or Communist, within each group there must be resemblances to justify using the same label. There must also be distinctions between the two groups and between them and the democratic group.

Irrespective of what one classifies, the technique of classification requires that certain features be selected for making comparisons and contrasts. If an anthropologist, for example, divides humanity into segments according to skin color alone, he may designate the races as black, brown, white, and yellow. The question is then raised whether pigmentation offers a significant index for differentiating between human beings, and, if so, whether this is the only factor of significance. Variations in hair, size of skull, length and breadth of nose, the shape of eyes and eyelids may also be meaningful. Consequently, the anthropologist may decide to combine many characteristics in some single-word description like Caucasian, Mongolian, Negro, or Polynesian. He will then make generalizations that are true of the group on the average and further include any feature for which the group is unique.

The political scientist faces the same kind of question. He too must make his selection from the various features that can serve as criteria for classification. He must decide whether only one criterion is meaningful or whether there are more than one. If the latter, he must then determine whether the states that are placed in their respective classes under one criterion fall into the same groupings or are reassorted when judged by another criterion. In other words, does the use of different criteria produce a cross-classification?

The problem is well illustrated by the classification of states that a succession of Greek historians and philosophers devised. Originally this was based upon a simple division in terms of the number of people holding supreme authority. Experience, as well as logic, seemed to show that there were three possibilities. Power could be lodged in the hands of one person, a few, or many. The advantages and abuses of each system were described by Herodotus, "the Father of History," in a passage[10] that entitles him to be considered a grandfather of political science. Since all three types could be productive of good or evil, the philosophers next introduced a second criterion with an ethical flavor. In whose interest, they asked, was government conducted? For the benefit of the rulers only, or of the whole community? If the former, power was being perverted; if the latter, the state was true to its intended purpose.[11] The final step was to superimpose this pair of alternatives upon the threefold distinction between the authority of one, few, or many. The result was the traditional classification which Aristotle presented in the following form:[12]

	IN THE INTERESTS OF ALL	IN THE RULERS' INTEREST
GOVERNMENT BY ONE	MONARCHY	TYRANNY
GOVERNMENT BY A FEW	ARISTOCRACY	OLIGARCHY
GOVERNMENT BY MANY	POLITY	DEMOCRACY

Not being the author of this way of classifying states, Aristotle felt free to criticize it. The difference between oligarchy and democracy, he pointed out, does not depend principally on a numerical division

[10]*Histories*, iii, Chaps. 80–83.

[11]This point is made by Plato in his dialogue *The Statesman*. Probably it had been advanced earlier by his master, Socrates.

[12]*Politics*, iii, Chaps. 6–7.

between a few persons and many, but on a division of wealth.[13] It is because the wealthy are few that they form an oligarchical government to protect their wealth. It is because the poor are numerous that they constitute a democracy in order to redistribute the wealth. Both systems in his judgment involve plunder—of the poor by the rich in an oligarchy and of the rich by the poor in a democracy. That is why he characterizes both kinds of government as "perversions," not as "true forms" where the rulers govern in the interest of all.

If the Greek classification involved two criteria, and if even this required the addition of a third, it is evident that any modern version must be still more complicated. After all, the history of the intervening centuries has exhibited fresh forms for which a classification must allow. The categories that embrace a wider experience have to be more complex. One of the numerous modern attempts to solve the problem was made by Robert M. MacIver, who proposed the following scheme:[14]

A	B	C	D
Constitutional Basis	*Economic Basis*	*Communal Basis*	*Sovereignty Structure*
1. Oligarchy	b1. Folk economy, primitive government	c1. Tribal government	d1. Unitary government
a1. Monarchy		c2. *Polis* government	d2. Empire colony dependency
a2. Dictatorship			
a3. Theocracy	b2. Feudal government	c3. Country government	d3. Federal government
a4. Plural headship	b3. Capitalist government	c4. National government	
2. Democracy		c5. Multi-national government	
a5. Limited monarchy	b4. Socialist government		
a6. Republic		c6. (World government)	

The need for formulas broad enough to cover a long history of politics emerges clearly from this classification. But the categories adopted are in some cases so vague that the result is confusing. Terms such as "communal basis" and "sovereignty structure" add nothing to

[13]Aristotle, *Politics*, Chap. 8. "The real ground of the difference between oligarchy and democracy is poverty and riches." (Barker trans.)

[14]*The Web of Government* (New York: The Macmillan Company, 1951), p. 151. By permission of the publisher.

clarity of discussion. Nor are "primitive government" and "country government" particularly helpful. Despite the effort to achieve breadth, some vital issues are omitted. For example, the problem of the functions of government, comprising the relation of the state to society and the choice between monism and pluralism, which is the central theme of *The Web of Government,* is not included in the table, save to the partial extent that the "economic basis" may imply the practice of state intervention or abstention where economic matters are concerned. The medieval experiment in church-state dualism involved more questions than economic and cannot be fitted into the chart. Furthermore, no reference is made to the choice between the separation or fusion of the branches of government, which is important to the operation of the state. Nor are the facts of modern totalitarianism,[15] a concept considerably wider than dictatorship, adequately explained by MacIver's headings.

The analysis of political problems presented in this book contains a plan of classification in itself, since forms of government can be distinguished by the way in which they settle each of the Great Issues. A summary of the various solutions discussed in previous chapters is contained in the table on this page. It should be used with the following caution in mind: No chart can possibly express the constant flow and movement from choice to choice, or the countless subtle gradations that a single heading embraces. The United States, for instance, has been a federal union ever since 1789. But the relation of the federal government to the states was far from identical in 1800, 1850, 1900, and 1950. Nuances and transitions cannot be revealed in a classification, whose categories necessarily look more clear-cut than they are in real political life.

1st ISSUE	CITIZENSHIP	FOR A PRIVILEGED FEW (elitism) (oligarchy)	FOR THE MAJORITY		FOR ALL (equalitarianism)	
2nd ISSUE	FUNCTIONS OF THE STATE	REDUCED TO BARE MINIMUM (pluralism) (laissez faire) (individualism)	CONSIDERABLE EXTENSION (includes welfare, regulation)		TOTAL CONTROL OF SOCIETY (monism) (collectivism)	
3rd ISSUE	SOURCE OF AUTHORITY	RESIDES IN THE GOVERNMENT (authoritarianism) (dictatorship)	RESIDES IN THE GOVERNED (freedom, responsible government)			
4th ISSUE	UNITY OR DISPERSION OF POWER	UNITARY STATE (centralization) FUSION OF BRANCHES (cabinet system)	FEDERALISM (decentralization) SEPARATION OF POWERS			
5th ISSUE	SIZE OF STATE	CITY-STATE (polis)	NATION-STATE	EMPIRE-STATE	? (REGION-STATE)	? (WORLD-STATE)

[15]For a discussion of this, see p. 420.

THE GREAT ISSUES APPLIED TO DEMOCRACY, TOTALITARIANISM, FASCISM, AND COMMUNISM

In the political conflicts of our century, the rival systems have been described as democracy, totalitarianism, fascism, and communism. Each of these connotes both concepts and institutions. Each is necessarily all-inclusive since it comprises the whole political system. For that reason each is difficult, if not impossible, to define. In lieu of definition, however, they can be identified and compared by reference to their solutions of the Great Issues.

Take democracy first.[16] There are plainly two issues for which only one kind of solution is permissible if a state is to be democratic. On the subject of citizenship, such a state must adopt equalitarian principles and allow to all a fair opportunity to participate in the conduct or control of their government. To the extent that any are denied this right, the state has fallen short of democracy's ideal. Likewise, in a democratic state the source of governmental authority must lie in the governed, who need effective means for bringing their representatives or officials to account. This is another way of saying that the essentials of democracy are equality and liberty. Fused together, these form the bedrock on which the foundations of democracy must always rest. With regard to the remaining issues, democracy is neutral. It has been associated with either pluralism or monism, with a concentration or dispersion of power, and with any size of territory or population.

Totalitarianism is indifferent to the size of the state. But on the other four issues its requirements are specific. It is the result of an alliance between privilege, monism, authoritarianism, and unity of power. When these are added together, the sum represents the most complete (that is, total) domination of society by the state and of the state itself by a few.

Fascism and communism are not easy to define or compare. For one thing, fascism did not take the same form in Italy under Mussolini as in Germany under Hitler or in Spain under Franco. For another, the realities of communism deviate in so many respects from the principles of Marxism that one must be careful to state whether the theory or the practice is being discussed. On the issue of citizenship, a Fascist state is dedicated unequivocally to the idea that, because of human inequalities, participation in government is reserved for the few.[17] Marxian theory is equalitarian, but Communist practice, as ini-

---

[16]On this subject, see my book *The Democratic Civilization* (New York: Oxford University Press, Inc., 1964).

[17]Hitler went much further than Mussolini in his racial doctrines and his exclusion of women from public life.

tiated by Lenin and developed by Stalin, has been oligarchical and has reestablished a society with sharp differentiations of rank and reward. The functions of the state know no limits in Fascist theory, since it is the state that to Mussolini embodied the supremacy of the nation and to Hitler the supremacy of the "Aryan race." In practice, however, both regimes encountered opposition from the religious quarter and had to live with a church they could not crush. Monism is more complete in the Communist state, where private ownership of the means of production is virtually eliminated, which is not the case under fascism, and where the church is subservient. Paradoxically, however, it was Marxism, from whose doctrines has emerged the most powerful state of all, which proclaimed that the state would wither away when socialism was achieved! Both Communist and Fascist systems, when they come to the problem of the source of power, are similarly authoritarian in theory as in practice. Each has aped the other in establishing the dictatorship of a single disciplined party ruling the masses by a mixture of propaganda and coercion. Likewise, the concentration of power has been pushed to the same extreme point by all these regimes. As to the size of the state, however, fascism and communism exhibit differences. The former is fiercely and inherently nationalist. Communism in principle and by preference is international, since its fundamental concept of the proletariat leaps across national boundaries. Yet, as Tito's Yugoslavia first demonstrated, and as other Communist governments have since manifested in varying degrees, communism too can be as permeated with nationalism as other political systems.

HISTORICAL PERSPECTIVE ON THE GREAT ISSUES

The classification of states in terms of the five Great Issues may serve another purpose. It can be applied to the successive broad periods in the political history of the West: the Graeco-Roman city-state, the Roman Empire, the Middle Ages, the nation-state, the twentieth century. Which solutions of the Great Issues were prevalent in those different periods?

1. The Graeco-Roman City-State. Citizenship at that time was severely restricted in the oligarchies but was considerably extended in democracies like Athens. Nowhere, however, was it perfectly equalitarian, since slaves and women were relegated to an inferior status. The functions of the state were everywhere considered coextensive with society. Examples occurred of authoritarian and of responsible government, of the unity and of the dispersion of power. Typically and ideally, the size of the state was the simple *polis*, but the largest cities departed from type and tried to found empires.

2. *The Roman Empire.* This state moved steadily from privilege towards political equality, though the latter was never granted to women or slaves. At the onset, the functions of the state were unlimited; but limits were accepted when Christianity was adopted. Under the republic, an unsuccessful attempt was made to locate authority in the governed. Later, power was placed in the emperor through his command of the army. Powers were centralized when the state was small; decentralized, when it expanded. At the center, powers were dispersed under the republic, but were integrated in the empire. In size, Rome was, of course, the giant of antiquity, forming an antithesis to the *polis.*

3. *The Middle Ages.* In the eyes of God, all men were equal. In earthly practice gross inequalities prevailed and politics was an arena for the privileged. The functions of the state were drastically curtailed by its copartnership with the church. Government was authoritarian in fact, though theories to the contrary persisted. Power was decentralized and dispersed to the maximum degree. The unit of government was as large as Christendom in the ecclesiastical sphere, but was localized on the temporal side.

4. *The Nation-State.* This period commenced everywhere with the rule of privilege, but many states have been moving toward a broader equalitarianism. The early nation-state was allied with monism in the guise of sovereignty. In the nineteenth century, however, the challenge of economics led to doctrines of dualism and pluralism. Nation-states have had either authoritarian or responsible governments. Their power structures have been either unified or dispersed. They have varied in size because of the difficulty of making nation and state coterminous, and several have been builders of empires.

THE UNIQUENESS OF TWENTIETH CENTURY POLITICS

World depression, two world wars, and the spread of revolutionary ferment are the evidence that this century is one of crisis. When the nature of the crisis is clarified in terms of the Great Issues, it becomes apparent that our age possesses a unique character unparalleled in any earlier period. Modern society is undergoing three major transformations simultaneously—in the relations of person to person, of state to society, and of state to state. What is happening in each of these fields is a drastic change of scale. The drive toward equalitarianism brings more people into the circle of political participation. Pluralism has steadily been giving way in favor of increased state activity. Meanwhile, under the stress of military and economic urgency, new units of government are being sought as replacements for the nation-state. It is this threefold expansion—the phenomenon of new government, both larger and smaller in scale, taking on more functions for a larger mass of citizens—that makes contemporary politics distinctive and gives our problems a quality without precedent. Any single one of these changes would be difficult to undertake with success. But when all three take place at the same time, and when each impinges on and complicates the other two, the task of finding a solution is thereby so much the more formidable. Never before have we confronted simultaneously the triple need to organize more equality, more functions of government, and states of new magnitudes. What is more, we are doing this not in one corner of the globe, or even on one continent. Tomorrow's solutions, if they are to work, have to be projected on a scale as large as the earth itself and eventually must embrace all humanity. To produce the ideas, the institutions, and the inspiration that will encompass such changes presents a political challenge to match the physical revolutions of electronics, nuclear power, and space rockets. Nor is there anything predetermined about the character of the solutions or the methods that will be used in reaching them. Any prediction of future trends, therefore, is hazardous. Nevertheless, the alternatives can be reviewed and their implications spelled out.

EQUALITARIANISM TODAY

The age-old choice between privilege and equality has assumed a new form in the twentieth century. The social consequences of industrialism, which brought more people into closer contact in crowded cities and required literacy and further education; the invention of improved and speedier communications; the spread of the printed word by the press and magazines; the extended range of eye and ear through radio, motion pictures, and television; these and like innovations have ushered in an era of mass politics in which the power that drives the wheels of government depends on what beliefs millions accept and what facts they have been told. The masses of mankind are ceasing to be the passive subjects of politics, as in the past. Instead, they are becoming active participants. Their participation, however, can be organized in alternate ways. The change of scale, tremendous though it be, has not removed the choice between privilege and equalitarianism. What it has done is to increase the complexity of achieving either solution. The competition between democracy and communism is a struggle between rival systems for the same objective—the allegiance of the masses.

The promise of communism is to pulverize the existing order and eliminate whatever social and economic inequalities it contains. But the result, because of the monopoly of power by one party, is to reestablish a new type of privilege to which political power provides the entrée. The chief concession that communism makes to equalitarianism, and a major difference between the Russia of today and the Russia of the tsars, is that communism recruits its privileged oligarchy from a much wider segment of society. The promise of democracy, on the other hand, is to cut the ties between political power and privilege by offering the masses alternative leaders and programs through two or more parties, thus preventing the formation of a permanent caste.[18] The impact of the numerical increase in participants produces a different response in the two systems. The one-party state attempts the organization of millions by demanding conformity and discouraging dissent. Outwardly this method gives an appearance of power by its display of solidarity. Inwardly, however, the intolerance to new ideas puts the brakes on progress. The democratic state organizes its inhabitants by tolerating multiformity and leaving a wide arena for political competition. This is a source of strength, because new thoughts may be freely expressed and discontents can receive an airing. But there are also some attendant risks. Conflict between groups may delay and even prevent discussion; private interests, uncontrolled, may capture public power; or two large organizations (for example, Democrats and Republicans, or a corporation and a trade union) may cease to function as rivals and instead, by sharing a monopoly of power, may exclude a genuine alternative.

If millions are to be organized for political action in a manner that keeps their loyalty, the performance of the system means more than the promise. A major difficulty for communism is the discrepancy between what it professes—a genuine equalitarianism—and what it practices—intolerance and inequality.[19] The rigidities of the one-party system with its power monopoly make it difficult for the underprivileged to challenge their masters. The latter, in order to explain away the contrast between their sayings and their doings, and justify perpetuation of their dictatorship, propagate the view that they face a hostile world which seeks to destroy them. This exemplifies the dictum that "Politics as a practice, whatever its professions, had always been the systematic organization of hatreds."[20]

---

[18]The promise is not always fulfilled, however—witness the Democratic and Republican nominating conventions of 1968.

[19]George Orwell in *Animal Farm* (New York: Harcourt, Brace & World, Inc., 1946) satirizes this inconsistency in the slogan: "All animals are equal. But some animals are more equal than others."

[20]Henry Adams, in *The Education of Henry Adams*, Chap. 1.

Democracies, too, depart at times from their own professed principles and permit substantial discrimination against women and against racial, religious, ethnic, or economic groups within their midst. Serious difficulties arise when a democracy omits to apply in other sectors of society the equalitarianism which it considers cardinal to politics. Thus, in Britain during the nineteenth century the equalitarian tendencies expressed in the broadening franchise ran counter to the privileged status of the aristocracy and the general stratification of people into upper, middle, and lower classes. Similar were the consequences that industrialism, allied with laissez-faire notions, produced in the United States and Britain. By the time World War I broke out, gross inequalities prevailed in the distribution of property and income. Indeed, the contrast then existing between the political power of the many and the economic power of the few supplied a disquieting repetition of the Aristotelian view that democracy is a struggle of the poor against the rich. During the last six decades, therefore, democracy has tackled and continues to confront a pair of associated problems: how to transfer the fundamentals of equalitarianism from politics to the rest of the social order, and, while leveling up, to avoid an excessive leveling down that would destroy incentive and deny recognition to talent. Suffice it to say that the democratic state, while it has accomplished much in the last hundred years, still has plenty left to be done.

The same verdict—that gains have been made, but much remains undone—can be rendered in the sphere of race relations. This problem constitutes an aspect of equalitarianism fully as crucial as the economic or social aspects. Indeed, it is only realism to point out that in many communities the ordering of relations between different races is the central problem on which everything else hinges. It is precisely the attitude toward race that governs economic development and molds the ethos of society in Hawaii and Brazil, in South Africa and Mississippi. Not only in domestic, but also in international, politics the spokesmen for racial exclusiveness are doomed to be the faction leaders of a losing minority. They can never be the statesmen to guide a majority. This holds true alike within the United States and the United Nations.

A further form of discrimination which has yet to be eradicated is as old as the dawn of history. This is the discrimination against one-half of the human race. It has been practiced persistently by the male sex at the expense of the female in virtually every culture. Today, throughout most of the world, these traditional modes of inequality continue with little substantial change. In certain societies, it is true, women have received equality in legal status and in the right to vote and to hold office. Even in these respects, however, and certainly in most matters which pertain to employment and careers, to social freedom and education, either inequalities persist or such equality as has been conceded turns out, upon examination, to be more formal than real. Seldom does a woman of equal, or even superior, abilities stand the same chance in life as a man. The double standard is still with us —a durable monument to the male sense of justice.

THE TWILIGHT OF PLURALISM

It is no accident that the age of the common man has witnessed everywhere an expansion of the functions of government, and that the politics of equality has provided an impetus toward monism. In the nineteenth century the nations that were foremost practitioners of laissez-faire in the relation of politics to economics, and of pluralism in the relation of the state to society, were of two kinds. A country like Britain led the field in industrialization; while in the United States, there was a vast territory to people and develop, and such was the distribution of property that private associations could finance an economic transformation with substantial independence of the state. In this century, however, circumstances have fundamentally altered. Intensified competition for foreign trade among industrialized states; the vanishing of the frontier in the once-New World; domestic political pressures for social and economic aid to the underprivileged; the need for regulation of overmighty private groups; and finally the mobilization of entire peoples for victory in war and their impoverishment afterwards; these facts have aggrandized the state and made the twentieth a century of monism.

Because a society in rapid flux requires a central focus for organization, the latter-day advocates of pluralism have been placed on the defensive and forced into retreat. Some, like G. D. H. Cole, who was a pluralist in the days when he argued for guild socialism, or Harold J. Laski, who wrote from a pluralist standpoint until the depression of the 1930's, reversed their positions and accepted the logic of monism. Others have maintained their original view, but with increasing difficulty. Robert M. MacIver, for instance, admits the need for society to be unified, but refuses to acquiesce in the state as its unifier. Instead—as a Greek playwright whose plot had become too tangled used to bring in a deity to extricate his characters in the last scene, or as Adam Smith relied on unseen hands to bring harmony out of competition[21]—he introduces his ideal of "community." This is a sense of belonging together

[21]See Chap. 2, p. 32.

which people are supposed to feel in sufficient force to prevent a plurality of associations from flying asunder. But how community is realized and made articulate is unclear, especially since MacIver will not concede that it should be organized and expressed through any association with power to override the rest—which would be tantamount to monism.

Other pluralists modify their basic theory and make such concessions to the state that, after denying admission to monism at the front door, they let it creep in at the back. Thus, Friedrich A. Hayek, who pleads eloquently against socialism and planned intervention by the state in economic matters, writes in favor of planning *for* freedom and insists that powerful private monopolies and combines must not be allowed to stifle genuine competition.[22] Inevitably, however, this ideal, to be enforced, requires a stronger state and more governmental regulation of the economy than fit his premises. Other pluralists endeavor to distinguish between the internal structure and external activities of private associations. They agree that the state should have the power to intervene in external conflicts (for example, a strike or lockout in a major industry) that disturb the peace and prosperity of the whole society. Then they perceive that the policies pursued externally by a big business firm or a big union may be connected with the character of its internal structure. Oligarchical tendencies, whether in corporation management or in trade union control, may sometimes lead a business executive or union boss on the path of aggression so that he may maintain his dominance within this organization by the victories he wins against opponents outside. Consequently, the pluralist may admit that there is a case for the state to prescribe the conditions that the government of a private association must satisfy. But all these expedients lead to the same conclusion. Any pluralist who holds that society is or should be a unity, or who recognizes the need to mitigate public clashes between private groups, must eventually admit the fundamental point of monism that society requires a coordinator, and must then face the political corollary that the state qualifies for that task more appropriately than any alternative organization. The only genuine pluralist would be the anarchist, who wants to be rid of government altogether. But his philosophy has never found a workable formula for its ideal of spontaneous, voluntary cooperation.

PROBLEMS OF THE MONISTIC STATE

A state that embraces monism avoids the weaknesses by which pluralism is beset, but confronts problems of its own. Monism may assume

[22] *The Road to Serfdom* (Chicago: The University of Chicago Press, 1944).

one of several guises. In its extreme form, as envisaged by Plato, the state settles the difficulty of rival associations by eliminating them and absorbing their functions. But the notion that a single institution could serve all the social needs of twentieth century men, though a logical possibility, is no more practicable, in view of the scale and complexity of the requisite organization, than the opposite extreme of anarchism. Of workable monism there are two alternatives. One is for the state to enforce its control over other groups by permitting no more than one association to serve each major need and interest. Thus organized, society would possess a single system of public education permeated by only one philosophy, a single state-established church intolerant of heterodoxy, a single state-directed economic structure professedly abolishing struggles between occupations and classes, and so on. Monism of this sort, unlike the Platonic variety, is not confined to the realm of speculation, since it is the goal to which the modern totalitarian regimes aspire.

The third kind of monism tolerates a variety of associations for each of man's needs. Thus, if people are left free to worship in the way that their individual consciences dictate, society will contain numerous religious faiths preaching different creeds. If opportunities exist for a person to learn various skills and move from job to job, or to own property and invest in a choice of enterprises, divergent economic interests will arise that reinforce themselves by establishing rival associations—corporations, trade unions, and the like. Under such circumstances, the principle of toleration or, in its wider sense, freedom, has the result of dividing society into competitive groups. Men who are pulled apart, however, by economic institutions, or organized religion, or cultural traditions, can be reunited through citizenship. In that case, as the monist sees its functions, the state serves as the binder of society. It then becomes irrelevant whether one is agnostic or Catholic, Jew or Protestant, black or white, male or female, manufacturer or employee, farmer or teacher, provided that all are equally citizens who share the same basic rights and duties, and owe the same allegiance. Thus on the political plane, through sharing the same citizenship, human rights, and governmental services, mankind can acquire a sense of belonging together and may achieve the unifying focus they otherwise lack.

Attainment of this goal through the politics of monism depends on avoiding certain pitfalls. For one thing, the possibility of unifying society by the state is qualified by the size of area and population to which the jurisdiction of a single government extends. When continents and people are parceled out among nation-states, the solidarity that each state achieves within its borders stops abruptly at international frontiers. The nation-state system unites the nationals of a state, but its existence separates them from nationals of other states. Pluralists point out, however, and with truth, that social relationships, though most numerous among persons of the same state, reach further afield. Religion is a bond that links the citizens of many countries. Trade relations create a common interest between the producers of one nation and the consumers of another. Scientific, professional, and cultural bodies draw their membership from the practitioners of different lands. The present boundaries of society are wider, therefore, than the boundaries of politics.

STATES IN SPACE

The state emerged historically[23] to organiz some basic services in response to universal needs. To give protection, maintain order, administer justice and welfare—for such functions as these are states created and governments instituted. It follows then that, wherever such activities are organized, the political process is *ipso facto* at work and the seeds of the state are being sown. In this present age every eye can see that the same tendencies which ushered in the nation-state are operating again to provide it with a successor. For ensuring security and prosperity, we have found our present units too small to be effective. Therefore, despite protestations to the contrary, we are turning for salvation not to national power alone but to international arrangements; not to sovereignty but to alliances, federations, and mutual commitments; not to the exclusive interest of a single state but to a wider community of interests. In the last liquidation of the older imperialism, we observe the disappearance of colonial systems, the recognition of new and often unsteady governments, and a need to reunite political clusters which are splitting off into separate fragments. Many of the most urgent problems of our age can only be solved, if they are to be solved at all, on a scale of territory and population far larger than even the greatest of nations now contains. Indeed it is evident that domestic politics have already reached a peculiar phase in some of the most advanced countries, such as Denmark, Sweden, Switzerland, and New Zealand. Fifty years ago the public was agitated over questions of further democratization, the extension of the suffrage, the attainment of socialism or social services, and so forth. Nowadays, most of these matters are accomplished facts. No longer is there debate over the broad principles. Argument now focuses on the details—which are appropriate to a legislative commit-

[23]See Chap. 3, pp. 60–71.

tee room or an administrative agency, but are tedious in public discussion and deathly in electoral oratory.

In their place, another crop of problems has sprouted from a fertile field of political controversy. Some of these are age-old conditions which only now are beginning to receive proper attention; some, however, are utterly unprecedented in human experience. The former include those still-continuing examples of social injustice, of man's inhumanity to man, to which I referred earlier—namely, racial prejudice, religious bigotry, discrimination against women, and the gulf between haves and have-nots. Certain of these stigmata on our civilization —for example, the contrast between affluence and poverty—are even becoming more acute rather than less. The significant new feature is the attitude now prevailing toward such conditions. Too many people either ignored them in the past, or, if they were aware of them, felt apathetic. This is no longer the case. Today there is not only awareness, but also concern—although admittedly the feelings of the concerned run the gamut from empathy with the underprivileged to hostility and fear.

A whole range of problems, however, have risen recently to beset us, which are novel in character and are terrifying in their potentialities for eventual disaster. The first and foremost of these is the population explosion, which threatens to engulf the planet with a tide of humanity and, if unchecked, will surely lead to mounting misery and recurrent wars. Coupled with this is the ever-present possibility of nuclear annihilation, since weapons are now lodged in men's hands which could exterminate the human species. Third is the increasing burden of expenditures for armaments, which become more complicated and more costly and yet have made nobody any safer. Next is the continuing pillage of our physical environment; the poisoning of air, land, and water; the reckless and wanton destruction of our habitat. Finally, we are afflicted by the onrush of technological innovation—the revolution which more and more subordinates man to the imperatives of his machines and has the social effect of enmeshing him in huge, impersonal bureaucratic systems which dehumanize, and deaden the spirit.

The cumulative result is far more than merely to transform our society. Whether we like it or not, and know it or not, we are undergoing a social revolution. Man once again is adrift from his wonted moorings. He feels himself floating helplessly on the ocean of an uncertain fate. He knows not into what whirlpool its currents may plunge him. Is it any wonder then that this century thus far has been the most violent in all history? From their rage or ignorance or despair, men react with passionate brutality—hoping either to unleash or to block the process of change.

And what implications does this have for government? One point at least can be affirmed with certainty. No social revolution of this depth and these dimensions can occur without a consequential revolution in our government system, and, since the changes sketched out above are truly global in scope and universal in character, no state anywhere and no species of politics will remain unaffected. Is it possible to discern the outline and direction of this revolution? And how is it related to the Great Issues which have formed the subject of this book?

Doubtless, the political responses will vary along the lines already discussed in the opening chapter.[24] Some persons will abandon the effort to understand or control. They will merely resign themselves to submitting to the dictate of events. In that case, as Emerson warned us, "things will be in the saddle and will ride mankind." Others, however, will seek to apply their reason and their faith to assist man in becoming the master of his fate. It is to these that I address myself.

One aspect of the contemporary revolution in society is the basic alteration in the scale and size of the problems we confront. Just as conditions which had once been local became national, so now have many of the latter passed to the international domain. But conversely, another and seemingly contradictory process is at work. Conditions which for long were too easily assumed to be national are now being redefined as subregional or even local. Let us explore these twin tendencies more closely, for their elucidation may offer clues to the solutions we seek.

For many centuries the community to which people belonged in fact and to which they felt attached was their immediate locality, bounded by the short radius of day-to-day contacts. This was true for practically all of mankind throughout the history of the *polis* and of the empire-state, which succeeded it. The advent of the nation-state, however, broadened the boundaries of political identification as it also enlarged the frontiers of human transactions. Centralized governments now emerged. They wielded strong powers which affected life and well-being, and they supplied services and performed functions on which more individuals came more to depend. In a sense that was by no means rhetorical, community and nation became increasingly coextensive.

The revolution now taking shape under our eyes has precisely the effect of breaking that connection. It is dissolving the links of the old-style community while it is creating new relationships whose boundaries are as vague as they are varied. Because of such relationships, communities are emerging in fact (objectively, that is) before the subjective attitudes and loyalties have been readjusted. Hence the

[24]See Chap. 1, pp. 4–9.

stresses and tensions, the dissent and demonstrations, the alienation and ambivalence, by which humanity, both young and old, is racked asunder.

A good way to envisage what is happening is to think of the sum total of our relationships with our fellowmen as a series of concentric circles. Quite a few circles would be needed at this time in history; and two of them comprising both old and new relationships would appear considerably more problem-ridden, and therefore more important, than they had in the past—the local community and the community which cuts across national frontiers. Both these aspects of our contemporary society were mentioned earlier, albeit separately. Now is the time to see their connection. At the international level, problems have now emerged which can no longer be resolved by Washington or Paris or London acting alone, but only by programs and arrangements conducted between them. Obvious examples of this occur in the military and economic spheres, where, to put it bluntly, national solutions are *no* solutions. When the range and extent of a problem is international, international policies are required—and, with them, their ultimate corollary: supranational institutions.

Simultaneously, however, at the local level—traditionally much despised and generally ignored—people find that life itself is now affected or afflicted by dangers which also are ungovernable by present means. Social injustices give rise to protests and then to civil commotion, which disturb the local peace and may threaten life and limb. At the same time, our cars and factories pollute the air we breathe, while domestic sewage and industrial waste poison the water of our rivers and oceans. Then, too, millions live in swarms which are ever more congested. Cities have expanded into metropolitan complexes which embrace suburban clusters and a sprawl of satellite towns. Residents of these towns may travel as far as 60 miles to work —plagued, more often than not, by substandard commuter railroads and inadequate highways.

How can we cope with all these situations rationally and intelligently? Obviously not through the machinery of government which has been traditional for the last hundred years or more. It cannot be asserted too emphatically or too often that this social revolution spells the doom of the sovereign, centralized, independent nation-state. This has become outmoded and obsolete because it is now too small for some of the problems which humanity must solve—and too large for others. Its foundations are being eroded and its roof is caving in. Many of its powers have to be redistributed by delegation, both above and below. The world cannot handle its emergencies of overpopulation, underdevelopment, and poverty, except through supranational agencies. Nor can it remedy the ills of congestion, pollution, inadequate transportation, and urban ghettos without recreating the community of the local region.

For the future, therefore, if we are to survive as a species—and nothing less is at stake—we must devise unprecedented institutions for these unprecedented conditions. We should be willing to experiment with new layers and levels of government simultaneously, and our concepts of citizenship must be readapted both to the smaller and more intimate and to the larger and more extensive. Men will be members henceforth of several communities, ranging from local to global, and our machinery of government—state boundaries included—must follow the geography of the problems. For unless they do, solutions will never be forthcoming. Expressed in terms of the Great Issues, all this signifies a change in the solutions to the fourth and fifth issues preferred during the last hundred years. We may expect in the future to see a flight from centralism at the same time as we shall witness the evolution of supranationalism.

THE METHODS OF POLITICAL CHANGE

Contemporary political trends are unmistakably leading in the direction of more equality, more governmental functions, and larger states. What happens then to the remaining issues when changes of this magnitude are occurring? The answer can be expressed in terms of the distinction between political ends and governmental means.[25] Of the five Great Issues there are three which act as the prime movers in relation to the processes of change because they provide the goals for action. Analyze the revolutionary crises of history and you find that the items in dispute have always included one or more of the following fundamentals: the extensiveness of citizenship, of state functions, and of the size of the state. A major increase or contraction in any of these is likely to start off a chain reaction of consequent changes. The two issues which deal with the subject of authority—the question of its source and its unity or dispersion—are not themselves the independent originators of political change. They resemble rather what statisticians call "dependent variables." Constitutions, institutions, and the distribution of power, to the extent that these are concerned with structure and procedure, are undeniably important, but their importance is most immediately felt by politicians and officials—that is, by the practitioners who operate the system. The mass of the people are most directly interested in the practical results which the framework

[25]See pp. 70 ff.

of government brings in their daily lives and lifetime dreams. They can understand the need for redistributing powers and redesigning institutions when there are substantial goals to be attained for which established methods are unsuitable. Anyone who doubts this should recall the worldwide effects of the economic depression of 1929-34 upon political systems. The historical record demonstrates that a change from dictatorial to responsible government, from unity of power to dispersion of powers—or vice versa—is likely to follow, and not precede, a shift of preference between equality and privilege, pluralism and monism, and a big and small area. Those directing the transition from any of these alternatives to its opposite have often employed authoritarian means, plus a concentration of power, to obtain their results. Especially does this happen when those who were influential under the older regime offer fierce resistance to change or when speed seems to the innovators a condition of their success. Contrariwise, the test of a mature and basically united people is their ability to absorb major changes without resort to dictatorship or loss of liberty.

THE NATURE OF REVOLUTION

In this capacity to absorb great changes, and in the manner of accomplishing them, a significant distinction may be noted between political systems. The role of government in the evolution of society is profoundly affected by the timing of the changes that occur as well as by their content. No social order is ever completely static. Most societies generally undergo continuous change which is imperceptibly absorbed. But there are occasions in the history of a community when the rate of change is sharply accelerated, and adjustments are attempted or accomplished with rapidity and urgency. Any kind of change, of course, imposes a strain, since it involves a departure from settled practices and a dislocation of established institutions. Excessive speed may make the strain intolerable and lead a society to the breaking point.

Changes can differ in depth, as well as speed. Some modifications of an existing order may be only surface deep. Others may reach far down and upset the foundations of society. When a party defeats its rival at a free election peacefully conducted, and a new administration and legislative majority replace their predecessors, the top personnel and some of the programs of government will alter. But the civil service, the judiciary, and most of the policies already in force continue to operate without change. This method of assimilating innovations gradually, and on the whole harmoniously, has become the standard practice in states which are democratically organized. A deeper change is one that alters not merely the government, but also the constitutional system under which it is organized. The Philadelphia Convention of 1787, for instance, had to reach decisions on more fundamental matters than are ordinarily settled in periodic elections. But the most profound changes of all, inducing the greatest disturbance and most intense controversy, are those that refashion the main structural pillars on which society reposes. The substitution of one form of property for another and basic modifications in ownership and distribution, a major religious upheaval, or any sharp challenge to long-cherished cultural values—such movements impinge on entrenched interests and arouse strong emotions. It is impossible to consummate changes of this sort without producing political repercussions.

The most extreme changes are revolutions. In the light of the preceding discussion, what does this term mean? When one group takes over power from another within the framework of the same constitutional system and by a procedure constitutionally defined and mutually accepted, that is no revolution. But when the constitution as well as the government is reconstructed, then a revolution occurs. If, besides constitutional renovation, society is transformed root and branch, the character of the revolution becomes still more thoroughgoing and the most turbulent disorders usually ensue. When finally changes of government, constitution, and social order are simultaneously achieved at breakneck speed, state and society suffer agony and convulsion under the momentum of the driving force. In this way it is possible to distinguish between the major revolutions that have taken place in the last three hundred years. The American Revolution from 1775 to 1789 involved a change of government and constitution, but conserved most of the social fabric—its economic system included—in much the same design as before. The English Revolution between 1640 and 1688 altered both constitution and government, settled the issues of Protestant-Catholic and church-state relations, and confirmed the prominence of a new urban commercial class. The French Revolution, which began in 1789, went much further than the English in the ferment—economic, philosophic, and cultural—that it evoked throughout society as a whole.[26] The Communist Revolution, inaugurated in Russia in 1917, probed the deepest of the four and has been responsible for one of the most penetrating and intensive overhauls of a social order of which history has record.

[26]This explains why Edmund Burke, who approved the principles, methods, and results of England's seventeenth century revolution, was aghast at the French Revolution and reacted to it conservatively.

All four revolutions, it may be noted, were accompanied by warfare, which in the English case took the form of civil war only, and in the other three cases involved conflict with foreign powers as well. While the constitutions that emerged from the English and American Revolutions successfully provided a peaceful method of governmental change for the future, it should be remembered that violence was initially required to lay that groundwork of constitutionalism. The three revolutions whose effects were not confined to the state but spread to society, namely the English, French, and Russian, produced the phenomenon of dictatorship with extraordinary powers concentrated in the hands of one man or a tiny clique. Significantly, the American Revolution, which was content to limit itself to a political change without transforming the social order, did not succumb to dictatorship; and while other countries had resort to Cromwell, to Robespierre and Napoleon, to Lenin, Trotsky, and Stalin, the needs of the United States were adequately served by Washington and Jefferson.

DICTATORSHIP IN A TIME OF CHANGE

Besides the cases just cited, there are many recent instances of peoples who spawn a dictatorship while undergoing drastic change. Witness the power acquired for a while by Hitler or Mussolini, by Ataturk or Nasser, by Castro or Perón, by Mao or Tito. The frequency of this occurrence suggests some further reflections on the subject of change. Undeniably a community in convulsions is prone to yield to a Directory, a Politburo, a military *junta,* or the dynamism of a "strong man," whose personality thrusts itself above the leading clique. The reason is to be found in the practical demands and the psychology of crisis conditions. A society that must decide major issues faces momentous, and perhaps irrevocable, choices. Collectively its members share the *élan,* the heightened tension, the sense of adventurousness, and with these the latent fears and anxieties concerning the outcome, which any period of rapid flux calls forth. It is always more difficult politically to chart a course for change than for conservatism. The former opens many avenues of choice. The latter prescribes one route —continuation, as far as possible, of the *status quo.*

To minimize the risks and uncertainties of change, and to offset the weakness that division produces, a society in crisis will be urged to submit to a pattern of discipline and thus reassert its unity and solidarity. Authoritarianism will be represented as a source of strength, because it is supposedly efficient, single minded, and fast moving. In our century many circumstances have appeared to set a premium on such factors. People who seek in warfare an outlet for their aggressions, or who smart under the humiliations of a defeat, have often acquiesced in dictatorship. A long-lasting and widespread economic depression brings loss of savings, unemployment, or bankruptcy to many individuals who then lend a willing ear to the advocates of desperate remedies. Or again, a technologically backward community, proud of its ancient memories, faces the challenge of a different culture equipped with superior machines and scientific knowledge. Forced to adapt themselves to alien novelties, yet wishing to preserve enough of their traditional ways so that their identity may not be lost, millions of people will attempt to combine the seemingly contradictory policies of heavy borrowing from abroad and a positive reaffirmation of their own cultural distinctiveness. The psychological result in this last case is a state of ambivalence. The dependent group admires and respects those whose techniques it copies, but is also fearful of them and resentful. The political result, not infrequently, is like a state of siege.

This helps to throw some light on one of the most interesting political problems of our century: the common association of dictatorship with nationalism. The building of a nation-state does not, in and by itself, necessitate either dictatorship or democracy. There are, however, two sides to nationalism, and they face in different directions. So far as its internal aspect is concerned, nationalism unites people with a common loyalty to their political association. It imparts a sense not only of belonging together, but also of belonging together as equals because nationality does not admit of degrees. In this way nationalism and democracy are compatible, and it is therefore understandable that many political leaders with perfect consistency have been both nationalists and democrats, for example, Lincoln, Mazzini, Masaryk. Viewed externally, however, nationalism asserts the individuality of the group and its separateness from others. When this emphasis upon uniqueness happens to be linked with the uncertainties of a time of troubles—due to military or economic reasons or cultural readjustment or a combination of these—the aggressions and frustrations that exist within the group are siphoned into the channels of dictatorship. That has occurred not only in European states which yielded to the embrace of fascism or communism, but also in Latin American and Asiatic countries that wanted to catch up with Western technology and at the same time rid themselves of colonialism.

FROM PROTECTION TO PERFECTION

Thus, for all its enlargement of scale, the search for solutions to humanity's political problems will require, both now and in the future, a continuing selection among the same perennial choices and an elaboration of the same basic patterns in presumably more intricate forms. As politics encompasses a wider embrace, the horizons of the state expand and governments assume more duties. It is a far reach from the fortification of a hilltop to walking on the moon, from control of a river valley or a city to the ordering of a planet, from participation by a few to equalized liberties for all. The mode and means may vary in all their richness of detail, but the principles at stake will not. Humanity still must choose, or allow a fraction of its number to make the choices for the rest. The risk is serious, since the penalties for bad government have increased in the same proportion as the potentialities for good. Hitler outdid Attila, as a future tyrant could outdo him.

The state originated in mankind's need for protection, which requires the organization of force. A government amasses force initially, and monopolizes it finally, in order to repel any threats, internal or external, to life and limb. But the history of the functions of the state consists in an advance from protection and order to justice and the good life. This does not mean that the state abandons or surrenders its duty of protecting its members. Far from it. The state that ceases to protect ceases to be a state. But, after ensuring the conditions that make life possible, the state must proceed toward the goal of the good life. It is precisely this changeover that presents a supreme challenge to the architects of government. For how does force or power fit in with welfare? The concept of welfare is broad. It embraces economic prosperity, moral well-being, and the whole system of values composing a civilization. Such considerations transfer the issues of politics from the starting point of physical safety to the terminus of an ethical ideal. The creation of the state resembles the construction of a dwelling to shelter the life of society. A house has foundations to stand on, just as a state is built upon man's fundamental need for protection. But people do not lead their daily lives in the basement of their homes. The living room is raised some feet above ground level, and it is here that the members of the household develop the relations that can give to life a quality of love, nobility and taste. And it is, or can be, the same with politics. The function of the foundations is to support the upper framework which houses the political life of man and makes him civilized.

That actual states do not always reach the ideal, and at times depart from it by deliberate decision, is true and obvious enough. There have been, and continue to be, many governments which build no higher than the basement and force their subjects to stay there. Also, when the warlike politics of an anarchic world compel all states, even those concerned with welfare, to reemphasize the priority of physical protection, humanity rushes to the refuge of the bomb shelter and scurries down from living room to basement. The state may fail, then, to subordinate the force it must employ to the ethical ideal for which men grope. What was the servant may emerge the master. The power that founded a government can become the means whereby the will of the governing group is forcibly imposed throughout society. In that case, their regime is a tyranny, and, when linked with monism, the product is totalitarian. Hence, the crucial test of the would-be monistic state is to keep its stock of power within bounds and sublimate power in the service of the good. Unless this is done, there is no superior merit in monism as against the pluralist alternative. For why should one flee from anarchy into the embrace of despotism?

The first problem, then, is to organize power, yet keep it under control and legitimize it as authority; to unify society through the state, but avoid the authoritarian means and the regimented end. That is the third of the great issues, which offers the choice between freedom and dictatorship. There is no certain way of guaranteeing freedom. It is possible, though difficult, to establish and operate a politically free society. It is not too difficult to suppress freedom entirely by a perversion of power. All that can be prescribed is a set of conditions which, if adhered to, tends to encourage the attainment of freedom and discourage its opposite. These conditions depend on planning a constitutional system that builds the right of criticism and opposition into the central structure of government. Applied in detail, this principle spells itself out into universal suffrage, periodic elections, the coexistence of two or more parties, and opportunities to form new political combinations. Where such requirements are met, liberty is better guaranteed than by the pluralist reliance on mutual conflict between private associations and their general rivalry with the state.

POLITICS AND THE GOOD LIFE

But the institutional checks just mentioned, while basic to the politics of freedom, do not ensure the good life. Though liberty may be assisted by procedural arrangements, the purpose of the latter is also to reach decisions about policies. The contents of such decisions, as well as the ways of reaching them, must be encompassed in the philosophy of the state, since the ends accomplished are more significant than the means employed. Hence, the state which seeks to integrate society must embody an ethical ideal. Otherwise, instead of the good life taking priority over power, power will steal the priority from welfare—in which case no reply can be given to Augustine's question: What else is the state but a great robber band if it lacks justice? But as it happens, two of the Great Issues, the first and second, have a direct bearing on the contents of policy. Whenever the state administers a program, a service is supplied for some or all of its citizens. This evokes controversies over the appropriateness of the service and the designation or selection of recipients. Should the state, for instance, pay and provide for large-scale schemes of low-cost housing? If so, to whom should houses be assigned? Should it embark on programs of social security, covering all major hazards, economic and physical, that flesh is heir to between birth and death? If so, who should be eligible for benefits, and how should the financing be apportioned?

Questions like these have other implications for society than that of freedom. They suggest that the state accept some responsibility for influencing the distribution of material goods; that it provide at least a minimum below which no person be allowed to sink, while encouraging everyone to raise his status above the minimum by his own efforts. To say this is to recognize that social and economic privilege —when expressed in a grossly unequal distribution of property, income, security, and living standards—is no more desirable than the political privilege of a limited class or caste. That, in other words, is an affirmation of the principle of equality. How can the state which assumes the direction of society organize the race of life so as to mix equality with liberty? It is possible to do this if the state ensures equality for all at the starting tape; if it provides fulfillment to the more talented; and if it guarantees some minimum to each contestant. These criteria would seem to satisfy the test of welfare. More than that, by blending the rights and duties of the individual with those of society, they point the way to a conception of social justice. It is only when this is achieved that power, besides being rendered safe by the politics of freedom, also acquires a moral legitimacy. The degree of approximation to this standard is some measure of the level of civilization that a people have attained. Conversely, a subordination of welfare to power and the disregard of social justice is an index of inhumanism.

Finally, it is through this concept that the difficulty stated in the beginning of this book may be resolved. Human beings, as was observed, associate in groups under the contrary impulses of cooperation and competition. But to reconcile the two has always posed a problem. Perhaps the answer is found, however, when liberty and equality are synthesized under the higher concept of the good life. It is in their concern for the human condition that men express their altruism, cooperativeness, and sense of solidarity. It is in the personal achievement of creative growth that they display their individuality. To maintain both principles in equilibrium and use them constructively in the solution of the Great Issues, to unite the good person with the good society, is the wisdom of statesmanship. When the power of government is directed in the service of that ideal, the good life emerges into the realm of the possible and the art of politics becomes a voyage of ethical discovery.

Bibliography

As soft, doughy bread is bad for the teeth, so soft, doughy books are bad for the mind. Indispensable for understanding politics are the classic works of eminent thinkers, which have stood the test of time. All these are easily accessible, in the original or in English translation, in a variety of editions—such as those of Everyman's Library (published by E. P. Dutton & Co., Inc., New York, and J. M. Dent & Sons, Ltd., London) or the Modern Library (publishers, Random House, Inc., New York). This bibliography will cite a particular edition of a classic only if it possesses some special advantage over others. In the Western tradition, political science is born in the *Histories* of Herodotus and Thucydides, and subsequently grows to maturity in the care of philosophers. The fundamentals of the subject are probed in four Platonic dialogues: *Crito, Statesman, Republic,* and *Laws.* Of these the *Republic* is the most famous because of its logical systematism, artistic and literary excellence, and analytical rigor. His uncompromising argument for absolutism in metaphysics and politics and his elitist assumptions have brought Plato equally strong admirers and critics. The *Republic* can be most conveniently studied in A. D. Lindsay's translation, published with his introduction in the Everyman's Library. A more moderate philosophy of the state is expressed in the *Politics* of Aristotle, which also introduces and employs in a masterly fashion, the method of a comparative analysis of actual governments. The translation by Ernest Barker, together with his notes and explanatory essays, is excellent (New York: Oxford, 1946).

The Romans, whose abilities lay in action rather than in thought, produced the raw materials for a study of government, but not the study itself. Many valuable insights, however, into the politics of an authoritarian regime are revealed in the *Annals* of the trenchant historian Tacitus. The Christian impact on political thought can best be observed in the treatises of Augustine and Thomas Aquinas. The former's *City of God,* written during the collapse of the western half of the Roman Empire, outlines the double standard of values which was basic to the philosophy of the church. Aquinas' *Summa Theologica,* the architectonic achievement of medieval philosophy, affirms the subordination of politics to ethics and to a hierarchy of law whose highest manifestations have to be taken on faith.

The sixteenth, seventeenth, and eighteenth centuries—a period of political ferment—were productive of fundamental political thinking in an altered vein. Machiavelli's *Prince* and *Discourses* (printed together in the Modern Library) are the distilled observations of a scholar and diplomat who truthfully mirrored his times, possessing loftier ideals than most of his contemporaries and fewer illusions than most of his predecessors. The *Leviathan* of Thomas Hobbes is an intellectual tour de force that combines psychology and ethics with a drastic political philosophy, but terminates in theological polemics. The political section includes assertions and assumptions about the basic issues on which each has to make up his own mind. Separated from the *Leviathan* by only four decades, John Locke's *Second Treatise of Civil Government* is worlds apart in temper and objectives. While his discussion of property has earned Locke a place in the ranks of conservative thinkers, his emphasis on individual rights—including the right to rebel against autocracy—and his justification of legislative rather than monarchical supremacy make him a founding father of liberal democracy.

The growing chorus of protest against absolute monarchy produced in the eighteenth century two books that have remained classics. Montesquieu's *Spirit of the Laws* is notable for its use of the comparative method and for its elaboration of the principle of the separation of powers. It should be consulted in the Hafner Classics (New York, 1949) along with the introductory essay by Franz L. Neumann. Rousseau's tempestuous writings reached their climax politically in the *Social Contract,* a work for the most part closely reasoned, yet containing illogical lapses and elusive concepts which have yielded equal inspiration to mutually incompatible successors.

The era that opened with the American, French, and Industrial Revolutions has been prolific with political speculation. Certain works stand out from the rest for their intrinsic quality or because they have had wide influence. A conservative attitude toward the process of change is eloquently expounded by Burke in his later speeches and in such booklets as the *Reflections on the French Revolution,* where many gems of political wisdom are enshrined in the incidental remarks. A philosophy of reaction, as distinct from conservatism, is contained in Hegel's *Philosophy of Right,* which is in essentials a philosophy of the far right. The *Federalist* papers, composed by Hamilton, Madison, and Jay to persuade New Yorkers to ratify the Constitution of the United States, are a blend of clear analysis, historical scholarship, and keen practical judgment. The noblest aspects of liberalism are nowhere better portrayed than in J. S. Mill's *Essay on Liberty,* a brief master-piece whose universal tolerance and even the internal contradictions testify to its author's open-mindedness and humanity. His *Considerations on Representative Government* bespeak the problems of giving institutional concreteness to general principles in an age of reform, when the extension of the suffrage and of governmental functions imposed new stresses on legislative, administrative, and party organization. These two works of Mill, along with his philosophy of *Utilitarianism,* are printed together in Everyman's Library.

The attacks on liberal democratic ideals and institutions that emanate from the extremes of left and right are in general dogmatically formulated. The *Communist Manifesto* of Karl Marx belabors the theme that economic relationships are fundamental to politics and intermingles historical generalizations with the distortion of the propagandist. Among his successors, Lenin's *State and Revolution* and Trotsky's *History of the Russian Revolution* explain, prospectively and retrospectively, the technique of violent overthrow of government as understood by two who proved themselves adept at the practice.

Fascism, repudiating thought in favor of action and reason in favor of emotion, produced little coherent philosophy—and that little grandsired by Hegel. Two statements have a certain significance because of the names attached to them rather than for their intellectual content. Mussolini's *Social and Political Doctrine of Fascism* concisely summarizes the ethos of the movement he led; while Hitler's *Mein Kampf* (New York: Reynal and Hitchcock, 1939), published several years before he came to power, is a lasting record to racial prejudice and to the dangers of underestimating an egomaniac with ability.

For a general review of the main currents of political thought, seen in relation to the ebb and flow of historical tides, a superb treatment in a single volume is George H. Sabine's *History of Political Theory* (New York: Holt, Rinehart & Winston, Inc., 1950).

Modern attempts to analyze the nature of politics begin with scholars who were not political scientists. The *Introduction to Political Science* by J. A. R. Seeley (London: Macmillan, 1919) is the work of an experienced historian, just as the *History of the Science of Politics* by F. Pollock (rev. ed., London: Macmillan, 1911) comes from the pen of an eminent jurist. Harold J. Laski wrote *The Grammar of Politics* (London: Allen and Unwin, 1925) in the period when he was still a plural-ist. Also composed from a pluralist standpoint are two notable volumes by the sociologist Robert M. MacIver: *The Modern State* (London: Oxford, 1926) and *The Web of Government* (New York: Macmillan, 1951). Harold D. Lasswell's *Politics: Who Gets What, When, How* (New York, London: McGraw-Hill, Whittlesey House, 1936) illustrates the use of Freudian psychoanalysis and the power approach to the study of politics. It should be read in conjunction with *The Power Elite* by C. Wright Mills (London: Oxford University Press, 1956). Charles A. Beard's *Economic Basis of Politics* (New York: Knopf, 1945) is an illuminating and sensible treatment of a problem which the Marxists made controversial.

Comparisons of the governments of a number of countries have been tried in alternative ways. One is to analyze the entire govern-ment of a country, then to do the same successively for others, and finally to compare them and draw conclusions. The best example of this method is James Bryce's *Modern Democracies* (New York: Macmil-lan, 1921). The second way is to analyze the subject into topics and discuss under each heading the experiences of various countries. In-stances of this approach are Carl J. Friedrich's *Constitutional Govern-ment and Democracy* (rev. ed., Boston: Ginn, 1950) and my work *The Democratic Civilization* (New York: Oxford University Press, 1964).

Finally, a few books require mentioning which are important to political scientists, either as treatments of a special topic or as offering the insight of a neighboring field. Tocqueville's *Democracy in America* is a profound evaluation by a gifted Frenchman of the American form of government—novel in Old World eyes—as it existed in Jackson's time. Walter Bagehot's *The English Constitution,* a pioneer of realism when first printed, contains many observations that are still challeng-ing. Because he wrote at the time of the American Civil War, he tended to be more impressed with the weakness than the strength of the American system. Yet, through Woodrow Wilson and others he exercised no little influence on thinking in the United States. The World's Classics edition (New York: Oxford, 1942) includes the pref-ace that Bagehot wrote to the second edition in 1872, and an essay by Lord Balfour. Howard L. McBain's *The Living Constitution* (New York: Macmillan, 1937) is a short outstanding analysis by a twentieth century scholar continuing in the same tradition and probing for the actualities that lie behind the forms.

Among the writings of modern philosophers whose interest em-braced the field of action as well as the realms of thought, both John Dewey and A. D. Lindsay have left behind them books which possess enduring qualities, for instance, the former's *The Public and its Prob-*

lems (New York: Holt, 1927) and the latter's *Modern Democratic State* (New York: Oxford, 1947). Abraham H. Maslow has expounded a humanistic psychology in *Toward a Psychology of Being* (Princeton: D. Van Nostrand Co., Inc., 1962). The issues that arise in the relations of politics to economics are masterfully handled in Joseph Schumpeter's *Capitalism, Socialism, and Democracy* (New York: Harper & Row), and more recently in *Modern Capitalism* by Andrew Shonfield (New York: Oxford University Press, Inc., 1965). Nor has the Muse of History been wanting. Two remarkable works by historians, one Swiss and the other British, are "musts" on any list. These are Jacob Burckhardt's essays and lectures, republished in English under the title *Force and Freedom* (New York: Pantheon Books, 1943) and Arnold J. Toynbee's *Study of History* (abridgment by D. C. Somerwell in two volumes, New York: Oxford, 1947-57).

Index

A

Adams, Henry, 425
Administration, public (see also Officials), 298-300, 305-06
Age, in relation to government, 104-05
Agriculture, 62-63, 68, 179 n. 2, 183, 188-90, 200-201, 233, 250, 281-82, 342-43
Akkad, 64
Alabama, 27, 142, 336
Albania, 394, 403
Albigenses, the, 354
Alexander VI, Pope, 373
Alexander the Great, 72-73, 106, 161, 347-48, 351
Alexandria, 281, 352
Algeria, 388, 389 n. 15, 391 n. 18
Amsterdam, 251
Anarchism, 38, 254, 428
Anarchy, 28-30, 32, 280-81
Anderson, William, 292-93
Anthony, Mark, 73, 247
Anthropology, 7-8, 62-63, 95-96, 100 n. 18, 139
Antoninus Pius, 118
Antwerp, 179, 251 n. 4
Apelles, 159
Arabs, the, 79-80, 222, 281, 312, 341, 352, 388, 390
Argentina, 74, 226
Aristocracy (see also Oligarchy, Privilege), 91-92, 100-04, 108-09, 115, 127, 168, 220 n. 6, 240, 249-51, 288-90
Aristophanes, 102 n. 23, 158
Aristotle, 29 n. 2, 48, 72 n. 21, 89-91, 96-97, 100, 120 n. 1, 122, 151 n. 2, 160-62, 293, 347-48, 356, 391, 418-19, 426, 443
Arkansas, 142, 336
Arnold Thurman, 194
Art, 16, 25, 34, 57, 86-87, 153, 369-70
Assemblies, popular, 64-65, 106, 244-46, 286-87

Athens, 63-64, 73, 102 n. 23, 159, 177, 243-45, 281, 286-87, 342, 343 n. 5, 345-46, 369, 372, 378, 406
Atlanta, 146
Atlantic, the, 9-10, 326, 358-59, 373, 378-79, 396, 401, 410
Attlee, Clement, 306
Augustine, 70, 72, 164, 167, 444
Augustus, Emperor, 73, 246-47, 349, 351, 369, 406
Aurelius, Marcus, 118
Australia, 129, 313, 320, 327, 363, 399, 414
Austria, 113, 131, 341, 360, 364, 378, 386, 394
Authority (see also Dictatorship, Power), 13-14, 53, 69, 76 ff., 215-42, 243 ff., 253, 339
Ayub Kahn, 226
Aztecs, the, 112, 220 n. 6

B

Babylon, 221
Bacon, Roger, 281
Bagehot, Walter, 132-33, 303, 446
Banda, H. K., 309 n. 32
Bandaranaike, Mrs. S., 106 n. 30
Barcelona, 313
Barker, Ernest, 443
Basel, 248
Batista, Fulgencio, 226
Beard, Charles A., 134, 446
Beethoven, Ludwig van, 51
Belgium, 69, 100 n. 18, 126, 208 n. 26, 211 n. 30, 364, 394
Belgrade, 238, 316
Benson, G. C. S., 327 n. 22
Bentham, Jeremy, 128, 147, 260
Beria, 235, 237
Berlin, 82
Bern, 313, 367

Bismarck, Otto von, 20, 131, 315, 360, 366, 369

Blumer, Herbert, 96 n. 11

Bodin, Jean, 173-74

Bolivia, 222

Boniface VIII, Pope, 167-68

Borodin, 233

Botswana, 394

Bourbons, the, 101

Bradley, A. C., 104

Brady, Alexander, 99 n. 16

Brazil, 27, 97, 226, 312-13, 333-34, 394, 426

Brezhnev, Leonid, 239, 403

Britain, Great:
  cabinet government in, 304-06
  centralization in, 321-23, 376
  churches in, 109, 172, 221
  constitution of, 20, 266-70
  democracy in, 129 ff., 239
  economic development of, 187-89, 192 ff., 198, 203 ff., 208 n. 20, 376-77, 388, 391 n. 18
  monarchy in, 73, 249 ff., 268, 290, 304, 415
  parliament in, 115-16, 130 ff., 172-73, 188-89, 198, 249 ff., 252-53, 256-57, 267-69, 283, 290-91, 304-07, 322-23, 373, 415
  premiership in, 304-06
  race relations in, 95, 146
  social classes in, 101, 115-16, 251

British empire, the, 92, 97-99, 111-12, 254, 309, 349 n. 12, 360, 372 ff., 384, 388-89, 408, 415

Brittany, 339

Bryce, James, 446

Bucharest, 238

Budapest, 236, 390

Buddhism, 220, 368

Bukharin, N., 233-34

Bulganin, N., 236-38

Bulgaria, 394

Burckhardt, Jacob, 91 n. 4, 110 n. 36, 447

Bureaucracy (see also Officials), 298-99

Burke, Edmund, 130, 153 n. 6, 436 n. 26, 444

Burma, 226, 368

Burnham, James, 279 n. 35

Business (see also Economy, the), 52-53, 143-44, 153 ff., 176, 187 ff., 260, 264

Butler, Bishop, 35 n. 12

Byzantium, 350, 358

C

Caesar, Julius, 73, 246-47, 314 n. 4, 348, 352, 415

California, 68, 205, 303

Calvin, Jean, 153, 220, 367

Campbell-Bannerman, Henry, 306

Canada, 27, 129, 254, 312, 320, 326-27, 363, 367-68, 373 n. 3, 396

Canning, George, 130

Capitalism, (see also Business), 32, 35-36, 184-214

Caracalla, 125-26

Carlyle, Thomas, 92, 153

Carthage, 123 n. 3, 348

Cary, M., 64 n. 8

Castro, Fidel, 437

Catherine the Great, 5, 106

Catholicism (see also Papacy), 27, 104, 109, 128, 163 ff., 252, 326, 362-63, 366-68, 373

Catullus, 349

Cavour, Camillo, 360

Centralism, 284 ff., 310-39, 354, 410-11, 414, 433

Cervantes, Miguel de, 112, 351

Ceylon, 106 n. 30

Chagall, Marc, 16

Chamberlain, Joseph, 323

Charlemagne, 167, 352-53

Charles I, 252, 290

Chase, Chief Justice, 325

Chiang Kai-shek, 226, 233, 388

Chicago, 74, 82, 406

Childe, V. Gordon, 64

China, 23, 62, 112, 223 n. 11, 226, 233, 239-40, 297, 314, 341, 360, 386, 388, 390 n. 16, 394, 401-03, 414-15

Chopin, Frederic, 369

Christianity, 57, 104, 108-09, 120, 125-26, 128, 158, 162-74, 176, 178-79, 212, 248 ff., 351 ff., 412, 444

Churchill, John, 373

Churchill, Winston, 147, 306, 406

Citizenship, 6, 13, 15, 52-54, 89 ff., 123-25, 225, 244-45, 349, 428-29

City, the (see also State, City-), 63, 138-39, 145 n. 28, 159, 190, 193-94, 197, 208, 251, 288, 315, 321-22, 328, 331, 339, 349, 423-24, 433

Civilization, 7, 25, 30-31, 64, 255, 396, 431

Civil liberties, 281-82

Civil service (see also Officials), 7, 298, 300-302, 303 n. 28, 308

Classes, social, 100-104, 127, 130 ff., 188, 229, 249-52, 314 n. 6, 391, 441

Cleisthenes, 343 n. 5

Cleon, 102 n. 23

Cleveland, 145

Cleveland, Grover, 194 n. 19, 300

Clive, Robert, 415

Clodius, 73

Colbert, 183
Cole, G. D. H., 35 n. 12, 43 n. 21, 187, 427
Collective security, 10-11, 61, 380 ff.
Columbus, Christopher, 359
Communism, 10, 36, 120-21, 140, 210-11, 226, 228, 229 ff., 275, 280, 308-09, 315-19, 388-90, 400 ff., 421-22, 424-25
Community, 311 ff., 337-40, 347, 360, 432 ff.
Competition, 32-40, 46, 57-58, 67, 149-50, 154, 184 ff., 192, 194-96, 206, 278, 381, 385 ff., 441-42
Confucius, 223 n. 11
Congo, the, 69, 390
Consent, 75-76, 83, 215 ff., 253-55
Conservatism, 100-107, 259, 437 n. 26, 444-45
Constance, 248
Constantine, 108, 162-63, 169, 176, 350, 412
Constantinople, 350, 356, 358
Constitution (see also Britain, Great, United States), 256-73, 276-78
Constitutionalism, 20, 182, 217, 246-47, 256 ff., 260-62, 278, 333-35, 437
Contract, the social, 44-45, 127
Coolidge, Calvin, 153
Cooperation, 30-31, 33-39, 46, 57-58, 61, 67, 149-50, 154, 278, 381, 385-86, 393 ff., 428, 441-42
Copernicus, 281
Corinth, 177, 345, 348
Corporation, the, 45, 51, 184, 188, 194-95, 200
Cortes, Hernando, 220 n. 6
Costa Rica, 286
Crassus, 351
Crete, 159, 380
Cromwell, Oliver, 128, 290, 437
Cuba, 226, 401, 403
Culture, 111-12, 349, 368-70
Custom, 3-6, 224, 259, 267 ff.
Cynics, the 123
Cyprus, 368, 390
Cyrus, 346
Czechoslovakia, 118, 208 n. 26, 211, 239, 365, 368-69, 397, 400, 403

D

Dalai Lama, the, 220
Damascus, 352
Dante, 112, 163
Darwin, Charles, 38, 46-47, 281

Defoe, Daniel, 29
De Gaulle, Charles, 17, 226, 272, 292, 396, 401
De Gobineau, Arthur, 97
Democracy, 109 n. 35, 114 n. 42, 129 ff., 136, 200, 205, 217-18, 228-29, 239, 243-83, 286, 300-301, 315 n. 8, 415-16, 419, 421, 424 ff.
Demosthenes, 159, 347
Denmark, 27
Descartes, 43-44
Deseret, 221
De Tocqueville, Alexis, 135, 165, 179 n. 2, 267 n. 24, 379-80, 446
Dewey, John, 32 n. 6, 446
Dicey, A. V., 267
Dictatorship, 15, 73-74, 83, 217, 224-42, 275, 280, 287, 308-09, 313 ff., 335, 408, 410-11, 413, 437 ff.
Diderot, Denis, 5
Diocletian, 350
Disraeli, Benjamin, 208, 306, 374
Dominican Republic, the, 226
Donne, John, 34, 42
Dred Scott case, the, 136, 262 n. 18
Drews, Elizabeth Monroe, 8 n. 4
Dubcek, Alexander, 239
Duguit, Leon, 187
Durham, Lord, 373 n. 3
Dutch, the (see Netherlands)
Dvorak, 369

E

Ecology, 1-2, 338-39, 431, 433-34
Economic theory, 7, 32, 50, 114-15, 178 ff., 188 ff., 375-76
Economy, the, 6, 18, 27, 51, 156, 175-214, 251, 288-89, 322, 387, 435
Education, 4, 52-54, 132-33, 136, 140-43, 207-08, 238, 244, 362, 369, 391 n. 18
Edward I, 249, 251
Egypt, 226, 341, 347, 369, 388, 390-91
Eire (see Ireland)
Eisenhower, Dwight D., 142, 203, 416
Elite (see Aristocracy, Oligarchy, Privilege)
Elizabeth I, 106, 172, 252, 360, 369, 374
Emerson, Ralph Waldo, 432
Empire, Holy Roman, 167 ff., 221, 353 ff., 365-66, 371
England (see Britain, Great)
Epicureans, the, 123, 161
Equality, 11, 13, 15, 19, 21, 108, 119-47, 162, 192 ff., 335-36, 408 ff., 421-22, 424 ff.

Ethics, 20-25, 34-39, 72-73, 86 ff., 160, 212, 216-17, 242, 254, 440-42
Ethiopia, 386
Europe, Council of, 396
Europe, Western, 9-10, 103-04, 171, 246, 353, 355-56, 360, 378, 380, 396 ff.
European Community, 70 n. 16, 211, 272 n. 30, 396
European Free Trade Association, 396

F

Family, the, 28-31, 39, 52-54, 56, 152 ff., 342-43, 362-63
Fascism, 73-74, 228-29, 233, 240, 275, 280, 308-09, 334, 421-22
Federalism:
  in Australia, 327
  in Brazil, 333-36
  in Canada, 326-27
  in general, 18, 154, 310-19, 320, 324 ff., 414
  in Switzerland, 326
  in the United States, 7, 12, 133-34, 190, 320, 324 ff., 327 ff., 367, 420
Fersal, 79-80
Ferdinand & Isabella, 358-59
Feudalism, 73, 103-04, 179 n. 2, 247, 251, 288-89, 354, 356-57
Florence, 251 n. 4
Force (see also Violence), 71-76, 81-82, 85, 111 n. 37, 158, 175, 215 ff., 221, 382
Fortescue, John, 73
France, 20, 73, 98, 109, 123, 126-30, 131, 167, 198, 208 n. 26, 211 n. 30, 226, 250, 252, 271-73, 286, 290-92, 320, 349, 353-54, 355, 358, 360, 367, 372-73, 378-79, 386, 388, 390, 394, 396, 401-02
Franco, Francisco, 74, 226-27, 240, 421
Frankfurter, Felix, 265 n. 22
Franklin, Benjamin, 368
Franks, the, 247, 352-53
Frazer, J. G., 104-05, 218 n. 1
Frederick the Great, 93
Freedom, 1-8, 15, 19, 21, 182, 188-91, 243-83, 319-20, 413, 440
Freud, Sigmund, 8, 38 n. 18, 46-47
Fribourg, 68
Friedrick, C. J., 446
Fulbright, J. William, 416 n. 9

G

Gaitskell, Hugh, 238 n. 22
Galileo, 281
Gandhi, 146

Gandhi, Mrs. Indira, 106 n. 30
Gardner, E. A., 64 n. 8
Gary, 145
Gelasius I, Pope, 164 ff.
Geneva, 153, 220, 367, 386
Genoa, 115
George I, 304
George II, 304
George III, 106 n. 29, 304
Georgia, 146
Germany (see also Prussia), 10, 65-66, 84, 97-98, 112, 126, 131, 139, 228-29, 233, 247, 271, 290, 297, 308-09, 315, 337, 341, 351, 353 ff., 360, 365-67, 378-79, 382, 386, 394, 401, 421-22
Germany, East, 239, 401
Germany, West, 208 n. 26, 211 n. 30
Ghana, 226, 309, 391 n. 18
Gibbon, Edward, 351
Gladstone, William E., 118, 306, 374
Goebbels, Joseph, 282
Goethe, 102
Gooch, G. P., 221 n. 8
Goodness, 8, 20-25, 439-42
Goths, the, 247, 352
Goulart, Joao, 334
Government (see also Politics, State):
  and area, 310-70, 432 ff.
  controlling the governed, 7, 14, 75 ff., 81-84, 217, 409
  costs of, 6-7, 250, 298, 323, 328 ff., 367-68, 393-94
  definition of, 59-60
  functions of, 11-12, 13, 15, 18, 60-71, 157-214, 296 ff., 303, 424, 438 ff.
  responsiveness of, 76-80, 121, 126-27, 217, 243-83, 250, 260 ff., 280, 409-10, 439
Governorship, the American, 302-04, 336
Grant, Madison, 97
Gray, Thomas, 319 n. 11
Greece, classical (see also Athens, Sparta), 63-64, 102, 106 n. 29, 110-11, 120 n. 1, 122, 161-62, 174, 218, 342 n. 2, 344-48, 371
Greece, modern, 226, 368, 398, 410 n. 1
Gregory VII, Pope, 166-67
Grotius, 382
Groups, social, 30-58, 72-73, 149-74, 255, 338-39, 362, 436
Guatemela, 226
Guilds, the, 51, 179-80, 187 n. 13, 251

H

Haiti, 309
Hamburg, 179, 251 n. 4

Hamilton, Alexander, 12, 106 n. 29, 191, 257 n. 14, 324, 445
Hammurabi, 221
Hanseatic League, 251 n. 4
Hapsburgs, the, 101, 108-09, 317, 360, 365-66, 386
Harada, Baron, 105 n. 27
Harding, Warren G., 337
Harlem, 146
Harty, Louis, 191 n. 15
Hayek, F. A., 428
Hawaii, 27, 146, 426
Hegel, G. W. F., 241, 348, 445
Henry IV, Emperor, 165-66
Henry VII, 358
Henry VIII, 172, 174, 252
Henry the Navigator, 359
Heraclitus, 37
Herodotus, 66-67, 71, 78, 384, 418
Herskovits, Melville G., 62 n. 1, 65 n. 11, 95-96, 100 n. 18
Hinduism, 107-08, 113, 146
Hitler, Adolf, 10, 74, 83, 93, 97-98, 100, 228-29, 232, 239-40, 269, 290, 309, 315, 369, 406, 421-22, 437, 445
Hobbes, Thomas, 22, 29-30, 32, 44 n. 22, 45 n. 23, 68, 169-70, 174, 354 n. 18, 383, 444
Homer, 28, 102
Honduras, 226
Honolulu, 146
Hoover, Herbert, 270
Horace, 349
Hughes, Charles E., 282 n. 36
Humanism, 21-25, 123, 242
Humanitarianism, 8, 147, 207-12
Hungary, 236, 365-66, 390, 397, 401
Huns, the, 247

I

Ibun, Khaldun, 222
Iceland, 341, 394
Imperialism, 345-52, 372 ff., 388 ff., 401
Incas, the, 112, 222-23
India, 23, 62, 99, 106 n. 30, 107-8, 112, 118, 146, 153, 312, 333, 349 n. 12, 360, 373, 391 n. 18, 394, 408, 415
Indians, American, 29-30, 68, 99-100, 139, 191
Individualism, 28-32, 35-38, 40-45, 151-52, 176, 183 ff., 193, 272-73, 337-39, 381
Indonesia, 226, 388, 391 n. 18
Innocent III, Pope, 369
Innocent IV, Pope, 167

Institutions, 52-54, 61, 70, 284 ff., 300 ff., 383 ff., 440
International Labor Organization, 384-85
International Organization, 383 ff.,
International relations, 9-11, 14-15, 39, 60, 161, 287, 340-404, 413 ff., 416
Iran, 388
Iraq, 226
Ireland, 188, 250, 312, 362, 367, 369, 376
Islam (See Muslims)
Israel, 34, 106 n. 30, 341, 368-69, 390-91, 394
Issawi, Charles, 222
Italy, 66, 73-74, 110 n. 36, 112, 125, 131, 208 n. 26, 211 n. 30, 220, 228-29, 233, 251 n. 4, 308, 315, 333, 340-41, 345, 349, 353, 355, 360, 365-67, 378, 386, 421-22
Ivan the Terrible, 232

J

Jackson, Andrew, 135, 300
Jackson, Robert, 319 n. 11
James I, 221
James II, 172, 252
Japan, 10, 66, 105, 110 n. 36, 113 n. 41, 155n. 7, 211, 220, 282, 297, 309, 337, 360, 380, 386, 388, 394, 396 n. 21, 398
Jay, John, 445
Jefferson, Thomas, 12, 46, 106 n. 29, 118, 127, 135, 189-90, 253-54, 293, 297, 368, 431
Jericho, 63, 135
Jerusalem, 354-55, 356 n. 19, 358
Jesuits, the, 153, 367
Jesus, 125, 156, 279, 281
Jews, the, 98, 109, 145, 220, 312 n. 1, 341, 368
Joan of Arc, 360
John, King, 165, 248-49
John XXII, Pope, 168
Johnson, Lyndon B., 277, 400, 416 n. 9
Jordan, 391, 394
Justice, 70-71, 80-81, 143, 192-93, 212, 222, 242, 439
Juvenal, 81

K

Kamenev, L. B., 233
Kansas, 68
Kant, Immanuel, 128, 148
Kemal Ataturk, 227 n. 13, 411, 431
Kennedy, John F., 7, 75, 105 n. 28, 142, 145
Kennedy, Robert F., 75

Kenya, 389, 391 n. 18
Kerensky, Alexander, 228
Khrushchev, N. S., 233-39, 402
King, Martin Luther, 75, 145
Kinship, 341-43
Kipling, Rudyard, 97, 374
Knowledge, 1-9, 16, 51-52, 117-18, 121-22, 132-33, 137
Konoye, Prince, 105 n. 27
Kosygin, Alexei, 239, 403
Krause, Lawrence B., 70 n. 16
Kropotkin, Peter, 38

L

Labor Unions, 51-53, 60, 197 ff.
Laissez faire, 32, 181 ff., 190-91, 195 ff., 206-07
Land (see Agriculture)
Laski, Harold J., 150 n. 1, 187, 427, 445-46
Lasswell, Harold D., 414 n. 4, 446
Law:
  common, 75
  enforcement of, 74-75, 78, 90, 142, 153, 175, 241, 267, 299, 301, 381
  international, 381-83
  natural, 127-28, 259-60, 444
  Roman, 123-24, 246, 348-49
  rule of, 217, 245 ff., 257-58
  written, 6
Lawrence, T. E., 29 n. 2, 79
Leadership, political, 76-78, 312 ff.
League of Nations, 384-87
Leakey, Louis, 62 n. 1
Lebanon, 226
Legislature, the, 130 ff., 249 ff., 290-93, 298 ff., 307-08
Lehman, Herbert, 303
Lenin, V. I., 83, 228, 230-31, 233-34, 236, 422, 437, 445
Leo III, Pope, 353
Liberalism, 12, 132
Liberty (see Freedom)
Lincoln, Abraham, 135, 361, 368, 406, 438
Lind, Andrew W., 96 n. 11
Lindsay, A. D., 35-36, 43 n. 20, 76, 81 n. 29, 122, 443, 446
Lipson, E., 288 n. 4
Lipson, Leslie, 204 n. 24, 446
Lisbon, 275
Lloyd George, David, 306
Localism, 284 ff., 310-39, 354, 411, 432
Locke, John, 44 n. 22, 45 n. 23, 46, 83 n. 31, 127, 182, 189, 253, 290-91, 293, 298, 300, 444
Lombards, the, 352-53
London, 63 n. 4, 179, 203, 313, 319, 322 n. 13, 323, 374

Los Angeles, 145, 313
Louix XIV, 183, 290, 373, 406
Louisiana, 142, 336
Ludwig, Emperor, 168
Luther, Martin, 358
Luxemburg, 211 n. 30, 341, 394

M

MacArthur, Douglas A., 7, 415
Macaulay, T. B., 132 n. 10
Macedonia, 346-47
Machiavelli, 23, 81 n. 28, 225, 358, 370 n. 30, 444
MacIver, Robert M., 14 n. 7, 150 n. 1, 187, 262 n. 16, 276, 419-20, 427-28, 446
Madison, James, 114, 151 n. 4, 293, 295 n. 16, 297 n. 20, 298, 300, 309, 445
Madrid, 275, 313
Mahomet, 156, 352
Maitland, F. W., 172
Majority rule, 224, 255, 278-82
Malawi, 309
Malaya, 100 n. 18
Malenkov, G., 234-37
Man, the nature of, 2-9, 21-26, 28-39, 41-50, 90-95, 119 ff.
Manchus, the, 113
Mao Tse-tung, 240, 437
Marathon, 346
Marius, 73, 247
Marshall, John, 257-58, 330
Marsiglio, 248
Martin, William, 68 n. 14
Marx, Karl, 7 n. 3, 46-47, 114-15, 196, 209, 234, 445
Marxism, 7, 36, 114-15, 210-11, 230 ff., 319, 421-22
Masaryk, T. G., 118, 438
Maslow, Abraham H., 447
Massachusetts, 145, 198, 258, 295 n. 18
Maurois, Andre, 352-53
Maxon, Yale, 105 n. 27
Mazzini, G., 360, 438
McBain, Howard L., 302 n. 26, 446
McKinley, William, 105
Media, 66-67, 78-79, 384
Meir, Mrs. Golda, 106 n. 30
Mellaart, James, 63 n. 6
Mendes-France, Pierre, 20 n. 10
Mercantilism, 180-81, 188, 191, 252, 289, 375-76
Merriam, Charles E., 31
Metternich, 365-66
Mexico, 190, 220 n. 6, 234 n. 18, 359
Mexico City, 82, 339

Michels, Roberto, 279-80
Mikoyan, A., 234
Milan, 251 n. 4, 315
Military organization and government, 10-12, 53, 61-66, 108-09, 123, 188, 203, 217, 226-30, 234-37, 287, 290, 335-37, 342-43, 347, 351, 376, 378, 380, 385, 387, 398, 403-04, 413-14, 424
Mill, J. S., 31-32, 132-33, 184-86, 445
Mills, C. Wright, 85 n. 33, 446
Milo, 73
Minnesota, 328 n. 25
Minority, the, 255, 278-82, 339
Mississippi, 27, 138 n. 23, 142, 146, 336, 426
Modernization, 227, 329 ff., 391 ff.
Molotov, V., 235-37
Monarchy, 64, 73, 78-80, 93, 109-12, 127, 168, 172-74, 189, 219 ff., 222, 246, 248 ff., 287, 289-90, 294, 352, 373
Monism, 15, 150 ff., 173-74, 177-81, 186, 196, 212-14, 407 ff., 410-13, 422, 424, 428 ff.
Monnet, Jean, 70 n. 16
Montesquieu, 294-95, 298, 300, 304, 324, 444
Montezuma, 28 n. 6
Montreal, 313
Mormons, the, 361-62
Morrison, Herbert, 323
Moscow, 232, 238-39, 275, 315
Moses, 156, 221
Mossadegh, 388
Mowrer, Richard, 169 n. 17
Mumford, Lewis, 193 n. 17
Murray, R. H., 5 n. 2
Muslims, the, 112, 312 n. 1, 352-53, 355-56, 359, 388
Mussolini, 73-74, 83, 151 n. 2, 228-29, 240, 309, 315, 340, 421-22, 437, 445
Myrdal, G., 362 n. 27

N

Napoleon, 126, 130, 279-80, 292, 297, 304, 326 n. 19, 360, 373, 376, 437
Napoleon III., 131, 153
Nasser, Gamal Abdel, 226-27, 388, 390-91
Natal, 99
Nation-state, 9, 170-74, 289 ff., 357-404, 432 ff., 438-39
Nature:
   law of, 127, 182, 185
   state of, 28-30, 37-39, 68, 182
Nazism (see also Hitler), 98, 138-40, 228-29, 233, 308, 315, 348, 380
Nebraska, 301 n. 25

Nehru, 118, 146, 406
Nelson, 297
Netherlands, the, 27, 98, 208 n. 26, 211 n. 30, 358, 369, 372-73, 388
Neumann, Franz, 295 n. 15, 444
New Delhi, 333, 388
New South Wales, 332
Newton, Isaac, 45-46
New York City, 82, 313, 331
New York State, 303, 332
New Zealand, 129, 203 n. 24, 280, 320, 363, 399
Nicaragua, 226
Nicholas von der Flue, 68
Nigeria, 147, 333
Nixon, Richard M., 105, 416
Nkrumah, Kwame, 226, 309
Nobility, the (see Aristocracy)
North Atlantic Treaty Organization, 396, 398
North Dakota, 203
North, Lord, 189
Norway, 280, 312, 372

O

Officials, 74-75, 77, 244, 250
Ogg, David, 186 n. 12
Oligarchy, 90 ff., 114-15, 224 ff., 232 ff., 278-81, 428
Ontario, 313, 326, 332
Order, 66-70, 75-76, 82-83, 251
Oregon, 322
Ortega y Gasset, Jose, 93
Orwell, George, 86, 425 n. 19
Otto the Great, 353
Oxenstierna, 117

P

Paine, Thomas, 127
Pakistan, 146, 226, 312
Palmerston, Lord, 374
Panaetius, 123
Panama, 394
Papacy, the, 165 ff., 179 n. 2, 196, 220, 353-57, 365-67, 369, 371
Papal States, the, 220, 340-41
Paraguay, 153, 226, 394
Pareto, Vilfredo, 279-80
Paris, 82, 183, 190, 313
Party, the single, 227-42, 275-76, 280, 408, 429
Party politics, 130, 200, 203-04, 266, 274-78, 300-306, 425 n. 18
Pascal, Blaise, 153 n. 5

Pasternak, Boris, 69
Paul, St., 125
Peisistratus, 73
Peking, 275
Penn, William, 173 n. 24
Pericles, 159, 161, 274, 406
Peron, Juan, 74, 226, 437
Perry, Ralph Barton, 21 n. 11
Persia, 162, 177, 346-47, 369
Peru, 226, 359, 391 n. 18
Peter the Great, 232
Peter the Hermit, 355
Phidias, 159
Philip of Macedon, 346-47
Philip the Fair, 167-68
Phoenicians, the, 372
Physiocrats, the, 183, 189
Piggott, Stuart, 4 n. 1
Pilate, 281
Pitt, William, 106 n. 29, 130
Plato, 22, 29 n. 2, 39, 42-43, 48, 73 n. 21,
    81, 84-85, 114-15, 117-18, 160-61,
    170, 347, 418 n. 11, 443
Pluralism, 15, 150 ff., 186 ff., 196, 273 ff.,
    276, 408 ff., 410-13, 423-24, 427 ff.
Plutocracy, 113-15
Pobyedonosteff, K. P., 109 n. 35
Poland, 239, 249, 315, 341, 360, 364, 368,
    401, 412
Police, 69, 74, 82, 99, 216-17, 232, 235
Political science,8-9, 12-25, 42-50, 59-60,
    405-42
Political theory, 19-20, 44-45, 53-54, 92-
    94, 164 ff., 261-62
Politics (see also Government, State):
    and age, 104-05
    and anthropology, 3-4, 62-63, 111-12
    and biology, 41-43, 46-47
    and economics, 32-33, 35-39, 46-47,
        175-214
    and ethics, 20-25, 34-39, 72-73, 86
        ff.,216-17, 254, 439-42
    and law, 262 ff.
    and philosophy, 19-20, 43-45, 116-18,
        405-06
    and physics, 45-46, 380
    and psychology, 30-31, 44, 93-94, 129,
        141, 191, 313-14
    and social groups, 27-58, 150-74, 361-70
    and sociology, 47-49, 111-12
    and wealth, 64 n. 8, 113-16, 125, 130 ff.,
        134-35, 194, 208-09
Pollock, Frederick, 445
Polybius, 123
Pompey, 73, 247
Pompidou, Georges, 292 n. 9
Pope, Alexander, 6, 100
Portugal, 358, 372-73, 410 n. 1

Power:
    economic, 176 ff., 195 ff.
    nature of, 75 ff., 82-87, 92 ff., 215-42,
        261, 422, 440
    separation or concentrations of, 14-15,
        244-46, 284-309, 323 ff., 409 ff., 415
    transfer of, 232 ff., 239
Prague, 239, 369
Privilege, 13, 15, 27, 89-118, 147, 193 ff.,
    391 ff., 395, 400, 408 ff., 425-26
Property, 70
Projection, 60-66, 81-82, 101 n. 37, 255,
    343 ff., 356-57, 380 ff., 398, 439
Protestantism, 27, 95, 98, 109, 128, 145,
    170-74, 252, 312 n. 1, 326, 362-64,
    366-68, 373, 376
Prussia, 110, 116, 131, 229, 249, 341, 360,
    366, 378, 412
Psychoanalysis, 8-9, 38 n. 18, 46-47
Psychology, 7-8, 30-31, 50, 93-94, 120-21,
    129, 141, 191, 313-14, 438
Pufendorf, Samuel, 382
Pushkin, 112

Q

Quakers, the, 173 n. 24
Quebec, 312-13, 326, 363

R

Race relations, 27, 57, 95-100, 111-12,
    137-47, 335-36, 362, 426
Reformation, the, 172-74, 176, 186 n. 12,
    252, 358
Regionalism, 10-11, 313-14, 395 ff., 411 n.
    2
Religion, organized, 52-54, 57, 60, 104,
    107-09, 152 ff., 159, 163-74, 195, 212,
    218-21, 260, 354-57, 363-64, 368, 412,
    422, 430
Rembrandt, 25
Renaissance, the, 176, 186 n. 12, 370 n. 30
Representation, 77, 130 ff., 248, 252 ff.,
    265
Revolution:
    the American, 126-28, 436
    the English, 120, 126-28, 131-32, 252-
        53, 290, 436
    the French, 20, 77 n. 24, 109, 120, 126-
        28, 271-73, 279-80, 291-92, 436
    general character of, 23, 83 n. 31, 120-
        21, 131-32, 216, 225, 227, 247, 253,
        255, 259, 276, 432 ff., 435 ff.
    the industrial, 129, 158, 175, 187 ff., 196
        ff., 297, 321-22, 373, 376-77, 423 ff.

the Russian, 69, 120-21, 210, 230 ff., 279, 297, 437
Ricardo, David, 184, 187
Romania, 239
Rome, 57, 63-64, 73, 101, 103, 105, 111, 117, 123-25, 158, 161-63, 166, 177, 218, 246-47, 279, 287-88, 293, 313, 341, 343 n. 4, 345, 348-52, 354-55, 359, 371-72, 406, 411-12, 415, 443-44
Roosevelt, Franklin D., 77, 269-70, 303, 306, 328-29, 406
Roosevelt, Theodore, 303
Rousseau, Jean Jacques, 8, 20, 35 n. 12, 43-45, 127, 183
Russia, czarist (see also Soviet Union), 10, 84, 97, 109, 221, 249, 308, 315, 341, 360, 368, 379, 412

S

Sabine, George H., 248, 445
Salamis, 346
Salisbury, Lord, 105
San Francisco, 313
Sao Paulo, 312, 333-34
Scalapino, Robert A., 155 n. 7
Schopenhauer, Arthur, 38 n. 18
Schumpeter, Joseph, 447
Science:
  behavioral, 7-8, 23-25, 47-50
  biological, 37, 41-43, 46-47, 281
  physical, 1-2, 23-25, 45-46, 281
Scipio, 123, 348
Scotland, 162, 250, 323, 339, 367, 377, 411 n. 2
Seeley, J. R., 17, 445
Sen, B. R., 391 n. 18
Shakespeare, William, 6, 28, 43, 102 n. 23, 104, 112, 221, 342 n. 3, 357, 360
Shaw, G. B., 376 n. 7
Shephard, W. J., 65
Shonfield, Andrew, 210, 447
Siegfried, Andre, 362 n. 26
Simon de Montfort, 249
Slavery, 11, 57, 68, 90, 96-97, 99, 108, 124, 135-36, 361
Smetana, 368
Smith, Adam, 32, 35-36, 180, 183-85, 187, 189, 427
Smith, Alfred, E., 303
Smith, Joseph, 221
Socialism, 187 n. 13, 202-11, 316 ff.
Social services, 207 ff., 323, 441
Society, 2-6, 26-58, 149-74, 361-70, 427 ff., 436 ff.
Sociology, 7-8, 48-49, 85, 112, 139
Socrates, 22, 159, 281, 418 n. 11

Solon, 64
Solothurn, 68
Soloveytchik, G., 68 n. 14
Somervell, D. C., 29 n. 2
South Africa, 27, 98-99, 108, 139, 144, 363-64, 368, 389, 426
South Korea, 226, 331, 390, 415
Sovereignty, 173-74, 180, 196, 251, 279, 289-90, 374 ff., 433
Soviet Union (see also Russia, Stalin), 10, 36, 84, 210-11, 228, 229 ff., 308, 315-18, 337, 341, 379, 386, 389 ff., 391 n. 18, 394, 397, 400 ff., 414
Space, 2, 238, 380, 398, 424, 439
Spain, 74, 109, 112, 123, 168 n. 17, 226-27, 252, 349-50, 353-54, 358, 360, 367, 369, 372-73, 378, 394, 410 n. 1, 421
Sparta, 64 n. 9, 105, 110-11, 159, 345 n. 7, 346, 378, 414 n. 5
Spencer, Herbert, 37, 186 n. 11, 187, 209, 212
Spinoza, 18, 281
Stalin, 10, 83, 228, 229-36, 240, 280, 282, 308, 315-16, 389, 400, 402, 406, 421, 437
State (see also Government, Politics):
  and church, 162-74
  city-, 14, 158-62, 178, 287-88, 344-48, 360-61, 369, 371, 403, 412-13, 422-23
  classification of types of, 417 ff.
  and the economy, 175-214
  and social groups, 149-74, 412
  empire-, 14, 348-57, 369, 423
  nation-, 9, 14, 170-74, 289 ff., 357-404, 423, 433, 438-39
  origins of, 59-87
  size of the, 14-15, 340-70, 414-16, 432
  use of force by the, 71 ff., 81-86, 157-58
Stenton, Doris Mary, 219
Stoddard, Lothrop, 97
Stoicism, 122-24, 161
Sudan, 92
Sulla, 73, 247, 348, 415
Sumer, 64
Sweden, 117, 208 n. 26, 210, 312, 412
Switzerland, 27, 65 n. 11, 67-68, 210, 280, 319-20, 326 n. 21, 344, 364, 367, 382
Sydney, 313
Sylvester, Pope, 163
Syria, 226
Systems analysis, 47-50

T

Tacitus, 65, 443-44
Taiwan, 226
Tawney, R. H., 108, 179 n. 2

Taylor, G. R. S., 186 n. 12
Tchaikovsky, 51
Technology, 10, 12, 23, 48, 187-88, 272 n. 30, 297, 337-38, 357, 373, 380, 387, 398, 403-04, 424, 431
Tennessee, 331
Tennyson, Lord, 395
Thailand, 226
Thebes, 345-46, 378
Theocracy, 218-21
Thermopylae, 346
Thomas, Aquinas, 356, 406, 444
Thucydides, the son of Melesias, 272 n. 33
Thucydides the Historian, 102 n. 23, 161 n. 11, 443
Tibet, 220, 401
Tito, Joseph, 232, 236, 316-19, 400, 422, 437
Tokyo, 82, 339
Tomsky, 233
Toronto, 313
Townsend, Peter, 208 n. 26
Toynbee, A. J., 29 n. 2, 62 n. 1, 150, 155 n. 9, 447
Trevelyan, G. M., 131 n. 9, 172 n. 22
Trotsky, Leon, 232-34, 437, 445
Trujillo, Rafael, 226
Truman, Harry S., 7, 415
Tunis, 222, 388
Turkey, 226-27, 317, 345, 351, 355-56, 358, 365-66, 398, 411-12
Tyranny, 83-85, 160, 214, 246, 255, 258, 260, 273, 279, 309, 314-15, 319-20

U

Ulster, 27, 312, 323
United Nations, the, 10, 140, 147, 341, 387-95, 403, 426
United States of America, the:
  business in, 12, 33 n. 8, 191 ff., 264, 391 n. 18
  Congress of, 134, 143, 145, 199-200, 263-65, 271, 297 ff., 306-07, 324-25, 335-36, 415-16
  Constitution of, 9, 20, 66, 106 n. 29, 134-37, 140-42, 146, 191, 256-58, 262 ff., 281, 295 ff., 324-25, 327 n. 21, 328-29, 361-62, 368, 445
  Declaration of Independence of, 11, 106 n. 29, 127, 135-36, 140, 189, 253, 368
  federalism in, 7, 12, 133-34, 190, 320, 324 ff., 327 ff., 367, 420
  foreign policy of, 9-12, 337, 360, 384, 386, 394, 396 ff., 415
  labor in, 198 ff.

  President of, 77, 105, 270-71, 297 ff., 302-04, 306, 415-16
  race relations in, 27, 97, 137 ff., 335-36, 362
  slavery in, 11, 108, 135-36, 361
  Supreme Court of, 140-41, 145, 199, 257 ff., 262-66, 282-83, 297 ff., 329-30, 335-36
  voting in, 133-38
Urbanism (see City)
Uruguay, 344, 394
Utah, 362-63
Utilitarians, the, 128, 260-61

V

Values, 19-25, 30-31, 255
Vandals, the, 247, 352
Vargas, Getulio, 333-34
Vatican State, 220, 340-41
Vattel, E. de, 382
Venezuela, 226
Venice, 101 n. 21, 115, 251 n. 4, 355, 358, 372
Vercingetorix, 348
Vespasian, 220
Victoria, Queen, 133, 188, 369, 374
Vienna, 365
Vietnam, 11, 147, 226, 239, 277, 337, 400, 416 n. 9
Violence (see also Force), 71-75, 81-82, 221 ff., 278, 338-39, 437
Virgil, 349
Virginia, 142, 190, 293, 336
Visigoths, the, 352
Voltaire, 127
Von Gierke, Otto, 186
Vote, the right to, 11, 116, 129-38, 265, 275-76

W

Wagner, Richard, 368
Waldenses, the, 354
Wales, 250, 323, 339, 367, 376, 411 n. 2
Wallas, Graham, 151 n. 3
Walpole, Robert, 304
War:
  American Civil, 57, 97, 135, 325, 326, 361
  class, 196 ff.
  English Civil, 252, 290-91
  and government, 61-66, 109-11, 177, 181, 250, 345, 358-59
  Napoleonic, 98, 188
  Peloponnesian, 111, 346

World War I, 10, 126, 133, 136, 378, 380, 384
World War II, 10, 139-40, 378, 380, 387, 415
Warren, Earl, 141, 303
Warsaw, 238
Warsaw Pact, 211, 397
Washington, D.C., 325 n. 17
Washington, George, 256, 274-75, 325, 368, 437
Welfare, 11-12, 207-14, 242, 439 ff.
Wheare, K. C., 19, 332 n. 27
William and Mary, of Orange, 252
William of Occam, 248
Wilson, Harold, 105
Wilson, Woodrow, 46, 118, 303, 385-86, 446
Wisconsin, 205, 303
Women in politics, 105-07, 133, 136, 139 n. 26, 426-27
Wordsworth, William, 358

X

X, Malcolm, 75
Xerxes, 346

Y

Young, Brigham, 221
Yugoslavia, 211, 231-33, 316-19, 364, 400, 402-03, 413, 422

Z

Zeno, 122
Zhukov, Georgi, 235-37
Zinoviev, G. E., 233
Zurich, 313, 332, 367
Zwingli, 361